CREATING A PUBLIC

CREATING A PUBLIC
People and Press in Meiji Japan

James L. Huffman

University of Hawai'i Press

Honolulu

02 01 00 99 98 97   5 4 3 2 1

Library of Congress Cataloging-in-Publication Data
Huffman, James L., 1941–
   Creating a public : people and press in Meiji Japan / James L.
Huffman.
      p.   cm.
   Includes bibliographical references and index.
   ISBN 0–8248–1882–2 (alk. paper)
   1. Press—Japan—History—19th century.   2. Press and politics—
Japan—History—19th century.   3. Journalism—Social aspects—
Japan—History—19th century.   4. Japan—History—Meiji period,
1868–1912.   I. Title.
PN5404.H78   1997
079'.52'0934—dc21   96–48431
                                                              CIP

Book design by Nina Lisowski

To Judith Huffman,
Whose work this was as much as mine

and to Robert and June Huffman,
Who showed me first the joy of exploring

Contents

Acknowledgments

I am a debtor. This study has been under way for two decades, and with each passing week I have become more and more aware of the crucial role played by those friends and colleagues who have plowed the furrows before (and sometimes beside) me, lightened my research load, prodded me to keep going, and provided unending sustenance. I must say a public thank you.

One important group consists of scholars of Japanese journalism, many of whom know Meiji press history far better than I. It would be impossible to express adequate thanks to Uchikawa Yoshimi, whose friendship and advice have cheered me even while keeping the study from wandering too far astray. I also am thankful to Yamamoto Taketoshi, Ariyama Teruo, and their colleagues (including Giles Richter) in the Medeia Shi Kenkyūkai, to Nagai Michio whose conversations so often raised fresh ideas or opened new doors, as well as to Koito Chūgo, Arase Yutaka, Kato Hidetoshi, Roger Purdy, and Gregory Ornatowski.

I also owe much to a number of scholar-friends outside the field of press history whose advice about matters large and small helped me in this study: the late Jackson Bailey, my mentor Roger Hackett, *Asahi Shimbun* executive Kobayashi Masayuki, John Dower, Sidney Devere Brown, Yamaji Hiroki, Kobayashi Toshio. I am especially in debt to several who agreed to read all or parts of the manuscript, dear friends whose suggestions I sometimes was too stubborn to take but who gave wonderful advice and saved me from considerable embarrassment: Mikiso Hane, Sally Hastings, Jane Bachnik, Barbara Sato, Fred Notehelfer and another anonymous reader at the University of Hawai'i Press—as well as to Sally Serafim and Susan Stone, whose editing of the final manuscript was not only meticulous but gentle. To the editor, Patricia Crosby, a special word is needed: more competence or graciousness I cannot imagine.

I also want to thank a number of colleagues and research assistants who have helped me find details, summarize materials, keep things organized, and maintain my sanity. I think of Kathy Schulz and Gina Entorf in the Wittenberg Library, Kitane Yutaka and Fujii Sachiko at the Meiji Shimbun Zasshi Bunko, Kimura Hiroshi at the University of Tokyo's Shakai Jōhō Kenkyūjo library, two marvelous secretaries, Margaret DeButy and Rosemarie Burley, and former student assistants Kaoru Abbey, Doug Buchanan, David Hewitt, Jeremy Hunter, Hideyuki Kikuchi, Kathryn Mensendiek, Michael Molasky, Josh Pifer, Tracy Pollard, Madoka Yamakawa-Ermarth, and Miho Yasukawa. And I must express my appreciation for undeservedly generous financial support to the Fulbright-Hays Commission (and Caroline Yang), to the Japan Foundation (and Murayama Atsushi), to the National Endowment for the Humanities for a summer travel grant, the American Philosophical Society and to Wittenberg's own Faculty Research Fund Board for help at key points along the way. I also am deeply thankful to the University of Tokyo's Shakai Jōhō Kenkyūjo and the National Institute for Multimedia Education in Chiba for providing a research home during two extended stays in Japan.

Finally, I must say a personal word to a particular group of friends whose fields range far from mine but whose ideas and values inform every page of this study: Eugene Swanger, Stanley Mickel, Fumiko Togasaki, and the other members of Wittenberg's East Asian studies program; Warren Copeland in the religion department; Charles Chatfield, Joe O'Connor, Bob Cutler, and *all* of my stimulating colleagues in the history department—and so many others I wish I could name. And then there are the members of my family: Jim, Kristen, and Dave, whose ideas and energy constantly push me in new directions, and my late wife, Judith, a partner and confidante beyond peer, who read every word of this study, kept me going when I might have quit, provided many of my freshest ideas, and was consumed by a passion not only for life but for helping peoples of the world understand each other.

INTRODUCTION

A popular government without popular information
or the means of acquiring it, is but a Prologue
to a Farce or a Tragedy; or perhaps both.
Knowledge will forever govern ignorance.
                                      James Madison[1]

Journalism is essentially a state of
consciousness, a way of apprehending,
of experiencing the world.
                                      James W. Carey[2]

Something remarkable happened to Japan's commoners, or *minshū*,
during the Meiji era. In 1868, at the period's outset, the vast majority of them were subjects and nothing more, as far removed from
the government, in journalist Tokutomi Sohō's words, "as heaven
is from hell."[3] When his august majesty died forty-five years later,
in 1912, their grandchildren were displaying the characteristics of
modern citizens: writing letters to newspaper editors to discuss
debates in the legislature, marching in the streets by the tens of
thousands to demand lower streetcar fares and an aggressive foreign
policy, using phrases such as "constitutionalism" and "the people's
will" as if they were second nature. And when they shouted, the
governors usually responded—despite the fact that most of these
minshū had no vote, no legal means for expressing their will, until
the 1925 enactment of universal male suffrage.

Scholars have looked in a number of directions to explain this
rapid transformation. The steady spread of education and literacy
often has been cited, as have the creation of modern political institutions, the early extension of communications networks to remote
towns, the successful efforts of political activists to get citizens to

1

demand "popular" rights, even the expansion of capitalist economic structures. This study focuses its lenses elsewhere. Without denying the importance of education, political movements, or economic transformation, it contends that no single institution did more to create a modern citizenry than the Meiji newspaper press, a collection of highly diverse, private voices that provided increasing numbers of readers—many millions, in fact, by the end of Meiji—with both a fresh daily picture of the world and a changing sense of their own place in that world. The papers also offered a repertoire of the ideas and actions that would be needed if commoner protests were to take on *public* significance. An understanding of the press' role in leading the "people" thus becomes a prerequisite to any full explanation of Meiji development. And, it seems safe to add, a study of the press' behavior in nineteenth-century Japan also should tell us much about the role newspapers can be expected to play in the evolution of modern societies more generally.

This study's second theme is the reverse impact the *minshū* had on the Meiji press. The change in the people's political consciousness was matched, perhaps even exceeded, by the dramatic evolution in Japan's daily newspaper world in these years. From beginning to end, the mainstream editors and publishers harbored elitist political values: a deep commitment to Confucian paternalism, a desire to strengthen Japan's age old symbols and creeds, a determination to extend the nation's influence to foreign shores. The way they gave voice to those values, however, changed dramatically from the 1870s to the 1910s. In the early years, the Confucian orientation produced small, erudite papers marked by endless gray columns of dense political discussion. By the turn of the century, those same Confucian-bred editors were turning out dailies full of sensational feature stories, exposés of corruption and officials' sex lives, serialized novels, and daily family columns. The late-Meiji papers had more political influence than ever, but their impact now stemmed from huge readership bases and the power of exposure more than from editorials and political discussions.

Fueling this change were the growing communities of urban *minshū*, people who had migrated from the countryside by the hundreds of thousands, bringing with them different skill levels, new values, new desires, and new markets. By mid-Meiji, nearly all of the newspaper owners and editors had become capitalists, made aware by experience that they could not put out a successful paper without resources sufficient to buy modern presses, pay reporters, and cultivate extensive communication channels. And since resources were available from just two places, advertising and circulation, even the most patrician editors had been forced to cater to plebeian reading tastes—which meant revising their approach to journalism. One of the prime driving forces of the Meiji press was thus the increasing symbiosis between the papers and the *minshū*. From the people flowed circulation fees and a definition of what kind of journalism was commercially acceptable; from the papers came a fresh view of the world and a new sense of what it meant to participate in the public life of the nation. The newspapers, in other words, turned the people into citizens; the people turned the papers into mass media.

The impact of the urban masses is a particularly timely concern in our own day, as increasing numbers of observers worry about the influence of ever more sensationalized media on the social and moral fabric of society. That issue stimulated endless debate in the late Meiji world, too, as paper after paper found itself forced either to "turn vulgar," as purist journalists contemptuously put it,[4] or to wither away. The results were mixed, some salutary, some troubling, but not always in the ways lofty standard bearers expected. The popularization brought new intellectual life to millions and fresh approaches to editing, even while it undermined the essay form of journalism and darkened the front pages with crime. It is not at all clear, however, that popular journalism had much to do with the *minshū*'s changing "morals," which upset so many of the old elites. And it is quite certain that the thought control patterns that began to haunt the last Meiji years stemmed less from the popularization of the press than from the strident nationalist rhetoric of elite essayists and the paranoia of the officials. Undoubtedly, an examination of the late-Meiji relationship between press and people will provide both new questions and new perspectives on the press-people issues that bedevil our own time.

This study benefits from several earlier accounts of how political consciousness developed outside the governing circles. Irokawa Daikichi, for example, has provided rich and provocative insights into the spread of constitutional ideas in the villages west of Tokyo and beyond; Roger Bowen's work on popular rights *(jiyū minken)* activities in regions such as Fukushima to the north shows that the movement had roots in the provincial commoner classes, and studies by Mikiso Hane and Patricia Tsurumi of the modern underclass show varying levels of political consciousness among miners, factory workers, and rebellious peasants. For the later Meiji and early Taishō years, Shumpei Okamoto, Tetsuo Najita, Andrew Gordon, and Michael Lewis all have published vivid accounts of riotous crowds extending political consciousness into the streets, with Gordon and Lewis in particular providing important insights into just how politically sophisticated these mass demonstrators often were. And Carol Gluck's masterful, meticulous study of late-Meiji ideology shows powerful, complex links between an elite world trying to integrate the country through a *tennōsei* (emperor-system) ideology and an ever larger, increasingly literate populace.[5]

Most of these works make occasional references to the press and include newspapers among their sources; several suggest in passing that the press had an impact on the process of citizen building; but none of them seriously analyzes the press' role as a political or social force. The same is true of the few English-language studies that have been produced on individual editors and specific institutional features of the Meiji press: John Pierson's and Sinh Vinh's studies of Tokutomi, Kenneth Pyle's look at Kuga Katsunan and Miyake Setsurei, my own account of Fukuchi Gen'ichirō, D. Eleanor Westney's examination of Western influences on the Meiji press' institutional development. Albert Altman has taken the press' socializing role more seriously than others have, but just for the early-Meiji years. The only possible exceptions, indeed the only substantial English-language studies to examine Meiji journalism as a whole, are press histories by Kisaburō Kawabe and Harry Emerson Wildes—and they appeared nearly three-quarters of a century ago and dealt very little with the press-*minshū* question.[6]

One of the reasons for this lacuna in the English-speaking world probably lies in the structures of academia, where press history has been undertaken largely by scholars in the field of journalism and communications rather than by mainstream historians. Although this does not gainsay the value of their works, it clearly affects the questions and perspectives that are raised. Histories of the American press, of which there are many, tend toward an institutional or intellectual focus, and the Japanese press has been ignored almost completely. Indeed, even in Japan, where press history remains fairly vibrant, the focus has been largely institutional. I am deeply indebted not only to the meticulous work of former historians of the Meiji press such as Ono Hideo, Yamamoto Fumio, Midoro Masaichi, and Nishida Taketoshi, but to the fresh approaches and penetrating insights of such contemporary press historians as Uchikawa Yoshimi, Yamamoto Taketoshi, Ariyama Teruo, Haruhara Akihiko, and Sasaki Takashi. Even they, however, have not addressed the press' role in creating a modern citizenry systematically or thoroughly.[7] Uchikawa wrote four decades ago that the most serious gap in the field of Japanese press history was a study of the papers' role as a social medium.[8] That study has yet to be done.

The one societal question that has attracted considerable scholarly work, both in Japan and in the West, is the issue of freedom. English-language works by Lawrence Beer, Gregory Kasza, Richard Mitchell, and Jay Rubin illustrate the high degree of interest in the freedom question, an interest that has been present among Japanese scholars since the beginning of the modern era.[9] Kasza in particular shows not only the continuous growth of government regulation across the prewar years but the comparability of Japan's case to increasing statism during that period in advanced countries everywhere. Beginning with the voluminous writings about *hikka* (press-law infractions) by Miyatake Gaikotsu,[10] a host of Japanese historians and students of the press, including especially Midoro, Uchikawa, Okano Takeo, and Okudaira Yasuhiro, also have done detailed studies of press laws and the struggle for freedom. Many of them have taken a polemical approach, arguing vigorously for the removal of shackles on expression. Okano, for example, uses Fukuzawa Yukichi to argue that the first requisite of civilized government is "free will" *(jishū nin'i)*,[11] and Ono declares unabashedly that "those who would snatch away freedom and popular rights first take away the freedom to publish."[12] One of the most forceful polemicists is Midoro, who opens his history of the Meiji and Taishō press with the declaration:

> In a constitutional government, freedom of discussion and assembly is the people's most important right. Without freedom of expression there can be no constitutional government. Freedom of expression brings constitutional government to perfection. . . . We must demand this freedom. A study of the history of the world's presses *(genron)* reveals clearly that people do not win freedom overnight.[13]

No one should belittle the importance of these press freedom studies; to be a scholar is, almost by definition, to care about such matters and to abhor restraints on expression. But one wonders how much this preoccupation with the question of freedom springs from an Anglo-American, or at least a Western, scholarly bias, a tendency to evaluate the Japanese experience by the rubrics of Western intellectual discourse. That those rubrics speak to universal concerns is emphasized by the fact that so many Japanese press historians have come to employ them too. But they are inadequate for anyone wanting to see Japan's historical development in its own terms. They prompt us too often to evaluate the Meiji press simplistically, as tamed and cowering (as it sometimes seems in Mitchell's telling) or as courageous and cantankerous (as Midoro would have it). And even more seriously, they prompt us to stop short of a full-bodied analysis of the role the press has played in the broader unfolding of modern Japanese history. To ignore free press issues is to present an incomplete story; to talk only about those issues is to tell very little of the story at all.

One of the ironies of this focus on institutional history and freedom is that scholars in more contemporary fields—social scientists and communications analysts, for example—have been discussing for decades the multifaceted nature of the press' role in a modern society. Newspapers, they have shown us, are first of all *organizers and disseminators of information,* shapers of public reality by the very news package that they put together each day. Journalists, says James Carey, "determine what the audience *can* think —the range of what is taken to be real on a given day. If something happens that cannot be packaged . . . in a fundamental sense, it has not happened."[14] Douglass Cater, studying the press in Washington, D.C., several decades ago, put it this way: "Each day hundreds of thousands of words are spoken, tens of dozens of events occur. The press and other media perform the arduous task of sorting out and assigning priorities to these words and events. This . . . constitutes a power far more formidable than the purely editorial preferences of the press."[15] The press, in other words, is a narrator, a storyteller whose decisions about what to ignore and what to include do far more to shape our vision of public reality than most of us realize, even as its tendency to marginalize "alternative, radical perspectives" leaves us with "the belief that the social and political structure is 'natural'—the way things are."[16]

Other communications students focus on the *newspapers' role as educators;* they are what Paul Hirsch calls the "gate-keepers" of a society's "ideas and symbols," the teachers who acquaint their readers with the events, facts, people and concepts needed to make life meaningful.[17] It was this role that so many of the early Meiji editors had in mind when they wrote editorials encouraging "civilized" people to eat meat and abstain from public nudity, this function the late Meiji writers were performing when they called the city's first labor rallies, described the invention of airplanes, and talked about themselves as *"shakai no bokutaku"* (teachers of society).[18]

Papers are *opinion shapers,* too, not so much through their editorials as through their news columns—through an *Asahi Shim-*

bun account of subway sabotage by Aum Shinrikyō (Supreme Truth) leaders, for example, which makes readers clamor for increased police surveillance, or through an Associated Press picture of a naked girl fleeing a soldier in Vietnam, which turns weary Americans against the war. While research by scholars such as Paul Lazarsfeld and Wilbur Schramm suggests that editorial opinion columns have only limited impact in changing people's well-entrenched ideas, other studies make it clear that the press plays a powerful role in shaping perceptions about *new* matters and issues, particularly in large urban areas.[19] Often the press' influence results in the reinforcement of existing values; at other times it nudges readers toward new values and options. But it never stops shaping our ways of looking at the world, whether we are conscious of that fact or not.

Scholars love to point out that the media also serve as *guardians of the public interest*. The nineteenth-century Irish parliamentarian Richard Brinsley Sheridan was grandstanding when he declared: "Armed with liberty of the press, I will go forth to meet [the minister] undismayed. . . . I will shake down from its heights corruption and bury it beneath the ruins of the abuses it was meant to shelter."[20] But his point was not a vacant one. The fundamental premise behind free press ideals is that public institutions need scrutiny from outsiders to evaluate their policies and to search out secret arrangements that violate public trust. It was this function that led to some of the Meiji press' brightest moments: exposing corruption in the sale of government lands in Hokkaido, detailing the effects of copper pollution in the mines at Ashio. And it was this function that created the most heated tensions between nervous officials and the private scribes.

Wilbur Schramm, one of this century's most thoughtful analysts of the press' social role, says that the newspaper in a healthy society has three fundamental functions. It is a watchman (guarding the public interest by disseminating news), a policy shaper (introducing ideas and channeling debates), and a teacher (providing information and opinions).[21] In other words, the press is one of society's more powerful social, political agents—not just a medium but an actor, a shaper, a mover—the kind of institution that caused 93 percent of Japanese households in the mid-1990s to subscribe to more than fifty-two million copies of newspapers daily.[22] To look at its institutional growth or to focus on issues of freedom and control, while crucial, is simply not enough; for those topics fail to explain the press' function in helping a modern society such as Japan to develop. It is with that fact in mind that this study sets out to examine the role the press played in creating a modern public as well as the way the new citizens changed the papers themselves.

Central to my argument is the contention that the Meiji press was, at its core, a popular medium—a tool of Confucian and capitalist elitists, perhaps; a mouthpiece for intellectuals and cabinet factions, certainly; what scholars have called an "equilibrium-sustaining, even conservative" legitimizer of conventional values much of the time[23]—but the only public channel available for timely, ongoing intercourse between the *minshū* and the national establishment. Before the advent of electronic communication, no private institution had more immediacy or greater range than the newspaper; no voice could reach so many people so quickly. Thus, it was understood that people out of power, in Japan as elsewhere, would use the press to voice their concerns and to maneuver for influence. Those who wanted to publish newspapers may themselves have come from the elite strata, but more often than not, being private citizens, they regarded the "people" as their base. As the influential journalist Baba Tsunego wrote in the 1920s, "A newspaper reporter's fundamental view of life *(jinseikan)* inculcates worship of the public and reverence for the people. Reporters dare not regard the people as fools."[24]

Thus, from the launching of the very first quasi-modern news sheets by diehard former Tokugawa supporters in 1868, editors talked about the need to write for commoners—or, as one put it, to publish materials, including illustrations, that would catch the attention of the "rustic public," even of women and children.[25] The first daily newspapers of the Meiji era were started as tools to speed the people along the path of "civilization and enlightenment" *(bunmei kaika)*. By the seventh year of Meiji, most dailies were in the hands of vocal proponents of "representative" government who lambasted the government for dallying in the creation of a popular assembly. And as the era progressed, it was newspaper essays that ignited and heralded nearly every popular movement and rebellion. All of the popular rights chapters in the 1870s and 1880s, for example, used newspapers to spread their messages; Tanaka Shōzō began the antipollution crusade in Ashio as a reporter;[26] the earliest socialist and labor crusades were promoted by reporters and editors; and in 1905 the press fueled the infamous rioting at Hibiya Park. In other words, leaders of all stripes—national and local, opposition and establishment—saw the press as a channel for reaching the people. And while the definition of "people" changed over time, coming to include ever wider segments of the populace, from the very first it was the nongoverning groups whose voice the press pioneers wanted to amplify.

Yet the Meiji press also was an establishment institution. If the Meiji editors clasped hands with the people on one side, they welcomed the support of powerful officials and tycoons on the other. Leaders of the profession in the early Meiji years were ambitious, politically oriented intellectuals (at least three of them eventually became prime ministers); at era's end, the press' best-known names were wealthy members of the business elite; and throughout the era all of the profession's leading lights were state-oriented, emperor-loving nationalists. The very fact that they had the wherewithal and connections to publish newspapers and write editorials indicated that they were highly placed in society. But, unlike other members of the elite, their livelihoods depended on the outsiders who bought and read their papers. They were not satisfied merely to argue their ideas within the councils of state; they sought a wider voice. That was why many of the early writers forsook safe positions in the bureaucracy for the tempestuous world of journalism. And by mid-Meiji, when city masses had become the major source of circulation and revenue, they articulated the issues of the outsiders or their papers folded.

Before I turn to the body of the study, a few words are needed about this work's particular emphases, limits, and contours. The study will concentrate, first, on the *political* role of the press. It will be necessary to include a good deal of discussion about the newspaper world's institutional and intellectual evolution: the impact of personalities and ideas, the influence of technology and organization patterns, the rise of commercialism. But these will be examined in terms of their effect on journalism's changing relationship with the *minshū*. Such discussions will serve, in other words, as a backdrop to the creation of a citizenry, not as the end of the story in themselves.

This focus on the press' leadership of the masses also requires an emphasis on the national press, rather than the provincial papers that sprang up across the archipelago after the mid-1870s. "National" will be defined broadly, to include the presses of both Tokyo to the east and Osaka to the west, since the western giants, *Asahi* and *Mainichi*, broke ground for so many of the important Meiji press developments, particularly in the last half of the era. But I will sketch journalistic developments in other regions only in the broadest of strokes. I must admit to a certain sense of regret in taking this approach, since provincial journalism played a significant role in the Meiji era. However, the central urban papers dominated early Japanese journalism both numerically and in terms of impact, more even than in other developing countries. Already in 1873, Japan had a "national" press, in the sense that the leading Tokyo and Yoko-hama newspapers were sent to every prefecture, where they shaped the political debate. The regions outside Kantō and Kansai, by contrast, developed their own newspapers more slowly.[27] And when the provincial papers did begin to grow, the urban giants held sway over most of them, defining what constituted news, competing for readers even in the provincial papers' own backyards, eventually swallowing up many of the smaller local newspapers. While serious study of strong regional and local papers such as the *Fukuoka Nichi Nichi* in Kyushu and *Otaru Shimbun* in Hokkaido is needed, space limitations and the dominance of the Tokyo-Osaka press preclude it here.

This study also focuses on the mainstream newspaper press. While using the word "press" for convenience, I concentrate on those publications generally categorized by Japanese scholars as *"shim-bun."* This classification includes some publications that came out irregularly in the early Meiji years, when terminology had not become fixed, but once technology had made movable type accessi-ble, the capital's *"shimbun"* nearly all became dailies.[28] The effect of this delineation generally is to exclude magazines *(zasshi),* the more occasional periodicals that tended toward specialization of audience and content. My reason, again, is both theoretical and practical. In the early years of Meiji, most political discussion was carried on in the newspapers, and, even later in the era when the numbers of *zasshi* soared, the newspapers remained the primary vessels for communicating ideas and news with the general popu-lace. There were exceptions, popular journals such as *Kokumin no Tomo, Taiyō,* and *Nihonjin,* but the magazines as a whole focused on more specialized groups (religious sects, politically conscious women's groups, literary circles, economic elites). Though large in number, most were small in circulation, often rather short-lived.[29] As a result, adequate treatment of the periodical press must be left for another study. The other news-oriented media, radio and televi-sion, simply did not exist in the period under discussion, with the dawn of radio broadcasting not coming until 1925 and TV not until 1953.[30] The focus on mainstream journalism also means that ex-tremist and fringe papers as well as the sensational, entertainment-oriented *koshimbun* of the early Meiji years are discussed only as they exerted an influence on what opinion leaders of the time saw as the more influential, respectable press.

A final delineator relates to time. The Meiji years form the core of the study. Since imperial ascensions and deaths create artificial boundaries, however, I begin with an examination of the Tokugawa publishing legacy, which was considerable in terms of both volume and ideas, then look at the press in some detail from 1861 onward, when the country's first private newspaper, the English-language *Nagasaki Shipping List and Advertiser,* appeared. The concluding date is more problematic, since the urban press in 1912 was a large engine gathering steam. For this reason, I also look briefly at the 1910s and early 1920s, a time in which most of the late-Meiji journalistic trends reached maturation. The heavy hand of the authorities during the 1918 rice riots, combined with the destruction of all but three Tokyo newspaper offices during the Kantō Earthquake of 1923, gave Japan quite a different press after the late Taishō years—and made mid-Taishō a somewhat more "natural" point of conclusion.

Moving to the smallest of detail, a few words about style may save the reader some mystification. Romanization of Japanese words generally follows *Kenkyusha's New Japanese-English Dictionary* (an exception being the word *shimbun,* where the "m" has been used long enough and widely enough to have become standard), with macrons used over long vowels except in such well-known geographical names as Tokyo, Osaka, Hokkaido, and Kyushu, in words that have attained sufficient English-language usage to be included in standard dictionaries (e.g., daimyo, shogun), and in quotations from which the macrons were omitted in the original. Dates, including those before Japan switched to the Gregorian calendar in 1873, have been rendered according to their equivalent in the Western calendar. Personal names are given in standard Japanese form (surname first) unless they were used otherwise in the source of the quotation. Notes omit translations of Japanese titles, since they can be found in the bibliography. And the names of newspapers have not been translated unless the translation has something special to tell us, on the grounds that English renderings of newspaper names usually are more quaint than useful.

CHAPTER 1

THE LEGACY

In Spite of the Authorities

> Morality is nothing but the necessary means
> for controlling the subjects of the empire.
>
> *Ogyū Sorai*[1]

Historians outside the mainstream occasionally argue that East Asia has a long-standing free speech tradition, that early-Meiji popular rights advocates drew inspiration not only from Western philosophers but from a long line of Eastern forebears. They point to quite a rich heritage in making their case: to Man'yōshū poets who defiantly proclaimed the dignity of paupers;[2] to assertions in the Chinese *Book of History* that "Heaven embraces the people and shall heed the wishes of the people,"[3] to seventh-century Korean practices that permitted commoners to communicate with their rulers, to Japan's "first press infraction" *(hikka jiken),* in A.D. 837, when Ono Takamura was banished for writing a poem opposing the traditional embassies to China[4]—and, in later centuries, to Priest Nichiren's refusal to bend before the Hōjō regents, to the resilience of early kabuki troupes, and to the courageous perseverance of the *rangakusha* or scholars of Western learning late in the eighteenth century. Some even contend that when Yoshida Shōin discussed the fundamental importance of "channels of expression" *(genrō)* during his mid-nineteenth-century prison lectures, he was drawing on a traditional East Asian equivalent of the West's free press theories.[5] And one journalism scholar suggests that the foundations of Japanese press freedom were laid nearly fourteen centuries ago in Shōtoku Taishi's constitutional declaration that "decisions on an important matter should not be made by one person alone. They should be discussed with many."[6]

With a history rich in such examples, these scholars contend, it is unfair simply to link democratic ideas to Western philosophers whose writings made their way to Japan in the nineteenth century. And they have a point; traditions of independence and dissent are real and deserve a good more study than they have received. Indeed, the central theme of this chapter will be the virility of the Tokugawa writer's world, the way in which countless forerunners of the modern journalist found means to communicate every conceivable kind of information and idea, official strictures notwithstanding.

THE TOKUGAWA THUMB

Before examining that lively publishing tradition, however, we must acknowledge that the mainstream scholars are essentially right, that the Tokugawa era's salient feature (at least when seen from the perspective of the center) was not freedom but control. Even the bravest and most independent pre-1868 writers operated in an environment suffused with regulations, threats, and prohibitions designed to maintain the existing regime and prevent subversive ideas. As one Meiji official said, "The fundamental principle underlying the written laws of the Tokugawa Dynasty was that the people should obey the law, but should not know the law."[7] Laws, as a result, generally were posted but not published, lest publication assist potential offenders—and lest the rules themselves stimulate debate and discussion. The official attitude was that "the ruling class should provide its subjects with only as much information as was necessary to maintain rule."[8] The people, in Ōkuma Shigenobu's words, were to "be stupid, be stupid."[9]

It is generally accepted, in fact, that the maintenance of order and control was the primary goal of *all* Tokugawa institutions and policies. Foreign intercourse was closed down completely in the 1600s, except for two Dutch visits allowed each year to the little island of Deshima in Nagasaki harbor, so that external ideas and loyalties could not be used to challenge the Tokugawa polity. Christianity was banished so thoroughly that the missionary Guido Verbeck found that when Western religion "was mooted in the presence of a Japanese," as late as the 1860s, "his hand would, almost involuntarily, be applied to his throat, to indicate the extreme perilousness of such a topic."[10] And the ban on study of the West was severe enough to cost more than a few daring souls their lives.

Nor was it merely alien thought that was controlled; every

aspect of Tokugawa life was regulated. Daimyo had to follow strictly prescribed regimens, no matter how large their fiefs. Citizens were required to register and stay in touch with local temples, whose responsibility it was to maintain social tranquility. Classes were rigidly divided, then coerced to follow strict codes of proper behavior. *Metsuke* or censors in the service of the Tokugawa served as intelligence agents, keeping an eye on the conduct of subordinates and employing "all the apparatus of secret services, black cabinets, informers and *agents provocateurs* that characterize an uneasy autocracy."[11]

At the local level, *gonin* and *jūnin gumi* (five- and ten-family groupings) were organized for mutual surveillance, leading to a situation where "there was little confidence between man and man."[12] While the Tokugawa regime allowed peasants to petition against the more egregious abuses of local authorities, villagers had no recourse at all against the most common and serious offenses, since direct appeals to higher authorities regarding taxes or land surveys generally were illegal. Indeed, when an individual peasant decided that he could take it no longer, that tax or land abuses had become unbearable enough to warrant a direct petition to higher authorities despite the prohibition on such appeals, he knew that he likely would pay with his life, even if his cause were upheld and the abuses corrected.[13] Individuals, in the words of press scholar Futagawa Yoshifumi, were "no more than objects responsible for paying taxes, subjects who simply served the authorities."[14] From the perspective of the authorities, people existed for the state alone; so it was necessary that control mechanisms reach every area of life.

This then was the world of the Tokugawa writer, a feudal world in which the dragnet of control was as near to complete as officials knew how to make it.[15] Rules and provisos regulated areas of expression as diverse as kabuki, puppet theater, translation, *ukiyoe* (woodblock prints), and books. Their aim was to prevent all communications of a potentially disruptive nature, including any unauthorized material about shogunal families past and present, any news about governmental or official acts, slander against members of the samurai class, revelations of scandalous priestly behavior, or erotic materials that might corrupt public morals. And the techniques used to prevent these unwarranted communications reached in all directions.

Booksellers guilds were used, for example, to extend the self-regulating principles of the *gonin gumi* into the worlds of communication and commerce. Though several guilds were banned by the

Tokugawa authorities after their initial appearance in Edo in the 1650s, they soon came to be seen by the same bureaucrats as useful surveillance tools. As early as 1673, an Edo official reportedly ordered a woodblock carver, Jinshirō, to create a guild that would report to authorities on "suspicious" materials. That effort appears to have failed,[16] but a quarter of a century later, in 1698, two dozen Edo booksellers were allowed to form a guild by officials in the Tsunayoshi administration who saw a chance for mutual benefit. When the guild's officers complained to the authorities about book piracy by other booksellers in 1699, the bakufu confiscated the pirated works; guild profits had been protected and the bakufu had a means of controlling what was being sold. By 1721, Shogun Yoshimune's officers were coercing publishers and sellers to form guilds, and in 1722 the government officially began to charge guilds with censoring publications.[17] Indeed, by the end of the 1700s publication laws regularly stipulated that guilds would be held responsible if anything unacceptable were published.

As the years passed, officials at all levels also made concerted efforts to monopolize the sources and channels of information. Already in 1633, Shogun Iemitsu had set up a book magistery *(goshomotsu bugyō)*, with four administrators charged with overseeing the acquisition and handling of books for the government itself.[18] In the eighteenth century, the shogunate and leading daimyo also developed networks of couriers, called *kihyaku*, who carried information, both rumors and substantial items, about all the "untoward occurrences . . . in the provinces," and most daimyo assigned the person in charge of their Edo residence to gather information and pass it on to them while they were off in the provinces during the home portion of *sankin kōtai* (alternate attendance) service.[19]

Over the years, the most intensive bakufu efforts at monopolizing communication networks lay in the field of Western knowledge. Apprehensive about the potential of foreign news for disrupting the domestic scene, yet ever mindful of the need to stay abreast of what was occurring in barbarian regions, the shogunate began soon after the closing of the nation to request reports from the Dutch captains at Deshima about the state of the European world in general and the movements of warships in particular. By mid-Edo, these reports had become full-fledged, regular *oranda fūsetsugaki* (Dutch news summaries), prepared by the Deshima colony to keep the bakufu informed of the major happenings in Europe and Asia.[20] The reports were not for public consumption, however. The news they contained was considered sensitive, fit only for the eyes of the Council of Elders *(rōjū)* and a few top officials until the very last years of the era.[21]

This two-sided effort, to both generate and restrict international news sources, was reinforced in 1811 by the establishment of a Bureau for the Translation of Barbarian Writings (Bansho Wakai Goyōkakari), which took over responsibility for compiling the *fūsetsugaki* and began translating important Western works for shogunal officials. The bureau's activities increased significantly once seclusion came to an end at mid-century, and in 1855 it was renamed the Institute for Western Studies (Yōgakujo).[22] Like the Dutch reports, the institute quickly became both a control mechanism and a news channel. The bakufu wanted enough information to assure informed responses to international events but not enough to stir up trouble should Yōgakujo reports seep into the public. Thus the generation of news itself became a method of keeping tabs on a carefully controlled world, both at home and abroad.

Equally useful in maintaining this control was the development across the Tokugawa years of a long list of direct regulations and punishments to deal with those who persisted in trying to make their own thoughts known. The first known Tokugawa censorship regulations, issued in 1673 during the reign of the fourth Tokugawa shogun, Ietsuna (r. 1651–1680),[23] required writers to secure permission from the city magistrate *(machi bugyō)* before discussing public matters, reporting unusual happenings, or writing about anything likely to be embarrassing. A 1684 edict, early in Shogun Tsunayoshi's reign, went even further and forbade the publication of broadsides (variously called *yomiuri* and *kawaraban*) about current episodes.[24] Then a five-article ordinance was issued by the conservative, reforming Yoshimune during the winter months of 1722, setting the framework for all subsequent Tokugawa publication laws. The ordinance forbade "excessively mendacious or heterodox discourses"; provided for the suppression of materials "of an erotic nature . . . deemed injurious to public mores"; called for "rigorous investigation" of any books alleged to "delve unfairly into the family lineages of other clans"; required colophons with authors' and publishers' names; and proscribed printed references to any Tokugawa family members.[25] Although censorship was relaxed slightly in 1735, with permission granted to mention the shogun's name in certain cases, it was tightened again in the autocratic era of Matsudaira Sadanobu, under Shogun Ienari, particularly with a 1790 decree reiterating earlier restrictions and adding that it is "forbidden to make baseless rumors into *shahon* (manuscript books) written in *kana* (phonetic script) or to lend such books out for a fee."[26] This decree added that since "books had long been published, no more are necessary; so there ought to be no more new books."[27] Responsibility for enforcement of these regulations was to be borne, at least in part, by the booksellers and publishers guilds.

These regulations were enforced rigorously. Even before the issuance of formal regulations, Yamaga Sokō was banished to Akō in the 1660s for writing that Neo-Confucianism was too far removed from the ancient teaching of Confucius himself. And the frequent, severe punishments of scholars who disseminated dangerous Western ideas have been described too frequently to warrant detailed discussion here: the posthumous beheading of Takahashi Kageyasu in 1829 for translating Philipp Franz von Siebold's Western maps, for example, or the jailing of Hayashi Shihei in the 1780s for writing about the need for better national defenses.[28]

It was not, however, just elite Confucian scholars and advocates of Western learning who were punished. Writers at every level, on every topic, and in every region, were subject to the authorities' harsh thumb, as were publishers, booksellers, guild representatives, even relatives of writers. And their punishments ranged from fines and manacles to jailing, banishment, and execution. The first person known to have been punished for what he wrote in this era was the Osaka bookseller Nishimura Denbei, who was decapitated in 1649 for selling materials that referred specifically to Shogun Iemitsu.[29] Four decades later, in 1686, the storyteller Shikano Buzaemon was banished to Izu Ōshima when one of his stories sparked a rush on the Edo plum market.[30] And during the generation that followed, shogunal authorities seldom flinched when it came to punishing potentially disruptive writers. Haga Eizō, whose specialty is modern press violations, lists forty-two well-known cases in which individuals were punished during the Tokugawa years for their writings, more than a quarter of them resulting in execution or forced suicide. Offensive writings, he says, included materials about Christianity, slanders against rulers, criticisms of Tokugawa policies, and descriptions of immoral and lewd practices.[31] The literary scholar Jay Rubin notes that in 1807 even the "unimpeachably respectable" writer Takizawa Bakin and his mentor Kyōden were required "to submit an affidavit promising to eschew current events or rumors, to follow the principle of Encouraging Virtue and Chastising Vice, to concentrate on good characters such as filial children and loyal retainers, and to do their utmost to write books instructive for women and children." The two men also promised to "correct offensive sections" in what they already had written and to turn their backs on profit-driven publishers who wanted them to pander to popular tastes rather than to Confucian propriety.[32] To write, in other words, was to adjust to the heavy hand of state control. As Kyōden himself said of the harried writer: "To do a hundred deeds he thought a thousand times. He feared officials like tigers."[33]

PUBLISHING ANYWAY

But that was not the entire story. While communication students have focused on the Tokugawa authorities' activities, painting a grim era, dark with the heavy colors of control, the reality was more complex, for a remarkable outpouring of news and ideas found its way into public channels during the whole of the Tokugawa period. If British press historians wrote merely of stamp taxes and libel laws, ignoring the impressive growth of relatively unfettered newspapers in the nineteenth century, or if American scholars merely discussed publisher James Franklin's 1722 prison term and said nothing about the country's free press tradition, they would not be much farther from the truth than are the Tokugawa historians who tell us about official controls and overlook the determination of so many writers to speak out anyway.

The untold (or at least inadequately interpreted) part of the tale resides in the impressive intellectual vitality of the Tokugawa era, especially of its last century, a vitality that gives the lie to suggestions that officials were capable of keeping ideas and information in check. There were the revolutionary Western studies of Sugita Genpaku and Takashima Shūhan, for example, the outspoken and pragmatic writings of Aizawa Seishisai and Honda Toshiaki, the openly expressed chauvinism of Hirata Atsutane, the radical and widely discussed ideals of Ōshio Heihachirō and Yoshida Shōin —all of them unorthodox and all of them influential. Beginning in the 1770s, says Donald Keene, Japan "entered a new age, that of modern Japan. One finds . . . a new spirit, restless, curious and receptive."[34] Indeed, even the commoners were partaking of this spirit by the 1850s, preparing their own memorials on how the Tokugawa government should deal with the encroaching foreigners, reading and publishing satires on the increasingly inept regime.[35]

Such a spirit would not have been possible had ideas and information not been communicated widely—and over a considerable expanse of time. The German observer Engelbert Kaempfer had commented already in the 1600s that "Liberty of Conscience" was permitted in Japan, "so far as it doth not interfere with the intent of the secular Government, or affect the peace and tranquility of the Empire."[36] Those were rather sweeping caveats, susceptible to restrictive interpretations by control-bent authorities, but his observation pointed nonetheless to a world in which spirited intellectual intercourse was indeed a reality, even in the early Tokugawa decades. By 1854, when Yoshida Shōin tried to stow away to America in order to learn enough about Western ways to create a more effective resistance, it seemed quite natural for him to be talking about the need for "open channels of communication" *(kai genrō)*, for he was reflecting a longstanding stream of native thought, not merely a new idea snatched from the incoming foreigners.[37]

The first condition necessary to the communication of news and ideas is a thirst for knowledge, and from all evidence this thirst was widespread in Tokugawa Japan. Thousands of schools, ranging from the elite domain-approved institutions to local academies run by temples, merchants, and private scholars, provided not only functional literacy but an acquaintance with the ideas of leading philosophers and scholars for hundreds of thousands of Tokugawa youths. Literacy rates are hard to calculate for the nineteenth century, but Ronald Dore estimates that at the end of the Tokugawa era some 43 percent of all boys and 10 percent of the girls were getting at least some sort of schooling, and among the samurai nearly everyone was literate.[38]

Moreover, several centralizing forces heightened people's awareness of—and desire to learn more about—what was going on around Japan. The bakufu's *sankin kōtai* system forced many thousands of samurai to move back and forth between the capital and their domains each year, bringing them into contact with people from other regions of the country. Castle towns and transit networks pulled large numbers into newly flourishing urban centers, while the onrush of commercialization led to a national trade and market system (for books, among other things). The bakufu also developed a wide-ranging postal system, with couriers who rushed from Kagoshima to Hakodate. Even villagers became part of this nationalizing trend, sending their fellows to jobs in town, their children to local schools, and their products off to markets. Indeed, by the early nineteenth century, a significant sector of the rural population had become almost as politically and socially aware as their urban counterparts, turning late-Tokugawa Japan into "a metropolitan network" where commercialization had become even "more significant in the hinterland than in the city."[39]

One result of this spreading sense of interconnectedness was an ever-rising perception by people in all classes of the need for channels of communication: for means by which farmers in Tano-hata could learn techniques that had worked successfully in Kuma-moto, by which the interpreters of Nagasaki could get word about Western trends to *rangakusha* on Honshu, by which the merchants of Kanazawa could find out about prices in Osaka. Thomas Smith, in his seminal *Agrarian Origins of Modern Japan*, shows how Miya-zaki Antei's pioneering ten-volume treatise on agriculture, *Nōgyō zensho* (Agriculture encyclopedia), was read by farmers all across Japan eager to improve their agricultural skills.[40] Similarly, Peter Kornicki, a student of Tokugawa-era lending libraries, attributes the spread of eighteenth-century publishing partly to "a growing awareness of a national rather than a local identity." By the Toku-gawa midpoint, he says, Japan was experiencing "an expanding demand for information of national . . . character."[41]

Another prerequisite for the spread of communication is appropriate technology; news cannot be disseminated without ade-quate printing equipment and effective transportation methods. It thus comes as somewhat of a surprise to learn that, in some cases, old rather than new technologies were used to propel the expanding Tokugawa communication industry. The shogunate did experiment with a new technology, movable type, early in the era, using presses confiscated from the Koreans by Toyotomi Hideyoshi's invading troops in the 1590s. The imperial family had copies of the *Classic of Filial Piety* and the *Nihon shoki* (Chronicles of Japan) printed on these presses, and Ieyasu reportedly gave 300,000 pieces of wooden, movable type to the Ashikaga family to reproduce old manuscripts and had another 200,000 copper types cast in 1614.[42] But the complexity of the *kanji* (Chinese characters) used in Japanese writ-ing and the aesthetic sterility of materials produced by interchange-able type fonts disturbed most Tokugawa-era printers; so after a few years they threw out the printing presses, just as they discarded the foreign guns and religions, and shifted back to the traditional slate and woodblock techniques. At the same time, they improved transportation networks and industrial organizational structures enough to sell hundreds of thousands of copies of individual wood-block editions all across the country by the mid-1700s. And as a result, the use of modern printing techniques was delayed until another era.

NEWS FOR SALE

Reluctance about the printing press did not prevent Tokugawa intellectuals and entrepreneurs from embracing, with ever-increasing enthusiasm, one of the era's genuine innovations: the idea of selling news. The actual roots of "news" publication antedate even the Tokugawa years, with some scholars placing them far back in the tenth-century stories *(monogatari)* and miscellanies *(zuihitsu)* of the Heian court and other students finding them in the *rakushu* and *rakusho* or satirical verses that commented wryly on medieval court affairs.[43] But it was not until the Tokugawa years that Japanese actually began publishing news intentionally as a means of making profit or spreading information.

The first person to take note of this kind of human activity apparently was Arai Hakuseki, who commented in his 1715 *Seiyō kibun* (Report on the Western world) that "it is the European custom, when something happens, to record and sketch it, then to make it known to the world by setting it in print."[44] But Arai was uninformed if he thought only the Europeans published news sheets; for while his compatriots would not begin producing actual newspapers for another century and a half, they had been making a profit off certain types of printed news since the earliest Tokugawa years. The most common form of Tokugawa-era news publication —indeed, the forerunner of Japanese newspapers—was the *yomiuri* (read and sell) or *kawaraban* (slate impression), a one-page broadsheet on which Tokugawa entrepreneurs printed information about sensational, topical events for hawking and selling. The oldest known *kawaraban* dates to 1615. Apparently commissioned by Tokugawa Ieyasu himself to "influence the feudal lords" across the country and "unify Japan," it reported on the siege and destruction of the Toyotomi family's Osaka Castle by Tokugawa troops.[45] And it launched a tradition.

Even more profit-minded than their Chinese Confucian counterparts, not a few Japanese businessmen saw the commercial potential of such sheets, and by the eighteenth century they were turning out *kawaraban* after nearly every significant or unusual event. As a rule, the sheets were printed from woodblocks, but when time was of the essence, printers were known to resort to wax plates or even to slabs of *mochi* (pounded rice cakes) for their "presses." Since speed was more important than quality or accuracy and since only a few hundred copies of any given *kawaraban* were likely to be run off, crude methods sufficed.

The content often was crude too. Forerunners of the mid-Meiji "red journalism" (*yellow* journalism in the West), the broadsides were full of scandal and sensation: news of fires and assassinations, sightings of ghosts, double-love suicides, pictures of festivals and sporting events, stories about the birth of triplets, tales of volcanic eruptions and mermaid spottings—"town gossip which was usually more interesting than accurate."[46] They supplied readers, in the words of one nineteenth-century commentator, "with that highly spiced sort of intellectual nourishment supposed to be afforded now-a-days by . . . the American *Day's Doings* or *Police News.*"[47] And they did so with a flair. As a scandalized seventeenth-century observer put it: "Some fool collected contemporary gossip and printed it," after which "noisy vagrant rascals of low breeding . . . roamed through the streets and alleys of the city," calling out, "Hey, it's incredible! Hey, it's curious! Hey it's awful! Hey, it's this and that!"[48] The more dispassionate press historian Yamamoto Fumio is not much kinder. The main purpose of the *yomiuri*, he says, was to make money off the urban commoner's thirst for the curious and the salacious; so they generally fell into three categories: picture broadsides, composed mostly of flood, fire, and earthquake sketches; musical *yomiuri*, in which hawkers attracted potential buyers by singing about sexual escapades and double suicides; and miscellaneous sheets devoted to reports of vendettas and even official acts.[49]

These publications were discouraged by the authorities, who enjoined repeatedly against those who "irresponsibly print and walk around selling short songs *(kouta)* and currently fashionable things *(hayari sōrō koto)*, and reports of unusual contemporary occurrences,"[50] but enforcement was made nearly impossible by the one-time, spontaneous nature of the publications. Ono Hideo, probably the most careful student of broadsides, has catalogued no fewer than three thousand separate *kawaraban* published in the Tokugawa years;[51] indeed, in 1853–1854 alone it is estimated that a million copies of five hundred separate *kawaraban* were circulated in Edo, many of them broadcasting the arrival of Matthew Perry's black ships and giving commoners their "first detailed view of the world outside Japan."[52] And their impact was wider yet, since readers frequently sent their own copies to relatives in the provinces.

Why was it that these broadsides appeared only in Japan, of all Asian countries? The answers are too complex for this introductory sketch, but they surely lie at least partly in the highly entrepreneurial instincts of Tokugawa townspeople who saw in the packaging of "news" a chance for profit. And they are likely to be found too in the eagerness of city dwellers across the country to pay for information and print-based entertainment. The *kawaraban* were, in the jargon of journalism scholars, Japan's first attempt at "mass communication."[53]

But they were not the only attempt. Scholars have catalogued an astonishing variety of media through which Tokugawa-era Japanese told each other about things curious and important: courier networks that linked the villages of each *han* and communicated not only official decrees but political messages people wanted to get to each other;[54] streetside sermons of Buddhist priests, called *dangibon*; kabuki and puppet theater shows; shadow plays *(kage e)* and the later *kami shibai* or picture card shows, which remain popular to this day; traveling storytellers; and *tozaiya* (town criers), who advertised all manners of merchandise. During the lively Genroku era (1688–1704), singing couples *(tsurebushi)* would roam the streets, hiding if necessary behind large straw hats or folding fans, and singing to a lively beat the juicy details of some illicit love affair or of the revenge of the forty-seven *rōnin*. When the ever-vigilant morality police tried to suppress the *tsurebushi*, the same material would appear in different media, particularly *sharebon* (jokebooks) and *kibyōshi* (yellow-covered storybooks), many of which disguised their salacious material about the court or bakufu in thinly veiled stories about "the past."[55]

Perhaps the most interesting of these "news" sources were the *jitsuroku mono* and *jitsuroku-tai shosetsu*, semifictitious accounts of indiscreet events, issued in flimsy manuscripts called *shahon* (manuscript books) because their subjects were too sensitive to be published in more permanent forms. A number of *jitsuroku* were written early in the nineteenth century, for example, about the Enmeiin affair, in which an actor-turned-priest used a secret chamber at the Nichiren temple Enmeiin to seduce a number of leading ladies from the shogun's house. He was executed "as much on account of the links with the shogun's household as of his moral shortcomings,"[56] and the *jitsuroku mono* writers could not resist retelling the incident often. Such news-based tales had become commonplace by the middle of the 1700s, and the 1771 list of forbidden books published by Kyoto booksellers includes more than one hundred *jitsuroku* manuscripts.[57]

The circulation of the *jitsuroku* and other publications was stimulated by another Tokugawa-era innovation, the *kashihon'ya* or lending libraries. By the end of the eighteenth century, Japan had hundreds, perhaps thousands, of these institutions, handling not only sturdier publications such as books but, often more than anything else, *jitsuroku*-style manuscripts.[58] As Kornicki has demonstrated in meticulous research on the lending libraries, the *kashihon'ya* had spread across the entire country by the late 1700s, into small towns as well as major cities, making the news-based *shahon* available to hundreds of thousands of people—and creating the sense of regional (or countrywide) connectedness necessary for successful newspapers in a later era.[59]

It is clear then that, legal restrictions notwithstanding, even the early and middle Tokugawa years produced an abundance of communication, some of it distributed quite widely to satisfy a growing popular appetite for news about contemporary society. In addition there was an impressive volume of publishing in the realms of scholarship, religion, agriculture, children's literature, and commerce. Indeed, already by 1710, Japan boasted more than six hundred publishers and booksellers.[60] And by the early 1800s, that solid flow of printed information had turned into something of a river, with increasing numbers of literate city dwellers demanding information about happenings in the society about them. At least one bookseller in the capital's Kanda area reportedly had begun charging fees by the 1840s for his records of current events,[61] and, about the same time, the political philosopher Yokoi Shōnan had commenced denouncing traditional scholarship as "useless" because it was not tied sufficiently to contemporary "world affairs."[62] "News" about society had begun to create its own markets.

NEW WORLDS, NEW MEDIA

Then in the 1850s the inscrutable Americans and Europeans came, and the thirst of Japan's educated elite for news grew insatiable. As the centuries of isolation ended and barbarians began moving into treaty ports, a national debate ensued over how to meet the challenges, and a surging Tokugawa opposition movement turned the Edo streets into cauldrons. One result was a large increase in the distribution of varied kinds of news sheets. Unsigned, satirical lampoons in the form of *rakugai* and *rakusho* soared in number, most of them placed in easily observable spots along roads or in public squares and filled with cryptic but obvious criticisms of the trembling Tokugawa regime. They served, in the words of one press historian, as forerunners of the popular Meiji-era newspaper correspondence *(tōsho)* columns.[63] Private citizens began to publish their own *fūsetsugaki,* too, based on rumors and news bits culled from the growing foreign populations. Quite a number of the keepers of Edo's daimyo castles also began to publish news about their lords' comings and goings.[64] And the number of *kawaraban* multiplied, many of them delving for the first time into satire and direct political criticism.

The new atmosphere also prompted the bakufu to revise its own policies regarding news, to begin a series of moves that finally would bring Japan its first *shimbun* or newspapers. First, the shogunate intensified efforts to secure news for itself. As leading officials came into increasing contact with the West, particularly after missions began traveling abroad in 1860, they talked more and more about how important it was to know what was going on elsewhere as well as about the social and political potential of news. In 1861, foreign office secretary Oguri Tadamasa returned from the first official mission to the United States determined that Japan must create a newspaper like those he had seen abroad.[65] And three years later another *gaikoku bugyō* (foreign office secretary), Ikeda Nagaoki, came back from France with a detailed report for his superiors that one scholar has labeled Japan's "earliest attribution of social value to news." He explained how papers could help a government "learn of conditions among the public" and serve as tools to explain Japanese positions abroad.[66]

At a slightly lower level, young bakufu translators such as Fukuchi Gen'ichirō and Fukuzawa Yukichi professed themselves amazed by the speed and the social impact of newspapers they saw in the United States and Europe. "I learned just how powerful a newspaper could be in shaping public opinion about domestic and foreign political issues," recalled Fukuchi regarding his trip to Europe in 1865, when he was just twenty-five. He was sure Japan needed its own papers; he even wondered, presciently, whether he might "become a newspaper reporter" himself.[67] And Fukuzawa returned from his first foreign trip reporting newspapers to be the best instruments he ever had encountered "for exposing what is seen and heard . . . and for studying the ways of the world."[68]

Prodded thus by domestic crisis and foreign pressures (as well as by foreign models), bakufu officials decided to reorganize their translation bureau in 1855 and rename it Yōgakujo or Institute for Western Studies. Then a year later they renamed it again, this time calling it the Bansho Shirabesho or Office for Studying Barbarian Writings. The purpose of the name changes was to highlight the

central aim of the reshaped office—namely, the increasingly extensive translation of Western newspapers into Japanese. The urgency
of this task was heightened in 1857 when the Dutch stopped sending their regular reports from Nagasaki on the state of the world.
They offered instead to send European newspapers themselves, and
the result was the development, over the next half dozen years, of a
full-fledged government effort to gather foreign news.

At the heart of this operation were more than thirty scholars
hired by the Bansho Shirabesho to translate important articles from
the leading English, Dutch, and French newspapers into Japanese.
Typically, one person would translate a piece orally; a secretary
would transcribe it, and the institute would have the article set into
wooden type and published for officials to read. Officials also began
looking to the fiefs themselves for information on the West, order-
ing each daimyo to "report all Western literature owned by the
clan, including titles, publishing data, and subject matter."[69] By the
late 1850s, news of what was happening in the West had become
crucial to national survival, and the Tokugawa had become serious
about securing it.

The focus of this newsgathering remained almost exclusively
on foreign affairs until 1863, when the brilliant young linguist
Yanagawa Shunsan (1832–1870) entered the bureau and its name
was changed to Kaiseijo (literally, Office to Carry Out the Opening).
After British and American attacks on Satsuma and Chōshū that
summer, Japan's domestic mood changed. The xenophobic popular
mood of the previous decade abated in the face of overwhelming
Western military strength, and its place was taken by a rapidly
spreading, increasingly virulent anti-Tokugawa spirit among Edo's
young zealots. What was worse for the government, those sentiments were being adopted now by growing numbers of scholars and
han leaders, people capable of effecting genuine revolution. As a
result, the bakufu ordered translators to begin paying more attention to news about domestic activities. Ironically, Kaiseijo translators still had to rely on Western newspapers, even for this task,
since the myriad *kawaraban, rakushu,* and ballads were hardly to
be trusted for reliable news, and Japan had no dependable news publications—or reporters—of its own.

The bureau thus began to turn out abridged translations of
entire issues of several Dutch and English-language papers. The prototype for this activity had come in 1860, when the office produced
the *Kanhan Batabia Shimbun,* a collection of excerpts of key articles from the foreign news columns of the Dutch *Javasche Courant,*

published on the island of Java. Although the series lasted just two months, it holds a secure place in Japanese history as the country's first sustained news publication. After Yanagawa's arrival, the Kaiseijo took on the newspaper compilation task in earnest. From May 13, 1863, until May 24, 1865,[70] the bureau published 107 issues of a journal taken primarily from the *Japan Commercial News,* which it called *Nihon Bōeki Shimbun.* When the *Commercial News* stopped publishing, the bureau produced *Nihon Shimbun,* based on *The Japan Times,*[71] and then, after September 30, 1865, it published the *Japan Herald*–based *Nihon Shimbun Gaihen* for exactly a year. During this time, the Kaiseijo also translated excerpts from several papers published by missionaries in south China, under names such as *Chūgai Shinpō, Hong Kong Shimbun,* and *Chūgai Zasshi.*[72] While these publications hardly could have been called newspapers, they gave to Japan its first examples of news published on a regular, ongoing basis. And while only specially placed officials were permitted to read them initially, this development meant that at least a few Japanese now were able to keep in touch regularly with the exploding domestic and international political scene—and a few bright young translators were inspired to dream of new communication possibilities in the private sphere.

Indeed, one of the most significant developments in the communications field from the 1850s onward was the government's loosening of restrictions on private news channels and the resultant creation of Japan's first nongovernmental news sheets. After the coming of Perry's Black Ships, it became clearer by the year that the Tokugawa no longer could control the flow of news systematically. So the shogunate began to focus more on accumulating its own sources and less on controlling those of others. In the very year of Perry's arrival, for example, the government decided to allow the keepers of the Edo daimyo estates to copy the Dutch *fūsetsugaki* for transmission to their own fiefs.[73] About the same time, officials also permitted members of several progressive *han* to create a Shimbun Kai (Newspaper Society) in which they would gather for monthly readings from the Dutch reports and discussions of their implications for Japan.[74] And when the Kaiseijo started turning out more translations after the mid-1860s, the financially strapped bakufu even began to allow ordinary citizens to subscribe to its "newspapers." The *Nihon Shimbun Gaihen,* for example, was offered to readers for two *bu* every six months. Issues were loaned, not sold, and anyone not returning a paper within a day after receiving it was fined, "except in the case of older papers that already have circulated for more than a month."[75] To subscribe, readers had to "join" the Kaiseijo formally.

Not surprisingly, this relaxation in bakufu policies prompted important changes in Japan's private news world. No longer would *kawaraban* and *rakushu* be the sole source of published news. Though most Japanese entrepreneurs remained wary of the idea of printing news on a regular basis, one or two decided to try their hands, and several foreigners began publishing papers, too, giving Japan its first privately produced newspapers. The very first nongovernmental paper written and published in Japan was the *Nagasaki Shipping List and Advertiser*, a two-page semiweekly sheet launched in 1861 by the Englishman Albert W. Hansard, a grocer who earlier had published the *Southern Cross* in New Zealand. Like the other foreign papers of the decade, it was printed in English, primarily for the benefit of the newly arrived Western merchants. Its content, however, was rich. Going beyond the trade lists that would serve as the staple of most early English-language papers, it attempted to introduce Japanese culture to the expatriate community.[76] After twenty-eight issues, Hansard moved to Yokohama and took his paper with him, changing its name to *The Japan Herald* and hiring a young businessman named John Reddie Black as its editor. Black, on his way home to Scotland after having failed in an Australian trading venture, had planned only a short stay in Yokohama. But the job and the place suited him, so he stayed to become one of Meiji Japan's foremost foreign journalists and the author of *Young Japan*, a two-volume, often-quoted description of life in the lively new capital.[77]

The *Herald*, which would itself endure until the end of the Meiji era, was joined soon by other English-language papers in Yokohama. The *Japan Express* was published in 1862 by an American grocer, Raphael Schoyer, who, in the view of one French diplomat, tailored his news to stimulate American profits.[78] The following year, in May 1863, a third paper came out. Named *The Japan Commercial News* and published by a Macao-born Portuguese, F. da Roza, it appeared on Wednesdays and concentrated on shipping lists. Press historian Ono Hideo speculates that it carried more domestic news than either the *Herald* or the *Express*, however, since it was the local paper chosen first for translations by the Kaiseijo. Unfortunately, it lasted a mere two months.[79]

When da Roza decided to sell the *Commercial News*, Charles Rickerby, a British banker with a flare for salesmanship, bought the printing equipment and launched Japan's first "sensational" newspaper, the *Japan Times*. Sometimes driving authorities to distraction with his free-wheeling approach, he ran exposés of the sultry activities of prominent port-town residents and publicized a call by the neophyte British embassy interpreter Ernest Satow in 1867 for the shogun to resign.[80] After the Satow incident, the Kaiseijo decided to stop translating the *Times* and to patronize the *Herald* instead, in the process triggering a *Herald-Times* rivalry that would enliven Japanese journalism until long after the *Japan Mail* had bought out the *Times* in January 1870. As Black commented, editor Rickerby "was a most capable individual but lacked finesse." He suggested that if Rickerby's "tact" had been "equal to his talent, the *Japan Times* might have become a power in the land; for, without question, it was well written and had excellent sources of information."[81] The residents of the Yokohama treaty port saw their news menu enriched still further in 1867, when Black decided, with the financial encouragement of several Western businessmen, to leave the *Herald* and start his own paper, the *Japan Gazette*. Calling it "the first attempt in Yokohama to furnish a daily paper with current news," he gave the Westerners the closest approach yet to a full-fledged newspaper and, as a result, enjoyed a "liberal measure of public support."[82]

The long and short of this sketch is that when the Tokugawa fell at the beginning of 1868, Japan already had a vigorous English-language press, with a dozen different newspapers and journals having made their appearance in Nagasaki, Hyōgo, Kanagawa, and Yokohama.[83] Few could boast more than a hundred subscribers; the majority lasted no more than a year; and their history remains essentially outside the sphere of this study, since their long-range impact on the development of Japan's domestic press was peripheral. They were important nonetheless, because they served as Japan's first ongoing newspapers—and because they became one of the most important windows for Tokugawa officials on the international events of the day and, to a degree, even on the rapidly changing domestic situation. And their role as models was crucial too. Seeing them and their potential for shaping policy, several Japanese were inspired to consider journalism as personal careers. They were, in a genuine sense, pioneer papers.[84]

It seems a bit surprising that very few Tokugawa-era Japanese were interested in following these Westerners into the world of the press, given the apparent financial success of many *kawaraban* and the growing public interest in the *bakumatsu* political world. One reason for the reticence probably lies in the rejection two centuries earlier of movable type; broadsides were easy to produce quickly with woodblocks; whole newspapers were not. Another is that while Tokugawa control policies may not have prevented thousands of efforts to sell "news" in *yomiuri*, ballads, and *jitsuroku*, they had precluded the development of a class of people who saw news dissemination on a regular basis as potential careers. Therefore, most of the pre-Meiji publishers of newspaper-style publications were foreigners. It is significant, however, that there were two exceptions, Japanese men with strong ties to Westerners or to the English-language newspapers, men who defied precedents and gave at least a few Edoites a taste of Japanese-language journalism during the waning Tokugawa years.

The first of these, Hamada Hikozō (1837–1897), had been shipwrecked while fishing in 1850, rescued by an American ship crew, and taken to California, where he took the name Joseph Heco. After converting to Christianity and becoming a U.S. citizen, he returned to Japan early in the 1860s as a diplomatic interpreter and opened an import-export business in Yokohama. Heco worked quietly at first, cautious about the highly charged antiforeign atmosphere. But after the xenophobia had passed its peak, he decided to begin acquainting his fellow-countrymen with Western ways through a regular news publication and so launched Japan's first native-language newspaper, the biweekly *Shimbunshi*, later renamed *Kaigai Shimbun*, in the spring of 1864.

To produce each issue, Heco, who had learned coarse Japanese in his childhood fishing village, prepared rough translations from British newspapers on the ships that docked regularly now in Yokohama, and two learned associates, Kishida Ginkō and Honma Senzō, polished the pieces into smooth Japanese. The articles then would be carved onto woodblocks, printed, and hand-delivered throughout Yokohama by Kishida, Honma, and Heco themselves. The paper attracted only about a hundred readers and survived for just twenty-four issues. It contained no news about Japan, forced as it was to draw exclusively on the foreign papers. But it was the first Japanese-language paper produced by and for private individuals on a continuing basis, and thus is typically evaluated by press historians as an important "step toward the rise of a modern domestic press."[85] It also was important in introducing Kishida to the world of journalism. A boarder and English student at the home of the missionary linguist Joseph Hepburn, he never had heard of newspapers prior to his encounters with Heco. But convinced by Heco and the *Kaigai Shimbun* of the potential "profitability of newspapers," he decided that someday he would try his own hand at publishing—a decision that would have great import for the world of Japanese journalism only a few years hence.[86]

Even more important were the contributions of the preeminent Kaiseijo translator Yanagawa Shunsan. The son of a Nagoya tool salesman, Yanagawa gained a childhood reputation for his skill at calligraphy, then at age nineteen, two years before Perry's arrival, published a manual on Western artillery, and half a decade later, in 1857, followed his ambitions to Edo, where a promising future seemed to beckon anyone who knew the tongues and ways of the West. He attracted attention quickly for his prolific translations of Dutch, French, and English writings into Japanese, reputedly at thirty times the speed of most other translators.[87] Then, in 1863, he entered the Kaiseijo and, almost at once, became a committed journalist, the man, in Ono's words, "who first introduced newspaper and magazine culture" to his countrymen.[88]

Yanagawa's genius was that he did more than translate news. He seems from the first to have sensed the inherent power of information. For that reason, in addition to preparing his Kaiseijo translations, he put together his own in-house paper at the Kaiseijo, pushing his colleagues beyond translation and into recording the events, intrigues, and personalities that were shaping life in this changing city. Calling his sheet the *Shimbun Kaisō* (Rich thicket of news), he sought his coworkers' assistance in compiling, both for bureau insiders and for posterity, as much of the news-behind-the-news as they could garner. As he wrote:

> Because my colleagues at the translation bureau have such a large circle of acquaintances, they have many opportunities to get scoops. Yet it is not uncommon for them to forget what they have learned, either because of neglect or because they do not write things down. So I have put a notebook in the office in which anyone may write down anything notable that he sees or hears. Information thus recorded will not be lost. I ask them to observe three rules when they do this.
>
> 1. Every news item is to be recorded, no matter how trivial—even gossip.
>
> 2. Anyone who has time is urged to participate in the project. Articles written separately, on other sheets of paper, may be pasted in the notebook itself at the bureau.
>
> 3. The notebook may be read, or even copied, by anyone. It is not, however, to be taken from the bureau.[89]

The *Shimbun Kaisō* was printed in four volumes, from 1865 until the Meiji Restoration, and was filled with the kinds of fresh, often confidential materials that journalists pride themselves on seeking, everything from the daily comings and goings of Edo society to reports on secret meetings between the French ambassador Léon Roches and bakufu officials.[90]

The *Shimbun Kaisō* hardly could be called a newspaper, intended as it was for official eyes only; it was more like a set of minutes. But Yanagawa's newsgathering approach revealed something significant: the mind of a man often called Japan's first true journalist. As if to prove that point, he undertook two years later, in 1867, to publish the first news-oriented magazine of the Tokugawa era, the monthly *Seiyō Zasshi*. Like most of the era's domestic news sheets, it had a short life—just half a year. But it too showed a bona fide journalistic spirit. As the company announcement in the first issue put it, "The purpose of this publication is to disseminate all the interesting news that can be gathered from the magazines *(magasein)* of Western countries."[91] The periodical contained material on the relationship between education and national wealth, the German standard of living, the discovery of aluminum, the state of the Dutch monarchy, and a translation of a history of the development of chemistry. It was, in short, a full-fledged news medium, which survived longer than any Japanese-language news medium to date.

READY FOR THE MODERN ERA

When the Tokugawa government fell on January 3, 1868, the news was reported widely to an urban population whose taste for information about contemporary society had risen significantly over the previous decade. Unfortunately, however, it had to be spread largely by word of mouth, by official decree, and by foreign publications, since Yanagawa's monthly *Seiyō Zasshi* was the only Japanese-published journal still alive. The *Kaigai Shimbun* had been dead three years, and the only newspapers being published for private citizens were English-language sheets such as the *Herald* and the *Gazette,* and the foreign-published *Bankoku Shimbun,* all produced in Yokohama. Japanese journalism was incubating; it can even be said to have been in the delivery room, but at the onset of the new era it had not yet been born.

Even in these late-bakufu years, however, several contours of a distinctly Japanese approach to the dissemination of news had become apparent. For one thing, nearly all agree that the Tokugawa years brought to maturity ideas and policies that would dominate the government's (and writers') approach to press control right up until World War II. At the heart of this approach lay the Neo-Confucian attitudes toward authority. Robert Bellah has argued that the "primary concern" of individuals in Tokugawa Japan was to serve "the system goal," to be faithful to "the particular system or collectivity of which one [was] a member"—hence "the enormous importance of loyalty . . . to the head of one's collectivity."[92] And intellectual historian Tetsuo Najita says the "central political legacy" of the era was "bureaucratism," which served to "sanction loyal bureaucratic action" and to give individuals "an awareness of . . . necessary limitations imposed by normative structures."[93] These values asserted that the key duty of all educated individuals was to serve society as a whole, to lead and teach others what was necessary for the creation of a stable, wholesome order. Thus, those who wrote tended to be checked automatically by an internal control mechanism. There simply was no intellectual tradition to suggest a clash between individual rights and the needs of the broader society. Even Najita's nineteenth-century "restorationists," or revolutionaries, acted in behalf of the greater political good, for the sake of "institutional utility."[94] Even they saw themselves as "true loyalists," and they fought the existing regime not to establish a new order but to perfect the old, eternal one. Thus it seems safe to conclude that the single most important control mechanism bequeathed to modern Japan by the Tokugawa experience was not so much any particular set of rules or structures but a mindset that put the good of the system above the interest of the individual. This deep-seated commitment to the established order may not have rendered regulations unnecessary, but it certainly made them easier to enforce.

The era also produced specific rules about communicating that would serve as the fundamental models for later press control laws: self-policing patterns enforced through guilds and mutual surveillance groups, proscriptions of all materials deemed likely to create social instability or to endanger either the existing order or the ruling class, the right of censors to suppress materials arbitrarily and without explanation or recourse to law, the use of sellers and distributors as a means of control, the right to suspend publication and directly punish offending writers and publishers, even the practice of lecturing and warning offenders about proper behavior and social responsibility. The rise of newspapers in the early-Meiji years would require many specific modifications and innovations in information-control laws. But the patterns were set by the Tokugawa state. As Haga Eizō comments, in a bit of hyperbole, the Tokugawa "era of fear" *(kyōfu jidai)* was simply a precursor to Meiji's "era of excess" *(kado jidai).*[95]

Yet, as we have seen, control was not the only Tokugawa legacy. At least as significant was the determination of thousands of persons to make their views known anyway, regardless of persecution and harassment. The regime's widely enforced publication restrictions may have made the broadside publishers and roadside satirists seem to later scholars more like annoying gnats than like fundamental threats to the regime. But clearly, by the nineteenth century, both iconoclastic thinkers and news conveyors constituted a significant, sometimes-threatening element in the national political body. And they gave rise to an energetic, if spotty, system of information gathering that in turn inculcated several of modern Japan's most important journalistic features.

First, the early attempts to translate Western papers bore evidence to an impressive elite awareness of the crucial role that information plays in a well-functioning society. This awareness was not simply a Western import. The early-Tokugawa system of censors, *fūsetsugaki,* and runners proves that. But the alacrity with which the bakufu took up the translations of foreign papers suggests that once the Western presence reached a certain mass, the leaders' comprehension of the importance of news grew dramatically. And that understanding would in its turn undergird many of the policies of their Meiji successors. Similarly, the pragmatism of *bakumatsu* officials in making the Kaiseijo translations available to a broader public once it was clear that the information stream no longer could be controlled hints at the realism of Meiji authorities, which prompted an often-contorted, yet relatively effective process of revising press regulations every few years. "Men of ability" apparently were adept, even in the Tokugawa years, at tightening screws only to the degree that was politically sensible.

Another late-Tokugawa legacy was the overwhelming establishment orientation of the bakumatsu writers who gravitated toward journalism. There may have been an incipient populism in the love stories and satire of the *kawaraban* and in many of the *shahon,* but for some reason the writers of those genres did not follow the Western editors into journalism. They kept making money on their occasional broadsides and titillating ballads, but they steered clear of systematic news publishing. Those who did try their hands at newspapering in the *bakumatsu* years, the Yanagawas and the Kishidas, were Confucian-educated public servants who felt a responsibility to educate their contemporaries. And the audience they envisioned was not so much a "public" as their fellow officials and educated opinion shapers, the people they thought most capable of guiding Japan into the new era. Thus, their prose was classical and hard to read, their content was elitist (foreign politics, scientific developments, essays on government, official regulations, the comings and goings of ships), and their circulations remained minuscule. Such elitism was hardly surprising, given the newness of their enterprise and the Neo-Confucian education these men (and they were all men) had received. But it is significant nevertheless; for the establishment orientation would persist well into the next century, uniquely shaping the interactions between the Meiji press and the broader public or *minshū*.

The years from Perry to Meiji thus marked a time of transition. If the first two and a half Tokugawa centuries had provided a tenuous balance between authoritarian control and the stubborn refusal of many private individuals to keep quiet, the final decade and a half brought into its own an important new idea: that the dissemination of information was one of the most important agenda items for any modern society. Seeing this trend, members of the elite both inside and outside the government began to create something without precedent in Japan, a news establishment. It was a tiny establishment when Tokugawa Keiki announced his intention to resign as shogun late in 1867, but its members included enough men of talent and vision to suggest something important afoot. With the dawning of the new era and the onrush of civil war, conditions would be ripe for the emergence of Japan's first modern-style press, the beginnings of a new bridge between the official world and a soon-to-expand "public."

CHAPTER 2

COMING INTO BEING
1868

> In prosperous regions where newspapers
> flourish, you can learn the strange
> stories and marvelous tales of far distant
> places, even while sitting at home.
>
> *Moshiogusa, June 1, 1868*

Seldom does real life give historians undisputed markers for organizing the past into chronological categories. The battle at Sekiga-
hara in October 1600, for example, seems at first glance to provide a
clear starting point for the Tokugawa era, but specialists have spent
careers arguing whether the new era really began then, or in 1603
when Ieyasu became shogun, or in 1598 when Toyotomi Hideyoshi
died, or even decades later when Tokugawa control was indisputable. So too with January 3, 1868, the day of the Meiji Restoration.
The palace coup provides a convenient milepost, especially useful
for undergraduate tests on modern Japanese history. But did Japan's
new era really begin then, or in 1853 when Perry's Black Ships
arrived, or earlier in the century when the Tokugawa regime came
under increasingly vociferous attacks? Some even start the "modern" era in the 1870s, after the Meiji leadership issue was settled, or
in 1889, with the promulgation of the Meiji Constitution.

But if even the clearest dates often are slippery, there is at
least general agreement among those seeking the origins of Japan's
modern press. The spring of 1868—a season that saw the new Meiji
leaders struggling to eradicate their opposition and take firm hold of

the state apparatus—produced a transition so dramatic in Japan's communications world that scholars unanimously cite it as the beginning point of the country's modern press. "Faction breeds print," says British press historian Anthony Smith;[1] and so it did in the Edo of 1868. Incited by political passions and driven by a desire to make information available about what was occurring on the battlefields, more than a dozen cerebral, mostly young samurai decided to start producing their own news publications. The sheets they put out were the first quasi-modern "newspapers" most Japanese, even within the elite, had seen.

None of the Restoration papers proved lasting. The longest-lived, Yanagawa Shunsan's *Chūgai Shimbun,* stayed in print for only four and a half months, from March 17 to July 27, issuing a total of forty-five issues; *Tōzai Shimbun* survived just twelve days and four issues in early July; and the shortest-lived of all, *Fūka Shimbun,* came out but once.[2] Neither did they appear daily or with absolute regularity. Small staffs and the time required to carve woodblocks precluded that. Nor did they look like newspapers as we know them. Instead, they resembled small books or pamphlets filled with a miscellany of opinion and "news." But they were Japan's first genuine attempts at what today we define as newspapers: privately produced publications containing both news and opinion, issued on a regular, continuing basis for a public audience. For this reason, historians are unanimous in seeing in them the first real prototypes of Japan's modern press.[3]

PASSIONATE EDITORS

The editors of these Restoration papers had two quite different sources of inspiration: foreign models and domestic crisis. Most of them got the idea of editing at least in part from their own acquaintance with the Western press, both at home and abroad. *Kōko Shimbun* editor Fukuchi Gen'ichirō, for example, had translated Western newspapers for the bakufu foreign office *(gaikoku bugyō)* as a teenager and, as we have seen, had marveled during his 1865 trip to France at "how powerful a newspaper could be in shaping public opinion," deciding then and there that he would publish his own newspaper some day.[4] Yanagawa, similarly, encountered newspapers at the Kaiseijo, as did quite a number of the other editors of that spring's new papers. And Kishida Ginkō, who launched *Yokohama Shinpō Moshiogusa* on June 1, 1868, had never heard of newspapers until Joseph Heco told him "about a thing in America called a 'newspaper' (*shimbunshi*), which pulled together each day's happenings and all of society's strange events and disseminated them to the public."[5]

As important as those foreign models were, however, they were not the primary reason so many news sheets came into existence in the spring of 1868. Even more important was the domestic situation. We already have seen how the news-for-profit *kawaraban* tradition and the growing popular desire for information after Matthew Perry's arrival inspired only two Japanese, Yanagawa and Heco, to create publications of their own. What seemed to be lacking was a cause, some issue that would impel others like them to seek a tool for communicating with fellow countrymen. The Meiji Restoration provided that inducement. The replacement of the bakufu with a group of young officials whose legitimacy and control were shaky at best, men who had not yet devised ways to control communication channels, provided new stimuli and fresh opportunities, and launched a period in which young samurai with a sense of mission could write without having to worry much about official supervision. The special conditions of that period did not last long, but for a few months they allowed a "public" of several thousand educated urbanites to read, for the first time, politically oriented, privately printed news sheets.

All told, about twenty Restoration papers and several official gazettes came out during the spring and summer of 1868,[6] the dominant ones being Yanagawa's *Chūgai Shimbun*; the *Naigai Shinpō* of Hashizume Kana'ichi, which published fifty issues; Fukuchi's *Kōko Shimbun*; and the *Ochikochi Shimbun* of Tsuji Shinji. None of the papers had large circulations by today's standards. Yanagawa claimed that *Chūgai* "had reached a circulation of 1,500" by the end of its first month, but the scholarly consensus is that he was counting the total number of issues published that month, which would have given the paper a still-impressive circulation of about two hundred subscribers per issue.[7] By his own testimony, each of the paper's first eight issues sold out and had to be reprinted.[8] The circulation for most of the other papers seems to have been similar or smaller. In format, the papers looked more like pamphlets than what we think of as newspapers today. They were octavo (book-page) in size, printed on a relatively cheap grade of rice paper, and ran about a dozen pages per issue. *Naigai Shinpō* came out daily most of the time, *Chūgai Shimbun* and *Kōko Shimbun* every two or three days, and most of the rest less frequently.[9] The content was overwhelmingly political.

The first thing that strikes one on reading these sheets has to be the passion with which the editors wrote. When Tokugawa Keiki had asked his supporters not to resist the new regime in February, many of them had been dismayed, even outraged, at the idea that a centuries-old regime would capitulate so easily. So when some of the Tokugawa followers defied Keiki and took up arms against the new government, a few others decided that they would fight with words; they would create *shimbunshi* in which they could use battles as the grist for news and enmity as the stimulus for editorials. There were, of course, a few pro-Meiji papers (the government's own gazette or *Dajōkan Nisshi*, the *Naigai Shimbun* in Osaka, and the *Tohi Shimbun* in Kyoto),[10] but most of the editors hated the new regime viscerally—and their news columns and essays alike reflected that fact.

Battle reports from the Boshin War between the Meiji army and recalcitrant Tokugawa supporters, for example, formed the core of the papers' news, and with few exceptions the stories described Meiji defeats and Tokugawa victories, sometimes even when the facts warranted a different report. The papers also printed government decrees and edicts, memorials to the new officials, pleading the Tokugawa loyalist cause, and essays criticizing new administration policies. Sometimes, they branched into less political news, including gossipy items about the entertainment world, commercial notes, and translations from the English-language papers about developments abroad. But for the most part they focused on domestic politics, on the war-related issues that had called them into being in the first place.

Moshiogusa alone defied this highly political approach, and though it was small and made hardly a ripple in Edo, it set precedents for later Japanese newspapers that demand notice. Published in Yokohama by Kishida and the swashbuckling Pennsylvania businessman Eugene M. Van Reed, its primary purpose was commercial. Kishida had not been able wholly to chill the newspaper fever that had infected him during the *Kaigai Shimbun* months, and during the Restoration struggles he jumped back into journalism, using Van Reed's standing as a treaty port foreigner to provide protection from authorities but doing all the editing and managing himself.[11] The paper's first issue described newspapers as "extremely profitable things" and promised to provide a full menu of both domestic and foreign news, proclaiming a desire to bring to Japan the kind of "flourishing newspapers" that graced other "civilized countries."[12] Although the first issue also promised at least ten papers a month, Kishida apparently was too busy with his other commercial and publishing ventures to deliver quite that much. In reality, *Moshio-gusa* averaged about two issues a month during its two-year life, publishing forty-two times altogether and never gaining much more than a hundred subscribers. Nonetheless, as the sole Restoration editor to publish for purely commercial reasons, the only one who took no particular political stand, Kishida has been called the pioneer of commercial journalism, a "people's teacher" *(sekenshi)* who established the first link between newspapers and commoners.[13] He also published Japan's first newspaper cartoon, in *Moshiogusa*'s sixteenth issue.

FORERUNNERS OF A MODERN PRESS

If their political orientation made most of the Restoration editors genuine forebears of the later, mainstream press, so did several other, quite specific features of their small springtime journals. For one thing, each one of these editors exhibited a self-conscious determination to reach as wide an audience as possible—and for that reason gave his paper a highly public flavor. We already have seen how, in the early 1860s, Oguri Tadamasa and Ikeda Nagaoki introduced the idea of using papers to bring the government's views to the people and how Fukuchi and Fukuzawa came back from Europe talking about the social and political impact of the presses there. But the pre-Restoration writers themselves had had little to say about the potential public utility of a press; they wrote for the rulers, and largely just for the rulers. Now, however, with new reasons for publishing, the Restoration editors gave not only lip service but genuine attention to a broader range of readers.

Chūgai Shimbun, for example, ran a foreigner's letter contending that "whenever the government is just and the people civilized, newspapers will flourish." *Soyofuku Kaze* noted that news was valuable to "widen one's knowledge."[14] *Kōko Shimbun* made much of the fact that its articles would be written not just for the elites but "for women and children" to read,[15] as did Kishida, who noted in his diary that he tried to write so that "even a farmer can read."[16] Even the new Meiji government, which countered the Restoration press with no fewer than a dozen *nisshi* or newsbook-style gazettes, announced in the *Dajōkan Nisshi* that it sought both "high and low" readers, that in order for announcements to have "practical expression" it was important that *everyone* "respectfully receive them."[17]

One of the more impressive efforts to reach a broader public came at *Naigai Shinpō,* where editor Hashizume published an appendix, called "*Naigai Shinpō* Jisū" (Glossary to *Naigai Shinpō*), intended to help poorly educated readers understand the characters used in each issue.[18] Something, it seems, had happened to make both the government and its opponents aware of the necessity of gaining support from a larger segment of the populace than before. The audience these writers had in mind still was small; phrases such as "even a farmer" and "even women and children" were frequently hyperbolic and always patronizing. But for those inside the intellectual and official establishment actually to be discussing a need to reach a wider public suggested a sea change in the elite mindset, a change with implications not only for the press but for Japan itself.

A pathbreaking characteristic of these months was the emergence of true and sustained advocacy journalism. In contrast to the *yomiuri* and *kawaraban* publishers, the Restoration editors had little interest in profit. Nor were they interested in serving, Kaiseijo style, as pure information channels. Their goal was political. Japan was split asunder in 1868, and like Milton in *Areopagitica* and James Franklin in the *Courant,* the Restoration writers wanted most of all to make a public case about what they saw as the illegitimacy of the new regime. As Kishida described it, their purpose was to "undertake a verbal war, with each editor expressing his own political opinions."[19]

Yanagawa was typical. He used the very first issue Of *Chūgai Shimbun,* on March 17, to argue that the Tokugawa had been the repository of true loyalty to the emperor and to attack the officials in the new government as usurpers, calling the Meiji administration an arbitrary creation based not on the loyalty about which its founders talked so glibly but on a bald grab for power by men from Satsuma and Chōshū (Satchō). "There is no reason for the regional lords to submit to them," he argued.[20] The very purpose of *Chūgai,* says historian Ono Hideo, was to "satisfy his grudges," one against the Meiji usurpers, the other against the Tokugawa decision not to fight.[21] Some papers carried their crusade so far as to make up erroneous stories about imperial army defeats.[22] A tiny paper, *Fūka Shimbun,* immediately found itself in hot water with the authorities for running a poem in the classical style *(waka)* vilifying the government. And so many of the other papers lampooned the new government with cartoons, letters, and essays that the British diplomat Ernest Satow was prompted to quip about how the Restoration papers were filled with "as much forgery of memorials, manifestoes and correspondence as in any other part of the world in a time of political excitement." He thought they also contained "a great number of interesting political documents."[23]

The most blatant and influential single example of press advocacy was Fukuchi's ringing eight-page editorial "Kyōjaku ron" (On strength and weakness), which appeared in *Kōko Shimbun* on June 24. The twenty-seven-year-old Fukuchi loathed the new government, signaling that fact first by naming his company Tori Naki Sato Zappō Kyoku, a play on the proverb "A one-eyed person rules in the land of the blind." From the initial issue, *Kōko Shimbun* had supported the Tokugawa cause; now, in the sixteenth issue, Fukuchi gathered his considerable debating skills to prove that the Satsuma and Chōshū forces were incapable of ruling a unified Japan. He went so far as to urge a new "representative government" led by a "great hero" from the Tokugawa family.[24] The editorial hit so hard that the new rulers threw Fukuchi in jail (an act to be discussed later), but it illustrated the determination of these new journalists to use their papers as platforms. Surely none of them had heard of the Irish politician Richard Brinsley Sheridan's irritated remark "Give me but the liberty of the press and I will give to the minister a . . . servile House of Commons."[25] But the idea of using a private print medium to fight an existing regime openly and consistently—an approach without precedent in pre-Tokugawa Japan—had taken root with a speed that would have been deemed impossible just months earlier.

Another characteristic of the Restoration press was the surprising degree of freedom its writers experienced in expressing their views. For a few months during the first half of 1868, the new government had neither the policies, the machinery, nor the degree of control necessary to enforce Tokugawa-style regulations. The relaxed atmosphere combined with the partisan commitment of the Hashizumes and the Yanagawas to give Japan its first free-press era. Although the new government had announced in January that "the good features of the traditional Tokugawa system and its laws will be left unchanged,"[26] little official attention was paid to the press' fulminations until June 18, about three months after *Chūgai's* launching.[27] What was more, a new approach to publication had at least been suggested in the Charter Oath, calling for "all measures" to "be decided by open discussion."[28] That meant that, throughout the spring, the angry, pro-Tokugawa samurai were left relatively unchecked to argue their cases. That was why Yanagawa could write in his paper's twelfth issue on May 22 that if the administration "wants people to follow the government, it must gather views widely, from throughout the nation, being careful not to bind itself to a single view."[29] This freedom was short-lived, but the vigor with which advocacy journalism burst forth along with the season's azaleas suggested not only a lively era to come but a vigorous native tradition of expressing one's own mind. Smith has noted that most of Europe's nineteenth-century nationalist movements began not on battlefields but in newspapers founded "to express a certain set of expectations of the nature of the new civic life."[30] He could have been speaking of early-Meiji Edo.

This determination to speak was not, however, a particularly populist phenomenon. At its core was a more conservative characteristic of the Restoration papers: a thoroughgoing national, in many ways establishment, orientation. Studies by Ronald Dore and many others have shown that the fundamental aim of Tokugawa-era education was to prepare youths for public service, to inculcate the Confucian idea that education should equip one primarily to lead others for the good of the larger society. Hence, Yamaji Aizan's declaration: "I love politics, I adore politics. . . . My fate is bound up with the fate of the Japanese nation."[31] All the young Restoration editors were reared in that tradition; and all of them wrote for a single overriding purpose: to create a better, stronger Japan wholly loyal to the emperor. They may have harbored personal ambitions; they were, after all, human beings. But their zeal was focused on the nation, at least as much so as that of the new leaders. Most of these opposition editors had left their own *han* during the *bakumatsu* years to join the Tokugawa bureaucracy and thus to serve the country as a whole, while many of the new Meiji leaders had continued to work within their own then-rebellious fiefs. So it was for the sake of the "nation" that these journalists railed against the new order. This is the reason that Yanagawa, in his May call for "gathering views widely," also asserted that "Japan must be forever independent." "It dare not submit to other countries," he wrote. "If Japan desires to remain free, it must foster adequate national strength." He even called for people to "follow the government" and to foster national unity. It was merely the current administrators, the impostors, whom he regarded as untrustworthy and thus in need of removal.[32] Similarly, Kishida declared at *Moshiogusa:* "If we want always to keep Japan in the hands of the Japanese, we dare not appear in the sight of foreigners to be on the decline."[33] And even Fukuchi's "Kyōjaku ron" made "loyalty to the emperor" the rock foundation of its proposed system, concluding: "My hope is that the entire country will work together, combining its forces and strengthening its prestige in the community of nations. All imperial servants must devote their primary efforts to this end."[34] In other words, the point of "rebellion" against the new regime was not rebellion per se but an incipient nationalism. Japan must be saved from the usurpers of true imperial authority. A salient feature of later Meiji and Taishō journalism was its boisterous patriotism even when editors fought a specific policy or cabinet. That overweening nation-consciousness already was there at the birth of the modern press.

The final feature of the Restoration press was the eventual onset of governmental control. After the three months of relative freedom, the government struck quickly, crafting new policies and carrying them out with a vigor that suggested considerable fear of the printed word. On June 18, 1868, a day after the publication of "Kyōjaku ron," the Council of State issued Dajōkan Decree 358, a fifty-six-character articulation of the regime's new approach to private publications; all "new books and reprints," it said, would henceforth require official permission before printing.[35] The decree included no enforcement provisions, but that did not prevent officials from launching strong punitive actions a few weeks later.

On July 4, Meiji troops destroyed the last of the pro-Tokugawa resistance forces in Edo, wiping out the Shōgitai in a pivotal battle at Ueno and prompting a bitter editorial by *Soyofuku Kaze* to the effect that "the most sacred spot in all of the Kantō Plain has been, in but an instant, reduced to flame," proof that "the workings of heaven know no right or wrong."[36] Barely more than a week later, on Sunday afternoon, July 12, Fukuchi, whose "Kyōjaku ron" had caused such consternation, was summoned to the Edo Castle from his home and office across from the former Shōgitai headquarters. There, he was thrown into what he described as a chaotic jail, threatened with execution, then released eight days later on the condition that he destroy his printing equipment and discontinue publishing.[37] On July 27, another Dajōkan decree (Number 451) specifically prohibited the unlicensed publication of newspapers *(shimbunshi)*, wiping out with a stroke all of the Edo Restoration papers not officially sponsored by the regime.[38] And on August 8, still another decree (Number 500) provided that all book publication be handled by the Gakkōkan or Education Office.[39] The July and August decrees also spelled out punishments for violators.

The upshot of this series of acts was the demise of the Restoration press. Using Tokugawa licensing precedents, the government initiated a press-prohibition *(hakkō kinshi)* policy that would change only in tone and degree of specificity during the next seventy-five years. The underlying philosophy of these regulations was that private communication would be permitted, but just for those registered with the authorities and then only if the authorities deemed a paper or journal beneficial to the national well-being, likely to encourage order, and supportive of traditional moral standards. The burden of proof lay—always—with the writers and editors; officials need not even give reasons for the permissions they granted or denied. As a result, by August only three tiny nongovernmental papers remained in all Japan: Yokohama's *Moshiogusa* and the foreign-edited *Bankoku Shimbun,* both protected by the fact that they were published in a treaty port, and the progovernment *Naigai Shimbun* in Osaka.

It would be a mistake, however, to place too great an emphasis on the emergence of restrictive governmental control techniques. There was, after all, nothing new about draconian approaches to control. For centuries, Japan's writers had had to work through and around the authorities, either satisfying or eluding censors in order to publish at all. What was new in 1868 was the emergence of a relatively free press, short-lived though it was. Never before had so many writers assailed an existing regime so openly or for so long. While those writers may have been disheartened as the *momiji* season approached that autumn, fearful that the spring liberation had been an aberration, a new era really had begun. Neither the need for broader dissemination of information nor the desire to express private views publicly could be stifled long. A new time demanded new channels of communication between the private and national spheres, between the center and the periphery; thus, within a few years the Yanagawas, Tsujis, and Fukuchis would be called pioneers, men who had led the way to a Meiji press more lively than the young officials ever could have dreamed (or feared) in 1868.

CHAPTER 3

SERVING THE GOVERNMENT
1868 to 1874

> At night I talked with Sugiyama and
> Yamagata about my purpose in opening a
> newspaper office. . . . I want to inform people
> of distant domains about the reforms that are
> taking place . . . to make them aware of
> the spirit of the present age.
>
> *Kido Takayoshi, April 5, 1871*[1]

> The newspapers simply will not touch upon
> a sensitive issue for fear of losing government
> favor. When there is a praiseworthy deed on
> the part of the officials, the papers will praise
> it to the skies with exaggerated language very
> much like a harlot with her customer.
>
> *Fukuzawa Yukichi, 1873*[2]

Government officials took more interest in newspapers than the original journalists did themselves in the years immediately following Fukuchi's 1868 jailing. *Chūgai Shimbun*'s Yanagawa went back to work at the translation bureau, which had been renamed again, this time the Kaisei Gakkō, or School for Carrying Out the Opening, to reflect its increasing emphasis on education in Western sciences and languages. He was assigned to continue work as a translator, then was made a senior professor, but though he accepted a government paycheck, he expressed his feeling about the new regime by working at home rather than going to the Kaisei Gakkō offices. After failing in an 1869 effort to start another newspaper, he began spending more and more time in the Yoshiwara pleasure quarters, "drinking until late at night," composing and dancing the drunken *kappa odori* with a young friend, Narushima Ryūhoku, who would himself become a journalistic star later. He died unexpectedly in 1870, a mere thirty-nine years of age, broken and disillusioned.[3]

Similarly angry and disillusioned, Fukuchi took off for the Tokugawa hometown of Shizuoka after getting out of jail, but finding the city crowded with more former samurai than jobs, he returned to Edo and defied a summons to become an official. He adopted the pseudonym Yumenoya (Dream Hut) and turned to the writing of cheap fiction.[4] A few other people tried to start papers, as did Kishida Ginkō, but none of them lasted for more than twenty or thirty issues.[5] As a result, Japan was without a single domestically produced, private newspaper until the launching of the country's first daily, *Yokohama Mainichi Shimbun*, three years into the new era.

AGENTS OF CIVILIZATION

If the journalists gave up their dreams of starting papers, however, the leading officials did not. While "big" issues such as defense and national unification may have demanded the bulk of most officials' time, a surprisingly large number of them wrote often about the issue of communication: how to get information to the people, the role of media in Western societies, whether the government should start its own newspaper office, how "private" newspapers might be established to serve the modernization process.

The first line of the argument on behalf of creating a press, as many officials articulated it, was that Japan's "backward" commoners or *heimin* needed to be educated more fully if the country were to join the ranks of leading nations. While technical literacy may have been relatively high by international standards, particularly in the major centers of Edo, Kyoto, and Osaka, functional literacy was low in the provinces—to the point that a full decade into the new era a third of the residents of Shiga and nearly half those of Gunma still could not write their own names.[6] Villagers all across Japan were ignorant not only of how to read and write but of the political life of their land and of their own roles as potential citizens. Itō Hirobumi described the general populace as "merely a numerical mass of governed units,"[7] while Fukuzawa groaned, "What could be done with this country of ours, when there were so many people as ignorant as this! . . . People themselves invited oppression."[8] Some popular rights editorialists in the mid-1870s described the *heimin* as "essentially ignorant, powerless fools who live in the realm of servitude."[9] Even the historian Irokawa Daikichi, who has worked hard to unearth evidence of political sophistication in the villages, has noted that the vehement debates that so enlivened Japan's political atmosphere after the late 1870s "seldom stirred even a ripple below the regional elite level."[10] A people so disconnected from the sources of power, a people so restricted by a village-first, village-only mentality could hardly be expected to help Japan march toward "civilization and enlightenment."

While the tools for fighting this ignorance were manifold—education, the military, more effective administrative structures, to name a few—several of the young Meiji bureaucrats were quick to grasp the unique potential of newspapers for reaching even distant peoples quickly. A set of official instructions in the summer of 1871 urged government allies, in this spirit, to create newspapers that would "foster people's knowledge" and "destroy the spirit of bigotry and narrow prejudice" that so often blocked the path to progress.[11] The next year, the governor of Yamanashi set up a newspaper conversation association *(shimbun kaiwa kai)*, "because people need to know the affairs of the world" and because newspapers "are helpful in knowing what is good and bad, as well as in improving morals."[12]

The most influential supporter of this view was Kido Takayoshi, the junior councillor from Chōshū who probably did more than any other individual to bring a democratic leaven to the evolving Meiji structure. Early in 1871, he wrote in his diary of an evening conversation with Yamagata Aritomo and Sugiyama Kōtarō about "opening a newspaper office . . . to inform people of distant domains about the reforms that are taking place in local administration, and about the reforms of the world generally, to make them aware of the spirit of the present age and to cross over the threshold to enlightenment."[13] That same year he wrote a letter describing similar plans to Shinagawa Yajirō, who was then in Europe observing the Franco-Prussian War, and added that the government's connection to such a paper should be covert, so people would not be suspicious about the writers' independence. Shinagawa responded enthusiastically, agreeing on "the indispensability of the newspaper to contemporary life."[14] And Kido maintained a deep interest in newspapers throughout the rest of his life. During the Iwakura Mission to America and Europe, for example, he visited presses in both the United States and Scotland and made detailed observations about the kind of equipment needed to produce a good newspaper.[15] His diary also records frequent visits both during the Iwakura Mission and afterward with the journalist Fukuchi.[16]

Balancing this sense of potential were the apprehensions of many officials about the social and political disruption newspapers were capable of causing. Had the previous Tokugawa regime not found it necessary to place communications control at the foundation of its plan for maintaining a stable society? Had it not been necessary ever so recently to crush the Restoration papers? As Kido's more autocratic counterpart Ōkubo Toshimichi was wont to say: If "we permit the people's feelings to get out of hand, the result will be . . . more fearful than an attack by a huge army."[17] Many, most surely a majority of early-Meiji officials, agreed with Ōkubo, and that is why the promise of "open discussion" in the April 6, 1868, Charter Oath referred to above generally was taken not to mean genuine "public discussion" but merely the need to avoid narrow control by "small cliques within the government."[18] It also is why the many discussions of news channels within the official world at the beginning of Meiji ran in two quite different, if not wholly contradictory, directions. If Ōkubo might agree that news channels were necessary, he would have to have Kido's assurances that they would be carefully regulated.

For that reason, the bulk of the government's press-related energies in the months after Fukuchi's jailing were given to preparing a legal structure to control communications. Early in 1869, orders were issued providing for the licensing of papers by the Education Administration Office (Gakkō Gyōseikan); then on March 21, that same office printed and distributed the Shimbunshi Inkō, the era's first "newspaper publication law."[19] The eight-article ordinance required that publishers submit two copies of each issue for inspection and that they publish paper titles as well as publishers' and editors' names in each issue. It also outlined quite specifically what could be published: articles about "changes in the heavens," prices, commerce, politics, fires, marriages, births, deaths, the arts and sciences, food, clothing, translations of Western literary works, and foreign news—all "as long as they are not harmful to society." At the same time, the law forbade "irresponsible criticism of the government" and "false accusations." And it placed responsibility for prosecution in the Tokyo area under the Gakkō Gyōseikan; newspapers elsewhere were to be examined by local courts.[20]

Thus, the authorities made it clear that publication would be "free" only so long as it operated within officially set definitions of what was good for society. At the same time, in what one scholar has called "a remarkable advance for this early stage of the Meiji period," the press law made it equally clear that private publication would be allowed, that there would be no prior censorship, and that officials would step in only when newspapers failed to censor themselves.[21] There probably were several reasons for the liberal aspects of the press law: the drafters' idea that advanced countries were expected by Westerners to have a relatively free press, the desire of some officials to use news sheets themselves to get their own views published, the Confucian tradition of expecting that educated people would be responsible for what they wrote and thus would not need external censorship. But most important, by any reckoning, was the commitment officials had made to the concept of *bunmei kaika,* to "civilization and enlightenment" policies that would bring Japan as quickly as possible into the ranks of advanced nations. If the people were to be enlightened, a press must be given enough flexibility to help lead the way in that process.

Some two dozen press regulations and decrees were issued by the Council of State over the next half decade, with supervision moving to the new Monbushō (Ministry of Education) in 1871 and newspapers being instructed specifically to "foster people's knowledge" and fight prejudice.[22] In August 1871, the Dajōkan insisted that newspapers print "authentic records" and avoid making "something out of nothing."[23] An 1873 decree articulated several things the press was forbidden from publishing, including essays that advocated foreign laws, materials that "slandered the national essence *(kokutai),*" "indiscriminate" criticism of political decisions, and disclosure of the political opinions of active officials.[24] But though the tone of these decrees was fairly severe, the general nature of press regulations stayed well within the spirit of the 1869 Shimbunshi Inkō during the first half of the 1870s. There remained no specific provisions for enforcement, no set list of penalties for offenses, no prior censorship. Editors would be expected to act as good Confucian-trained public servants, requesting permission to print in the first place, then taking responsibility for upholding community standards. And by and large, it should be noted, that is just what they did in these years, thus rendering stricter laws unnecessary.[25]

SERVANTS OF THE OFFICIALS

The biggest reason for the compliance of editors probably lay in the fact that the press until 1873 remained, at heart, a semiofficial medium. If the cautious approach of the Ōkubo camp led to restrictive press codes, the activist orientation of those like Kido prompted several ministries and bureaucrats to create their own newspapers or to encourage friends in the private sphere to go into publishing, so that the government would have links to the populace. One of the better-known newspaper tales of the era has Etō Shinpei, the soon-to-be justice minister, doing just that in his own rather surreptitious fashion. One day after work early in 1872, the story tells us, he ordered his carriage driver to the home of Jōno Denpei, a forty-one-year-old fiction writer who lived along an alley near what would become Asakusabashi train station. There, Etō handed over several gold pieces and promised that Jōno's new paper, *Tōkyō Nichi Nichi Shimbun*, would be granted permission to publish court news. The import of this action, according to the gossip of the day, was that the ambitious young bureaucrat had "snared" in a single visit what would become the decade's leading newspaper.[26] The capture actually did not help Etō much, since he quit the government the next year in a pique over Japan's policy toward Korea, then was executed in 1874 for leading a rebellion of disaffected samurai in Saga. But his action illustrated both the attitude and the approach of a number of early-Meiji officials. Newspapers were tools to be used, not just adversaries to be controlled. As a result, bureaus and bureaucrats alike "financed and established newspapers" quite generously,[27] and the early 1870s saw the emergence of a press that was, essentially, an arm of the government.

As noted in the previous chapter, the first government-sponsored paper was the *Dajōkan Nisshi*, an official gazette of the Council of State, inaugurated less than two months after the Restoration and made available by subscription to private individuals. During the next three years, several other minor papers also were given government assistance, including the British merchant John Hartley's *Kakkoku Shimbun*, which lived but a single day during the tumult of the Restoration spring,[28] and the *Kaigai Shimbun*, published in 1870 by the Daigaku Nankō.[29]

The first successful government effort to launch a "private" paper came on January 25, 1871, with the appearance of Japan's earliest daily newspaper—and the first to be printed with metal type—the *Yokohama Mainichi*.[30] Actually, the paper was not supported directly (or overtly) by the authorities; rather, following Kido's idea of publishing a paper "as if the government had nothing do with it,"[31] Governor Izeki Morikata of Kanagawa Prefecture, a friend of Joseph Heco, induced several wealthy investors to underwrite the

venture, selected Koyasu Takashi, a book inspector in the Yokoyama customs office, as editor, and had foreign ministry officials in
Yokohama do many of the editorial tasks.[32]

A few months later, on June 18, the newsbook *Shimbun
Zasshi,* which was to become one of the period's leading journalistic voices after changing its name to *Akebono Shimbun* in 1875,
was launched in similar fashion, amid a flurry of rumors that it was
to be Kido's mouthpiece. As it turned out, the rumors were accurate. The young junior councillor had given a thousand gold *ryō* of
his own money to Yamagata Tokuō, one of the paper's first editors.[33] The *Shimbun Zasshi* retained the appearance of independence,
just as Kido wished, occasionally even expressing criticism of official actions, but it was Kido's organ, a tool for spreading enlightenment to the people and for arguing on behalf of his own positions
within the bureaucracy. It was vigorous, for example, in calling for
the abolition of the old feudal fiefs and faithful in reporting on his
activities abroad during the 1871–1873 Iwakura Mission. Kido lost
control of the *Shimbun Zasshi* during the intense fights over foreign policy and a popular assembly in 1873–1874, but not before it
had served him in the early factional wars.

Actually, the *Shimbun Zasshi*'s eventual defection probably
was rendered less painful for Kido by that fact that by 1874 he had
made another catch, having nurtured close ties with Etō's old paper,
the profitable and ever more respectable *Tōkyō Nichi Nichi.* The
paper's early operations had been simple, even crude, with Jōno and
Nishida Densuke doing all the editing, managing, and accounting
in a second-floor, six-mat room of a "house propped up by slightly
crooked poles."[34] But the combination of patronage by men with
close ties to the Finance Ministry and skillful editing by Jōno and
Nishida had turned *Nichi Nichi* into Tokyo's most influential
paper, with a reported circulation of eight thousand and offices in
the Ginza.[35]

And both the influence and Kido's connections had been
heightened in 1874, when Fukuchi Gen'ichirō agreed to become the
Nichi Nichi editor. Fukuchi had been enticed out of private life in
1871 by Kido and Itō Hirobumi, who asked him to join a mission to
study banking systems in the United States. Following that trip, he
had served as an interpreter on the Iwakura Mission, then as an
Ōkurashō (Finance Ministry) official, but he grew frustrated with
the insipid routines that characterized life in the bureaucracy. So,
when an offer came from Jōno, he ignored the advice of friends who
saw journalism as a second-rate profession, and accepted. The

promise of a 150-yen monthly salary (twice what top editors normally received) and a share of monthly profits may have helped him make up his mind.[36] For Kido, Fukuchi's decision was nothing short of a coup, since Fukuchi was both a friend and an ideological ally, the sort of concealed mouthpiece he needed. When *Nichi Nichi* subsequently proclaimed itself the *goyō* or "patronage organ" of the state council, people in the know assumed, correctly, that it was not so much a Dajōkan vehicle as a Kido-led Chōshū organ. As Fukuchi himself later put it, "I would discuss my views with Kido, and find that we agreed on many things."[37] He insisted always on his right to disagree, but that seldom was necessary.

One of the most interesting examples of government patronage in these early-Meiji years was John Reddie Black's *Nisshin Shinjishi,* founded on April 24, 1872, less than four weeks after the *Nichi Nichi,* for the purpose of "educating" the Japanese about "what a newspaper was."[38] Black maintained that he had been promised no outside support at the outset, that he just wanted to do in Japanese what he already had done in English at the *Gazette* and the *Herald.* Pressed for finances, however, he accepted an offer of aid in return for making *Nisshin Shinjishi* a semiofficial organ, a *goyō,* of the Sa'in or Chamber of the Left of the Dajōkan. His paper gained a reputation as a model of the "modern" newspaper, one of the best published, with Japan's first editorial columns and a broader range of articles than could be found in other newspapers. It also was respected for the reliability of its Sa'in-connected news stories, but even Black could not escape the close financial ties that bound newspapers so closely to the official world in these years.[39] Indeed, when the paper began showing too much independence in the mid-1870s, it was killed by the very officials who made it a paragon of government-press symbiosis in the early 1870s.

A final example of the press' early reliance on official initiative was the *Yūbin Hōchi Shimbun,* which would stand near the forefront of Tokyo journalism throughout the entire Meiji era. Launched on June 10, 1872, *Hōchi*'s very name, "Postal Reports," suggested its ties to officialdom. The reality was that Maejima Hisoka, minister of posts and telecommunications and the father of Japan's new postal system, had his own personal secretary start the paper. As Kishida Ginkō (who became a writer at rival *Nichi Nichi* that same year) recalled it, "Maejima was an old friend of mine who would talk repeatedly, in a bookstore we knew, about the need for a newspaper. Finally, he decided to publish one."[40] Maejima's particular dream was to accelerate the process of nation building by having mail handlers all across Japan send news items to the capital for dissemination through a newspaper. So he persuaded his secretary, Konishi Gikei, to assume the editorship and Ōta Kin'emon, a friend who ran a bookstore, to become publisher. He also helped *Hōchi* cultivate a national network of writers by allowing it to send and receive manuscripts postage-free.[41] And in the process, Maejima secured for yet another government office not only a special pipeline to the public but, of even greater importance to him, a way to spread modern ideas more quickly.[42]

This pattern of official stimulation and support also extended to the provinces. While provincial papers generally developed later than those in the capital, they too were brought into being, by and large, by ambitious, visionary officials intent on improving communication and speeding modernization. And a few of the regional papers were launched almost as soon as those at the center. *Nagoya Shimbun,* for example, began near the end of 1871, assisted by a prefectural order that each village and ward subscribe to it in order to "spread knowledge, establish the foundations of industry, and stimulate civilization."[43] In Fukui, a prefectural newspaper office created the *Satsuyō Shimbun* in 1872, reportedly the "thirty-seventh newspaper in all Japan,"[44] while in Niigata the prefecture established its own printing plant in July 1873 to produce the *Niigata Kenji Hōchi.*[45] This pattern repeated itself scores of times across the decade—in the *Kainan Shimbun,* established in Shikoku in 1876 by the second governor of Ehime prefecture;[46] in the *Aichi Shimbun,* founded in 1877 with secret ties to the prefectural office;[47] in the *Aomori Shimbun* to the north, which appeared in 1879 at the hand of the prefectural printers, with government assistance;[48] and in the *Kumamoto Shimbun* far to the south, launched with the assistance of local officials in 1876.[49] Officials' motives for starting papers ranged from ambition and an eagerness to tighten control to a desire to spread enlightenment, but the end result was the same: by the 1880s nearly every prefecture had taken a hand in the creation of one or more newspapers. If *bunmei kaika* was the official goal, newspapers represented a consensus means of achieving it.

There was no consensus, however, on just how newspapers should be assisted and used. The cases outlined here, for example, differed significantly from each other. The *Dajōkan Nisshi* was actually published by the government, *Yokohama Mainichi* was started with private financial assistance from friends of Governor Izeki, *Tōkyō Nichi Nichi* and *Shimbun Zasshi* received covert funds from officials, *Yūbin Hōchi* was launched by a minister himself, and Black's *Nisshin Shinjishi* became a Sa'in organ six months after its establishment. In other words, there simply was no official press policy beyond the laws regulating what the papers could say.

To a large degree, this lack of consensus reflected the fact that the Meiji government was itself so divided. Both bureaus and individuals regarded information—its acquisition as well as its dissemination—as crucial to the accumulation of power, but they had no unified information policy. Instead, they competed with each other to secure their own voices, their own channels to the public, their own newspapers. It can be argued, in fact, that the control of papers was a result not of government unity or strength, certainly not of governmentwide foresight, but of official infighting, of individual and factional competition within the varied branches of the growing bureaucracy. In the long run, that press-related factionalism would give the Meiji press one of its more distinctive and enduring characteristics, a propensity for divisions among the papers themselves that reflected the fissures that rent the government as a whole. In the short run, it led to the creation of the first daily press, then undermined the press-government ties when the intragovernmental squabbling went public in 1873 and 1874.

Before turning to that story, however, we need to look at some of the other forms that press-government ties took in these early-Meiji years; for while direct control of individual papers and editors may have been the most obvious way to influence the press, it was by no means the only one. It probably was not even the most effective. And it certainly did not have as much long-range impact on national development as a number of less direct measures instituted to encourage the overall growth of this new communication channel.

Of first, and perhaps greatest, import were the decisions made by Maejima's postal service to accept newspapers for delivery through the mails, then to extend the *Yūbin Hōchi* perk of free manuscript delivery to all newspapers on July 1, 1873. Maejima's aim seems to have been twofold: to encourage the rapid spread of information and, more practically, to publicize his new postal system by showing how it could be used to distribute newspapers.[50] He would claim in later years that no newspapers had yet begun publishing when the free delivery went into effect and that his aim in drawing up beneficial newspaper regulations was to encourage would-be editors. When even the new rules did not stimulate publication, he said, "I got impatient and went ahead and tried putting out a newspaper myself." Actually, Maejima's memory failed him;

there already were several newspapers in existence when the regulations were announced and when *Hōchi* was launched.[51] But he was right about the most important thing: the postal service's favored treatment of newspapers had a profound effect in encouraging the early success of the country's press.

As Maejima also said, this time correctly, if newspapers had not been declared "postal matter," private delivery from Tokyo to the Kansai region would have cost at least ten yen per package, a daunting expense in a day when subscription to a major paper cost less than ten yen for an entire year and when editorial writers generally were paid about fifty yen a month.[52] Undoubtedly, the early emergence of a national press owed much to his initial decision to assist not only *Yūbin Hōchi* but all newspapers through favorable laws. The postal exemption ended in 1882,[53] and in 1889 the Kuroda Kiyotaka cabinet actually tried to restrict newspapers through postal regulations.[54] At the beginning of Meiji, however, the press and the government were allies, and Maejima's assistance helped keep them that way.

Government assistance also took the form of official purchase of daily copies of certain favored papers. On May 4, 1872, less than two months after the appearance of *Nisshin Shinjishi* and *Tōkyō Nichi Nichi*, Inoue Kaoru of the Ōkurashō ordered that the government purchase three copies each of *Tōkyō Nichi Nichi*, *Shimbun Zasshi*, and *Yokohama Mainichi* for each of Japan's seventy-two prefectures and three city *(fu)* governments. Two months later, on July 8, *Nisshin Shinjishi* was added to the list. The practice lasted just a year,[55] and the total of 225 subscriptions per paper sounds paltry today. But most papers' overall circulations were tiny at first, and the impact of Inoue's directive was to increase circulation of these papers by more than a fifth, enough to make the difference between success and failure.[56] Moreover, the prestige that accompanied selection for governmental purchase was immensely important, attracting still more individual subscribers to the favored papers.

Of further assistance was the liberal approach most bureaus adopted in making news accessible to reporters. I already have noted how Maejima urged local postal employees to send items to *Yūbin Hōchi* as well as the important place that government notices played in most papers' "news" columns. Beyond that, well-connected editorialists were granted almost total access to the officials and activities of the bureaus in which their patrons worked. And several specific official rulings resulted in brighter, more interesting publications. At its inception in 1872, for example, *Nichi*

Nichi was granted the right by Etō to publish court rulings,[57] and some three months later, on July 7, the Justice Ministry gave general permission to newspaper reporters to attend court hearings in Tokyo.[58] The following summer, government expenses and revenues were made public for the first time, and early in 1875 the Dajōkan ruled that the public could attend civil suit hearings.[59] Nothing mattered so much to the early Meiji papers and their readers as political news; editors and subscribers alike focused on what was happening in government bureaus and councils. As a result, this access to official decisions and activities assured the viability of Tokyo's leading papers. It could have been otherwise; the officials might just as easily have concluded that secrecy would serve them best. That they provided relatively easy access was crucial in the early spread of a healthy press.

One other, equally important and far more unusual, means of support lay in the encouragement many officials gave to newspaper reading by creating "newspaper discussion associations" *(shimbun kaiwa kai)* and "reading rooms" *(shimbun jūransho, shimbun etsuransho)* here and there across Japan in these years. In a move reminiscent of northern England half a century before, where towns would establish "subscription rooms" in which the poor could read the local and London papers,[60] Japanese officials began early in the 1870s to create forums and locations where villagers and townspeople could read the Tokyo papers—or, if they were unable to read themselves, where they could have the news read and explained to them. One of the best known of these was instituted in Yamanashi Prefecture in November 1872, just after the founding of *Kyōchū Shimbun,* the forerunner of today's *Yamanashi Nichi Nichi Shimbun.*[61] Alarmed by a local peasant uprising over taxes, prefectural officials sent out an order to village headmen, blaming popular ignorance of "what is going on in the world" for the unrest. Describing newspapers as unsurpassed sources "for getting this knowledge . . . a short cut to improving manners," they decreed that, "henceforth, in all villages qualified persons from among the Shintō priests, Buddhist monks and farmers shall be selected to serve as reading masters to explain (at lectures held six times a month) what is printed in newspapers."[62] Similarly, *Shimbun Zasshi* reported that same month on a program set up by town officials in Nishinokyō near Nara, for people to come to the local elementary school on the evening of the twenty-seventh of each month, to have newspapers read in order to "nurture the young people of the area."[63] On November 22, 1874, a *Tōkyō Nichi Nichi* article described government-sponsored newspaper discussion groups in Niigata Prefecture on the Japan Sea coast, and the same fall reports reached Tokyo of similar groups to the northeast in Miyagi Prefecture.[64] Rural youths who eventually moved to Tokyo to become national leaders also reported with surprising frequency that newspaper reading, often at the local *kaiwa kai*, played a pivotal role in awakening their consciousness to a world beyond the village.[65] Made respectable by official patronage, newspaper reading (and listening) spread in the 1870s even to the valleys of distant regions.

IMPACT OF PATRONAGE: GROWTH

The first question that comes to mind as one looks at the central role the government took in launching the Meiji press relates to impact: How did this intermingling of the official and the nonofficial, the public and the private, influence Japan's route toward modernity? And, of even greater pertinence to this study, how did the symbiosis shape the press itself; in what ways did it make Japanese newspapers different from what they otherwise might have been—or from what their counterparts were in other lands?

The most obvious answer is that the government's patronage helped to trigger the rapid growth that Japan's newspapers experienced in the early Meiji years. In 1870, Japan had not a single daily newspaper; by the middle of the era papers existed in every corner of the country, many with circulations running into the tens of thousands.[66] Indeed, already by the time that the government began to draw back from its heavy support of the press in the mid-1870s, something of a "newspaper boom" had enveloped the major cities and, to a lesser degree, some of the provinces.

A writer for the *Japan Weekly Mail* near the end of the 1870s suggested that Tokyo now had more newspapers than London and surmised (in an understatement) that there must be "considerably over one hundred newspapers" throughout the country. In fact, he noted: "In much the same way as they were seized with a violent fancy at one time for queerly marked rabbits, the Japanese in Tokyo and other places appear to have gone into rapture over the news-paper press."[67] Similarly, a Japanese scholar has noted that this period saw small, poorly financed papers "appear and disappear like foam" on water, so great was the enthusiasm for publishing.[68] One sign of the popularity of the newspaper fad was the appearance on Tokyo streets in the mid-1870s of popular woodblock prints, called *shimbun nishikie*, that reproduced illustrations and descriptions of popular fashions under the mastheads of leading papers. An article in *Chōya Shimbun* noted that these *nishikie* had become popular souvenirs for tourists returning from Tokyo. "My god!" said the writer. "What a sign of civilization! What a sign of culture!"[69]

Another sign of the spreading newspaper culture was the appearance of privately sponsored communal reading projects throughout the country during the early 1870s. Nihonbashi, Kanda, and the Asakusa nightless quarters, for example, saw the growth of newspaper tea rooms, in which women would either read to customers free of charge or provide papers for the customers to read themselves, at about half the cost of a cup of tea.[70] In other regions, joint reading was promoted for social or intellectual reasons. Yamamoto Taketoshi tells of a gentleman in Hachiōji, west of Tokyo, who sought to improve the local intellectual level by calling together women and children for newspaper readings.[71] Irokawa describes village leaders along the Tama River discussing articles by popular writers to learn what the latest ideas were.[72] Inukai Tsuyoshi, later prime minister but now a youth in Okayama to the west, said that every copy of a newspaper in his village was read by many people, so that "it might . . . take nine or ten days" for the community to get through a single issue.[73] And *Tōkyō Nichi Nichi* in 1876 reported on one village in Nagano Prefecture where more than thirty literate villagers formed their own club to discuss the contents of newspapers and develop political proposals based on the articles they read.[74]

None of these examples should be taken to suggest that *most* Japanese were reading newspapers by the mid-1870s. The majority of commoners were incapable of reading a newspaper; the participants in reading circles represented a small minority of the population, members of the intellectual elites in their own regions. And the understanding of the very concept of newspapers remained highly limited well into the 1870s, even among many in the elite. Black relished recounting the time when he urged a merchant who had bought a copy of *Nisshin Shinjishi* to subscribe regularly:

> "Why?" [the merchant] asked. "I've got it—what more do I want?"
>
> "Yes, you have one day's issue; and it comes out every day."
> "So I understand," he replied, "but having it already, why should I take it everyday?"
>
> And all the *banto*s (clerks) laughed, thinking it an excellent stroke of wit, no doubt.

Only after careful explanation did Black convince the gentleman that each day's paper contained "something new."[75] *Tōkyō Nichi Nichi* editors encountered an even more basic kind of ignorance when they decided to place newspapers in attention-getting containers on street corners; not knowing what the receptacles were for, some people used them as urinals.[76]

The fact remains, however, that newspapers had begun to grow rapidly by the middle of the 1870s, at least by the standards of a country that had not had a single private, Japanese-language paper to report on the emperor's initial arrival in Tokyo in late 1868. By 1877, Japan had 225 newspapers by some counts, and a decade later as many as 470 separate papers were being published.[77] In Tokyo itself, there were at least seven newspapers in the mid-1870s with individual annual circulations of 1.5 million and daily circulations above five thousand; the largest, *Yomiuri Shimbun*, was selling nearly 5.5 million yearly copies by 1877.[78] And the regional papers, though much smaller, were spreading nearly as rapidly. In 1872 alone, papers were launched in fourteen provinces, and by the end of the decade nearly every prefecture had its own newspaper.[79] Kumamoto, for example, imported the country's first provincial printing press in 1873 and a year later saw the birth of the *Shirakawa Shinshi*.[80] In 1877, a Fukuoka druggist named Fujii founded the *Tsukushi Shimbun*;[81] in October 1878, *Yūbin Hōchi* reported that the *Ise Shimbun*, launched in January, already had published ninety-eight issues and was "greatly flourishing";[82] by 1879 the radical Komatsubara Eitarō was editing the *San'yō Shimbun* in Okayama.[83] And so it went: officials lent their support to newspapers as instruments of enlightenment, and all across the country they spread with impressive speed, just like every other artifact of Western culture. This expansion probably should not surprise us, since early-Meiji society already had advanced well beyond the 20 percent literacy, 10 percent urbanization standard that scholars accept as the threshold for a journalistic "takeoff."[84] But the rapidity of the growth was remarkable nonetheless. And at its core lay the sponsorship of key officials and bureaus, who gave papers not only financial and editorial support but respectability.

IMPACT OF PATRONAGE: CONFUCIAN ELITISM

At least as important as the fact of growth in the early 1870s was the kind of press that this symbiotic government-press interplay stimulated. Nothing stands out more boldly in an examination of these papers than their highly political, unabashedly elitist tone. While they sometimes used populist rhetoric, everything about the content and style of the major papers suggests that the early journalists were Confucian-bred, self-conscious leaders of their generation, intellectuals who were, at their very core, political beings.

The first evidence of this establishment-oriented elitism shows up in their attitudes toward government sponsorship. Japanese journalists a century later would be as vociferous as their Western counterparts in decrying hints of financial links between the government and private papers. But not so their early-Meiji forebears; close relations with the official world never bothered Nishida, Black, or Koyasu. In fact, they encouraged the ties. The Confucian ethic in which they had been reared rested squarely on the concept of *jōi katatsu:* popular subordination to the imperial will. Private institutions, according to the Tokugawa intellectual presuppositions, were tools for cultivating the state-determined public good. Words and phrases such as "free press," "independence," the "public's right to know"—indeed, the very idea of "rights"—were not in the vocabularies of these first journalists.

Their core philosophy grew instead from concepts such as obligation, loyalty, and harmony. It was for those traditional concepts that the Restoration papers fought in 1868, and now that the new government had become legitimate, it became quite natural to seek—and return—the blessing of the official world, without any self-doubt in doing so. As Yamamoto Taketoshi says, to be labeled a *"goyō shimbun,"* or patronage paper, at this time meant protection by the "all-knowing, all-powerful government that was stimulating the growth of industry and production and pushing forward civilization and enlightenment. Everyone in the fields of education, industry, and commerce strove mightily to acquire this symbol. The newspaper world was no exception."[85]

These editors preferred influence to freedom, a platform to independence. *Yūbin Hōchi* writers, for example, repeatedly said that "the sole aim of newspapers is to encourage people along the forward path of development, down the shortest route to culture."[86] *Nisshin Shinjishi* began each issue with an announcement that it aimed "to spread human knowledge, help develop civilization *(kaika),* and in every way possible promote the national welfare."[87] Even the nonpolitical, much more plebeian *Yomiuri Shimbun* said that the purpose of journalism was to pave a "rapid road" that would "lead the people to enlightenment."[88] And at the end of the decade, when the *Ōsaka Asahi Shimbun* sought a license to publish, its editors discussed their intent in the Confucian terms of social utility, declaring that their sole aim was to aid in "the enlightenment of common men and women, in order to promote virtue."[89]

This did not mean that these editors thought of themselves as kept people; they would have rejected such a label vociferously. As Carol Gluck has reminded us, even "so-called 'government scholars' *(goyō gakusha)* were not court ideologists but academic consultants who prided themselves on their intellectual independence."[90] In the same vein, the early editors made it clear that they wrote only what they genuinely believed (a fact that soon would drive a wedge between them and their sponsors). It was just that they saw themselves as members of the same society-shaping elite as the officials, and in the press' first years they took it as a given that their goals of fostering national strength and enlightenment were, in the essentials, synonymous with those of their official patrons. If government sponsorship magnified their influence, then *goyō* status should be nurtured.

Another result of the elitist Confucian breeding was the overwhelming political orientation of these early-Meiji journalists. Like the Restoration papers' editors, the men who founded Tokyo's *ōshimbun* or mainstream, "prestige papers" knew no love greater than politics. Fukuchi voiced many of their aspirations when he announced, on assuming the *Nichi Nichi* editorship, that if he "could not be prime minister," he would be a journalist, "the uncrowned king" of society.[91] The number of aspiring (or former) officials who went to work for newspapers, either to gain a springboard to official prominence or simply to find a personal mouthpiece, includes several future prime ministers and scores of parliamentary and bureaucratic leaders.[92] This was what press historian Ono Hideo calls the "era of the all-powerful editor" *(shuhitsu bannō jidai)*,[93] the period when, in Uchikawa Yoshimi's words, editors were "star players . . . engaging in the sport of battle." Not until decades later, in the late-Meiji and Taishō years, would the journalists become mere spectators, reporting rather than creating the stories.[94]

The effect of this political orientation was obvious even in the layout of a typical early-Meiji *ōshimbun.* Page one would begin with items, often decrees, from the Council of State or specific government offices. If these did not take the entire page, the rest and much of the next two pages would be given to editorials on political issues and news reports about governmental affairs, followed most often by politically oriented correspondence and foreign news (generally summarized from the English-language papers in the treaty ports). Only after these sections would general-interest news be printed, in a *"zappō"* or *"zatsuwa"* (miscellany) section that had neither headlines nor typographical divisions, except for an open circle indicating each change in topic. The last page typically would contain price lists, small advertisements, and publication data. What news was included most often related somehow to enlightenment issues: how civilized people ate, political developments in European countries, the latest foreign books, and inventions.[95]

Nothing dramatized the political orientation more clearly than the contemptuous way in which staff members responsible for gathering news were treated. At the top of each paper's hierarchy were the editors; then came the *kisha* or writers, who specialized in essays rather than reportage; and at the bottom were those who handled news. The actual newsgatherers usually were poorly educated, underpaid menials, called *tanbōsha* or *tanbōin,* who went into the streets to listen to the gossip at police offices, brothels, and government bureaus, then came back to the office with notes or oral reports that cheap fiction writers *(gesakusha)* would turn into "news." Their items sometimes were more interesting than accurate since, in the generous telling of one Meiji editor, they "were not unusually capable and needed only an ability to record correctly what people said in order to be hired."[96] Their reports, after all, were little more than filler. The use of *tanbōsha* declined during the third Meiji decade, as papers moved away from their overwhelming political orientation, but some of them still were in use at *Asahi Shimbun* at the end of Meiji, still "a step lower in rank than people in the political bureau," still regarded by everyone as "lightweights."[97] In a Confucian world where serving the country was a journalist's highest duty, the ability to write political analysis was what counted. That attitude undermined effective news treatment in the first Meiji years, and its residue would influence the press for most of the era.

A British press historian noted that an 1830s editor of the *Manchester Times* "had a greater purpose in journalism than to make money: he wished to make opinion."[98] The same could have been said of the early-Meiji editors, because a third result of their Confucian elitism was that they paid very little attention to ledger books, or to the office facilities, layouts, and promotional side of journalism that became so important in later years. These were not, in other words, commercial newspapers. If their content was political, their formats were gray. There were no real headlines, only a slightly bolder, barely larger typeface to indicate section changes. There were no pictures and few sketches. Type was small and sometimes smudged. And the overall effect was a dullness even more severe than Horace Greeley's pre–Civil War *Tribune* and the late-century *Times* of London. The *ōshimbun* were, in other words, elitist and political, and their typography screamed that anyone unable to find pleasure in the prose and the argument should look elsewhere.

Moreover, the physical operations at most companies revealed a seat-of-the-pants simplicity possible only in a world of small circulations and meager profits. We already have noted the tiny, flimsy office in which *Nichi Nichi* began publishing. Suehiro Tetchō's paper, *Akebono Shimbun,* operated out of a seven- or eight-mat room, with four editorial staffers and "two or three *tanbōsha* of the lower classes." And the other Tokyo papers in mid-decade were much the same, "exceedingly pitiful things"[99] with small quarters and even smaller budgets, manned by writers most of whom received a pittance. If typical editors earned little more than fifty or sixty yen a month, the *kisha* most often earned just twenty yen and the *tanbōsha* as little as seven yen a month. For that reason, one might well launch a paper for a mere four thousand yen.[100] A yen may have been worth a good deal more then than it is now, but even in early Meiji the sums were almost trifling.

Nor were early circulations very large. Growth may have been impressive for a country just launching a modern press. But in contrast to the populist New York and London papers, whose circulations ranged above 150,000 now, Japan's leading *ōshimbun* were minuscule. In 1874, only two of the *ōshimbun* had more than three thousand subscribers: *Tōkyō Nichi Nichi,* with 7,430, and *Yūbin Hōchi* with 6,881. Black's highly reputed *Nisshin Shinjishi* had 1,762 daily readers, *Yokohama Mainichi* a mere 978.[101] And their readers came from sharply restricted levels of society. In later years, the journal *Chūō Kōron* would call this the press' "high society" *(jōryū shakai)* era, when only officials, educators, and politicians were reading newspapers—in contrast to subsequent years when lower officials, then clerks, and finally commoners became readers.[102] And that evaluation jibes with the early journalistic self-image. Our readership, said *Chōya,*[103] comes from "people above the middle class." Similarly, *Tōkyō Nichi Nichi* estimated not long after Fukuchi became editor that 80 percent of its readers were officials.[104]

The news and content base was limited too. Until the 1880s Tokyo and Yokohama not only furnished Japan with its only influential newspapers, but that region provided nearly all of the events and developments that editors deemed worthy of coverage. Papers might circulate throughout the country; small local sheets might spring up across the land. But the things that happened in the provinces were beneath serious notice. "Hardly anyone had reporters in the provinces," noted Suehiro. And Fukuzawa Yukichi declared himself "dumbfounded" at the inadequate treatment of regions beyond Tokyo when he entered the press world with *Jiji Shinpō* early in the 1880s.[105]

This narrowness upset few, given the elitist proclivities of the major newspapers. A bemused John Black observed that the singular characteristic of the patrician he had hired to edit his own *Nisshin Shinjishi* was his unwillingness to write prose that ordinary people could understand. Trained in the classical styles of the educated, he sought only to influence his own kind. "Everyone said how beautiful was his language," Black quipped, "but I had many convincing proofs that it often took some of its professed admirers a long time to understand it. It had the effect, however, of placing the paper very high in the estimation of the highest and most cultivated classes."[106] Soon, another kind of newspaper, known as a *koshimbun* or vulgar (literally, small) paper, would become available for those whose tastes were less erudite. But for now, in this world of Confucian elitism, refinement and well-honed argument remained much more important than readability or zest.

IMPACT OF PATRONAGE: *BUNMEI KAIKA*

This narrowness and elitism did not, however, mean that the press' impact was limited to the upper reaches of society in these years. The readers may have come from a circumscribed circle, but that circle exerted a powerful outward influence on the less educated and less political classes. In part, this was because the papers' political articles and essays helped to stimulate policy changes that affected readers and nonreaders alike. Even more, it resulted from the fact that the papers supplemented their heavy political menus with a decent serving of "news" in the "miscellany" sections, items thought likely to assist in the enlightenment process. And while few commoners read these stories directly, the chances were that they heard about the more interesting and significant ones, perhaps through a hawker, possibly in the columns of a *koshimbun*—or, most likely, through word of mouth channels that linked inner and outer worlds.

Reporters wrote often about what "civilized" people did: they drank beer and coffee, ate meat and Western candy, took new medicines, read Samuel Smiles and John Bunyan. Readers were admonished to eat onions with beef and to avoid public nudity, so as to "prevent ridicule by prudish aliens."[107] *Tōkyō Nichi Nichi* reported in its early issues on train rides from Yokohama to Shinbashi, a distance of perhaps twenty miles, which arrived, "amazingly," by nine in the morning,[108] and in February 1875 it ran a dazzled-yet-approving account of Mori Arinori's Western-style wedding in which the couple actually embraced. A typical *Yūbin Hōchi* article in the fall of 1872 told of a postal worker who found an envelope on which an ignorant commoner had attached 1.1 *sen* in coins instead of a stamp.[109] The worker, who stole the money and replaced it with a canceled stamp, was sentenced to sixty strikes with a cane. At the end of the story, the writer admonished readers to learn a lesson: if they followed postal regulations carefully, they might save postal workers from falling into temptation.[110] Even more directly tied to the enlightenment theme was a *Nichi Nichi* article at the end of 1872, which used a chart to explain the government's plan to change from the lunar to the Western, Gregorian calendar. The piece proved so popular that the paper had to issue 20,000 reprints.[111]

Material of this sort, backed up by the weight of official patronage, clearly played a role in acquainting ever larger numbers of people with what Japan's leaders meant by *bunmei kaika*, even as it also helped to spread political consciousness. Only months into its first year of publishing, *Nichi Nichi* made this point with a letter from a Kobe resident, praising the paper for making capital news available so quickly in the provinces.[112] Similarly, *Kyōchū Shimbun* in Kōfu, to the west of Tokyo, ran an article in its very first issue about a local man who had bought several dozen photographs of the Emperor Meiji to give to his friends—to help people worship the emperor "even in such a remote corner of the country."[113] And a few years later, the plebeian *Yomiuri* received a letter from a resident of Chōshi on the eastern tip of Chiba, urging editors to be more diligent in printing official decrees, because of the guidance they provided for people in the provinces. "Several newspapers have failed lately to publish some of the items issued by the Council of State," he wrote. "I do not know why they have not published them. There are instructions in these decrees that we need to know;

so I implore our newspaper editors to be diligent about publishing such decrees."[114]

While evidence of this sort is anecdotal, the point is unassailable: from their inception, newspapers were significant tools of a paternalistic establishment intent on speeding national consciousness and civilization both horizontally, across the nation, and vertically, down through the classes. According to Yamamoto Taketoshi, the leading student of readership in this era, "Newspaper readers became the political opinion leaders of the *mura* and *buraku* communities, passing on to the nonreaders their own interpretation of the news and ideologies that they garnered from the papers."[115] In other words, actual readership might be limited to the well educated, but influence was not. Yamamoto adds that credit for increasing provincial support for the early-Meiji policies "belongs to the papers that were patronized by the government."[116] Over the years, schools, armies, and elections would help mightily in spreading national consciousness; but none of these could equal the press for the combined breadth and immediacy of their impact. Newspapers were, as *Yūbin Hōchi* said, "guides to enlightenment and shortcuts to civilization,"[117] especially when they worked in such comfortable tandem with the official world.

It could not be expected, however, that this easy cooperation would last long. Meiji officials themselves were far from unified in their approaches to national policies, and the more important editors were anything but mindless mouthpieces. The idea of some melodic, government-directed harmony was naive, suited better to official rhetoric than to the day-to-day practices of a faction-ridden government. As a result, few were surprised when bureaucratic infighting about finances and foreign policy in 1873 began to cause cracks in the press-government bond. When Inoue Kaoru's bureaucratic supporters took on Ōkuma Shigenobu over budget requests in the spring of that year, it was quickly obvious that his faction also would take on any *papers* that backed Ōkuma—and that the result would be as dramatic for press-government relationships as it was for the official winners and losers of the budget struggle. The press had served its first government-initiated role well, helping to spread ideas of enlightenment and national loyalty more widely and quickly than any Tokugawa-era leader might have imagined possible. Now, with a shift at the government's own center, the press itself would take on a new—more independent and more powerful—role almost overnight.

CHAPTER 4

FINDING ITS OWN VOICE
1874 to 1881

> Punished on the first, they reenter the
> fray on the second. Withdrawing on
> the third, they advance on the fourth,
> ceaselessly fighting and tormenting the
> courts. Such is the stubbornness and
> idiocy of newspaper essayists.
>
> *Narushima Ryūhoku*[1]

Political crises propelled much of the press' evolution during the first two Meiji decades. Thus, when ugly government squabbles were leaked to the public in 1873, then again when scandals rocked the Council of State in 1881, the official world's own troubles sparked a different, but equally significant, set of upheavals in newspaper circles. And those upheavals in the end helped the press evolve from its early role as a tool of the authorities into a relatively independent medium of public discussion—indeed, into the first private medium with a public voice that Japan ever had experienced. Out of the rumblings of internal strife, one might say, came the stirrings of civil society.

The first of these political episodes was ignited in April 1873, a year and a third after the Iwakura Mission had departed Edo on its international fact-finding mission, leaving Saigō Takamori and Inoue Kaoru in charge of day-to-day government operations. The public face of the government had been fairly tranquil until then, despite factional and philosophical differences behind the scenes. But when the ministries began to maneuver during that spring's budget discussions, several officials decided to build support for their own positions through the city's young newspapers and, in the process, changed the role of Japan's press for all time.

The budget struggles actually had cropped up first in 1872, when the education and justice ministries fought with Inoue, who as vice-minister was presiding over Ōkurasho (Finance Ministry) affairs in Minister Ōkubo Toshimichi's absence. Plagued by spreading red ink, he had vetoed their requests for increases then;[2] so there was little surprise when the budget struggle reemerged the next spring. Justice Minister Etō Shinpei and Education Minister Ōki Takatō again requested more money than Inoue would approve. But they were intransigent this time; so a third party, the rising young Ōkuma Shigenobu, was asked to moderate, and when he sided with the education and justice ministries, Inoue resigned.[3]

Although there was nothing particularly remarkable about the squabble, the way it was handled was precedent setting, because this time the combatants took their fight into the public arena, an action that would have been unthinkable in feudal Japan. Inoue's side initiated the new tack by leaking to *Shimbun Zasshi* and Black's *Nisshin Shinjishi* a Shibusawa Eiichi memorandum that supported the Finance Ministry. Their leak raised eyebrows far and wide, not just because it was unprecedented but because the government had issued an order only the previous month forbidding the unauthorized disclosure of official matters to the press.[4] Ōkuma responded by having his own budget figures published, and before the issue was settled the papers had launched into Japan's first journalistic discussion of an internal governmental dispute.[5] The result was a press that changed, almost overnight, from an official mouthpiece to an instrument of political debate. It would remain an elitist, establishment institution, with individual editors who nurtured ties to powerful officials and factions, but never again would the newspaper world appear to speak for the government per se. As press historian Yamamoto Fumio sees it, "The divisions that suddenly developed within the government . . . took the press in a completely new direction."[6]

It is conceivable that this new course might have been temporary, a short detour away from what until now had been a steadily tightening press-government relationship, had it not been for a second, even larger crisis that hit Japan later that year and rendered full-fledged press-government cooperation impossible forever. This crisis centered first on the government's relations with Korea, then, more generally, on the long-term directions of foreign and domestic policy as well as on the fundamental question of how decisions would be made. The Crisis of 1873, as it sometimes is called, needs no elaboration here, since it has been covered in detail by many historians of the Meiji era.[7] Suffice it to say that when members of the Iwakura Mission returned to Japan that autumn, several of them succeeded in overturning a belligerent Dajōkan plan to force Korea into diplomatic and economic relations with Japan. Saigō, who had designed the plan, left the government in protest and took with him a number of leading officials, including Etō Shinpei, Foreign Minister Soejima Taneomi, and State Councillors Itagaki Taisuke and Gotō Shōjirō. His angry withdrawal marked a watershed for the evolving Meiji regime, sparking several violent rebellions by disaffected samurai, leading to the rise of Japan's first "popular" (or at least privately led) political movements and prompting the rulers to focus their modernizing efforts on the maintenance of domestic order—at the expense, some said, of progress toward democracy.

The most significant result of the political schism for the press was the fact that it inspired several editors to turn their papers into more forceful vehicles for shaping opinion. Stephen Koss, historian of Great Britain's political press, sees the "transition from official to popular control" as one of the major steps in the development of modern journalism,[8] and while that transition would occur gradually in Japan, its beginnings clearly lay in the press' response to the 1873 crisis. Papers that had been well-tamed chroniclers of enlightenment became organs of public dialogue, participants in a "press debate of unprecedented vigor."[9] As Nishida Taketoshi saw it, "Eight or nine of every ten Tokyo and Yokohama papers now became completely politicized."[10] They retained their Confucian orientation as vessels of educated leaders seeking "to inform the ruler . . . of how his subjects fare,"[11] but the editors now took up the added task of advising the ruler, on their own and through a public medium, about how he should respond to the subjects' situation.

The new approach was not simply the result of a change in the journalists' attitudes, though that was an important part of the mix, as we shall see below. At least as important in triggering the change were the activities of the officials themselves. As the bureaucratic world grew increasingly factionalized and as it became clear that opinionated editors could not easily be controlled, the various ministries began taking steps to separate themselves from the very papers they had created. In October 1873, as if in anticipation of the furor to come, the government issued a new newspaper regulation, forbidding indiscriminate criticism of political affairs.

And during the next several months officials cut back on the distribution of newspapers to the prefectures, first giving regional administrators freedom to choose which papers to buy, then, in 1875, cutting off newspaper-purchase funds altogether.[12] Similarly, the postal bureau and the Sa'in severed ties in the fall of 1874 with their respective press allies, *Yūbin Hōchi* and *Nisshin Shinjishi,* and refused from that time onward to give them special assistance in securing news.[13]

The reasons for the government's severance of ties appear to have been both political and financial. In part, bureaucrats were motivated by the serious budgetary concerns that had prompted the bitter infighting in 1873. If one could save a few yen by dropping subscriptions, that was the thing to do.[14] Of greater importance was the fact that the papers were becoming less reliable. More and more, dailies that served their patrons on one day were running the views of a competitor on another. No longer could anyone pretend that there was a single government voice to be amplified, now that some of the highest officials had begun using newspapers in their own turf struggles, now that the popular official Saigō had made the most vicious internal struggles public by going home to Kagoshima. Close, open ties between officials and newspapers were rendered not only expensive but increasingly impractical.

DEBATING STATE POLICIES

The negative side of this development, for the press, was the loss of revenue and of the stamp of authority that accompanied official ties; the positive side was increased independence and influence— and the emergence of a more interesting press. Well-honed editorial debates began to crowd official announcements for top billing on page one. Political essayists throughout the capital discovered a new outlet for communicating with more people than they ever had thought possible. And, in perhaps the most significant development of all, several talented and opinionated bureaucrats were induced by the new atmosphere to take up careers in journalism themselves. Narushima Ryūhoku, a trenchant writer who had served in the shogunate then traveled in Europe after the Restoration, assumed the editorship of the upstart government critic *Chōya Shimbun* on October 1, 1874.[15] Another former bakufu official, Kurimoto Joun, stubbornly anti-Meiji and famous for his "incorruptibility . . . integrity and scholarship," became editor of *Yūbin Hōchi* and allied that paper with the forces demanding wider representation in the government.[16] And as we have seen, Fukuchi left the Finance Ministry to take over *Tōkyō Nichi Nichi* in October 1874, a move that energized the press debates at least as much as it tightened *Nichi Nichi*'s ties to the government's Chōshū faction.

The new proclivity for debating issues was given a special boost early in 1874, when *Hōchi* began running frequent political opinion pieces and when most of the other *ōshimbun* responded with combative essays of their own. The essays did not appear daily; nor did they take consistent positions. Indeed, many of them appeared in the correspondence *(tōsho)* section, and the views expressed in a given paper varied as much as the range of political opinion itself. One day, a "letter" (quite possibly written by a staff member over a fictitious name and address) might support Itagaki's demands for wider representation, and several days later another piece of "correspondence" might take the official line. Only at the end of 1874, when Fukuchi began daily editorials with a fixed *Nichi Nichi* position, did consistency become the norm.[17] But already at the beginning of the year, the "op-ed" piece had moved to the center of Tokyo journalism, no matter what it was called or where it was run, making the press an instigator as much as a conveyor of political ideas.[18]

And there was plenty to debate; for by this time the entire elite world was engulfed in disputes over so many controversial issues that the press probably would have become a debating medium even without the impetus of new journalists and irritated officials. Chief among these was the question of whether—and when—Japan should create a popular assembly and thus bring outsiders into the national decision-making process. This debate, which sprang directly from the overturning of the original Dajōkan decision on Korea, exploded almost overnight on January 17, 1874, when Itagaki and seven other Saigō supporters petitioned the government for the immediate creation of an assembly. They claimed that governing power had been taken away from the "Imperial House above" and the "people below" by arbitrary officials. "The manifold decrees of the government appear in the morning and are changed in the evening," they wrote; "the channel by which the people should communicate with the government is blocked, and they cannot state their grievances." Invoking the idea that those who pay taxes should participate in rule, the petition cited the Korean episode as an example of official arrogance and predicted that "if a reform is not effected the state will be ruined." The country must find a means to develop "public discussion in the empire," the petitioners concluded; it must create "a council-chamber chosen by the people."[19] The result of this memorial, once Black published it in *Nisshin Shinjishi,* was Japan's first sustained, *public* debate of a specific government policy: "the raising of the curtain on a golden age of discussion."[20]

Nisshin Shinjishi was not only the first to publish Itagaki's petition; it also launched the discussion, first in a progovernment piece by Katō Hiroyuki on February 3 questioning Japan's readiness for popular participation in government, then in responses from Itagaki and his supporters, and still later with Katō and the populist Ōi Kentarō debating the issues across successive weeks. Soon, other papers took up the issue, and by late winter the discussion had gained sufficient momentum to carry it for a full year, with supporters of Itagaki calling for the immediate creation of an assembly and *zenshinshugisha,* or gradualists, on the other side insisting that an assembly was premature. And while most papers presented the views of both sides throughout 1874, the preponderance of essays in all but *Tōkyō Nichi Nichi* fell in the antigovernment, pro-assembly category, with *Chōya* arguing most vigorously in behalf of an early assembly.[21]

At the core of the *minken* (people's rights) or pro-assembly argument was the contention that an assembly would keep officials from becoming tyrannical. As Ōi put it in February 1874,

> If we wait for a distant day when the people have achieved knowledge and enlightenment, I fear that we will experience nothing but official despotism until then. As a result, the people will have no confidence in the laws, and if they have no faith in the laws, they will not submit to them. . . . People will uphold laws that they themselves create.[22]

Challenged by Katō Hiroyuki, who feared that hasty movement toward assembly government might threaten national stability, Ōi replied, with Confucian-bred logic, that an assembly would bring "the emperor's thoughts above into contact with the masses below," then added that "a country rich in popular rights is a free country" and that an assembly was "right for the spirit of our times *(jisei).*"[23]

Supporters of the assembly cause included Kurimoto, Narushima, Furusawa Shigeru, and Suehiro Tetchō, who had become an editorial force at *Tōkyō Akebono.* Hayashi Mokichi at *Minkan Zasshi* argued that "it is hard for a nation to be independent" unless the people *(min)* "develop a free and independent temperament."[24]

And Soejima, the former foreign minister who had left the government with Saigō, published a powerful response to Katō in Black's *Nisshin Shinjishi,* calling the alarms about potential popular disturbances "absurd" and saying that the real danger lay in the "evil of official despotism." Drawing on John Stuart Mill, Soejima declared: "Barbarism needs tyranny. Slaves need tutelary government. For people advanced beyond these stages, an independent assembly system is appropriate. . . . Those who want the people to be wise must support their right to handle public affairs and engage in discussions of the pros and cons of national issues."[25]

The government's side of the argument—that an assembly should indeed be created, but only after the groundwork had been laid deliberately and carefully among the people—was taken up most forcefully by Katō and Fukuchi. On January 23, 1874, *Nichi Nichi* ran an essay deriding the Itagaki petition as an "emotional outburst" grounded in "pure suspicion," and on the twenty-sixth it called for the government to spend at least a full decade preparing the people for representative government. In early February, *Shimbun Zasshi* ran Katō's argument that to establish an assembly "too rapidly in a nation not yet enlightened or merely to seek to copy other countries' systems . . . would be to hinder progress."[26]

The most sustained statement of the gradualist view came after Fukuchi took the *Nichi Nichi* editorial reins in October 1874. He called his opponents "radicals" *(kyūshinshugisha)* and argued that "no nation tending to radicalism has long been able to maintain national tranquility."[27] He agreed that an assembly must be created eventually but maintained that giving an early vote to people reared under feudalism risked confusion at best, anarchy at worst. And then he turned the argument on the *minken* proponents, noting that they were calling for an assembly made up of former samurai and noblemen alone. The legislature must encompass not just the upper classes, he argued; it also must include the *heimin* or commoners, who deserved a voice just as much as did the former samurai, who for two and a half centuries had been mere "parasites sustained by the people."[28] "The *heimin* were not born without spirit and power," he wrote; their problem was just that "they have been oppressed by the so-called spirit and power of the *shizoku* (former samurai)."[29] It would take time to train them to participate in government, and the assembly should be delayed until they were ready, until local assemblies and joint commercial enterprises had taught them to "snatch their rights" and "increase their spirit."[30] He also noted the irony inherent in another of his opponents' demands: the fact that they insisted on the continuation of the elitist, Tokugawa-era government stipends for former samurai even while calling themselves *minken* or popular rights advocates.

Although the views articulated by both sides in this debate are important in and of themselves, the key point here is the way they changed Japan's *ōshimbun* press. Having taken up weighty and controversial matters with such passion, the Tokyo journalists never again would settle for subservient relations with those running the government bureaus. The popular rights debate itself would cool off in the spring of 1875, when the government set up an assembly of local officials (chihōkan kaigi) to consult on public affairs, and created a Senate (Genrōin) and Supreme Court (Dai-shin'in).[31] But a full sixteen months of debating national policy had given the press a new self-image, a new understanding of the role of journalism. Writers no longer saw themselves as mere scribes of enlightenment; they had become participants, men compelled by training and profession to help determine what was best for their "people."

PUSHED TOWARD INDEPENDENCE

This was, for the rulers, a menacing shift; indeed, it was a menacing *time.* Not only had Saigō led his disaffected fellows out of the government; samurai by now had rebelled in Saga, and they were growing restive in Hagi and Kumamoto. Moreover, by the spring of 1876, many in the press had moved beyond theoretical descriptions of governmental forms to direct attacks on the officials themselves. Narushima at *Chōya,* for example, had likened the bureaucrats to "captains" sailing "their craft full-speed into a mountain,"[32] while Soejima had raised the clique-government *(hanbatsu)* issue, noting that nearly two-thirds of all higher officials came from the four domains that had led in the Restoration,[33] and radical journals such as *Sōmō Zasshi* and *Fusai Shimbun* were going so far now as to call for the assassination of corrupt officials and for "liberty" to be "earned with blood."[34] In one notorious editorial, *Sōmō Zasshi* likened officials to "clerks" and the people to "masters," commenting that any master who did not "rebuke and fire" an errant clerk was a "damned fool."[35]

To officials determined to keep Japan strong in the face of foreign threats, Confucian-bred rulers who feared nothing so much as a breakdown in public order (à la French Revolution), attacks of this sort went beyond the pale. It did not really matter that the mainstream journalists were themselves committed to an orderly transition to modern government or that the writers were closer to the Confucian paternalism of their official peers than to a Robespierre or even a Jefferson. They saw the willingness to attack officials and their positions publicly, in print, as threats not only to their own personal authority but to the stability of the country. And so, they increased the tempo of bureaucratic directives designed to limit press comment. Midoro Masaichi lists eight press-related official notices between February 1874 and March 1875, ranging from prohibitions on publishing news about military operations in Saga to a proscription of the use of official funds for purchasing newspapers.[36] The Justice Ministry took up the press-control issue in March 1874, instructing the Education and Home ministries to begin work on a comprehensive set of new press regulations.[37] And fifteen months later, on June 28, 1875, their work culminated in a far-reaching newspaper law *(shimbunshi jōrei)* that closed the door forever on any kind of thoroughgoing press-government cooperation.[38]

Drafted by Inoue Kowashi and Ozaki Saburō with the advice of the French legal specialist Emile Boissonade, the law created Japan's first comprehensive framework for regulating newspapers.[39] It adhered to the paternalistic philosophy of Tokugawa-era control patterns and followed precedent in requiring prior approval, now by the Naimushō (Home Ministry), for the publication of any paper. But most of the law's specific measures were new, and many bordered on the draconian. They limited ownership of vernacular papers to Japanese citizens; editors, who now bore primary responsibility for violations of the law, were required to print both their own names and the names of the printers at the end of each issue, and writers were instructed to sign their articles "in every case where the discussion turns upon foreign or domestic politics, finance, the feelings of the nation, the aspect of the times, learning or religion, or matters affecting the rights of officials and people."[40] Moreover, papers were required to print corrections or explanations if someone "mentioned by name" in an article requested it. They were forbidden to publish judicial deliberations, preliminary criminal proceedings, unauthorized petitions to the government, and criticisms of laws. They also were instructed explicitly to refrain from advocating revolution, reviling "existing laws," confusing "the sense of duty of the people," and justifying "offenses plainly contrary to the criminal law." And writers deemed guilty of provoking a crime were to be considered "equally guilty with the person who has been caused to commit it."

Perhaps the sharpest break with the earlier Meiji regulations came in the list of punishments. No longer would journalists be left to follow the laws out of their own Confucian sense of honor; now the law had teeth, sharp ones. Failure to specify editors or proprietors carried a one-hundred-yen fine for each person unnamed; the use of "feigned names" was to cost ten yen and up to thirty days in jail, and those who signed someone else's name would spend seventy days in prison. Papers with no editor would be suspended, and those printing matters deemed likely to incite crimes would be fined up to five hundred yen and jailed for as much as three years. The government, said one indignant press historian, had decided to treat reporters "like swindlers and thieves in the night."[41] Another called the law a "literary prison" *(moji no goku).*[42] And the journalist Suehiro said he felt suddenly like a "caged bird" or "a wild horse that had been tamed." People, he explained, "had come to regard the newspaper as a necessary agent in correcting social and political evils, as a kind of scolding drum"; so the shock of the new restrictions "was extraordinary."[43]

Actually, the law should not have surprised the journalists. Official press restrictions held sway in most countries, including the "enlightened" states of France and Germany, and while liberalization had been under way for several decades in Europe, it had been erratic even there, with many countries still exercising greater control than the Meiji officials had until now. Moreover, Japan's newspapermen knew that a comprehensive code was being written and during the previous year had frequently written articles or sent petitions urging officials not to circumscribe their freedoms.[44] So when it was issued most writers voiced less shock than caution. Unable to get the new law in type for their Tuesday (June 29) editions, the editors generally printed it verbatim on page one on Wednesday. But, with the exception of *Tōkyō Akebono* and *Chōya,* which launched early attacks on the law, most of the papers refrained at first from commenting on it directly. In a world where average reporters earned under twenty yen a month and top editors made only eighty or one hundred yen,[45] jail terms and five-hundred-yen fines were threat enough to make discretion the norm.

Minoura Katsundo thus wrote at *Yūbin Hōchi* on August 30 that "the former practice of speaking frankly in editorial columns has become rare; important items that should be discussed now are ignored, and those who do discuss them employ allegory or fantasy.

They write vaguely or use circumlocutions, and thus are terribly weak in moving readers."[46] As if to prove his point, a typical *Nichi Nichi* editorial in early September argued that the real intent of the new system surely was "not to suppress just and fair arguments" but merely "to prevent the destruction of social peace and tranquility."[47] And *Meiroku Zasshi*, the elite journal through which many young opinion leaders debated the day's policy questions, was cowed to the point of discontinuing publication. Though not a newspaper by ordinary definitions, its leading lights decided that the new law would diminish its vigor, and so on September 1, 1875, following Fukuzawa Yukichi's argument that "free scholarly expression is not compatible with last June's press and slander laws," they voted, nine to four, to disband it.[48]

The reticence of leading writers to fight in public did not mean that they accepted the restrictions without a challenge, however; nor did the smaller journals keep quiet even in their editorial columns. In July, for example, the feisty little *Hyōron Shimbun* urged people to defy the law "with all their might" lest it turn the "whole country into deaf mutes."[49] And the more prestigious, establishment editors devised another, more discreet—and creative— means of struggling. Frustrated and unsure about how to proceed under the new rules, several of them called together the country's first "newspaper reporters' association" *(shimbun kisha no rengo)* to discuss the law's meaning and to form a joint response.[50] Gathering in Asakusa's Sensōji at 9:00 A.M. on the Thursday following the announcement of the law, they represented all of the major papers, including in their number Fujita Mokichi of *Yūbin Hōchi*, Kishida Ginkō and Fukuchi from *Tōkyō Nichi Nichi*, Narushima from *Chōya*, Suehiro from *Tōkyō Akebono*, and Yokose Fumihiko of *Hyōron*. After a good deal of discussion, they decided to draft hypothetical essays on a series of sensitive topics, then to submit the essays to the authorities, asking whether "an article such as this constitutes a violation of the new law." Each writer drafted a single, anonymous essay; then at a subsequent meeting Kishida agreed to edit them and present the complete package to the government, with the affixed seal of each of the cooperating newspapers.

One of the articles chided the Monbushō and Tokyo's city education bureau for hiring a classroom teacher who made numerous writing errors. Another called for the dismissal of unskilled plaintiffs "who make a nuisance of themselves." A third demanded the creation of a popular assembly, because "an authoritarian government cannot forever rule Japan in peace." A fourth labeled official favoritism toward the former samurai class "a disgrace." And still another urged "quick abolition" of the press law, which was "incompatible with free speech."[51] Officials accepted the submissions but refused to respond, commenting only that the government had "neither a responsibility to make refutations . . . nor any instructions to give."[52]

The official response was predictable, the editors' aggressiveness less so. The fact that highly connected journalists were willing to question the new legal approach, even if cautiously and through official channels, suggested that something significant was afoot in Japan's press world. Confucian or not, Japan's editors were finding it more and more difficult to identify with the government. Most of them probably regarded the dispute as somewhat intramural, the struggle of differing camps within the elite, educated establishment. But clearly many of the editors were moving toward greater identification with *external* forces, with ideas such as "popular rights" and "free speech," if only as a means of struggling for greater influence within the elite world. And that shift would, in time, have profound results.

Even more surprising in the short run, given the establishment press' close ties to the government mere months earlier, was the willingness of a few of the *ōshimbun* to defy the government quite directly once the more discreet group approach had failed. Suehiro and Narushima in particular took vigorously to the attack. An impetuous young twenty-seven-year-old Shikoku native who had quit the Finance Ministry when he found his work spiritually constricting, Suehiro launched a series of daily attacks on the new code with a July 20 editorial labeled simply "On the Press Law" *(Shimbun jōrei o ronzu)*. He declared himself willing to go to jail for the cause of press freedom, and on August 7 the authorities obliged with a twenty-yen fine and a two-month prison sentence for confusing "the sense of the duty of the people to observe the existing laws" (Article 14).[53] Prison did not, however, tame him. After being released on October 7, he resigned from *Akebono* rather than accept his editor's insistence on greater moderation and joined the combative Narushima at *Chōya*. There, in December, he got himself in further trouble by writing an editorial about two "little men" who had "created a law that oppressed the people." He described an ambitious, greedy pair named "Inoue Saburō and Ozaki Kowashi" who "toadied to authorities while pretending to be gentlemen." These men, he wrote, "do everything they can to silence us and to repress our lofty intentions." Were they to die, their sinister reputations would precede them to hell. It was clear that Suehiro actually was describing Inoue Kowashi and Ozaki Saburō, the ministry officials who had drafted the press law. So back he went to jail, this time for eight months, with a two-hundred-yen fine.[54]

Nor was he alone. Narushima was a dozen years older than Suehiro but only slightly more circumspect. He weighed in with his own discussion of the law on July 23, saying that even if criticism of the law were illegal, surely analysis was not. On August 9, he ran an essay praising Suehiro's defiant courage as "an auspicious omen of the age of enlightenment."[55] And six days later he referred to Suehiro's "folly and stubbornness," writing: "Why do people continue to violate the law even after they are punished for their crimes? Can they not help themselves? Or is it that they have unshakable integrity? Maybe they simply are determined to see our government become enlightened. I really do not know."[56]

Other editors too, emboldened by Suehiro and Narushima, began to express mildly critical questions about the press law as the summer and autumn moved along. The government-oriented Fukuchi at *Nichi Nichi,* for example, ran an essay saying that while the law's intent ("keeping people from stirring things up and preventing agitation") was proper, if it "caused servility or cowardice," it would mark a "severe retreat" for Japan.[57] In November, Hasegawa Gikō of *Tōkyō Akebono* argued that "one cannot discuss morality in the abstract," after officials had cracked down on him for an exposé of the "scandalous behavior" of Governor Mishima Michitsune of Tsuruoka. How could the educated elite be expected to lead society, he asked, if they could not discuss morality in terms of actual deeds by real people?[58] And other reporters, as varied as Hokiyama Kageo of *Nichi Nichi,* Oka Keikō of *Yūbin Hōchi,* Tsukahara Yasushi of *Yokohama Mainichi,* and Sakai Kisaburō of *Akebono,* also ran essays questioning either the law or its enforcement.[59]

These criticisms were rendered particularly impressive by the government's almost paranoid response to them. All of the writers just noted, except Fukuchi, paid for their audacity with fines or jail terms. Junior councillor Inoue Kaoru, one of the more moderate officials, illustrated the government's nervousness about critics in his own personal efforts to deal with the Suehiro case. First, he put behind-the-scenes pressure on the *Akebono* editor, Aoe Shū, to tone down his young reporter. Then he met with Suehiro himself, granting that the law might be a bit severe but chiding him for overreacting. He succeeded only in goading Suehiro into more determined resistance, but the time he gave to trying to tame a young writer showed the official nervousness over public criticism.[60] And many of Inoue's less moderate colleagues decided that it was time to bring the press to heel. If papers would not serve as arms of the government, at least they should be prevented from becoming weapons against it.

THE LAW'S HARSH ARM

Thus began what the Irishman J. R. Black called a time of "persecution,"[61] a time in which a zealous government turned recent allies into what some scholars have called *"giseisha"* or martyrs.[62] Black knew whereof he spoke, because he was the first martyr, since the *shimbunshi jōrei* stipulation that only Japanese subjects could own Japanese-language newspapers was aimed directly at him. This was the era of extraterritoriality, when foreigners were not subject to Japanese laws, which meant that his *Nisshin Shinjishi* had been able to ignore Japanese press rules and publish materials unavailable to other newspapers.[63] Now, he was removed from *Nisshin Shinjishi* altogether, and though he reacted vigorously, first trying to start another paper, then demanding compensation, his pleas were ignored and the paper died.[64]

Black's fellow editors did not complain about his martyrdom; they had long resented his special privileges and had promoted the rule against foreign ownership of vernacular papers. But perhaps they should have, because the next few years saw the Naimushō and other ministries engage in unrelenting efforts to bring their own papers under control too. In some cases, the efforts were subtle, as when they brought ambitious writers such as Ōi Kentarō of *Akebono,* Inukai Tsuyoshi and Yano Fumio of *Yūbin Hochi,* and Furusawa Shigeru of *Nisshin Shinjishi* into the bureaucracy.[65] More often, however, they were direct. When Black said, "uneasy lies the head of him who wields an editorial pen," he was referring not so much to his own plight as to the large numbers of writers who went to jail or paid heavy fines over the next few years for insisting on the right to speak.

We already have seen that Suehiro was jailed twice. So was the more influential Narushima, for five days in the fall of 1875, then again for four months the following year. In all, according to Nishida Taketoshi, a cautious student of such matters, at least eleven journalists were jailed in 1875, eighty-six in 1876, and another forty-seven in 1877. Their ranks included such men as Oka

Keikō, Minoura Katsundo, Ueki Emori, and Yokose Fumihiko. And they wrote for the era's leading papers—*Chōya, Nichi Nichi,* and *Yūbin Hōchi*—as well as for such smaller sheets as *Saifū Shimbun* and *Hyōron Shimbun.*[66] Nor were their prison terms insignificant. While some got off with a few weeks or a month, several spent upwards of a year in jail, and Katō Kyūrō of *Saifū* was imprisoned for a full three-year term.

The most serious offender, in the eyes of the government, was *Hyōron,* founded in March 1875 by Ebihara Boku of Aichi Prefecture and edited by the irascible Komatsubara Eitarō.[67] Disgruntled by the plight of former samurai and enamored by the democratic ideals of Rousseau, the *Hyōron* writers flailed away, issue after issue, often in extreme language, at the authorities. Japan was being oppressed by "despotic government" *(sensei seifu);* "oppressive regimes deserved to be overthrown"; the rulers should "put their energies into reforming national laws in accordance with the people's will."[68] The official response was consistently harsh. On September 4, 1875, Yokose Fumihiko was fined five yen for violating the press laws; on January 29, 1876, Komatsubara received a two-year jail sentence; on March 2, Yokose was convicted again, this time with a three-month, fifty-yen penalty. And that conviction unleashed an onslaught, as *Hyōron* editors and writers were fined or jailed no fewer than nine times in March and five times more in April and May. When one editor was convicted, says Midoro, "a second would rise from his corpse, grieving over the predecessor's loss even while continuing his bitter attacks on the government."[69] By summer, the officials had had enough, and on July 5 they shut *Hyōron* down altogether, under a new Dajōkan decree permitting the banning of papers that disturbed national tranquility. "To support national tranquility," said the paper in its final issue, "does not mean what the authorities think it does"; it means "expanding freedom and popular rights."[70]

Prison conditions themselves were relatively moderate. At first, they involved little more than house arrest, because the government had inadequate prison space. One court officer told Suehiro he found it "disgraceful to imprison newspaper writers" and let him receive visitors freely.[71] By the time of Suehiro's second indictment late in 1875, however, officials were clamping down. He was bound with a rope for delivery to court this time, then held in a cold and smelly cell.[72] And by the time he and Narushima were sentenced at the beginning of the next year, the government had a new jail ready. As Narushima recalled:

> The judge suddenly raised his voice and gave Suehiro and me a total of one year in jail and 250 yen in fines. . . . The jailer took us to a prison and shut me up in Cell 22 in the northeast section; then he put Suehiro in Cell 24. The northeast section held only regular prisoners *(kingokunin)* who were treated a bit more lightly than those under preventive custody *(kōryūjin)*. The jail, which had been completed at the end of the previous year, was copied after Western-style prisons and was in the shape of a cross.

He said his section contained several other journalists, including Yokose, Komatsubara, and *Saifū Shimbun*'s Katō. Prisoners were bound by ropes and had to go barefoot, even on icy winter days, and they were given only limited opportunities for bathing. They did, however, have plenty of leisure and were allowed to write; so Narushima produced both a famous memoir, *Gokunai banashi* (Prison talks) and what surely was Japan's first prison newspaper, the *Kingoku Eiri Toto Ichi Shimbun*.[73]

Narushima was released from jail on June 11, just seventeen days short of the first anniversary of the *shimbunshi jōrei*. On the anniversary itself, more than a hundred writers from Japan's leading papers gathered beneath the Sensōji's massive red pillars for a satirical memorial service, to commemorate their success in surviving the previous twelve months. It was a curious event. Assisted by nearly forty sutra-chanting priests and several musicians, the journalists read prayers and made speeches by the incensed light of flickering candles, confessing their professional faults, mourning departed colleagues, and asking for mercy for writers still in prison. The opening speech was made by Ōuchi Seiran of *Meikyō Shimbun*, the closing address by Fukuchi. But the most quoted of the talks was delivered by the irrepressible Narushima, who addressed his remarks to the "Newspaper Spirit" *(shimbun no rei)*. He thanked that presence for coming from the West to enlighten a Japanese public yet "indistinguishable from potato worms, unable to speak a word or to write a line of argument," a public incapable of anything better than "revering official speeches and government decrees as paragons of truth and reason." He thanked the spirit for a press that had enabled the Japanese people at last to raise their voices on behalf of their own well-being. Then, unbowed by his recent days in jail, he sarcastically chided the journalists present for their brash opposition to the authorities and thanked the "wise government" for limiting the penalty for press violations to a "mere three years in prison and a thousand-yen fine."[74]

The service was a fresh breeze to a press that for a full year had felt itself under attack, a curious mixture of courage, religious symbolism, and high spirits. On one level it showed the remarkable sense of fraternity bestowed by an oppressive government on a press corps whose philosophical differences heretofore had engendered only conflict. On another level, it announced to the public that the press would not be stifled. The bureaucratic infighting of the last three years had combined with heavy-handed legal controls to turn Japan's newspapers into vehicles for the open discussion of public issues. There, more than in Western ideas, lay the source of the press' newfound vigor.

I do not mean to suggest that the press had lost all inhibitions or that it had become recklessly outspoken. Only a few of the smallest papers flailed away unabashedly at the government. As we already have noted, all of the mainstream editors were born and reared Confucian, imbued with what Irokawa Daikichi calls the "conventional morality" that posits the good of the state above that of the individual and focuses above all on "communal conformity."[75] Their language had not even contained words for concepts such as "rights," "civil liberties," or "political freedom" prior to the invasion of Western culture.[76] Even the outspoken Suehiro claimed, as his core value, an "amalgamation of divergent elements for the common good . . . the Confucian ideal of a harmonious, unified society."[77] And the populist Narushima would write just a few months later, during the Satsuma Rebellion, that while press freedom should be the norm in a fully civilized society, Japan was not quite ready yet for complete freedom. Hence, "if the government finds it necessary at times to interfere with the freedom of the press, to suit the emergencies of a partial civilization, it is but taking care for the true public interest."[78] Was he being sarcastic? One never could be quite sure with Narushima, but the tone would suggest not. Even he was, like all his fellows, committed to the good society above all.

But the remarkable—and new—thing was that this Confucian acceptance of authority had begun to loosen its grip as more and more journalists took the risk of confronting official pronouncements and laws in an open, public manner. In the words of Fukuzawa, journalists such as Kurimoto and Narushima were beginning to demonstrate "the middle-class spirit of independence that created Western civilization," beginning in a fundamental sense to "modernize Japan."[79] Thus, a year after the Asakusa service Black would write about the "irrepressible boldness" that had come to characterize Japan's journalists. "They will write," he said, "and regardless of all consequences they refuse to avoid criticism of the Government and the officials. It has never once been found that when one writer or editor has been incarcerated, there were no men of ability to step at once into his place, and run the same risks."[80]

The journalists' motive may have varied. Some opposed the government because they thought errant officials had disrupted Confucian harmony by cutting off the flow of opinion between subjects and rulers. Others felt called upon by their education to advise the ministers. Many another, in the words of Meiji journalist Shimada Saburō, saw themselves as "ministers without portfolio." Only a few really believed in freedom as an end in itself. But, for nearly all editors, the sense of separation from the government as an institution had become palpable. Journalism had become, said Shimada, its own "citadel for political discussion."[81]

A MODERN, IF MODEST, INSTITUTION

Given this evolving posture, it is hardly surprising that Tokyo's *ōshimbun* took up an ever-widening range of issues over the next half decade. More and more, the newspapers became agenda-setters, covering not only policies initiated within the bureaucracy, but all the issues—economic, political, diplomatic, educational, religious —that they thought important to a changing Japan, and doing so with an erudition and vigor that seems remarkable from today's vantage point. Before turning to that coverage, however, we need to pause for a brief examination of the institutional side of the press, to the evolution in operations, management, and circulation that gave shape to the political and editorial developments.

It is striking how small these papers still were. Newspapers had become major enterprises in Europe and the United States by now, with some London papers boasting circulations of 300,000 by the 1850s,[82] and New York's leading papers recording Civil War–era press runs in excess of 100,000.[83] But Japan's papers remained small in all categories: staff and salaries, publishing operations, profits, circulation. In 1877, for example, the largest paper, *Tōkyō Nichi Nichi,* had just 150 total employees, most of them engaged in the labor-intensive work of printing the paper, while *Yūbin Hōchi* had 116 workers and *Chōya* only 108,[84] and during the next few year those numbers increased only marginally. The numbers of editors and reporters were downright minuscule: twenty-seven at *Nichi*

Nichi in 1875, eleven at *Ōsaka Asahi Shimbun* in 1879, only three that year at the tiny *San'yō Shimbun*, ten at *Chōya* in 1880.[85]

Wages also remained low, with average newspaper salaries well below those even of low-ranking government workers. At *Yūbin Hōchi*, Japan's best-paying paper, the average wage for all but the half dozen top editorial writers in 1877 was barely over 13 yen a month; at *Nichi Nichi* it was 11.6 yen, and at the sensational paper *Tōkyō Eiri Shimbun*, just 5.29 yen a month.[86] Lead writers were paid well, with stars like Fukuchi receiving more than two hundred yen a month after the middle of the 1870s—a figure that compares favorably to the high-ranking *chokunin*, or imperial appointees just below the ministerial level. But many of the working staff in newspaper plants received as little as five yen a month, in contrast to government employees, who received twenty yen per month all the way down to the fifteenth rank.[87] Even a prominent writer like Shimada was regarded as "highly paid" in 1874 with a salary of thirty yen a month; when he became a coeditor in 1875, his monthly pay advanced to fifty yen.[88]

The meager salaries reflected the fact that employee recruitment was quite informal too. For top writers, publishers and owners usually either sought out well-known acquaintances they knew to be good writers or turned to graduates of the growing numbers of colleges administered by their friends, especially Fukuzawa's Keiō Gijuku and Niijima Jō's Dōshisha in Kyoto. The innovative *Asahi* in Osaka began limited experiments with entrance tests for reporters in 1880. But for lower-level employees, there was little system to the hiring process.[89] When a position opened up or a new job was created, employers took anyone available.

Many papers also continued to operate out of small, almost primitive plants during these years. There were exceptions. *Nichi Nichi*, for example, became profitable enough to move in 1877 into an impressive brick building in the Ginza that reminded Narushima of "the golden cavern of a heavenly hermit,"[90] as did *Chōya* and the upstart *Yomiuri*.[91] But the majority still had small quarters and limited assets. One scholar has noted that an ambitious person could launch a newspaper in this period for as little as four thousand yen, and as late as 1883 one journalist said a circulation of five thousand "should yield a profit."[92] We already have seen how *Akebono* carried out all of its work in a single room at the time of the 1875 press law. By 1880, it had fixed assets of a mere 8,950 yen, while *Chōya* had 23,000 yen and the well-endowed *Nichi Nichi* just 45,000.[93] As Edward Morse commented on visiting a newspaper office in 1879, "I had expected to see an immense room, knowing the number of characters used to set up a piece of printed matter, and was astonished to find a room not over thirty feet square." The result, he said, was such crowding that "the room reminded one of an ant hill with the black ants ceaselessly passing each other to and fro."[94] Since even the prestige papers owned only hand-operated printing presses until 1881—often only two or three at that—the buzz of human energy demanded to get out papers of even a few thousand circulation is easy to imagine.[95]

And a few thousand is all that most of them did publish each day—partly because of their limited technical capacities and partly because most of these early editors were interested more in influencing an elite inner circle of intellectuals than in making profits by selling to commoners. While figures are rough at best in these early years of the press, on one thing they all agree: only a few major papers ever reached a daily circulation of more than 10,000 until the 1880s. *Chōya* exceeded that briefly, with nearly 18,000 subscribers in 1876, apparently because of the popularity of Narushima's prison writings, then dropped to 7,076 the next year. *Tōkyō Nichi Nichi* rose to 11,000 in 1877, the year of the Satsuma Rebellion when the Tokyo public quested after the latest battlefield news, then fell to 8,231 a year later. The commercially oriented *koshimbun Yomiuri* also boasted circulations of around 20,000 after 1877, but no other paper ever exceeded 10,000 subscribers in these years.[96] While the press of the late 1870s was lively and influential, packed with potential, it remained small and distinctly premodern in a material sense, made up primarily of "miserable publications . . . to the eye of the foreigner accustomed to the broadsheets of London or New York."[97]

But it hardly was a stagnant institution, even in institutional terms. As the very writer who called the papers "miserable" said, by the end of the 1870s the press had begun growing "at a rate almost alarming from its rapidity."[98] While circulations of individual papers rose gradually and spasmodically, the total numbers of newspapers kept increasing steadily, with a resultant rapid rise in readership and awareness in these years. Figures compiled by Ukai Shin'ichi show that total national newspaper circulation quintupled from 8.3 million in 1874 to 44.5 million in 1879, with the number of subscriptions for every 10,000 citizens rising from 6.7 to 34.1.[99] Certainly this increase affected the capital; a *Japan Mail* correspondent talked about the people there going "into raptures over the newspaper press."[100] But at least as important was the fact that people increasingly were reading papers in the provinces too.

Almost at its inception, *Nichi Nichi*, for example, had signed a contract with an Osaka shop to distribute the paper in Kansai, while the other Tokyo papers were quick to begin selling papers at bookstores and picture book stores (ezōshiya), first in the capital and then in the regional centers. Late in 1874, *Nichi Nichi* also began selling its Tokyo papers through corner newsstands of the type Fukuchi had encountered on his travels in France. And all of the major papers soon took to using home deliveries, with writers themselves sometimes dropping off papers on the way home and typical deliverymen carrying papers in boxes on the ends of poles with a jangling bell attached to attract attention.[101] The first big boost in regional sales came in 1877, when individual stores in provincial centers were allowed to begin selling several different papers at the same time. Until then, no given store had been permitted by the editors to sell more than a single title. Once individual shops began signing simultaneous contracts with several newspaper companies, says Yamamoto Taketoshi, there was a marked increase in the sale of Kantō papers in regional Japan.[102]

These years also saw a significant rise in the number of papers actually published in Japan's provincial regions. Though figures used by students of the press vary considerably, it is clear that while only about two dozen papers were publishing at any one time during the years of close press-government ties, that number had at least quadrupled, probably multiplied six or seven times by the end of the 1870s. On the high side, some estimate as many as 225 papers in existence by the late 1870s, while the most conservative scholars put the figure at more like 100, and a safe estimate would seem to be somewhere between 150 and 175.[103] A study of local histories shows that all but a half dozen of today's forty-seven prefectures had newspapers by 1881. Among the papers that came into existence in 1876 alone were the *Nishin Shimbun* in Iwate Prefecture, the *Ibaraki Shinpō* in Ibaraki, *Matsumoto Shimbun* in Nagano, *Aichi Shimbun* and *Aichi Nippō* in the Nagoya region, *Futsū Shimbun* in Tokushima, *Ehime Shimbun* in northwestern Shikoku, *Saikai Shimbun* in Nagasaki, *Kumamoto Shimbun* in that prefecture, and *Inaka Shimbun* in Ōita. Those born two years later, in 1878, included the *Hakodate Shimbun* in Hokkaido, *Yamagata Shimbun* to the north, the *Gunma Shinshi* in central Honshu, *Mezamashi Shimbun* in Fukuoka, and *Ise Shimbun* in Mie.[104] Taken together with the diffusion of reading rooms, public newspaper readings, and newspaper discussion groups described in the previous chapter, the profusion of new papers makes it clear that the press' impact had become national as Japan moved toward the middle of the second Meiji decade.

These years also provided new variety in the kinds of reading material available to the public. For one thing, magazines intended for more specialized audiences appeared in the late 1870s, and while some of them were political in tone, others focused on fields as varied as health, education, religion, literature, music, satire, and the arts.[105] For another, the second half of the 1870s saw the emergence of a popular, commercially oriented nonpolitical press that, while lying outside the parameters of this study, must be noted briefly because of the impact it would have on the establishment papers themselves.

The genesis of this press lay in the rising class of literate but apolitical urbanites who populated the cities in increasing numbers after the Meiji Restoration, people who had an interest in reading easy and lively material but not in plowing through intellectual, political discussions or in the heavy Chinese-style prose of the *ōshimbun.* Recognizing the market these people represented, several entrepreneurs of the old *kawaraban* mindset experimented with easy-to-read, sensational papers in the first Meiji years, including the 1873 *Mainichi Hirakana Shimbun,* which eschewed Chinese characters and used only the *hiragana* phonetic symbols in a failed effort to simplify reading.[106] The first paper to succeed in developing a sizable plebeian readership was *Yomiuri Shimbun,* which published its first issue on November 2, 1874, under the editorship of dictionary publisher Koyasu Takashi, the former editor of *Yokohama Mainichi.*[107]

Financed by a yarn merchant, the two-page paper was not a great deal more attractive visually than *Yūbin Hōchi* or *Yokohama Mainichi,* though it did include *furigana,* the phonetic aids intended to make Chinese characters easier to comprehend.[108] From the first number, however, it showed a keen understanding of what merchants and clerks wanted to read. The November 2 issue included a story on a fire in Nagasaki, an account of forty-eight people bitten by mad dogs near Kuwayama, the tale of a farmer's wife who recovered the use of a lame arm by praying to the local *kami,* advice on how properly to show respect to the Meiji Emperor when he traveled through Tokyo the next day, and, of course, the obligatory official notices.[109] The paper came out every other day, sold for just one *rin,* and by the end of 1875, after becoming a four-page daily, had the largest circulation in Tokyo.[110] Its forte was mass-oriented news, and even its daily opinion column, launched in 1879, was titled "Yomiuri Gossip" *(Yomiuri zōdan).* The *Yomiuri* editors sent special reporters to cover major events such as imperial tours and the 1878 conference of local governors, and after

Yanagawa Shunsan, *Shimbun Kaisō and Chūgai Shimbun.* (Courtesy Mainichi Shimbunsha)

Eugene Van Reed, *Moshiogusa,* and Joseph Heco, *Kaigai Shimbun.* (Courtesy Hajima Tomoyuki, Tōyō Bunka Shimbun Kenkyūkai)

The young Fukuchi Gen'ichirō, *Kōko Shimbun, Tōkyō Nichi Nichi Shimbun.* (Courtesy Mainichi Shimbunsha)

Koyasu Takashi, *Yokohama Mainichi Shimbun* and *Yomiuri Shimbun.* (Courtesy Yomiuri Shimbunsha)

Narushima Ryūhoku, *Chōya Shimbun.*
(Courtesy Mainichi Shimbunsha)

A youthful Murayama Ryōhei, *Asahi
Shimbun.* (Courtesy Asahi Shimbunsha)

Fukuzawa Yukichi in the early days of *Jiji
Shinpō.* (Courtesy Mainichi Shimbunsha)

A youthful Tokutomi Sohō, *Kokumin
Shimbun.* (Courtesy Mainichi
Shimbunsha)

The editorial offices of *Yomiuri Shimbun*, newly built on Tokyo's Ginza Street, 1877. (Courtesy Yomiuri Shimbunsha)

Woodblock print by Hiroshige III of *Tōkyō Nichi Nichi*'s Ginza offices, latter 1870s; owner Jōno Denpei looks out the upper window, far right, while cofounder Nishida Densuke works at the second first-floor window. (Courtesy Mainichi Shimbunsha)

sensational events like an 1875 fire in Sakurada and the 1878 assassination of Ōkubo, they were among the first to get extras onto the streets.[111]

Yomiuri was followed by a number of other commercially oriented papers, all of them known as *koshimbun* or "small papers," partially because they were printed on smaller sheets but mainly because they were not respectable in elite society. According to Ono, these *koshimbun* generally had ten characteristics:

1. They were printed on smaller sheets of paper.

2. They avoided politics and editorials.

3. They appended *furigana* to most articles to make for easier reading.

4. Their reporters focused on human interest news—the willow world, sensational and scandalous events, touching incidents in people's lives—with only brief articles on politics.

5. They used vernacular prose, avoiding the classical styles of the *ōshimbun.*

6. They ran serialized novels.[112]

7. They cost about half as much as the *ōshimbun:* from .8 to 1.5 *sen* a copy, compared to two *sen* or more for the prestige papers.

8. They were sold by hawkers on the street, much like the Edo-era broadsides.

9. Their readers came from the ordinary class of urban dwellers and included many merchants and housewives, in contrast to the intellectuals who made up the bulk of the *ōshimbun* audience.

10. They drew their writers mostly from the literary world, especially from the circles of cheap fiction writers *(gesaku-sha)* and *haiku* poets.[113]

Many of the *koshimbun* had short lives, but some proved as permanent as the leading prestige papers. And, despite the derisive "small paper" name, by the end of the first Meiji decade several also rivaled the *ōshimbun* in readership. In 1876, *Yomiuri's* average daily circulation of 18,189 dwarfed *Nichi Nichi's* 10,951 and *Yūbin Hōchi's* 7,978. By 1879, both *Yomiuri* (20,822) and *Tōkyō Eiri Shim-*

bun (14,381) had at least five thousand more daily readers than any of their "prestige" rivals.[114] They wrote about things that appealed to an ever broader audience, and while they may have charged less, their careful attention to management made the best of them quite profitable.[115]

Nor were the *koshimbun* limited to the Tokyo area. By the late 1870s, the Kantō successes were being emulated in the provinces, with commercial papers emerging in Kyoto, Sendai, Osaka, Fukui, Wakayama, Kumamoto, and Nagoya, among other places. The most important of these regional papers was Osaka's *Asahi Shimbun*, whose styles, while not widely noted at the time, eventually would change the face of Japanese journalism. The paper was launched with an investment of 30,000 yen on January 25, 1879, by the sake brewer Kimura Heihachi, with his playboy son Noboru serving as "proprietor," the literary light Tsuda Takashi as editor, and Murayama Ryōhei as manager. When Tsuda got the paper into financial troubles by trying to make it more political, a bitter control struggle ensued. By 1880, Murayama was in charge, and in January 1881 he and the accountant Ueno Riichi purchased *Asahi*.[116] They turned it into something of a middle-ground newspaper, committed to profit and readability, heavy on business news, and managed with a close eye to both accounts and editorial reliability. Over the next two decades, all of the country's successful *koshimbun* and *ōshimbun* would begin moving toward a commercialized middle ground that included both politics and profit. It is significant that a Kansai *koshimbun* pioneered this approach.[117]

One other development outside the mainstream newspaper press that demands note, if only for the influence it exerted on the political consciousness of the elite journalists, was the emergence in these years of a handful of satirical journals, which combined the politics of the *ōshimbun* with the vigor of the *koshimbun*. Drawing on the cartoon-based style of the English-language *Japan Punch*, which provided foreigners with some fifteen sheets of humor a month from 1862 to 1887, the Hiroshima native Nomura Fumio launched the satirical *Marumaru Chinbun* in 1877. Within two years, he was selling an astounding 15,000 weekly copies of comment on current affairs, and by the time the paper died three decades later it had made cartoonists such as Honda Kinkichirō, Kobayashi Kiyochika, and the Frenchman Georges Bigot national figures. The *Marumaru* writers poked fun at the pretensions of the elite, tweaked Japan's slavish imitation of foreign customs, and lampooned the hypocrisy of so-called democratic government policies. In 1880, its editor was jailed for besmirching the imperial family, and the paper was suspended for a year. The popularity of its political and social wit was sufficient, however, to inspire several other satirical magazines, including Miyatake Gaikotsu's *Tonchi Kyōkai Zasshi* and Bigot's *Toba-e,* and to provide grist for the mainstream political essayists.[118]

AMPLIFYING THE POLITICAL MOVEMENTS

The most influential cudgels of these years, however, were wielded by the *ōshimbun* writers, who saw politics, and politics alone, as worthy of serious journalism. While *Akebono* or *Tōkyō Nichi Nichi* might occasionally alert readers to a sensational murder or a financial impropriety in the miscellany columns of the late 1870s,[119] the prestige papers generally gave themselves more fully than ever to undergirding enlightenment and debating policy issues—and thus limited news coverage to matters deemed important and weighty. In 1877 they focused on war and the disestablishment of the old samurai class, in 1878 on assemblies and assassinations, in 1880 and 1881 on issues of sovereignty, the timing of a constitution, and government scandal. And throughout these years, all the papers chronicled (and often participated in) the spread of political activities through the rising popular rights, or *jiyū minken*, movement. An examination of the press' handling of three of these issues should help us see just how important the *ōshimbun* press had become in the evolving political process of a country stumbling toward constitutional government.

During 1877, no issue so thoroughly occupied the Japanese press as war. Several of the papers already had built their circulations partly through the coverage of earlier conflicts. *Tōkyō Nichi Nichi,* for example, had seen a significant rise in popularity when it sent the much-respected Kishida Ginkō to cover Japan's battle against Chinese forces in Taiwan in 1874.[120] And Tokyo residents had avidly bought papers to read about the rebellions of former samurai in Saga and Hagi at the middle of the decade. The first important chance for the press to deal with a war of genuine scope, however, came when Saigō led his Satsuma followers in a full-scale uprising against the government in January 1877. And the press generally proved itself up to the challenge.

The government put severe restrictions on coverage of the Satsuma Rebellion, first issuing an order prohibiting the "publication in newspapers of material about the Army for Subjugation of the Kumamoto Rebels," then following up in February and May with modifications that required "authorization" or "permission" prior to publication.[121] When editors violated the restrictions, they typically were fined. *Chikushi Shimbun* was assessed three yen for an inaccurate report that the rebels had taken Kagoshima, and the nominal editor of Osaka's *Kōmin Shinshi* was fined in September for reporting rumors of the deaths of several officers on the government side.[122] By and large, however, there was only a minimal need for enforcement; for while editors carped occasionally about restrictions on coverage, all but *Chōya*'s Narushima supported the government side—even its "right" to curtail coverage—wholeheartedly.[123] A February editorial in *Akebono*, for example, cited Bismarck's comment that "a single article in a newspaper might cause the ruin of a hundred thousand souls," then called the heavy censorship "reasonable and proper," even while urging the government to make "reliable information" available to the public.[124] A week later, the lucid American ally of several top officials Edward H. House wrote in his *Tokio Times* that while many foreign observers had expected these editors to use the war as a chance to retaliate against a government that had sent so many of their fellows to jail, the journalists had acted instead with "wise moderation . . . evincing a deep and genuine loyalty and a pure and fervent patriotism."[125] And *Yomiuri* typified the editors' disappointment in the once-popular Saigō with a mid-March editorial comment that despite his "bright and talented spirit," he "seemed now to be befuddled."[126]

This did not mean that the Tokyo editors simply accepted the official restrictions. They complained a good deal about the initial ban on coverage, then devised ways either to circumvent it or to work within the official limits, and by late winter, reports on the civil war were appearing regularly in the major papers. Fukuchi at *Nichi Nichi* secured the biggest scoop, getting permission from his friend Field Commander Yamagata Aritomo to accompany the troops as a secretary and clerk. During the spring and summer, his reports caused the *Nichi Nichi* circulation to soar, especially after the emperor himself summoned Fukuchi on April 6 for a two-hour personal audience to discuss the war—an invitation that Fukuchi called "an honor for all newspaper reporters."[127] Stung by the *Nichi Nichi* coup, *Yūbin Hōchi* managed to get its own reporter to Kyushu: Inukai Tsuyoshi, a young Keiō Gijuku student, who first sought appointment as a soldier, then, when that request was denied, went "trooping along with the army and sharing all dangers" as Japan's second domestic war correspondent.[128] No other papers succeeded in actually getting their writers to the battlefront, but several sent them to the military headquarters in Kyoto. All told, seven persons were dispatched to cover the civil war,[129] and the papers without correspondents used information from officials with whom they had connections or from other papers to keep readers abreast of battlefield developments.

The reports sometimes strayed from later standards for accuracy, but what writers missed in precision they made up in patriotic vigor. Typical was Fukuchi's tone in describing the troops he had accompanied on March 23: "Consider, my reader, how bitterly they fought by day and by night, even while enduring three days of continuous rain. It is impossible to imagine their hardships. This company's blood speaks the glory of patriotism. Its deaths speak the righteousness of national service."[130] A few observers thought the war reporters went overboard in their progovernment rhetoric. Fukuzawa, for example, expressed dismay about the many writers who "disgorged virtueless, redundant words" and were "guilty of abuse and slander" in their attacks on Saigō.[131] But most newspaper readers did not share his qualms. They may have revered Saigō, but they had rallied around the national cause, and they wanted to know what was going on; so they purchased papers like *Nichi Nichi* and the news-oriented *Yomiuri* (which also despatched a correspondent to the army's Kyoto headquarters) in record numbers. And the result was that the war left what Yamamoto Fumio has called a "revolutionary" mark on Japanese journalism, tying writers more closely to their readers and introducing the idea that at least some events must receive the same serious attention that ideas did.[132]

Once the rebellion had been quashed, the press moved on, to the major policy debates of the period. There were discussions of the emerging civil code; a heated debate between Inukai, now at *Tōkai Keizai Shinpō,* and *Tōkyō Keizai Zasshi*'s Taguchi Ukichi over Taguchi's advocacy of free trade; emotionally charged arguments about treaty revision; discussions of the role the military should play in a modern society; a debate about whether Japan's attorneys were making the country litigious; a series of *Tōkyō Nichi Nichi* arguments against the use of torture in the penal system;[133] and occasional articles on women's issues. In a single month, December 1877, one paper ran essays on the recently ended Satsuma Rebellion, the worrisome spread of selfishness and personal jealousy, treaty revision (seven columns in all), the new stock market, the court system, freedom of speech and press, the rice exchange,

people's rights (three editorials), the practice of murder by stran-
gling, the issuance of national bank notes, inheritance laws, the
meaning of responsible journalism, the legal system, the connection between social customs and modern laws of commerce, and
the relationship between personal virtue and national tranquility.[134]

The prestige papers' focus in the late 1870s, in other words,
was overwhelmingly on national policy and the political process
that shaped it. If an event or development related to Japan's political life, it would be discussed at length, as often in heated letters to
the editors as in the original essays that prompted the correspondence.[135] But if the "news" had no obvious political element, there
was a good chance it would be ignored. Two developments in these
years—one a concrete incident of limited duration, the other an
ongoing story—evoked more journalistic interest than others and
should serve to illustrate both the way the papers covered politics
and the changing role the press was assuming in political life.

The first was the assassination on May 18, 1878, of forty-
nine-year-old Home Minister Ōkubo Toshimichi. A native of
Kagoshima whose childhood home was mere meters away from
that of Saigō, Ōkubo represented the antithesis of those things cherished most by the former samurai factions who had been crushed in
Satsuma the previous autumn. He was cool (frigid, some said), calculating, completely committed to making Japan a strong nation,
even at the expense of oldtime values, and he was generally thought
to be the most powerful operator in the government. All of which
meant that he was deeply hated by both the Saigō loyalists and the
majority of those in the *jiyū minken* movement. Thus, when six
former samurai stabbed him to death as he was being driven toward
a meeting at the palace on that overcast Tuesday morning, they
touched a national nerve. The fact that they slashed the legs of his
horses, killed his coachman, and ignored Ōkubo's pleas for mercy
heightened the dramatic impact, as did their resort to traditional
bushi values by turning themselves in and using the trial as a platform for defending their righteous motives. Ōkubo, they said, had
become an obstruction to channels of communication between the
people and the emperor. If he were removed, the emperor would see
the agony of his people and move to expand popular rights. The fact
that they wanted political "rights" for former samurai alone and
not for commoners was glossed over in their statements.[136]

Of particular interest here is the role the press played in making the assassination as well as the tension-packed ideas behind it a
public issue, and in ensuring that the views of the perpetrators

would receive a full public airing. The terrorists' apologia was written by Kuga Yoshinao, a journalist who already had been punished several times for press law violations.[137] It was delivered to several leading papers, and *Chōya* in particular gave it full play, including its suggestion that other officials also deserved death and that "corrupt officials" were leading Japan to destruction. As the assassins' document said of those officials:

> Their first sin is that they ignore public opinion and suppress people's rights while profiting personally from politics. The second is that they use deceit in carrying out laws and ordinances, even while expanding their own authority arbitrarily. The third is that they waste national finances in useless construction projects. The fourth sin is that they stir up rebellions by alienating fervent, loyal samurai and displaying hatred toward their patriotic enemies. The fifth is that they have made mistakes in discharging foreign relations, failing to preserve our national strength.[138]

That *Chōya* should have sympathized with the assassins was not too surprising, given Narushima's attachment to Saigō and his record of antagonism toward the government, even during the Satsuma Rebellion. More surprising was an editorial in *Minkan Zasshi* by Fukuzawa downplaying the seriousness of the episode. He wrote that while Ōkubo's assassination was "truly tragic," it was no worse on the personal level than the tragedy of commoners who "are murdered daily and monthly" but die in obscurity. "There is no reason to express special pity for him as a person," he wrote. Only because Ōkubo was a high official did his "misfortune become the nation's misfortune." Therefore, it was important for officials to act moderately, to avoid turning the assassins into martyrs and thereby undermining popular support for the government.[139]

The officials' response to accounts and discussions of this sort was harsh. Fukuzawa was too prominent for direct censure, but the police informed his editor, Katō Masanosuke, that the essay was "extremely disquieting" and demanded an assurance that *Minkan* would not run such an editorial again.[140] *Chōya* was shut down for ten days.[141] The editor of *Tōkyō Shinji Shimbun*, a small antigovernment paper, was fined thirty yen and jailed for two months for running material supporting the assassins; then his paper was shut down permanently on August 3. The journalist Kuga, who wrote the assassins' apologia, was sentenced to life in prison.[142] And the press chronology of that summer and autumn is filled with papers and writers punished for unacceptable material.[143] Quite clearly, public discussion of events such as assassination, particularly if the discussion showed any sympathy toward the perpetrators and their ideas, posed a threat in the official mind to Japan's tranquility, even when that discussion occurred in small and insubstantial papers. Just as clearly, the country's press corps now included more than a few, even among the larger and more respectable papers, who were willing to damn the risks and take up the discussion anyway.

Probably the best evidence of the rising assertiveness lay in my second example of late-1870s press coverage, the all-consuming attention journalists gave to the *jiyū minken* movement. This movement, born in 1874 at the time of Itagaki's memorial on representative government, was the most important stimulus of political activity outside the government itself in the 1870s and 1880s. Supported by out-of-power activists at various levels of society, it served as the primary medium through which people could demand "natural rights," a constitution, and a popular assembly. More than that, the movement provided the primary public platform for discussions of political philosophy during the late 1870s. And at its heart lay scores of journalists who used their columns not only to disseminate information about *minken* activities, but actively to propagate the movement's ideas.

The *jiyū minken* movement was neither coherent nor unified; its leadership, philosophies, and supporters changed significantly during the decade of its greatest activity, 1874–1884. In its first years, the leading advocates of freedom and rights came largely from the ranks of discontented samurai activists, many of whom had fought for the Restoration and now felt abandoned. Its activities then centered on political clubs or societies such as the Aikokusha (Society of Patriots) and the Risshisha (Self-Help Society), whose primary goal was to counter the Satsuma and Chōshū hold on the government by establishing a representative assembly. They were not particularly liberal; certainly they were not democratic. As late as 1882 Itagaki made it clear that he would grant the franchise only to "the samurai and the richer farmers and merchants" who had "produced the leaders of the revolution of 1868."[144] Fukuchi was not wholly off base, in fact, when he wrote in the summer of 1876 that "intelligent people smile on them with pity" because of the transparent opportunism of their views.[145]

But if the movement's early leaders were opportunists, they also were effective publicists, people whose rhetoric inspired genuine seekers after popular rights just as much as they did the more partisan types. The *jiyū minken* thus had broadened by the late

1870s to include both prominent Tokyo intellectual organizations, such as the Ōmeisha and the Tōyō Giseikai, and the regional groups that had given Itagaki his first support.[146] Its proponents continued to concern themselves with issues of local power and finance, but by now they also had developed a well-focused *national* issue, which created a sense of commonality, no matter whether they hailed from Toyama or worked the fields of Okayama. And that issue was the creation of a popular assembly.

What Irokawa Daikichi calls a "unique period in our history" clearly had dawned, a period in which political clubs sprang up all across Japan, drawing on a longtime village tradition of "enthusiasm for study and learning," to draft their own versions of what form Japanese polity now should take.[147] Organizations with quixotic names such as the Gakuyōsha (Mountains and Oceans Society) in Tosa and the Tokushinsha (High Spirits Society) in Yamagata held frequent *jiyū minken* meetings, where landowners, teachers, and petty merchants echoed Ueki Emori's assertion that "all people are created equally by Heaven . . . so if you cannot have freedom, die and be done with it."[148] And when the government in 1878 published the conservative British jurist Peter Brougham's *Institutional Maxims* supporting strong central authority, a local teacher west of Tokyo rewrote the maxims from a *jiyū minken* perspective, declaring: "When the right of the People and the right of the sovereign conflict, the right of the People takes precedence."[149] So potent had the movement become, in fact, that Ono Azusa felt compelled to warn fellow officials in an 1879 memorandum that the people, having become "overly enthusiastic about freedom," might rise up in a French-style revolution if their demands were not recognized,[150] and a year later no fewer than 21,000 of those people signed a petition in mountainous Nagano Prefecture claiming that "over half of . . . Japan's more than seven million households support the opening of a national assembly."[151]

The press played a central role in making the *jiyū minken* era possible, spreading information about the movement's key activities, providing a rationale for its central positions, and agitating directly for wider support. The most obvious, or at least the most traditional, press role was informational. Movements depend on communication channels to make their views known and to make interaction between members possible, and the press played a pivotal role in this regard. Once the Satsuma Rebellion was over, the *jiyū minken* activities became an important source of news for all of the major papers. Irokawa's estimate that these years produced "well over a thousand" local *jiyū minken* organizations—groups in which people "were really able to breathe the air of the new age . . . and to dream of their future in an ideal Japan"—is based primarily on the abundant reports in the press of the day, particularly news accounts of well-known journalists invited to speak at local meetings across the country.[152] And the reports appeared almost as often in the conservative dailies as they did in liberal papers. One particularly fascinating account of populist political fervor was printed in *Tōkyō Nichi Nichi* early in 1881. The writer described a political speech made on a train in the Kansai region. The speaker, he wrote, insisted on his right to "freedom of speech" when officials tried to quiet him, persisting until train personnel finally gave in and let him continue his oration. "There always is a lot of commotion on a train," commented the writer, "but this is the first time we have heard of a political speech on one."[153]

The press also provided the basic "research materials" for most local *jiyū minken* clubs. The newspaper reading rooms discussed above served as a focal point for many regional political activists. *Tōkyō-Yokohama Mainichi Shimbun* reported in April 1880,[154] for example, that public reading stalls, with "newspapers and periodicals from all over the country . . . piled high as a mountain," were in heavy use in Itsukaichi, a center of *jiyū minken* activity.[155] Similarly, *Yūbin Hōchi* reported that in the aftermath of the Satsuma Rebellion, when government critics concluded that violent resistance would not work, local political groups often would study opposing editorials in *Yūbin Hōchi* and *Tōkyō Nichi Nichi*, then stage local debates on the issues. "In some people's rights regions, however, there were so many more *Hōchi* readers that supporters of the government's paper just kept silent."[156] Probably the best-known account of newspaper essays being used as grist for movement lectures was Fukuzawa's series of editorials in *Yūbin Hōchi* in the summer of 1879. According to his own exaggerated retelling, they set off a debate that "spread through all the Tokyo newspapers, even into the provincial press, until enthusiasts from the provinces began to come up to Tokyo to present petitions for the opening of the Diet. . . . My whim had unexpectedly shaken the whole country."[157]

It was not just in providing channels of communication, however, that the press of the late 1870s spurred on the freedom and rights activists. When Anthony Smith wrote that "the language of agitation" often employed by presses in a developing society "is a language of emotion, of overstatement and, necessarily, of frequent inaccuracy,"[158] he was describing quite precisely many Japanese journalists in this period. They saw themselves as political actors, not merely as recorders. As Numa Morikazu, one of the period's half dozen most influential journalists, put it: "In order to develop the people's hearts and minds, to spread the ideas of freedom, one must mobilize the weapons of discussion. How dare one neglect the skills of persuasion!"[159] Journalism, to him, was not merely a reporter's trade; it was an educator's podium. And most of his *ōshimbun* peers, feeling the same way, became active participants in the day's debates, organizing their own popular rights clubs and using their papers' columns to promote "freedom and rights."[160] As Nishida put it, now that violence had been ruled out by the failure of Saigō's followers on the battlefield, the "two wheels of the *minken* movement were political speeches and newspapers," with the journalists serving as speakers almost as often as they did as writers.[161]

Numa is a good example. He had entered journalism because, as a bureaucrat, he felt frustrated by his inability to reach a wider audience. He purchased *Yokohama Mainichi* in 1879, moved it to Tokyo, and renamed it *Tōkyō-Yokohama Mainichi Shimbun*, all in order more effectively to fight the government ally Fukuchi and to raise the political consciousness of the commoners.[162] Making the paper into an organ of the pro-*minken* Ōmeisha, he published a continuing chorus of essays demanding assembly government in order to curb what he saw as the increasingly arbitrary clique or *hanbatsu* government. And his approach was emulated widely in the provinces. Across the nation, in mountain valleys and on the plains, regional papers were created to fight for *minken* causes. In Kōchi Prefecture on the southern coast of Shikoku, two different papers, both named *Kōchi Shimbun*, were launched with the sole aim of promoting the movement, and when the latter *Kōchi Shimbun* was banned by the government, the surrogate *Dōyō Shimbun* took its place.[163] North and west of there, in Okayama, the *San'yō Shinpō* was launched on January 4, 1879, under the influence of Komatsubara Eitarō, the radical liberal who had been jailed for his strident editorials at *Hyōron Shimbun*. Nearer to Tokyo, in the old Tokugawa hometown of Shizuoka, the *jiyū minken* banner was carried by the *Shizuoka Shimbun*. And to the north of the capital, pro-assembly crusades were encouraged by the *Tochigi Shimbun*, founded in June 1878, then revived after a spluttering first effort, on August 2, 1879.

Sometimes the tone of the writers was radical and revolutionary, with calls for "overthrowing tyrannical government"[164] or holding the emperor's ministers to account. One writer expressed the more extreme view this way:

> Government is the joint property of the people, not the exclusive property of the officials. If officials devise cunning tricks to serve their own interests, or to block the people's rights and curb popular freedom, the people should discuss the situation and improve the laws. If this is not possible, they should bring the government to an end and set up a new, just administration.[165]

More often the tone was more moderate, in the manner of *Shinano Mainichi Shimbun,* which argued in an 1880 editorial that progress toward national civilization and strength "will not come about accidentally but only in response to the stimulation of outside forces *(gaibutsu no shigeki)";* or in the manner of Narushima, who wrote that "the one thing to be remembered regarding national movement is that *progress must be for the sake of the people, just as retreat also must be for the sake of the people."*[166] But always, whatever the tone, these writers demanded, first and last, the early creation of a national assembly.

As Irokawa tells us, it was primarily through the newspapers in these years that scores of "young men developed the bases for their thought and their spirit of freedom, as well as the writing styles that distinguished them throughout the remainder of their lives."[167] An exasperated Fukuchi found the tone of these papers irritating, noting in an 1876 editorial that "newspapers today . . . have lost the essential quality of impartiality. They merely attack the government, having lost any inclination for independent public discussion. . . . Intelligent people smile on them with pity."[168] But a greater number of readers liked the fighting tone. "Readers and reporters felt a common bond as they worked together toward a common destiny," says Yamamoto Taketoshi of Hitotsubashi University; "it was one of the happiest periods in press history."[169]

GOVERNMENT AND PRESS: THE JOCKEYING CONTINUES

A telling example of this happy, if precarious, union between papers and readers came with the launching early in 1881 of the *Tōyō Jiyū Shimbun,* one of the era's shortest-lived, most intriguing *jiyū min-ken* papers. The first issue, on March 18, looked rather ordinary. A mere four pages long, it was as gray as the other elite papers, beginning with an editorial followed by official decrees and miscellany. Page two contained a foreign news column and essays by the editor and company president, and the other two pages combined essays, publication data, and a few small ads. But if the format was ordinary, the impact of the paper was extraordinary, because its tone was pungent, its editor was Nakae Chōmin, one of Japan's best-known *minken* spokesmen, and its president was none other than Saionji Kinmochi, the thirty-year-old son of a court nobleman and brother of the Emperor Meiji's grand chamberlain.

Saionji had embraced Rousseau's idea of the social contract in France, where he studied law for the entire decade of the 1870s, and on returning to Japan in 1880 had determined to support the *minken* cause. As a result, the *Tōyō Jiyū* became, during its brief existence, one of the country's most articulate and, to the officials, threatening supporters of assembly government. The first issue stated that the paper intended to "cultivate the strength of public opinion and spread freedom," asserting in Rousseau's name that "people without freedom are not people at all" and that "the creators of a nation must work solely to expand the people's right of freedom *(jiyū no ken)*."[170] Issues two and three ran editorials on the "joint rule of emperor and people *(kunmin kyōchi),*" arguing that while many nations have used that rhetoric, only the truly advanced adhered to its spirit. And subsequent issues demanded "freedom of the spirit" *(shinshi no jiyū)* and the creation of a national assembly to end the "abuses of clique government."[171] One of the later issues declared that "there is no greater evil than for those who govern to prevent freedom of expression." Citing Locke, Rousseau, Aristotle, and Plato, the editorialist asserted: "When rulers block free speech, we cannot express our true feelings, no matter how fine our ideas; we cannot record our innermost thoughts in books. In such situations, our subtle reasoning remains trapped in our minds, wholly removed from articulation to the world at large. Even later eras are precluded from the benefit of these ideas."[172]

The official world was dismayed by this new *jiyū minken* paper, particularly by its close ties to the highest reaches of the aristocracy. Prince Iwakura called on Saionji personally, to dissuade him from involvement with the paper, but to no avail. Then another prince, Sanjō Sanetomi, summoned the young zealot to report the emperor's "deep anguish" that someone so highly placed was assisting the antigovernment forces. But Saionji responded by writing an appeal to the throne, arguing the case for freedom of expression and requesting a personal audience with Emperor Meiji to explain his views more fully. That request was ignored; Saionji was served with an imperial order to leave the newspaper, and in early April the paper ran an editorial announcing his departure. "But shall we cower in fear and change our course?" asked Nakae, the writer of the editorial. "We can say only that we are the more determined to be persistent in behalf of the great cause of freedom."[173] And to make the point of its determination, another editor, Matsuzawa Kyūsaku, sent Saionji's appeal to three other papers, *Yūbin Hōchi, Ōsaka Nippō,* and *Kōchi Shimbun,* each of which printed it in its entirety or summarized it for readers.[174]

The bluster was greater than the *Tōyō Jiyū's* staying power, however; late in April it was shut down after its thirty-fourth issue, and Matsuzawa was sent to jail for seventy days for making Saionji's appeal public. Years later, Saionji the elder statesman would call the entire episode "a bit of fun," maintaining on reflection that he "was not a strong advocate of people's rights."[175] The events of the time, however, suggest a different reading of his attitudes. They show a young idealist who believed in the *minken* cause strongly enough to persist against intense pressure as well as a government that took his role seriously indeed. They also show how deeply and widely the *jiyū minken* ideas had penetrated into the consciousness of those both inside and outside the circles of power.

And they make clear just how bitter the press-government struggle continued to be, as the Meiji era entered its second decade. We already have seen the contrast between the pugnacious and timid editors in the months immediately after the *shimbunshi jōrei* of 1875. Now, as the *jiyū minken* spirit spread in the late 1870s, the press' fractious element seemed to become dominant, certainly loudest, even though a few government allies like *Nichi Nichi* continued to hew a cautious path. As the establishment-oriented E. H. House described it two years after the law, some papers had begun "to display a license which would have been intolerable in any country," printing the "wildest and most vindictive invective," considering "themselves a newly-constituted supreme authority in the land."[176] The result was an era in which officials, bent on controlling discussion, were as harsh in their treatment of writers as the *minken* faction was obstinate.

It should not be assumed that the Meiji regime was more authoritarian than other governments at a similar stage of development. Nearly all the countries of Europe had engaged in heavy press control during the early nineteenth century, with France, for example, enforcing a nearly impenetrable set of "crippling restrictions" until the end of the 1860s.[177] And it can be argued quite fairly that the Meiji government went as far as might reasonably have been expected, given the times and the Tokugawa legacy, not only to maintain the laws but to countenance a growing diversity of viewpoints and to bring increasing numbers of people into the governing process.[178] The government never even considered doing away with the right of private individuals to publish newspapers; indeed, officials began in these years actually to assist independent journalists in some cases, by setting up rudimentary press rooms and issuing the country's first press releases.[179] Nor did the officials execute their opponents for what they wrote or go beyond legal limits in attempting to quiet the opposition. As in Tokugawa, so in Meiji: officials adhered carefully to their written law codes. Even *Akebono* commented during the Satsuma Rebellion that Japan's press control was not "the worst in the world."[180]

Nevertheless, there is no gainsaying either the harsh quality of the press code enforcement in these years or the willingness of officials to make the codes even more severe. On July 5, 1876, for example, the Dajōkan issued provisions whereby papers could be suspended administratively by the Home Minister *(hakkō teishi)* or even shut down completely *(hakkō kinshi)*, without so much as an explanation of why, for printing items that threatened to disturb public order.[181] An 1878 decree prohibited soldiers from subscribing to any papers except *Tōkyō Nichi Nichi, Yūbin Hōchi,* and the official *Naigai Heiji Shimbun,*[182] and in 1880 the Council of State added "subversion of morality" to the offenses that could evoke suspension or banishment. The result was that these years saw a constant flow of writers to jail, and a number of papers ended up on the chopping block. Saitō Shōzō, an early student of press control, recorded some 138 *hikka* or press violation episodes between 1876 and 1880, in contrast to just nine in the half decade before the press law.[183] And his list was on the sharply conservative side. More recent scholarship has pushed the number of punishments ever higher, with Okano describing 349 cases between 1875 and 1880, and Nishida listing 694 cases for the three years 1878 through 1880 alone.[184] Even the establishment *Nichi Nichi* had writers fined or jailed at least eight times in these years—possibly, some scholars suggest, when careless editors failed to catch material inserted by more liberal writers.[185]

Sometimes the episodes that evoked official wrath had a quirkish quality, as in the case of a five-yen slander ruling against

Yomiuri for reporting that a government clerk named Fukugawa had received a thrashing for misappropriating rice cakes intended as alms for the city's poor,[186] or the coverage of the celebrated pet shooting by the vacationing German prince Heinrich in 1880. In that case, several papers were punished for reporting on the fact that the sixteen-year-old grandson of Emperor William I had been detained by local police after he mistook a pet near an Osaka-area pond for a wild duck and shot it. Officials, nervous about Japan's standing with European governments, decided to treat the case as if Heinrich had been a member of Japan's own royal family. They apologized profusely to the German government, punished the police officer who had apprehended the prince, and cracked down almost ruthlessly on the papers for reporting the episode. The editors of *Ōsaka Nippō, Ōsaka Shinpō,* and *Kyōto Nichi Nichi Shimbun* were fined as much as three hundred yen each and given jail terms ranging from five months to a year, and the more influential Tokyo papers, *Chōya* and *Akebono,* were suspended for four days.[187]

Most of the time, the punishments in these years related directly to discussions of the *jiyū minken* movement. Early in 1880, for example, a *Yūbin Hōchi* editor was fined one hundred yen for running a memorial by sixty-four people from Fukuoka calling for a national assembly. That same month, a *Tōyō Jiyū* writer was sentenced to a year in jail after warning that "without a national assembly the popular mood will become agitated."[188] And the writer of a sarcastic article in *Kinji Hyōron,* suggesting that officials might as well be selected by lottery, drew four months and eighty yen.[189] Punishments were frequent in the regions away from Tokyo too: thirty days in jail for a *Hiroshima Shimbun* editor who ran the Fukuoka memorial about a national assembly, a monthlong jail term for a Kumamoto writer for complaining in print that a local government receptionist was arrogant,[190] jail for an Osaka editor who wrote that "the government belongs to the people, not the monarch."[191] So frequent were the punishments, according to *Hyōron* in 1876, that "going to jail became just like breaking wind."[192]

Even so, fines and jail terms were regarded by most editors as the least noxious of the potential punishments in these years, because after the 1876 ordinance providing for suspension and banishment, many papers had to fear for their very existence. The primary targets of the decree were the small, extreme, and unrelentingly irritating papers; so there was little surprise when three of them—*Hyōron, Sōmō Zasshi,* and *Kōkai Shinpō*—were permanently banned within a few days of the issuance of the new regulation. To the chagrin of the Home Ministry, however, all three editors submitted applications a few days later to begin new journals with different names (in one case, merely reversing characters so that *Sōmō Zasshi* became *Mōsō Zasshi*). Since the regulations provided no grounds for disallowing the "new" journals, the radical editors continued to goad the official world until the Council of State at last drew up additional guidelines forbidding press permits to papers that once had been proscribed.[193] Although the government shut down no major papers in these years, it gave *hakkō kinshi* orders to several minor papers each year.[194]

The major *ōshimbun* were, however, subject to increasingly frequent suspensions, or *hakkō teishi* orders, as the period progressed. The first temporary suspension of a major paper was levied against *Chōya:* ten days, beginning May 15, 1878, for publishing the apologia of Ōkubo's assassins.[195] A total of four papers were suspended the next year, and sixteen in 1880. Then, in late January of 1881, the regional *Ōsaka Asahi* was closed for three full weeks for publishing a serialized essay on the creation of a national assembly. Although the series was accused of spreading "dangerous ideas among the common folk," many scholars think the real motive behind this suspension lay in the fact that the enterprising, ambitious Murayama Ryōhei and Ueno Riichi had just purchased the paper; cautious officials wanted to warn the new owners against dipping too freely into the waters of political journalism. The last half of 1881 would unleash the first real onslaught of suspensions of major *ōshimbun,* but that story must await the next chapter.

During the years from 1874 to 1881, the press, newly independent and increasingly self-confident, refused to be cowed. The strata gems by which editors avoided suppression were multifarious: hiring surrogate editors for five yen a month for the sole purpose of going to jail,[196] using circumlocutions to throw off the censors, and finding patrons within bureaus who might help secure leniency, among others. But the most important technique was simply the consequences-be-damned approach that many writers took. Freed from the constraints imposed by the bureaucrats' early financial largess, the press by 1881 had become a voice for public-spirited outsiders who desired to shape policy by debating ideas. There still were editors who served the establishment cause, and the reality was that most writers maintained their Confucian sense of loyalty to the greater (national) whole even as they fought for change. But scores of journalists now took on themselves the role of fighting authoritarianism by demanding constitutional government. And try as it might, the official world could not shut them up.

The key development of these years thus lay in the press' role as a politicizing agent, a force that brought increasing numbers of people, or *minshū*, into the political process even as it taught the ways of civilization and amplified commoners' voices within the inner circle. Standard analyses of Meiji Japan continue to focus largely on the initiatives of the center and the top, giving the impression that political change originated almost exclusively in the government, that the moves toward even a limited form of democracy were generated largely by astute leaders in the upper reaches of power. Edwin Reischauer typically says that the period's "real question" is "why the oligarchs gave the elected representatives of the people a share in political power"; it was "certainly not," he says, "because of the strength of the demands for popular government, which the oligarchs could have disregarded with impunity."[197] Increasing numbers of scholars have studied the provincial political movements of these years, but their accounts have yet to be incorporated adequately into mainstream histories of the period as a whole.[198] The *ōshimbun* press' experiences in the late 1870s, however, provide telling evidence that they should be.

Admitting that everyone—even the Nakae Chōmins and the Suehiro Tetchōs—looked to the center, admitting that the Meiji rulers were astute, admitting even that those out of power often fell victim to government control and manipulation, there simply is no denying the impact of the outsiders' pressure on the center or the press' role in intensifying that pressure. It was those little Tokyo newspapers that turned internal bureaucratic squabbles into an open, public issue in 1873; it was the press that placed outsiders' views about a popular assembly at the heart of public debate in 1874, the press that so effectively empowered and broadened the *jiyū minken* movement and struck fear into official hearts in succeeding years. *Yūbin Hōchi* was not far off the mark in 1877 when it called the press "an army that mobilizes people's ideas . . . a force that sways people's most prized thoughts."[199] Those were heady words, uttered by a writer impressed by a young institution's new role as a popularizing force. Just how accurate—and prescient—they were would become increasingly obvious in the next few years.

CHAPTER 5

SERVING THE POLITICAL PARTIES
1881 to 1886

A political party without a newspaper
is like an army without weapons.
> *Jiyū Shimbun, June 25, 1882*

The ancestral spirits must have returned troubled from Tokyo's *bon* festival in the summer of 1881. Japan's economy was staggering under stringent retrenchment policies aimed at countering years of serious and debilitating inflation; junior councillors were waxing venomous in their debates over what kind of governing system Japan should have; unrest over taxes and political impotence was spreading like a fever in the towns and villages; and officials were whispering behind closed doors about the "land scandal" in Hokkaido. What only the most prescient among those spirits could have known, however, was that all the troubles would erupt soon in a crisis chaotic enough to goad officials into drawing up Japan's first constitution. What even those prescient ones probably would not have guessed was that this event, known to historians simply as the *seihen* or "political change" of 1881, would be even more cataclysmic for Japan's press, that while it would energize Tokyo's journalists and dramatize their growing influence, it also would trigger a wave of editorial partisanship bitter enough, in the end, to destroy the *ōshimbun* brand of editing and require a wholesale reshaping of the entire journalistic institution.

THE CRISIS OF 1881

Two quite different developments, one political and one economic, led to the Crisis of 1881. On the political side, a debate had gone on for months already over the timing and nature of Japan's coming constitutional system. The junior councillors had been ordered late in 1879 to prepare written memorandums on what kind of a constitution Japan should have, and most of them complied, recommending deliberate movement toward an authoritarian document that vested power primarily in the emperor and his advisors. Ōkuma Shigenobu, the powerful finance minister, by contrast, had held off on submitting his written opinion until March 1881, and when the young Meiji Emperor insisted that he delay no longer, he complied with a proposal that touched off a storm.

Ōkuma, it turned out, had broken ranks. In contrast to Itō Hirobumi and Inoue Kaoru, to whom he was thought to be close, he outlined a constitution that would create a British-style system, with the head of the Diet's majority party serving as prime minister. He also called for speed; the constitution was to be issued forthwith; legislative elections would be held in 1882 and the Diet convened "early in 1883." In defense of popular government he wrote: "Constitutional government is government by political parties." And about the more conservative proposals of his colleagues he sniped: "Love of power is the origin of the loss of power."[1] In other words, Ōkuma wanted a constitutional system that transferred considerable power to the public, and he wanted it soon. To say that his fellow councillors were aghast is to state the superfluous. The fact that Ōkuma was from Saga rather than Satsuma or Chōshū already had made some of them nervous about him; this breach of ideology was a major challenge. Itō reportedly "exploded in anger" and called him a "deputy" of Fukuzawa Yukichi.[2] As Mikiso Hane puts it: "Ōkuma had violated one of the cardinal principles of Japanese politics, that is, the need for each individual to work with the group to which he belongs without departing radically from the consensus."[3] The German physician Erwin Baelz, likely unaware of the struggle going on behind the closed doors of the bureaucracy, observed in June that Ōkuma, "though a man of cheerful disposition . . . has changed a good deal of late, and suffers from a persistent cough."[4] One suspects the reasons were more than physical.

The summer's second unsettling development related to agricultural lands in Hokkaido. For a decade a Colonization Bureau had been pouring public monies into land reclamation and improvement there in an effort to spur the economic growth of one of the country's most undeveloped regions. By 1881, more than fourteen million yen had been spent, and when officials began looking for ways to reduce heavy government deficits, the Hokkaido project emerged as an obvious target. So when Kuroda Kiyotaka, head of the Colonization Bureau, proposed that the project be disbanded and the lands sold, everyone agreed. Eyebrows were raised, however, when he urged that the sale be made to the Kansai Bōeki Kaisha (Kansai Trading Company), headed by his friend and fellow Satsuma native Godai Tomoatsu, for a mere 387,082 yen (one thirty-sixth of the cost), to be repaid over thirty years, interest free. Under the terms of the proposal, Godai and his colleagues would receive the products and supplies accumulated by the colonizers, the lands that had been developed, their experimental stations, and a number of commercial projects, including silk farms, iron works, beer factories, canneries, a net factory, hunting fields, and vineyards. Thrown in would be several boats and ships used on the project.[5]

Ōkuma opposed the proposal as unsound and unethical, but coming on the heels of his constitutional faux pas and a series of acrimonious debates over Japan's economic policies, his opposition was disregarded as a political gambit, and the Dajōkan approved Kuroda's plan. The episode did not end there, however. Someone leaked word of the sale, and a public uproar ensued. For two months, in fact, few other issues were discussed in the teahouses and shipyards of Japan's cities and towns, either inside or outside the government: Was the sale a sign of broader bureaucratic corruption? Could it be stopped? How could the system be changed to prevent abuses of power? What were the implications of Ōkuma's new role as insider gadfly? So heated were the discussions that the normal operations of state ground nearly to a halt until October 12, when it was announced that the sale would be rescinded and that by 1890 a constitution would be promulgated. On the same day Ōkuma resigned from the government on the grounds of "rheumatism," commenting to friends that "the situation had changed so radically that I was reduced to being treated as a criminal."[6] With him went some fifteen supporters and protégés, including Yano Fumio, Inukai Tsuyoshi, Ono Azusa, Shimada Saburō, and Maejima Hisoka.

The *seihen* represented, by any reckoning, the most tumultuous turn of affairs in Tokyo since Saigō had gone home to Satsuma eight years before. And a central role was played by the press. The journalists initially had little to say about the squabble over Ōkuma's constitutional opinion; that was a discreet dispute, intended for the ears of those inside the house. But when the press got word of Kuroda's plan late in July, it jumped on it emotionally. For two months, editorials dissected the details of the Kuroda plan, news stories described the rallies and crusades that were being organized against the *hanbatsu* government that had agreed to the sale, and journalists went on organized lecture tours to discuss what the Hokkaido scandal meant for Japan's political future. Most significantly, not a single prominent journalist—not even those in the progovernment camp—supported the government side.

The press' alacrity on this issue should have surprised no one. We already have seen the energy that editors had thrown into the *jiyū minken* movement over the last several years, and by 1881 a number of the leading papers had begun devoting major amounts of space to constitutional questions. Prodded by the knowledge that the councillors were drafting opinions, most of the *ōshimbun* ran weighty discussions of constitutional theory in the spring of that year. At *Tōkyō Nichi Nichi*, for example, Fukuchi published his own proposed constitutional draft in a March–April series that stretched on for nearly three weeks. Moderate conservative that he was, he advocated absolute imperial sovereignty, "equal rights before the law, regardless of rank or social status," a popularly elected bicameral legislature, an executive branch responsible to both the emperor and the Diet, and an independent judiciary. The emperor, however, was to hold final authority for sanctioning laws.[7] The next month, *Yūbin Hōchi Shimbun* produced its constitutional proposal, based on an early draft by the Kōjunsha, an 1800-member political and social club with close ties to Fukuzawa. It wanted a more democratic constitution, and called for a cabinet wholly responsible to the legislature, as in the British system—a proposal that Prince Iwakura found "radical and extreme."[8] And during the summer one of the more important *minken* papers, the *Kōchi Shimbun* in Tosa, published Ueki Emori's even more liberal constitutional ideas, proposing strict limits on the prerogatives of the emperor.[9] Even in the villages of Nishitama, farmers such as Chiba Takusaburō were discussing "deep into the night and to the sound of a crackling fire the matter of drafting a national constitution."[10] The press and its readers, in short, already were fully attuned to constitutional issues when they learned about the Hokkaido land scheme. And since all of the editorialists had proposed constitutional drafts more popular than that envisioned by the councillors, they were ready to pounce on the land sale's broader political implications.

What is more, Ōkuma had been cultivating close ties to the press for some time now and was thus ready to use journalists, much as Inoue had in 1873, as allies in this new bureaucratic struggle. Joyce Lebra, his American biographer, has noted that one reason that several members of the Satchō clique mistrusted him was that he "showed a very early awareness of the implications of mass media, making him a precursor of mass democracy."[11] Some of his official enemies spread rumors now that his friends at Mitsubishi were providing money to journalists who supported him,[12] and they probably were right. Certainly no one saw it as coincidence that several of those who left the government with him in October took jobs at either *Yūbin Hōchi* or *Tōkyō-Yokohama Mainichi*.[13]

Nor did it come as any surprise that Ōkuma's camp triggered the press assault over Hokkaido in late July. The first newspaper account of the land sale appeared in *Tōkyō-Yokohama Mainichi* on July 26, and it was based on "detailed information" provided, it appears, by Ōkuma's intimate in the bureaucracy Ono Azusa.[14] Under a page one headline, "Kansai Bōeki Shōkai no kinjō" (Recent events at the Kansai Trading Company), it reported the receipt of "various accounts" regarding Kansai Bōeki's conduct, including news that the firm had attempted unsuccessfully to secure a government loan of five million yen to set up a merchant association in Osaka. "The officers in the company," said the article, "then turned toward Hokkaido and contracted with land reclamation officials to secure products from Hokkaido." The proposed deal, which had not been approved at this point, would be monopolistic, the writer said, because the goods "would be sent to this company and no other."[15] A day later, *Yūbin Hōchi* began a four-part series on the continuing official discussions of the proposed sale. And when rumors spread that the proposal had been approved at the end of the month, *Mainichi* ran a two-part editorial titled "Kan'yūbutsu haraisage no hō ikaga" (Questions about the methods of selling government holdings), analyzing the entire episode.[16]

Then the dam broke. Across the next two months, every one of the *ōshimbun* ran constant articles explaining and damning the sale as well as the system that had produced it. *Tōkyō-Yokohama Mainichi* published no fewer than seventeen major essays on the issue after the beginning of August. An August 12 piece openly suggested corruption; a two-part essay in mid-September called the episode a "major disaster" for Japan,[17] and when the government finally reversed the sale in October, the paper welcomed an act "for which all thirty-five million of us have been craning our necks in hope."[18] *Tōkyō Akebono Shimbun* was equally vocal, with a typical editorial on August 30 discussing how disturbing the sale was to the public and another on September 21 calling the government "calloused," suggesting that the scandal was an indictment of the entire Dajōkan system. *Yūbin Hōchi* ran one of its many essays under the heading "Aode ten ni nageku" (Looking up, we cry to the heavens). *Akebono* proclaimed Kansai Bōeki's "monopoly inconsistent with the prosperity of Hokkaido,"[19] and *Chōya Shimbun* ran one derisive editorial after another. On August 5, it reported on growing disagreement within the government itself about Kuroda's plan and sniped about selling property for one percent of its worth. On August 8, it described Hokkaido as "Japan's treasure chest" and pleaded with officials to abandon the sale, "not just because of its connection to the interests and welfare of the people of Hokkaido but because of its fundamental importance to the well-being of all Japan."[20]

The most noteworthy attacks came from Fukuchi Gen'ichirō at *Tōkyō Nichi Nichi*. Abandoning years of intimate ties to the government's Chōshū faction, Fukuchi went on the attack against both Kuroda and Itō, with even more energy than the others. On August 10 and 11, he explained his early silence by incredulity, writing that he had found it impossible to conceive of such a deal in a government run by people he trusted. Once convinced, he was outraged. Even more ominously for his official friends, he refused to accept the sale as an aberration or a display of individual greed. Like a lover spurned, he took the act bitterly, as a symptom of a system gone awry. "It is natural that scandalous things will occur in an oligarchy," he said, and then added, "I am firmly convinced that even if my own tongue should fail me and my brush be broken, public clamor still would not die down."[21]

On that point he surely was right; for the clamor continued to rise throughout August, with members of the press not only writing editorials but giving speeches—in Osaka, in Kyoto, in Wakayama, throughout all of Japan, stimulating popular interest until, by one telling, even the corner rickshaw drivers, "people who never had heard of people's rights," were busy discussing the issue.[22] The most dramatic lecture meeting came on August 26, when an audience of nearly five thousand crowded Tokyo's Shintomiza to hear several leading lights in the opposition flail away at the government. According to *Tōkyō Nichi Nichi*, temperatures near ninety degrees drenched people with perspiration but did nothing to dampen enthusiasm. The three thousand printed tickets had sold out four days ahead of time; more than a thousand additional partisans had arrived by 10:00 A.M., and when the gates opened at 1:00 P.M. the rush of people to secure good seats was "like a great, billowing wave." The final, "climactic" speech, by Fukuchi, lasted an hour and a half and was interrupted no fewer than sixty times by applause and standing ovations.[23]

Fukuchi began his talk with an explanation of his first reactions to the rumors about the sale. He recalled his inability in 1877 to believe Saigō capable of leading a rebellion, and declared the current episode "identical" in the way it "awakened me from a long night's delusion."[24] After discussing how secrecy had undermined trust, he detailed the steps leading to the sale and evoked sustained applause with a series of reminders of just what the deal entailed: "It's unimaginable! Three hundred thousand yen. Interest free. To be repaid in thirty yearly installments. With no guarantor." He suggested that his listeners might not mind a deal like that, then prompted shouts of agreement when he linked the sale to taxes and the national assembly question:

> These taxes, the property of all the people, were transferred to new custodians with no discussion at all by those to whom the money belonged. (Sustained applause.) It is shameful that a national assembly has not yet been formed and that we therefore cannot discuss this issue directly with the Cabinet Council. The people may want to deliberate, but they have no way of preventing the sale, either by rational debate or by passing laws. I covet a means of expressing my suspicions, just as you in the audience do. We need not fear people's rights; our rights should be limited only by the free boundaries of our inborn, natural abilities.[25]

Fukuchi concluded with a ringing tribute to the power of the people's voice. He noted that rumors had it that the sale might be rescinded because the government was worried about "the boisterous nature of public opinion *(yoron)*." "If that report is true," he declared, "the nation should rejoice. Public opinion should be hailed for exerting this kind of political influence, for exerting a check" on government. He predicted that the power of public opinion would "grow greater" until "patrician politics *(kajin seiji)* will be terminated and a constitutional system created." And he concluded: "Public opinion, grown strong, seeks just that. My number one goal is to work to this end, with all my compatriots in this audience!"[26]

His predictions were on target. The official world struggled to maintain control of events throughout September, with Iwakura writing on September 6 that any change in the official position would provide "regrettable evidence of the government's weakness"[27] and Sasaki Takayuki arguing three days later that "if we are compelled to give in to their demands, violent and perfidious men will have their way."[28] But by the end of the month bold fronts had become insupportable. Sensing that the Dajōkan system itself was in danger, the officials waited until the emperor returned from a Tōhoku trip, then announced on October 12 that the two central popular demands would be met: the land sale would be rescinded, and a constitution would be granted by 1890. It was also announced that Ōkuma would leave office.

Evaluations of what the settlement meant are as complex as the maneuvering that preceded it. Whether the narrowing Satchō clique won more than the *jiyū minken* forces did remains an open question, though scholarly consensus rests with a clique victory, since the Satchō leaders were able to narrow their power base and gain nearly a decade to prepare for constitutional government. More important for this study is the question of what impact the press had on the *seihen* developments and what impact the crisis had on the press.

The standard interpretation, especially among press historians, has been that the newspapers' role was pivotal in speeding up the country's movement toward democracy and that the crisis marked a major—and positive—turning point in the press' own evolution toward modernity and influence. Without papers to publicize the issue, the argument goes, officials would have felt less pressure to rescind the sale and draft a constitution, and without the crisis, the press would have been slower to recognize and assert its own political power. George Akita, by contrast, thinks the journalists and the *minken* forces they represented played "at best a secondary role in the final resolution of the question."[29] He quotes Ōkuma's ally Ono Azusa to the effect that the people's influence was "negligible" and says the land sale was a minor issue in the entire crisis, a diversion. It was essentially a dispute over constitutional issues, and the trigger of the struggle lay in Ōkuma's rash moves and the question of who was in control.[30]

While Akita is right in placing the constitutional issue at the center of the *seihen*, his dismissal of the popular forces' impact simply does not square with much of what happened in the late summer and early autumn of 1881. Ōkuma may have been the trigger, but his weapon of choice in attacking bureaucratic rivals was the press. That the journalists' editorials and lectures fanned an unprecedented level of public interest in an internal government decision is a matter of record, as is the fact that the resultant clamor frightened the officials and prompted them to drop a land sale that already had been approved over Ōkuma's objections. Perhaps the most significant development of these weeks was the writers' astute decision to portray the sale not simply as an isolated outrage but as a symptom of broader problems, a sign that governments without legislatures are almost certain to run roughshod over the public interest. They turned the discussion, in other words, from the concrete and specific to the theoretical and systemic—and in doing so they forced the promise of a constitution. To diminish the importance of that act is to deny the facts and to demean the rising influence of an expanding public.

Japan's press historians are unanimous in calling 1881 a seminal year in the evolution of the press' political role. Midoro Masaichi calls Hokkaido and constitutionalism "the issues that perfectly demonstrated the power of the press."[31] Haruhara Akihiko sees in the Hokkaido *seihen* coverage the press' first exercise in "campaign" journalism.[32] Okano Takeo describes the episode as a precedent-setting victory of "discussion rooted in justice."[33] And Haga Eizō, one of Japan's earliest students of press control, waxes eloquent about journalists who "sacrificed their own tears and blood" and "combative press heroes who rose like clouds."[34] The prose sometimes is purple, but the historians undoubtedly are right on the central point: the press in this instance exerted a more direct, more obvious impact on the country's political life than it ever had before and as a result gained new respect in the eyes of rulers and ruled alike.

It is seldom noted, by contrast, that the *seihen* also had a negative longterm impact on the life of Japan's *ōshimbun*. Heady with a feeling of success and eager to influence the constitutional drafting process, the *jiyū minken* forces became more organized in the aftermath of the October 12 decree than they ever had been before. And most of the leading papers joined them, tying themselves not just to the ideas of freedom and rights but to the specific parties that espoused those ideas. It was a predictable and logical development, given the new sense of political efficacy that journalists and *jiyū minken* leaders felt after the *seihen* struggle, but, for the press, it was also a troubling development. It turned the papers into mouthpieces and organs of outside parties, dependent not simply on the ideas of writers and the skills of editors but on the exigencies of partisan politics. And those exigencies would, sooner rather than later, undermine the very foundations of the *ōshimbun* press. Before turning to that story, however, we must look briefly at the remarkable changes in Japan's political scene as the Meiji era entered its fifteenth year.

IN LEAGUE WITH THE PARTIES

One of the most dramatic results of the 1881 *seihen* was the upsurge in organized political activity, which occurred not just in the Kantō-Kansai corridor but in scattered regions all across the country. In the last months of the year, the *jiyū minken* movement caught fire, on a scale heretofore unseen in Japan. And it was not just an elite movement. Though scholars long have pictured the people's rights groups as dominated by urban merchants, former samurai, disgruntled former bureaucrats, and wealthy landowners (in other words, by a relatively small elite who "strove primarily for democracy, for people's rights, for freedom of enterprise—*all for the respectable classes*"),[35] recent studies have shown a different dimension. The movement, according to these works, spread not only across the nation but up and down the social ladder. Shimoyama Saburō, for example, describes a melding of the classes in popular assembly petitions drawn up, early in the 1880s, in nearly three dozen prefectures in every part of the country;[36] Roger Bowen describes at length the "democratic" characteristics of the movement;[37] Shimura Akiko tells us about women such as Fukuda Hideko and Kishida Toshiko who became involved with journalism first through *minken* activities.[38]

And Irokawa Daikichi shows the popular rights campaigns resounding loudly in rural regions all across Shikoku and Honshū, with significant political "rumblings among the people."[39] He quotes a *Tōkyō-Yokohama Mainichi* writer who likened the political energy then to "torrents of water running downhill," so forceful even in "small and remote mountain communities" as to be "almost impossible to control by human power."[40] He also tells the story of "hundreds and thousands of anonymous teachers" who had far more impact on the people than any of the national intellectuals did.[41] And he describes people who attended political lecture meetings by the hundreds, competing "in their eagerness to go to the rostrum to present their ideas" and arguing viewpoints well into the night.[42] "I have perused massive quantities of historical documents," he says, "but in no period of Japanese history have I encountered evidence of the same kind of enthusiasm for study and learning that existed in mountain farming villages in the 1880s."[43]

His picture is corroborated by numerous other studies of the era as well as by scores of accounts in the day's press. In the Aizu region to the north, for example, more than a hundred political lecture meetings attracted crowds of up to 1,200 people during the spring of 1882 for discussions of popular political ideas.[44] In Niigata on the Japan Sea, said a mid-1882 issue of *Jiyū Shimbun*, local villagers were reading all the major urban papers—*Tōkyō Nichi Nichi*, *Jiji Shinpō*, *Meiji Nippō*, *Chōya*, as well as journals such as *Kinji Hyōron* and *Fusō Shinpō*—in order to develop their own political views. It reported that readers of the "liberal" papers would argue so heatedly with subscribers to the progovernment journals that "they nearly all came to see each other as bitter enemies."[45] From coastal Kōchi Prefecture as well as from mountainous Gifu came reports of growing political activity among women.[46] And the Tokyo papers carried frequent stories of new political clubs being formed, youth groups joining together to discuss political ideas, parties springing into existence and lively lecture-rallies held in Shizuoka, Hiroshima, Shimane, Okayama, Ibaraki, and Kumamoto, among other places.[47]

Just how lively these rallies could be was reflected in a *Tōkyō Nichi Nichi* account of a meeting in Kōchi, where the son of Jiyūtō (Liberal Party) leader Itagaki Taisuke was supposed to speak to a large, early-afternoon crowd of antigovernment partisans. Before Itagaki began, the reporter said, hired henchmen nabbed a suspected "spy" and started to toss him out of the hall, whereupon the assembled enthusiasts went wild, raising clenched fists, throwing objects at the suspected intruder, and shouting, "Kill him! Kill him!" Only after repeated assurances that the security men had made a mistake did things quiet down. Throughout the afternoon, the meeting was interrupted repeatedly by other outbursts over sensitive issues.[48] *Jiyū minken* supporters were activists, fighters for rights the establishment was loathe to give, so it is not surprising that their activities sometimes went beyond the polite and the politic.

Indeed, while most *jiyū minken* activities were orderly, these years also saw a marked increase in extremist, even violent movements that gave the phrase "freedom and rights" a new meaning and confirmed the worst fears of an order-oriented establishment. In Fukushima, for example, a coalition of priests, farmers, craftsmen and teachers carried out a protest movement late in 1882 against the autocratic governor Mishima Michitsune that included rallies, tax boycotts, work stoppages, massive demonstrations, and litigation. And when Mishima had nearly two thousand of them arrested, antigovernment groups sprang up elsewhere.[49] Some three thousand farmers attacked a moneylender's home and captured a police station in May 1884 in Gunma. Four months after that, a handful of liberal leaders attempted an unsuccessful revolution near Mt. Kaba near Utsunomiya. And in November 1884, more than six thousand peasants were brutally put down after rising in rebellion against taxes and insensitive officials in Chichibu, northwest of Tokyo. Indeed, more than eighty clashes between police and impoverished, tax-burdened peasants were recorded between 1882 and 1885. And in almost every case, rebel leaders were affiliated somehow with the *jiyū minken* movement and the journalists who carried its torch.

What concerned officials even more than the uprisings, however (since rebellions often strengthened the government's hand by stirring up public indignation against extremism), was the increasingly organized, institutionalized nature of the political opposition in 1881 and 1882. One of the unanticipated results of the October 12 constitutional promise was the emergence of Japan's first full-fledged political party movement—and of a press with close ties to each of the new parties. Before the month of October was out, Itagaki, that old nemesis from the Saigō days, announced formation of the Jiyūtō as an organ to bring *minken* ideals to fruition. The party's purpose, according to the announcement, was to "work for the expansion of freedom, the preservation of rights, the spread of happiness, and the reform of society," all of which would be brought about through a "good and beautiful constitutional system."[50] A few months later, on March 14, 1882, Ōkuma announced the creation of the Rikken Kaishintō (Constitutional Reform Party), to push for the development of a British-style constitutional system, which would balance the "glory of the imperial family" with the "happiness of the people." Despite a slightly more conservative tone, its antigovernment stance was just as clear as that of the Jiyūtō, committed to "wiping away the corrupt practices of the central government" through a system of elections and regional power.[51] And a few days after the Kaishintō's launching, Fukuchi announced the creation of a third, thoroughly conservative party, the Rikken Teiseitō (Constitutional Imperial Party), devoted to "the parallels of order and progress."[52]

Fukuchi's announcement was the most controversial. After becoming a *jiyū minken* celebrity during the clamorous days of

August and September, he had reversed himself again following October's imperial decree, announcing that the concrete promise of a constitution had restored his confidence in the officials and that *Nichi Nichi* henceforth would serve as a true *goyō* or organ of the administration. Now, in March, with the rise of two antigovernment parties, he declared that a progovernment party was needed to keep public opinion from becoming "democratized to the extreme." As he put it: "I shuddered at the radical democracy being advocated by the newspapers and society at large. . . . The parties seemed on a collision course with the constitutional monarchy."[53] These shifts, first to the popular cause, then back to the government side, set off a wave of public condemnation from which Fukuchi would never fully recover; they also made the political debates a great deal more lively for the next couple of years.

During 1882 and early 1883, the three parties dominated Japan's political life, providing the speakers for the lecture-discussion rallies described above, inspiring the ideas and programs of local activists, serving as umbrellas for scores of regional parties, providing organizational experience for ambitious young men anticipating the eventual creation of a national legislature. And—of greatest relevance to this study—each one of them depended first and foremost on at least one major *ōshimbun,* as well as on several smaller papers, for its ideas, leadership, and publicity. Stephen Koss, historian of the British press, calls newspapers the "gears which kept the party machinery in motion" in nineteenth-century England.[54] He could have said the same for Japan in the early 1880s.

One of the most eloquent statements of this fact came in the "publishing goals" *(hakkō shii)* of the *Jiyū Shimbun,* which was founded on June 24, 1882, to serve Itagaki's party. Asserting its intention of "expanding the freedom of the people, promoting the advance of culture, and increasing happiness everywhere," the paper issued this assessment of the role papers should play in the political process:

> A political party without a newspaper is like an army without weapons. With what else could we hope to topple our rival parties or exert our influence throughout society? We already have organized the Jiyūtō, a major organization through which we hope to become a powerful, active force. The primary task now is to spread knowledge, to exchange ideas, to strengthen party unity, and to bring the public together in support of our fixed, invincible philosophy. The weapon for accomplishing this is the newspaper.[55]

The leaders of the other parties were equally forceful in describing their reliance on the press. The journalist and Kaishintō leader Yano called *Yūbin Hōchi* the "headquarters" of his party, adding: "We engaged in war through the medium of print. When we would take control of some prefectural paper, the government would respond by creating a publishing company of its own or attaching itself to an allied newspaper. Never in my recollection has there been another era of such brilliant editorial confrontation."[56] And Fukuchi said much the same shortly before the launching of the Teiseitō, though from quite a different perspective:

> We must give great care to the preparations for the establishment of a national assembly, bringing into harmony the officials above and the people below. If newspapers really are the eyes and ears of public opinion, the self-appointed leaders of society, they must be diligent about these preparations. . . . They must help the public to lay the groundwork carefully, through the formation of political parties and the nurturing of political thought. These are the true responsibilities of a newspaper reporter.[57]

Newspapers, in the view of each of these men, were the most important, perhaps the only, tool available for stimulating and institutionalizing popular political activities. It is little wonder that *Ise Shimbun* referred to the new union of papers and parties as "a major revolution in journalism history,"[58] or that press historians now call this the *seitō kikanshi jidai:* "the era of political party organs."[59]

The use of papers and magazines as official mouthpieces was not new, as this study already has amply demonstrated; that practice had begun in the first year of Meiji, when the officials created the *Dajōkan Nisshi,* and it had continued in the early *jiyū minken* period, when journalists were persuaded to speak out for popular rights causes. Early organs of political groups included the Meirokusha's *Meiroku Zasshi,* the *Doyō Zasshi,* which articulated the demands of the Risshisha for a national assembly, treaty revision, and lower land taxes, and the *Ōmei Zasshi* of the anti-*hanbatsu* Ōmeisha. But while these journals represented rather informal, intellectual political associations aimed more at winning debates than at securing converts, the post-*seihen* party atmosphere gave rise to something new: mainstream papers that were doctrinaire mouthpieces for full-fledged political parties. And in that atmosphere, "the newspaper world became completely divided between the establishment *(taisei)* and antiestablishment sides."[60]

Indeed, in early 1882 only one of the *ōshimbun (Chōya)* even so much as hesitated before tying itself to a specific party. Studies of the press show about three-fourths of all the newspapers in Japan, large and small, serving as a voice for the political parties by the middle of 1882. Similarly, a *Tōyō Shinpō* list of fifty-three leading papers in the summer of 1883 included not a single exception to the party organ pattern.[61] And Ono Hideo's study of 187 newspapers in this period found sixty-two serving as Jiyūtō mouthpieces, forty-three articulating Kaishintō positions, and thirty tied to the Teiseitō. Other scholars have used different samples, but the breakdown is always similar: about a third of the papers tied to the Liberal Party, a fourth to the Reform Party, and a fifth to the Teiseitō.[62] The remaining group consisted of some (but not all) of the *koshimbun*, a few new, nonpartisan papers that will be discussed below, and a handful of politically active, generally antigovernment papers that simply did not affiliate with a specific party.

Two papers that stood out in the last category were the *Kyōto Shinpō*, founded in the spring of 1881 to espouse a liberal, antigovernment but independent position,[63] and Tokyo's energetic *Chōya*, which became the source of some derision for its inability to decide which of the antiestablishment parties to support. Its ambivalence resulted from the fact that Suehiro Tetchō and several other *Chōya* writers were vocal Jiyūtō supporters, while president Narushima had close ties to Ōkuma and the Kaishintō. When Suehiro invited the Jiyūtō activist Baba Tatsui to write a guest editorial in March 1882, he told him not to worry about the lack of affiliation, because "our employees support the Jiyūtō philosophy." *Chōya*, he said, was something of an "allied army" of the Liberal Party.[64] Not so, said fellow *Chōya* writer Inukai Tsuyoshi: *Chōya* "remained true to the Kaishintō."[65] The squabbling prompted *Tōkyō Nichi Nichi* to snip sarcastically that while *Chōya*'s editorials were written by Kaishintō adherents, its *zatsuroku* (miscellaneous notes) were written by the Jiyūtō faction. The paper "may have announced . . . that its editorials are fair and impartial," the *Nichi Nichi* writer commented, "but who on earth believes that?"[66] The *Chōya* editors were irritated enough by the criticism to respond, saying that the important thing was not having ties to a given party but having a "fixed philosophy," and that, they said, it clearly had: "freedom and rights for the people" *(kokumin no kenri jiyū)*.[67] The Jiyūtō also got into the bickering, accusing *Chōya* in July 1883 of "belonging tacitly to the Kaishintō."[68] The overall effect seems to have been a weakening of the paper's influence.

In the partisan press, the Jiyūtō flagship was the *Jiyū Shimbun*. Founded with 20,000 shares worth five yen each, its staff included most of the big names of the liberal world: Itagaki as president, and an eleven-man editorial board with Baba, Nakae Chōmin, Taguchi Ukichi, Gotō Shōjirō, and Suehiro on it—and Ueki Emori as an editorial researcher. The opening issue, after pledging to fight for the rights and welfare of the people, declared that this path had "long been the path of the emperor," whose ascension to the throne had been accompanied by issuance of the Charter Oath and who had only recently shown his intent to share power with the "common people" *(shūsho)* by promising a constitution. Public opinion, said the essay, could not be quenched; efforts to block the popular voice would be like trying to "quench the roaring flames of a blazing sky with a drop of water.... Rather than quenching it, such measures would just make it spread."[69]

The *Jiyū Shimbun* never became a major paper, even though it was promoted optimistically by several *minken* intellectuals as a successor to Saionji's feisty *Tōyō Jiyū Shimbun*.[70] Its late arrival on the *ōshimbun* stage put it at a disadvantage in attracting readers, and it was hurt by the disinclination of its activist editors to pay attention to managerial affairs. But most of all it was undermined by its wholly partisan tone. It had no raison d'être except Jiyūtō politics; so when the party was rent by internal schisms after the middle of 1883, the paper's already modest circulation declined, and in March 1885 it folded after a mere thirty-three months of existence. For two years, however, its political essays articulated all the issues of Japan's feverish political wars, and in the end its demise symbolized the quickly changing nature of the country's newspaper world.[71]

Other Tokyo newspapers and journals tied to the Jiyūtō included the *Seiri Sōdan, Tōkyō Keizai Zasshi, Kinji Hyōron, Kōko Shinpō,* and *Kokuyū Zasshi*.[72] The most interesting—very possibly the most important, in the long run—was the *Eiri* (Illustrated) *Jiyū Shimbun,* founded on September 1, 1882, to bring Liberal Party ideas to the growing numbers of shopkeepers and workers who were educated enough to read but were intimidated by the heavy styles of the prestige papers. It used the editorial techniques of the so-called minor papers (illustrations, phonetic aids, a more colloquial writing style, greater amounts of gossipy news) but departed from them in giving full play to the political concerns of the *minken* movement. The approach worked. Its circulations grew quickly, and by 1884, when the *ōshimbun* had gone into decline, *Eiri Jiyū* was the largest politically oriented paper in the capital.[73] There also were a number of party papers in the Jiyūtō's second center, Osaka, the most important being the *Nihon Rikken Seitō Shimbun*, which served as a successor to *Ōsaka Nippō* and lasted until the fall of 1885, when it was shut down by the government.[74] And in Kōchi, another liberal center, at least eight papers were formed to fight the Jiyūtō cause, including the influential *Kōchi Shimbun*, which made a national reputation with its vigorous, lucid editorials. Similarly, in nearly every region—Aichi, Wakayama, Fukuoka, Fukuyama, Fukushima, Toyama, the Hokuriku provinces, Shimane, Yamaguchi, Kumamoto, and the rest of Kyushu—small papers sprang up with ties to the Jiyūtō or one of its prefectural affiliates.[75]

It is important to note that few of these papers lived long or attracted large numbers of readers. The flagship *Jiyū Shimbun*, for example, had fewer than five thousand daily subscribers at its peak, and the regional papers usually numbered readers in the hundreds rather than the thousands and in some cases lasted fewer than ten issues.[76] The Jiyūtō may have had more papers than any of the other parties, but those papers were the smallest and the flimsiest. With the exception of the ambivalent *Chōya*, none of the established papers seriously considered lending its name to this most liberal of the parties; so the Jiyūtō had to create new organs with a less affluent, less influential base. The typical pattern was for a party unit to launch a small paper with little capital, then for that paper to fight vigorously with the established newspapers and regional officials. Before long, the paper's spirited editorials would draw penalties, and within a year or two it would fold, killed either by its inability to pay the bills or by the government's press-control policies. This pattern should not be taken to suggest that the Jiyūtō papers were unimportant or irrelevant. On the contrary, it highlights the growth of a political press closer to the "people" than anything Japanese journalism had seen before. It also means that the Jiyūtō press' role, while pathbreaking, was unusually dependent on the vagaries of regional politics. As a result, when the party movement went into a winter chill after the middle of 1883, the Jiyūtō papers withered too.

The Kaishintō, by contrast, was supported by most of the established antigovernment press, both in the capital and in the provinces. Perhaps because Ōkuma presented an option that was anti-*hanbatsu* yet much more clearly within the Confucian mainstream, an option where they could fight the existing regime without wandering too far from the elitist center, the press' dominant editors were drawn to his party. Kaishintō papers thus were generally larger, more affluent and more influential. And as a result, when the country's political fever subsided, most of them fared better than their Jiyūtō counterparts; they were hurt but they remained viable.

Foremost among the Kaishintō papers was *Yūbin Hōchi*, year in and year out one of the "big three" among the *ōshimbun*. It had led the moderate opposition ever since the days of Kurimoto Joun, and now it became the center of Ōkuma's supporters, with Yano Fumio as editor and such articulate, rising stars as Inukai Tsuyoshi and Ozaki Yukio as chief writers. *Hōchi* had particularly close ties to Keiō Gijuku, Fukuzawa's school, and to the Tōyō Giseikai, one of the Reform Party's forerunner organizations. And, through Fukuzawa, it had access to Mitsubishi connections. In other words, it represented the full range (and leverage) of the anti-*hanbatsu* establishment: its leading university, the most articulate people, the leading business circles. So well established were these forces at *Hōchi*, in fact, that Hara Kei, an ambitious young journalist with a less combative style who had joined *Yūbin Hōchi* two years earlier, now "felt swamped" and decided to quit—with little resistance from Yano, who distrusted his opportunism.[77]

Nearly as influential was Numa Morikazu's *Tōkyō-Yokohama Mainichi*, which had been battling the more conservative *Tōkyō Nichi Nichi* ever since a petty 1879 dispute over Fukuchi's use of public funds to stage the Tokyo reception for America's touring former president Ulysses S. Grant.[78] Numa had a well-deserved reputation for independence, having resigned his Genrōin post rather than endure the frustrations of a law that prohibited officials from speaking at public gatherings. And, as a member of the Tokyo Assembly *(fukai)*, he had become a popular advocate of lower taxes, more legislative bodies, and freedom of speech. *Mainichi* waited a while before tying itself to the party movement, partly because Numa had been courted by Itagaki, with whom he had worked in Tosa before the Restoration. But Itagaki seemed too radical, or at least too erratic, to Numa now, and since he actively disliked Baba, another Jiyūtō leader, he decided to throw his lot in with the Kaishintō. When he hired another Ōkuma ally, Shimada Saburō, as an editor, *Mainichi* could boast that its staff now included 40 percent of the men "popularly referred to as the five *bugyō* (commissioners)" of the party.[79]

The forty-odd Kaishintō papers in the provinces also tended to be more influential than their Jiyūtō peers. The *Ise Shimbun* in Mie, *Gifu Nichi Nichi Shimbun* in the Japan Alps, *Akita Nippō* and *Yamagata Shimbun* to the north, *Rikuu Nichi Nichi Shimbun* in

Miyagi, *Futsū Shimbun* in Tokushima, *Nanhō Shimbun* in Ōita, *Tottori Shimbun* in Tottori, and *San'yō Shimbun* in Okayama all were leading provincial papers that supported the Kaishintō in 1882–1883, then continued as relatively healthy papers after the party movement subsided.[80] Typical of the provincial Reform Party papers was the *Niigata Shimbun*, which had been founded in 1877 by prefectural officials eager to promote enlightenment. The paper began running editorials on an irregular basis in April 1878, then became an opinion leader "with great influence" after the arrival of Ozaki Yukio as a writer in 1879. By the beginning of 1882, although Ozaki had gone off to assist Ōkuma in Tokyo, the paper had established itself solidly in the Kaishintō camp, with a number of Keiō graduates as writers, including Minoura Katsundo and Tsuda Kōji.[81]

Ōkuma's party also was supported by two of the capital's leading plebeian papers, *Yomiuri* and *Ukiyo Shimbun*—a fact that meant more to the evolving history of the press than it did to the establishment-oriented Kaishintō leaders at the time. The *koshimbun*, as we have seen, had eschewed politics until now; so *Yomiuri* editor Maeda Genjirō's decision in 1882 to move his mass-oriented paper in a partisan direction suggested that something was happening to the gulf separating urban commoners from the world of the elites.[82] *Yomiuri* would remain less political than the *ōshimbun* for decades to come, but no longer would it seriously slight government and politics. It would not be long before the prestige papers, in turn, would begin to realize that they no longer could afford to ignore the masses in their own editorial policies, indeed, that they would have to include more news along with their political discourses if they were to survive financially. It is significant (and typical), however, that the profit-oriented *koshimbun* responded first to the changing interests of the commoner readers.

Japan's third party, the Rikken Teiseitō, focused even more heavily on the party's capital-city flagship paper than did the other parties. This was not because the Constitutional Imperial Party lacked regional organizations or papers; indeed, it had at least two-thirds as many newspapers as did the Kaishintō. It stemmed rather from the fact that the party actually was founded by the *Tōkyō Nichi Nichi* editor, Fukuchi, who in the minds of many simply *was* the Teiseitō, as well as from the fact that the other major Teiseitō leaders, Maruyama Sakura of *Meiji Nippō* and Mizuno Torajirō of *Tōyō Shinpō*, saw themselves as Fukuchi lieutenants.[83] Thus, from the first, *Nichi Nichi*'s editors took to the lecture circuit on behalf of the party's stated aim—preserving "the parallels of order and progress, so as to preserve national stability and carry out reforms"[84]—and the paper's editorials were given almost wholly in these months to fighting Teiseitō battles. The paper's most sensational association with the party movement came early in April 1882, when a young Gifu school teacher who supported the Teiseitō stabbed Itagaki with a sword after one of his lengthy antigovernment speeches. Itagaki was not hurt seriously, but the episode was reported widely, and when it became clear that the teacher had been provoked by a *Nichi Nichi* editorial, Fukuchi himself came under attack, especially after he ran a defensive essay accusing Itagaki of slandering the emperor.[85]

One of the Teiseitō's more intriguing supporters was the capital's *Tōyō Shinpo*, an offshoot of the once-radical *Tōkyō Akebono Shimbun*. After Suehiro left that paper when the editor capitulated to government pressure in 1875, it lost much of its spark but continued as a *jiyū minken* supporter. Then on March 1, 1882, just as the party movement was gaining force, it was taken over by conservatives. Mizuno became editor and changed its name to *Tōyō Shinpō*. The ties between the conservative Teiseitō and a once-lively voice of liberalism raised more curiosity than support; the paper never developed a wide following, and a mere 154 issues later, toward the end of 1883, it folded.[86] Even weaker was the party's other leading Kantō paper, the *Meiji Nippō*, which never had much more than a thousand subscribers and lasted only until November 29, 1885.[87]

In the Kansai area, the party was supported by the *Daitō Nippō*, founded in April 1882 for the single purpose of fighting party wars and edited by the *Yūbin Hōchi* refugee Hara Kei. Hara left *Daitō* in October to begin his government career, and the paper labored, to the very end, under the shadow of the more established Kaishintō papers and Murayama Ryōhei's better-edited *Asahi Shimbun*, never securing much more than eight hundred readers and lasting less than three years. Other regional Teiseitō papers included the *Shinano Mainichi Shimbun, Shizuoka Shinpō, Yamanashi Nichi Nichi Shimbun, Akita Nichi Nichi Shimbun, Fukushima Shimbun, Okayama Shinpō*, and the *Kyōtō Shiga Shinpō*.[88] Unfortunately for the party, the one characteristic that linked these regional newspapers together was their inability to secure a large or diverse readership. If the Jiyūtō press was plagued by a lack of readers with money and influence, the Teiseitō press was undermined by the fact that nearly all of its readers were well-off and well connected. Commoners exhibited little interest in papers known to express the party line of the political establishment, particularly when those papers did not provide them with much news either. So readership remained limited to bureaucrats, priests, school teachers, and some businessmen with close government connections of their own.

There was one class of non-Kaishintō, politically oriented newspapers that did prosper in these years, and that was a small group of papers that eschewed partisanship yet devoted large amounts of space to political issues and made no apologies about seeking profits. These probably were the period's most important papers, in fact, because while they remained on the edges of the *ōshimbun* world during the partisan years, they already had begun pointing the way to the kind of journalism that would dominate Japan after the middle 1880s. Before looking at their contributions, however, we must glance briefly at the specific issues over which the party papers argued—the issues that made the era especially lively—and at the government's efforts to curb the press's spreading influence.

DEBATING THE ISSUES

The most pronounced characteristic of the *ōshimbun* press' essays and articles in this period was, not surprisingly, their overwhelming preoccupation with political news and ideas. The papers did not wholly abandon nonpolitical issues,[89] but even more than in the late 1870s, politics—*partisan* politics—dominated. And the range of political issues the editorialists debated ran the gamut: *hanbatsu* machinations and the need for a Diet system to curb them, whether a Diet should be unicameral or bicameral, what foreign models should be studied in writing the constitution, the appropriate relationship between the cabinet and the legislature, who should be in the assembly, the role of the emperor in day-to-day affairs of state, the government's handling of treaty reform. Freedom also was a major debating point, with Jiyūtō papers asserting the "need for human freedom now" and predicting that Japan soon would "reap liberty's harvest."[90] But above all, and certainly most heatedly, the party papers argued about the nature of Japanese sovereignty and fought over the foibles—both ideological and personal—of their rivals.

The roots of what Ono refers to as "the famous sovereignty debate" between *Tōkyō Nichi Nichi* and *Tōkyō-Yokohama Mainichi* extended back to 1880, when several of the papers began discussing the divergent sovereignty statements found in the many constitutional proposals then being drafted.[91] In the fall of 1881, as the *seihen* crisis wound down, nearly all of the papers took up the sovereignty question, with a focus on the nature of Japan's polity and the practical demands of the modern world. On October 7, for example, *Kōchi Shimbun* ran an editorial asserting that "sovereignty must reside in the people."[92] On November 9, *Tōkyō-Yokohama Mainichi* posited it in the abstract concept of *seiri* or justice. And on December 3, *Tōkyō Yoron Shinshi* contended that it lay "both in the people and in society." Then, with the coming of the new year, the dispassionate tone of the debate changed. *Tōkyō Nichi Nichi* weighed in with quite a different set of arguments, and the discussion turned into a full-scale battle.[93]

In a series of lengthy, mid-January editorials titled "Shuken ron" (On sovereignty), the paper shifted the ground of the debate. While the other papers had focused their arguments on universal principles, *Tōkyō Nichi Nichi*'s Okamoto Takeo now argued that if sovereignty represented "the chief, the highest, the supreme, the free and independent authority of the country," if its role was to "express a nation's independence and to preserve its honor abroad," and if its core was "the exercise of legal, administrative, and judicial functions at home," then universal principles were not adequate for determining where it lay. Instead, he argued, a nation must look to its own *kokutai* or national essence. And in Japan's case that meant looking to the emperor and to the emperor alone. Having been ruled for more than two millennia by a unique, benevolent imperial family, Japan must take its place in the modern world as a constitutional monarchy *(rikken teiseikoku)*, with "sovereignty residing in the ruler." This was not an excuse for despotism, Okamoto added: "In exercising sovereignty, the imperial will must encompass the mind of the people." But to depart from the principle of imperial sovereignty would violate the country's very nature.[94]

Mainichi's response was fervent. On January 18, just a day after the last *Nichi Nichi* editorial, Numa's paper began a series titled "Doku *Nippō* kisha shuken ron" (On reading *Nichi Nichi*'s discussion of sovereignty), supporting a constitutional monarchy but urging Japan to emulate England, where the king and the people had learned to rule together, where "the assembly discusses and agrees upon the bills, the king approves ... and society is kept in order."[95] *Tōkyō Nichi Nichi* came back with its own five-part response, chiding *Mainichi* for "violating the shining spirit of our *kokutai*" and "delighting recklessly in the systems and customs of Europe."[96] And *Mainichi* responded again to *Tōkyō Nichi Nichi*'s "false doctrine," calling once more for the joint exercise of authority by emperor and people.[97]

Japan's other party newspaper quickly joined this spirited debate. *Chōya* ran a lengthy refutation of "the Nippō reporter's fallacies" in mid-February, contending that Okamoto's emperor-alone argument misapplied its own logical premises and arguing that only joint rule would succeed in Japan.[98] And the next month *Kōchi Shimbun* took up the issues again, with Ueki criticizing all of the other papers, defining sovereignty as the "fundamental power of a nation," something at once more abstract and broader than the mere legislative, administrative, and judicial functions of a government. He made a distinction between the state, where sovereignty actually lay, and the government or ruler who carried out the state's functions. Sovereignty, he contended lies in the state—and the state consists, quite simply, of "the people."[99]

Although the arguments were nuanced and intellectual, they also were emotional, filled with levels of passion typically associated with true believers. Debating political ideas had, by now, become a mania in Japan's educated circles, and the fighting grew as vicious as *sengoku* territorial battles. Miyake Setsurei recalled that editorialists would "slash in every direction," with *Nichi Nichi*'s Watanabe Asaka, for example, striving to "completely mow down" *Mainichi*'s Koizuka Ryū.[100] Something of the fervor that lay behind the arguments was captured in Seki Naohiko's recollections of an afternoon experience at *Nichi Nichi* early in 1882. A Tokyo Imperial University law student working part-time at the paper, he was perusing a book in the office when Fukuchi demanded to know what he was reading. Seki replied that he had found an interesting defense of the idea of imperial sovereignty in "Austin's jurisprudence." Fukuchi, recalled Seki, became excited, "pounded the desk and exclaimed, 'Now I understand!'" Then, said Seki:

> Ōchi Sensei began writing newspaper editorials about sovereignty. He ran them for several days in the *Tōkyō Nichi Nichi* editorial columns, catching public attention for quite a while. To tell the truth, I only read the first few pages of Austin's sovereignty theory to Sensei, and the beginning of the book was hardly enough to provide an understanding of his whole argument. But Ōchi really liked the chapter that posited sovereignty in the emperor; it was as if, hearing a tenth of the argument, he conjectured the whole of it.[101]

One wonders if the *Chōya* writer knew this when he argued that Fukuchi had missed the heart of Austin's argument, which, taken as a whole, called for the king and the people to share rule.[102]

In the end, no one gave any ground in these debates and before long, purely partisan attacks began to crowd aside the theoretical discussions. Moreover, quite often the tone became personal and mean. When the patriotic Gifu teacher stabbed Itagaki in the spring of 1882, for example, Jiyūtō papers jumped on Fukuchi as if he were personally responsible, even though the stabbing troubled him as much as it did his more liberal rivals. And when Itagaki and his party ally Gotō Shōjiro left Japan late in 1882 to study European constitutions, all the non-Jiyūtō dailies lambasted them as greedy opportunists who had deserted the party movement during a crucial season.

Tōkyō-Yokohama Mainichi's Numa took the lead on this particular issue, with editorials accusing his old friend Itagaki of ignoring party interests, succumbing to personal ambition, and accepting bribes from officials who wanted to destroy the Jiyūtō. "One cannot say clearly that he is a gentleman of honesty and integrity," sneered Numa. *Yūbin Hōchi* made similar charges,[103] and *Nichi Nichi* ran an interview with Ōkuma lamenting Itagaki's propensity for attacking "officials and policemen without regard to right and wrong."[104] Other Kaishintō leaders described Itagaki's followers as "illiterate and boorish" men who did not understand the political theories they espoused.[105] Later years would give credence to the rumors that Itagaki and Gotō had received government funds, but the tone of the invective suggested that rival editors were concerned with a good deal more than the integrity of the system and the health of the party movement; they wanted to destroy Itagaki personally.

The Jiyūtō faithful returned as much as they received. Beside making frequent, sneering references to "elegant gentlemen" who wore European clothes, former officials (i.e., Ōkuma) who had depleted Japan's "national treasury by four million yen,"[106] and leaders of "false parties," the Liberal Party papers focused particularly on their progressive rivals' ties to Mitsubishi money. Not long after the *seihen,* the anti-Ōkuma press had run articles accusing the young shipping company of benefiting from suspiciously large government grants during Ōkuma's tenure as finance minister.[107] Then, following the attacks on Itagaki, Jiyūtō papers began a string of harsh pieces on the "vices of Mitsubishi," accusing the company of duplicity in secretly underwriting a party that now opposed the very government that had made it so successful, and lambasting

Ōkuma for the personal financial gain he allegedly had received from his close ties to Mitsubishi.[108] That the Kaishintō and the Jiyūtō sought essentially the same kind of constitutional system would have escaped most readers of these partisan attacks; the struggles were as much personal as they were ideological, and few accusations were considered too extreme in discrediting the opponent.

THE PRICE OF PARTISANSHIP

For about a year after the *seihen*, the overall impact of the lively debate was quite positive, bringing ideas into wider circulation and pulling new groups into the public conversation. Yano looked on these years as the time of Japan's most "brilliant editorial confrontation."[109] And Fukuzawa wrote in the summer of 1882 that people across Tokyo were reading newspapers "like birds let out of a cage one day a week." He said he found people in lounges more interested in reading newspapers than in bantering with each other. "What is this?" he asked. "Has culture progressed to its very limits, without our even noticing it?" He added that newspapers had inspired a new "understanding of freedom and rights that, in its turn, had generated a mysterious life force."[110]

But if the partisan struggles brought new energy to Japan's political world, their long-term impact had a disruptive side. The mean-spirited bickering obscured the common interests of the parties and obfuscated the arguments of many of Japan's best minds. And the fighting helped, all too soon, to undercut party politics and seriously to undermine the *ōshimbun* press. After the middle of 1883, the energy went out of the party debates with the whoosh of a punctured balloon, and by the New Year that followed, popular political discussion was largely dead. Partisanship was not the only reason for its demise; government harassment of the press and the politicians played a role, as did the difficulty of sustaining political momentum when elections were years away. But there is no gainsaying the fact that the petty bickering alienated more than a few readers, especially those who had believed deeply in the parties' ideals. So after the spring of 1883, many of the new readers and even some of the old ones began to drop their subscriptions to the party organs.

The disaffected sometimes blamed new prepayment subscription policies for prompting them to cancel,[111] and sometimes they said the frequent suspensions of their favorite papers had made it too hard to keep up with the news. But those were "just excuses," says Yamamoto Taketoshi; the real reason most people deserted the papers was that petty partisanship had alienated them.[112] As a result, circulations declined and many of the smaller papers had to shut down, while even the well-established *ōshimbun* lost up to a third of their subscribers during 1883, with greater losses occurring in the years that followed.[113] More will be said later about the details of this decline; what seems clear—and pertinent—here is that while partisanship may have been a natural, even inescapable, outcome of the fevered political struggles surrounding the political crisis of 1881, it created a narrow approach to journalism that simply could not be sustained in a modern, industrial society.

Intensifying the troubles were the unending efforts of officials in these years to control the press, even to eradicate those parts they could not control. There is no question that the outbreak of popular rhetoric and the proliferation of opposition groups struck fear into the hearts of an official world that had for generations operated on the assumption that the sharp divide between *kan* and *min*—official and popular—spheres was not only natural but essential to the maintenance of order.[114] Surely, that is why Inoue Kowashi wrote to Iwakura in 1881 that the popular agitation had to be brought under control or "we will see incalculable disturbances."[115] The same assumption accounts for Itō's instructions to the Bureau of Police Protection in 1883 to devise some means for punishing cartoonists whose brushes were too sharp.[116] And it helps explain the fact that Home Ministry officials prohibited more than a thousand proposed meetings and talks a year between 1882 and 1884,[117] as well as the scheme to coopt Itagaki and Gotō by sending them abroad. The idea of "popular rights" in the abstract did not particularly disturb the officials, but the spread of *taji sōron*, or contentious debates, among the people frightened them thoroughly, sending them, in the hyperbole of one scholar, into a "truly indescribable panic."[118] They also prompted officials to devise ever more forceful means to control expression.

The authorities' most effective approach lay in ongoing efforts to win press allies—and thus, they hoped, to render heavy-handed coercion less necessary. Sometimes they did this through the old method of creating progovernment news organs, sometimes by coopting journalists (Tokutomi Sohō referred sneeringly to the "officialization" or *kanka seraru* of once-liberal leaders),[119] often by channeling covert funds to selected papers. *Yūbin Hōchi*'s Yano noted how hard officials worked to balance *minken* papers with their own mouthpieces. "Whenever we would get hold of a paper in a given prefecture," he commented, "the government would establish its own paper there, or designate an existing one as an 'allied paper.' "[120] The most obvious effort of this sort was the launching of an official gazette, the *Kanpō*, on July 2, 1883. During the first Meiji decade, official notices and decrees had been publicized in the *Dajōkan Nisshi*, but that publication died in 1880 and several efforts to create a successor proved unsuccessful.[121] The most active supporter of an official gazette was Yamagata Aritomo, who wrote a memorial now lamenting "the extreme resentment and agitation" being stirred up by the party newspapers. "Most of them attack the government and libel the court," he wrote. "The government should assist the people in following correct ways . . . it should disseminate its philosophy and general aims" through an official paper.[122] His plans came to fruition, ironically, just as the party press had begun its own decline. Even more ironic—and telling—was the fact that one of the two *Kanpō* editors was Komatsubara Eitarō, the irascible Okayama native who had gone to jail for damning officials in the 1870s, a man who had decided that life was easier in a ministry than in a jail.[123]

More insidiously, the government now launched an extensive, secret program of distributing money to a surprisingly wide range of journalists, including several in the opposition camp. Under a plan drawn up by Itō, apparently in late 1881, more than 75,000 yen was earmarked for assistance to what were regarded as influenceable papers: 30,000 for creating the *Kanpō*, 20,000 for winning the support of *Meiji Nippō* and *Akebono*, and smaller payments, usually monthly, to *Tōkyō Nichi Nichi*, *Chōya*, *Yūbin Hōchi*, *Tōkyō-Yokohama Mainichi*, and *Yomiuri*. The money earmarked for *Akebono* apparently was used to shut it down and launch the new *Tōyō Shinpō*, noted above.[124] An additional plan was worked out with Fukuchi, following his return to the government camp, where *Nichi Nichi* was purchased for 75,000 yen by a group of official loyalists, then reorganized under Fukuchi's complete personal control.[125] In May 1882, government assistance of five hundred yen a month also was earmarked for Osaka's *Asahi Shimbun*.[126] No strings, apparently, were attached to any of these payments, and Fukuchi claimed "complete freedom" and "pure independence."[127] We already have seen, moreover, that several of the papers argued vociferously for assembly government and for Kaishintō positions. But Ariyama Teruo has found evidence of behind-the-scenes understandings that *Asahi*, for example, would go lightly on the government in return for assistance.[128] And it stretches credulity to deny the moderating influence of the "gifts" on the other papers, especially after they began to experience financial difficulties in 1883.[129]

Funds of this sort also were distributed widely by provincial administrators to local papers and, when funds alone were inadequate, papers were created or purchased outright. The editor of the *Ōsaka Nippō*, for example, reportedly received 13,000 yen when his paper ran into financial difficulty. The loyal *Daitō Nippō*, also in Osaka, received six hundred yen a month from its founding until 1886.[130] When officials failed to bring the *San'yō Shimbun* in western Japan under their control, they bought out another Okayama paper, *Kibi Nichi Nichi Shimbun*, and made it their own.[131] Indeed, said the nonpartisan *Jiji Shinpō* in the spring of 1882, "there are schemes in every prefecture and city to create official papers." It reported that new *goyō* papers had been created, among other places, in Nagano, Kōchi, Ōita, and Miyagi.[132]

Despite all the efforts at securing supporters and buying out opponents, however, papers remained feisty; so when the sweeteners failed, officials resorted to more traditional solutions: censorship of specific articles, fines, jail sentences, suspensions, and banishment. Armed with the penal provisions of the 1875 *shimbunshi jōrei* and its later supplements, the Home Ministry was more active against the press in these years than at any other time up to the Sino-Japanese War of 1894–1895. Occasionally, when offensive material happened to be caught before the paper was printed, the censors would simply tell the editors not to run it. On January 19, 1885, for example, *Jiji Shinpō* ran a terse notice stating that "at 10:30 last night we suddenly were prevented from running our intended editorial." The following day's issue explained that the editors had planned an essay on Korea (where Inoue Kaoru was negotiating following an anti-Japanese coup attempt) but that Naimushō authorities had censored it, too late to allow for a substitute essay.[133] More often, the unacceptable materials found their way into print—and resulted in heavy penalties for the offending journalists. Altogether, more than six hundred journalists were fined or jailed between 1881 and 1884,[134] and though a careful analysis of the cases lies outside the scope of this particular study, three or four examples should illustrate the severe response when writers exceeded the ambiguous bounds of what was acceptable.

In the autumn of 1881, the editor of *Tōkai Gyōshō Shinpō* was sent to jail for three years and fined nine hundred yen for reporting on a speaker who compared Japan's first emperor, Jinmu, to the sixteenth-century warrior Hachisuka Koroku, a mere mortal.[135] The next June, a writer for the frequently offensive *Ukiyo Shimbun* was given seven days and a three-yen fine for maligning the character of a Shintō priest.[136] And in the spring of 1884, both the editor and the printer of *Gifu Nichi Nichi Shimbun* were sentenced to five months in jail and fined thirty yen for an article criticizing Dajōkan regulations that allowed governors to select provincial officials without consulting anyone.[137] One of the more novel cases occurred in November 1882, when the *Okayama Nichi Nichi Shimbun* set in type an essay heralding the approaching "day for singing the victory song of freedom." Worried that the passage might offend censors, the editor had inked it out before the paper was distributed. Officials were not impressed, however; they said the passage still was readable and sent him to jail for nine months for advocating a change in the *kokutai*.[138]

Nor did the authorities stop with punishing individuals. Armed with the *hakkō teishi* and *hakkō kinshi* (suspension and banishment) additions to the 1875 law, they focused increasingly on the papers themselves, sometimes even on the bigger ones. One reason for the increasing popularity of suspensions and banishments was that they did not have to be defended legally. Fines and prison sentences had to go through the courts, but the Home Ministry could suspend or banish papers on its own, without so much as a word of explanation. As a result, an average of fifty-five papers a year were suspended from 1881 to 1884, and sixteen were shut down completely.[139]

It goes without saying that the Jiyūtō papers were hit most often by *hakkō teishi* and *hakkō kinshi* orders, though Kaishintō organs also received a number of such punishments.[140] When *Eiri Jiyū Shimbun* ran an essay on May 8, 1884, describing violent methods used by certain Russians to wipe out red light districts, it was shut down for three weeks, even though the editors tried to protect themselves by commenting that "not even the most obstinate and foolish leaders could agree with such a simplistic approach."[141] *Nihon Rikken Seitō Shimbun*, the leading Jiyūtō paper in Kansai, was suspended six times, for a total of twenty-three weeks;[142] *Hokuriku Nippō*, the Etchū Jiyūtō organ, was banished in 1883, then banished again when it reemerged as the *Jiyū Shinron*,[143] and when the *Tōkyō Shinshi* ran an article in the winter of 1883 alleging an illicit affair between Inoue Kaoru's daughter and a stable keeper, its doors were closed forever.[144]

One of the more vivid examples of the government's determination to bring papers under control, no matter how the editors resisted, came at *Kōchi Shimbun* during the heated spring debates of 1882. When the paper resumed publication in mid-March, after its third suspension, it ran an essay exclaiming: "Do we get no explanation? Government suspensions of our paper have become more severe, but official statements provide no explanation of what we have done wrong or why we are shut down."[145] The paper was suspended again on March 25. Then on July 14, after continued defiance of official threats, it was handed a *hakkō kinshi* order. In its last issue, the following day, it ran a lively essay, addressed to "thirty-six million fellow citizens," in which it proclaimed: "Five times we were given the death sentence, and still we refused to die." Soon after that, the prefecture's liberal journalists held a "funeral service" for the paper, with deliverymen carrying the coffin and reporters following in its wake. Some 2,727 people signed the *Kōchi Shimbun* memorial tablet.[146]

As energetic as enforcement procedures were, however, the laws were not adequate to the Home Ministry's goal of silencing the opposition; no matter how vigilant enforcers might be, the opposition writers managed to skirt the law through dummy editors, circumlocutions, and surrogate papers.[147] As a result, a new Law of Assembly was proclaimed in 1882, sharply restricting people's freedom to hold political meetings. And on April 16, 1883, a revised *shimbunshi jōrei* was issued, designed to close loopholes and render evasion of control mechanisms more difficult. Universally decried by press partisans as a "newspaper extermination law," it contained forty-two articles (compared to eighteen in the 1875 law), and made enforcement simpler and publication more difficult. It also brought to maturation the pre–World War II Japanese approach to press control.[148]

A linchpin of the new law was a security deposit system, not unlike that found in France's Publishing Act of 1819, under which papers had to deposit a fee with the government when they sought permission to begin publishing. The amount varied, depending on the location and frequency of publication, ranging from one thousand yen for a Tokyo daily to 175 for a thrice-monthly provincial paper, and officials claimed that their intent merely was to make sure that papers could pay fines if they violated the law. The actual purpose, however, appears to have been to eradicate the small, poorly financed papers that published the shrillest articles. Indeed, one official, Mizumoto Shigeyoshi, said as much when he greeted the law with an expression of hope that "journalism now would improve" because Japan at last would be rid of "those vicious newspapers edited by groups of outrageous individuals who have no resources."[149]

Other features of the law included a broader definition of who could be held responsible for legal infractions; a direct prohibition on the creation of *migawari* or surrogate newspapers, which so often had risen to take the place of suspended publications; and a significantly expanded list of proscribed materials. It was forbidden now to publish matters discussed at government meetings, to print criminal writings, to run anything proscribed by the navy and army ministers, and to publish slanderous caricatures. To discourage the hiring of dummy editors, the law prohibited foreigners, women, and minors from publishing. And it made it illegal for owners and employees of a publication under suspension or banishment to publish another journal or paper.[150]

The impact of this law was immediate. Just as its designers had intended, a significant number of smaller, more extreme papers went under at once, unable to raise the security deposit. Just two months after the code's publication, *Jiji Shinpō* reported that thirty-two (nearly 40 percent) of Tokyo's newspapers and journals had been forced to cease publishing.[151] A similar number of papers and periodicals (thirty-one) had to shut down their presses in Osaka and the provinces.[152] Even those papers that could afford the fees faced added financial pressures when their printers, worried about the new legal risks, raised the printing rates.[153] And, probably most serious for the now-struggling political movements, many editors found in the law one more reason to dampen the political fires that had scorched their columns for the last year and a half.

Yūbin Hōchi's Ozaki Yukio commented in retrospect that the new law made apostates of some "party advocates,"[154] while Jiyūtō supporters put it more graphically. The new press and assembly laws, said one, "pull out the people's tongues and hearts; they make them deaf and dumb. It is as if they had killed all the people, as if Anthony had taken out Caesar's tongue."[155] Said another:

> Thanks to the press and assembly laws, the press no longer can be called free. . . . We have no choice now but to keep our mouths closed about political issues. You become nervous whenever you feel like making a speech or writing an article. You feel as if you are walking on thin ice or standing on the edge of a precipice. Your mouth hesitates; your hand withers; your heart and stomach feel completely exhausted.[156]

The law certainly did not silence all the editors. Nor should one give too much credit to the new regulations for the decline of the party movement after the middle of 1883. As we already have seen, a number of personal and institutional developments combined to undermine political passions. It is undeniable, however, that the tone of the *ōshimbun* press changed—and that the revised *shimbunshi jōrei* was one of the reasons. The most radical papers died; the rhetoric of the remaining papers cooled; economics, culture, and international affairs began to crowd politics for space in the papers' lead articles; and—most important—the prestige papers went into the precipitous circulation and financial decline noted above. So serious were their problems, in fact, that by 1885 *Nichi Nichi, Yūbin Hōchi,* and *Chōya* all had been pushed from the ranks of Japan's largest newspapers and dwarfed by both the upstart *Asahi* in Osaka and several of the long-scorned *koshimbun. Asahi* had more than five times the circulation of any of the old prestige papers by 1885: nearly 32,000 daily, compared to 5,700 at *Yūbin Hōchi* and 4,300 at *Nichi Nichi.*[157] And sales revenues were declining too—from 72,834 yen in 1883 at *Chōya* to 45,934 in 1885, and from a high of 76,427 in 1882 at *Nichi Nichi* to 38,550 in 1885.[158] Even more dramatic was the decline in *Nichi Nichi*'s total monthly income, from 8,316 yen in 1880 to a mere 3,112 in the first half of 1886.[159] And the *Jiyū Shimbun* no longer could make ends meet, dipping into the red by more than 2,300 yen in a mere five months, from June through October in 1883.[160] That all of the leading political papers would survive was far from certain as the 1880s reached their midpoint.

HARBINGERS OF A NEW JOURNALISM

At least as significant as the decline of the *ōshimbun* press in the middle 1880s was the nature of the papers that had begun to replace them as Japan's circulation leaders. They were, in every case, less partisan, more news-oriented, and more popular. The country's second largest paper in 1885, with a daily circulation in excess of 15,000, was *Yomiuri,* which by now had become more political without sacrificing readability or its populist approach, and the third largest daily (13,799 readers) was *Jiyū no Tomoshibi,* a Tokyo paper that retained its serious *minken* flavor but, like *Yomiuri,* catered to the more lowbrow interests of the city's working people. While most of these challengers were denigrated by the establishment as cheap and vulgar, unworthy of serious consideration, their popularity suggested that something new was afoot in Japanese journalism. Their brand of editing would not be accepted as the norm for some time to come, but their financial success could not be ignored by the Yanos, the Narushimas, and the Fukuchis. And two of the newcomers, *Jiji Shinpō* and *Asahi*, already were beginning to be taken seriously, even by the *ōshimbun* scions, as exemplars of a centrist kind of journalism, neither flagrantly partisan nor crudely commercial, that might suggest a way out of the partisan disaster.

Actually, *Asahi* had been in deep trouble when Murayama Ryōhei and Ueno Riichi took control of it at the beginning of 1881. Osaka's *Sakigake Shimbun*, published by the former *Asahi* editor Tsuda Takashi, boasted better writers and threatened to drown *Asahi* in its wake; readership was half of what it had been at the end of 1880, and the company had over four thousand yen in debts.[161] Murayama and Ueno, in fact, had to put 30,000 yen of their own money into the paper when they assumed command.[162] And to make matters worse, just weeks after their takeover local officials tried to intimidate them with a harsh, unexplained suspension. So threatening and worrisome did the paper's employees find the punishment that, when publishing resumed, more than thirty donned red happi coats and paraded through the streets shouting, "Asahi Shimbun! Released from Suspension!"[163]

But Murayama was not one to let a project sink. Unlike his counterparts at the Tokyo *ōshimbun*, he was a businessman first, a journalist second, and a politician third. A skilled swimmer and swordsman of samurai origins, he already had become one of Osaka's most successful entrepreneurs, building a merchandising business with outlets across western Japan and in the Japan Sea regions of the northeast. Once he decided to concentrate on helping the founding Kimura family save *Asahi* rather than expanding his own business into Korea, he had no intent of letting the paper sink. At the same time, he was not interested in taking *Asahi* down the purely commercial road of a typical *koshimbun.* Very much the Tokugawa Confucian, he seems to have taken quite seriously the paper's original promise to "seek the public good and eschew private benefit"[164] and to "use illustrations, attach *furigana* and make ideas easy to understand, because our chief aim is to educate infants, women, and children."[165]

As a result, Murayama and Ueno brought a new and highly successful journalistic style to the Kansai region after 1881. As serious proprietor-managers, they paid close attention to everyday busi-

ness operations, for one thing. Murayama became involved personally in managing *Asahi,* meeting daily with his executives, yet generally keeping business and editorial operations separate, so long as
the editorial content supported sound fiscal policy. He created a
department structure in which section heads were responsible for
their own areas, and he allowed his editors relative autonomy in
handling news and editorials while he and Ueno concentrated on
the business side. "Not once," notes Iwai Hajime, "did he ever take
up the pen or write a manuscript."[166]

The content of the paper was different too. It contained the
serialized novels and easy-to-read prose of its *koshimbun* beginnings, but it also took seriously the reporting of significant news
and gave full play to the political issues of its times. Unlike *Jiji,*
whose forte was opinion, it concentrated on news. And unlike the
prestige papers, it refused to support any given party, insisting on
neutrality despite daily visits from Jiyūtō leaders who wanted the
paper's allegiance. A mid-1882 *Asahi* editorial explained its insistence on independence this way: "The newspaper is not merely a
vehicle for carrying on political discussions; nor is it simply an
implement for discussing statecraft. Its purpose is to record the
world's new expressions, to describe the mysteries of society, to
assist in spreading knowledge among the people."[167] One of the the
paper's strengths, not surprisingly, was the coverage of Kansai commercial and business developments, particularly after the editors
began in the spring of 1881 to hire university graduates as business
reporters and to have them gather their own material rather than
relying on *tanbōsha* for content.[168]

Murayama also was aggressive about sales and technology. He
moved more quickly than other editors to secure the presses needed
to expand the paper, increasing the number of cylinder presses from
one in 1882 to eight in 1885.[169] And he showed a practical, common-
sensical side by reviving old circulation methods when the new
technologies failed him. To increase readership outside of Osaka,
for example, he hired rickshaw pullers, unemployed runners from
the old Tokugawa postal relay system, and even palanquin bearers
as deliverymen—because the postal trains, which *Asahi* had been
using, ran too infrequently to get papers to readers on the morning
of publication.[170] He also raised the cost of a subscription in April
1881, from one *sen* to 1.5 *sen* a day, yet kept the price low enough
to compete with the *koshimbun* and to undersell all of the prestige
papers.[171]

The outcome of this new, results-oriented approach was successful beyond what anyone might have imagined. Within weeks, *Asahi*'s circulation had returned to its earlier peak. In 1882, its daily circulation passed 13,000, making it Japan's second largest paper after *Yomiuri*. In 1883, it became the largest in the country, with 21,565 daily readers, and by 1885 its 32,000-person readership was more than double that of any other paper.[172] And its income from sales that year was 68,768 yen—more than 20,000 above its nearest competitor.[173] Was *Asahi* an *ōshimbun* or a *koshimbun*? No one was quite sure. Its pages were nearly as gray as the Tokyo political papers and it paid a great deal of attention to politics, but its writing was simpler, it used *furigana* and ran novels, and it covered news more fully than did its counterparts. What was more, it stayed aloof from partisanship, and it marketed its product with the zeal of an American Pulitzer or a British Northcliffe. Whatever it was, it had to be watched.

Significantly, the paper with the second highest sales revenue in 1885 was the other upstart, nonpartisan innovator: Fukuzawa Yukichi's *Jiji*, which was launched in Tokyo on March 1, 1882. This certainly was not Fukuzawa's first experience with journalism. We already have seen his essays at several papers, including *Minkan Zasshi* (which he published in 1874 and 1875), as well as his role in *Meiroku Zasshi*. He also had agreed in 1881 to serve as editor of a government *kanpō*, though the project was dashed by bureaucratic infighting, to his disappointment.[174] *Jiji*, however, represented his first attempt at editing a daily newspaper and, as in nearly everything else he tried, he was immediately successful, partly because of the influence of his name, partly because of the financial circles that supported him, and partly because of his editorial and management skills.

Few people in Japan were better publicists than Fukuzawa, and he captured the public imagination immediately by proclaiming *Jiji* a *dokuritsu fuki* (free and independent) newspaper. There really was nothing new about claims of editorial independence. *Chōya* had used the phrase *fuhen fuki* (impartial and independent) the previous year in describing the way public figures (and newspapers) should behave; *Tōkyō Nichi Nichi* often had used the phrase *futō fuhen* (nonpartisan and impartial), and others used labels such as *kōhei fuhen* (just and impartial), *fuhen chūritsu* (impartial and neutral), and *kokuritsu dokkō* (independent and self-reliant) to describe themselves.[175] But in 1882, coming from Fukuzawa's pen, the phrase had a fresh ring. In the overheated atmosphere of the day, it suggested a conscious determination to avoid pettiness and narrowly partisan affiliations. As Fukuzawa himself explained it:

> Society today has a government; it has many parties; it has a variety of businesses and industries; it has numerous scholarly associations. If we are to be true to our spirit, we will favor none of these, but will assist them all as friends. We will oppose only those who stand against this approach. . . . Our primary aim in taking the name *Jiji* will be to record developments in recent civilization, to discuss goals and events related to the progress of that civilization, to keep abreast of each day's new currents, and to report them to the world.

"The world for us," he added, "has neither enemies nor friends. We render judgments solely on the basis of whether something helps or hurts the nation."[176]

This did not mean that *Jiji* would avoid politics. To the contrary, its columns were filled with political essays. Indeed, one of the main reasons people subscribed to it was to read Fukuzawa's opinions about the political world.[177] It cannot even be said that *Jiji* was wholly nonpartisan, since Fukuzawa's views were quite close to those of the Kaishintō and its Mitsubishi friends. What it meant was that the paper would accept no formal or binding relationship with any party; it would insist on the importance of journalistic independence. And that assertion itself was highly appealing in a society that saw undue partisanship as impure. As Carol Gluck has noted, "repeated assertions of impartiality kept neither the government nor the newspapers free from political alignments, but they did reinforce the contention that any overt pursuit of partisan interests was of questionable moral value."[178] That Fukuzawa had correctly divined the mood of Tokyo's reading public was illustrated vividly when Seki Naohiko took over the *Nichi Nichi* reins several years later and immediately committed that paper too to "independence and freedom" *(fuki dokuritsu).*[179]

Another *Jiji* innovation, this one very much in keeping with what Murayama was doing in Osaka, involved broadening the definition of respectable journalism to include a better balance between news and opinion. The paper usually ran a political essay on page one, just as the *ōshimbun* did, and it continued the dull gray format of respectable papers. But its contents differed. The happenings of society, particularly the economic developments, became a *Jiji* forte. The very first issue contained nearly three dozen news articles in its *zappō* section and another eight in the foreign news section. The second had a similar offering, and by 1883, news coverage had become a major feature. Like Murayama, Fukuzawa hired college graduates (mostly from his own Keiō Gijuku) to do the reporting, and he encouraged them to report especially on news likely to be useful in Japan's ongoing modernization process. The March 2, 1882, issue, for example, contained an item about *Jiji*'s own plans to begin making Sundays a holiday for its printers, since Sunday work schedules at other papers led to "much sickness." Science and cultured living became popular subjects. In the fall of 1882, the paper ran the first of numerous controversial pieces on the craze for patent medicines, which, it claimed, had fewer curative powers than "drinking water or tea."[180] In the summer of 1886, the paper ran a story on the hiring of a Western-style cook at the Keiō dining hall, indicating that students liked his dishes more than the old rice-based fare. Other articles urged people to drink milk and eat meat, since Japan's traditional vegetarian diets made people look "like dogs at a funeral" and led to mental indolence and early aging.[181] News was as important to Fukuzawa as politics as a means of civilizing his people; its publication became one of *Jiji*'s distinguishing traits.[182]

A third *Jiji* feature was an unapologetic commitment to making a profit. Fukuzawa declared in his autobiography that it was not in "my usual nature" to enter "into the minute accounts of the treasury; I leave all that to the men in charge."[183] He was not, however, averse to making sure that his editors kept an eye on the balance sheet. He had little respect for Confucian ideologues who disdained profit or saw political debate as the sole legitimate activity of a paper. It was in this vein that he wrote to Ōkuma, even before the paper was launched, that a financially solid newspaper would be a boon to jobless Keiō graduates, many of whom "are living shamefully, like *ronin*, worn out in the search for work, sometimes frustrated enough to think of settling for the world of commerce—or even of literature."[184]

Partly for this reason, Fukuzawa put heavy emphasis on advertising revenues. Just six months after *Jiji* was launched, he published a defense of aggressive newspaper advertising policies, and in March 1887 he wrote that "advertising is as important to a business as weapons are to an army." He said he wanted a "high-class" readership because "merchants will find advertising most useful in a paper read by the highest class of people." Advertising, he added, was necessary to make the paper profitable.[185] Following that philosophy, his editors placed ads for just about everything imaginable

in a typical *Jiji* issue: lectures, insurance, books, shipping companies, telephone poles, roofing, industrial exhibitions, tobacco, wine.
One catchy shipping ad in the January 6, 1886, issue took up three-
quarters of a page, and the January 16 paper gave over half of its six
pages to advertisements. Moreover, by 1887, page one was used
exclusively for ads, many of them well illustrated. Typically, advertising provided a quarter of *Jiji*'s annual revenue.[186]

Like Murayama five hundred kilometers to the west, Fukuzawa turned this combination of serious news, modest profit-seeking, and nonpartisanship into a model for the struggling establishment press. *Jiji* never attained the circulation heights of *Asahi*; it
probably was too serious for that; certainly Fukuzawa was not
Murayama's business equal. But it grew steadily, even as the *ōshimbun* were going into decline, hitting a daily circulation of nearly
five thousand in 1882, increasing to 7,500 in 1883 and approaching
10,000 in 1886, well ahead of *Nichi Nichi, Chōya, Yūbin Hōchi,*
and *Tōkyō-Yokohama Mainichi*.[187] *Jiji*'s sales revenues were the
second highest in Japan by 1885. A year later, they remained second
but the gap between *Asahi* and *Jiji* had been cut by two-thirds.[188]
That a public figure of Fukuzawa's stature had been willing to defy
the politics-only path of Japan's respectable press meant a great
deal. That he did so with such success held tremendous importance
for the future of journalism.

By any reckoning, Japan's establishment press quivered at a cross-
roads in the middle of the 1880s. The *ōshimbun* political press—
still the only press that mattered in the minds of the nation's
elite—was in serious trouble. On the one hand, its editors' obses-
sion with shaping national politics had made it influential beyond
what once had seemed imaginable, enabling journalists to spawn
popular movements and bring down administrations. On the other
hand, that very power had driven the prestige papers into a partisan
cul-de-sac. When the parties sprang into being, it was natural, probably inevitable, that the papers would become their engines. But
when the parties went into decline, so did the papers. In the process
of bringing a once disconnected class of readers into the political
process, the *ōshimbun* press had laid the seeds of its own demise.
For when that new class lost interest in the petty party squabbles, it
was not about to continue reading the more philosophical, erudite
political essays of the previous decade. It gravitated instead to new
kinds of papers—either to the *koshimbun* with a popular rights ori-

entation like *Eiri Jiyū Shimbun* or *Yomiuri*, or to middle-of-the-road papers such as *Asahi* and *Jiji*.

How the prestige papers would respond was far from clear at mid-decade. Continuation along the former elitist lines was impossible; the rising costs of publishing and the soaring circulations of their rivals would not permit survival with such small circulations. Emulation of the *koshimbun* was not feasible either. The *ōshimbun* editors were public servants by self-definition; to have turned their papers into money-making machines was, for them, unthinkable. That a third approach had emerged thus was as important as it was fortuitous. In Fukuzawa's and Murayama's middle way lay elements that held promise for editors on both sides of the *ōshimbun-koshimbun* divide: a nonpartisan approach to politics, a balance between news and opinions, profit-based management policies held in check by a sense of social responsibility. It was those elements that would give Japan, in the very next years, a truly modern press.

CHAPTER 6

DEVELOPING
A NEW PERSONA
1886 to 1894

> In the 1880s, all over the world,
> the newspaper was ready for a new formula.
> *Anthony Smith*[1]

> The people look no longer to the military
> class for guidance. The samurai's place has
> been taken by the newspaper.
> *The Times, April 19, 1889*[2]

Monday, February 11, 1889, was a reporter's dream (and night-mare)—full of promise at daybreak, disastrous by mid-morning, glorious later, and brimming with news enough to fill a month of papers. It snowed in the villages of Gunma that morning, and silk merchants piled barrels of sake into high monuments, while house-wives cooked special rice for those who had not trekked off to Tokyo to join the capital celebrations. Before the day was out, the Emperor Meiji had given his people a new constitution; a Shintō nationalist had assassinated Education Minister Mori Arinori, an amnesty had given freedom to scores of *minken* political prisoners, and Kuga Katsunan had launched Japan's newest newspaper, *Nihon*.[3] At the close of the day, people celebrated the constitution and mourned Mori with fireworks.

The day was particularly symbolic for Japan's established newspaper world, which covered the constitutional promulgation like it had no event before it. *Tōkyō Nichi Nichi*'s new president, Seki Naohiko, was at the court at 8:00 A.M., and his paper was on the street with a text of the document at 10:00 A.M., the very hour at which the imperial ceremonies began.[4] *Jiji* was selling copies by mid-afternoon. And *Asahi* spent an incredible 7,300 yen for a telegram to get a two-page extra containing the entire constitution onto the Osaka streets that same day. "We spared no expense," said editor Murayama; "our brash use of such a long telegram dumbfounded people."[5] At least as dumbfounding was the unabashed competition and rivalry that marked the day's news coverage. The papers jostled for the ten press spots at the promulgation ceremonies,[6] used insider connections to get advance texts of the document, and printed flashy ads to promote their reportorial exploits.[7] They also ran editorials overflowing with patriotic pride, declaring the constitution the symbol of a new and modern Japan, a document filled with "glory enough" to justify a bit of national "boasting to the world."[8]

Something quite clearly had happened to Japan's press since the descent into partisanship seven years earlier. Reporters from all types of papers and journals, big and small, came together now at the promulgation ceremony, with each of them interested both in politics and in winning readers through speedy, lively reportage. If the years just after the emperor's constitutional promise had produced a press consumed by politics, the years surrounding the promulgation inspired a press committed to news and profits. They pushed both *koshimbun* and *ōshimbun* toward the middle, in the most significant transformation Japan's press had known since its break from the government early in the 1870s. And the most striking characteristics of this new press were the same things that made the February 11, 1889, coverage symbolic: a renewed focus on the political life of the nation, an emergent willingness by all the papers to seek profits through fast and attractive news coverage, and the appearance of a new kind of nationalism.

THE REVIVAL OF POLITICAL PASSION

The painful failure of the party press may have caused the *ōshimbun* to wither, but it did not kill the political interest that had brought them into being in the first place. Politics, after all, continued to dominate the national life throughout the 1880s, as Itō, Yamagata, and their cohorts prepared the country for life under a constitutional monarchy. And even the new, more profit-oriented editors and publishers, who disdained partisanship and turgid editorials, had been trained in Confucian schools that focused on the need for effective, morally sound central political institutions. So the papers never stopped discussing political issues altogether, and as the promising days of assembly government approached, political news and opinion came once again to dominate the daily news and editorial offering. By the late 1880s, indeed, all the leading newspapers were concentrating on the key issues of governance, both diplomatic and domestic, some of them even dipping again in the broiling waters of partisanship. As the German physician Erwin Baelz commented in his journal near the end of the decade, the Japanese "seem made for party life."[9] "Public opinion, public opinion, they shout and the echo is political," agreed the *Tōkyō Shinpō*; "the government, the government, they call, and their wails too, are political. Are the people of Japan to live by politics alone?"[10]

One clear sign of the rejuvenated political interest was Tokutomi Sohō's dramatic entry onto the national journalistic stage with the launching in 1887 of the politically oriented *Kokumin no Tomo*, a journal that championed a distinctive, rather nationalistic brand of internationalism and *heiminshugi* ("commonerism") and shocked the establishment by quickly garnerning 12,000 subscribers.[11] Another was the way papers began giving more space again to the issues of the "people": the rights of women and the poor, the necessity of establishing free speech, the need for lower taxes, even popular rights.[12] But the primary sign of renewed political passion was the reappearance of constitutional essays, especially those on the relationship between the coming Diet and the executive branch. *Yūbin Hōchi*, for example, set off a lively debate early in 1886 with an editorial titled "A Way to Cure the Evils of *Hanbatsu* Politics" *(Hanbatsu seiji no hei o tamuru ni hō ari)*, calling for the cabinet to be responsible to the legislature in order to empower the *minshū*. *Nichi Nichi* replied that legislative dominance could destabilize the government, because an "assembly system is synonymous with a political party system" and political parties are too prejudiced to rule impartially.[13] "Why shouldn't we have legislative cabinets?" demanded *Doyō Shimbun* in response; they would assure that the people's will be taken seriously.[14] One of the most lucid discussions appeared in the April 1888 issue of *Kokumin no Tomo*, when one of Nakae Chōmin's famous "three drunkards" argued that a constitution would be good only if it assured the *heimin* of both freedom and power. As he put it, "All enterprises of human society are like alcohol, and liberty is the yeast. If you try to brew wine or beer without yeast, all the other ingredients . . . will sink to the bottom of the barrel and your efforts will be in vain." And again: "Constitutionalism is not bad but democracy is better. Constitutionalism is spring with a faint touch of frost or snow; democracy is summer with no trace of frost or snow."[15]

Giving special energy to the renewed political discourse was the Daidō Danketsu Undō (Movement of Like Thinkers), created by *jiyū minken* types in the latter half of 1886, purportedly to prepare the public for constitutional government. Led by Gotō Shōjirō and Hoshi Tōru, among others, it demanded freedom of speech and assembly, lower land taxes and, especially, revision of Japan's unequal treaties with the Western powers. Its leaders declared that "if the people are not free to associate and discuss issues, a vigorous public opinion cannot be nurtured," and warned that any curtailment of free speech in the new system would foment "secret plotting" among those out of power and "even internal domestic rebellions."[16] And they emphasized the power of joint action—*their* joint action. "We, fellow citizens, will not oppose the government as individuals," wrote *Seiron;* "we will respond to unfair, unjust government decrees as a united body." One of that body's strategies, the writer added, would be "to wear out the government by refusing to pay taxes."[17]

The movement was neither well organized nor long lived, but it stirred up regional political passions in a manner reminiscent of the popular rights campaigns at the beginning of the decade. It organized chapters in more than three dozen prefectures and cities and late in 1887 brought nearly one hundred political leaders to Tokyo to demand directly of Itō that the people's will be protected in the constitution that he and his colleagues were then drafting—a move that inspired near panic in some of the government's more conservative corners. At the center of the movement, moreover, was the press, with all the papers reporting on Daidō Danketsu activities and quite a number of journalists organizing or speaking at its rallies. The movement collapsed prior to the opening of the national assembly in 1890, partly because of heavy-handed government suppression, which will be discussed below, and partly because of factional disputes among its leaders.[18] But during the late 1880s it provided the grist for a great deal of copy—both editorials and news reports.[19]

The actual promulgation of the constitution also played a major role in shaping the press' changing persona. It was no accident that Kuga chose promulgation day to print the first issue of *Nihon.* No group had been more intellectually, or emotionally, involved than the journalists in the creation of a constitutional system; so it is not surprising that they now consumed large quantities of ink in publicizing its symbolic value and analyzing its contents. Many, of course, pronounced themselves essentially pleased—gratified that Japan now was "worthy of being called a nation."[20] But a number took a skeptical stance once the excitement of constitution day had worn off. Gotō, for example, focused in a *Seiron* editorial on the need to turn the constitution into an instrument of the popular will. "To fulfill it," he said, "we must first of all seek the opinion of a cooperating public *(kokumin kyōdō no yoron)*." And he called on the people to "come forward, on their own, to expand the scope of the law" in accordance with Article 37, which said: "Every law requires the consent of the Imperial Diet."[21] Nakae took the same tack, arguing that only practice would clarify the question of whether the constitution was "gold or dross."[22]

The dominant journalistic approach in the months after the promulgation thus was to express basic support for the fact that a constitutional system had been created, then to analyze endlessly what it would—or should—mean in practice. Much space was given to the question of ministerial "responsibility" and what was intended by the ambiguous Article 55, which said that ministers of state "shall . . . be responsible" for their advice to the emperor, with the majority of editorialists, including those at the progovernment *Nichi Nichi*, contending that the article implied responsibility to the Diet and, through it, to the people.[23] Many writers also raised questions about the proper role for the emperor in declaring war (Articles 12 and 13), creating the army and navy, and concluding treaties. *Tōkyō Asahi Shimbun* argued that it was essential that the Diet be included in decision making even in sensitive areas such as this,[24] and Tokutomi noted at *Kokumin no Tomo* that none of the European nations gave treaty-making authority solely to the emperor.[25] On balance, even the Jiyūtō camp liked the document but nearly every journalist worried about what an increasingly conservative oligarchy would do with it.

Far more divisive—and even more lively—was the press' handling of the other central political issue of these years: treaty revision. These discussions were not new; the unequal treaties had been a source of bitter dispute and endless negotiations ever since Townsend Harris' 1858 commercial treaty robbed Japan of tariff autonomy and provided extraterritorial rights for Americans residing in Japan. The government had tried continuously to push the Western powers toward more equal treaties, encouraging the Iwakura Mission to negotiate toward that end in 1872, building the

Rokumeikan in downtown Tokyo in 1883 to encourage social intercourse between Japanese and foreign diplomats, holding conferences among the leading Western countries in 1886. But as the 1880s
progressed and a newer generation of opinion leaders began to move
onto the lecture stages, the lack of progress on the issue increasingly was taken as a sign of national weakness. As a result, by the
late 1880s, the treaty revision issue was stirring up the kind of zeal
among political activists that the elimination of the samurai class
had generated a decade earlier.

The Normanton disaster of 1886–1887 was a case in point.
When the British ship by that name sank in a November accident
off the coast of Wakayama, and the British consular court declared
its captain innocent of wrongdoing even though the entire British
crew had been saved while all twenty-three Japanese passengers
drowned, Japan's press reacted noisily. Osaka's *Asahi* sent several
reporters to cover the consular court deliberations in Kobe and Yokohama and ran numerous supplements to keep its readers informed
of Normanton developments.[26] *Jiji* called the court's acquittal "in-
comprehensible," and Fukuchi predicted at *Nichi Nichi* that the
episode would unify the Japanese as never before in their opposition
to the unequal treaties. He accused the British captain of "treating
his Japanese passengers like luggage."[27] The heat from the public
reaction was so intense that a retrial was held in Yokohama and on
December 8 the captain was sentenced to three months in jail. But
that did not assuage an angry public. As a British writer observed, in
a bit of exaggeration: "Public opinion then asserted itself with a
force before unknown in Japan; and at the same time gathered new
strength from so practical a proof of its own power."[28]

Another press explosion occurred in the spring of 1889, when
reporters learned that Ōkuma, now back in the government as
foreign minister, had been negotiating secretly with the Western
powers to terminate extraterritoriality. That Ōkuma, the onetime
popular hero, would negotiate secretly was one thing; the details of
his proposals (leaked to *The Times* of London) were another. They
provided for the gradual elimination of extraterritoriality in return
for freedom of residence for foreigners anywhere in Japan and the
acceptance, during a transition period, of foreign judges on Japan's
Supreme Court when foreigners were involved in the litigation.[29]
While some journalists found that an acceptable compromise,
many saw it as demeaning and potentially debilitating. And because the issue spoke so directly to Japan's sense of self-definition
and place, it sparked an unusually emotional debate. Three papers

alone—*Ōsaka Asahi, Ōsaka Mainichi,* and *Shinonome Shimbun*—
ran 319 editorials on the issue between June and October 1889.[30] Of
twenty-three papers examined that summer by *Nihon Shimbun,*
fifteen wrote in feverish tones, only eight dispassionately.[31] And
the public reaction was equally heated; by the end of the year, at
least 583 memorials had been delivered to the authorities on treaty
revision.[32]

Yūbin Hōchi ran several essays praising Ōkuma for his
shrewdness, arguing that the concessions were a fair exchange for
the abolition of extraterritoriality. Most of the other papers from
the Kaishintō faction—including *Tōkyō-Yokohama Mainichi, Yomiuri, Chōya,* and *Kaishin Shimbun*—took a similar stance. But though
these papers were influential, they were in the minority, overwhelmed, at least numerically, by a raucous chorus of anti-Ōkuma,
antigovernment papers. Kuga Katsunan's new journal, *Nihon,*
warned that foreigners would buy up Japanese farmland, take over
the mines, and humiliate the country by sitting in judgment on its
highest courts. Allowing foreigners on the court, the paper added,
would violate the constitution.[33] The journal *Fusō* discussed the
terrible consternation that left even children "pensive and in tears"
because "Japan's administrative and legal authority will not enable
us to control Westerners."[34] And one of the most impassioned, *Shinonome Shimbun,* warned that "any country that would preserve
its solemn independence must prevent foreigners from intruding
into its lawmaking and administrative procedures."[35] It agreed with
Nihon's view that mixed courts would violate the constitution and
warned that the next step might be the naturalization of "foreigners, who do not subscribe to our customs and morals, are not accustomed to our laws and system, and cannot share our thoughts and
feelings."[36] Some of the writers also took note of Herbert Spencer's
Social Darwinism, then quite popular in Japan, warning that mixed
residence might result in intermarriage and undermine the Japanese
race. Among the leading voices on this side—which one foreign
journalist accused of having an "awkward and ungracious disposition to kick over the vessel with the milk and cream of long sustained persistence"[37]—were *Eiri Jiyū Shimbun, Asahi, Jiji Shinpō
Nihonjin, Tōkyō Shinpō, Tokyo Kōron,* and *Kansai Nippō*.[38]

The motives of the treaty revision combatants were as partisan as they were patriotic, with papers dividing along Kaishintō-
Jiyūtō lines. Even the anti-Ōkuma writers favored revision of some
type, just not along the lines that had been negotiated; so at least
part of their fervor clearly was opportunistic. Diet elections were
approaching, and this issue was ready-made for stirring up an anti-

government constituency ready to vote for them a year later. "People are too excited to think calmly about the matter," wrote diarist Baelz.[39] A British journalist told his *Times* readers that the mood had taken on serious implications for Japan's political future. "The people had now become the arbiters of the situation," he wrote, because the oligarchs knew "that to meet the first Parliament without having obtained Western recognition of the country's rights would be to forfeit all credit for other achievements."[40]

Even Itō apparently was intimidated by the clamor and withdrew his support from Ōkuma's plan. On October 18, an impassioned reader of Kuga's chauvinistic *Nihon* threw a bomb at the foreign minister's carriage, causing Ōkuma to lose a leg and to leave the government. And when the cabinet resigned as a result, the extraterritoriality agreement was withdrawn, a victim of press-inflamed public opposition. As in 1881, politics not only energized an opposition press; it turned the journalists themselves into full-fledged shapers of public policy, feared not just by their own press rivals but by officials bent on order and control.

Underlying the treaty revision discussions was still another theme new to this era, a theme that had been latent during the early-Meiji years but that came, from the early 1890s onward, to influence a major portion of Japan's news and opinion. That theme was nationalism. One hardly could have doubted the deep national loyalty of the earlier journalists. Fukuchi, after all, had based his constitutional ideas on Japan's own special *kokutai*; Fukuzawa talked about citizenship and what Japan needed to be a vibrant modern country; the popular rights activists "tended to give preference to building a strong state over securing wider political participation,"[41] and even the radical *Hyōron Shimbun* based its calls for democracy on what was "acceptable to the emperor."[42] But there was a minimum of chauvinist rhetoric in the early *bunmei kaika* years, when the need to "become modern" dominated people's thinking and love of country lay *beneath* the arguments.

By the end of the 1880s, that had changed. More and more, editorials were being written by a younger generation, men like Shiga Shigetaka, Tokutomi, and Kuga, who had not experienced quite the overwhelming sense of Western dominance that Numa, Fukuzawa, and Kishida had. Nor were the younger journalists as deeply impressed as their seniors had been by Western ideals; the treaty revision fight had undermined any sense that advanced nations acted more nobly; the powers, for them, had become as much rivals as models. And the Meiji Constitution had given them new reason for pride and for confidence about their ability to confront those rivals.[43] As a result, a new tone was heard in the journalistic world in these years: a pride in the country's achievements, a need to assess Japan's role on the world scene, and an eagerness to talk about both in print. "The main trend in Japan's press and intellectual world after 1886," says Nishida, "was the appearance of nationalism."[44]

The evidences of this new attitude were everywhere. We already have seen how the treaty revision essayists worried about the "imminent danger of the overrunning of their fair land by foreigners"[45] and how eager writers were to show the world Japan's "glory" when the constitution was promulgated. Journalists also began talking a great deal now about the difference between *kokumin*, or citizens, and what Carol Gluck calls "unpatriots" *(hikokumin)*, who had no "sound sense of nation."[46] They praised the 1890 Imperial Rescript on Education as a tool to instill loyalty, and many railed against the journalist-educator Uchimura Kanzō in 1891 when he would not bow before a signature of the emperor during a ceremony at the First Higher School. There was another outcry in the press a year later after *Tōkyō Nichi Nichi* published a conversation with the Tokyo University historian and former Iwakura secretary Kume Kunitake, who had written an article calling Shintō "outmoded" and criticizing the idea that emperors were divine.[47] And the leading journalists wrote increasingly about Japan's role in Asia. Even Uchimura wrote paeans to his homeland as a bridge between East and West. "We stand in our relation to Asia as did the ancient Greeks in relation to Europe," he wrote in an 1892 newspaper essay. "To reconcile the East with the West; to be the advocate of the East and the harbinger of the West; this we believe to be the mission which Japan is called upon to fulfil."[48]

The most vivid example of the rising nationalism may have been the launching of Kuga's *Nihon* in 1889 for the express purpose of creating "nationalism from below."[49] A leader of the cultural nationalist organization Seikyōsha (Society for Political Education), Kuga had founded *Tokyo Denpō* a year earlier to argue for a more forceful stance toward the Western powers. Now he chose promulgation day for *Nihon's* first issue, to symbolize his belief that the press must be a tool for turning the people into loyal citizens, since there could be no nation in a state where the people "lack patriotism."[50] He was backed financially by several conservative opponents of the government's "weak" foreign policy, and in the first issue he proclaimed, beneath a distinctive map of Japan, that his would be a new kind of paper, neither partisan nor commercial but dedicated "to restoring Japan's national spirit *(kokumin seishi)*, which temporarily has been lost."

Kuga called for his journalistic colleagues to rise above partisanship and profit and to fight for "Japan alone." He derided most political papers for the "blight of being partial to a single party's philosophy" and the commercial papers for "pandering to the ideas of their readers." *Nihon,* he said, "neither belongs to a party nor allows itself to be a commercial product; but it does have a fixed vision, and that is to represent and encourage public opinion."[51] His editorialists accepted the merits of Western civilization but hit hard against the " 'Eurocentrism' *(ōkashugi)* of the intellectual world and the 'Eurocentric policies' *(ōka seisaku)* of the clique government," calling for "the revival and proclamation of the unique spirit of the Japanese people, handed down across the generations." The best label for *Nihon*'s philosophy, they said, was *"Nihonshugi"* or Japanism,[52] and at the heart of that philosophy were calls to preserve the country's ancient, emperor-centered culture and enact stronger policies against other nations. So persistent were the paper's criticisms of "weak" *hanbatsu* policies that it was suspended thirty times, for a total of 230 days, during its first eight years.[53] The specifics of several of those suspensions will be discussed later; for now it is sufficient to note that most resulted from articles calling for a stronger Japan.

Of special significance is that fact that *Nihon*'s chauvinistic approach found a ready public. Although it never attained the circulation peaks of the commercial papers, its daily circulation rose to a healthy 21,000 during its first five years, compared to 22,000 at *Yūbin Hōchi* and 18,000 at *Nichi Nichi.*[54] And it was influential with Japan's opinion leaders. Several other nationalist papers were founded in its wake, including *Tōyō Shinpō* and *Keisei Shinpō,* and the press historian Ono Hideo was sufficiently impressed to call it "the leader of Tokyo's newspaper world" in the early 1890s.[55] Spurred by resentments over unequal treaties, by increasing Japanese activities on the Asian continent, and by pride in the country's rapid transition to modernity, patriotism had become fashionable in the press by the onset of the 1890s. And when it came to patriotic styles, no trendsetter was the equal of Kuga's *Nihon.*

THE GOVERNMENT: A WATCHFUL EYE

Given the press' unending preoccupation with political issues in these years, it should not surprise us that the officials were as vigilant as ever to keep the journalists under control. It might be argued that these years marked as much of a transition for the authorities charged with maintaining order as for the press itself, for it was in the years surrounding the promulgation of the Meiji Constitution that the general Meiji approach to social and political control finally reached maturity. It was in these years, for example, that the Monbushō reshaped the education system "to place it at the service of the state rather than the individual,"[56] in these years that central control over cities and prefectural governments was at last made solid, and at this time that the Home Ministry's responsibility for overseeing the press was rendered untouchable. And the one behind most of these policies was Yamagata Aritomo, a man who "instinctively thought in terms of harsher controls and greater restrictions on the life of the people,"[57] so the fact that the focus was on ever greater authoritarianism should come as no surprise.

One of Yamagata's first acts in this period was the issuance of the *hoan jōrei* (peace preservation law) on Christmas day 1887 to quiet the dissent over treaty revision and local economic conditions that we observed above. Yamagata had grown increasingly agitated throughout the months of Daidō Danketsu activity, and when the movement sent scores of regional leaders to the capital to question officials directly about treaty revision and the constitution, Yamagata decided to have the Police Bureau draft a speedy law that would "put into effect my stubbornly held old-fashioned idea of expelling people from the capital."[58]

The ordinance went farther than any previous official action in its efforts to stifle dissent. It proscribed secret societies and secret meetings, prescribed stiff penalties for those who created disturbances or published material that might stimulate unrest, allowed the cabinet to ban unauthorized meetings, and permitted police to stop open-air meetings. It also included certain measures aimed directly at the press: officials could confiscate any printed material deemed likely to create a disturbance, and they could stop the publication of "all newspaper and printed matter" that had not undergone "a preliminary examination by the police authorities." The most dramatic clause was Article 4, which gave police the right to ban from the Tokyo area anyone suspected of inciting trouble or disrupting public order. Such persons, the article stipulated, were to be prohibited for up to three years from living within seven and a half miles (three *ri*) of the imperial palace.[59]

Within hours of the law's announcement, Yamagata's forces rounded up more than 570 Tokyo residents, giving each a few hours to pack up personal belongings and leave the capital area on threat of stiff jail sentences for refusal. The variety of people named in the roundup suggested either a hasty job of drawing up the list or, in a few cases, quixotic criteria. *Jiji* reported that while many of the victims were well-known government opponents, others had little in their past to explain why they had been singled out, except, perhaps, for being from the *minken* hot spot of Kōchi Prefecture. An evangelical Christian named Kataoka Kenkichi, for example, appeared to be guilty primarily of "propagating his religion," hardly the kind of activity encompassed by the peace preservation law. Similarly, the only thing that distinguished Keiō Gijuku student Mori Shigee (beside being from Kōchi) was that he "generally declined all visits from acquaintances, so that he could pursue his single-minded goal of mastering his scientific research." When an apolitical farmer named Okimoto, who had come to Tokyo to find menial work, received a summons, "he appeared at the police station in a state of great fright and inquired about the summons, only to learn that he had received a deportation order." He thereupon decided, reported *Jiji,* that a life of farming "was preferable to returning to the frightful capital." Still another victim, Hayashi Hōmei, had founded Tōkyō Eigakukan, a language school with more than seven hundred students, but hardly appeared to be a political threat.[60]

The deportations were carried out with a chaotic sense of urgency. "There was confusion everywhere," said one press account.[61] Markers were placed along transportation routes at spots seven and a half miles from the palace, and emergency telegraph cables to the various Tokyo branches of the military police were installed during the night of December 27.[62] Telephone technicians were instructed to work "day and night" to set up new lines to handle all the calls connected with the deportations. Leading officials each were assigned as many as eight bodyguards, some of whom "carried billy clubs up to three feet long."[63] And the intensity of the surveillance sometimes turned the evacuation into a circus. All of the 237 evacuees who left Tokyo for Yokohama during the early morning hours of December 27, for example, were accompanied by their own police officers. The press reported that sixty-six of these evacuees (all from Kōchi) stayed at a single inn, the Matsui, and "with one police officer for each deportee, the inn was virtually surrounded by officers." In another episode, an activist named Yagiwara had to be persuaded by his accompanying officer, who was short of cash, not to buy a first-class train ticket, because it would be "difficult to guard Mr. Yagiwara from a different section of the train."[64] One of the more novel incidents found a police escort accompanying his assignee to a string of brothels, so that the deportee could spend his last Tokyo evening "with one of the 'flowers of the Yoshiwara.' " The rickshaw puller reported that "the courtesans were terrified by the appearance of the policemen," and the man returned home dejected and unfulfilled "after what amounted to a thorough tour of the area."[65]

It goes without saying that the impact of the *hoan jōrei* on the press was considerable. For one thing, the lists of evacuees included a large number of journalists, many of them well known. The prominent exponent of democracy Nakae Chōmin, who had written for *Kōron Shinpō* after the 1884 death of his *Obei Seiri Sōdan*, was sent packing to Osaka. Ozaki Yukio of *Chōya*, Hoshi Tōru of *Mezamashi Shimbun*, and Shimamoto Nakamichi of *Jiyū Shimbun* all were banned for a full three years; Yoshida Masaharu of *Kōron Shinpō* and Fukui Kōji of *Okayama Mainichi Shimbun* were ordered to stay out of the capital for two and a half years; *Konnichi Shimbun*'s Sakazaki Saken received a two-year expulsion order, and Wada Izumi, also of *Konnichi*, was evacuated for just one year. Ozaki resisted at first, demanding an explanation for his surprising inclusion on the list, but when he received no satisfaction he left, grumbling that he "must write something about this mess."[66] All told, the numbers of writers deported extended into the dozens.[67]

The effect on the papers for which these men wrote was, needless to say, severe. Pro-Kaishintō papers such as *Yūbin Hōchi* and *Mainichi* remained largely unscathed, as did the progovernment *Nichi Nichi*, but the more liberal papers suffered badly—despite *Chōya*'s sarcastic observation that the more outspoken papers had so often "gone to war rashly . . . that they would not be concerned about the loss of just one battle."[68] *Mezamashi*, for example, found it impossible to maintain its readership after Hoshi's departure and in July 1888, barely half a year after the *hoan jōrei* clampdown, it was forced to sell out to Murayama Ryōhei, who wanted to launch a Tokyo branch of *Asahi*. *Konnichi*, which seemed to lose focus now, lasted just eleven months before being taken over by *Miyako Shimbun*, which sought readers by serializing novels. Even *Chōya*, devoid of Ozaki's talents, struggled for a couple of years for a sense of direction before regaining some of its earlier vigor after the promulgation of the constitution.[69] A sense of intimidation also filled the post–*hoan jōrei* atmosphere, at least for a while. The mainline papers began attacking the *minken* advocates for precipitating the law by their inflammatory writings, with *Mainichi* chastising journalists "who swagger about in the world of politics, using brute force." Those, the paper said, are the real "enemies of free and representative government."[70]

Not all of the papers succumbed to the pressure, however. Some journalists, like Nakae, simply changed their base of operations and spread the *jiyū minken* ideas elsewhere. On January 15, 1888, just two and a half weeks after being banished, he founded the *Shinonome Shimbun* as a Liberal Party voice in Osaka and quickly turned it into a rival of Murayama's prosperous *Asahi.*[71] Others watched what they said (and how they said it) for a few months, then took up the cudgel again fairly unreservedly after the constitution was promulgated fourteen months later. And nearly all of the papers, including even those nearer the center, found ways from the first to express their views through factual reports when essays seemed too direct. *Jiji* in particular described with relish the way Ozaki badgered officials for an explanation of why he was being ordered out of Tokyo, then followed with an account of bureaucratic ineptitude in sending the subpoena of another offender, Hayashi Yūzō, to the wrong person. It also made a great deal of the treatment of a "well-respected" Mr. Ikuta who was on the verge of graduating from Keiō and had committed no apparent offense. The *Jiji* writer's sympathy was obvious as he described Ikuta protesting the punishment, "filled with righteous indignation," being jailed for the protest, then having to bear the further banishment of a friend who came to the Police Bureau to try to help him.[72] As in the earlier crackdowns, the writers found it necessary to watch their tone, out of respect for the authorities' paranoia, but they never ran out of ways to show what they really felt.

The upper hand, however, clearly had been gained by the authorities at the end of 1887. Roger Hackett, Yamagata's biographer, may overstate the case somewhat when he says that the crackdown "was so unexpected and so sweeping that the momentum of the popular movement was decisively broken."[73] But it is indisputable that the officials were determined now to keep the lid on what they deemed "extreme" political expression, and measures such as the *hoan jōrei* helped them do just that. Gifts, political pressure, cooption, and intimidation all had been used in tandem with the laws to restrict opposition debate during the early Meiji years, and when the press had remained defiant, the officials had wasted little time in enacting new measures that gave the Home Ministry even greater scope for cracking down. That clearly was the reason for the 1887 peace preservation law, and it also was the reason for the issuance just three days later of a new thirty-seven-article Press Law *(shimbunshi jōrei)* that largely completed the pre-war legal structure for managing newspapers.[74]

Scholars differ on whether this new law increased or lightened the legal burden on the press,[75] but they agree that its primary role was to fine tune the press-control system that they had been developing for nearly twenty years and that, as a result, most of the oppressive features of earlier press codes remained intact, while some control mechanisms were strengthened and a few added. On the one hand, the clear improvements for the journalists included the addition of truth as a defense in libel cases and the removal of the rights of governors and the foreign minister to suspend papers administratively. The old licensing system also was abolished, with owners now required simply to notify the government of their intent to publish. And the requirement that reporters reveal sources was erased. On the other hand, both the army and the navy ministers now were granted the right to prohibit the publication of material they deemed a threat to security, the heavy security deposit (which already had driven more than seventy small papers out of business) was left intact, and the right of the Home Ministry to suspend *(hakkō teishi)* or banish *(hakkō kinshi)* papers without explanation was reaffirmed. Foreigners, women, and minors continued to be barred from publishing papers, and maximum prison sentences remained at three years.[76]

The unrelenting harshness of this approach dismayed Japan's more popular, *minken*-oriented political leaders almost as much as it did the editors. Ozaki Saburō, one of the drafters of the 1875 libel law, was especially critical, arguing that while curbs on speech had been necessary at the outset of the Meiji era, successful implementation of constitutional government would require greater freedom of expression. "Preserving a law that shackles debate," he argued, "curbs the steadfast and patriotic debaters on the one hand, even while it stirs up dangerous and radical agitators on the other."[77] Several attempts were made by those who agreed with Ozaki to lighten the restrictions in the early Diet sessions. In 1893, in fact, the Fourth Diet came within a single conference committee vote of agreeing on a bill to eliminate both the security deposits and the administrative suspensions and bannings,[78] but a combination of bureaucratic strategies and national crises finally doomed such efforts. The press did win one legal victory in these years, when powerful editors successfully pressured the government in 1889 to reject Kuroda Kiyotaka's costly, restrictive plan to require that all papers send out-of-town subscriptions through the national mail system.[79] And its supporters in the Diet kept the cabinet early in the 1890s from regularizing a policy of prepublication censorship, as we shall see later. But the general tone of the press codes remained as restrictive as ever, right through to the end of the Meiji era.

Actual enforcement also continued to be similar to that of earlier periods. "The relationship between the press and the government actually was quite subtle," says Yamamoto Fumio, with the government balancing poison and palliative.[80] When possible, officials tried to win journalists over to their side; when that did not work, they used coercion and control. Financial gifts to key papers were reduced after 1888 but were not cut off.[81] When Seki Naohiko took *Nichi Nichi* in a more independent direction after Fukuchi's departure in 1888, Yamagata tried to buy him off with the offer of a new rotary press, and when that did not work, Seki was forced out in favor of the reliable Itō Miyoji.[82] In 1891, Itō Hirobumi, Yamagata, Inoue Kaoru, and others developed a far-reaching, concrete plan to create a political affairs bureau *(seimu bu)* in the cabinet, responsible for coordinating government press policy. The bureau, as outlined in a draft by Mutsu Munemitsu, was to provide financial assistance to key papers and strategic writers, sign contracts with cooperative regional papers, assist monetarily in the printing of loyal foreign newspapers—and to allow these papers the right to criticize the government mildly so that readers would not suspect that they were controlled. The plan was undermined, and finally dashed, by Home Ministry bureaucrats worried about losing their own power over the press, but its expansive vision illustrated dramatically just how far top officials were willing to go, in Itō Miyoji's words, "to protect clique government from the attacks of the popular party forces."[83]

For those who resisted blandishments, there was, of course, the more direct approach. Scores of journalists continued to be fined and imprisoned in these years, with Miyatake Gaikotsu, for example, fined fifty yen and sent to jail for a full three years after writing a satirical account of the constitutional promulgation ceremony in the February 28, 1889, issue of *Tonchi Kyōkai Zasshi*,[84] and the editor of the *Nohi Nippō* being sentenced to jail with hard labor for an 1890 essay ridiculing the idea that Jinmu Tennō was divine.[85] Suspension and banning cases numbered in the hundreds, with at least nineteen suspensions issued during the debate over Ōkuma's treaty revision policy and the 1892 Diet elections bringing

The eruption of Mt. Bandai, Japan's first published newspaper photograph, *Yomiuri Shimbun,* August 8, 1888. (Courtesy Hajima Tomoyuki, Tōyō Bunka Shimbun Kenkyūkai)

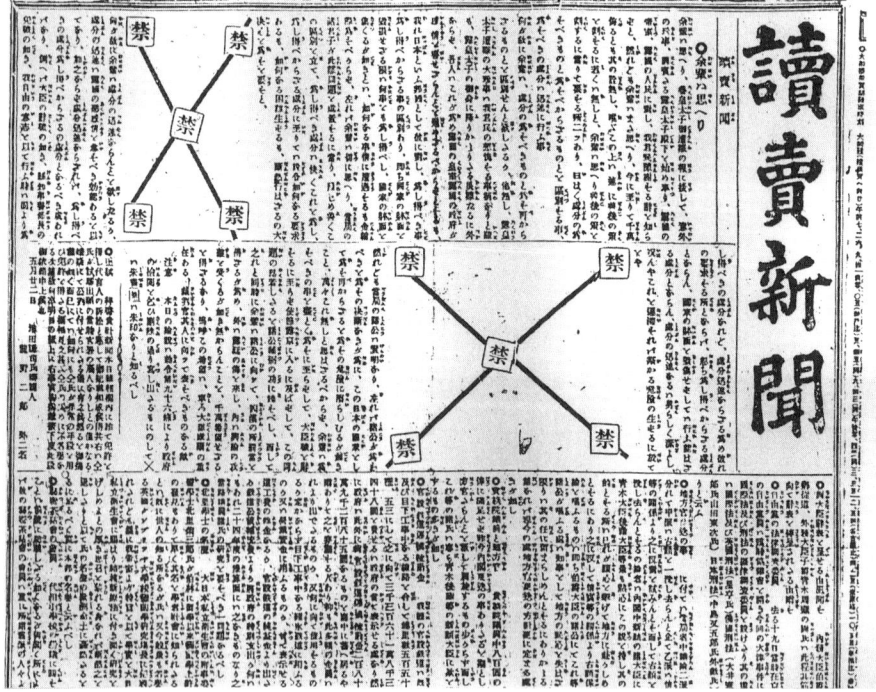

Yomiuri Shimbun article, May 23, 1891, on the shooting of Russian Crown Prince Nicholas, which precipitated the Ōtsu affair; small boxes are marked "prohibited." (Courtesy Yomiuri Shimbunsha)

hakkō teishi orders to thirty-eight different papers.[86] The years 1892 and 1893 saw eighty-seven suspensions each, almost all of them for "disturbing public order,"[87] and *Nihon* alone was shut down for nearly three full months (eighty-three days) during the tumultuous Diet struggles of 1892.[88] As Kuga reminded readers in 1891, only Japan and Russia among the modern nations still allowed bannings and suspensions of newspapers, and only in Japan could they be carried out without judicial review.[89]

THE ŌTSU AFFAIR

The legal situation was not wholly dismal, however. To some, the crackdowns themselves suggested that the journalists were doing their jobs well—and it was in that spirit that Kuga hung his *hakkō teishi* orders on the wall of the *Nihon* reception room.[90] Moreover, if the *hoan jōrei* showed the extremes to which the authorities were willing to go in enforcing order, and the 1887 law showed their determination to keep the control structure intact, another event later in the period illustrated the equally important fact that officials sometimes were limited by their own laws. That episode was the Ōtsu or Konan affair in May 1891, an incident well known for helping to establish the independence of the courts in the Meiji constitutional system. Less well known was its role in fixing the principle that direct prepublication censorship would not be accepted in Japan, except in extraordinary situations. It also highlighted, in new ways, the sharp differences that exist between journalists' and governors' purposes as well as the continuing, indeed expanding, power of public opinion in checking central power.

The incident was precipitated when a patriotic policeman, Tsuda Sanzō, stabbed Russian Crown Prince Nicholas in the town of Ōtsu on May 11, after a royal boat ride across Lake Biwa. Tsuda feared that Nicholas' trip presaged Russian aggression in East Asia, and he abhorred the idea of a Russian prince being received by the Emperor Meiji.[91] He surely had not envisioned the embarrassment his act would cause to the emperor he so revered. The future czar was not hurt seriously, but the event caused panic in the cabinet, which feared Russian military retaliation. After frantic discussions, the ministers decided to send Meiji himself to meet with Nicholas in Kyoto and to try patrolman Tsuda under Article 116 of the criminal code, which would call for the death penalty for anyone who attacked the crown prince. The article clearly had been intended to apply only to the Japanese imperial family, since it used the word *tennō* in describing the offense,[92] but an unsuccessful attack on a normal citizen would not allow a death sentence, and the cabinet feared, said Saigō Tsugumichi, that a lesser sentence would provoke a Russian fleet to "come over to the Shinagawa coast and bombard our capital." As Prime Minister Matsukata Masayoshi summed up the government's case: "The nation's existence comes before that of the law. . . . If there is no nation, there will be no law."[93]

The problem for Matsukata and his colleagues was that many of Japan's judges did not see the case quite that simply. The issue was remanded to a special court of cassation that ruled six-to-one, despite pressure and threats from the cabinet, that Article 116 did not apply to foreign royalty. Chief Justice Kojima Iken was not on the special court, but his role in standing up to cabinet members and articulating a powerful case for judicial independence was pivotal in the court's ruling. Tsuda thus was tried under normal criminal rules and on May 27 was given a life sentence; he died five months later of pneumonia in a Hokkaido prison. The Russians accepted the decision without protest, and Japan's courts survived a major political challenge.[94] In these months, says Barbara Teters, Japan "took a small but significant step toward constitutionalism."[95]

The press took a significant step, too, in its case toward legal acceptance of the right to be free from prepublication censorship. That step came only after quite a bitter struggle with the authorities over what could be printed, and when, in cases such as this. Although detailed news of the stabbing was permitted in the Tokyo papers the very next morning,[96] the Kansai papers were censored heavily, thanks in part to the generally stricter approach of officials in that region and in part to the tensions in the areas where the attack had occurred. When the Kansai reporters covering the crown prince tried to cable descriptions of the stabbing back to their home offices, they were prohibited by censors from including anything more than enigmatic phrases such as "Russian Crown Prince ill . . . forced to return to Kyoto . . . trip to Osaka postponed." Then, when their papers received the full story and prepared articles later that night, local authorities forbade anything except vague comments about the "prince's illness."[97] Five days later, on May 16, the Home Ministry issued a special decree (Order 46) for all papers and magazines across the country, requiring that any "writings (or drawings) concerned with diplomatic affairs be approved in draft form by the censors, prior to publication." Violators were to be subject to up to two years in jail and three hundred yen in fines.[98]

The result was a difficult month for most of the papers. News about the actual episode had to be conveyed carefully, often by nuance and suggestion and always by "the exercise of special restraint in selecting each word and phrase," as the editor of *Ōsaka Mainichi* put it.[99] The papers, most of them patriotic to a fault, were universally critical of Tsuda, whom they called a "madman" and accused of putting his country's existence in jeopardy. And they expressed sympathy for the crown prince. But the line between what information was "sensitive" and what was acceptable was a fine one, and papers sometimes arrived on the street with large blank spaces on page one and the word *kin* (prohibited) stamped where there should have been news.[100] Many suspension orders also were enforced, sometimes for up to a week.[101]

The most important part of the struggle related not so much to the event itself (or even to censorship) as to the writers' astute attention to the legal struggle between the courts and the cabinet as well as the questions of national sovereignty implied by all the maneuvering. The antigovernment press in particular vigorously supported Kojima's views on the necessity of following the country's laws precisely, even in a time of emergency. On May 17, the nationalistic *Nihon* deplored Tsuda's crime but said the country's laws must not be altered to meet the whims of diplomats. "Japan has law, it has courts, it has judges," said the editorial.

> Criminals, whether their crimes are great or small, grave or trivial, all are judged by the court which has jurisdiction. . . . There is no criminal law by which men can be judged except the statutory law. Therefore, no matter how heinous the crime . . . not even the slightest encroachment by others must be permitted. The statutory law must not be distorted by farfetched interpretations for the sake of other considerations.[102]

Tokutomi Sohō's *Kokumin Shimbun*, hardly a radical paper, also invoked questions of national sovereignty and dignity, writing on May 17: "We should apologize for our faults; we should regret our failures; we should shed tears of sympathy and grief; but we dare not forget the dignity and standing that go with being a great Eastern nation."[103] For their temerity, both papers were suspended, as were most of the major papers at one time or another before this episode had ended.[104]

Equally important to the papers was the question of the prepublication censorship that was invoked throughout May in the name of national security. There was little they could do about that question during the crisis, beyond leaving blank spaces on page one to show readers what the censors had done to them, but once the furor over Ōtsu had subsided, both the journalists and their political supporters took the issue up in ways that would affect the press throughout the entire prewar era. The issue was propelled onto the public agenda a few months after the special court ruling, when Home Minister Shinagawa Yajirō asked the Diet to make prepublication censorship the permanent norm for news related to diplomatic affairs. His request was approved by the Upper House in the Second Diet (November–December 1891) but ran into a storm of opposition in the Lower House, with antigovernment representatives lambasting the cabinet's willingness to subvert justice to politics during the Ōtsu crisis and attacking the vagueness of clauses such as "writings concerned with diplomatic affairs." When the proposal failed again in the 1892 Diet, the Home Ministry gave up and accepted the longstanding Japanese practice of penalizing papers only after publication.[105] The opposition of the young Diet on this issue, says Uchikawa Yoshimi, "must be recorded as one of the important chapters in the history of free speech and publication in Japan."[106] The government still had the upper hand in the struggle to control information, but at least papers would not have the added burden of dealing with censors and bureaucrats while they were getting copy ready for press. And that was signally important.

CHALLENGED BY A NEW WORLD

Politics may have continued to dominate Japan's newspapers at the dawning of the third Meiji decade, but no longer in quite the way they had in the past. By the time the first Diet opened in 1890, news reports had surpassed editorials at the center of most papers' political coverage. Circulation figures for the country's largest papers had reached 50,000 a day by then. Nearly every paper had a theater critic, along with columns for special interest groups such as students and housewives.[107] Even the staid ōshimbun were competing vigorously for sales and profits. And the old ōshimbun-koshimbun order was under attack. By the end of the Sino-Japanese War half a decade later, that order had given way to a more commercial middle path that made the press more powerful than ever yet emphasized what was interesting and profitable over what was edifying and ideal. There still were opinion papers in the mid-1890s, but they had lost their dominance, and the variety of journalistic styles now hawked on the streets of Tokyo and Osaka rendered neat divisions into "prestige" and "popular" categories impossible.

This change did not occur overnight. We already have seen how, already in the mid-1880s, the descent into narrow partisanship had undermined the prestige papers, then pushed them toward a broader center. We also have observed changes in government-press relationships, the fresh blood that flowed into many of the old papers, and the emergence of new models in Fukuzawa's *Jiji* and Murayama's *Asahi* early in the decade. All of these trends gained momentum now, as Meiji entered its third decade. And along with them came two other developments that made radical change all but unavoidable in the major papers. One was the transformation that occurred in the country's urban settings, particularly in the kinds of people who had an interest in reading the daily press; the other was the increase in technologies available to facilitate rapid dissemination of news to ever larger numbers of people.

The change in readership was a natural result of the Meiji era's modernization policies. Nearly every government program from 1868 onward was aimed in one way or another at bringing the masses into the national sphere. First samurai daughters, then peasant girls were sent off to factories to "serve the nation" by spinning silk; village girls and boys were enrolled in new schoolhouses under the 1872 compulsory education decree and taught that they were "Japanese"; peasant draftees were trained in the virtues of patriotism and good citizenship; modern literature and art talked about the issues of a "nation" in transition; factories and higher schools enticed people from the countryside to new opportunities in cities, where they had little choice but to develop new self-identities as parts of a bigger, more cosmopolitan whole. The result of this process was the creation, particularly in those urban areas where the major newspapers flourished, of a larger and noticeably different readership pool by the early 1890s.

That these were years of unabated urbanization is beyond denying. Tokyo's official population more than doubled between 1872 and 1894, from about 800,000 to more than 1.8 million; Osaka went from 531,000 to 1.2 million, Kyoto from 567,000 to 902,000— as "destitute farmers streamed into [the cities] after losing land or livelihood" in the Matsukata deflation of the mid-1880s.[108] And the life in these cities was radically different from anything most immigrants had known in their distinctly premodern villages. In 1887, for example, public lighting was introduced in Tokyo by the Tokyo Electric Light Company, and five years later it came to Kyoto.[109] The late 1880s brought Western clothes and the first female clerks to the cities' dry goods stores.[110] And the factories of Kyōbashi, Honjo, and Shiba wards in Tokyo or ports like Nishi-ku in Osaka provided employment and salary opportunities unthought of back home. The number of factory workers in Japan as a whole would not reach the millions until the next century, but the takeoff really began now, as worker totals nationwide grew by more than 600 percent, from a mere 61,025 in 1882 to 418,140 in 1895.[111] And incomes rose in this period too, from a per capita average of about $120 in 1886 to $190 in 1899, hardly enough to lift slum dwellers out of the poverty that *Chōya* reporters had found endemic in an 1886 series but sufficient to keep attracting more rural immigrants.[112]

Moreover, the migrants were moving in from rural areas that were themselves more attuned to modernity and to the national "whole" than would have seemed possible a mere twenty years before, increasingly tied together by a growing communications network that put people everywhere in touch with each other—and made newspapers from cities hundreds of miles distant accessible within a few days at most. The Tokyo-Kobe railway line brought the capital and western Honshu together in 1889; a Ueno-Aomori line tied the capital to the far north just two years later. Railway mileage increased eight times in the decade of the 1880s, from 122 to over a thousand miles; both telegraph and telephone lines linked Japan's major cities in the 1880s; the numbers of letters and postcards handled by the new postal service grew ten times between 1874 and 1892. And the number of newspapers handled by the post office in those years simply soared, from 2.6 million a year to 52.2 million![113]

The people moving to the cities and using these communications networks also were increasingly literate. Arai Naoyuki notes that a major reason for press changes in this period lay "in the gradual spread of the 1872 compulsory education system." "When you reached the third Meiji decade," he notes, "you generally had a fairly high level of school attendance. Nearly all of the population had entered the literate class."[114] Scholars argue about the meaning of the word "literate," but there is no doubt that Arai is right about the spread of school attendance and literacy of at least some sort. By the beginning of the 1890s, school attendance had reached 52.4 percent for Tokyo men and 42.6 percent for its women—and by the end of the decade it was up to 86 percent for men and 80 percent for women, with similar percentages in the provinces.[115]

What this meant for Japan's newspapers was that hundreds of thousands of newly educated people—workers, college students, shopkeepers, apprentices, housewives—were becoming part of urban life and, as a result, eager to read the day's events. They were not the Confucian sophisticates of the old Tokugawa schools, not self-impressed scholars willing to struggle through the ponderous political prose of the old *Nichi Nichi* or *Yūbin Hōchi,* but neither were they satisfied with the sensational pablum of the early *Yomiuri.* They wanted to learn about the new world they had entered: the latest fads, the squabbles with foreigners, the fire in Kanda, yesterday's sumo winners—*and* the most recent fight in the Diet. And they wanted to gain their information through columns that were readable and lively. They were the kind of people Lord Northcliffe described in London at the same time, people who "will read anything which is simple and is sufficiently interesting."[116] They were, in *Yorozu Chōhō* editor Kuroiwa Shūroku's words, "people who are busy, people who work in the daytime and pay their oil bills in the evening, people who need reading that is easy."[117] They were, to put it quite simply, the often-derided "lower-class readers" who did more than any others to swell newspaper circulations and change the press' persona in the early 1890s.[118]

Closely tied to this urban demographic transformation came changes in technology that would have inspired major journalistic shifts even without the rise of a new readership, changes that made the process of adapting to the new population a good deal easier. The most important of these in the newsgathering area was the telegraph. Samuel F. Morse's invention had arrived in Japan first on Perry's Black Ships in 1854 and had spread through most of the country during the 1870s, albeit under tight government regulation. In 1879, Japan had become a member of the Universal Telegraphic Union.[119] The use of the medium by newspapers had been held back, however, by both the editors' preoccupation with political opinion and the cost and limited availability of the cables. Even the most aggressive *news* paper, *Asahi,* used telegraph but sparingly in the early 1880s: for the transmission of brief items, for spectacular events such as the imperial promise of a constitution in 1881, and for in-house messages.[120]

But the year 1889 changed that. Murayama had taken an increasingly aggressive approach to newsgathering throughout the mid-1880s, sending correspondents as far away as Hakodate, Nagasaki, and Shanghai and setting up permanent *Asahi* branches in Kyoto, Tokyo, and Kobe to get the news quickly and completely. Once the February constitutional promulgation had demonstrated the possibility of sending longer cables, the telegraph became indispensable, especially for the Kansai papers. Many editors still worried over the fact that the Morse code rendered cable transmissions susceptible to more errors than manuscripts did, and the costs sometimes seemed staggering, "beyond what any Tokyo paper would have dreamed."[121] But the availability of the telegraph now made speedy reporting feasible—and presaged the war coverage of the early twentieth century, when cables finally would become a staple of Japanese journalism.[122]

The press transformation also was assisted in these years by the spread of railroad networks, by new methods for reproducing and publishing photographs, and by the telephone. The Ueno-Aomori trunk line, noted above, facilitated not only regional distribution of capital newspapers but the collection of news from wider areas after the end of the 1880s. The first photograph ever printed in a Japanese newspaper appeared just six months before the constitution, on August 8, 1888, when *Yomiuri* ran a picture of the eruption of Mt. Bandai in Fukushima Prefecture, with an explanation that the likeness had been "reproduced by an improved copperplate."[123] It was not the first photograph used by a Japanese paper; editors had experimented since the 1870s with pasted-on photos.[124] Nor was the reproduction very sophisticated. But photographic reproduction was exciting enough to prompt *Yomiuri* to publish the Bandai picture again—and again, and again, for more than a month—and it ushered in a medium that would transform newspaper formats as well as their advertising campaigns in the decades ahead.

The telephone too came somewhat late to the press, though for different reasons. It had appeared in Japan in 1877, just a year after its invention by Alexander Graham Bell, but the construction of lines was costly and slow, with the first general-use line (between Tokyo and Atami) not going up until 1888. The first newspaper use of the telephone came in 1887 when (typically) Murayama's *Asahi* used an experimental phone line in covering Ōi Kentarō's trial for participating in an abortive plan to foment rebellion in Korea.[125] Two years later, *Jiji* used a special line to speed its reporting on the constitutional promulgation ceremony.[126] Like the telegraph, the phone would not be used widely in the press until the Sino-Japanese War years, but the fact that several editors saw its potential well before Japan's first regular lines had been installed in the 1890s suggests how technology was changing the press' approach to news. It also is significant that it was the middle-road entrepreneurial papers, rather than the established *ōshimbun* or *koshimbun*, that tried it first.

One of the most important determinants of change was the

typesetting and printing process, where the complexities of the Japanese writing system yielded constant frustration. The first dailies had been printed by woodblock, with carvers working right alongside writers, because Chinese characters and the phonetic *kana* were so difficult to obtain in metal type.[127] By 1876, *Yomiuri* had purchased a steam-powered cylinder press, and a year later it was using stereotype. Most papers also switched to Western paper, which held up better in the printing process, but very few of the papers had advanced beyond the use of flatbed presses with movable wooden, then metal type by the early 1880s. In 1881 and 1882, for example, *Chōya Shimbun* had two presses, both hand-operated; *Nichi Nichi* had eight hand-operated and one steam press; and *Asahi* had one cylinder press, one foot-operated press, and seven hand presses.[128] Since it took even a cylinder press more than twelve hours to print ten thousand copies of a four-page paper, printing limitations necessarily held down circulation in the press' first two decades.[129] That began to change, however, in 1889, when *Ōsaka Asahi* used Murayama's connections to get one of its employees, Tsuda Torajirō, included in a press-purchasing trip to Paris by the head of the government *Gazette*. There, he purchased a Marinoni press for the paper and took lessons at the daily *Le Petit Journal* on how to operate it. It took some time for Tsuda and Murayama to get the press into full operation because of problems with ink, but by the spring of 1891 it was printing a full 15,000 copies an hour.[130] *Asahi*'s rising rival, *Ōsaka Mainichi*, also secured a Marinoni press in 1893,[131] and by the latter half of the decade all the leading papers were using them.[132] Even then printing capacity was limited, due to the ongoing difficulties of setting the Chinese characters and their accompanying *furigana* into type.[133] As with telephones and photographs, the most significant thing about the use of print technology was, first, the slowness with which the early editors adapted the Western presses and, second, the serious efforts nearly all the editors put into improving their printing capacities after the onset of the 1890s.

THE PRESTIGE PAPERS: WHAT TO DO?

The surest sign that change was more than ephemeral was the response of the established *ōshimbun* to the new environment at the end of the 1880s. That Murayama at *Asahi* and Koyasu at *Yomiuri* would have grasped new opportunities was a given; that *Nichi*

Nichi's Seki and *Yūbin Hōchi*'s Yano would do so said a great deal more about the changing press. Doing something was, of course, necessary. The *ōshimbun* had verged on the brink of disaster after the cooling of the country's political fever in 1883. Not only had their circulations dropped by as much as 40 percent,[134] their quality had declined too, as lost revenues forced them to use cheaper paper that smudged the ink.[135] And that in turn pushed subscriptions and revenues down even further. *Chōya*'s sales income plunged from 70,892 yen in 1881 to 36,881 in 1886; it was even worse at *Nichi Nichi*, where revenues went from 72,209 to 36,200 in the same years; at *Yūbin Hōchi* they dropped from 66,099 to 40,474; and *Akebono* simply died.[136] It was, said Fukuchi, a time of "great perplexity."[137] And an employee of the political *Ōsaka Shinpō* echoed plaintively, "The number of people seeking newspapers decreases daily."[138]

Multiplying the prestige papers' problems was the appearance of rival papers whose success made it abundantly clear that people had not lost interest in newspapers per se, but simply no longer wanted the traditional sheets. *Jiji*, for example, quadrupled its own revenues between 1882 and 1886, while *Asahi* became the richest paper in the country.[139] Other Tokyo upstarts such as the popular *Yamato Shimbun*, founded in 1886, and *Minato Shimbun* (1888) siphoned off more than 20,000 readers a year between them.[140] And most ominous of all for the established press scions was the decision in 1888 by Murayama and Ueno to enter the Tokyo market with a Kantō edition of *Asahi*. Their purchase of the faltering *Mezamashi Shimbun* instantly touched off the fiercest circulation/distribution war the city had yet seen.[141] But the established papers, still struggling for ways to satisfy readers without betraying the values that had drawn them to journalism in the first place, were not up to the aggressive Kansai management styles, and within a year *Tōkyō Asahi* was the capital's second largest paper, within two years its largest.[142]

In more ways than the beleaguered editors would have recognized, however, the *Asahi-Jiji-Yomiuri* challenge was a blessing; for it dramatized the necessity of change. In this same period, half a globe away, London's established dailies were experiencing similar stagnation—and most of them failed to adapt. "Ponderous leaders expressed opinions about which few cared a straw," commented one observer of those British papers. "Columns were dull and heavy and the news set out with little art. A thing was done because it had been so done for thirty years."[143] He might have said the same of the

Tokyo *ōshimbun*, except that, in the late 1880s, they began genuinely to stir themselves; and by the end of the decade most of them had become vital once more: no longer the sole arbiters of established journalistic norms, no longer known as *ōshimbun*, but changing, growing, and influential in wholly new ways.

The first *ōshimbun* to take the new environment seriously was *Yūbin Hōchi*. Already in 1884, it had gone to an advance payment plan for subscribers to fight the revenue decline, a move that probably helped make its decline a bit less precipitous than that of its peers.[144] Even more important was Editor Yano's trip to the United States and Europe two years later, which brought him back to Japan convinced that *Yūbin Hōchi* must "popularize" *(tsūzokuka)* if it were to survive. He thereupon announced a reform plan: *Yūbin Hōchi* would reduce its page size by about a third (to 49 × 36 centimeters), slash its price (from 83 to 30 *sen* a month), and change its contents by incorporating more stories from the provinces, using simpler prose, avoiding difficult *kanji*, including more *furigana*, and printing more feature materials as well as serialized novels.[145] He also pledged that the paper would avoid partisan politics, and he reorganized its management, to give more weight to the business side under the direction of Miki Zenpachi, who would be known for his skill at improving circulation and creating sales networks.[146]

The other prestige papers followed suit, more out of desperation than because they wanted to. At the end of September, *Nichi Nichi* lowered its monthly circulation rates from 85 to 50 *sen*; in early October *Chōya* did the same (from 60); and Numa Morikazu's *Mainichi*, which was nearing collapse, lowered its price all the way to 25 *sen* a month. Then at the beginning of 1887, still struggling with only two-thirds of its pre-*seihen* readership, *Nichi Nichi* joined *Yūbin Hōchi* at 30 *sen*, only to see Yano and Miki drop the *Hōchi* price further, to 20 *sen*.[147] These papers might have sneered at the cheap *koshimbun* in an earlier day when political passions garnered readers regardless of price. But they could afford snobbery no longer, especially when the price-slashing strategy turned out to be effective. After hitting bottom in 1886, readership began to rise, until by promulgation day in 1889, most of the old prestige papers had passed—in the case of *Yūbin Hōchi* more than doubled—their previous readership peaks.[148] It would take several more years for profits to catch up with rising sales, since subscription prices had been cut by nearly three times, but all but *Akebono* continued to reform, and the result was an impressive, if gradual, return to viability.

NEW METHODS AND A NEW PERSONA

At the core of the papers' restoration was a fundamental change in the entire industry's approach to newspapering. And it was not only the prestige paper editors who carried out the changes; all of the papers underwent a revolutionary transformation. The old prestige papers remained more political than some of their rivals; a few new papers focused on opinion more than on news; other dailies, both new and old, made reporting and sensation their forte. But regardless of each paper's individual formula, the distinctions between ō and *ko* newspapers grew fuzzy in these years, as all the papers joined in the effort to balance profitability and social responsibility. As a result, the salient feature of the entire journalistic world in the years that surrounded the promulgation of the constitution was the emergence of a truly popular press, a press in which papers of all stripes paid attention to readers along the full educational and social spectrum.

The old press streams, in other words, came together in these years, and the one thing that joined the publishers and editors, more than any other, was a commitment to financial viability. Very few of the publishers had reached the point yet of seeking profit for its own sake. At the least, they gave lip service to the responsibility of journalists to improve society and encourage morality. But no longer were Japan's journalists—not even the most Confucian of them— willing to edit for influence and ideology alone. And that fact, more than anything else, accounts for the press' transformed self-image. Following the middle-road example of Fukuzawa's *Jiji*, Murayama's *Asahi*, and Yano and Miki's *Yūbin Hōchi*, editors were more and more willing to agree, at least grudgingly, when *Ōsaka Mainichi Shimbun's* Motoyama Hikoichi called newspapering "a business enterprise."[149]

This acceptance of economic realities showed up with special force in the struggles to keep circulation high, which became a passion with most editors. Haunted by the desertion of *ōshimbun* readers earlier in the decade, nearly every newspaper staff worked tirelessly now at improving sales and distribution methods. *Tōkyō Nichi Nichi*, for example, launched the *eki*, or station, sales system (an approach that still is central to Japanese journalism) by placing salespersons at prominent bus stops, beginning with Shinbashi, in 1885.[150] The papers also began to replace their own home delivery systems, which had required scores of menial workers,[151] with agreements with booksellers who would buy the papers wholesale and resell them to newspaper retailers and delivery people. *Yūbin Hōchi's* Miki led the way in the process, and when he succeeded in increasing efficiency and saving money that way, the other papers followed, keeping a few of their own delivery agents but signing contracts with the same distributors to handle the bulk of their distribution. As a result, by the latter 1880s, five major booksellers had become the central distribution agents for the city, responsible for getting an increasing proportion of the daily papers to the hundreds of retailers and home delivery agents across the capital.[152] The new system robbed the papers of some control over just what was charged to the actual customer, but it went far in helping the press expand and "rationalize" sales procedures and "expand its geographic scope . . . without having to assume directly the burden of distribution."[153]

Just how seriously the editors took the task of expanding sales was vividly illustrated by the Tokyo editors' reaction about a year and a half after Murayama and Ueno made the entry into the capital referred to above. As *Tōkyō Asahi* grew, the sixteen Tokyo papers began worrying that the Kansai assault might invite financial disaster if they did not respond. Their first move was an 1890 plan to fix prices so that *Asahi* could not drive subscription rates any lower. The Tokyo editors invited Murayama to a March meeting where they proposed a citywide minimum sales price for newspapers. When he refused to accept that idea, they formed an anti-*Asahi* alliance and tried to undermine him through the new distribution system. On March 12, they informed their five central wholesale agents that they were not to sell or distribute *Tokyo Asahi*. But Murayama was ready for their tactic. He retaliated with a vivid account of their "monopolistic" scheme on the first page of *Tōkyō Asahi's* March 16 issue, then met with the five distributors personally to discuss the situation.[154] In the end, his ability at persuasion, strengthened by "a large amount of cash in his pocket,"[155] won out, and four of the five sellers refused the alliance's exclusionary demands.[156] But the willingness to play financial hardball revealed just how important financial stability had become to this new press.

One of the more colorful features of the new fixation on sales was the introduction of aggressive, often unorthodox, promotional schemes to win subscribers. Papers began to publish more and more extras and to put out picture supplements to attract readers. The arts-oriented *Miyako Shimbun* tried placing issues on seats at leading theaters. Often papers sponsored contests or surveys, requiring people to send entries in on ballots printed in the newspaper. *Kon-*

nichi Shimbun ran a contest to choose Japan's "ten most outstanding men" (Fukuzawa ranked first, followed in order by Fukuchi, Itō, and the jurist Hatoyama Kazuo).[157] Others had readers vote on top plays, top actors, and top businessmen.[158] Another gimmick was the charity drive—an 1886 campaign by five Tokyo papers to collect aid for families of the victims of the Normanton tragedy, for example—which, says D. Eleanor Westney, "served the dual purpose of arousing the reader's concern and presenting the newspaper as an effective agent for translating that concern into useful activity."[159] And at other times newspapers would promise gifts to subscribers: gold watches to announce *Miyako Shimbun*'s fifth anniversary in 1893, free horsecar rides to celebrate *Tokyo Asahi*'s release from suspension in 1891.[160] Not until the latter half of the 1890s would the press pull out all the stops in the promotional gimmick war, but its entry into this arena showed, again, just how much journalistic values had evolved by the early 1890s.

The emphasis on profitability also increased the importance of advertising in this new press. As newspaper managers around the world have long known, advertising makes money more efficiently than subscriptions do. And Japan's editors began taking that truth seriously in these years. It was not that selling ads was new; Japan's first native-language paper, *Kaigai Shimbun*, invited ads in its initial issue, and in 1867 *Bankoku Shimbun* was running about ten ads each time it came out. The early-Meiji papers all ran ads too, especially on page four,[161] though they were called *kōkoku* only at *Yokohama Mainichi*.[162] It was not until the mid-1880s, however, that many papers became serious about advertising as a significant part of annual revenue.

Jiji Shinpō was a leader in this area. Early on, Fukuzawa had written an editorial on the usefulness of ads to businesses.[163] In 1886, his paper launched the practice, eventually followed by most of the other papers, of giving page one entirely to ads. The stated reason was that rain and delivery agents sometimes damaged the first page, and it was better to ruin ads than news; it did not hurt that page one ads sold well. *Jiji* tried the page one experiment nine times in January of 1886, repeated it eleven times in February, and made it standard in May.[164] *Jiji* also set up an advertising agency, Sanseisha, the same year, with its lead followed in 1890 by the *Ōsaka Mainichi* advertising company, Mannensha.[165]

By the beginning of the 1890s, papers were filled with ads for nearly everything imaginable: books, patent medicines, cigarettes, soaps, property, foods, clothing, "approved" textbooks, sporting events, cosmetics, candies, beers, wines, and concerts. Private individuals also began purchasing spots for personal death notices in the early 1890s. A typical New Year edition of *Jiji* in the early 1890s saw all of page one given over to advertisements, many of them splashy display ads, page two filled with cartoons, and more than half of the rest of the paper taken up by ads for everything imaginable.[166] And on October 26, 1893, the *Niroku Shinpō* took the unprecedented step of buying space in several other papers to advertise its own birth.[167]

Ads also became more expensive in these years, thus increasing their profitability. From 1886 to 1908, in fact, ad prices increased almost six times.[168] The reason merchants were willing to pay for the increases was that the ads were effective. By the late 1880s, people had learned to turn to them when they needed to locate services or buy products. Hani Motoko, the country's first woman reporter, tells how her grandfather, "an avid reader of *Chōya Shimbun*," chose a school for her in 1889 through a newspaper advertisement and how she herself turned to "newspaper ads" when she needed work several years later.[169] The need for profits had brought respectable papers a long way from the starchy early days of Kurimoto and Fukuchi, not quite to Lord Thomson of Fleet's view that "editorial matter" was "the stuff between the ads,"[170] but well along the way.

The drive for profitability also prompted many changes in the newspaper formats and content. It led to the standard use of *furigana* by all major papers after the early 1890s, to the serialization of novels by even the most respectable publications,[171] to a few experiments with evening editions,[172] to a movement to publish almost every day of the year,[173] to the replacement of news-collecting menials with competent, well-trained reporters, and to the creation of special interest columns on everything from household needs to theater and literature. Probably the most important innovation in newspaper content was the elevation of news to the first rank now by all but one or two of the leading papers. There had been nothing self-evident to Japan's pioneer journalists about the media's responsibility for providing information; none of those first editors had shown any propensity for printing "all the news that's fit to print." The early press leaders had edited for political purposes, for influence, and reporting was subsidiary. But now, following the lead of the Murayamas and the Koyasus, and listening to the demands of less-educated readers, even the most traditional papers became serious about reporting.

This change was evident institutionally in a number of new structures created now to facilitate accurate and efficient news coverage. Most of the papers followed *Jiji* and *Asahi* in the late 1880s, for example, in starting to hire only well-educated reporters and having them write their own stories—a sharp break from the old *tanbōsha* system. They also began encouraging their writers to work together with reporters from other papers when efficient news-gathering called for it. Already at the beginning of the 1880s, some government offices had begun setting up on-site offices to help reporters gather news; now such offices became commonplace, and in September 1890, after the election of the first Diet, three dozen reporters themselves created the Gikai De-iri Kisha Dan (Diet Reporters Association) to assist each other in gaining information about the legislature.[174] Similar clubs were created within the next several years at various political parties and cabinet ministries, all of them forerunners of the establishment-oriented reporters clubs that exerted such influence in twentieth-century journalism. A few worried that these arrangements tied the reporters too closely to their sources, but most editors were willing to risk that in their new determination to get news fully and quickly.

The papers also began turning to news agencies in these years. Japan's first news service, Jiji Tsūshinsha, was created by Mitsui interests with government assistance in 1888 to distribute news two or three times a day to the Tokyo and provincial papers. Two years later, Police Bureau Chief Kiyoura Keigo created the Tokyo Tsūshinsha for the same purpose, and that same year Yano Fumio at *Yūbin Hōchi* launched the country's first journalist-sponsored press agency, the Naigai Shimbun Yōshi Kaisha, which set up branches throughout Japan to collect and distribute news. By 1893, six such agencies had been formed, three of them with government funds, two with ties to the Kaishintō, and one—the Naigai Tsūshinsha—independent.[175] The papers also began to use Reuters, the British agency that monopolized news distribution in East Asia. At first, at the outset of the 1890s, they would translate Reuters material from the Yokohama-based, English-language *Japan Mail*, which had the country's only contract with the European news firm.[176] In 1893, however, *Jiji Shinpō* signed its own contract with Reuters, and a few years later so did *Asahi.* All of these attempts at creating and using news services were quite limited, mere suggestions of the powerful role networking would play in the coming decades, but the fact that the news agencies got their start now, in the years surrounding the constitution, illustrates again the crucial character of this period.

It also helps explain the fact that even though the format of most papers remained gray and dull on all but special occasions, the columns themselves now began to overflow with daily news. Sports (especially sumo) became a staple, as did weather and natural disasters.[177] The rise of new religious groups and the outbreak of family squabbles were detailed by *Yorozu Chōhō*, protest movements against the spreading copper pollution problem in Ashio by Tokyo's *Mainichi*,[178] and scandals—both political and sexual—by a number of the papers. One story that typified the new approach was the seventeen-month, Berlin-to-Vladivostok horseback ride of Lieutenant Colonel Fukushima Yasumasa between February 1892 and June 1893. The ride may have been less than compelling in strategic importance, but the papers all covered it extensively, as an affirmation of the Japanese spirit. When Fukushima reached Vladivostok on June 9, a *Tōkyō Asahi* reporter was there, waiting to interview him. And some interview it was, providing copy for 120 successive stories that lasted until November 26![179] It was this kind of coverage that prompted Uchikawa to note that Japan's leading journalists, who once had been the "star players" of the political world, now had become "spectators, standing on the sidelines" and reporting the news.[180]

Nothing better illustrated the preoccupation with news than the election and Diet coverage of the early 1890s. Japan's first national election was held on July 1, 1890, and the enthusiasm it generated would be difficult to exaggerate. The journalist Ubukata Toshirō recalled the "political excitement" at the school that fall, when students created their own song, begging for three things: that their dormitory supervisor die from cholera, that the school burn down, and that the Diet be convened.[181] The excitement among journalists was heightened when sixteen of their own number (5 percent of the entire body) were elected, most of them as members of the dominant, antigovernment Jiyūtō and Kaishintō parties.[182] And the interest grew even more intense when lively Diet politics, combined with government infighting, precipitated Prime Minister Yamagata's disgusted resignation during the spring of 1891.[183]

It should not surprise us then, in this new journalistic atmosphere, that the press fed the country's ever-growing political appetite with lavish, detailed reports on every nuance of Diet and electoral maneuvering. After the election, papers published extras, with lists of the new Lower House members and their affiliations.[184] They did the same when the body convened to elect its officers, reporting in bold type the election of Jiyūtō leader Nakajima Nobuyuki as speaker, 161 to 158 over Tsuda Mamichi.[185] When the

legislature convened for the first time, they gave large amounts of
space to Diet seating charts, sketches of the opening session, and
reports on the speeches.[186] And the press gave full play to the size of
the budget, military spending, the government's handling of the
Ōtsu crisis, land taxes, election interference, and a host of other
issues. When Shimada Saburō of the Kaishintō attacked the officials' May 1892 decision to recess a Diet bent on censuring the cabinet, even onetime (and future) government lackey *Nichi Nichi*
reported his speech zestfully.[187] Later that year, when the Jiyūtō
shifted positions on a land tax and thus triggered a charge by Ozaki
Yukio that its leaders "seemed to have become drunk with some
drug," *Chōya Shimbun* gave a good two columns to the squabble.[188]
Diet struggles were among the most interesting stories of the time;
they received full treatment in every paper.

The reports may not always have been evenhanded, but they
certainly were lively, and often they were courageous. With a tone
that harked back to the narrowly partisan press of the early 1880s,
many of the papers flailed away nonstop at "corrupt officials" and
"venal politicians" in their rivals' camps, at political shenanigans,
and at Itō's "wirepulling" behind the curtains of the Matsukata
cabinet. "Out front, we have a prime minister with responsibility
but no real power," sniffed *Chōya* in the summer of 1891; "but if
we look behind the scenes, we see the actual prime minister, with
no responsibility but the real power."[189] And they left the officials
themselves seriously shaken. Itō reportedly told the emperor that
he feared assassination if he were to accept the prime ministership
proffered him after Yamagata's resignation,[190] and Police Bureau
Chief Kiyoura Keigo recalled that his office in those days would
"thoroughly inspect" all of the newspapers before dawn each morning and "place a red circle around points that especially demanded
attention." Several cabinet ministries did the same thing, he said,
and the bureau then issued an opinion on which articles should be
censored.[191] *Chōya Shimbun* said the "failure to cultivate public
opinion," which necessitated such rigid control, had been "the
greatest mistake ever committed by the government since the Restoration."[192] And Yamamoto Fumio noted that controlling the press
became "the cabinet's most important work" in these years.[193]

The issue that agitated both the officials and their journalistic
critics the most was the February 1892 election, called by Yamagata's successor, Matsukata, in an effort to secure a more cooperative Diet. By all accounts, it was a brutal election, with Home
Minister Shinagawa Yajirō's minions guilty of intimidation, vio-

lence, bribes, press suspensions, and every other device imaginable in their efforts to assure the election of a more "amenable" legislature. Before February ran its course, in fact, the government-induced campaign violence resulted in at least 388 injuries and twenty-five deaths.[194] That the tactics did not work was in many ways a testament to the press' new emphasis on reporting—and on keeping people informed about the oligarchs' abuses.[195] *Jiji,* for example, ran a detailed story on February 2, less than two weeks before the election, about Home Ministry orders to its "election couriers" *(senkyo tanbō)* in the provinces to influence the vote. Several papers published vivid accounts that same week of a violent clash between Jiyūtō and government forces in Kōchi Prefecture, in which "weapons shone brightly in the sun," "the earth shook," and a number were injured.[196] *San'in Shimbun* in Shimane wrote, caustically: "We know of not a single case yet where the government has shown consideration in defense of a people's party."[197] And just three days before the election, *Nihon* ran a lengthy report on the upcoming vote under the headline "Election interference extremely acute" *(Senkyo kanshō kiwamete rokotsu).*[198]

There were many impressive things about the opposition's tenacity during this election, and one of them was the stubborn refusal of several of the most respected papers to keep quiet.[199] Before the election season had passed, papers had been suspended a total of thirty-eight times;[200] yet the reporters kept telling the story. One reason lay in the antigovernment political alliances that journalists had formed in the early days of Diet competition. But that was not all there was to it; for papers such as *Jiji* and *Nihon* were essentially nonpartisan. Another factor was the fact that stories about dramatic struggles attracted readers and swelled profits, as did the reputation for courage a paper received after being issued a *hakkō teishi* sentence. And a third was that reporting really had become central at most papers. They were *news*papers, and when something as newsworthy as violence on the campaign trail occurred, they would not leave it unreported. The "public's right to know" had, for that central group at least, become a new creed.

One other result of the Diet struggles was the rekindling, at least temporarily, of the spirit of press partisanship. Ties between leading papers and specific political organizations already had revived somewhat during the treaty revision fights of the late 1880s. Now, with the onset of electoral politics, the old elite papers began to take sides again. In nearly every prefecture too, at least one paper made itself the mouthpiece of either the Liberal or the Progressive forces.[201] And in the major cities, the lineups made one wonder if it were 1882 all over again—except that there were more papers now, they changed alliances more frequently, and several of the former *koshimbun* had become as partisan as the *ōshimbun*. Even the invective returned, with *Chōya* and *Yomiuri* in one mistaken binge accusing the neutral (but generally antigovernment) *Nihon* of accepting government funds in "a massive breach of etiquette."[202]

Although the loyalties changed from time to time, depending on who was editing a paper and whether Satsuma or Chōshū men were heading the administration,[203] the general breakdown of affiliations this time was as follows:

- Jiyūtō: *Jiyū Shimbun, Eiri Jiyū Shimbun, Tōzai Shimbun, Kōko Shimbun* (later named *Rikken Jiyū Shimbun,* then *Minken Shimbun*), *Azuma Shimbun.*

- Kaishintō: *Yūbin Hōchi Shimbun, Mainichi Shimbun, Yomiuri Shimbun, Minpōtō Shimbun, Chōya Shimbun* (until 1890), *Kaishin Shimbun.*

- Conservative but neutral: *Chūsei Nippō.*

- Progovernment (Satsuma faction): *Yamato Shimbun, Chōya Shimbun* (after 1890), *Chūō Shimbun.*

- Progovernment (Chōshū faction): *Tōkyō Nichi Nichi Shimbun, Tōkyō Shinpō.*

- Neutral: *Nihon, Kokumin Shimbun, Jiji Shinpō, Yorozu Chōhō, Tōkyō Asahi Shimbun, Niroku Shinpō, Kokkai.*[204]

One thing that gave this partisan revival a particularly familiar ring was the fact that the best-edited party papers were tied, as in the early 1880s, either to the Kaishintō or to the government. As a rather blunt, not quite accurate, English-language observer put it: "The Kaishin-tō journals . . . occupy front rank in the press of the capital; while the single organ of the Jiyū-tō, the *Jiyū,* is regarded at best as a second rate paper."[205] Another link to the earlier decade was the fact that several of the most innovative and successful papers stayed out of the partisan fray. Although *Nichi Nichi* and *Yūbin Hōchi* had ridden their newly popular, news-oriented approach back to profit and acceptance, partisanship kept them down toward the middle of the circulation charts in the early 1890s, and their old places at the top were taken by the newcomers. Indeed, the largest Tokyo paper by 1893 was Murayama's *Tōkyō Asahi,* and the third largest was the upstart *Yorozu Chōhō.*[206] Neither of these new sheets avoided politics; they both reported political happenings with relish. But they handled politics as news, avoiding partisanship and the pitfalls it entailed. And the rising middle class of news-oriented readers rewarded them for it.

THE NEW JOURNALISTS

The clearest sign that a new press age had dawned was the founding of several highly distinctive—and remarkably successful—papers in the capital just before and after the constitution took effect. In a development unique to these heady years, the press gave birth now to what some press historians call the "era of personal journalism" *(pūsonaru jiyūnarizumu),*[207] a time when several aggressive, opinionated individuals created a group of highly distinctive newspapers that quickly came to dominate Tokyo journalism. Some of these men edited for nationalistic reasons, some to espouse personal philosophies, some to provide news for commoners, some to get rich, and some just to make a name for themselves. What they shared was a combination of zeal, nonpartisanship, and managerial skill sufficient to change the face of Japan's press.

One of these newspapers, the highly literate, nationalistic *Nihon* of Kuga Katsunan and Shiga Shigetaka, has been discussed above. Another was *Miyako Shimbun,* which replaced the failing *Konnichi Shimbun* in November 1887 and soared to a daily circulation of more than 30,000 early in the 1890s, thanks in part to the novels and editorials of chief writer Kuroiwa Shūroku.[208] A third was *Niroku Shinpō,* founded late in 1893 by the iconoclastic, often opportunistic twenty-six-year-old Akiyama Teisuke. A bombastic champion of "the rights and benefits of the average masses" *(ippan kōshū no benki oyobi kenri),* the paper lasted only two years and forced Akiyama to auction off everything but his frock coat to satisfy creditors, but it set crusading precedents that he himself would revive with great success half a decade later.[209] There also was the revived *Ōsaka Mainichi Shimbun* off in Kansai, which changed its format late in 1891 to provide more compact news and clearer headlines to make stories attractive,[210] and rode Motoyama Hikoichi's unapologetic "publishing-is-business" philosophy into a spirited rivalry with *Ōsaka Asahi.*[211] Each of these papers, whether new or newly invigorated, showed that there was a growing market for

lively, popular, yet solid journalism. All of them focused on literate and readable prose; all paid attention to the financial bottom
line, and all reflected the personal influence of strong personalities
at the helm. But even more important than any of this group
(except perhaps *Nihon*) were three other newcomers to the Tokyo
scene that dominated their own spheres of the new press world in
the early 1890s and influenced the rest of the press for decades into
the future.

The first was *Tōkyō Asahi*. We already have seen the consternation caused by its aggressive entry into the Tokyo market in the
summer of 1888. On one level, the anxiety was caused by sincere
opposition on the part of some editors to the introduction of the
aggressive, profited-oriented Kansai brand of journalism into the
Kantō region; Murayama's journalism, they feared, would "lay
waste" to the venerated journalism of ideas and political opinion.[212]
The challenges of *Jiji, Yomiuri,* and the increasingly respectable
koshimbun had provided more than enough of the "new journalism," as far as older Tokyo editors were concerned; further progress
down that road would take the press where it should not go. For a
greater number of the Kantō journalists, the consternation grew
from more mundane concerns; they understood just how competitive—and effective—Murayama could be, and they were not sure
the Tokyo papers were up to the challenge. And their fears were
well placed, because Murayama was serious about making his news-
oriented *Tōkyō Asahi* the most successful paper in the city. To
demonstrate that resolve, he and his wife moved to Tokyo, leaving
Ueno in Osaka, and commenced immediately to take charge of
every aspect of his new paper. On arriving at the office early each
morning, the reports say, he first would visit the business offices,
next would consult with his editors about the next day's articles,
and then would discuss the paper's general policies with whomever
happened to be appropriate. Evenings he often spent talking with
section chiefs about what was going on in their areas. And when
there was time he would set up personal meetings with important
news sources—or do his own proofreading and editing of reporters'
articles.[213]

The *Tōkyō Asahi* forte, as in Osaka, was news, carefully gathered, well written, and cheaply delivered to readers. Though the
paper proclaimed an affiliation for Jiyūtō politics at the outset,
apparently over the opposition of the business-minded Ueno,[214] it
moved quickly to a centrist stand: nationalistic but skeptical of
both the *hanbatsu* government and its doctrinaire opponents. Across

the years, it hired the best writers available, including the well-known patriots Ikebe Kichitarō and Torii Sosen, and secured the services of stars like Tokutomi Sohō for specific essays. And its reportage was the most complete and spirited in the city. Within a week of its founding, for example, it dispatched one reporter and two artists to the scene of the Bandai eruption and printed their accounts and sketches of four hundred deaths in impressive detail.[215] The next year, it hurried onto the streets with extras, complete with graphic sketches of collapsing houses, following a Kumamoto earthquake.[216] Its aggressive coverage of stunts such as the Siberian ride of Lieutenant Colonel Fukushima already has been noted.

Tōkyō Asahi's preoccupation with news and with self-promotion of its many scoops may have brought a frown to the brow of the established editors. But, clearly, it was a frown of worry more than of contempt. They already had capitulated to the necessity of gathering both news and readers, as we have seen; and Murayama was good enough at it to threaten their own positions. In 1887, *Mezamashi*, the *Asahi* forerunner, had had a daily circulation of 7,960; in 1889, *Tōkyō Asahi's* first full year, its circulation more than doubled to nearly 18,000; and by 1890 it was nearing 24,000—far more than that of any other paper in the capital.[217] The statesman Mutsu Munemitsu once commented: "Murayama is Japan's best newspaper manager; Tokutomi is Japan's best journalist. If the two of them would join forces, it would be wonderful not only for Japanese journalism but for the two of them."[218] Their approaches to journalism were too far apart to permit that kind of union. It would have been foolish, however, to question Mutsu's evaluation of Murayama the press manager.

The year 1890 showed just how right he was about Tokutomi too. On January 20, Tokutomi and several of his friends held a convivial newspaper-launching party at a restaurant in Shiba, complete with violin and *biwa* music;[219] then ten days later, on February 1, he brought out the first issue of *Kokumin Shimbun*, a paper too lofty in tone to compete with *Tōkyō Asahi's* circulation figures but stylish and passionate enough to make it one of Japan's most influential dailies over the next three decades. Tokutomi was only twenty-eight at the time, not all that long out of L. L. Janes' Yōgakkō in his native Kumamoto or Niijima Jō's Dōshisha in Kyoto, but no one in the intellectual world was surprised at either the paper's appearance or its impact. His book *Shōrai no Nihon* (The future Japan) had been a bestseller when he was just twenty-four, and he had started the successful opinion journal *Kokumin no Tomo* at twenty-five.[220] Moreover, he had planned his entry into the newspaper world with a care and precision of which few others were capable. He honed his business skills at Min'yūsha, the publishing firm that produced his books and journal; he persuaded his friend Fukuda Wagorō to take a job at *Kyōto Nippō* and learn "practical journalism."[221] And when the time was right he bought some Ginza land with five thousand yen of *Kokumin no Tomo* money, borrowed another six thousand yen from Kumamoto backers, and launched his paper.[222]

Kokumin Shimbun's forte was excellent writing. Tokutomi wielded a brilliant brush, perhaps the best of the era. In the words of Kido Motosuke, the later president of *Ōsaka Mainichi:* "He was born to write. There never was a day he did not write. Newspapers, magazines, new books *(shinkansho)*; foreign works or Japanese works: it did not matter what they were. He read like a glutton. Always reading. Always writing. This was his life. He literally disgorged articles."[223] Indeed he did! During the next decades, he produced more than 350 works, including a one-hundred-volume history of early modern Japan *(Kinsei Nihon kokumin shi)*. He also hired a number of other talented writers: Fukuda (as chief editor, or *henshūchō*), Tokutomi Rōka (his brother), Hitomi Ichitarō, Miyazaki Koshiyoshi, Matsubara Iwagorō, Yamaji Aizan, and the artist Kubota Beisen. And he had the distinction of publishing what appears to have been Japan's first newspaper article by a woman, an essay by Takekoshi Takeyo in February 1890, arguing the unprecedented position that journalism was an appropriate field for women.[224] He was the stingiest of managers, paying his brother Rōka, for example, a mere eleven yen a month, but his personal energy and the influence that being associated with *Kokumin Shimbun* gave them were enough to keep most writers loyal.[225]

A second *Kokumin Shimbun* forte was breadth. "A newspaper should not limit itself to politics and economics," Tokutomi said.[226] It should be "the mirror of society."[227] The paper's aim was explained in detail in a prepublication announcement in the companion *Kokumin no Tomo*, which included the obligatory pledge to make articles readable for young people, women, city dwellers *(tokai no hito)*, and country folk, then declared:

> We will run both reports and commentaries on recent events. We will invite experts to evaluate developments in agriculture, industry and commerce, in education, in the arts, in crafts and skills, and in

the world of culture. We will report both provincial and foreign news, quickly and often, and we will describe regularly the real conditions of the Japanese people, exposing especially the hidden realities of the lower classes. . . . Thus, we will nurture mutual affections among the Japanese people.[228]

By all accounts, the paper did just that.

Its third strength was commentary, both by its own writers and by the people about whom it reported. Taking a nonpartisan but essentially popular, anticabinet philosophy that Tokutomi labeled "commonerism" *(heiminshugi)*, it ran shorter, more topical editorials than those in the old prestige papers, had its writers do interviews with opinion leaders on timely issues, and included some of the best sketches and portraits in Tokyo. It opposed Itō Hirobumi vigorously in its early years as "a weak individual and statesman, a man without self-confidence, uncertain of his own abilities and lacking any clear perception of how the nation should proceed."[229] It joined *Nihon* and others in demanding revision of the unequal treaties. And it won quite an audience among students and political activists, probably coming closer to bridging the old chasm between prestige and popular papers than any other paper yet published.

As Ono Hideo put it, *Kokumin Shimbun* was "less elegant than *Tōkyō Nichi Nichi*, less bookish than *Nihon Shimbun*, and without the maturity of *Yūbin Hōchi*; it was popular with young people and easy for families to subscribe to—a model newspaper."[230] And since Tokutomi was a good manager and promoter too, an editor who knew how both to sell papers and to gain his colleagues' respect,[231] the paper was successful from the first. It attained a circulation of nearly nine thousand its first year and grew steadily after that, reaching 36,000 in 1896.[232] Tokutomi's penchant for skimping on salaries assured that it would turn a good profit too.

The last of the new papers, Kuroiwa Shūroku's *Yorozu Chōhō*, went even further in demonstrating what a new world journalism—and Japan—had entered. A native of Tosa, reared by a judge, and brother to a doctor, Kuroiwa had moved to Tokyo in 1879, at seventeen, to study at Fukuzawa's Keiō. He never graduated, however, because he became enmeshed quickly in the energizing worlds of journalism and politics, writing essays (including one that landed him in jail for sixteen days for attacking Kuroda Kiyotaka over the Hokkaido land schemes), translating European novels,[233] speaking, and editing. He was connected at one time or another with *Dōmei Kaishin Shimbun, Yoron Nippō, Nihon Tai-musu,*[234] *Eiri Jiyū Shimbun* (as chief editor for ten yen a month), *Konnichi Shimbun,* and *Miyako Shimbun* (as editor, for fifty yen a month).[235] His frequent moves may have indicated a restless spirit but hardly a lack of talent. Wherever he went, his essays and novels sparked a rise in circulation, and he left *Miyako* primarily because of a near breakdown, precipitated by a combination of frenetic work patterns and political disagreements with the owners.

When a doctor told him after leaving *Miyako* that his nerves were too weak for him to reenter journalism,[236] he took up ink-making. But newspapering was in his blood, and when Murayama offered him 150 yen a month to join *Tōkyō Asahi,* he decided he simply had to return to the field he loved—but not for *Asahi.* He had had enough of working for others; he would start his own paper. His first inclination was to enter the Osaka market, where his swashbuckling style would fit quite naturally. But after examining the Osaka competition, he concluded that Tokyo offered more opportunities.[237] So he pulled together 1600 yen in startup capital, rented a "very small and dirty" room in Takabashi,[238] began publicizing his determination to publish,[239] and on November 1, 1892, joined his seven-person staff in issuing *Yorozu's* first edition. He promised his readers "a newspaper with dependable and detailed articles and opinions that can be read and trusted in every matter." The paper would come out more than 360 times a year and would provide "daily zest that never will tire you" as well as an "inexhaustible store of interesting and profitable material." In a phrase (Kuroiwa loved phrases), he would give them, each day, a "solid journalistic meal" *(shimbunshi naka no kome no meshi).*[240]

If *Kokumin Shimbun* was a literary feast for students and middle-class readers, *Yorozu Chōhō* was a bowl of rice for the working person. When Max Pemberton said that England's Lord Northcliffe was "born with an instinct for understanding the great reading public which has never been surpassed,"[241] he might as well have been talking about Kuroiwa, who seemed to comprehend the tastes of the rising urban classes almost intuitively. Like a sound bite TV producer a century later, he said that his sole purpose in publishing was "to help the average masses know the times thoroughly at a glance,"[242] adding later that "I could not be satisfied unless *Chōhō* reached all classes of Japanese society, in all places, and had the confidence of everyone in the entire nation."[243] He came close to achieving his desired readership (if not the universal respect!), using the skills of business, promotion, and reporting to make his paper rival *Tōkyō Asahi* in circulation within a year, pass it within two years, and double the readership of any other Tokyo paper by 1898.[244]

Yorozu Chōhō's early impact was based on at least five characteristics, all of which would influence most of Japan's other papers in the later Meiji years. It was cheap, its articles were short, it read easily, it gave special place to serialized novels, and it remained aggressively independent. The paper sold for one *sen* an issue, less than any of the other papers in Tokyo then. "Newspaper prices have been gradually rising, until even the cheapest now cost more than 1.5 *sen*," he wrote; "even 1.5 *sen* is a big sum in today's society, more than the cost of an indispensable daily trip to the bath, more even than the price of a precious postcard." To assure that the "average *(futsū ippan)* person" could buy a paper, he pledged to keep prices as low as possible."[245] And he did just that, charging only about two-thirds of what even the popular *Tōkyō Asahi* and *Yamato* did well along into the 1890s.[246] One advantage of keeping prices low was that it enabled Kuroiwa to insist on payment at or before delivery of the paper, even to gain some of that much desired notoriety at one point for denying delivery to a rich Tosa patron who fell behind in payments.[247]

On the matter of length, he noted that "long articles are a waste of time and simply tire one's mind and eyes." "Big newspapers," he explained in defense of *Yorozu Chōhō's* four-page limit, "are like unwelcome guests who stay at your place forever. Anyone who has put up with a troublesome guest can appreciate a simple and concise paper."[248] As for writing, he said a paper's articles should possess three characteristics—simplicity *(kantan)*, clarity *(meiryō)*, and incisiveness *(tsūkai)*—because it was important that everyone, male and female, highly educated and poorly educated, read the paper.[249] Actually, he noted, "the paper becomes quite cheap if the entire household—including the wife, the butler, the clerk, the maids and servants—reads it."[250] And he saw no need to construct a defense for his publication of novels. His translations had boosted sales mightily at *Miyako*, and as many as half of that paper's readers switched to *Yorozu Chōhō* now for the novels alone.[251]

All of this showed Kuroiwa's keen sensitivity to the changing readership of Tokyo, but the thing that probably did more than anything else to assure his success and to prompt scholars to compare him with America's "penny press" founders, Benjamin Day and James Gordon Bennett,[252] was the paper's fifth characteristic: a stubborn, often abrasive independence. Other papers were cheap; nearly all ran novels by the mid-1890s; many had come to emphasize brevity and simple writing. But none showed *Yorozu*'s zest, its ruggedness (and often raggedness), or its willingness to take on establishment tastes. "We do not have any lovers," said Kuroiwa, "no government, no political parties, no politicians, no commercial interests. We go our independent way. We simply are honest and sincere."[253]

It was not a unique claim; "independence" and "nonpartisanship" had become part of the standard rhetoric of new papers, as we have observed several times already. But *Yorozu Chōhō* went further than others in making good on those claims, and the result was lively, sensational, and sometimes inaccurate reporting. Almost at once, for example, the paper took on the issue of taxes on pharmaceutical drugs, which increased what the poor had to pay for medicine. It criticized the political establishment, other newspapers, and the "corrupt" leaders of the religious organization Renmonkyō. One of the best examples of hard-hitting, iconoclastic news coverage was its handling of the "Sōma affair" in 1893. When the highly respected Sòma family of the old Nakamura *han* north of Tokyo accused one of their servants, Nishikiori Takekiyo, of kidnaping their family head, the entire press had supported the legal charges that landed Nishikiori in jail. Kuroiwa saw the case differently. He took up Nishikiori's side, arguing day after day in *Yorozu* that family members had themselves "imprisoned" the family patriarch in a mental hospital, poisoned him, and then bribed the judges. *Yorozu* stood absolutely alone on this side of the case, accepting suspension four times for its attacks on the establishment. But it never stopped playing the case as a rich-versus-poor drama, even when an autopsy failed to reveal any poisoning, and it won a great deal of support from the *futsū ippan* city dwellers as a result.[254]

To say that coverage of this sort made Kuroiwa controversial is to repeat the obvious. The establishment hated him, accusing him, apparently falsely, of accepting secret money himself,[255] labeling *Yorozu* the "blackmail newspaper" *(yusuri shimbun),* and calling him "Shūroku the pit viper."[256] But the plebeian classes for which he wrote loved him, and Ono thinks that there was more than mere commercial savvy in his identification with the commoners. "He wanted to think as the general public felt, to feel anger with them and solve problems with them. He wanted to help the poor, the weak," he says.[257] Their label for *Yorozu Chōhō* was *"Edokko Shimbun,"* the paper of Tokyo's masses.[258] They bought an amazing seven thousand copies of its very second issue,[259] and before long even the upper classes and the oligarchs themselves were reading it, albeit sometimes on the sly.[260] As a Buddhist university student described his own experience with the paper: "Once I finished reading sutras each morning, I would take up the red newspaper, *Yorozu Chōhō*. And I was not alone; all of the 250 students at my university were ardent *Yorozu Chōhō* readers."[261]

Very few would have called the paper much more than a third-rate daily during its first years. It was too cheap, too sensational, too often inaccurate. But it was different from anything Japanese journalism ever had known: more brazen, more seriously committed to the interests and needs of the city's new commoner classes, filled with better writing than the old *koshimbun*, and edited by a man who had the gift of being able to combine business acumen, journalistic skill, and social commitment in roughly equal parts. Within a few years it even would gain respectability, much like Northcliffe's *Daily Mail* and Bennett's *Herald.* For now, it merely demonstrated how rapidly Japanese journalism was changing.

IN TRANSITION

Not everything had changed in the early 1890s. Political struggles continued to form the core of most papers' news and editorials. Although treaty revision, elections, and Diet explosions had replaced constitutional theory as the meat of controversy, questions of governance remained at the forefront even of papers such as *Kokumin Shimbun* and *Niroku Shinpō*. The struggle over freedom of expression had not diminished either. As in the earlier years, the cabinet kept revising the legal system for controlling the press, with another major newspaper law in 1887 and various minor revisions after that, and the majority of journalists kept fighting: sometimes toning down their coverage or keeping quiet about proscribed materials but just as often haranguing officials, expressing controversial views, then loudly advertising their own spunk when they were suspended or sent off to jail. There had been some shift in the deeply Confucian, heavy sense of social responsibility felt by most journalists, but not much. Editors still employed the Confucian rhetoric about using their papers to lead the people, and, as we have seen, most of them genuinely believed it. Even the gray formats remained largely unchanged, probably as much because of typesetting and printing limitations as from predispositions of taste.

Offsetting the constants, however, was a set of fundamentally important transformations that made this a revolutionary period in the press. Modernization was giving birth to a new urban environment in these years, a world populated by hundreds of thousands of people from the old, barely literate subject classes who had now learned to read, people developing a new sense of connectedness to their country's public institutions, people too tired or poorly educated to suffer kindly the heavy prose of political theorists but nonetheless eager to buy lighter and simpler reading materials. And the papers responded to this changing environment with the same alacrity that seemed to characterize everything else in the Meiji years.

Most dramatic among the changes was the narrowing of the gap between the ōshimbun and koshimbun. Some papers retained their dominant political orientation; a few slighted politics; some nurtured ties to the political parties; others eschewed them. but all of the papers came toward the center. The "small," popular papers paid more attention to accuracy and politics, while the prestige press cut its prices, simplified its prose, and worked to increase circulations through richer news offerings and appeals to the lower strata. Ono describes eleven major characteristics that almost all of the papers came to share in these years, including the downplaying of editorials, an increase in society news, the addition of art, and the widespread staging of promotional events.[262] I would argue that three changes were fundamental.

First, the press became more overtly nationalistic. The political theorists of journalism's first fifteen years, men who thought deeply about what would make Japan strong but saw no need to employ very much blatantly patriotic rhetoric, were replaced by a younger generation with different upbringings. Among this new group were intellectuals such as Shiga, Kuga, and Tokutomi, who had come to grapple not only with the West's technological and military supremacy but also with its unequal treatment of Asian nations, men who saw Japan's own rapid progress toward modernity as a sign of national strength and were ready to talk openly about its role vis-à-vis the rest of the world. The new group also include the Murayamas and Kuroiwas, whose patriotism was less intellectual but at least as intense. With issues such as treaty revision to goad them, both of these groups introduced a new, more militant and nationalistic rhetoric to the newspaper world in the late 1880s and early 1890s. In the next decade, their tone would grow sharper still, moving both the press and the country in new and imperialistic directions.[263]

The second major shift of these years was the rising respectability of the word "profit." It had taken Fukuzawa to make open discussion of newspaper finances respectable in the previous period, early in the 1880s, but despite his prodding, the *ōshimbun* editors, Confucian to the heart, preferred to leave economic issues in the closet. The mid-decade crises combined with the successes of the new papers, however, to change that. Circulation wars, self-promotion, splashy ads, and easier reading all had one essential purpose from the late 1880s onward: to increase a paper's profitability. It would be inaccurate to say that the press had become thoroughly commercial yet. Motoyama's bald pronouncement that "publishing is a business enterprise" still made much of the journalistic world uncomfortable. But the day of unalloyed commercialism was on the horizon, because these years had made profitability not only essential but respectable.

The third major shift was in the content of papers. With only a few exceptions, the dailies truly became *news*papers in these years. *Nihon* continued to focus on opinion, and *Kokumin Shimbun* was better at criticism than at reporting. But all of the papers now accepted accurate reporting of public events as one of the essential characteristics of responsible journalism. For the first time, the established editors began hiring competent reporters and letting them write their own stories. They expanded their coverage to include culture, sports, society, and the arts. They tried to outdo each other in speed, sometimes at the cost of printing extras. And a few of them began dipping into sensationalism. As with commercialism, the tendency toward expanded coverage and the focus on news would not approach maturity until the Sino-Japanese War. Indeed, one of the strengths of this era was the balance many papers were able to achieve between news and opinion. But the mindset clearly had changed toward newsreporting as a paper's central function, and that was of signal importance.

A final point that deserves emphasis is the deep relationship that existed between all these changes and the public that the papers served. We noted in earlier chapters how seriously the pioneering journalists and officials took their responsibility for bringing "civilization" to the people or *minshū*, how constantly they wrote about "modern behavior" and fanned political interest in a conscious effort to expand and tutor Japan's public sphere. Now the editors' relationships with their readers began to take on a new dimension. There was no diminution of the press' efforts to bring enlightenment to the people, to "nurture mutual affections among the Japanese people," in Tokutomi's phrase.[264] But the people had now begun to have as much impact on the press as the papers did on the people. Brought into the cities and into the public life by a combination of modernizing forces (of which the press was an important part), they now expressed tastes and interests to which the editors had to pay attention, at the risk of survival itself. And that fact lay behind most of the journalistic changes that dominated this era. It was, in other words, both a new citizenry and a new press that were propelling Japan in the early months of 1893, as it moved toward conflict on the Asian continent. Many elements in this new world would be stimulated to even more rapid change by the war at mid-decade, and the press would emerge from that war altered forever.

CHAPTER 7

REPORTING
A WAR
1894 to 1895

The Press is responsible for this war.
Yorozu Chōhō, October 18, 1894

If Diet quarrels stimulated a public thirst for news at the beginning of the 1890s, rising tensions with Korea and China had the same effect, multiplied several times, in the summer of 1894. Japanese officials had regarded Korea as crucial to their own security since the first Meiji years and twice had seriously considered going to war there to assure Korean cooperation with Japan's Asian plans. The first episode, in 1873, resulted in Saigō Takamori's dramatic departure from the government, and the second, in 1885, produced the Tianjin Convention, in which Japan and China, Korea's other dominating neighbor, agreed to notify each other before sending troops to Korea. Although the Convention produced several years of relative tranquility, many Japanese began looking to the possibility of eventual war in Korea to eradicate China's paternalistic influence and strengthen Japan's own standing in the broader imperialistic world. Thus, when a secretive Korean religious society, the Tonghaks, launched several uprisings in the spring of 1894, the situation turned explosive. And when the conservative Korean government asked the Chinese on June 4 to send troops to help them quell the Tonghaks, Japan's more expansionist writers declared it was time for action of their own, to stop Chinese "meddling" and assure Korean "independence."

PREPARING THE PEOPLE FOR WAR

Popular Japanese attitudes toward Korea's Chinese patrons had had a schizophrenic quality from the dawn of the modern era. On the one hand, most educated Japanese found it hard to think ill of a country that had provided the foundations of their own writing system, numerous administrative structures, two of their three major religious systems, and many of their aesthetic norms. "The China we children envisioned before the Sino-Japanese War," recalled the journalist Ubukata Toshirō, "was noble, romantic, and heroic. China never was disparaged, never regarded spitefully, in any of the things we saw or the stories we heard."[1] On the other hand, the Japanese had watched with increasing contempt as China struggled unsuccessfully to meet the challenges of modernity and Western imperialism. And the leaders of Japan's political opposition had become quite bitter about China's involvement in Korean affairs. By the mid-1880s, in fact, *jiyū minken* forces had made Japanese strength in Asia one of their central goals. Thus, when Seoul turned yet again to Beijing for military help in the spring of 1894, many of Japan's most articulate opinion leaders were ready to demand a strong response.[2] A number of journalists, led by Tokutomi Sohō, already had been squabbling with the Itō Hirobumi administration over a variety of domestic issues; now the warming Chinese-Korean ties gave them reason to attack the cabinet for weakness on the continent too.[3] Debt to a glorious past, they reasoned, did not obviate the need to correct China's inept and meddlesome ways in the present.

The actual arrival of thousands of Chinese forces troops at the Korean port of Asan on June 8 prompted the quick dispatch of several hundred Japanese troops in response—and a serious debate within the cabinet between the moderate allies of Prime Minister Itō Hirobumi and Foreign Minister Mutsu Munemitsu, and a clique of expansionists who wanted to send upwards of seven thousand troops and perhaps even go to war. Particularly galling to the expansionists was a line in China's June 7 troop-dispatch notification that included the phrase "China protects its dependencies."[4] The interventionists won the cabinet debate and more than five thousand troops soon were on the Korean peninsula, but even that was not enough for the government's increasingly jingoistic critics, most of whom genuinely believed that China must be taught a lesson.[5] When Japan's forces won a battle against the Chinese on July 9, the clamor for decisive action increased. And by the time Ambassador Ōtori Keisuke installed a pro-Japanese regime in Seoul on July 23, the talk at home was all of Japanese dignity, sovereignty, and opportunities. And of war. Many of the discussants harbored a good deal of apprehension because of China's assumed superiority and the widespread perception that Great Britain might assist the Middle Kingdom if war came.[6] But even those doubts were greatly assuaged after the Japanese defeated China's fleet outside Asan on July 25.

Leading the rising public clamor were almost all of the nation's newspapers. Newly attuned to the importance of providing an abundance of *news* even for intellectual readers, editors now found themselves confronted by richer story possibilities than ever before. Moreover, they were stories that dramatized the issues of national sovereignty and strength, stories sure to attract nationalistic readers and increase profits. And they were stories on which writers might (at least so they thought at the time) find common cause with many of the officials whose anger had made editing difficult in recent years. It is doubtful that many journalists thought consciously of all these issues when the Korean conflict erupted; their reactions generally were more visceral. But all of these factors combined to turn the press into the country's loudest prowar trumpeters in the spring and summer of 1894—and to secure forever the newspaper world's new *minshū*-oriented, news-dominated persona.

When the reports of China's troop dispatch reached Tokyo in early June, the leading papers demanded an immediate, strong response. Already in May, *Jiji Shinpō* had called for a nonconfidence vote against the Itō cabinet because of its failure, among other things, to act forcefully against those responsible for the March assassination of Kim Ok-kyun, one of Japan's most forceful Korean allies.[7] Now, on June 7, *Jiji* went to the streets with a scare-inducing extra, reporting in bold headlines: "Korean Government Seeks Chinese Assistance . . . Nearly 10,000 Chinese Troops Dispatched . . . Chinese Soldiers Already Heading for Korea."[8] A day later the paper's regular columns carried several stories explaining the "reports from Tianjin,"[9] and a day after that, on June 9, fifty-nine expansionist writers from twenty-two companies in the Osaka-Kyoto area called a Kansai Journalists' Rally in Support of Aggressive Foreign Policies (Kansai kōha shimbun zasshi sha taikai) to urge more vigorous Japanese action in Korea. The following week, their peers in the Tokyo press world did the same.[10]

Never, not even during the Satsuma Rebellion or when the

constitution was promulgated, had the press become more exercised over a single story. *Niroku Shinpō*'s editor, Akiyama Teisuke, sailed from Nagasaki to Korea the third week of June, disgusted with what he regarded as the "dilatory and indecisive methods" of Itō and Mutsu, whose cabinet was operating as secretly as possible, and determined to get material from the scene that would prompt "a rapid opening of war" and "strike a blow against China first."[11] Other papers followed suit and published so many extras about events in Korea that a *Jiji* reporter quipped: "They never stop coming out. They come out in the morning; they come out at noon; they come out in the evening. It has reached a point that some salespersons now specialize in extras."[12] They reported on every aspect of the situation on which they could get information: the locations and capacity of China's ships,[13] the late-June arrival of Japanese naval forces in Seoul and army troops in Inchon,[14] the speeches given at prowar rallies in Tokyo,[15] revisions in the Japanese army's weapons procedures,[16] efforts to get the Korean government to "reform" and loosen its ties to China,[17] the increasing possibilities of full-scale war with China,[18] and the "opening of hostilities *at last*" off P'ung Island near Asan on the morning of July 25.[19]

But it was not just reporting of developments that characterized their coverage. As the journalists' early-June rallies suggested, these journalists were propagandizing patriots, men for whom abstract principles such as objectivity and journalistic independence faded before the concrete cause of national expansion. So from the first the vast majority of the papers began agitating, each from its own particular perspective, for war. Tokutomi Sohō's *Kokumin Shimbun* demanded that Japan take a "stand on the stage of world politics,"[20] calling this a "golden opportunity" for his beloved homeland "to be recognized by the world as an expansive Japan . . . to take her place alongside the other great expansionist powers . . . and internally, to strengthen national unity, to deepen the national spirit, and to promote the positive, progressive, and expansive vigor and vitality of the state."[21] *Tōkyō Keizai Zasshi* worried that letting China suppress the Tonghaks unilaterally would hurt Japanese economic interests, because "the whole country of Korea will be owned by China."[22] One of the regional papers, *Gifu Nichi Nichi Shimbun*, saw the coming war as a way to restore the dignity and prosperity of the country's ailing former samurai.[23] *Jiji*, the "most zealous" expansionist of all, lambasted China for its failure to "recognize Korean independence"[24] and emphasized the need to bring civilization to Asia, with Fukuzawa Yukichi himself writing a July

27 editorial calling for private donations to undergird what he saw as the imminent war effort—and pledging to give the first 10,000 yen.[25] Two days later, Fukuzawa called for a war to force the Chinese into the world, since they "are ignorant of proper international methods" and "do not want the progress of civilization." "This is not a war between people and people and country and country," he said, "but it is a kind of religious war."[26] And *Ōsaka Asahi* talked about the danger of lost opportunities, writing about the cabinet moderates:

> They never devise far-reaching policies; they miss heaven-sent opportunities. If we lose this chance, all ages will regret it. . . . We should take the lead in recognizing Korea's independence; instead we look on in a daze. This is not the way to preserve the nation's dignity and progress, not the way to fulfill our friendship with neighboring countries.[27]

As would happen so often across the next half century, the press' loud jingoism outpaced even that of cabinet and military activists, making reasoned or measured decision making difficult. Although official plans were laid already in June to react with force—to use the Korean confusion to strengthen Japan's own position on the continent—and although the dispatch of troops actually came quite quickly, the press' outcry threatened to take the initiative out of the hand of the bureaucrats. So the officials tried almost as soon as they received word of Chinese activities to clamp down on public discussion. On June 7, the war and naval ministers invoked Article 22 of the press law, prohibiting press reports on Japanese "troop or fleet movements, military secrets, and military strategies."[28] That very day, they temporarily suspended *Tōkyō Nichi Nichi* and *Shō Nihon Shimbun* for "violating public security" by publishing a report that Japanese troops would be sent to Korea,[29] and the same week they also handed out suspensions to *Tōkyō Asahi, Jiji, Yūbin Hōchi, Chūō Shimbun,* and *Kokumin.*[30] *Shō Nihon* responded by sending postcards to its readers to explain why it had not appeared on the streets.[31] And *Nichi Nichi* complained indignantly, after resuming publication, that errant censors had lifted the suspension "as soon as they came to their senses" and realized that the *Nichi Nichi* report was both correct and responsible.[32] The effect of the suspensions, however, was to prompt at least a modicum of caution in what the papers reported about sensitive developments throughout the rest of the summer.

There was little the government could do, however, to

dampen the war fever itself or the tone of editorialists who re-mained convinced the cabinet was moving too cautiously. Ubukata recalled one evening in his Gunma village when he "saw a neighbor on the other side of the street fanning air into his sleeves and hold-ing a copy of *Tōkyō Shimbun* in his hands. 'It looks like we are going to have a war on our hands,' he was murmuring."[33] By late July even *Nichi Nichi*, the only paper to have expressed some reser-vations about rushing prematurely into conflict, was calling for a "great war, a decisive war."[34] So when formal hostilities with China were announced on August 1, it took no one by surprise. It merely set up a new frenzy of patriotism and jingoism—and enhanced the press' growing role as a conduit and broker between government actions and the popular will.

COVERING THE WAR

To understand the public mood one must remember that this was Japan's first modern war with another country and that it followed four full decades of humiliation at the hands of the rich, advanced imperialist countries. Historians might fairly label Japan's actions greedy and aggressive, but few Japanese saw them that way at the time. To a people eager to be rid of the unequal treaties, a people proud of their own modernizing successes and determined to gain the respect of the Western powers, this war was not only just, it was holy. The Chinese, in their minds, had violated both Korean inde-pendence and Japanese-Chinese reciprocity; to let them get away with it would sully national honor and call into question Japan's ability to defend its own sovereignty. Heightening the mood as the months passed was the fact that it was such an easy war, a war in which Japan won every battle—and often with greater ease than expected: at Pyongyang on September 16, just six weeks after the declaration of war; against the larger Chinese navy in the Battle of Yalu a day later; at Port Arthur on November 21; and eventually in Chinese waters not all that far from Beijing, at Weihaiwei where the Japanese fleet destroyed China's navy in mid-February.

It should come as no surprise then that the public appetite for information about the "glorious war" was beyond satisfying. An *Illustrated London News* essayist wrote with amazement in Octo-ber about the "enthusiasm in Japan" and the "spectacle" of an "Eastern nation fighting and maneuvering and organizing with a *verve* and intelligence worthy of a first-class European war."[35] Ubu-kata recalled of village life early in the war:

> News came to the police station before the newspaper received it. All news was put up on a message board in front of the police station, and we children ran there several times a day to check for any change in the war situation. The excitement generated among the Japanese people was beyond imagination. China, after all, was thirty times as big as Japan, and its population was more than two hundred million, compared to thirty million in Japan. . . . Every adult, every child, every elderly person, every woman talked day and night of nothing but the war.

When news came of the victory at Pyongyang, he said, "a cleaning woman threw her broom down and jumped up with joy," and a shop clerk "ran out of the house like a madman . . . and did not come back for some time."[36] "News of the outbreak of war," Donald Keene tells us after a survey of the period's literature and art, "was greeted everywhere with enthusiasm, and . . . there was virtually no trace of anti-war feeling at any later stage."[37]

Certainly there was no significant antiwar mood in the press,[38] where editors vied with each other to defend Japan's cause. Kuroiwa Shūroku expressed special pride in the newspapers' role in hastening the war. The press "crushed the national lethargy," his *Yorozu Chōhō* wrote in an eloquent if awkward English-language column. "It awoke . . . patriotism to the fervent height, which, if not stirred for another quarter of a century, might be extinguished and the whole nation reduced to the impotent mass of imbeciles, intellectually and physically."[39] Tokutomi, who was irritated that some young people were more interested in gossip "than in the fierce battle fought at Liaoyang,"[40] focused on the new international stature he expected the war to give Japan. "The attack on China opens a new epoch in our history," he wrote; "it moves us from the national stage to the world stage. . . . Our Great Japan *(waga dainihon)* now becomes tied to the world, militarily, commercially, and politically—in our national actions, in our personal actions, in the material sphere, and in the spiritual sphere."[41]

To several journalists, particularly the noted Christian Uchimura Kanzō and *Jiji* editor Fukuzawa, the important issue was Japan's destined role as a leader and as a civilizer of Asia. Uchimura called the conflict a *"righteous war"* that "shall mean free government, free religion, free education, and free commerce for 600,000,000 souls that live on this side of the globe." He added, with no hint of the pacifism of his later years: "What friend of humanity shall not wish God-speed to Japan and her cause?"[42] Fukuzawa predicted happily in an August editorial that Japan was about to become an Asian England, where "if you are not British, it is bad; if you do not speak English, it is unfortunate; where non-English clothes are not worn, and if the food is not English it is not tasty." Japan, he said, had become "the leading civilization of the East," a nation destined to fight for the progress of the entire hemisphere. "No matter what the conditions, no matter what the difficulties," he added, "all forty million of us will pledge ourselves, without a single step backward, to win." And then he reiterated his June pledge to contribute personally, and generously, to the nation's military expenses.[43]

Fukuzawa's paper also called on people to set aside partisanship during the war and to discontinue their tendency to criticize cabinet policies.[44] But that did not mean that he and his fellow editors would see eye-to-eye with officials as the war progressed. Much to the contrary. Just as in the heated weeks that preceded the declaration of war, the editors' and officials' common desire for victory cloaked but scantily their quite different understandings about how the Japanese citizens should be informed of the battlefield developments. War always produces censorship, and this one was no exception. On August 1, the day that hostilities officially opened, the authorities issued emergency regulations for the journalists. The provisions of Article 22 of the press code forbidding news about troop movements, military secrets, and military strategies were to be carefully followed. War correspondents would be allowed to go to the front but only under the supervision of a high-ranking military officer. And, most significantly, "when a magazine, newspaper, or similar publication desires to publish material about military or diplomatic events, it shall submit a draft to the authorities and receive permission before publishing."[45] Responsibility for the inspection of articles was given to the Home Minister, and punishment was set at a month to two years in jail, with fines ranging from twenty to three hundred yen. The emergency provisions were replaced on September 13 with a regular military law that transferred responsibility for censorship to the war and navy ministers.[46]

None of the papers disputed the government's right to control news that might assist the the enemy or make prosecution of the war more difficult, but there was a great deal of complaining about the interpretation of what should be kept secret and the manner in which censorship was enforced. Battle reports were sharply edited or even suppressed completely on numerous occasions, sometimes when there was no apparent reason for secrecy, and most of the Tokyo editors were called in by the authorities for questioning at one time or another.[47] Wartime controls accounted for the fact that suspensions soared by nearly two-thirds in 1894, to a record 140.[48] *Yorozu* wrote in October about "the artificial barriers erected by the official red-tapism" that kept people from knowing what was going on.[49] A case in point was the censors' refusal to release information about Japan's dealings with the now-compliant Korean cabinet, headed by the Taewongun.[50] Although Seoul signed an agreement on August 26, promising to assist Japanese troops in maintaining Korean "independence" from China, no reports were allowed in the Japanese newspapers until September 12.[51]

Most galling of all, for the journalists, was the inconsistency of the censorship, the way some papers would be prohibited from printing while others would be allowed to go ahead with the same item, or the way officials would change their minds from time to time. *Tōkyō Nichi Nichi* complained at one point in the war about "directionless" *(hōshin no nai)* censorship policies that allowed "various foreign-language newspapers in Japan" to publish "with impunity" items that had been kept out of the Japanese-language press. In some cases, censors would decide that a certain story was a "military secret" several days after it had been published elsewhere "and the Tokyo papers alone would be prohibited from printing." The *Nichi Nichi* writer declared that the whole prepublication censorship process had "rendered editors unnecessary," then implored the cabinet to "establish a consistent policy and determine precisely what constitutes 'military secrets.' "[52]

The frustrations over censorship never ended, but neither did they become a major problem in this war, because while they slowed information down and prevented occasional items from reaching the readers, the timing and nature of the war assured that more actual news would be published than ever before in Japan and that press control would remain a relatively peripheral issue. The press, after all, had but recently entered its "news era"; so reporters' prerogatives and the "people's right to know" were not sufficiently established even in the minds of the journalists to propel a wholesale questioning of censorship policies. Moreover, the war's developments were so favorable to Japan as to render sharp disputes between reporters and authorities generally unnecessary. Thus, the big story in the newspaper history of 1894–1895 was not press control but the solidification of the role of news as the core of Japanese journalism.

Papers across the country exerted unprecedented efforts to get the story of what was happening in Korea and China to their readers. Some sixty-six papers sent correspondents either to the army headquarters in Hiroshima or to the continent to cover the war, often under excruciating conditions. Tokutomi's Min'yūsha used all of thirty men to report on the war;[53] *Asahi* had more than twenty correspondents gathering, writing, and sketching its stories of battle;[54] *Yomiuri* sent four correspondents to the continent and one to Hiroshima;[55] *Tōkyō Nichi Nichi* dispatched a full dozen reporters to cover the war; and *Yūbin Hōchi* and *Ōsaka Mainichi* sent at least four each. All told, more than three hundred people were enlisted by the papers to work specifically on war coverage, at least 114 of them as correspondents, eleven of them as artists, and four as photographers.[56] Among the more prominent of those who went to the continent were the Nishimura brothers, Tenshū and Tokisuke, as well as Yokogawa Yūji and Yamamoto Tadasuke from *Asahi*, Takaki Toshita of *Ōsaka Mainichi*, Yamashita Shizumi of *Chūgoku Shimbun*, Fujino Fusajirō and Ochi Shūkichi of *Yomiuri*, Kuroda Kōshirō of *Tōkyō Nichi Nichi*, Harada Nobuyoshi of *Yūbin Hōchi*, Matsubara Iwagorō and Kunikida Doppo of *Kokumin Shimbun*, and, after the hostilities had stopped, *Kokumin*'s energetic nationalist editor, Tokutomi himself.[57]

The enthusiasm with which the battlefield reporters took up their tasks was matched only by the difficulty of their assignments. These were Japan's first regular foreign war correspondents, and the military had had no previous experience with regulating men who were not in the military yet not quite out of it either, which meant that tensions between journalists and field commanders were frequent, and procedures for handling correspondents ranged from disorganized to erratic in the early weeks.[58] And marching with the troops, especially in the rugged terrain of northern Korea, was often tortuous, as was sleeping without adequate blankets, in tents on rough soil or on shipboard, after the war stretched into the bitterly cold months of December and January. Fujino told *Yomiuri* readers that his backpack on the trek with troops to Pyongyang contained "blanket, overcoat, three or four days' worth of biscuits, dried bonito and dried cuttlefish, a satchel (with reporting equipment), oil paper, a Japanese sword, and other such items totaling around thirty pounds." "Bearing that kind of weight up the long road," he added, "was unspeakably tiring."[59]

Sanitation was a serious problem too. Reporters following the First Army in northern Korea suffered frequent and severe attacks of dysentery. *Asahi*'s Nishimura Tokisuke was sidelined in Seoul by malaria, and *Ōsaka Mainichi*'s Tsuji Shinnosuke died from bronchial problems contracted at the front.[60] Others, including Yamashita Shizumi of *Chūgoku Shimbun* and Endō Bun'ei of *Niroku*, were killed in the fighting itself.[61] Compounding the problems of terrain and health was the fact that no system yet existed within the press for compensating reporters who performed special feats or were injured, or the families of those killed in the line of duty. As a result, more than a few gave all they had to offer, only to become embittered (or have their survivors embittered) by an apparent lack of appreciation back home.[62]

One of the correspondents' most daunting challenges was the need to get news back to readers expeditiously, under conditions that defied communication. No military mail system existed until the war was well along.[63] And while a telegraph system was operative from the continent, through a Shanghai-Nagasaki underwater cable, access was difficult from the front, and transmission costs were too high for use in sending full-length newspaper reports.[64] So while terse outlines of battle results usually arrived back in Japan promptly by cable, then hit the streets through extras within hours, delivery of correspondents' personal dispatches was dependent on a combination of horseback, foot, mail, freighters, and military ships.[65] Reporters frequently would have no option but to entrust a dispatch to a soldier or officer traveling to headquarters or going home. *Asahi*'s Yokogawa reported that he sometimes would secure passage himself on ships carrying wounded soldiers, after agreeing to help load ammunition. This meant, of course, considerable confusion and inevitable delays in getting news into print. Some reports were lost en route.[66] Almost never did a correspondent's account get into the paper in less than a week after its dispatch; usually it took a good two weeks, often more than a month. On one occasion, a *Yomiuri* story about fighting in the Liaodong Peninsula came out thoroughly confused, because different segments of the article arrived at the paper on separate days and in the wrong order.[67]

The difficulties of getting stories through did not, however, check the editors' commitment to providing readers with every imaginable detail about the war effort, both at home and abroad. Indeed, the newspapers of these months contained little else. They were filled with stories of money-raising campaigns and support-the-war-rallies in Tokyo, artists' efforts to raise money for the soldiers, and the emperor's activities in the Hiroshima headquarters. They described soldiers' living conditions in the north Korean trenches, the praise French observers were heaping on the Japanese military,[68] the Chinese soldiers' treacherous behavior, the difficulty of obtaining cigarettes and alcohol, what it felt like to have "shells . . . skimming only ten meters above my head."[69] Above all the dispatches waxed eloquent about the bravery of his majesty's loyal battlefield servants.

It was the stories in this last category, the detailed accounts of the grime and grit of life at the front, that readers cherished most, because they gave the war its flavor and tone. Osaka readers had been thrilled to read factual accounts of victory at Pyongyang on September 17, a day after the battle. But what really pushed up the *Asahi* circulation was Ogawa Jōmeyō's lengthy "war correspondent's diary" *(jūgun nikki)*, which made the Pyongyang fighting concrete, even though it did not appear in the paper until November, more than a month and a half after the pivotal battle. Reading its accounts of "exhausted, thirsty soldiers who descended to the rivers and ditches, drank heavily of the filthy water and were felled by an epidemic," subscribers began actually to identify with their compatriots. Ogawa wrote in first person, explaining his own bout with dysentery and how it felt when famished troops had to defeat not only the Chinese but high fevers and diarrhea.[70] Similarly, when Matsubara Iwagorō joined a cavalry patrol and rode behind enemy lines, his *Kokumin Shimbun* descriptions of the danger and the enemy's situation drew thousands of readers eager for drama as much as for knowledge of how their sons and friends in the military camps were living.[71] A typical *Yomiuri* report by Ochi Shūkichi provided details about the "wickedness and cruelty" *(zangyaku budō)* of Chinese soldiers—"in contrast to the loyalty and bravery *(chūyū)* of our troops."[72] And in late January, Yokogawa managed to get himself aboard a torpedo boat in China's Weihaiwei Bay, from where he wrote a vivid participant's account of that crucial battle, which consumed an unprecedented fourteen columns when it finally reached *Tōkyō Asahi* in mid-February.[73]

It was not enough, however, for these reports to be vivid and detailed; they also had to be nationalistic in tone. Seeing no need to restrain either their patriotism or their commercial instincts, editors employed every imaginable device to help Japan win the war. And more often than not, the articles they printed exuded one of three attitudes: contempt for the Chinese enemy, respect for the valor of Japan's own troops, or a deep belief in the righteousness of Japan's cause. The journalists sneered, for example, at the first Chinese war prisoners, who arrived in Japan in October. "If that's what the Chinese soldiers are like, I could kill a couple of them myself," a reporter quoted a female onlooker as saying, then added: "This is

true. They would be no match even for the women of our country."
Another suggested cutting off the Chinese queues and selling them
to wig makers, "though Japanese women might, of course, object to
wearing wigs made from the hair of *tombikan* (pigtails)."[74] In a similar vein, *Yūbin Hōchi* sponsored contests for songs that would
"arouse feelings of hatred against our national enemy."[75]

The contrasting valor of Japan's own troops was detailed in
every conceivable journalistic genre. Many of the papers turned
their popular poetry sections over to verses praising the soldiers'
exploits. They also serialized novels by famous writers about troop
bravery. Izumi Kyōka, for example, provided *Yomiuri* readers with
the story of Nogawa Kiyozumi, who dies in battle, refusing to give
up his sword to a sympathetic fellow soldier lest, in doing so, he
sully his "duty as a military man."[76] The popular novelist Kunikida
took employment as a navy correspondent for *Kokumin Shimbun*
and turned out patriotic prose that, in Keene's words, overflowed
"with a childish enthusiasm and patriotism."[77] And Emi Suiin wrote
popular war novels for *Chūō Shimbun* as a means of "giving my all
for the nation, with a pen instead of a sword."[78]

The papers also ran endless reportorial accounts of the
exploits of battle heroes: Matsuzaki Naoomi, the war's first battlefield casualty, who supposedly continued fighting even after he had
been shot; Shirakami Genjirō, the bugler, who, fellows said, still
had his instrument at his lips when rescuers found his corpse;
Harada Jūkichi who scaled a wall and opened the gates for his
fellow troops at Pyongyang; an anonymous sailor who died at the
battle of Weihaiwei, urging his comrades to continue the attack.
"Of the countless soldiers who died in battle, some received more
recognition than others," recalled Ubukata; these famous ones "appeared in all of the imaginable media: the newspapers, the magazines, the picture card shows, and the dramas. Their names were
everywhere."[79]

By contrast, when the Japanese soldiers carried out a massacre
following their victory at Port Arthur in November, "firing and
slashing" with "unbounded joy" and leaving behind "mountainous
piles" of "bodies of Chinese men and women,"[80] the Japanese press
was restrained. Most papers reported on the heavy killing but obscured the outrages against civilians, laying any suggestions of improper shootings down to revenge for Chinese atrocities and confusion caused by the Chinese soldiers themselves, who allegedly
disguised themselves in civilian garb. The Japanese papers also
wrote a good deal, and quite candidly, about many of the difficulties

the troops encountered: the lack of socks, food, blankets, or fire-
wood, confusion in lines of command, anti-Japanese acts by Korean
civilians. But these reports were laced with the rhetoric of gal-
lantry, of patriots overcoming odds, so that implied criticisms were
lost on readers.

And the editorials and articles acclaiming the glories and
opportunities of Japan's cause itself, along with the dedication of
the citizens who were supporting it, appeared endlessly. *Yorozu* ran
a typical mid-October report on people who were pledging private
contributions to uphold the "heroic Yamato spirit."[81] *Tōkyō Nichi
Nichi* reported at length on the work of patriotic dramatists, particularly its own former editor, Fukuchi Gen'ichirō, who prepared a
kabuki play about the Sino-Japanese War that put the venerable
Ichikawa Danjūrō the Ninth in sailor suits and had gunpowder
going off onstage at the Kabukiza.[82] *Jiji* gave multiple columns in
mid-December to Tokyo's "first victory rally," explaining how each
city household earlier "had hoisted the national flag on every report
of a victory" and how Tokyo's citizens had decided, now that victory was assured, to come together "as a single body . . . to express
thanks for the army's and navy's distinguished services and offer an
imperial *banzai.*"[83]

At the heart of many articles about the rightness of the war
was a growing sense of just how much the military campaigns had
changed Japan's place in the world—and what opportunities they
offered for national profit. The word "Japanese," said Tokutomi at
Kokumin Shimbun, "now signifies honor, glory, courage, triumph,
and victory. Before we did not know ourselves and the world did
not yet know us. But now that we have tested our strength, we
know ourselves and we are known by the world. Moreover, we
know that we are known by the world!" War had become a "spiritual deliverance," he said, its "true meaning" found in the fact that
Japan's people had shown "a patriotic spirit that is unsurpassed in
the world," that they had sacrificed and won.[84] That this new
renown might be accompanied by material profit also occurred
more than once to the editors at *Yomiuri,* who noted as early as
December that the peace settlement ought to include both territory
and an indemnity designed to spur on the Japanese economy. "If we
do not extend our commercial rights and assure long-term profits,
our imperial land will have no right to express satisfaction," said a
January editorial. And what would assure the long-term profits?
"Taking land and obtaining money."[85]

There is no question that the editors were deeply sincere in these expressions of patriotism: national strength was a cause of long standing; calls for continental expansion had attracted many journalists for almost two decades. But it did not hurt that stories of battle victories also were useful in attracting new readers. For that reason, most of the editors went to every length not just to publish but to sell their stories and paeans. War coverage was expensive, the idea of making profits had become respectable, and everyday citizens were more eager than ever to buy the papers; so the editors competed vigorously for sales. They put out unprecedented numbers of extras (*gogai*), "giving birth to salespeople who specialized in extras" (*gogai senmon no uriko*) in Tokyo,[86] and simply attempting to attract increased readerships in Osaka, which had a long tradition of distributing extras without charge. *Ōsaka Asahi*, perhaps the most entrepreneurial of all the papers, put out no fewer than 146 extras in the eight and a half months of the war—nearly two every three days.[87]

They also made their pages more lively, with sketches, black borders, bolder type, cartoons, and even occasional headlines. The ranks of war correspondents included eleven artists, among them the *Kokumin*'s famous Kubota Beisen,[88] and four photographers, whose work served as source material for sketchers back in the home office. And editors broke up the once-gray editorial space often now with these men's dramatic sketches of saluting soldiers, battlefield fires, and battlefield maps.[89] They also ran lively cartoons, designed to inspire hatred of the enemy and respect for Japan's own troops even while boosting sales. The 1995 New Year issue of *Jiji*, for example, included large editorial cartoons on pages two and three, one of a Japanese citizen standing over a Chinese soldier and giving a "great imperial banzai," the other of the Japanese flag flying over several bowing Chinese in Beijing. Half of page five was given to a cartoon labeled "crisis," depicting a huge air balloon falling from the sky with desperate Chinese inside. And in mid-February, the paper ran a page one cartoon showing four frowning Chinese faces topped off by queues forming the figures 1895. The caption read, "Not a Very Happy New Year."[90]

Because headlines still were not used for most articles, the formats would have appeared dull even yet to a twentieth-century reader. But by the standards of Japanese journalism until then, they had become lively. Entire stories might be set in heavy, large type if the news was exceptional. Headlines were used on occasion, to call attention to a particularly important item, and it became customary to highlight individual words and phrases by printing them in darker, larger characters. The result often was more cluttered than spirited—but it showed a new commitment to weighing news and attracting readers by visual devices. *Yūbin Hōchi* made perhaps the most dramatic changes in format, announcing four months into the war, on November 26, 1894, that it was becoming a "high-class illustrated newspaper" *(kōtō naru eiri shimbun)* that would hew an independent, middle road between the old *ōshimbun* and *koshimbun.*[91] But all of the papers followed a similar course, setting editing off in a livelier direction that would render the unrelieved grayness of the political years unsalable forever.

DAMNING THE PEACE

It may have seemed strange for papers such as *Kokumin* to be talking about victory as an accomplished fact already in early December, so soon after the war began, but in fact the nature of the fighting was even more striking than Tokutomi's optimism suggested. The war indeed had been won. It had gone so disastrously for China that Li Hongzhang, China's preeminent statesman, had asked the British and Americans to intervene for peace by September and had proposed a peace settlement, with Japan as victor, in November. Japan, not eager to halt the hostilities while victories were coming so easily, deferred, saying that only full negotiations could bring the war to an end, then sent China's initial plenipotentiaries back home and refused to accept anyone of a status lower than Li himself as head of the negotiating team. The result was that when Li reached Shimonoseki to negotiate in mid-March, he encountered a public euphoric over victory, enthralled with the prospects of an immensely profitable peace settlement, though disappointed that Itō had not let Japan's forces "march right into Beijing, as Bismarck did into Paris."[92] Only when Li was wounded in Shimonoseki by an ultranationalist gunman did an embarrassed public calm down.

The mood made negotiations difficult. While all agreed that Japan would come away with major gains, there was uncertainty over the specifics, particularly over what kind of balance could be struck between a public that wanted a large indemnity and a significant continental land acquisition, and foreign powers such as Russia who were determined to keep Japan from taking "too much." In particular, there was the question of Liaodong, the peninsula northwest of Korea, that was to trigger so much East Asian animosity over the next fifty years. Itō and Mutsu were sure that some of the Western powers would oppose its cession, but they also knew that a raging public was determined to have it.

There was, after all, no place more important symbolically to the Japanese. It was there that a good deal of the Japanese blood had been spilled; and it was a part of China proper. In early April, *Kokumin*'s Tokutomi went to Liaodong personally, to see firsthand the land for which his compatriots had fought. He reported that "as I traveled about and realized that this was our new territory, I felt a truly great thrill and satisfaction." And on preparing to leave, he picked up a handkerchief of gravel from the beach at Port Arthur, a souvenir of territory that, at least for a moment, belonged to his homeland.[93] Such was the national feeling about the peninsula. As Mutsu recalled:

> It was a time when the entire nation seemed delirious with victory, when ambitious and vain hopes ran at a fever pitch. Imagine how chagrined the public would have felt if the treaty had omitted that one clause relating to the cession of the Liaodong peninsula, an area taken at the cost of so much blood! The nation's feelings might well have run beyond chagrin; quite possibly, the prevailing spirit of the moment would have prohibited the implementation of such a treaty.

He feared that a failure to secure Liaodong would produce a "domestic reaction of such scope and intensity that it would have been far more menacing than any conceivable international incident."[94]

And when the peace was signed on April 17, it included most of what the people wanted: independence for Korea, a commercial treaty granting Japan four new Chinese treaty ports and navigation rights on the Yangtze River; the right to occupy Weihaiwei until China had met all of the treaty's terms; a 200 million tael (about 350 million yen) indemnity, and the cession to Japan of Taiwan, the Pescadores, and the Liaodong Peninsula. Many critics of the government were not satisfied even with all this, feeling that Japan should have insisted on more of Manchuria and a larger indemnity, and they said so in print, only to have their papers suspended for several days.[95] But the general public tone was one of exaltation. Japan had received most of what it sought, and the agreement had made it the first imperial power in Asia.

The exhilaration soured a week later, however, when news appeared in the press that Russia, supported by France and Germany, had raised official questions about the treaty. On April 21,

Ōsaka Asahi informed its readers of Reuters accounts that Russia would oppose the cession of certain Chinese lands.[96] *Niroku* published reports three days later of rumors that "Germany, France, and Russia have agreed on united action to protect their interests in the Orient"—and warned two days after that that France and German politicians should not "follow such a stupid course," since "the only one to benefit from it will be Russia."[97] The warnings were moot, however, because by then the three powers already had informed Japan officially that the "advisable" course of action would be to return Liaodong to China, lest East Asian stability be threatened. The real reason for this Tripartite Intervention was transparent: Russia had its own designs on the region and did not want a strong Japan there. But the reason was irrelevant as far as Mutsu and Itō were concerned. The possibility of armed Russian intervention in the East was real, they thought, so on May 5 they agreed to give up Liaodong in return for an additional thirty million taels in indemnity.

The officials tried to keep their decision quiet, but rumors spread immediately, speeded along by reports such as those in *Niroku,* and when it finally was made official on May 14, the result was an explosion of public and journalistic indignation. "Just when the country was drunk with victory, there came the Tripartite Intervention," said one observer. "Our shop's old Dr. Hōgō, said to me, 'The Tripartite Intervention is like their complaining to us, 'Hey, you Japs, you've been too selfish.' . . . We were awakened from the sweet dreams of being conquerors."[98] Mutsu's fears of a public outcry, it turned out, had been no exaggeration; what he had called a "jingoistic mood" just weeks before turned angry. And the press led the way, in a month of bitter denunciations by journalists and harsh crackdowns by authorities. Indeed, the sense of unity that had marked the eight months of fighting was shattered now with a speed that suggested that the incriminations of the early Diet years were more "normal" than the unity was.

Tōkyō Nichi Nichi departed from its standard gray format and announced the return of Liaodong in huge black type.[99] *Nihon* reported the official capitulation under the declaration: "What living soul can read this without weeping?"[100] *Ōsaka Asahi*, which used almost the same expression on May 14,[101] began its coverage the next day with the headline "Whole nation in mourning" *(kyokoku kyosō).*[102] The people, said Mutsu, "suddenly gave vent to all of the feelings of irritation and discontent. . . . Soon the air was filled with charges that the fruits of victory gained on the battlefields had now been lost at the negotiating table."[103] Nearly every paper joined the outcry, lambasting the cabinet for weakness, decrying Japan's loss of face, expressing resentment of the Western imperialists, and declaring that Japan never again would let itself be put in such a position.

Akiyama Teisuke's *Niroku* was especially harsh in its attacks on government ineptitude. After being released in early May from its third suspension in a month, its editorialist asked sarcastically why the authorities had been so quick to throttle it: "Is it because our errant reporting has touched on the limits of our government machinery? Or is it because the major diplomatic policies of our officials are not fixed?"[104] The next day the paper criticized the government for secrecy that "made it impossible for newspapers to carry out their responsibilities"—and received another suspension. And three weeks later it said that three things were necessary for Japan to avoid similar diplomatic embarrassments in the future: "Barriers between the emperor and his people must be removed, responsible cabinets must be established, and the people's rights must be solidified."[105] The fault, in other words, lay in unprincipled leadership that ignored the popular will.

Loss of face and resentment of the Western powers fueled many of the writers, especially at the superpatriotic *Nihon*. Kuga Katsunan asked in a late-May editorial: "What happens to the *honor* of a country that listens to the demands of a third country about the needs of the defeated nation, then gives in and returns the land that it already has divided, even as it is in the process of petitioning the emperor to ratify the acquisition?"[106] Earlier, *Nihon* already had attacked the Russians repeatedly for the hypocrisy of their alleged "secret" agreements with China. And Miyake Setsurei added on May 15: "Not since feudal days has our nation been covered with such disgrace. It is hard even to imagine a people so rich in patriotism being taken in this way by foreigners."[107] A West that had served as a model to many of these journalists had robbed Japan of what they thought it rightly deserved; illusions had been replaced by cynicism and anger.

The most emotional, most significant editorials in the long run talked defiantly of the future and what Japan must do to avoid being placed in such a position again. Miyake continued the May 15 editorial by calling on his fellow citizens to wait for the day when Japan would be able to stand up to the world.

> If we want to start a war in Asia, we must consider, of course, the strength of the West. To muster the necessary military strength, we have to have resolution too. . . . If we want to defeat China, we must

have resolution sufficient to defeat powers greater than China. . . . One's pride often is crushed, if not in one situation then in another. Having been crushed now, we will have our chance to succeed another day.

Two weeks later, *Niroku* urged: "Fellow Japanese! Do not be discouraged! Do not despair!" The day would come, it said, when Japan would "fully utilize its national mission as a world leader."[108] *Kokumin*'s Tokutomi, who declared himself "vexed beyond tears" by the Tripartite Intervention, wrote a July editorial arguing that the only way for Japan to recover its national honor was to develop military strength sufficient to lead other societies and keep the peace in Asia.[109] This was something of a shift for Tokutomi, who had opposed militarism in earlier years, but as he himself said: "It is no exaggeration to say that the retrocession of Liaodong dominated the rest of my life. After hearing about it, I became almost a different person psychologically. Say what you will, it happened because we were not strong enough."[110] Even *Tōkyō Nichi Nichi*, which typically had maintained a more moderate tone throughout the spring, responded to the crisis with an editorial asserting that the root cause of the intervention lay in Japan's military weakness: "Would a nation sacrifice its friends and loved ones to defend its sovereign rights and interests? That nation must understand that the will to defend rights and interests has to be grounded, above all, in military preparedness."[111]

This wave of vituperation prompted a predictable response from the government: suspensions on an unprecedented scale. Authorities, as we have seen, had been straining every muscle for a year now to keep the press from undermining what they regarded as the rational and orderly prosecution of foreign affairs, suspending even moderate papers such as *Nichi Nichi*, censoring reams of news from the front, and prompting *Yorozu* to retort at one point: "Does the government question our patriotism!"[112] Even after the hostilities ended, the Home Ministry suspended several papers whose emotional demands were seen as obstructing the negotiating process. But most of these suspensions had been occasional and specific, levied against individual papers for individual violations. Now they came in a wave. And they came quickly.

It would appear, in fact, that the officials, worried about the impact inflamed opinion could have on the peace process, already had thought through plans for a crackdown, because on May 15, just a day after the imperial announcement of the final treaty settlement, they acted in wholesale fashion, shutting down several of the most influential critics. *Mainichi Shimbun, Ōsaka Asahi,* and *Nihon* all were suspended until the twenty-sixth,[113] giving the authorities ten days' respite from the most incisive and influential of its critics. *Niroku* received a similar punishment, then was halted again on May 31 for "disturbing the peace"—its fifth suspension since the end of the war.[114] In all, more than thirty papers were suspended in these weeks, including *Kokumin, Yūbin Hōchi, Mezamashi, Jiyū,* and *Kokkai.*

The most vociferous of the papers, *Nihon,* was shut down a staggering twenty-two times for a total of 131 days during the Sino-Japanese War months, with the most intense suppression resulting from its handling of the Tripartite Intervention.[115] Typically, when it was allowed to resume publication on May 27, after ten days on the sidelines, it led the next issue off with an explanation of the *hakkō teishi* ruling and an apology for inconveniencing its readers, then, remorseless, renewed its attack on the government's ineptitude—and received another full week's suspension, until June 3.[116] On June 4, it took Liaodong up again, still unbowed, in a strong lead editorial. By now, the public fever had cooled somewhat, however, and Kuga and his colleagues were allowed to continue publishing, since the officials did not want to turn *Nihon* into a martyr. In all, Japanese newspapers were handed 222 suspensions between March and December 1895—almost a third of the total *hakkō teishi* penalties meted out across the entire decade of the 1890s.[117] It was little wonder that Kuga wrote about this period:

> A newspaper is a tool; to be deprived of one's tools is agonizing. A newspaper is a job; to have one's work halted also is agonizing. A suspension order hurts in two ways: it takes away one's freedom and destroys one's property. And there is no recourse. Can one deny that Article 19 of the current newspaper law gives officials an antiquated, special right to behead, to banish, or to dismiss? Punishment that may be, but not a punishment appropriate to the present age.[118]

The antitreaty furor subsided with the coming of summer, but not because the press had been cowed. Time had cooled passions and provided new foci for journalists and officials. But as the whole episode made clear, neither rising nationalism nor increased profitability would make the press-government relationship easy. *"Gashin shōtan"* (perseverance and determination) was the phrase of choice when editors talked about foreign relations that spring; they insisted that privation and persistence now would lay a foundation for revenge later. The phrase said as much, however, about their approach to editing as it did about foreign affairs.

A CHANGED PRESS

On rare occasions institutions, like individuals, encounter experiences that change their entire way of looking at themselves and the world. The Sino-Japanese War was that kind of episode for Japan's press. Not only was it a bigger, more intense event than anything the journalists ever had covered, it was, for twelve hurried months, so all-consuming that it redefined the very meaning of journalism for most of the country's leading editors. If the immediate prewar years had unleashed the forces of populism and profit, the war months made the editors strain so hard at getting colorful news to their readers quickly that, when it all was over, it was as if they never had known any other approach to newspapering. At least three attitudes had become central to Japan's journalists by the spring of 1895—the idea that news lay at the core of journalism, a commitment to Japan's expanding international mission, and a desire to satisfy the demands of readers—all of them attitudes that would remain dominant for decades to come.

As we saw in the last chapter, the role of news in the journalistic mix already had increased significantly in the prewar years, under the influence of Fukuzawa's *Jiji*, Murayama's *Asahi*, and Kuroiwa's *Yorozu*. Now, the centrality of news became fixed. Readers may have enjoyed the jingoistic editorials, but it was reportage that they desired most: news of victories, accounts of how the troops were living and dying, information about Japan's changing international stance. And they wanted it as quickly as possible. That was why more than sixty papers felt it necessary to send correspondents to headquarters or to the continent. As the war progressed, Nishida tells us, the gap between papers with enough capital to provide solid reporting and those that had to cut corners widened significantly. The good ones added pages, increased the number of editions, put out frequent extras, and overwhelmed their opposition with lively, detailed reporting.[119] Even the best-endowed papers staggered under the heavy costs of supporting battlefront correspondents and printing extras, and those without the capital to keep pace were hurt even more.[120] Thus, while the oldtime opinion-shaping leaders such as *Tōkyō Nichi Nichi* and *Yūbin Hōchi* may have held their own in circulation, it was the news-oriented newcomers that soared. Even the opinionated *Kokumin Shimbun* passed the oldtimers in readership, with its intense use of war correspondents, while *Yorozu* and *Ōsaka Asahi* tripled and quadrupled their readerships.[121] By the end of this war, says Oka Mitsuo, even the "opinion-oriented (*genron shūshinshugi*) papers had become believers in the centrality of reporting (*hōdō chūshinshugi*)."[122]

The war also stimulated a newly aggressive brand of nationalism that went beyond the old eagerness to serve and publicize the nation and demanded that Japan take its "rightful" place, by force if necessary, on the world stage. These years did not give birth to aggressive nationalism; we already have seen the rise of chauvinist rhetoric during the treaty debates of the late 1880s and early 1890s. But the tone and content of patriotism changed in these months. Journalists had talked about Nihon and Nihonjin (Japan and the Japanese) in earlier years, and terms such as *kokumin* (citizen) and *kokutai* (national polity) had showed up in their writings with increasing frequency during the 1880s, but seldom had they talked about an active Japanese role in the world. That was what changed with this war; the phrase *waga teikoku* (our empire) appeared in some articles now, along with *waga kuni* (our country), *dainihon* (great Japan), and the aggressive *gashin shōtan*. Exaltations in Japan's achievements as an international leader and talk of territorial possibilities had, in other words, replaced the more modest earlier discussions of how to make the country strong and how to gain international respect.

The new brand of patriotism did not make the journalists easier for officials to work with; if anything it made them more irascible, because writers began making sharper distinctions than ever between the "emperor's country," which they loved, and its political leadership, which they often despised. Japan and its emperor were grand, glorious, and above reproach; the politicians were venal, wishy-washy, and inept. Thus, the very act of promoting the country often inspired criticism of rulers who talked too much about moderation and compromise when they dealt with other nations. The press had become more expansionist than the cabinet. As Midoro Masaichi puts it, these months produced among Japan's journalists unified support for "a vigorous foreign policy that praised militarism and inspired patriotism."[123] Inspired by victory, emboldened by China's pliability at the peace table, then infuriated by having the fruits of victory snatched away, Japan's journalistic spokesmen crafted a new rhetoric that was imperialistic to the core. That Tokutomi, a pacifist in the 1880s, would now be "convinced that, without power, justice and morality had no value at all" says volumes about the nationalizing impact of this war.

The most important thing about the journalists' new chauvinism probably was that it was influential—and it was influential because the editors and writers were so deeply in tune with their readers. If Joseph Pulitzer and William Randolph Hearst in New York helped bring America the Spanish-American War during this same decade by "cultivating public opinion in a favorable atmosphere,"[124] Kuga, Fukuzawa, and Tokutomi did the same with the Sino-Japanese War. That they believed in aggressive action is indisputable, but so is the fact that their ideas were shared by a rising populace at least as eager for a show of national force as they were, a populace chomping to buy any paper that would provide speedy, newsy stories about Japan's rising strength.

Few results of the Sino-Japanese War were more crucial, at least in the world of journalism, than this continued strengthening of the press-people ties. People turned immediately to the papers for news of what was going on and for explanations of what it all meant. "We people in the provinces could not comprehend why this war had occurred until we learned about it in detail by reading the newspapers," said Ubukata.[125] The people also sought the papers for affirmations of their changing views of the world, of the rightness of Japan's cause, the injustice of Chinese attempts to control Korea, the sheer hypocrisy of Russia's pressures after the war. And the editors tailored their papers as never before to the readers' desires, with their poetry and song contests and their sales promotions, with patriotic novels, with extras and supplements—with a popular style of journalism, in short, that made the ōshimbun-koshimbun gulf a dream from the past.[126]

This symbiosis produced remarkable jumps in circulation for the most patriotic papers. The nation's eight largest newspapers before the war increased their readership by more than 25 percent in 1894 and 1895, to an average daily circulation of more than 50,000 each.[127] Ōsaka Asahi rose to a new peak of 95,000 daily readers during 1894; its Tokyo sister paper increased from 43,000 to nearly 54,000; Yorozu doubled its readership to more than 66,000 a day; and Kokumin Shimbun, which had not been among the largest dozen in 1893 before the war, had become the seventh largest at the end of the conflict, with a daily circulation of more than 22,000.[128]

This growing closeness between the papers and their readers touched off something of a circular process. Producing news and formats good enough to satisfy readerships of 50,000 or 100,000 demanded capital investments unimaginable a decade and a half before: money for larger staffs and correspondents' expenses, for better presses and physical plants, for telegraph transmission and telephones, for more efficient delivery methods. And those capital investments in turn demanded an ever more attractive product that would keep the readers coming back and keep the ledger sheet in the black. The editors thus came to need reader support as much as readers needed their own daily dose of information and entertainment. The symbiosis thus created would produce Japan's first truly mass newspapers in the next few years—and make the press' political and social impact greater than ever.

CHAPTER 8

BUILDING A MASS BASE

1895 to 1903

> Printers . . . like the clergy, live by
> the zeal they can kindle, and the schisms
> they can create.
>
> *Thomas Jefferson, 1801*[1]

> Of what good are novels to the country?
> . . . Newspaper editors use them to capture
> the fancies of mindless men and women and
> thus to increase sales, without considering
> how they corrupt the moral order.
>
> Nihon *correspondent, July 1898*[2]

Wars produce unanticipated consequences, for the winners as well as the losers. They touch nerves, change relationships, and create social forces that generals and diplomats never foresee. Certainly that was the case in Japan after 1895, at the end of the Sino-Japanese War, for the journalists as much as for the political and military leaders. Any editor who expected the end of fighting to bring back a more relaxed style of journalism must have received a shock, because if the war months had created a maelstrom of change, the late 1890s found the press in an unstoppable typhoon, produced in roughly equal parts by the war and its settlement, by the Meiji modernizing processes, and by the growing urban population. It was a storm with a great deal of potential for innovative, profit-seeking editors, a storm destined at length to turn the country's most successful papers into mass mediums, a storm strong enough and of sufficient duration to render a final, irrevocable judgment on the long struggle over whether pride of journalistic place would go to the essayists and editorialists or to the reporters and feature writers. The victory, of course, went to the latter.

READERS AT THE TURN OF THE CENTURY

An 1899 *Mainichi Shimbun* article calling the Sino-Japanese War "a forerunner of today's labor problems"[3] suggested the kind of change that had gripped Japan's cities by the end of the 1800s. The entire quarter of a century prior to the war had produced a mere fifteen labor disputes in Tokyo, and that was precisely the number that gripped Japan in 1899 alone.[4] What had happened is too complex a story for an adequate telling here, but, as the *Mainichi* writer suggested, both the kinds of people who lived in the cities and the attitudes they brought to their workplaces had undergone a fundamental shift by the turn of the century. There were more of them than ever before; they had more (and usually better) schools; jobs were more plentiful if not more humane; and the gap between rich and poor was increasing.

Among the country's most important changes in these years was the continuing transformation of the urban economy. The indemnity from the Sino-Japanese War had pumped an immense 360 million yen into the Japanese coffers (or 4.5 times the entire national budget the year before the war), and much of it was used to boost the steel and shipping industries.[5] Trade rose rapidly as a result, with exports jumping from less than 100 million yen in 1892 to nearly 300 million a decade later, while imports grew from about 75 million to more than 300 million in the same period.[6] And the goods traded reflected a modernizing, industrializing society, as the raw materials brought into Japan spiraled from a minuscule 3.5 percent of all imports at the beginning of the 1880s to nearly a quarter at the turn of the century, while the proportion of finished goods imported dropped in the same period from roughly half to a third. And precisely the reverse occurred in exports—a sign of the growth of industries that needed raw materials from abroad to make their products.[7] Little wonder then that four out of every five Japanese factories operating in 1902 had been formed since the Sino-Japanese War,[8] or that the income produced by the industrial sector nationwide grew by more than 50 percent in the last half of the 1890s, to more than 1.5 billion yen a year.[9]

All this meant that, as new industries arose and old ones expanded, more jobs were created, the demand for laborers soared,[10] and people came to the cities in even greater numbers than in the earlier decades, moving more often than not into poverty-stricken slums where conditions were at least as bad as those they had known in the provinces and finding themselves awash and disconnected, without either the familiar customs or the human support networks of the old village. Tokyo alone had 24,961 industrial wage workers by 1896, a figure that would grow by more than four thousand a year during the next two decades.[11] And living alongside them by the beginning of the century were hundreds of thousands of rickshaw pullers, streetcar workers, builders, shop apprentices, bar keepers, custodians, restaurant waiters, umbrella makers, fish hawkers, and newspaper deliverers: more than half of them immigrants from the countryside,[12] and most of them barely able to make ends meet on salaries that averaged a mere 16.25 yen a month for a family of three.[13] These new residents had not yet turned Japan into an urbanized country; indeed, as late as 1920, two-thirds of all Japanese still lived in towns and villages of fewer than 10,000.[14] Their increasing numbers did mean, however, that low-city Tokyo and industrialized Osaka were overflowing by the late 1890s with new peoples, new values, new problems, and new markets.

Of particular importance to the press was the fact that more and more of these new urbanites were able to read. We already have noted the significant growth of literacy before the Sino-Japanese War; now, according to all observers, it grew even more rapidly. Fees for the four years of elementary school were abolished in 1898, and attendance rates increased. Nationwide, the percentage of males able to read went from 67 in 1891 to nearly 94 a decade later, and the growth for females was even more dramatic: from 32 to 82 percent. And in Tokyo, where rates had lagged behind the rest of the country throughout the first half of the Meiji era, literacy jumped to nearly 80 percent for women and more than 86 percent for men.[15] Across the country, there were more than a million students in Japan's schools by 1901,[16] and by 1905 more than 95 percent of school-aged girls and boys were in the classroom on a regular basis—compared to just over 50 percent in the early 1890s. And that was true in Tokyo, as well as elsewhere.[17] The statistics grow tedious, but the point behind them is that the forces of modernization, intensified by the Sino-Japanese War, had produced a mass of people who, while hardly ready to pick up a Nishimura Shigeki tome or even a Dickens translation, were increasingly eager to lay their hands on lively, simply written reading materials.

What was more, this new urban working class was experiencing the kinds of problems and struggles in the late 1890s that were sure to make them interested in the news of their world. Low wages, long and tedious work days, and wretched living conditions undermined whatever illusions they had had about benevolent employers. And officials usually seemed less a help than a part of the problem. An 1896 national business tax, for example, based not on profits but on a complex set of factors such as company sales and assets, riled up the workers almost as much as it did the owners; they, after all, would have to pay the higher prices. So did new indirect taxes in the late 1890s on everything from camphor and drugs to tobacco and cloth. The fact that the proportion of government revenues that came from land taxes dropped from 60.6 percent in 1890 to 32.5 percent at the end of the decade[18] may have made for greater equity but it did not sit any better with the city folk, from whom so much of the new revenues came, than did the doubling of rice prices in a mere five years. And the fact that the country was hit by a recession just as the old century ended stirred even more discontent and interest in public issues. Little wonder, given the spreading poverty and alienation, that a full 82 percent of the 7,701 workers who left textile jobs in 1900 did not bother even to give notice.[19]

It also was little wonder that the post-1895 years gave Japan its first ongoing experience with serious labor disputation. Tokyo had averaged but one significant labor struggle every two years during the early Meiji years; yet the decade after the war produced seventy-six such disputes, the largest share of them in heavy industry, printing, binding, and artisans' companies.[20] Across the nation, the same period experienced more than 150 labor struggles, involving nearly 20,000 workers, with the late 1890s bearing the brunt of the discontent.[21] The year 1897, for example, saw one dispute at the Yokosuka Naval Arsenal, three of them at the Yokohama Dock Company, and one at the Ishikawajima shipyards in Tokyo; 1898 found Tokyo locomotive engineers struggling with their employers, and 1899 brought disputes by capital machinists.[22] The workers still had not formed any permanent unions at the beginning of the new century,[23] and their disputes tended to be relatively mild, conditioned as most workers were by traditional norms against resisting authority. But the late 1890s saw what, for Japan, was an unprecedented willingness of laborers to work together against management, sometimes even in strikes and occasionally by violent means. And that meant that growing numbers of working-class citizens were eager to understand what was going on in the broader world and to communicate somehow with those who influenced what they earned, determined what taxes they paid, and drew up the rules they had to follow.

Society, says Ariyama Teruo of Seijō University, was dividing into classes by the dawn of the new century, with the former elites (including even the old *minken* crusaders) at the top and a rising city class of students and laborers far below. Members of this bottom class, most of them "estranged from the ladder of success," were more than ready to grab any new tool available to express their "indignation at society."[24] Indeed, when newspapers began inviting readers to express their views through "postcard correspondence columns" *(hagaki tōsho ran)* in 1898, the members of this new plebeian class did so in droves, because, according to the journal *Chūō Kōron*, they found in the postcards "a public platform" for the expression of views that no one outside their own families ever had seemed to care about, a stage on which they "could express personal opinions and talk openly about injustices."[25] I will have more to say about the postcard columns later; the important point here is the evidence they bore to the growth, in the wake of war with China, of a vocal, publicly attuned class of commoners ready to support newspapers or any other medium that might make life more livable. That a significant number of the Tokyo and Osaka editors responded positively, even innovatively, to this new "public" is the major press story of the period.

PLAYING TO THE MASSES

Driving most editors' daily decisions now was the question of how to make a profit. Established papers needed ever larger capital resources, first, to recover from the expenses of covering the Sino-Japanese War and, second, to meet the unending demands of state-of-the-art machinery, modern facilities, expanded coverage, and circulations now ranging upwards of 50,000 for average papers and nearing 150,000 for the largest. And the newer papers were desperate for quick investment capital, since they had not been adequately funded even before the war brought all of its new pressures.[26] This meant different things to different papers, depending on the specific audience they targeted, but for most it meant finding ways to increase circulations: speedier reporting, more interesting (though not always more accurate or consequential) news and feature stories, fewer editorials, more novels and entertainment news, sometimes wild promotion schemes, anything, in short, to make people buy the paper. *Hōchi Shimbun*, for example, created a *Hōchi* Trust and Confidence Office (Hōchi Anshinjo) in 1900 to respond to readers' needs.[27] A few editors such as *Nihon*'s Kuga Katsunan resisted popularization, but the vast majority now made reader-oriented profitability their number one goal. As Hanazono Kanesada put it: "Newspapers . . . became a paying business"—though not necessarily an independent business, since they now came under the control "of investors or advertisers" instead of censors.[28]

One outcome at most companies was a continuation of the efforts begun in the early 1890s to make their pages more appealing and to make sure readers *knew* they were appealing. While a few like *Nihon* continued generally to avoid headlines, most employed them with increasing frequency in these years, in addition to cluttering specific articles with heavier or larger type to call attention to important facts within the story. *Yorozu Chōhō* experimented in 1897–1898 with printing on red paper in order to see "if we could get large numbers of people to read it." Editor Kuroiwa Shūroku dropped the experiment after twenty-two months because the colored paper made for hard reading and led to derisive charges of "yellow *(iero)* journalism,"[29] but he did not lose his determination to use any gimmick likely to increase readership. Papers also worked to improve *furigana*, the tiny phonetic symbols printed alongside Chinese characters *(kanji)* to facilitate understanding, and *Ōsaka Asahi* developed a system in 1901 of setting *furigana* and characters in type simultaneously to speed typesetting and improve the paper's appearance.[30] Most editors increased the number of columns on page one in these years too, from the five or six that had been standard to at least seven.[31]

The papers also sought to attract readers by publishing more issues every year in the late 1890s than they had before, with all but two of Tokyo's leading dailies coming out more than six times a week by 1899, in contrast to the three hundred issues typical at the beginning of the decade. Indeed, *Yorozu, Chūō Shimbun, Yomiuri Shimbun, Nihon,* and *Jiji Shinpō* all had given up press holidays altogether by the end of the century, while only *Hōchi* and *Miyako Shimbun* still were coming out fewer than 325 times a year.[32] And *Hōchi* sought to counter its less frequent publication schedules (309 issues in 1899, for example) with catchy formats, using many sketches and breaking new ground for Japanese journalism on January 27, 1902, by beginning to print each Monday's edition in three colors (red, blue, and black); by autumn, it was printing the masthead in red or blue on most days and frequently running colored sketches and maps.[33] When one added to these innovations the increased use of flashy display ads, cartoons, and new, bordered features like *Niroku Shinpō*'s "People's Column," one found a much livelier package in 1903 than even *Hōchi* would have imagined when it brashly renounced its dull elitism a decade earlier.

That formats were not invigorated even more was due less to a lack of desire than to technological problems the Japanese language and tight budgets imposed on even the most powerful papers in these years. The rapid Marinoni cylinder press, which cost *Ōsaka Mainichi* a fifth of its total capital stock in 1893, was purchased by *Jiji* and *Hōchi* late in the 1890s and by most of the other major Tokyo papers in the next few years. *Yorozu* imported an even faster press from the German Albert firm in 1902, capable of printing 30,000 copies an hour, and the regional leader *Fukuoka Nichi Nichi Shimbun* secured its own Marinoni that year.[34] But less expensive Marinonis were not manufactured in Japan itself until the beginning of the Russo-Japanese War, meaning that the smaller papers had to struggle along with older, slower presses, and the truly modern Hoe presses used by leading American papers after the late 1800s did not arrive until *Ōsaka Mainichi* decided to buy three of them in 1921.[35]

The biggest typographical problem faced by Japan's editors—and the reason they were not more aggressive about finding funds to import Hoe presses—lay in the complicated system of Chinese characters, which made typesetting a nightmare by the standards of countries with phonetic writing systems. Even had adequate presses been financially feasible, their use would have remained problematic, because there were no typesetting machines capable of dealing with the *kanji-furigana* system until well after the end of the Meiji era. Indeed, it took large, often frenzied staffs so much time to compose type that only *Jiji* had expanded to more than ten pages per issue by the end of Meiji. The giant *Ōsaka Asahi* did not increase to eight pages until 1896, and *Yorozu*, Tokyo's circulation leader for much of the period, stayed at four pages throughout the era.[36]

To offset this size problem, all of the papers published frequent supplements to advertise special events or commemorate anniversaries, since these could be prepared and composed during less hurried postdeadline or nighttime hours. They also began the practice now of putting out multiple editions, sending early news, ads, and features off to the more distant provinces, then rushing late-breaking materials into a local edition that was printed at the last possible minute. By the beginning of the 1900s, *Jiji, Tōkyō Asahi*, and *Yorozu* all had three such editions, with a 4:00 P.M. deadline for Kyushu to the south and Tohoku to the north, a 9:00 P.M. deadline for places as far away as Osaka, and a midnight deadline for Tokyo.[37] Some also experimented with dividing the paper itself into two separately printed parts, with the latest news delivered to readers in a morning edition and features and softer materials in an evening edition. In most cases, however, the distribution system was inadequate for twice-daily deliveries; so when subscribers began complaining about getting their papers late, that system was scrapped.[38]

If editors and sales managers continued to be frustrated by technical problems in these years, they compensated with aggressive management and sales techniques. Advertising continued to grow in importance, with ads themselves produced largely by advertising agencies from the mid-1890s onward and readers encouraged to submit their own classified ads after the late 1890s. *Ōsaka Asahi*, for example, increased advertising revenue from 33,435 yen in the Sino-Japanese War year of 1894 to 118,006 yen in 1901— more than a 350 percent increase while total company revenues were not quite doubling.[39] Far and away the most successful generator of advertising revenue was *Jiji*, which not only sold more ads than any other paper but charged higher fees for them. It "overwhelmed the other papers in advertising," both by aggressive promotion and by being able to point out to advertisers that its pages reached Tokyo's most affluent, most business-oriented clientele.[40]

Even more aggressive were the efforts of most papers to sell *themselves*, to convince all those new residents of the urban whirlpool that they should become newspaper readers—and that they should read *Hōchi* (or *Yorozu*, or *Miyako*, or . . .) in particular. We already have seen how bitterly the Tokyo newspapers competed to keep *Asahi* out of their market late in the 1880s; now, a decade later, they struggled just as bitterly to outdo each other. It was not uncommon in the late 1890s for someone who had contracted to deliver, say, *Kokumin Shimbun* to the city's sales shops to snatch a rival newspaper such as *Tōkyō Asahi* from the racks and replace it with *Kokumin*, or for competing deliverymen to hide each other's carts.[41] Physical fights between deliverymen were not unheard of. In the early 1900s, *Hōchi* tried to end the chaos, for itself at least, first by establishing an exclusive delivery system in which six major dealers across the city took responsibility for distributing *Hōchi* alone to retailers, then, in 1903, by creating an extensive network of retailers under the direct control of its own managers. Other papers gradually began to follow this new model over the next dozen years, but not before a fiercely competitive mentality had become fixed in the urban press.[42]

One weapon in the sales war was pricing. Each editor struggled to balance the demands of ever-expanding costs with rates that his particular market would bear. If a paper charged too little, it undercut production revenues and profits; if it charged too much it threatened circulation. As a result, there was constant jockeying in the field of subscription and sales prices. A paper such as *Jiji* could afford to charge the city's highest monthly rates (50 *sen*) at the turn of the century, because its affluent readers attracted such high advertising revenues. *Yorozu,* by contrast, depended on a large readership among the city's poor classes and found it necessary to hold subscription rates to 24 *sen* a month and a mere one *sen* for an individual issue.[43] This effort to balance readership, product, and prices did not mean that editors accepted rivals' rates with equanimity. They competed with the passion of battlefield generals, because they knew that price was crucial in attracting readers—a fact borne out by the socialist Ōsugi Sakae's recollection that he began reading *Yorozu* in this period "merely because it was the cheapest newspaper," not because of what was in it. "Having just come from the provinces," he said, "I did not know its name, much less what kind of paper it was."[44] "Reasonable prices were extremely attractive to people in every class," says Yamamoto Taketoshi, "especially to the lower classes with meager incomes."[45] That was why the leading Tokyo papers schemed in 1896, for example, to get the city's sales shops to raise the prices on *all* their papers and thus rob the *Yorozu* of its price advantage. The shop owners could have done that, since retailers were not bound by a paper's officially stated sales price. But Kuroiwa had few peers when it came to fighting for readers. He bribed more than a hundred shopkeepers with gifts of two hundred yen each; so they continued selling *Yorozu* at a lower rate and he maintained his circulation supremacy.[46] To the end of the era, price and sales remained vital—and bitter—points of struggle among the urban papers.

The most creative attempts at attracting the cities' new readers came in a proliferation of the gimmicks, stunts, and promotion schemes that had surfaced first during the pre–Sino-Japanese War years. Some publishers, for example, sponsored contests: a competition among *Miyako* readers to determine Japan's most popular actors, another at *Yamato* for the most accomplished artists,

Yorozu drives to get readers to write the best desk mottos and esti-mate "the number of grains of unhulled rice in a half-gallon mea-sure,"[47] and an *Ōsaka Asahi* campaign to select the best amateur Nō actor. A Kuroiwa treasure hunt, which sent *Yorozu* readers dig-ging in famous temples and parks for a buried gold piece, earned a Waseda University student one thousand yen in stock and boosted attendance at popular spots right along with newspaper readership. And *Niroku*, which sprang back into existence in 1900 after a five-year lapse, sponsored lotteries, with gold tea kettles and kimono as prizes, and promoted huge labor rallies in a strikingly successful effort to win a working-class readership.[48]

One of the more socially productive schemes was the deci-sion by a number of papers in 1901 to form social and discussion clubs among their readers for altruistic purposes such as stimulat-ing the newly literate to talk about public issues and encouraging young thinkers to come up with ways to improve society.[49] *Nihon*'s group was called Nihon Seinenkai (Japan Young Men's Associa-tion), *Mainichi* formed the Speech Club or Enzetsukai, *Niroku* created the Rōdōsha Daikonshinkai (Great Laborers' Social Club), *Hōchi* the Shōka Yatoinin Shōreikai (Business Employees' Encour-agement Association), and *Yorozu* the Risōdan or Ideals Club.[50] Edi-tors touted the high-mindedness of the groups, pointing out quite accurately that a person need not subscribe to the paper to belong. But while the associations did indeed bring together people with similar aims, and while they obviously promoted productive dis-cussion and solidarity, they also had a more earthy goal. Each club, says one who has studied them in detail, "conformed in both char-acter and content with its own class of readers and was developed as a means to expand sales."[51] Profit seeking and public-spiritedness may not be mutually exclusive, but it is doubtful that the latter alone would have prompted the papers to create them.

The editors also worked tirelessly to come up with new kinds of articles and features that would attract readers. *Yomiuri*, for example, put out large commemorative issues filled with ads and feature stories for its eight thousandth issue (October 15, 1899), its nine thousandth issue (July 12, 1902), and its thirtieth anniversary (November 3, 1903). *Hōchi* ran personal advice columns on hygiene and how to handle disputes, and distributed monthly stereotype-produced collections of photographs of famous people, spectacular Chinese landscapes, and other photogenic materials. And most of the papers helped to spread a "correspondence fever" *(tōsho netsu)* between 1898 and 1900 when they invited readers to answer surveys and submit brief opinions on postcards for publication in the papers. The invitation touched a nerve among the urban working classes, providing people whose lives were circumscribed by social convention and poverty with a risk-free way to make their voices heard in public. They responded by the thousands, sometimes anonymously, sometimes with pseudonyms, sometimes using their own names. And they responded from every class, with menial workers and students sending in more letters than the businessmen and teachers did.[52] As one *Tōkyō Asahi* writer put it: "Although life has many pleasures, none brings as much enjoyment as the rare experience of having my poor piece of writing published in a newspaper."[53] Like the clubs, the postcard correspondence drives provided an important social outlet for the urban poor. They rivaled the clubs in driving circulation up too.

PUTTING NEWS AT THE CENTER

There is no denying the importance of these promotions; they enlivened the papers, fortified the commercial instincts of the journalists themselves, and played a pathbreaking role in bringing the cities' expanding working classes into Japan's public life. It would be a mistake, however, to give stunts and campaigns too much credit for the rapid growth in circulation and influence of papers like *Yorozu, Niroku, Kokumin,* and *Jiji.* These were, after all, newspapers, and though promotions made people aware of a given paper's special character or cheap price, it was the editorial product itself that in the end defined each daily and kept subscribers coming back. It is thus no exaggeration to say that the most important promotion mechanism in these years was the news column. And it was the journalists' evolving attitude toward this side of their profession—the gathering, writing, and editing of news—that more than anything else made the papers what they were in the interwar era.

These years, says Ariyama, saw a shift in the press' self-perceived center, as the "focus on political discussion *(seiron chūshin)* gave way wholly to a reporting orientation *(hōdō chūshin)."*[54] Press historian Arai Naoyuki, agreeing, notes that the papers had little choice: "They had to divest themselves of their political image, which had become an economic liability; so news became their raison d'être."[55] As never before, they began to hire people with college degrees and some particular expertise as reporters, men with knowledge of the stock exchange to write financial columns, for example, or educated women to report on family affairs. Staffs became more diverse, with *Ōsaka Mainichi* employing fifty-three people in its editorial division in 1902 to staff not only the time-honored political section, but correspondence, society, economics, features *(gakugei)*, general editing, and copy editing departments. It also maintained branch news offices in Tokyo, Kyoto, and Kōbe. And in addition to the local writers, the editorial division supervised more than 120 domestic and foreign correspondents.[56] Similarly, a 1903 sketch of the *Tōkyō Asahi* office shows the politics and economic sections occupying parallel spaces near the entrance, with the society department taking up considerably more space in the center.[57]

It was hardly surprising then, given the press' changing sense of purpose, that the front pages of the time were filled as often with tidal waves, fires, floods, earthquakes, rainstorms, volcanic eruptions, and blizzards as they were with Diet debates—and a great deal more frequently than they were with editorial comments. *Minshū* readers were more likely to be gripped by *Jiji*'s account of stranded trains, villagers who froze to death, and 209 soldiers fighting Aomori's "worst storm in thirty years"[58] than by the creation of a new party by Itō or Ōkuma. If the political development involved scandal, assassination, or intrigue, it received full coverage; if it involved complex issues or reasoned argument, its fate was less certain. Japan's press was becoming commercialized.

The only thoroughgoing holdout was *Nihon,* which continued every day, 365 days a year, to offer a loyal but gradually declining readership that oldtime, patriotic blend of opinion and analysis.[59] But even that paper had its moments of doubt. "Things grew severe after the Sino-Japanese War," said *Nihon* writer Kojima Kazuo; "even we were pressured by this force. If you did not run news, you could not make it."[60] The news that was covered varied from paper to paper. *Jiji* and *Tōkyō Asahi* emphasized economics; *Yorozu* focused on political activities; *Niroku* looked to labor and industrial affairs; *Yomiuri* concentrated on literature and the arts; and *Hōchi* worked assiduously to attract families.[61] But for nearly every paper the heart of journalism lay now in reporting and entertainment; people wanting political opinion and analysis had to turn to *Nihon* or to the magazines.

One thing this meant, quite naturally, was increasing attention to newsgathering methods. At the bigger papers, correspondents now were placed throughout the world. The enterprising Hara Kei, who became president of *Ōsaka Mainichi* in 1898, pushed not only to simplify the paper's prose and enliven its contents but to improve its international coverage. In February 1900 he established Japan's first permanent foreign correspondent system, and by 1902 the paper had no fewer than thirteen reporters stationed abroad and 111 working as correspondents at home.[62] Telephone also was used increasingly to speed reporting, especially at affluent papers like *Jiji,* and on April 24, 1897, *Tōkyō Asahi* initiated the use of carrier pigeons to scoop other papers with a detailed report of a major fire in Hachioji.[63] These years also brought increasing efforts by several papers to link up with news networks. *Ōsaka Asahi,* for example, followed *Jiji*'s lead in 1897 and became the country's second Japanese-language paper to sign a contract allowing it to use Reuters materials. Several domestic news agencies also were formed in these years, though the majority had ties to political parties or to business, which limited their usefulness to the press. Among them were the Meiji Tsūshinsha, formed in 1899 by the Liberal Party (Jiyūtō); the Nihon Denpo Tsūshinsha, created in 1901 by Mitsunaga Hoshirō with close ties to Itō's Seiyūkai; and independent Dokuritsu Tsūshinsha (1903), which concentrated on diplomatic and military news.[64] It would take another, bigger war to stimulate the next major spurt in the creation of news networks, but the growing competition of these years assured serious steps in that direction even as the new century dawned.

One of the most significant newsgathering developments at the end of the 1800s was the employment of Japan's first full-fledged women reporters. Actually, Takekoshi Takeyo had paved the way in 1890 with a three-month stint as an interviewer-writer for *Kokumin,* where she wrote that "no one in the world is better qualified for reporting than women" who have such "precise powers of observation" and an "astute ability to evaluate."[65] The English-language *Japan Gazette* also had employed Mildred Vaughan Smith —as editor—for a time in the early 1890s.[66] And there was a great deal of discussion of women's issues in the early-Meiji press as well as coverage of women stars in the *jiyū minken* movement.[67] But it was not until profit-seeking editors began seeking broader markets after the Sino-Japanese War that women were able seriously to breach the male journalistic domain.

The pioneer was Hani (*née* Matsuoka) Motoko,[68] who went to work in 1898 for *Hōchi.* A graduate of the first class at Tokyo Women's Normal School in Ochanomizu and an employee and protégé of the pathbreaking woman physician Yoshioka Yayoi, Hani first applied for a copy-editing job at *Yamato,* where a "sleepy-eyed" male receptionist made it clear "that no woman would ever be considered." Shortly thereafter, she saw an announcement of a similar position at *Hōchi* and after lying her way past a janitor was given an interview with the "unsmiling" editor, Miki Zenpachi, who proceeded to hire her.[69] Although Hani was the best copy editor Miki ever had seen, her ambitions lay in writing; so she took it on herself to interview the wife of Tani Kanjō, who had defended Kumamoto Castle from Saigō Takamori's forces during the 1877 Satsuma Rebellion, and submitted a seven-segment article to the editor of the paper's popular column "Portraits of Leading Women" *(Fujin no sugao)*. He decided to publish it; readers and editors both liked it, and Hani's days as a copy editor ended.

Hani worked for *Hōchi* for less than three years, until marriage to one of her juniors on the reporting staff, Hani Yoshikazu, caused the editors to push her out. In that brief span, however, her writings became popular among the paper's family-oriented readers. As she described her approach:

> I searched for worthy projects for the paper on my own, eager to contribute creative ideas, and I found more than enough. Not only everyday social notes, but even information brought back by police reporters often yielded items that begged for the woman's touch, the woman's point of view and the woman's pen. Reader responses proved me right, and I was rewarded with the satisfaction of knowing that I filled a vital role in society.[70]

A weeklong set of interviews in Shizuoka with an aging, charismatic monk named Nishiari produced more than a month's worth of articles (and almost persuaded Hani to become a nun), and other stories on a relief organization, the Okayama Orphanage, and the aristocratic political leader Prince Konoe Atsumaro brought her wide recognition.

The key to Hani's pioneering role, according to Chieko Mulhern, was not only her vision and self-confidence but pure hard work. "Instead of popular society news, which often amounted to little more than gossip concerning upper-class women," Mulhern says, "Motoko sought expressions of wisdom in mundane settings. After thorough search and research, she wrote in a straightforward, succinct style that contrasted sharply with the pedantic bombast then prevailing in newspaper style."[71] She was, in other words, a serious reporter. Even after being forced out of newspapering, she gave much of her life to journalism, writing all thirty-two pages of a new family magazine, *Katei no Tomo*, which appeared in 1903, just a day after the birth of her first child.[72] In 1908, she and her husband launched *Fujin no Tomo*, a women's magazine still popular at the end of the twentieth century.

Skillful as she was as a reporter, the most important thing about Hani's work undoubtedly was that it marked a beginning. Women journalists would not be treated with general respect until well after the end of the Meiji era, but once *Hōchi* broke the taboo, other papers also began to hire women. In 1899, Ōsawa Atsuko entered *Jiji*, "the sole woman on an editorial staff of a hundred" and the first Japanese woman to spend a full career as a reporter.[73] A year after that, Hara Kei hired Ōta Kaoru and Kishimoto Ryūko to write for the special family page that *Ōsaka Mainichi* had launched in 1898.[74] Then, in 1901, Matsumoto Eiko joined *Mainichi Shimbun*, where she, Kinoshita Naoe, and others wrote a ninety-five-part series on the human tragedies produced by copper mine pollution in Ashio to the north of Tokyo. The series angered the authorities enough that they forced her to leave journalism altogether. Other women who entered the arena of the press early in the 1900s included Kanno Suga, who worked for *Ōsaka Chōhō, Murō Shinpō,* and *Mainichi Denpō* prior to being executed with other socialists in the famous high treason case of 1910; Hirayama Oshieko, hired in 1903 by *Kyūshū Nichi Nichi* as the first known woman reporter on a provincial paper; Isomura Haruko and Ono Kiyoko at *Hōchi*; Kawagoe Teruko, Hattori Keiko, and the prominent socialist Fukuda Hideko at *Yorozu*; Suzuki Gen at *Shakai Shinpō*; and Honjō Yūran at *Chūō*.[75]

With the exception of Ōsawa and Hattori, none of these women gave full careers to newspaper reporting, though several continued writing for magazines or for women's and other political groups after leaving the newspaper world. The pressures against them were immense, ranging from the fact that women were late in being granted educational opportunities[76] to traditional prejudices against women working in the public sphere. Even their fellow reporters often made life difficult. Hani recalled hearing printers in the next room calling out, "Hey, there's a woman in the zoo now" during her first weeks at *Hōchi*.[77] As late as 1913, *Chūō Kōron* wrote that women reporters had few opinions and needed little "talent to run errands for the newspaper."[78] And in the autumn of 1909, *Tōkyō Asahi* writer Matsuzaki Tenmin summed up the view of many male colleagues in a piece about the way "women reared in the world of civilization and enlightenment" had "violated the male sphere." He said the instinctive male reaction was to see such women "acting boastfully, like uncrowned rulers," and to wish they would "go back to acting like women." The women reporters' actual performance, he added, made those wishes anachronistic.[79] It was not an easy atmosphere in which to work; the fact that so many women found a home in the country's increasingly commercial press probably says more about the women's own determination and about the kinds of news demanded by urban readers than about the attitudes of male editors.

Editors who were willing to hire women, in other words, had accepted the necessity of giving readers the kinds of news they wanted, even when it demanded hiring writers and publishing materials that no "respectable" editor would have considered a generation earlier. At some papers, this now meant beefing up business coverage in response to the "commercial fever" that gripped urban Japan after the Sino-Japanese War; at others, it entailed new literature and arts sections; at several, it resulted in sensational campaigns for everything from working rights to the liberation of prostitutes; and at most papers, it gave a new prominence to the page-three society stories of gossip, romance, scandal, and violence, commonly known as *sanmen kiji*.[80] *Yūbin Hōchi* had made the phrase *sanmen kiji* popular when it dropped the *ōshimbun* approach in December 1894,[81] and by the late 1890s, most of the papers were running their liveliest news on that page. In the early years of the new century, sensational stories came to be labeled *sanmen kiji*, no matter where they appeared in the paper.

This did not mean that Japan's urban newspapers became clones of each other now. Most papers actually worked more consciously than ever at creating their own individual styles, in order to attract the specific classes and groups of readers needed to assure profits. It simply meant that, whatever the audience or orientation, each paper put news at the center. Most of them continued to mouth the old Confucian axioms about the responsibility for providing moral examples and leading the people toward civilization, but while this once had produced erudite discussions of political theory, it now meant giving the readers interesting, palatable news stories. A brief look at the distinctive features of several of this period's largest and most influential papers illustrates just how completely news and profit had won the day.

DIFFERENT PAPERS, DIFFERENT APPROACHES

It is important to note at the outset that not all of the papers responded to the masses with equal skill in these years; a number of them went on much as they had before, while others had trouble grasping the demands of the new era even when they tried, and the financial results for these papers were grim. *Tōkyō Nichi Nichi*, for example, retained its close ties to the *hanbatsu* cabinets, first under Itō Miyoji, then under Asahina Chisen—and lost its place as a preeminent paper. *Yamato*, which had grown into one of Tokyo's more widely read papers at the end of the 1880s as a glorified *koshimbun* with good novels and society news, bucked the trend and turned in a more political direction now, with ties to the government's Satsuma clique—and its readership stagnated as a result.[82] *Yomiuri*, the forerunner of *sanmen kiji* journalism as Japan's first important *koshimbun*, gave its columns primarily to novels and poetry in this period, skimping along on third-rate coverage of politics and fourth-rate economic reporting—and paying the price with the lowest circulations in its history.[83] *Kokumin* declined steadily in readership through the late 1890s, after Tokutomi gave up his independent stance and threw the paper's weight behind leading clique bureaucrats such as Yamagata Aritomo, Matsukata Masayoshi, and Katsura Tarō.[84] And *Nihon*, as we already have seen, obstinately ("courageously," its partisans said) refused to remove highbrow essays from page one. Urged to make the paper more readable, Kuga had sniffed, "I do not want subscribers who cannot read without *kana*."[85] He also refused to give his readers much news. The intellectuals, military officers, and patriots who made up most of the paper's readership applauded Kuga's principles and sneered at all those other editors who pandered to society's lowest denominator. But the relative numbers of such readers declined steadily, and Kuga was forced to sell out in 1906 to Itō Kinryō, who turned *Nihon* into a Seiyūkai party organ.[86]

The papers that persevered in old patterns, however, were in the minority. More typical were *Niroku*, which sprang back to life in 1900 and used a combination of cheap prices, effective promotions, and sensational news to push itself briefly to the top of the Tokyo circulation charts, and *Maiyū Shimbun*, which pioneered evening journalism after its founding in 1899.[87] Among the established papers, *Mainichi Shimbun, Jiji, Tōkyō Asahi, Hōchi, Yorozu,* and the Osaka giants *Asahi* and *Mainichi* all rode intensified news coverage of one sort or another to an increasingly loyal—and increasingly large—readership. The kinds of news they featured varied, as did the audiences they targeted, but every one of them threw their energies into providing solid, interesting, and often controversial news for the city's growing pool of literate masses.

Shimada Saburō's *Mainichi* in Tokyo was the oldest and the most political of the established papers[88]—but in a highly independent, populist way that made it every bit a part of the new journalistic world. Shimada himself had been a fiery, antiestablishment member of the Diet since its first session, and he used his paper in these years to support a host of antimainstream causes, ranging from the organization of labor and the liberation of prostitutes to the reduction of military expenditures and the closing of the polluting copper mines in Ashio. His *Mainichi* attacks on Tokyo Assembly chief Hoshi Tōru for taking bribes, for example, were blamed by many for inciting Hoshi's assassination in 1901,[89] and he was the first journalist to raise the "social problem" *(shakai mondai)* of urban poverty in an ongoing, systematic way. Giving unfettered editorial freedom to socialist and humanist writers such as Matsumoto Eiko, Kinoshita Naoe, and Ishikawa Yasujirō, he declared in a 1901 editorial: "*Mainichi Shimbun* stands unshakably on principle. The powers that be cannot move us from our views; nor can money buy us off. Freedom, equality, charity, justice, humanity, and peace: those are the life force of *Mainichi Shimbun.*"[90] Shimada's revelations and attacks won him many establishment enemies, but they also incited reader interest, and though *Mainichi* eschewed the gossip and entertainment that attracted plebeian readers, its hard-hitting (sometimes scurrilous) campaigns, rooted in vivid human-interest reporting, caused its circulation nearly to double in the last half of the 1890s.[91]

Far more dramatic was the growth of *Jiji:* from fewer than 20,000 daily readers at the end of the Sino-Japanese War to 86,279 at the end of the decade.[92] Edited now by Fukuzawa Yukichi's second son, the Boston-educated Sutejirō, it developed an even more aggressive approach to reporting than that of the founder.[93] But while Fukuzawa promoted the paper with abandon, he paid little attention to format and gave very limited space to either *sanmen kiji* materials or political opinion; his innovative energies were focused instead on the solid commercial news likely to attract affluent businessmen across the country: reports from the stock markets and rice exchanges, conditions in the silk thread trade, general business trends. The paper also ran the most—and, as we have seen, the most expensive—ads. And as a result it attracted half again as many readers from outside the Tokyo region as any other paper.[94] Students could not afford it; scholars usually found it too economically oriented; but landowners, upper-class merchants, and even wealthy farmers across the nation took it by the tens of thousands, despite the fact that its 50 *sen* monthly price was a full ten *sen* above that of any other paper and more than twice that of *Yorozu*.[95]

Tōkyō Asahi took a similar, but lower-brow, approach in these years, and with only slightly less success. Like *Jiji*, it avoided third-page stories of chivalry and scandal, though it did include fairly large doses of what a snobbish reader of the journal *Taiyō* called "useless articles on the third and fifth pages."[96] It was weaker than *Jiji* on foreign economic news, and it avoided political opinion, but it was superb in reporting domestic economic news, particularly from the Kansai region where its sister paper had a stronghold. The result was that, like *Jiji*, it drew nearly half of its readers from the business classes, though generally from a lower stratum, since its subscription prices were only two-thirds those of the Fukuzawa paper. The lower rates and solid reporting also made *Tōkyō Asahi* the paper of choice for significant numbers of soldiers and students. And the bland, apolitical style, says Yamamoto Taketoshi, made it a "prototype for today's newspapers, if one takes their distinguishing characteristics to be a lack of individualistic content and an adherence to 'impartial' *(fuhen futō)* editorial policies."[97]

Hōchi's forte in these years was family journalism. It was less business-oriented and more political than *Tōkyō Asahi*, with close ties to the progressive, mildly opposition political elements represented by the Ōkuma Shigenobu's Kaishintō and later the Shinpotō.[98] But from the days of its self-proclaimed rejection of elitist journalism, it strove above all to attract a middle-level urban readership through simple prose, liberal use of reading aids such as sketches and *furigana*, and the publishing of novels, features, and news stories with an appeal to families. The paper's goal from the mid-1890s onward, said reporter Shinoda Kōzō, was to attract "parents and children."[99] For that reason, editorials were slighted and salacious items avoided, while domestic news and police blotter items were emphasized. It was also for that reason that *Hōchi* led the way in hiring women, ran stories on how to sew and manage a household, and sponsored a forum in 1901 for more than three thousand shopworkers on how to be successful employees.[100] And it was the family emphasis that prompted editor Murai Gensai to publish, for six years running, the exceedingly popular novel "Island of Dawn" *(Hinodejima)*, about the daily lives of ordinary people. One reader wrote in 1899 that he read *Hōchi* aloud to his family each day; "it is good for us as a family," he said; "it is part of our education."[101] Readers of the earlier, more elitist *Yūbin Hōchi* sometimes derided this new approach; indeed, Yamamoto's study of postcard correspondence shows that very few educators and only a limited number of officials or business leaders now read it. But the lower middle class of shopworkers, students, soldiers, and farmers took it in increasing numbers, and as a result it had become one of Tokyo's largest papers once again by the turn of the century, with a daily circulation in 1904 of almost 140,000.[102]

More successful yet in reaching the working classes was Kuroiwa's *Yorozu*, the capital's largest daily in terms of circulation and, by almost all counts, the representative daily of the era. If Kuroiwa had caught fellow journalists off guard with his rapid success after launching the paper in 1892, he swamped them now, pushing the *Yorozu* circulation from 68,554 in 1895 to 95,876 at the end of the century, nearly 10,000 more than its nearest Tokyo rival, *Jiji*, and more than 40,000 above all the others. By 1904, it was selling well over 150,000 copies a day.[103] And, most remarkably, while officials and educators scorned it as vulgar, its champions spanned the entire range of other readers, from rich businessmen and their shopworkers to poor students and poverty-stricken day laborers living in Tokyo's low-city margins.[104]

Yorozu probably was best known for its unembarrassed attention to the city's commoners. It boasted the cheapest prices, adhered religiously to its four-page, simple-reading format, ran the country's richest selection of *sanmen kiji* news, and fought the establishment with abandon. While several of its specific antiestablishment crusades will be discussed below, the point to be made here is that Kuroiwa used his news columns as levers for pushing the mighty and the rich off their perches, and his readers loved him for it. The journal *Chūō Kōron* referred to him as a man who "takes on as cnemics all of thc world's indcccnt pcoplc: thc cliquc politicians, the government officials, the noblemen, the capitalists," a man who "remains unafraid of anyone."[105] Many establishment figures loathed his approach, especially when he named names, but their hatred made the poor love him, and the sheer mass of their support made *Yorozu* powerful. Journalist Masaoka Geiyō described Kuroiwa as a "bartender who pours alcohol into his customers' glasses to trap them. . . . He makes people drunk" with his poison pen revelations, and "they have to have more."[106]

Perhaps the most remarkable thing about *Yorozu*'s approach in these years was its capacity to innovate and change with the times. The reporting of salacious material had been a Kuroiwa hallmark from the first. But in the years after the Sino-Japanese War, strengthened and emboldened by a stronger financial base, he began to improve *Yorozu*'s quality and expand its appeal. Like Joseph Pulitzer, his American contemporary, Kuroiwa "stooped for success and then, having achieved it, slowly put on garments of righteousness."[107] For him, this improvement meant adding editorials and polished writing to attract intellectuals and social activists, even while continuing the populist, labor-oriented efforts to create a better life for the masses. In 1899, he began hiring more skillful writers—and putting their essays on page one. He also initiated literary prizes for outstanding pieces submitted to the paper, published his own translations of European novels,[108] and launched a widely read English-language column.

The writers he induced to join or write for *Yorozu* included some of the day's brightest, most articulate champions of populist causes: Uchimura Kanzō, probably the country's best-known Christian intellectual; Kōtoku Shūsui, the brilliant young socialist who one day would die with Kanno Suga for a plot against the emperor's life; Sakai Toshihiko, who became one of Kōtoku's closest allies, and Kawakami Kiyoshi, whose lucid prose eventually would make him one of Japan's most widely published internationalists. All of these men shared Kuroiwa's passion for social justice, and all of them flourished under a generous editorial hand that encouraged them to attack privilege or injustice wherever they saw it, even when their views differed from those of Kuroiwa. Almost as soon as he entered the paper, for example, Kōtoku launched a series arguing that no "just" society would allow the continuation of "poverty and destitution."[109] And Uchimura ran endless attacks on everything from political venality and diplomatic hypocrisy to militarism and alcohol.

Uchimura, who was credited by another *Yorozu* reporter, Matsui Hirokichi, with turning "Shūroku the viper . . . into a saint," clearly was the brightest of the new stars.[110] And he wrote with a vigor that left few leaders unscathed. When Ōkuma wrote an article for the *New York Independent* asserting that Japan had never intended to keep the Liaodong Peninsula permanently, Uchimura suggested sarcastically that Japan prove its "innocence" by "evacuating" Taiwan, the other territory won in the Sino-Japanese War.[111] And a few days later when someone suggested that criticizing officials in *Yorozu*'s English-language column might give Japan a bad name abroad, he wrote:

> When I write for this column, I must (according to this patriotic advice) call Marquis Ito a saint, Count Okuma a learned philosopher,

Baron Iwasaki a great philanthropist, etc. etc. As if to imagine that foreigners can get no news from vernacular accounts of these and other gentlemen from multitudinous papers published in this country! But then, I confess, that it is not very pleasant to call devils even by their true names.[112]

A telling piece of evidence of just how much Kuroiwa's approach to journalism had changed as his paper had grown more influential lies in a seven-part series he personally wrote for *Yorozu* in June 1901 on "newspaper morals" *(Shimbun dōtoku ron)*, attacking the untempered capitalism that motivated newspaper owners of the day.[113] In the past, he said, "newspapers were called the disseminators of civilization; they were seen as society's upright ones; they were regarded as vessels of wisdom. Indeed, they were accorded special respect, because they differed in so many ways from the private companies that sought only to expand their 'profits' *(ri)*." Today, by contrast, respect for journalists had evaporated. "Some people even call newspapers and reporters 'horse shit.' Why on earth is this? It is for one reason only: newspapers have forgotten the difference between justice and profit."[114]

Never one to hide behind generalities, Kuroiwa blamed the Osaka papers for pioneering the "money is best" approach to journalism that "simply tries to please, entertain, and flatter people" and praised *Nihon* as the only paper still adhering tenaciously to principle.[115] It was time for papers to return to days when their editors put the "good of others" above their own profits." It was not too late to change course, he told his fellow editors near the end of the series: "The path of morality lies not in the profit seeking *(rishugi)* that you pursue today but in humanity and justice *(jingi)* alone, in producing newspapers worthy of being called newspapers. If you will give yourself wholly to that path, the respect you have lost will return to you."[116]

It was a remarkable series, coming from a man who had pursued large circulations and commercial success so ruthlessly. Yet it somehow rang true to the philosophies that always had undergirded his approach to newspapering. He may have sought profits and power, but from the first he had sought them by championing the poor and the powerless. What had changed most was the public reflectiveness, the new conviction (influenced by Uchimura, many suspected) that thoughtful discussion of the press' social role was needed—and the concern about respectable behavior. The series showed a man who had evolved into a public leader, a man still willing to fight in the trenches but ever more aware of the press' powerful establishment role.

The effect of Kuroiwa's willingness to keep innovating in these years—to improve the paper's writing and editorializing without sacrificing its mass orientation, to continue limiting each edition to four flimsy pages while running a mix of hard-hitting editorials, *sanmen kiji*–style news, and page-four advertisements—was both profitable and influential. It brought together the major features of both the *ōshimbun* and the *koshimbun* in a "two-faced strategy" *(ryōmen sakusen)* that was unprecedented.[117] "Isn't *Yorozu* a despicable paper," quipped an admirer; "it not only sends out its own poison, but its success inspires the creation of many 'little *Yorozu*s, which produce poison of their own.'"[118] A quarter of a century earlier, Fukuchi or Narushima would have blanched to have heard such a sensational paper described as Japan's "representative daily," but now, at the beginning of a new century, that was what *Yorozu* had become.

Even in the provinces, in fact, news and readability were becoming the journalistic norm in these years, although most readers and publishers there would remain too poor, or too restricted by political connections, to allow for thoroughgoing commercialism until the Shōwa era. Circulations of papers outside the Kantō and Kansai urban centers continued to be small, and the percentage of families taking their own subscriptions remained low in the years before the Russo-Japanese War.[119] As late as 1898, in fact, only five prefectures had more than five newspapers, while six had one or none,[120] and the average daily circulation of the 152 papers outside Tokyo and Osaka was a mere 3,237. Indeed, 70 percent of Japan's prefectures then could boast no more than one newspaper subscription for every one hundred residents—compared to one for every 5.6 citizens in Osaka and Tokyo.[121] The regional papers also were slower to sever ties with the political organizations that so often had given them birth.

But even those daunting facts were not enough to hold off the spread of news and profit as the defining characteristic of journalism, in the provinces as well as the center. Nishida Taketoshi, who has surveyed the late-Meiji regional press, notes that while many provincial editors used their papers to cultivate personal political bases, the times demanded that even they proclaim political "neutrality," at least in print, and that they edit for profit, which meant paying increasing attention to news and entertainment.[122] Moreover, the news-oriented dailies from Tokyo and Osaka were read as widely as the local papers in most provinces. *Yorozu,* for example, was being read across the whole country by 1899, from Nagasaki to Hakodate—with a full 40 percent of its circulation going to the regions beyond Tokyo. Papers selling at least a third of their issues in the provinces at the end of the century included *Tōkyō Nichi Nichi, Hōchi, Jiji, Yomiuri, Nihon, Kokumin,* and *Chūgai Shōgyō Shinpō.* Indeed, three of every ten papers taken in the regional areas were published in Tokyo.[123] And by 1905, *Ōsaka Asahi* was selling a full third, or 49,608, of its daily copies outside the Osaka-Kyoto-Kobe area, with nearly eight thousand going to Kyushu.[124] While rural and regional Japan may have changed more slowly, the commercial values of the central newspapers had become pervasive there too by the beginning of the twentieth century.[125]

"CAMPAIGN JOURNALISM"

Nothing better illustrates the dominance of news and profits at the leading papers now than the many reportorial campaigns that populist editors initiated from the late 1890s onward to fight for their causes and gain readers. Kuroiwa had hewed the path for these campaigns, with his early 1890s attacks on the aristocratic Sōma family and the corrupt Renmon religious sect. It was only after the Sino-Japanese War, however, that crusades became endemic in the mass-oriented press and that writers started going after corruption and seaminess in the world of the high and the mighty with a zest that would have done America's muckraking Ida Tarbell and Lincoln Steffens proud. In this period, moreover, the papers launched, for the first time, sustained efforts to form public opinion not by writing editorials but by exposing facts. That is why some press historians, Ariyama in particular, call this the "era of campaign journalism."[126]

The campaign themes were as numerous, sometimes as curious, as the issues that propelled and bedeviled society then: Uchimura's diatribes against the abuse of alcohol,[127] *Niroku*'s paeans to filial piety, *Mainichi*'s extensive articles on reporter Yokoyama Gennosuke's investigations of poverty among Japan's laboring classes and the sustained treatments at various papers of the rising labor movement, the sex lives of famous men, the pollution disaster along the Watarase River—even a set of short, self-promoting *Niroku* "revelations" in 1903 of how it had soared to the top of Tokyo's circulation charts.[128] Taken as a whole, they had two major

Kuga Katsunan, *Nihon*. (Courtesy Mainichi Shimbunsha)

Shimada Saburō, *Mainichi Shimbun*.
(Courtesy Mainichi Shimbunsha)

Kōtoku Shūsui, *Yorozu Chōhō, Heimin
Shimbun*, and Kanno Suga, *Murō Shinpō,
Mainichi Denpō*. (Courtesy Asahi
Shimbunsha)

Akiyama Teisuke, *Niroku Shinpō*.
(Courtesy Mainichi Shimbunsha)

Kuroiwa Shūroku, *Yorozu Chōhō.*
(Courtesy Mainichi Shimbunsha)

Ikebe Ichitarō, *Nihon* and *Asahi Shimbun.* (Courtesy Hajima Tomoyuki, Tōyō Bunka Shimbun Kenkyūkai)

Motoyama Hikoichi, *Ōsaka Mainichi Shimbun.* (Courtesy Asahi Shimbunsha)

The elder Murayama Ryōhei, *Asahi Shimbun.* (Courtesy Asahi Shimbunsha)

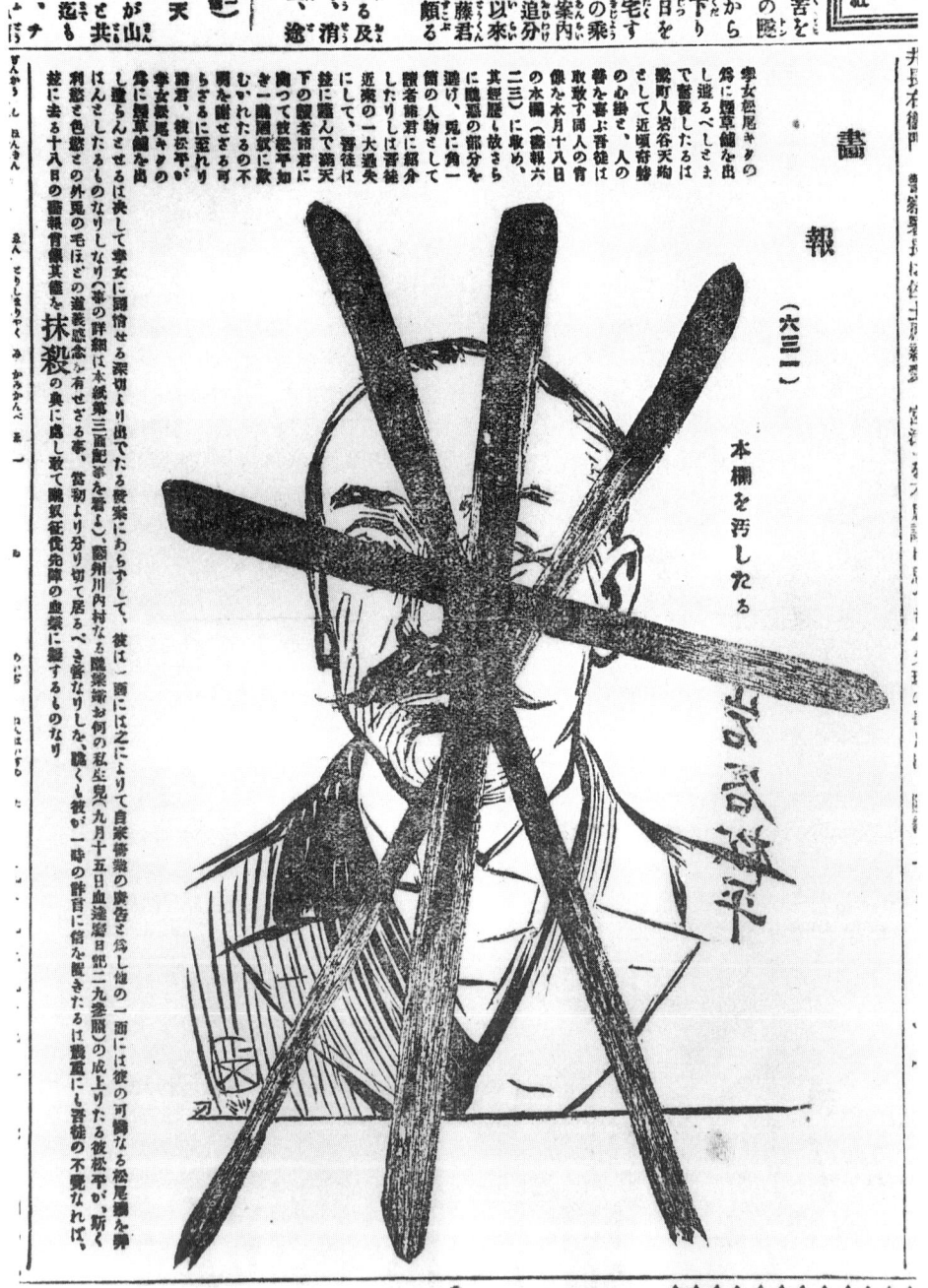

Sketch of tobacco mogul Iwatani Mappei, accompanying *Niroku Shinpō*
attack on his "heartless" business practices, October 26, 1901. (Courtesy
Hajima Tomoyuki, Tōyō Bunka Shimbun Kenkyūkai)

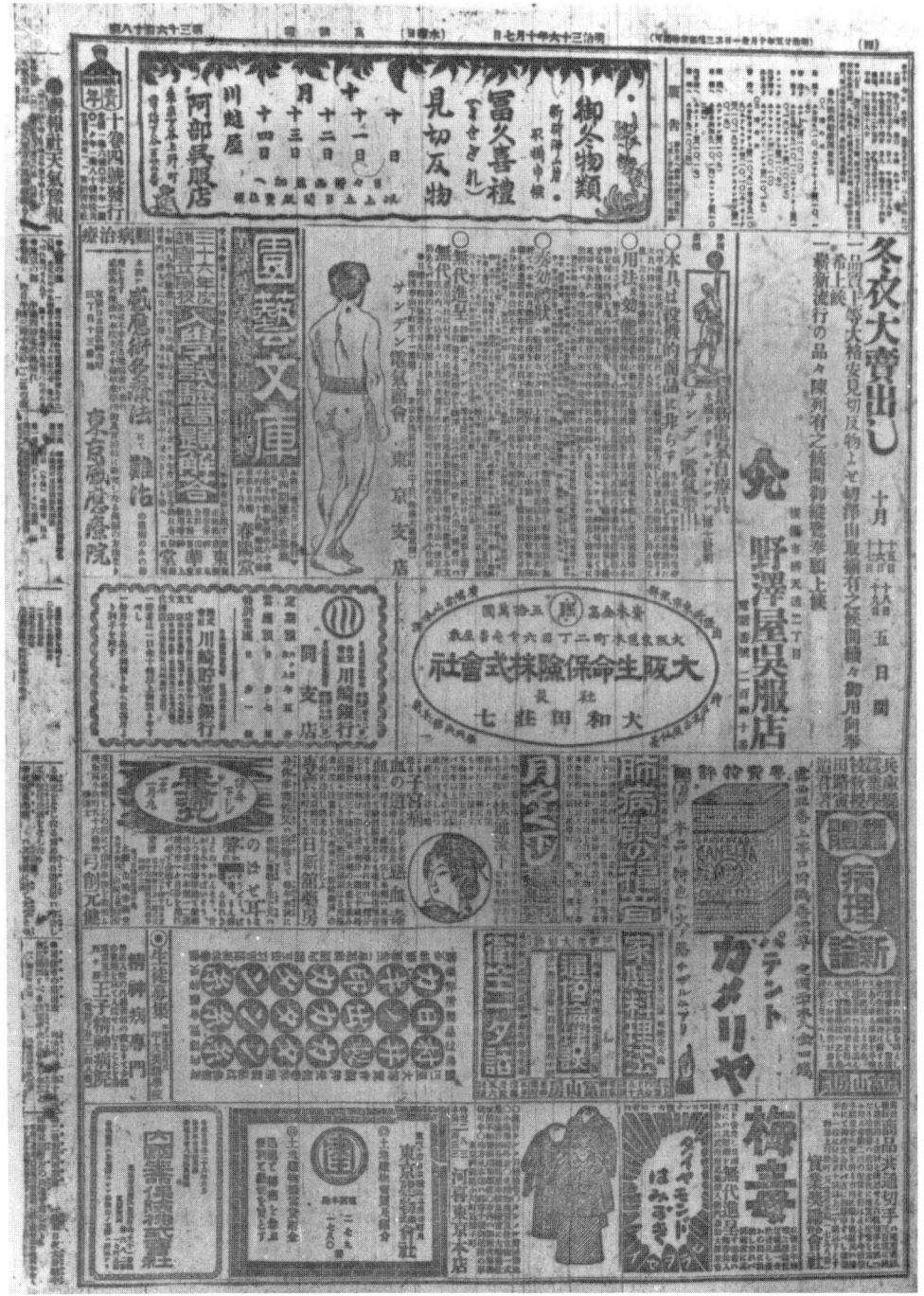

Typical page of *Yorozu Chōhō* ads, October 7, 1903: everything from insurance and electrical products to cigarettes, banks, and hospitals. (Courtesy Meiji Shimbun Zasshi Bunkō)

themes: the unscrupulous behavior of those in power and the problems of urban commoners.

In the former category, *Yorozu* and *Niroku* particularly reveled in pricking the self-righteous facades of leaders. Not long after resurrecting *Niroku*, Akiyama Teisuke began a three-month series of attacks, for example, on the financial shenanigans of the giant Mitsui family.[129] In the fall of the next year he took after Iwatani Mappei, owner of the firm that produced Tengu tobacco products, when it was revealed that his firm was employing a school-aged girl who was working to support her sick parents. Iwatani, he said, was a "brute of a man" who "tries to ensnare filial young women." When Iwatani announced that he would let the girl leave the plant and pay for her schooling, Akiyama attacked him again, as a hypocrite who was "trying to advertise his own business on the one hand and trifling with poor Miss Matsuo on the other."[130] On October 26 he ran a sketch of Iwatani with the face marked over by black ink strokes, and on November 27 he urged readers: "Let those who love Japan avoid Mappei's products!"

One of the most widely read onslaughts on elite hypocrisy was *Yorozu's* investigation in 1898 of the concubines and mistresses of some 480 of the country's best-known leaders. On July 5, the paper promised revelations that would "astonish people," then on the seventh it launched a series of more than fifty installments, titled "Heifū ippan chikushō no jitsurei" (Glimpses of evil habits; cases of concubinage), with the declaration:

> No situation is more to be pitied than that of Japanese wives, who are turned by men into playthings, in the name of time-honored custom. . . . It does not matter what a man's position or philosophy is; he still is likely to have multiple wives. We have seen a collapse in moral habits toward wives. We ourselves know of several hundred situations that can be regarded as nothing other than a social disgrace.[131]

The series ran for nearly two months, detailing what men visited which women (of what age) at what places—and, often, what children came from the liaison. July 8 brought news of the politician Inukai Tsuyoshi's dalliances, July 9 of novelist Mori Ōgai's, July 11 of Yamagata's. The series described not only politicians but journalists, photographers, doctors, educators, businessmen, actors, artists, and revered Restoration leaders. Among those whose sex habits were exposed: cabinet ministers Inoue Kaoru (July 12) and Itō Hirobumi ("about whom stories of lewdness are anything but rare"—July 13), the entrepreneur Shibusawa Eiichi (July 15), *Tōkyō Nichi Nichi* president Itō Miyoji (July 16), the early-Meiji leader Ōkubo Toshimichi (July 25), *Ōsaka Mainichi* president Hara Kei (July 26), *Yomiuri* writer Takada Sanae (August 14), former communications minister Suematsu Kenchō (August 23), oligarch Saigō Tsugumichi (September 1)—and the German physician Erwin Baelz (August 17).[132]

On founding *Yorozu*, Kuroiwa had commented that "to approve [misbehavior] by silence is to do a disfavor to our entire society. . . . Newspapers must attack the unjust to preserve society's good customs."[133] More than a few of the offended suspected that his motives were a bit less pure, since the attacks were wonderful for circulation. To the end, he claimed otherwise, asserting that evil merited no favor. It clearly did not upset him, however, that bombastic, righteous crusades also boosted sales.

Far more serious, at least in its immediate impact, was the 1900 campaign of Shimada Saburō at Tokyo *Mainichi* against corruption in Tokyo city politics. A mid-October article alleged that "shameless, corrupt, evil" men on the city council had demanded bribes from Nihon Enkan Kabushiki Kaisha (Japan Lead Pipe Company) prior to awarding Water Bureau contracts. "Is this not a scandal!" the writer fumed.[134] Over the next weeks, the paper hit away at the "crimes of the city council," focusing particularly on council head and communications minister Hoshi Tōru, whom it labeled "the leader in shame."[135] The rest of the press took up the issue too, and the resulting furor led to the arrest of several council members and Hoshi's resignation from the cabinet on December 21. The resignation was not enough for his journalist pursuers, however; the very next day, Shimada sniffed that "neither his legal problems nor his troubles in the city administration are over yet."[136] This particular campaign came to a tragic end the following June 21, when Iba Sōtarō, a fencing master agitated by the *Mainichi* attacks, stabbed Hoshi to death when he was resting in his city assembly offices. "Shimada's pen," said biographer Katakozawa Chiyomatsu, "brought Hoshi's death."[137]

The second major theme of the turn-of-the-century campaigns, the need to grapple with the social problems of the poor and powerless, said even more about the changing nature of urban society than the attacks on the establishment did. One of the most important developments of journalism in this period was, as I have noted, the willingness of several editors to take up Japan's emerging *shakai mondai*, to identify their papers with the interests of the rickshaw pullers, factory workers, prostitutes, and restaurant clerks of

Tokyo's low city, and to trust even their balance sheets to expanding sales among those classes. And nothing, not even pricking the powerful, served better to win the laborers' allegiance than accounts of how hard and unfair life was for the poor, followed by demands for an improvement in their lot.[138]

We already have taken note of *Hōchi*'s 1901 job fair, a rather middle-class effort to bring businessmen and employees together. For the populist papers, mass-oriented campaigns meant more radical approaches to labor and social injustice. Shimada, for example, became active in 1897 in the early efforts to organize workers and even accepted the presidency of the Printers Union in 1899. He also wrote continuously about urban problems and gave wide play throughout the late 1890s to Yokoyama's devastating investigations of living and working conditions among Japan's tenant farmers, slum dwellers, and "urchins in the match factories who find themselves jammed between spindles while most of the nation's children are in school struggling to master the Japanese syllabary."[139]

At *Niroku*, Akiyama gave overt encouragement to the idea of worker solidarity by sponsoring Japan's first mass laborers' rally on April 3, 1901, at Mukōjima. The paper publicized the gathering vigorously and sold a reported 70,000 10-*sen* tickets, giving more than a little pause to security-conscious police officials who informed Akiyama that only five thousand would be allowed to attend.[140] The paper, not particularly eager for a fight with the authorities, bought back thousands of tickets, but when 20,000 workers and family members showed up, the police had little choice but to let them in. The rally, billed as a simple "friendship meeting" *(konshinkai),* was primarily social in nature, with participants enjoying sword dances, *koto* music, and *rakugo* comedy, along with plenty of sake and food, and taking home commemorative towels that had been donated by Tokyo stores.

But it had an activist side too, in an address by the pioneer social worker Katayama Sen, who had edited Japan's first labor journal, *Rōdō Sekai.*[141] Although Katayama avowed that the sole purpose of the gathering was fun and fellowship for people "whose sweat-drenched work never ceases, 360 days a year," he went on to ask that the government recognize its responsibility to "protect laborers," give them the vote, and assure them a good education.[142] He was careful not to raise "radical" issues, such as the right of workers to organize and strike, and he avoided saying anything vindictive about the authorities. But the implications of the rally were quite serious, nonetheless, because the massive turnout demonstrated to officials, in a highly concrete way, just what kind of energy could be generated by an alliance between Tokyo's working classes and a sympathetic press. As a result, when *Niroku* announced plans for a similar rally the following year, the police banned it as a threat to public order.[143]

A second social issue on which several of the papers combined their efforts was the plight of Japan's prostitutes. Christian groups such as the Salvation Army and the Women's Christian Temperance Union had fought since early Meiji against a system that forced many girls and young women into brothels, then placed them under such heavy debts to owners or agents that they could never leave. The ecumenical Protestant journal, *Japan Evangelist,* ran a regular column on the problems of prostitution titled "The Social Evil." Shimada, himself a Christian, began speaking out against the "slavery system" as a "humanitarian issue" *(jindō mondai)* in 1889 and launched a *Mainichi* campaign against forced prostitution in 1900 at the urging of the Nagoya missionary U. G. Murphy, who found poor girls dropping out of his English-language school because they were indentured to the pleasure quarters. He wrote a series of articles demanding that the Home Ministry enforce its own 1872 law granting prostitutes the right of "self emancipation" *(jiyū haigyō)* and declaring that "the perpetrator of this rape, this prostitution against the holy reign of Meiji, must be judged to be the Home Minister" himself.[144]

Shimada's fulminations angered the officials, but it was *Niroku*'s Akiyama whose genius for the symbolic gesture provoked public outrage and forced official action. Early in September 1900, his paper blasted the government for failing to enforce its own *jiyū haigyō* regulations,[145] then, acting on a letter from a young woman named Ayaginu who wanted to leave the Shinmanrō brothel in Tokyo's Yoshiwara district, the *Niroku* editors decided to make (and report) their own news. They sent two reporters, Sakurai Kumatarō and Date Kitarō, to Shinmanrō as "customers" and had them secure a power-of-attorney from Ayaginu. The next day, they returned along with several others, including Akiyama himself, and led her away. Unfortunately for the reporters—and fortunately for *Niroku* sales—the liberation then took a dramatic turn. Several of the Yoshiwara proprietors saw the action, in Akiyama's words, "as a precedent-setting fatal blow to the brothel business" and assaulted the *Niroku* liberators, who proceeded, blood flowing, to take Ayaginu first to police headquarters to make her emancipation official, then to the newspaper offices.[146]

Niroku, of course, reported the episode in dramatic detail. Even the establishment papers such as *Jiji* now took up the issue, and within a week the country was in an uproar over the plight of girls and women trapped in houses of prostitution.[147] The Home Ministry, alarmed, issued new regulations on October 2, forbidding the employment of anyone under eighteen as a prostitute and reenforcing the right of the women to quit their work voluntarily.[148] Within the month, the press reported that 107 girls and women had left the Yoshiwara brothels, four-fifths of them by "self-emancipation," and by the following February some 1,100 of Tokyo's 6,835 registered prostitutes reportedly were gone from the profession.[149] Again, motives for the crusade were mixed, ranging from Shimada's humanitarianism and *Jiji*'s reportorial orientation to Akiyama's blend of populism and salesmanship. More important than motives were the new relationships such campaigns were forging between Japan's poorer urban classes and its populist newspapers.

The longest-running and most divisive of the campaigns focused on Japan's first public pollution crisis, the Ashio Copper Mine controversy. Furukawa Ichibei's mine in Tochigi Prefecture near the Watarase River had become a public issue by the beginning of the 1890s, when floods, which once had been welcomed for the rich silt they brought to the rice fields, increased massively in scale, owing to the deforestation of nearby mountains, and began carrying copper refuse in quantities sufficient to kill not only the fish in the river but the crops along its banks. "As the flood waters receded," notes one scholar, "it was as if the hand of death had passed over the land."[150] Furukawa's stewardship was criticized in the 1891 Diet session, particularly by the area's leading activist, journalist–political leader Tanaka Shōzō, and by writers from *Nihon* and *Mainichi.*[151] The problem triggered new public interest in 1896, when the largest flood in four decades killed more than three hundred people and dramatized the continued deterioration of the environment: withered willows and bamboo, mothers who could not produce milk for infants, dying crickets and birds. This time some eight hundred farmers began a march to Tokyo, a number of papers took up their cause (while *Tōkyō Nichi Nichi* and *Jiji* argued that Furukawa was doing the best he could),[152] and the Matsukata cabinet ordered that Furukawa clean up the pollution or close the mines. The government meant business this time, and debaters on both sides pronounced themselves satisfied with a plan designed to assure the continuation of "industry without pollution." Protests continued in the Ashio region when the plan produced limited results, but for the rest of Japan and the press the issue became, in the words of Kōuchi Saburō, "a dead rat."[153]

The dead rat roared back to life in February 1900, however, after 180 sword-wielding police clashed at the village of Kawamata with two thousand farmers who were making another march on Tokyo. When the confrontation turned violent, with serious injuries on both sides, the police arrested more than a hundred farmers, and during the lengthy trials and appeals that followed, Ashio became a major press issue: a symbol of government oppression for some editors, a sign of radical extremism for others, and a major news source for all of them.[154] As Alan Stone puts it, the combination of farmers' clashes and subsequent trials "became the key to the final success of their movement. It won them the headlines and the public sympathy they had sought. . . . The Tokyo press took up their cause, and Japan's last peasant rising became one of Japan's first 'social problems.' "[155]

It would not be accurate to say that all of the press, or even a majority of the dailies, saw Ashio as a cause worthy of a news campaign, even now. While *Tōkyō Asahi* and *Jiji* reported extensively on the trials, for example, they expressed scant sympathy for the farmers, referring to them as "unstable and shifting in spirit," disdaining the activists' habit of "excessive exaggeration," and praising the "scientific principles" that underlay the findings of an investigative commission created by the Tokyo Court of Appeals.[156] *Hōchi* was more sympathetic toward the plight of the Ashio victims but hesitated to blame either side.[157] And *Niroku*, somewhat surprisingly, showed little interest in the issue at all.[158]

The two papers that took up the Ashio case most vociferously were Kuroiwa's *Yorozu* and Shimada's *Mainichi. Yorozu*, though neither as thorough in its coverage nor as wholehearted in its expressions of support for the victims, typically humanized (and demonized) the story whenever it could. After the suppression of the Kawamata marchers,[159] it suggested that the mine be turned over to the pollution victims themselves, and when Furukawa's wife committed suicide by drowning during the court proceedings, it tied the tragedy to Furukawa's own sins, declaring that his greed had caused "thousands, tens of thousands, yea hundreds of thousands living downstream to lose their rice fields and their businesses." It described Furukawa's insatiable greed for "three million yen in annual profits" as no different than the "self-indulgent, lustful adultery" that had prompted him to take seven concubines and had driven his wife to suicide. "If Ichibei grieves over his wife's suicide by drowning," the writer concluded, "he should lament the difficulties of those whose plight is even worse."[160]

If *Yorozu*'s coverage was emotional and occasional, *Maini-chi*'s was thoughtful and relentless. Shimada had taken on the Ashio issue early, as an example of how citizens could be expected to fare in a capitalist society, and once the Kawamata defendants appealed their cases to the Tokyo Court of Appeals, he and his writers brought all their reportorial and editorial skills to bear, both on keeping the issue before the public and on analyzing its deeper meanings. *Mainichi* encouraged the Women's Christian Temper-ance Union to organize a charity campaign for the victims and ran lists of people who gave money; it ran scores of vivid, concrete reports by Kinoshita Naoe and Matsumoto Eikō on the actual extent of pollution suffering; Shimada worked with Kinoshita and Uchimura Kanzō to send five hundred college students on a tour of the Watarase valley;[161] he brought the issue up repeatedly on the floor of the Diet—and above all he published hundreds of articles and editorials damning a system that put private economic gain ahead of the people's welfare.

A set of January 1902 articles illustrated *Mainichi*'s incisive, no-holds-barred approach. On the second, the paper focused on the social meaning of official indifference to the victims, noting that while modernizing officials had made much of their determination to follow Western democracies in "letting the people express their pent up energies," the Ashio response represented a return to the benighted ways of traditional China and Korea, "where officials treat citizens *(kokumin)* like rubbish." A January 8 editorial in-voked Rousseau's "social contract," labeling officials who tax peo-ple without serving the public "parasites" and suggesting that the Tochigi region be given self-rule so that its residents could deal directly with the Furukawa firm. Two days later Shimada accused officials of ignoring their own laws by allowing pollution to con-tinue. And on January 24, he again took up the systemic implica-tions of the problem, writing:

> As individuals, officials are not all evil; nor are public men all back-ward wolves. But after living for so many years under a system that makes them kowtow to higher officials in order to protect their own position, they no longer can shake off their own inertia. . . . People are concerned only about themselves; they care little about the joys and griefs of others. They have no sense of responsibility toward, indeed no concept of, the public community *(shakai kōkyō)*.[162]

Although the press was not unified in this campaign, the *Mainichi* attacks exerted a significant influence. Its readership, though less than half that of *Hōchi* and *Yorozu*, included large numbers of progressive intellectuals who used the ammunition provided by the Matsumoto-Kinoshita reports and Shimada's editorials to fight for the Ashio victims in the broader, more established public forums. Kenneth Strong, Tanaka's biographer, gives credit to the influence of the *Mainichi* stories for the creation of a "Pollution Group" of Dietmen, lawyers, and journalists to demand purification of the Watarase, compensation of the victims, and the closing of the mine. He also shows Tanaka himself thanking Kinoshita for the ammunition he had provided for the "cause." And others see the *Mainichi* crusade as pivotal in the 1901 creation of a commission to investigate the Ashio situation.[163]

The most important point for this study, however, is the new role the press assumed in these campaigns. Where once its most articulate writers had employed erudite prose to debate theories about the nature of government, now several of the largest papers were attempting to shape policy through *news*-based articles and editorials. Journalists had become Japan's most active, effective fighters for populist social causes. In the Ashio case, in fact, Stone tells us that the "Left" was "almost exclusively a movement of popular journalists," men who had "come out of the editorial office and joined in the hurly-burly of practical politics, with considerable success."[164] There was nothing new about journalistic involvement in the hurly-burly of politics; that had characterized Japanese journalism since its early days. What was new was the way several leading journalists had begun using sensational, fact-centered reports to precipitate change—and the way they made their papers "organs of the weak."

PRESS AND GOVERNMENT: A CHANGING RELATIONSHIP?

Reading the populist crusade articles at the turn of the century, one is prompted at times to ask what had happened to the authorities. Where were the Home Ministry officials who had sent scores of early-Meiji journalists to jail and issued hundreds of suspensions in the first half of the 1890s? How was it that *Yorozu* could write with seeming impunity in 1901 that Japanese officials were "devoid of morality, engaged in murder, adultery, indolence, fraud, and perversity"?[165] What about Richard Mitchell's observation that when journalists stirred popular indignation, "the authorities' instinctive feelings . . . bubbled to the surface and in a Tokugawa manner they tightened the screw on the repressive vise"?[166] Quite clearly, something had happened by the onset of the century to the bureaucrats' approach to the press; while journalists' criticisms had been frequent and press-government tensions high in the past, never before had the writers been able to criticize the government so constantly or in such mass-oriented rhetoric.

This is not to suggest the press-government relationship had changed wholly. In many respects the tug of war went on as before, with twenty-five suspension orders given out in 1896, for example, and more than fifty official actions taken yearly against the press in 1899 and 1900.[167] Papers such as *Kokumin, Tōkyō Nichi Nichi, Yamato,* and even *Yomiuri* continued to maintain close ties either to cabinet cliques or to one of the political parties, even while publicly proclaiming their nonpartisan *(fuhen futō)* stance, and others like *Jiji* and *Tōkyō Asahi* had close liaisons with the business establishment. Moreover, the government kept on using its usual range of methods, from cooption and subsidies to intimidation and legal enforcement, to prevent excesses and maintain social unity. Nevertheless, as the foregoing pages have made clear, the Tokyo and Osaka journalists were publishing with more apparent freedom in these years than at any time since the 1875 press law. Something had changed.

One of the changes undoubtedly related to the institutional transformation of the press. As the papers grew larger and their bases expanded, suspensions became more costly and affected more people, likely making the enforcement authorities a bit more cautious about taking major actions against them. The enlarged papers also had become more powerful in their own right, prompting officials to treat them somewhat more carefully. The style of most criticism had changed too; while crusaders like Shimada and Kōtoku continued to make direct editorial attacks, a great deal of the criticism now came by way of reporting scandalous facts, which were more difficult to censor than expressions of editorial opinion. And public pressure against administrative suspensions increased after the Sino-Japanese War, particularly among members of Ōkuma's opposition party, the Shinpotō. Many officials seem to have concluded in the postwar years, in fact, that unduly harsh methods were counterproductive, that it was preferable, in Peter Duus' words, to enforce "a gentle tyranny, supported by fetters of red tape, not bayonets."[168] Even Matsukata Masayoshi, key villain of the journalists in the early 1890s, was forced to ease up on the press during his second cabinet (1896–1898), in order to keep his alliance with the Shinpotō intact.

One important factor in the changing atmosphere was a progressive revision of the press law in 1897, bringing to an end the Home Ministry's right to suspend and ban papers. This revision, which had failed several times before in the Diet, was precipitated by the *Twenty-sixth Century (Nijūroku Seiki)* Affair, which polarized the worlds of press and politics in the fall of 1896.[169] *Nijūroku Seiki*, an aggressively nationalistic magazine published by Takahashi Kenzō, with close ties to both *Ōsaka Asahi* and Kuga's *Nihon*, had been under suspension for its attacks on the Itō cabinet (1892–1896) almost half the time since its founding on February 11, 1894. When the new Matsukata cabinet announced on October 12, 1896, that it "valued the freedom and rights that fittingly belong to the people" and would "try to strengthen the guarantee of these rights,"[170] journalists looked to a brighter future for the press, particularly since Shinpotō supporter Takahashi had agreed to become Matsukata's chief cabinet secretary and Home Minister Kabayama Sukenori had promised to stop suspending and banning papers.[171]

Whether *Nijūroku Seiki* writers wanted to test the new atmosphere or really believed the Matsukata rhetoric is unclear, but, on October 25, the magazine published an unusually vicious attack on Itō's protégé, Imperial Household Minister Hijikata Hisamoto, titled "Kunai daijin" (The Imperial Household Minister). The article accused Hijikata and Vice-Minister Yamada Akiyoshi of manipulating the ministry to their own political and financial gain; they had arranged, it charged, imperial payments of 100,000 yen to Itō and 80,000 yen to Foreign Minister Mutsu Munemitsu following the Sino-Japanese War, along with 50,000 yen for Hijikata himself. *Nijūseiki*'s readership was too small for the piece to have much impact, but when it was reprinted by *Nihon* on November 9, it touched off an uproar, with *Tōkyō Nichi Nichi Shimbun*, *Chūō Shimbun*, and others calling for suspension of both *Nijūroku Seiki* and *Nihon* for bringing the imperial household into disrepute, while *Mainichi*, *Tōkyō Asahi*, *Kokumin*, and *Yomiuri* defended *Nihon* under the constitutional right of free speech and publication.

Matsukata's cabinet debated what to do about the articles for nearly a week, whether to offend Shinpotō supporters by breaking its pledge to stop suspending papers or to alienate powerful conservative allies by allowing such a specific attack on the imperial household to go unpunished. On November 14, it bowed to pressure from the Itō forces and shut down *Nijūroku Seiki* altogether, while giving Kuga another suspension order (this one for a week) to hang on his wall.[172] The action was something of a Pyrrhic victory for the conservative forces, however. The public energies unleashed by the controversy, combined with the Shinpotō's eagerness to strengthen freedom of expression, gave fresh momentum to the movement for liberalizing the press laws, and the result, the very next year, was the dismantling of the hated *hakkō teishi–hakkō kinshi* system.

The end of administrative suspensions and banishments marked the culmination of years of struggle between the journalists and conservative officials. Every Diet had seen bills introduced by representatives like *Hōchi* president Minoura Katsundo and *Kokkai* editor Suehiro Tetchō to halt this "useful tool for a clique government trying to preserve itself."[173] Several times their bills had passed the Lower House, but they always lost in the Upper House or in joint committee. In 1894, a compromise to replace suspensions with fines came within two votes of victory even in the conservative Upper House, but no amount of public pressure seemed capable of pushing the free press campaign over the top. Now, however, clumsy official high-handedness achieved what journalist legislators could not. Moved by the greater liberality of an Ōkuma-supported government and the embarrassment of the *Nijūroku Seiki* affair, the 1897 Diet swung behind repeal, and administrative suspensions and banishment came to an end.[174]

The journalists' victory hardly ended censorship though. Although suspensions now were illegal except by court action, the despised security deposits continued, as did most of the other restraints on the press. Moreover, the legislature added a specific prohibition on the publication of anything that demeaned the dignity of the imperial house (apparently in response to the *Nijūroku Seiki* episode), and the law made it possible now for the Home Minister to stop the sale and distribution (*hatsubai hanpu kinshi*) of individual issues, to impound the questionable issues, and to prohibit publication of any articles about the topics in question while the courts were considering charges against a paper.[175] Uchikawa Yoshimi, leading student of press laws, argues that while most journalists hailed the abolition of administrative suspensions as a victory,[176] the change was not all that it appeared. The growing commercialization and news orientation made the right to criticize officials less valuable than it had been, and the new sales and distribution provisions meant that writers still could be prevented from writing anything that unduly displeased the officials. "From the vantage point of free expression," he says, "what appeared to be a victory simply was not a victory at all." He quotes Miyake Setsurei, who likened the post-1897 climate to "a flying dove that wishes to get rid of air resistance but falls to the ground when the resistance is removed."[177] And Midoro Masaichi agrees, contending that the bottom line regarding this law was that it, like all those before it, continued to allow "an autocratic *hanbatsu* government to oppress popular movements."[178]

Not everyone agrees with those evaluations, but it cannot be denied that the government's efforts to control expression continued, quite unabated even if in revised form, after 1897. The use of subsidies and cooption, for example, was, if anything, more successful than ever. It was about this time that a Privy Council official wrote that the way to shape public opinion was "to get more than half of the newspapers and magazines under control . . . to form a strong inner citadel among the newspaper companies."[179] There was nothing particularly Japanese about efforts to woo and coopt journalists; Andrew Jackson had, after all, given federal appointments to at least fifty-seven of his favorite American journalists in the 1820s and 1830s.[180] But the Tokyo administrations had become as skillful as any in the world at covert press controls, and the officials used their cooption skill now with considerable effect.

The close ties of so many of the papers to political parties became a particularly serious threat to press independence after the Sino-Japanese War. Nearly all of the urban papers had railed against the early Matsukata and Itō cabinets (1891–1896), strengthening a reputation for moral fervor in the process. Now, when so many of those papers—including *Mainichi, Tōkyō Asahi, Yomiuri, Kokumin,* and *Miyako*—cooperated openly with Ōkuma's Shinpotō in helping Matsukata form a cabinet, many of their readers became cynical. The journalists' alliance with the new administration probably should not have surprised those readers, since the papers had been supporters of the Shinpotō's forerunner, the Kaishintō, when it was in the opposition early in the 1890s. Not only was Ōkuma the journalists' longtime champion, his espousal of party government and greater press freedom made support for a cabinet that he had helped to form quite natural. But supporting an administration in power represented a departure; it forced editors to waffle, to make compromises, and to defend (or ignore) some policies they once might have denounced. And many readers, used to a press that damned all rulers in clear, moralistic tones, did not like the change.

It was one thing for *Tōkyō Nichi Nichi* and *Tōkyō Shimbun* to support an administration; they were known to be progovernment papers. But this self-imposed quieting of once-critical voices raised serious questions now about all those pronouncements of neutrality and independence. Not all the papers were suspect; upstarts such as *Yorozu* and *Niroku* remained vocally antigovernment, and *Mainichi* hewed to its humanitarianism sharply enough to avoid most criticism. Nor were the links between papers and political factions as complex and pervasive as they would become after the Russo-Japanese War. But the support so many of the oldtime papers gave the Matsukata-Ōkuma cabinet marked a turning point for Tokyo journalism, the onset of a trend in which profit-driven, mainstream papers would identify increasingly with the impure establishment.[181] And few newspaper subscribers were pleased. Said a letter writer to the journal *Bunko* on January 15, 1903: "When you hear the two characters *go yō* (patronage), you think of false and unfounded writing, without integrity, without a philosophy, without any independence of thought."[182]

The most widely discussed case of government cooption in these years was that of Tokutomi, whose *Kokumin* had been such an outspoken critic of the earlier Matsukata and Itō cabinets. Tokutomi had played a key role in negotiating the alliance between his longtime friend Matsukata and Ōkuma's Shinpotō before leaving for a trip abroad in 1896. Then, when he returned to Japan in June 1897, he agreed to take a post in the Matsukata-Ōkuma administration as advisor to the Home Minister,[183] and set out to make *Kokumin* a more specialized paper, dedicated to reporting and analyzing political, international, and economic news for the nation's elite. The move alienated both the masses he once had championed and his independent-minded readers, much as Fukuchi's defection to the government side had done after the 1881 crisis, and the paper's circulation plummeted, prompting Tokutomi to quip that "if one were to cut out the abuses [directed against me] for just this one month alone and sell them to a scrap dealer, they would bring more than twenty *sen*." The criticism made Tokutomi bitter and paranoid, but from that point on he never severed his ties to the ruling establishment.[184]

He carried on an intensive correspondence with Yamagata Aritomo, quite clearly letting himself be used for the aging oligarch's own political ends at least as much as he used Yamagata to boost his own personal influence.[185] And while his close connection to the Katsura Tarō government at the beginning of the 1900s brought back some readers because of the paper's authoritative news sources, it alienated others by its apparent sycophancy. He defended his post–Sino-Japanese War approach to government as a way of seeing his views realized in society. "Great men through the ages have relied upon a variety of means, such as military power, wealth, or religion, to try to save the world," he wrote; "I take the newspaper as my means for this." He said his quest for influence was "for the purpose of pushing Japan forward on the stage of the world, not an effort to try to gain personal profit or to achieve individual glory."[186] Critics were not so sure about the denial of personal ambition, noting that the government ties muted *Kokumin*'s voice as often as they gave it authority.

If velvet gloves worked with many journalists, officials were not averse to using the old bare knuckles with others, in their largely unsuccessful efforts to tame the more populist papers. Fines, jail sentences, security deposits, legal proceedings, and the confiscation of offensive issues all were allowable under the 1897 law—and while the authorities went lighter in some areas, such as enforcement of the requirement that papers print readers' complaints about offending articles,[187] control measures remained relatively strict. Between 1897 and 1903, journalists were fined 738 times (an average of 105 times a year) under the press law and sent to jail twenty-five times.[188] When Kinoshita covered prefectural elections too vigorously in his native Matsumoto in 1898, for example, he was fined ten yen (about half a month's salary) and given eight months in jail.[189] A *Yorozu* editor was sentenced to a five-month jail term for injuring public morals with a series on the use of actors as male prostitutes.[190] And anyone who reported on the infant socialist movement at the turn of the century was almost sure to provoke a harsh response from the authorities. When a number of papers, including *Hōchi*, *Yorozu*, and *Mainichi*, published the party declaration of the new Socialist Democratic Party (Shakai Minshūtō) at its founding in May 1901, the government not only proscribed the party but fined the papers for threatening public order.[191]

Sometimes the fines and admonitions seemed to represent an effort to intimidate or harass recalcitrant journalists more than a belief that laws really had been broken. It was not unusual for administrative actions against papers to be overturned or disallowed on appeal to the courts—but only after the paper's operations had been interrupted and its editors given pause about what they would write the next time. Akiyama's feisty *Niroku* was a particular target of this sort of harassment. In 1902, for example, when the paper announced plans for a second labor friendship rally at Mukōjima, the authorities did not stop at prohibiting the rally; they also called seven *Niroku* employees to police headquarters for interrogation and took company officers to court for failing to account adequately for 108 yen in receipts at the 1901 rally. When *Niroku*, which had spent thousands of yen of its own money on that rally, was found innocent, Akiyama toasted employees with a keg of Ebisu beer; he also ran an editorial saying the labor rallies would be postponed "until the collapse of the Katsura cabinet."[192]

The most difficult feature of the 1897 law probably was the provision allowing the Home and Colonization ministries to prohibit sales and distribution *(hatsubai hanpu kinshi)* of specific issues of papers. Enforcement of this proviso was cumbersome, since it had to be carried out after a paper had been published but before readers had received copies. That meant that ministry employees had to read the papers early, that their orders most often would be issued without warning, and that publishers then would have to send people out to pull issues off the streets, at considerable inconvenience and cost to everyone.[193] *Hatsubai hanpu* prohibitions were issued sparingly during the first years of the new law (at a rate of eighteen per year between 1898 and 1903),[194] but when added to provisional seizures of daily issues and censorship of related articles, they brought considerable pain to Tokyo and Osaka journalists. They also set a fearsome precedent, for within a few years the prohibition of sales and distribution would increase dramatically, as we shall see below. The combined effect of all of the press control measures, both soft and harsh, clearly was to dampen reporting and discussion, to make many editorialists "wishy-washy," or *moshiwaketeki*, in the words of one journal.[195]

But, as we saw earlier in the chapter, that was not the whole story. While a proclivity for questioning anything that restrains free expression has prompted most journalists and scholars to focus on government rules and harsh enforcement procedures, there was another reality that we dare not ignore. By the dawning of the twentieth century, several of the largest papers were publishing daily stories as well as frequent editorials that unmasked hypocrisy, encouraged rising popular opposition movements, and criticized official policies—and doing so with relative impunity. There were areas that these writers knew (and usually preferred) to avoid: the imperial household, socialism, the national polity. But they published critiques of other areas of national life quite freely, and they got away with it. One reason lay in the shift from editorials to news as the papers' main product; another quite clearly was the 1897 press law revision. No longer needing to fear being shut down, or even suspended, without full court hearings,[196] the populist papers took on the officials with a consistency and intensity heretofore unknown. They still were far from free; in fact, most of them would have said they were anything but free. But the truth was that, by the early 1900s, they were getting by with stronger, more consistent attacks than ever before.

ALMOST A MASS MEDIUM

The salient characteristic of the press' overall development between the Sino- and Russo-Japanese wars was its evolution into a modern, near mass institution dominated by news and profits. By 1900, 944 newspapers and magazines had placed security deposits with the government; in 1901 the figure rose to 1,181; by 1913 it approached 1,500.[197] And while the majority of these numbered their readers in the hundreds or lower thousands, several had developed truly substantial readerships. In 1899, two Tokyo papers, *Yorozu* and *Jiji*, were approaching daily circulations of 100,000, while the Osaka *Asahi* already had surpassed that figure.[198] And by the end of this period, the largest paper, *Niroku*, was selling more than 140,000 copies a day,[199] with at least seventeen of the provincial papers boasting circulations of 10,000 or more.[200] It probably would be stretching definitions to say that this made the circulation leaders "mass" papers, in an era when New York's *Journal* and *World* each boasted more than 500,000 readers,[201] but it clearly would have placed them among the world's larger newspapers, poised on the edge of the mass media era.

The instincts of most editors had turned thoroughly commercial by the turn of the century: garnering ads and readers had replaced editorializing as their central occupation, copy had to be interesting and readable, audience interests were kept constantly in mind. America's famous "country journalist" William Allen White wrote on the death of chain newspaperman Frank Munsey in 1926: "Munsey contributed to the journalism of his day . . . the morals of a money changer and the manners of an undertaker. . . . May he rest in trust."[202] Many an onlooker felt much the same about the slide into sensational, crowd-oriented journalism in Japan, where stories of Hachioji fires and Itō's mistresses now rivaled Diet proceedings and ministerial pronouncements for daily space. Kuroiwa, no slouch with the account books himself, bemoaned the way his fellow editors had "forgotten justice in the pursuit of profits."[203] And Hana-zono Kanesada deplored the way "commercialization of newspapers set in after the close of the Sino-Japanese War" and "sensational-ism was the motto"; editors tried now, he complained, to satisfy "the taste of the majority of the readers, which is always slightly vulgar."[204]

If the rise of profit seeking and sensationalism was the most dramatic characteristic of the interwar years, however, at least four other developments were equally important. First was the peaking in this period of "independent journalism," a process that had begun in the 1880s with Fukuzawa's *Jiji*, Tokutomi's *Kokumin*, and Kuga's *Nihon*, then had reached a crescendo in the 1890s in Kuroiwa's *Yorozu* and Akiyama's *Niroku*. Each of these papers rep-resented the unique vision of a single founder; each attracted pas-sionately loyal readers who identified as much with the editor's forceful views and personality as with the news or opinion in the paper, and each dominated Japanese journalism for its own span during the 1890s and early 1900s. Some of them *(Nihon* and *Kokumin)* nurtured an intellectual, political base; others *(Jiji)* sought to shape the business world, and *Yorozu* and *Niroku* found their home among the masses. But all of them led the press through a time of transition, from an age of editorial dominance to an era of news reporting, from political elitism to a time when the *minshū* inspired the innovations. And all of them lost at least some of their luster with the passing of this era.

A second development lay in the increasing segmentation of the newspaper world in these years. Nearly all press observers have discussed the disappearance of the *ōshimbun-koshimbun* divide in the first part of the 1890s; fewer have noted the more complex channeling that was occurring now. While all but *Nihon* put news at the center, they did not all concentrate on the same kinds of news. Recognizing the good business sense of creating well-defined bases, the majority of papers developed sharper individual identities than ever before. Older papers such as *Tōkyō Nichi Nichi*, *Ōsaka Mainichi*, and *Hōchi* continued to run a fairly traditional blend of middle-road news, politics, and opinion. *Jiji* and the two *Asahi*s con-centrated on the business worlds. And *Yorozu* and *Niroku* roared to the top of the circulation charts with the mass-oriented *sanmen kiji* approach, while papers like *Yomiuri* and *Yamato* catered to readers with literary interests. Classification of this sort does an injustice to the rich complexity that characterized most papers, but there is no denying that compartmentalization had become a central feature of the newspaper world by the middle of the century's first decade. To decide which paper to take, readers now needed to decide where to place themselves in the intellectual, economic, political, and social spheres.

A third development was the changing way in which journalists exerted influence in these years. From the earliest years, "influence" had been a prime reason for entering the profession, and that had not changed, as Tokutomi's defection to the government camp and Matsuzaki Tenmin's evaluation of the new women journalists who acted like "uncrowned rulers" made clear. What had changed was the manner of exerting influence as well as the kinds of impact the journalists actually had. Whereas early-Meiji writers most often tried to change policies directly, by arguing the pros and cons of government policies in page-one opinion essays, now they increasingly exerted their pressure through the news columns. There were direct editorial campaigns, of course: the drive to get the press law amended, the calls for a more aggressive foreign policy early in the 1900s, *Ōsaka Mainichi*'s eleven-part series in 1898 assailing the Itō cabinet and demanding party government.[205] But the innovative hallmark of these years was the effort to shape policy through news, to *show* corruption or political failure through a series of investigative articles and thus to stir up a public clamor. The judicial decision to create a commission to study pollution in Ashio probably resulted less from Shimada's editorial comment than from Kinoshita's poignant reportage, and the regulations allowing for the self-emancipation of prostitutes were prompted by the uproar following *Niroku*'s stories of Ayaginu leaving her Yoshiwara brothel, not by the speeches of Christians and feminists.

A final development was the emergence of a group of commoner-oriented social reformers among the press' best writers. Popular advocates in earlier years had focused on political theory and the creation of a citizenry, on the need for a constitution, a popular assembly, and voting rights, what Carol Gluck calls "a litany of nation."[206] Now, awakened to bleak living conditions in the expanding cities and propelled by new classes of readers, journalists became a vanguard for social change. When press historian Koito Chūgo says that "the Meiji journalists had more guts,"[207] he is referring to the Shimadas, Kōtokus, and Akiyamas, who took up the whole range of *shakai mondai* afflicting the city masses: low wages, inadequate housing, lack of organization or influential connections, inhuman working conditions, inadequate child care and nutrition in the home, pollution of the rivers, prostitution and concubinage, the need for labor organizations. The populist journalists dealt with these issues in every section of the papers, in novels about everyday problems, in ads for solidarity rallies, in editorials about corrupt politicians who robbed the poor, in news articles about dead fish in the Watarase.

Duus notes that the journalists now "became tribunes for what they conceived to be the interests of the masses," writers willing to "criticize politics from the standpoint of the 'people.'"[208] This new approach troubled the old elitists, who could do no better than to moan about vulgarization. But it made the city papers more powerful than ever, influential not only as shapers of official policy but as nurturers of the working classes. "By sheer chance it fell to *Yorozu News* to take me by the hand and lead me out of blindness," said the socialist Ōsugi Sakae, newly arrived in Tokyo at the beginning of the century. "Through the *Yorozu News*, for the first time I was exposed to life as it was lived in the world outside the military. It especially made me see society's unjust and immoral aspects."[209] Society, for these new social prophets, was darker than it had been for their early-Meiji forebears, but they fought the "social problem" with hope as much as with indignation. And the impact of their revelations and fulminations would be every bit as profound as the changes wrought by Fukuchi's or Kuga's editorials about constitutions and foreign policy.

Fukuzawa Yukichi wrote in *Jiji's* five thousandth anniversary edition: "We get ever more kinds of newspapers, and there is no end to their changes; *Jiji* alone has remained fixed in purpose across these fifteen years."[210] His analysis of his peers was on target. The implied criticism, however, suggested less than a complete understanding of what was going on. Modernization had produced a new urban society, a world with too few affluent businessmen to support more than one *Jiji*. Seizing the needs and potential of the new era, the Kuroiwas and Akiyamas had brought the press to the threshold of the mass media stage. And while bringing it there, they had shown the world not only how to attract commoners as readers but how serious the *minshū* problems were that Japan must face as it entered the new, industrial era.

CHAPTER 9

COVERING A BIGGER WAR

1903 to 1905

Liaoyang occupied! Liaoyang occupied!
The news echoed through even the dingiest
back street, the humblest dwelling in the
remotest mountains, and the most isolated
island out across the roughest sea. Bell
ringing newsboys spread the new reports about
it almost hourly across the whole country.
                              Tayama Katai[1]

Yorozu Chōhō hawkers must have had a field day on October 12, 1903. At the top of that morning's issue were editorials by three of Japan's best known journalists—Uchimura Kanzō, Sakai Toshihiko, and Kōtoku Shūsui—explaining their decision to leave the paper. Uchimura, who had argued in an editorial a few days earlier that "supporting war with Russia was tantamount to supporting the destruction of Japan,"[2] wrote now that for him to remain at *Yorozu* would make the paper "lose society's confidence." Sakai and Kōtoku declared in a joint essay that "keeping silent" about their own opposition to war "would be an act of irresponsibility toward our fellow patriots," but that speaking out in *Yorozu*'s columns was no longer possible. And their editor, Kuroiwa Shūroku, told readers on the same page that while these three were his favorite writers—"the paper's bright lights if it has any"—he had no choice but to accept their resignations, since their views had become untenable.[3]

It was not just the public airing of disagreements that made the resignations shocking but also Kuroiwa's own advocacy of war with Russia. For months he had supported his antiwar writers, standing almost alone among the nation's leading publishers in urging negotiations to lessen tensions between the two pretenders to power in eastern Asia. Now, he said, he could support pacifism no longer—and since the paper was his, not theirs, Kōtoku, Sakai, and Uchimura would have to go. He enlarged on his shift the next day, in a lengthy editorial asserting that while he did not seek war, Russian actions on the continent (particularly the refusal to withdraw troops from Manchuria after the 1900 Boxer Rebellion)[4] made it unavoidable. "Since taking on another country in battle is a task for all of the country's people, not just for the army and navy," he said he saw no choice but to come out for a more aggressive foreign policy.[5] Journalists at other papers debated his motives, suggesting that the loss of readers and profits in an increasingly war-minded public prompted the conversion. The important thing for his country, however, was that, with *Yorozu*'s shift, the voice of restraint disappeared almost wholly from public discussions of foreign policy.

A CHAUVINIST MOOD

The pressures on Kuroiwa had been building for a long time. Throughout the 1890s, conservative *minkan* or private opinion leaders throughout the land had spoken with increasing fervor of the need to educate the people in "a sound sense of the nation" in order to make genuine "citizens" of them.[6] Operating in every field —politics, law, journalism, business, education—they ranged across a broad spectrum of political ideas, including advocates of civil morality like Inoue Tetsujirō and pan-Asianists such as Ōi Kentarō. Many of them detested the "corrupt" world of bureaucrats and politics; some made that world their home; many took up the cudgel of people's rights and social reform; others grimaced at "radical" issues of that sort. But with the passing years increasing numbers of people in every political camp espoused a litany of nation-centered ideas and phrases deemed necessary to foster unity and make Japan strong: national ethics and morality, *kokutai* or the national "essence," Shintō as a national "faith," and, above all, the centrality of the emperor as the embodiment of everything Japanese. As Education Minister Mori Arinori had put it before his assassination in 1889, the only way to assure national strength was for all Japanese to be " 'taught,' to the very marrow of their bones to feel a fervent spirit of loyalty and patriotism *(chūkan aikoku).*"[7] *Nihonshugi* or Japanism, in other words, had replaced *kokuminshugi* ("citizen-ism") and *kokkashugi* ("countryism") at the heart of nearly all public figures' ideological systems by the end of the 1890s, no matter where they stood on other political issues.[8]

Of particular importance to this study are the international tones that colored this new patriotism for many journalists in the decade following the Sino-Japanese War. Spurred by the end-of-the-century European land grabs in China, the heavily reported Boxer Rebellion of 1900,[9] and Russia's expansion into eastern Asia, more and more editors and journalists began linking discussions of *kokutai* and national strength to the need for Japan to stand strong on the international stage. And it was not just the old-time conservative chauvinists like Kuga Katsunan at *Nihon* and the expansionist founders of the Gen'yōsha (Dark Ocean Society) who moved in this direction. We already have seen Tokutomi's increasing preoccupation with international strength. Similarly, when the journal *Sekai no Nihon* (Japan in the World) was launched in 1896, the former *jiyū minken* champion Saionji Kinmochi suggested its name.[10] And Fukuzawa too had by the end of the 1890s taken up his "cast off Asia" *(datsu a)* stance, arguing that Japan should stop seeing itself as "Asian" and join the Western imperialist powers; its Asian role, he argued, should be that of leader or civilizer. "The main trend in the world of thought," says press historian Nishida Taketoshi of these years, "was imperialism *(teikokushugi)*."[11]

The ground thus was well prepared, as Russia expanded rapidly eastward during the fourth Meiji decade, for most Japanese papers to write in increasingly threatening terms about the Russian "problem." Particularly vexing was the fact that Russia had signed agreements with China in 1898, leasing Port Arthur and Dairen in the Liaodong Peninsula and thus gaining control of the same territory it had denied the Japanese in the Tripartite Intervention just three years before. When the Russians left thousands of troops in Manchuria after the 1900 Boxer episode, the press expressed grave suspicions about their intentions. The Anglo-Japanese Alliance quieted the rhetoric briefly in 1902, particularly when St. Petersburg agreed in April to a three-stage, eighteen-month withdrawal of its forces from Manchuria and began actually removing them in October. But when the second withdrawal date passed on April 1, 1903, without any more Russian soldiers being removed, the press began calling for Japan to force the issue. And when Russian negotiators refused to concede to Japan the rights in Korea that they themselves claimed in Manchuria, then ignored another troop with-

drawal deadline on October 8, the country's journalists were outraged. Russia's eastern expansion, they wrote, threatened not only
Japan's continental holdings but its very sovereignty.

Leading the attack in the press now were many of the mainstream journalists who had denigrated the populist writers' bombast over domestic social issues at the century's turn. Fukuzawa,
the most establishment of them all, had set the tone for his fellows
near the end of his life when he commented to a friend: "I do not
worry whether *Jiji* editorials are wholly on target or not, or even if
they hurt our reputation. If they give the Russians a fright . . . they
will have achieved their purpose."[12] When the Russians first missed
their troop withdrawal deadline in April 1903, nearly all of the centrist papers—both *Asahi*s, *Ōsaka Mainichi, Jiji, Yomiuri,* and *Hōchi*
—went Fukuzawa one further: they demanded war.[13] On April 19,
Tōkyō Asahi reported breathlessly on a series of troop actions on
the Manchurian plains, allegedly observed by Chinese citizens,
which clearly indicated to the writer that the decision for war
already had been made.[14] The fact that the assumptions were wrong
did not diminish most journalists' conviction that Russia must be
challenged militarily. A few weeks later the same paper declared
that a recent entry of thirty "insolent Russian troops" *(bōjaku bujin)*
into Korea to protect lumbering interests made it "impossible any
longer to accept noninterventionist policies."[15]

An important stimulus to the rising prowar fever came in
mid-June, when *Niroku Shinpō* published a confused version of a
document drawn up by several Tokyo Imperial University professors advocating a Japanese advance into Manchuria. The scholars,
known as the *shichi hakase* (seven professors), had been stirring the
political waters since 1900, working with journalists such as *Nihon*'s
Kuga Katsunan to get the Japanese government to accept not only
the necessity of pushing Russia out of Manchuria (as far back as
Lake Baikal, some of them urged), but the inevitability of war as a
means of doing that. When Tomizu Hirondo, the group's leading
spokesman, made a speech in the spring of 1903 demanding war,
Tōkyō Asahi reported that "frightened" military bureaucrats had
asked the Education Ministry to rein him in.[16] The professors themselves were upset when *Niroku* issued a garbled version in June of
what was supposed to be a secret memorandum they had prepared
for several officials.[17] When the progovernment *Tōkyō Nichi Nichi*
then criticized the professors for "lacking discretion" and stirring
up public opinion, they were furious, because the paper's direct
quotes from their memorandum suggested that Prime Minister

Katsura Tarō had leaked it to his ally *Nichi Nichi* president Itō Miyoji.[18] They called a press conference of their own on June 24 to criticize Katsura and explain their own analysis that Japan was ready for war economically as well as militarily, and from that point on the prowar clamor of *Nihon, Tōkyō Keizai Zasshi, Jiji, Ōsaka Mainichi*, and the two *Asahi*s never subsided.[19]

    Niroku described the Russian "mischief" and said it was time for Japan to "rouse herself from her medieval lethargy" and claim the "Promised Land." "In peace," the writer said, "be mindful of war. The time is fast approaching for Japan to play the part of young David against Goliath."[20] On June 27, *Tōkyō Asahi* blasted Katsura's "stupid plan" of relying on diplomacy to tame Russia, and on July 8 it ran an essay by one of the seven professors titled "We Definitely Must Begin War."[21] By fall, *Tōkyō Asahi*'s leading prowar editorialist, Ikebe Kichitarō (Sanzan), had declared, "The Japanese government dare no longer delay intervention," *Jiji* was writing that the long-standing relationship between Japan and Russia could not continue if Russia did not stop its illegal actions, and even the still cautious *Yorozu* was warning that most Japanese had "now reached the limit of our endurance."[22] And when the Russians still had not removed their troops in October, the cries reached a crescendo, prompting even Tokutomi's *Kokumin Shimbun*, a staunch Katsura cabinet ally, to declare that if Japan's negotiators made "further concessions to Russia, the righteous indignation of our people could not be held back . . . our nation would fall into confusion like a broken-up nest of a thousand bees."[23]

    The journalists also had begun moving beyond the editorial columns by then. *Asahi, Ōsaka Mainichi, Kokumin*, and *Jiji* sent reporters to Korea and China during the autumn months to observe the situation first hand.[24] And many reporters and editors took to the parks and lecture halls to agitate for military action. Already in 1900, more than two hundred journalists, led by *Asahi*'s Ikebe, Minoura Katsundo of *Hōchi*, and Enjōji Tenzan of *Yorozu*, had formed the National Association of Like-Minded Reporters (Zenkoku Dōshi Kisha Kai) to push for aggressive steps against Russia; in 1902 a similar Anti-Russian League (Tairō Dōshi Kai) was created,[25] and when tensions began to peak late in 1903, so did the reporters' activities. Scores of reporters joined well over a hundred lawyers, legislators, and businessmen at a press-sponsored Gathering for Consideration of the Current Situation (Jikyoku Mondai Rengō Konshinkai) at the Imperial Hotel on November 10, to hear a series of prowar speeches and adopt a demand that "our national leaders take quick and decisive action" to end a situation that "does not bode well for maintaining peace in Asia or protecting our own national interests."[26] Nearly two weeks later, on November 22, a similar meeting in Osaka drew a crowd of 2,500 to hear reporters from *Ōsaka Mainichi, Niroku, Miyako, Yorozu,* and *Ōsaka Asahi* demand action.[27] "The people of Japan reject détente," declared *Tōkyō Asahi,* "and we reject the methods of détente."[28]

Chauvinistic rhetoric was not universal. We already have seen *Yorozu'*s earlier calls for moderation, marked by declarations that "war means murder" and that a fight with Russia would bring "dire consequences to the life, progress, and happiness of the entire nation."[29] While editor Kuroiwa allowed individual writers like Enjōji to express hawkish views, he himself supported negotiations right up until his October 8 about-face, more than once criticizing the Japanese public's propensity for "becoming confused and losing its rationality" when the phrase "foreign problem" *(gaikō mondai)* came up.[30] Shimada Saburō's *Mainichi Shimbun* also expressed consistent opposition to conflict throughout the summer and fall, in part because of Shimada's Christian humanism, in part because he feared war would increase military influence in the government, and in part because of *Mainichi* reporter Kinoshita Naoe's socialism.[31] Less wholehearted in its support of conciliatory policies was *Kokumin,* which took a weakly noncommittal line most of the summer and fall, because the hawkish Tokutomi's close relationship with the Katsura cabinet gave it no other choice.[32] And then there was *Tōkyō Nichi Nichi,* which urged moderation right up until the beginning of hostilities, again less from belief than from its ties to the administration.

But voices of moderation had become lonely indeed by the time the maples lost their fall color. Even Shimada came out for war in November, and Tokutomi expressed his ambivalence through silence. Only *Tōkyō Nichi Nichi* labored on among the mainstream papers, persisting into early 1904 in calling the war advocates "noisy and crazy fellows," labeling the seven professors "sick Russophobes," and urging a negotiated settlement.[33] It was joined at the end of 1903 by *Heimin Shimbun,* a new socialist paper founded by Kōtoku and Sakai when they left *Yorozu.* But *Heimin'*s circulation was a minuscule 4,500, its voice a chirp in a typhoon. When Taguchi Ukichi of *Tōkyō Keizai Zasshi* boasted in February 1904 that his fellow journalists bore "great responsibility" for giving Japan a war, for " 'forcibly' pulling the authorities and causing them to begin fighting,"[34] he was not speaking idly. If the press' buildup to the Sino-Japanese War had been brief and spontaneous, its advocacy of this war was bombastic, tireless, and sustained.

WAR—AND THE THIRST FOR INFORMATION

War began on the battlefront on February 8, 1904, with a relatively ineffective surprise bombing of the Russian fleet at Port Arthur; it began officially on February 10, when the Japanese declared war. And though it would take nearly three months of often vicious fighting for Japanese troops to work their way up the Korean peninsula and across the Yalu River, by May General Nogi Maresuke's Third Army was engaged in a drawn out battle for the heavily fortified Port Arthur. The fighting there was costly almost beyond belief, with Japan losing 20,000 men in one week alone during August and the two nations suffering nearly 90,000 casualties before the Russian surrender on January 2. Next came a ten-day March attack on Mukden to the north, pitting 300,000 Japanese troops against 350,000 Russian soldiers in the largest single battle humankind had known.[35] By the time the Russians surrendered there, nearly 160,000 had been killed or wounded, about 45 percent of them Japanese. The war's last major battle came at sea, when the emperor's navy destroyed Russia's Baltic Fleet as it sailed through the Straits of Tsushima late in May. But though the Japanese won the major battles, only at Tsushima did they do so decisively or easily. Indeed, by the end of winter in 1905, Japan found its resources almost wholly spent, even as Russia was beginning to get new troops into East Asia over the long and sometimes disconnected Trans-Siberian Railroad. So when U.S. President Theodore Roosevelt agreed to mediate early in the summer of 1905, Japanese officials were more than ready for peace talks. A continuation of the fighting, they knew, could lead in worrisome directions.

Few Japanese citizens, however, knew that the situation in Manchuria had an ambiguous side. The Russo-Japanese War, for those at home, had consisted solely of a string of costly and sometimes slow, but always smashing and exhilarating victories, a glorious confirmation that the more modest triumphs of the earlier war with China were not a fluke, that Japan had become a power worthy of the name imperialist. Victory had been more than sweet; it had been delicious. And the central reason for this triumphalist, simplistic understanding—indeed, the most important thing about the press' own behavior in these months—was the way the newspapers handled their war coverage. Deep patriotism, a growing willingness to work with the authorities, and an intensified determination to report detailed news quickly took the journalists in fresh directions in these months. The experience of this war made the press simultaneously more populist and more nationalist than it ever had been before.

To say that the people were thirsty for war news is to understate the case twentyfold. The military had been building for a struggle with Russia ever since the galling Tripartite Intervention, spending some 40 percent of the annual national budgets between 1896 and 1903 on the army and navy. And the press had prepared the public thoroughly for a *righteous* struggle, as much by its silence about Japanese misconduct in Taiwan and Korea as by its 1903 fulminations against Russian imperialism and its breathless accounts of the opening hostilities. Even a champion of democracy like Nakae Chōmin would argue with his pacifist disciple Kōtoku now that "if we defeat Russia, we expand to the continent and bring peace to Asia."[36] And Japan's citizens, whether they lived in the shadow of Mt. Aso, in an Osaka slum, or in one of the capital's elite professional districts, thirsted like rice planters under a midday sun for information from the continental struggle.

The young student Ubukata Toshirō recalled how news of one battle made him feel "suddenly warm, unable to stay patiently at home"; so he went looking for friends and found them gathered around a newspaper extra, talking about the war. They kept right on discussing it, well into the night.[37] The novelist Tayama Katai described a similar mood in the Saitama village of his "country teacher" Hayashi Seizō, where each family agreed to take a "separate newspaper and circulate them around," so that they could get as many different reports as possible. "Every time the newspaper extras arrived," he recalled, "the eaves of the country towns would be bedecked with Rising Sun flags, there would be cheering in the stations, and around the straw-thatched houses . . . there would be children playing war games." When Seizō lay dying, the one thing he would not give up was newspaper reading, even though the doctor said it sapped his strength. "He couldn't keep hold of a paper for more than five minutes at a time. . . . Sometimes a half-read page would fall across his pale, unshaven face, with him unable to stir for a while." But he kept reading, because "this was an epoch-making war."[38]

The efforts Japan's editors and publishers exerted to satisfy this thirst were impressive. They both cooperated and competed with each other as never before to cover the war fully and profitably. Following the American journalist Roy A. Roberts' rule that "keeping the home front unbroken . . . is the newspapers' first function in war,"[39] rivals such as Kuroiwa and Tokutomi worked together now in organizing civic support for the war effort and coordinating press responses to governmental policies. At the same time, they fought each other in news coverage, promotion, and circulation. For if the war presented Japan's editors with fearsome challenges in logistics, scale, and cost, it also offered them unprecedented opportunities to blend their reportorial skills, managerial acumen, and promotional talents into a mix that would demonstrate their patriotism even while it attracted record circulations.

The editors' first response was to do what editors always do when a big story breaks: assign large numbers of reporters to cover it. As we have seen, the strongest dailies in war reportage—particularly *Jiji*, the *Asahi*s, *Ōsaka Mainichi*, and *Kokumin*—already had dispatched reporters to the continent prior to the outbreak of hostilities; now they sent them in larger numbers. Military regulations stipulated that no newspaper company would be allowed more than one reporter per army, but the major dailies got around that by subcontracting correspondents out to provincial papers.[40] In all, fifteen of Tokyo's sixteen dailies sent correspondents to the Asian continent, as did another thirty-seven regional papers. *Asahi* and *Ōsaka Mainichi* sent more than thirty reporters and artists each, while *Jiji*, *Yorozu*, *Hōchi*, and *Tōkyō Nichi Nichi* each sent nearly a dozen.[41] And they sent their most energetic, highly regarded writers: Torii Sosen and Ueno Iwatarō from *Ōsaka Asahi*; Okumura Shintarō,[42] Wada Tsunehiko, Shibahara Kameji, and Matsuuchi Norinobu of *Ōsaka Mainichi*; Kuroda Kōshirō (of Sino-Japanese War renown) from *Tōkyō Nichi Nichi*; and Fukushima Taimin from *Hōchi*. The reporters also were better cared for than they had been a decade earlier in the war against China, with *Asahi*, for example, having devised by now a full-fledged system of compensation for service abroad, special merit awards, injury and recuperation fees, and special payments to the families of employees killed in service.[43]

Of particular importance to the wartime journalists was the matter of getting the news back home quickly, partly because readers were so eager to hear what was going on and partly because doing so was so difficult. As in the previous war, cable lines were available from the major continental cities to Nagasaki, but getting reports to those centers was not easy, and the cables themselves were so clogged that military officials permitted only terse reports to be transmitted, which meant that detailed accounts of life in battle had to be delivered, once again, by mail or by hand.⁴⁴ And since the military mail service refused special treatment to newspapers, articles sent that way ran a risk of getting lost amid all the letters and reports.

As a result, reporters and editors resorted to all the clever schemes they could devise for speeding their reports to Tokyo and Osaka. Ōsaka Mainichi's Okumura, for example, scooped the nation with a detailed report on the army's first major engagement along the Yalu River in early May, by writing his article quickly at the battle scene, then persuading a reporter friend, Andō Hanji from Nakatsu Shimbun, to take it by ship to Shimonoseki, where a waiting Mainichi editor cabled it (at a startling cost approaching one thousand yen) to his superiors in Osaka, who in turn gave much of the next two days' issues to that story alone.⁴⁵ The other reporters carried their reports of that battle back personally, writing aboard ship as they went, and found on arrival that the story was old news. Following the battle of Liaoyang later in the month, Okumura returned to Shimonoseki himself, planning to cable his correspondence from there again. When he found that the telegraph office now was holding articles for inspection by the military censors, he took a train to Okayama, the end of the long-distance telephone line, and phoned in the piece, in seventeen successive calls.⁴⁶

Few editors had correspondents as resourceful as Okumura, but the efforts they employed to get the news to readers quickly were intense and innovative. To the degree possible, they used telegraph. Jiji and the Asahis were able to use their longstanding contracts with Reuters to get news from the continent to Nagasaki and then, by cable, to Tokyo and Osaka. Ōsaka Mainichi was known for its aggressive use of Chinese telegraph offices to get materials from the front. And sometimes reporters developed cable codes to speed accounts back. When Admiral Tōgō Heihachirō's ships demolished Russia's Baltic Fleet at Tsushima on May 27–28, 1905, for example, Asahi reporters scooped their rivals by telegraphing the code "What products did you sell?" (nan no shōhin o utta) to their editors in Osaka. The use of coded messages represented a violation of military regulations, but the rewards, in terms of reader confidence and sales, apparently were worth it.⁴⁷ Telegraph lines were too few and too crowded to carry any but the biggest (and shortest) stories, but they gave the affluent papers—the Asahis, Ōsaka Mainichi, and Jiji—a major advantage in the race for speed and readers.

Papers that could afford it also tried several schemes involving ships to enhance coverage and speed. After the navy announced that it would not allow correspondents to accompany its troops at all, *Asahi* decided in March 1904 to rent a small ship of its own, the seventy-five-ton *Shigetaka Maru*, to observe the war at sea. On its maiden voyage in the waters north of Yantai (Chefoo) on the Shandong peninsula, however, the boat's crew drew close to a Russian squadron, mistaking it for Japanese, and was sunk. The Russians captured *Asahi*'s Yantai correspondent, Miyamura Asajirō, and threw him into the military prison at Port Arthur, where he remained until General Nogi's capture of the city the next January. After three survivors swam to Yantai and reported the incident, *Asahi* decided not to buy any more ships. Their north China correspondents did, however, secure the services of several Chinese boats to observe naval activities in the area.[48]

Jiji gained a reputation for the best overall naval reportage, largely because of a contract with *The Times* of London, which had a state-of-the-art communications ship, the *Haimun*, in the waters off China. *Times* correspondent Lionel James placed one wireless system on the ship and another onshore in Shandong; he also secured an agreement from Japanese navy authorities to protect the *Haimun* in exchange for allowing a naval intelligence officer aboard. The ship went into operation just miles from Port Arthur shortly after the declaration of war and soon was "watching the war's progress from the very midst of the naval battles."[49] It barely escaped capture by the Russians on several occasions, and after the summer of 1904 Japan's own naval restrictions made it impossible for it to get near enough to the war zone to learn much; so it discontinued operations. But in the early months of the war, when many of the crucial naval engagements occurred, it was sending stories regularly to the wireless station in Shandong, which relayed them by underwater cable to London. And *Jiji*, with its exclusive *Times* contract, was able to get the details that won readers and irritated rivals.[50]

One of the most important devices for getting materials to readers quickly during this war was the issuance of extras or *gogai*. I have noted in earlier chapters the important role extras and supplements had long played in offsetting the problems of Japan's print technology; we also saw their use as information sources and publicity tools during the earlier war with China. Now, they became central to the press' modus operandi. More than a few scholars refer to this period, in fact, as the "era of the extras war" (*gogai sensō*),[51] a time when leading papers were putting out extras an average five times a week, when editors even began spying on rivals to be sure

they did not fall behind in the race for speed and pizzazz. The first
wartime extras came out the day the war began, February 10, 1904
(Ōsaka Asahi issued four gogai on that event alone),[52] and the
battlelike competition began immediately thereafter with a Hōchi
extra that scooped the other papers with news about the capture of
Russian ships at Inchon.[53] As the weeks proceeded, nearly every
paper in the country, regional as well as urban, populist as well as
mainstream, got into the competition, even when doing so was
financially foolish. The novelist Kunikida Doppō wrote a short
story titled "Gogai" several years later, looking nostalgically back
to the Russo-Japanese War months as "a time when you felt like
talking to passing strangers on the street" because everyone was
reading the same extras.[54]

The most active Tokyo participants in the gogai war were Jiji,
Yorozu, Tōkyō Nichi Nichi, and Tōkyō Asahi;[55] in Osaka they were
Asahi and Mainichi. And the intensity with which they fought
hardly could be exaggerated. Editors decorated the special issues
with eye-catching graphics: large, bold type, flags, sketches, and
shouts of teikoku banzai (a thousand cheers for the empire!). They
put them out in unprecedented numbers: 385 at Ōsaka Asahi during the war, 498 at Ōsaka Mainichi.[56] They put out specially edited
gogai for readers of different geographic regions.[57] They even advertised extras. And they did everything in their power to beat their
rivals to the streets. Ōsaka Mainichi's Okumura recalled that the
editors would have an employee with a stopwatch "run to the
Asahi entrance and take down the hour and minute when their first
extra came out."[58] Kiryū Yūyū, known for his later resistance to
ultranationalism, recalled an even more surreptitious way of checking, in which

> someone from the editorial department would go to the third (top)
> floor of Ōsaka Mainichi with binoculars and a stopwatch and scout
> out the Asahi chimney. They had a cylinder press already, but since
> it was powered by coal rather than electricity, you could tell if they
> were working on an extra by whether or not there was smoke. If the
> patrol saw smoke, he would rush in a frenzy to the second-floor edi-
> torial office and shout, "There's smoke coming from Asahi's chim-
> ney!" Then someone from the Tokyo-Osaka Communications De-
> partment would call our Tokyo branch office in a panic . . . to ask if
> they had material for an extra. If the branch officer said no, there
> would be a big commotion and someone would bark, "What are you
> doing up there, you damned idiot!"[59]

The Osaka papers drew up guidelines for cooperation early in the war, to prevent the expense of excessive *gogai* competition, but the rules were broken almost before the ink dried.[60] Even regional papers such as *Miyazaki Shinpō* and *Nishū Dokuritsu Shimbun* in Kyushu and *Kōchi Shimbun* in Shikoku fought each other and curried favor with readers through "extras wars," as did the people who hawked *gogai*, particularly in Tokyo where they stood to make a *sen* or more per copy. It was not unusual for 1500 sellers to go out from a single newspaper office, each wearing up to two dozen bells around the waist and shouting "Extra! Extra!" to crowds of city workers eager for the latest from the continent.[61] As Kiryū put it, papers felt compelled to report every bit of new war information "as quickly as possible," so when normal publication schedules stood in their way, they resorted to "news by detour" *(ukai no sata).*[62]

The newest technique in the war months for getting news to readers more graphically was the printing of photographs in the news columns themselves. By the turn of the century, American journalists had at last developed the technology to print photographs with copper plates attached directly to cylinder presses,[63] and by 1903 their Japanese peers had followed suit, so that on New Year's Day 1904, *Hōchi* was able to "stun" its readers by running pictures of court ladies and actresses on each page. By April of that year, *Yomiuri* also was running occasional pictures, as was *Tōkyō Nichi Nichi* by July. *Tōkyō Asahi* used the war as the subject of its initial photograph on September 30, printing a column-and-a-half photo by the pioneering Ueno Iwatarō, who used a hand-held Kodak camera. The picture showed three imperial soldiers standing near a Japanese flag on the Liaoyang battlefield where the Second Army recently had triumphed.

The technology for developing and reproducing photos remained primitive throughout the war (newspapers still did not even have their own darkrooms), and the Osaka giants lagged behind their Tokyo peers in this field, since they had no local company to develop and prepare the film for publication. As a result, it was early 1905 before *Ōsaka Asahi* was doing much with photography, while Tokyo's *Yorozu* was unable to run its first regular photo until May 1905, when the war was winding down. The war nevertheless pushed the papers toward what soon would become a revolutionary medium. By 1905, many of them were running frequent photographs of generals, of officers departing for battle, and of soldiers who died in battle, the most famous shot probably being Nakarai Sentarō's *Tōkyō Asahi* picture of General Nogi meeting General

Stossel after the capture of Port Arthur. And by the end of Meiji, photographs were used daily in the press.[64]

ALL THE NEWS THAT EDIFIES

If Japan's papers were unified in their determination to satisfy the popular demand for information about the war, they were less consistent when it came to the balance, honesty, and reliability of what they wrote in these months. There is no question that the editors felt a heavy responsibility toward their readers and their country; nor is there much question that they believed in the journalist's responsibility for presenting news accurately and fully. But in these months the conflicting demands of professionalism, patriotism, and profit sometimes shoved professionalism toward the end of the line. There was, for example, a constant temptation to curry reader favor by reporting unconfirmed rumors and ignoring, or slighting, war news that revealed anything other than victories or progress. It was easy to argue that it was proper to tailor battle accounts or omit troubling information in order to build morale and elicit public support for the war effort.

A telling example of the tension between professionalism and profit came in the response of *Asahi*'s Shanghai correspondent Hori Fusō early in 1905 to his editors' insistent demands for more (and speedier) reports on the whereabouts of Russia's Baltic fleet, then sailing from the North Atlantic toward Vladivostok. He replied testily that he knew that public curiosity was insatiable, but that he would not report what he did not know. As he told his editors:

> There are a lot of falsehoods in the other papers' cables, because they talk to reporters for the English-language papers in Hong Kong and Shanghai, then send their reports back without confirming their accuracy. As for me, I cannot sully *Asahi*'s honor with that kind of irresponsible reporting. If we really wanted to verify the Baltic fleet's whereabouts, we would need to hire two or three high-velocity ships and sail a hundred miles or so out into the ocean. . . . But I have no intention of wasting company money that way.

The restraint must have made his satisfaction the deeper when his Singapore contacts soon thereafter sighted thirty-two Russian ships on their way to East Asia, allowing *Asahi* to publish Japan's first extra on the actual "sighting of enemy ships."[65] But the editors' nagging and the paper's 385 wartime extras make it clear that double-checking for accuracy was more important to Hori than it was to his editors. A *Hōchi* editor revealed the same conflict between professionalism and profit when he told one insistent salesperson that he was not issuing as many extras as the sellers wanted, because he would not sully the paper's reputation by "putting out the same issue twice."[66]

That did not keep *Hōchi* or any other paper, however, from covering every aspect of the war—except its ambiguities—in numbing detail. Official decrees and statements were relayed to the public without fail, even when they were repetitious or of little significance. A survey of the front pages of these months shows that even the tiniest war detail merited coverage. There were reports on the setting up of military camps in Hakodate and Nagasaki, full-page maps of battle areas, stories about press regulations, as well as articles on innumerable "fierce attacks" by Russian troops (sometimes with casualty figures), on the battle deaths of other papers' correspondents,[67] on the Russian soldiers' fear of coming "out to pick up their dead comrades" at Port Arthur,[68] and on the changing strength of enemy forces. A *Kokumin* story informed readers that young German men, impressed by Japan's soldiers, wanted to secure Japanese brides, while *Yorozu* ran a letter from an anonymous foreigner praising the way the "noble Japs have acquitted themselves" and offering to serve himself as an officer in the emperor's army.[69] Endless stories appeared about spies and suspected spies, the cost of war (both human and material), and foreign evaluations (always glowing) of Japan's battlefield performance. There were poems about the war in the classic *hyakunin isshu* style,[70] accounts of riots among Russian evacuees in Harbin, descriptions of prison conditions on both sides, rumors from "well-informed circles" that the "fall of Port Arthur is now imminent,"[71] and reports on the occupation of Sakhalin and the nature of life in the camps. In the spring of 1904, *Jiji* reported on thousands of flag-carrying demonstrators, who marched in support of the war, sang patriotic songs, and shouted *banzai*s.[72] And at the end of that year a *Yorozu* reporter acquainted readers with the daily privations suffered by soldiers during a Manchurian winter. "Although it is cold," he wrote, "they do not have the luxury of *tōfu* (bean curd) boiled over a brazier." He outlined several days' diets:

> November 22. Morning: nothing but pickles seasoned for five short minutes in sake *(narazuke)*. Noon: a few dried sardines. Evening: *sengiri* (small, short vegetable pieces), *daikon* (white radish) and hot canned beef. . . .

November 23. Morning: two *umeboshi* (pickled plums). Noon: *sen-giri* and *daikon* with one ounce of beef. Evening: the same.[73]

As in the Sino-Japanese War, editors and readers lusted most avidly for announcements of victories and descriptions of their men's lives at the front. After the long-delayed victory at Port Arthur at the beginning of 1905, all of the dailies issued jubilant extras, followed by reams of reports on the nature and meaning of the victory. *Ōsaka Asahi* was on the streets almost as soon as the Russian white flag was raised, with an extra declaring, "Telephone report from Tokyo: Stossel surrenders (terms of surrender settled this morning)." *Yomiuri Shimbun* issued two extras on January 2, the first sandwiching a fifty-nine-character victory announcement between two banner headlines proclaiming, "Port Arthur falls," and the second providing a few more facts in large black type. *Tōkyō Nichi Nichi* also issued multiple extras that day, but typically used less flashy type and provided more detail. By January 4, *Tōkyō Asahi* was putting out longer extras, describing the months-long, exhausting efforts of Japanese soldiers that led to victory.[74] And the same kind of detailed, emotional stories followed each major success.

The stories the papers promoted most heavily were their correspondents' personal accounts of life among the troops. In May 1904, *Jiji* reported on the deadly battles for the Nanshan Heights on the isthmus north of Port Arthur, which the Japanese took only after consuming more ammunition than they had used in the entire Sino-Japanese War.[75] One reporter described the "fierce fighting" of the Russian troops, then explained the impact of the heavy casualties on his countrymen's own spirit. "It is said that our casualties numbered around three thousand," he wrote in a bit of understatement; but anyone who expected the heavy losses to undermine their fighting spirit "did not really know the true nature of the Japanese warrior *(bushi)*. The fact that each company lost almost half of its men simply prompted the healthy soldiers to draw on their combat skills and fight even more effectively, with a vigor and bravery that prevented even the slightest deterioration in our military strength."[76]

The *Asahi* correspondents were especially known for their meticulous descriptions of the ins and outs of life at the front. Miyamura's reports of his own life in the Port Arthur military prison, noted above, drew many readers, as did *Tōkyō Asahi* correspondent Konishi Kanau's almost scientific accounts of the attitudes of soldiers living under the "rain of bullets and crossfire of arms."[77] One of the most effective war correspondents was Torii Sosen, who wrote of the First Army's spring movement north through Korea:

> In this war, we had to fight first for the army's route. . . . The wretchedness of Korea's roads defies even the specialists. There are more mountain inclines than one can count, and most of them are little more than muddy seas. A horse has a hard time freeing itself if its foot slips off the trail. If an axle sinks in the mud, there is no moving, either forward or backward. As a result, the army has to move ahead step by step, through rugged rice fields and uneven mountain terrain, clearing the road as it goes. No matter how fast the infantry moves, it cannot fight without provisions; and even when the provisions arrive, it still cannot attack the enemy's stronghold until the gun carriages come. Will we ever have the heavy artillery we need for this fight?

Torii proceeded to describe the roads' ice cover on cold days and their spongy defiance when it rained. "The real victors in these hardships are the transport soldiers," he said; "they are the ones who deserve the first credit in the battle for the Yalu River."[78] This was the detail mothers and fathers back at home wanted, and while lengthy stories of this kind took a long time getting from the battlefront to the office, the editors gave them special play when they arrived.

The single most consistent characteristic of all the coverage—of long battlefield accounts, terse *gogai,* and tedious official announcements—was the writers' untempered patriotism. It seemed that correspondents were incapable of writing anything during this war without noting the sacrifice, the discipline, the faithfulness of the Japanese soldier—or the glory of the national cause. Shortly after the declaration of war, *Yomiuri* declared on page one: "We must have unalloyed resolution. In truth, forty million of us, fellow countrymen all, dare allow ourselves but a single purpose. Although we were fortunate enough to win a great victory in the first naval battle, our enemy is one of the world's great powers; it will not surrender after a loss or two." It called on each citizen to devote every bit of energy to the war cause, even if it meant "dying or falling into personal ruin."[79] Sometimes the enthusiasm took the form of reports on "the fervent patriotism of groups throughout the country"; sometimes it showed up in self-congratulations that "the nation has suffered no embarrassment whatever";[80] often it came in gushing expressions after battle victories about the "pride fathers and brothers must feel toward their family members at the front";[81] and sometimes it produced condescending reports about what weak patriots or overconfident strategists their Russian rivals were. As *Asahi*'s Ueda Sentarō reported on returning from St. Petersburg on April 10, 1904: "Of course the Russians know in their heads that they must fight Japan, but they are so strongly self-confident that it never occurs to them that they might personally have to fight or that they really are being attacked by Japan."[82] The foreigner who said "the whole country is sending its flesh and blood without a whimper or a murmur to feed the war" may have been exaggerating, as we shall see below, but only slightly. As Uchimura Kanzō, one of the few murmurers, said in exasperation at the patriotic, one-sided quality of the coverage: "There was no newspaper worthy of the name in Japan. Not one reported the truth." That was an exaggeration too. But he was right when he added that the papers usually "covered up unfavorable news . . . and reported small events unfavorable to the enemy."[83] The journalists saw themselves as soldiers of a kind, warriors for their country's noble cause, and the content and prose of their articles invariably reflected that fact.

UNEASY ALLIES OF THE STATE

This unleashing of patriotism did not mean that the reporters and editors always were happy chauvinists, however. As in the earlier struggles over treaty revision and constitutionalism, the journalists' patriotism took quite different forms from that of the officials, and though the war muted their antigovernment rhetoric, the struggles between writers and authorities continued, not so much over general government policy or the officials' right to censor as over the harshness and inconsistencies of enforcement. At the heart of the differences lay an official decision to control war news even more rigidly than in the Sino-Japanese War—more rigidly, by most evaluations, than it ever had been controlled anywhere, East or West, in any war. Elmer Davis wrote thirty years later as head of America's World War II Office of War Information that to win a war "the people should know as much about it as they can."[84] Japanese authorities in 1904 would have been aghast at such a view. Their attitude, in the words of Tokutomi, was that any facts that might even suggest vulnerability must be kept "completely secret so as not to undermine the people's spirit." Tokutomi admitted that critics might have had reason to question the censors' sincerity at times, but added that "given the seriousness of the upheaval then, the authorities decided it was best to keep things as confidential as possible, even if that might mean provoking popular outrage later on."[85]

Even before the war began, regulations were issued prohibiting the sending of coded telegraph messages from sensitive locales, and when war was declared on February 10, the Army issued a fourteen-article set of "rules for war correspondents" *(jōgun kisha kokoroe).*[86] It required that all Japanese correspondents and their aides (1) register with the Army Ministry,[87] (2) wear Western-style clothes and identifying badges at all times, (3) show their correspondent's certification when asked, (4) follow the orders of their military superiors, and (5) accept trial in military courts for the violation of any regulations. The most restrictive provision, Article 11, prohibited the use of secret codes in correspondents' reports and required that all articles be censored by military authorities before transmission back to Japan. Two days later, on February 12, the navy published a seven-article code with essentially the same provisions, as well as the all-purpose statement: "Regulations for handling the war correspondents of newspapers and news associations are the responsibility of squadron and troop commanders" (Article 5).

With these codes as a framework, the authorities put into place a censorship system that can only be called draconian, a system that the German physician Edwin Baelz said "sometimes borders on the absurd" and keeps even foreign diplomats from having "the slightest inkling where the different armies are and how strong they are."[88] News transmissions over the military telegraph system were limited to five lines. Reporters were allowed to observe specific campaigns only on the condition that they send no detailed reports on the fighting until after a battle's conclusion—which meant an eight-month blackout of anything but the vaguest news about the attack on Port Arthur. The navy allowed no reporters at all aboard its ships. Journalists from other nations who had come to Japan for certification as war correspondents were pampered, wined, and dined in Tokyo, then, in a situation one called "unique in the annals of journalism," prohibited for weeks from going to the continent itself. When loud protests resulted in their finally being allowed into Manchuria in tightly controlled groups, their access to battlefronts was strictly limited.[89]

And the pervasive, inconsistent censorship system, which often forced a reporter's piece through three or four levels of inspection only to be killed by the dreaded "military secret" *(gun no himi-*

tsu) stamp, prevented just about anything from being published that even suggested what difficulties Japan was experiencing on the battlefield or in its supply systems. Though papers could report the names of solders injured or killed, for example, they were not allowed to identify their divisions or units, lest readers learn too much about troop strength in specific areas. Detailed reports of what happened in the fighting areas were delayed for weeks and months when they were allowed to be discussed at all. And everyone had to grapple with gross inconsistencies in censorship policies, which saw urban dailies generally (but not always) handled more rigidly than provincial papers and often prevented the publication at higher levels of what lower-level inspectors would have regarded as acceptable. Only by reading between the lines of reports about the "fierceness of Russia's resistance" or the "high cost of the war" could readers get a sense that this was anything but a complete and smash-ing Japanese victory. And few readers were equipped, by either training or inclination, to do that kind of reading. Even Russian censorship, said one irritated foreign observer, "was more liberal than the Japanese."[90]

Patriotic or not, the journalists did not always accept these heavy-handed restrictions with gentle grace. In the war's first summer, reporters from all the major papers formed a Hiroshima Resident Reporters Club (Zaihiro Kisha Kurabu) to fight the rigid headquarters' controls and declared: "Even when we reporters act docilely, we receive a frigid response; we are treated like slaves. In the name of preventing military secrets from leaking, officials have become more and more oppressive of late. It has become an insult to public understanding; we can keep silent no longer."[91] Occasionally a suggestion of their frustration would seep into print, as when Yugeta Seiichi wrote in *Tōkyō Asahi* that "the material that is acceptable for writing is not particularly interesting" or when *Yorozu* asked its readers, "Are the army's censorship authorities really using common sense?"[92] Some reporters also devised ingenious schemes to circumvent the regulations that made it so hard to get reports back quickly, as described above. As a general rule, however, correspondents saw little choice but to grumble behind the scenes, accept the censors' rulings, and focus on the victories, neutral facts, and atmosphere of military life.

Particularly disturbing was a tendency of officials to range beyond the straightforward application of regulations into the world of intrigue when they felt strongly enough about a journalist's work. Early in the war, for example, a group of Katsura allies launched a mean-spirited, devastating attack on their longtime nemesis, Akiyama Teisuke of *Niroku*, that nearly drove him out of public life. Members of both the cabinet and the Diet were embarrassed and infuriated in December 1903 when it was discovered that Akiyama and several legislative cohorts had slipped a denunciation of the Katsura cabinet into the supposedly pro forma call for a new Diet to be convened.[93] Then, when he was elected to a third Diet term on March 1 by supporters who, in his own evaluation, "would not allow me" to withdraw from the election,[94] several officials decided he had to be checked. And when he published an editorial on March 16 (a full five weeks into the war), calling for the impeachment of the Katsura cabinet for increasing the national debt by handling war bonds ineptly, they decided to drive him out of public life.[95]

In what came to be known as the *Rotan* (Russian spy) affair, rumors were spread that the Nagasaki police chief had received a pencil-written postcard accusing Akiyama of "giving domestic secrets" to Russian War Minister Aleksei Kuropatkin while Kuropatkin was on a diplomatic visit to Japan the previous June.[96] The rumors' plausibility was supported, whispered Akiyama's antagonists, by the fact that *Niroku* had published a mistaken report that same month about a breakthrough in Russian-Japanese negotiations.[97] And even though Akiyama long had been a member of the prowar faction the allegations caused such a ruckus that the Diet finally set up a committee to investigate. The committee found "no evidence to prove the rumors," but added that Akiyama had "acted in a way that was beneficial to Russia," presumably through his stinging anti-Katsura editorials and parliamentary maneuvers.[98] When Katsura's Diet ally, Ogawa Gen'ichi, continued to push for his ouster from the Diet, Akiyama finally agreed to resign, not because of the *Rotan* allegations, he said, but because of the trouble stirred up by his paper's recent impeachment editorial. To announce his decision, he went to the platform for his first and last Diet speech, in an atmosphere "filled with the silence of ill will." He reminded his fellows that even baseless rumors destroy people. He said the face of Home Minister Yoshikawa Akimasa looked especially worried now, as well it should since he had it on good authority that Home Ministry funds had been spent to defeat Akiyama in the March election, and since "the one who knows the most about the *Rotan* problem is you, Mr. Home Minister." Then he concluded abruptly, noting that the Diet members had found the spy talk more "like a detective novel" than credible: "So there is no need for me to defend myself now. If asked to take responsibility for my newspaper, however, I shall be happy to do so." And with that he resigned.[99]

Unfortunately, the resignation did not end Akiyama's problems. The Home Ministry brought charges against *Niroku* for disturbing public order with its March 16 editorial, and on March 22, the Tokyo District Court issued an astounding banishment *(hakkō kinshi)* order and sent the paper's nominal editor, Shirano Masami, to jail for four months. Akiyama appealed unsuccessfully, and on April 14 one of Tokyo's largest, most influential newspapers was dead. Feisty as ever, Akiyama came out the next day with a new paper, the *Tōkyō Niroku Shimbun,* but it never approached the strength of the old *Niroku.* As he wrote in later years: "The government figured that, at this time, anyone linked to Russia would lose public popularity, even if the rumor were a lie. . . . It seems stupid . . . but this gave me the reputation of a hateful rogue and took away my standing in society."[100]

The most disturbing aspect of the *Rotan* affair may well have been the rest of the press' response. No one was overly surprised at the methods of the authorities, who had used muscle before when finesse failed, but the journalists, who had spoken often through the years about the importance of free speech, might have been expected to come to *Niroku's* defense. They did not, however. In the telling of Ariyama Teruo, the *Rotan* affair represented "an unprecedented level of newspaper oppression, the banishing of the city's largest-circulation paper; yet the other papers expressed little concern about the suppression. Only the fires of war stirred them."[101] The other editors may have feared similar persecution, but the greater likelihood is that they were not all that troubled by Akiyama's persecution. While journalists and scholars have damned the authorities repeatedly across the years for their heavy-handed control policies during the Russo-Japanese War, the truth is that most journalists were abettors of censorship. They had become self-confessed soldiers in the war themselves, and an iconoclast such as Akiyama made them more uncomfortable than the authorities' high-handed methods.

The most obvious group of abettors consisted of the *goyō* papers whose editors had close ties to the cabinet. The other, larger group was made up of the majority of the dailies, whose staffs kept the official world at arm's length yet, for reasons both financial and patriotic, did very little to counter the harsh censorship. The best-known of the former were Tokutomi's *Kokumin* and Itō Miyoji's *Tōkyō Nichi Nichi,* whose ties to officialdom stretched back for years. *Nichi Nichi's* relations with the official world became a bit more complex in this period, when it was purchased midway through the war by Katsura's rival, Katō Kōmei, with 100,000 yen of Mitsubishi money. But Katō turned out to be less antagonistic toward the cabinet's military policies than Itō had become, and the paper gave the war its full support.[102] And *Kokumin*, which received both money and scoops from the officials, aggressively took up the job of mobilizing the public on the government's behalf, a task that left Tokutomi exhausted but exhilarated. As he wrote a friend then: "The *Kokumin* is immensely popular. . . . There is influence. There is trust. . . . There is nothing like labor to dissipate one's anxieties and to overcome one's fears. I have discovered the paradise of the coolie laborer's Heaven!"[103]

That *Nichi Nichi* and *Kokumin* exerted a good deal of influence as official mouthpieces is indicated in the fact that both enjoyed significant jumps in circulation during the war months; their ballyhooed access to official sources gained them respect in these months.[104] It can be argued though that the general compliance of the other, supposedly more independent papers had even more impact on the general public than *Kokumin* and *Nichi Nichi* did. While it was true that the "independent" writers and editors grumbled over the troubles censors gave them and organized to get better treatment, it is equally true that they simply accepted the overall control system, submitting to the blackout on concrete battle news during the days or months that fighting was going on in a specific location, underreporting casualty figures, discussing battlefield difficulties only in terms of the immensity of the challenge and the heroism of the emperor's troops, vilifying anyone who dared raise a voice of dissent. *Asahi*'s Ōmura Kinka said afterward that he had held back voluntarily on letting even his editors know about the war's darker side when officials warned him that passing on such information might hurt national morale.[105] When the journalists cursed or circumvented the censors, it was because they wanted permission to get dispatches back more quickly or to print what they regarded as harmless material, rather than because they wanted to report on the war's complexities. They never complained about the general philosophies behind the censorship system, only about petty and inconsistent enforcement. And in the end, as we shall see, the price for that servility was high.

A MURMUR OF DISSENT

Fervent and pervasive as the press' support for the war was, it was not quite total. For the first time in modern Japanese history, the country experienced a whisper of public dissent over a foreign war, and though voices of caution and opposition remained at the fringes, they added an element to the world of journalism that demands a recounting. Yosano Akiko, for example, touched off a storm of mainstream journalistic retorts with a poem in the literary magazine *Myōjō*, begging her soldier brother not to die.[106] In a less well known case, Midorigawa Kikuo, a twenty-seven-year-old writer for the Hokkaido *Otaru Shimbun,* expressed a certain war weariness in the fall of 1904 and questioned the cavalier talk about dying for the homeland. His article was particularly noteworthy because the *Otaru Shimbun* had demanded war lustily in 1903. But eight months into the conflict, with no victory in sight, Midorigawa wrote "A Battlefield View of Life and Death" *(Senjō ni shishō kan),* urging soldiers to seek life, not death. "If I am to fulfill my responsibility as your friend," he wrote, "I must pass on a single word: Live well. That is it. To you who have resolved to die, I would say, Live!" He recalled how the old women of Sparta sent their sons off to war with the warning that they should come back carrying their swords lest they be borne back on a sword, and concluded by noting that foreigners had an appropriate epithet for Japanese battle bravery: "the lunatic passion of war" *(sensō kyōnetsu).*[107]

Midorigawa's voice was exceptional among mainstream journalists; that it was raised at all, even in far northern Hokkaido, was significant. Even more significant were the activities of a small group of nonmainstream journalists, the socialist companions of Kōtoku Shōsui, who gave Japan its first genuine, if limited, encounter with pacifism. Actually, socialist writings first had been discussed in the Japanese press well before the end of the Tokugawa era, in an 1863 series of *Kanhan Kaigai Shimbun* articles about revolutionary movements in Russia,[108] and the Japanese word for socialism, *shakaishugi,* had been popularized by Tokutomi in his early years at *Kokumin no Tomo* and *Kokumin Shimbun.*[109] By the late 1890s, several bright young thinkers concerned about the mushrooming urban social problems had created Japan's first significant socialist organizations, with names like Rōdō Kumiai Kiseikai (Association for the Formation of Labor Unions) and Shakaigaku Kenkyūkai (Association for the Study of Socialism), and in 1901 Japan's first socialist political party, the Shakai Minshūtō (Social Democratic Party), was founded—only to be shut down by the authorities a few hours later.[110]

There also were many lively, if generally unsophisticated, discussions of socialist views in the pre–Russo-Japanese War press, particularly in the three populist papers, *Niroku, Mainichi,* and

Yorozu. Niroku was concerned with the actual plight of the laboring classes more than with theories, but it raised the workers' standard with a kind of zest of which only Akiyama was capable. "Laborers also are Japanese! Like other Japanese their freedom to assemble is constitutionally protected," it declared on March 19, 1902, when police were threatening to shut down its second annual labor friendship rally. And two days later: "Tears for the Police interference! Cheers for the coming Reunion! Tears for all idlers and vagrants! Cheers for all hard-working order-loving laborers!"[111]

Christian humanism underlay *Mainichi*'s interest in socialist thought, and editor Shimada gave full play not only to Ashio's "innocent people receiving treatment that prisoners should not receive," but to the overtly socialist treatises of Kinoshita Naoe. He also serialized Kinoshita's socialist novel *Hi no hashira* (Pillar of fire), which described pacifist meetings, anticapitalist labor struggles, and the need "to construct a new era after a thoroughgoing destruction of the old," then had his hero, Shinoda, call socialism the "heart of God . . . which Christ declared."[112] The paper that ran the most socialist material was *Yorozu*, which included Kōtoku, Sakai, and Kawakami Kiyoshi among its writers. Already by the beginning of the century, Kōtoku had begun writing frequently about socialist and anarchist ideas, proclaiming a "requiem for the Liberal Party," raising questions about the need for governments,[113] and declaring that "neither war nor weapons . . . are compatible with a healthy society, a civilized society, a progressive society, or a peaceful society," since the use of such weapons was "like forcing powerful medicine on a people who are not sick."[114] Arahata Kanson, one of the the century's leading socialist thinkers, recalled that he began reading *Yorozu* "simply to experience Uchimura Sensei's prose" but in the process discovered Kōtoku, "the one who brought me under the influence of socialist thought."[115] And Sakai himself noted that "*Yorozu* evidenced rich socialist tendencies" right up until Kuroiwa's about-face on the war. Indeed, he said, with writers such as Kōtoku, Kawakami, Sakai, Shiba Teikichi, and Ishikawa Sanshirō, "all of them socialists . . . *Yorozu* at that time seemed like a semi–socialist organ."[116]

The authorities generally ignored these writings in the prewar years, partly because their proposals were either theoretical or relatively moderate and partly because socialist intellectuals were seen as marginal.[117] When the socialist writers lost their bases, with *Yorozu*'s and *Mainichi*'s conversion to the prowar factions late in 1903, however, that situation changed. Within weeks, on November 15, 1903, Kōtoku and Sakai launched Japan's first socialist newspaper, the weekly *Heimin Shimbun*.[118] And while it enjoyed neither a large circulation nor a long life, it drew enough attention from security-conscious officials and took positions sufficiently in advance of its time to prompt one press historian to call its appearance "the most notable journalistic development in the last half of the Meiji era."[119] That evaluation surely overstates *Heimin's* impact by several times, but no press history of the era would be complete without a look at its contributions.

The twelve-page initial issue, put out from Katayama Sen's home with the financial backing of the physician Katō Tokujirō and former Nakae Chōmin student Kojima Tatsutarō, ran a profile of the London labor leader Will Crooks ("From Slums to Parliament"); declared its commitment to "liberty, equality, and fraternity," and included more than thirty advertisements, for everything from Ebisu Beer to English-language schools and the works of Plato. The five-thousand-copy printing sold out quickly at 3.5 *sen* each; so the publishers printed three thousand more. The brands of socialism expressed in *Heimin* were multifaceted, reflecting the movement's nondoctrinaire makeup in Japan at the time. As Sakai recalled it, "The first issue's manifesto, which was shaped and drafted by Kōtoku, exhibited three tendencies: French liberal thought *(jiyū minken shisō)*, German democratic socialism *(shakai minshūshugi)*, and Christian socialism."[120]

The paper created much larger waves in Tokyo's intellectual circles than one might have expected from its limited circulation, in part because of its novelty and even more because of the virility of its intellectual life, what Kinoshita called the "whirling gaseous passions of those young people."[121] Overwhelmingly male as its staff was, for example, it provided relatively more place for women than any other paper, including among its writers and editors Kanno Suga, Fukuda Hideko, and Itō Noe.[122] It ran articles by nearly all of the country's best-known socialists as well as by other liberal thinkers: Nakae Chōmin, Katayama Sen, Abe Isoo, and, of course, Kōtoku and Sakai. And during its fourteen and a half months, it provided almost the only national vehicle for the expression of unorthodox views, including pacifism.

The theme that united the *Heimin* writers above all was opposition to violence in general and to the Russo-Japanese War in particular. Just before the war started, the paper blamed the tensions between the two countries on the "monied interests" of both nations: the desire to expand markets and secure colonies. A week after the bombing at Port Arthur, it observed that the fruits of victory would include not only the rise of militarism but "millions, nay trillions, of yen in interest on the public debt." "How long," the writer asked, "will you and your posterity have to work to pay off this burden?" And the next month the editors wrote to their Russian socialist counterparts:

> Dear Comrades: Your Government and our Government have plunged into fighting at last in order to satisfy their imperialistic desires, but to socialists there is no barrier of race, territory or nationality. We are comrades, brothers and sisters and have no reason to fight each other. Your enemy is not the Japanese people, but our militarism and so-called patriotism. . . . We object absolutely to using military force in our fighting. We have to fight by peaceful means; by reason and speech. . . . We cannot foresee which of the two governments shall win in the fighting, but whichever gets the victory, the results of the war will be the same—general misery, the burden of heavy taxes, the degradation of morality and the supremacy of militarism.[123]

The *Heimin* view was not popular with the war-impassioned public. Indeed, by the end of January 1904 it was selling only 4,500 copies, and once the war began that figure dropped to 1,700. Financial support withered too, with the number of ads per issue falling to about ten by May.[124] That did not, however, keep officials from worrying about the paper's influence. At the end of March, the Tokyo District Court slapped a *hakkō kinshi* or banning order on the paper for its antitax editorial and sentenced Sakai to three months in jail. When the Higher Court overturned the ban and reduced Sakai's sentence to two months, the police and Home Ministry officials began harassing the paper in other ways: searching newsstands where it was sold, warning Kōtoku that his activities were being watched, and sending policemen to "advise" readers to take a different paper.[125] "If one thinks that there are not more than two hundred professed socialists in Japan, it seems strange that the government is rather nervous about our propagandism," complained one *Heimin* writer. "None can better tell the government that we are harmless people than its own detectives, yet, the government is too nervous to let us alone."[126]

The battle between the officials and the editors climaxed in November, after the fighting at Port Arthur had stalled and the paper ran a call for primary school teachers to become socialists and promised a translation of the Communist Manifesto in the next issue. The Home Ministry forbade the sale and distribution of that issue, for corrupting the morals of young people, and when the Manifesto appeared on November 13, the paper's anniversary issue, the officials began new legal proceedings to shut the paper down and brought charges against Kōtoku and Ishikawa Sanshirō, the writer who had urged school teachers to embrace socialism. The paper's editors reacted defiantly, leading off the November 20 issue with the pronouncement *"Hatsubai teishi mata kuru!! . . . hatsubai teishi mata kuru!!!"* (Sales and distribution prohibited again!). The courts were not so kind this time, however. Nishikawa went to jail for seven months, Kōtoku for five, and the paper's appeal was disallowed.[127]

Heimin's final issue, on January 29, 1905, which was printed entirely in red, began with Kōtoku's lament, "Shedding tears, we now declare the discontinuation of *Heimin Shimbun.*" He apologized for letting his readers down, then insisted that socialist ideas were not dependent on this particular organ and that he was resolved to fight in other ways. His conclusion, however, was morose: "Alas! The life of *Heimin Shimbun* was brief and eventful. Who would have dreamed at its founding just how brief and eventful its life would be? Our solitary light is extinguished. With this last issue, the heavens turn cold; the night lengthens; the wind is dreary."[128]

His desolate metaphors were not far off the mark. The mainstream papers gave scant attention to *Heimin*'s passing. *Tōkyō Asahi,* for example, merely noted on January 30 that the paper's editors, "buffeted by one calamity after another, found it extremely difficult to keep *Heimin Shimbun* going and finally shut it down yesterday," without a word about the official order that forced the closing.[129] Heiminsha, the paper's parent company, started another paper, the weekly *Chokugen,* but by October it too was dead, victim of a government—and a society of fellow journalists—not yet ready to include "extremists" among those deserving free speech. As a *Heimin Shimbun* essay noted toward the end:

> It is not the government alone this time that persecutes us, but many papers and magazines are criticizing us as if with one voice. One of the magazines goes so far as to say that it would have socialists beheaded if it only had the power of executing them. It is not an unusual thing for them to urge socialists to go out of country, because by their presence uniformity of opinion is supposed to be violated.[130]

And uniformity was the goal above all goals in this time of war, for journalists as much as for officials.

REAPING THE WHIRLWIND OF PATRIOTISM

Socialism frightened Katsura and his fellow officials but, as they were to learn at war's end, uninformed, passionate patriots could be even harder to handle. As the last weeks of war approached and the peace negotiators and journalists converged on Portsmouth, New Hampshire, in the summer of 1905, the Japanese press was ready either for a grand settlement or for fighting to continue. Most writers actually favored the latter course, to assure that Russia's defeat was complete and that peace would be lucrative, but if negotiations were to be held they insisted that Japan should accept nothing less than what the "seven professors" of 1903 notoriety were now demanding: the cession of Sakhalin in its entirety, the maritime provinces in southeastern Siberia, Kamchatka, the East China Railroad, all of Russia's Manchurian rights—and a three billion yen indemnity. Only the "redemption of our wartime sacrifices" would do.[131]

As soon as the peace talks got under way in early August, the Japanese papers, nearly all of whom sent correspondents to cover them, began to express increasing frustration, first because it was so hard to get concrete information about the negotiations, second because of the direction they sensed the talks were taking. While Russia's chief negotiator, the popular Sergei Witte, was keenly sensitive to the importance of public opinion in negotiations of this sort and thus quite open with reporters on all sides,[132] the Japanese diplomats, headed by Komura Jutarō, were as closemouthed as their censors had been during the war. Russian views and interpretations of the proceedings (including the czar's alleged statement that Russia would not "pay one kopeck of indemnity nor cede an inch of territory")[133] thus were easy to secure, while the Japanese positions and activities remained hidden. As a result, even the Japanese reporters were hard-pressed to avoid putting a Russian slant on information.[134] Indeed, the only papers not thoroughly frustrated in their efforts to cover the conference were *Kokumin,* which secured inside information through Tokutomi's ties to Katsura; *Ōsaka Asahi,* which had unusually good sources among Western reporters, and *Ōsaka Mainichi,* which had hired as its correspondent John Callan O'Laughlin, a Washington journalist who had served as mediator Theodore Roosevelt's private secretary and knew Witte personally.[135]

The resentment over lack of access, however, was nothing compared to the Japanese reporters' rising anger about the direction negotiations seemed to be going. Sensing that their negotiators were not insisting on all they thought Japan had won in Manchuria, reporters adopted a critical tone now that had been impossible during the months of actual fighting. After the Russian statement about not giving up a kopeck, *Tōkyō Asahi* wrote that "only swords settle that which neither speech nor reason can arrange,"[136] and even the once circumspect *Tōkyō Nichi Nichi* urged readers repeatedly to push the government to stand up to the Russians. Japan's official demands, which appeared in the press on August 13, actually were not far from what most people had desired,[137] but by the waning days of that month, aggressive reporters had ascertained that some of those demands, including the indemnity and the cession of the whole of Sakhalin, had been dropped, and their papers responded sharply, with *Jiji* stating that Japan should either force Russia to pay an indemnity or help itself to more land on the continent, and a group of Tokyo reporters issuing a joint pledge "to work for the removal of the present cabinet."[138]

One of the most aggressive correspondents in teasing news out of reluctant sources was *Ōsaka Asahi*'s Fukutomi Masanori, who secured most of his news from the famous *Times* of London war correspondent George E. Morrison and friends in the Boston press. Like the other reporters, he found cable transmission maddening, complicated by the scarcity of lines as much as by hawklike censors. But he was clever, sometimes sending his reports to private homes and using codes couched in business language to fool the inspectors. When he learned that the demand for an indemnity was about to be dropped, for example, he cabled his superiors, "Prospects for rice harvest among Japanese immigrants in Texas are poor." His editors, knowing that Texas stood for Russia, rice for the indemnity, and Japanese immigrants for the country's negotiators, published an extra reporting that "demands for an indemnity have been rejected." Censors caught on to such codes quickly, and coups of this sort were unusual, but only one or two were needed.[139]

The Japanese cabinet officially agreed to give up its demands for an indemnity and the whole of Sakhalin on August 29, and by that time the journalists and public were primed. The press informed the public about the decision in apocalyptic prose, and with the signing of the peace treaty on September 4, the people erupted in violent protest.[140] It hardly mattered that many outsiders thought the Japanese diplomats had acquitted themselves well at Portsmouth or that many of Japan's own war correspondents and editorial writers long had known that their country's victory was incomplete and that some compromise would be necessary. The crusade had been holy; Japan had won all the major battles; the rhetoric had been of victory alone; and belief in the "rightness" of Japan's demand for an indemnity was universal. Now, despite victory on the battlefield, the negotiators had compromised, and Russia's East Asian presence had not been eradicated. The outcome had to be changed or the officials would be made to pay with their political lives.

The first full press fusillades appeared on August 31, a day after the extras had reported the official terms. "Rise, rise, rise!" shouted *Yorozu*. "Endeavor to solve this great question. Rise, Rise, our people!"[141] "We must abolish the peace treaty and continue fighting," declared *Ōsaka Asahi* on September 1, alongside a stark page-one cartoon of a weeping skull and broken sword captioned "the tears of bleached bones." "We will not allow the flesh and blood of our slain soldiers to turn to scorched earth." Its Osaka rival decried a peace process typified by "delay after delay, humiliation upon humiliation," a "corpselike peace" in which Japan's negotiators had abandoned not only requirements for limits on the Russian navy and the cession of the entire island of Sakhalin but "the single most important condition of all, the demand for a settlement of our war expenses." In Tokyo that same day, *Yorozu* wrote: "Full power belongs to the all-victorious people, whose faces are stained with tears," and *Hōchi* sneered, "The officials of the country that won the war have submitted to the demands of the country that lost; . . . they have discarded our great victory."[142]

The tone of the rhetoric escalated, if that was possible, in the next days, and a press-inspired antitreaty movement came into existence. *Yorozu* called on September 2 for people to greet the returning negotiators "with flags at half mast" and then to "erase" the treaty. The next day it said that "the world never before had witnessed a spectacle so astounding as this peace conference, in which the victors were so completely humiliated." *Ōsaka Asahi* reported that it had received 569 letters to the editors in a single day demanding that the treaty be rejected. *Hōchi* declared that day that, if the cabinet were allowed to retain power, "the debauchery would continue to spread." And on the fourth, *Jiji* weighed in with a less emotional but equally firm attack on Saionji for suggesting that the treaty was the best deal Japan could have secured, noting that "if this is only his own personal opinion it should raise serious questions, but if he represents the Seiyūkai, people surely must have grave doubts indeed." The writer added that he had heard that most of the party's leaders "were absolutely opposed to his speech."[143]

As in the prewar months, many journalists felt so deeply about this issue that they began agitating for their views beyond the pages of the papers. When a group of angry intellectuals and public opinion leaders organized the Kōwa Mondai Dōshi Rengō-kai (Council of Fellow Activists on the Peace Question) in July to lobby for a strong stance in Portsmouth, the opening speech was delivered by none other than the onetime peace advocate Kuroiwa. At least eleven of the council's members were journalists, as were seven members of its executive committee. During August, Rengō-kai members went on speaking tours, and after September 1, they worked aggressively to turn their fellow citizens against the treaty, sending 30,000 copies of a letter to opinion leaders across the nation, delivering an antitreaty memorial to the Imperial Household Agency, and calling for a massive rally at Tokyo's Hibiya Park on September 5, the day after formal treaty ratification.[144] The leading papers supported the Rengōkai, with calls for people to participate in the rally, just as the Osaka press supported a five-thousand-person rally against the treaty on September 4 at the Nakanoshima City Hall.[145] One *Tōkyō Asahi* reporter, Muramatsu Koichi, was arrested the morning of September 5 for his leadership role in Rengōkai.[146]

The overall story of the Hibiya rally and its aftermath has been told too often to merit much space here. Suffice it to say that a perspiring, crepe-carrying crowd of 30,000 angry patriots defied police efforts to keep them out of the park late on the morning of September 5, then after hearing speeches and shouting *banzai*s, several thousand of them went on a violent rampage when the officers interrupted the playing of *Kimigayo,* the de facto national anthem. By September 7, when heavy rains came, the damage they had done was staggering: more than 350 structures destroyed, including 70 percent of Tokyo's small neighborhood police stations and thirteen Christian churches; fifteen streetcars demolished; more than one thousand people injured (about half of them police officers and fire fighters) and seventeen killed; some two thousand arrested; and attacks on the prime minister's residence, the foreign ministry, the Imperial Hotel, the American embassy, and Tokutomi's *Kokumin* offices. During the next week, riots also occurred in Kobe and Yokohama, and by the end of the month more than two hundred rallies in forty prefectures had passed resolutions against the treaty.[147]

From beginning to end, Japan's journalists were at the center of the Hibiya explosion, first in helping to organize and publicize the rally, then in participating (on both sides) in the tumult, and finally in struggling with the government over the right to report and editorialize about what was going on. Speakers at the rally included a *Yorozu* reporter who called the police's efforts to barricade the park "unconstitutional" and bemoaned the negotiators' inability to secure a treaty that would "do honor to the lives of a hundred thousand people" and pay for the "two billion yen" lost in the war.[148] Over the next two days, the papers reported on the violence in sympathetic and minute detail, summarizing the speeches, graphically describing the police barricades, running artists' sketches of the attacks, and reporting ward-by-ward what damage the angered citizens had caused.[149] *Tōkyō Asahi* wrote that the fires at official buildings would be worth it if they led to a recovery of "our original peace conditions."[150] And when mobs attacked the protreaty *Kokumin* offices, the rest of the newspaper world approved quite openly, having strayed, in Tokutomi's distressed rhetoric, "from its usual path and run together with criminals."[151] During the following days the papers also reported with obvious approval on antitreaty rallies, some of them violent, in Kyoto, Kobe, Yokohama, Kokura, Chiba, Nagano, Yamanashi, Nagasaki, Saitama, Miyagi, Niigata, and Hokkaido, among others.[152]

Certainly the most important crowd activity, from the standpoint of press history, was the violence against *Kokumin*. Journalists from the city's other papers had stirred people up against Tokutomi with denunciations of his close ties to the "traitorous" cabinet and his editorial characterization of the antitreaty forces as "illogical" zealots who "would prolong the great war endlessly."[153] As a result, his editorial offices became one of the mob's first targets. Shouting "destroy the government newspaper" and "let's get the traitor Tokutomi," nearly five thousand of them laid siege to the company well into the next day, throwing stones, bricks, and tiles, trying to set it afire while Tokutomi and his staff remained inside. As Tokutomi described the incident:

> Mr. Hibino (a former employee who had heard of the company's danger and rushed there to help) was struck while standing behind the telephone at the entrance. Though hit in the forehead and bleeding, he did what he could to protect us, but the mob's rocks and stones came like rain. Inside the compound, some people were climbing onto the eaves, trying to take down our signpost, while others were

scaling the branches of trees near the window and trying to get into the second floor. It was quite a commotion.

Still, the police did not come. The office was completely trampled and crushed by the mob. Having no choice, Kurihara Busanta, Abe Mitsue, and others quickly took out swords and slashed into the mob, causing them gradually to give way.[154]

Tokutomi never left the office, having "resolved that since I could not escape quickly, I would just take my fate, whether it was to live or to die";[155] nor did the paper miss a day of publishing. But the public anger over Tokutomi's support for the treaty caused a precipitous decline in its paid circulation, which had grown to 65,795 in August because of Tokutomi's inside news sources. By October, it was down a full third, to 43,612, and a year later it had declined still further to less than 37,000. *Kokumin* advertising also fell sharply in September (though it climbed back to earlier levels in October),[156] prompting Tokutomi to complain a month after the attack that "the greater part, if not all, of the financial base of the past five or six years has been destroyed."[157]

The editorial outburst surrounding the peace negotiations represented quite a shift for a press that had accepted censorship and restrictions so lamely for a year and a half now, a bursting of the dam that was terrifying to the authorities. As a result, on September 6, Emergency Imperial Ordinance No. 206 was issued, permitting either the Police Inspector or the Home Minster to issue a suspension order *(hakkō teishi)* along with jail terms and fines to any publication running articles that incited disorder, encouraged criminal activities, desecrated the imperial honor, threatened to destroy the existing political system, or violated the constitution.[158] The crackdown was the most severe since the aftermath of the Tripartite Intervention a decade earlier. Some papers, such as *Jiji, Hōchi, Tōkyō Nichi Nichi,* and *Ōsaka Mainichi,* quickly abandoned their critical stance and avoided the authorities' wrath and the heavy financial cost of losing publication days, but a number of others refused to back off—and paid a heavy price for their independence. Nearly thirty papers and magazines were suspended across the next ten weeks for a total of 333 days. *Ōsaka Asahi* was shut down three times, on September 9, September 21, and October 24, for thirty-five days altogether. The longest individual suspension went to the revived *Tōkyō Niroku Shimbun* (twenty-eight days, beginning September 11), and those receiving multiple suspensions included *Miyako, Kyōto Chōhō, Ōsaka Nippō,* and *Tanshū Jihō.*[159]

The last suspension (*Jinmin Shimbun* for eight days) came on November 20, by which time all but two of the leading Tokyo papers had organized in the Shimbun Tsūshinsha Dōmei (Newspaper Correspondents Alliance) to lobby for an end to the emergency order. They drew up a five-point case for press freedom, which was published across the country, and on November 29, the decree was lifted.[160] By then, however, the Katsura cabinet was on its way out, the fevers of the riot season had subsided, and the press was ready to give its attention once again to broader issues and to the profit-oriented editorial policies that had marked the prewar years.

WHAT THE WAR WROUGHT

Scholars assert unanimously that the Russo-Japanese War changed Japan's press. It forced editors to go to greater (and more expensive) lengths than ever to get news and to get it quickly. It speeded the movement toward livelier formats, with more headlines, sketches, editorial cartoons, and even photographs, although content still was valued over appearance, and the Japanese papers had not yet approached the attention-grabbing style of Pulitzer's and Hearst's New York giants.[161] The period also gave Japan its first taste of anti-war journalism and highlighted in new ways the complex relationships between reporters and the state. And it increased the public dependency on the press to define what events "really mattered" in the life of the country.

While all of these developments were highly significant, even more pertinent to the press'—and Japan's—twentieth-century evolution were two other emergent characteristics that are less often discussed, one of them institutional and one philosophical. The first was a loss of the rich diversity that had marked the interwar years and a spreading conformity of editorial styles precipitated by the economic pressures of wartime journalism. The scale of this war was many times that of the earlier conflict with China, not only in duration but in manpower, numbers of battles, geographical expanse, and complexity, and for that reason it cost more to cover than any endeavor undertaken by the press until then. It demanded tens of thousands of yen for correspondents' salaries and living expenses, nearly as much for the telegraph, telephone, and shipping fees to get the news back to the home office, and heavy outlays for reproducing sketches and photographs, printing larger daily runs than ever before, and running offices adequate to the demands of mass journalism. And then there were the extras, so many of them, some claimed, that they alone forced publishers to begin importing newsprint from Wisconsin. In Tokyo, extras largely paid for themselves, since the papers could charge as much as four *sen* a copy in the affluent central city; but in Osaka, where extras always had been free, they were a serious financial drain on two of the country's most powerful papers. The *gogai* "champion," *Ōsaka Mainichi*, in fact, spent 86,500 yen on extras alone during the war—nearly half the capital required to start a major paper a few years earlier and more than a fifth of its total wartime costs.[162] And the budgets of the larger papers soared well beyond what anyone would have thought possible in earlier years. At the end of the 1890s, the two *Asahi*'s together reported a capital base of 210,000 yen, and in 1903, Kuroiwa Shūroku had observed that 200,000 yen was about what it took to get a solid paper going. Yet two years after the Russo-Japanese War the *Asahi* capital base had nearly tripled to 600,000 yen, and *Ōsaka Mainichi*'s was 300,000.[163]

The result was an increase in the gap between successful and unsuccessful papers, along with a redefining of what was required to be successful. Those with the wherewithal to satisfy readers' insatiable thirst for news saw their circulations rise rapidly, while those lacking the budget for correspondents, cable messages, and constant extras declined, sometimes sharply. The press as a whole actually enjoyed a huge circulation increase during the war, with total national circulation jumping 30,000 the week war began and many papers almost doubling in size.[164] But the smaller, poorly funded papers did not share in that growing wealth. *Nihon*, for example, was in such bad shape at the end of the war that it had to be shut down a year later.[165] The fact that the revived *Tōkyō Niroku* never reached its former strength had more to do with its lack of financial wherewithal to cover the war well than with government opposition. *Yomiuri* too slipped. As one of its readers wrote to the magazine *Shin Kōron* early in the war: "I am a fan of *Yomiuri*. It has been especially lively of late and is said to have increased its sales in the last year. Because of the war, however, I have had no choice but to switch from *Yomiuri* to *Jiji* and *Asahi*. Ah, has the newspaper business become a question of telegraph charges?"[166] Even a paper like *Yorozu*, which had been near the top of the circulation charts for a decade, now lost its edge. "Try as we might, we could not put adequate equipment into covering the war," lamented Kuroiwa. So the paper became "a follower rather than a leader" in battlefield reportage, a daily for "those who read two or more papers."[167] If an editor could not afford something approaching the 350,000 yen that *Ōsaka Mainichi* spent during the war,[168] his paper fell behind, in readership as well as quality. The result was that the feisty, opinionated papers like *Niroku, Mainichi,* and *Nihon* that had given such color and variety to the press for two decades lost either their distinctive voice or their impact, if they survived at all. The press would continue to be filled with energy, and the relationship between journalists and commoners would in many ways grow even closer. But never again would Japanese journalism see the individualistic, varied voices that had enlivened it at the turn of the century.

The second major change grew from the chauvinistic brand of nationalism that now engulfed the press. Even to comment on this development smacks of discussing the obvious, so constant was the barrage of patriotic rhetoric. But to ignore it would be a mistake, because even though it went to the heart of the most important issues that confronted Japan in the twentieth century, several of its most important journalistic implications still have been been examined only slightly. What did it mean to be a Japanese? What was the relationship between the "country" and the "government," between the practical, impure world of politics and the sweet, pure world of emperor and nation? What led the country's brightest minds, almost without exception, to elevate patriotic loyalties and feelings over rational discourse—to vent their indignation about perceived international injustices to the point of ignoring their own commitment to free speech and stirring up riots? Full answers are beyond our reach here, but three developments in the press of this period have significant things to say about the questions.

First, the most important single characteristic of Russo-Japanese War journalism probably was the almost total merging of populism and nationalism. We have seen how appeals to the *minshū* entered mainstream journalism in the early 1890s, in the highly successful consumer-oriented approaches of papers such as *Yorozu* and *Hōchi*. We also have seen the large followings secured by the populist papers at the beginning of the new century, with their appeals to sensationalism and to social idealism. And at the same time, we have observed how effectively the oldtime newspapers appealed in these same years to their own elite readers' loyalties to emperor and country—first in treaty revision struggles, next in the Sino-Japanese War, then in the debates over Japan's role on the Asian continent. Now, for a full twenty-four months, these forces came together. Populism had turned the Shimadas and the Kuroiwas into the government's loudest critics until the fall of 1903. By 1905, however, their stance had changed; they (particularly Kuroiwa) had joined the *Jiji* and *Asahi* editors as Japan's loudest exponents of aggressive, imperialistic nationalism.

Populist journalism thus became wedded to nationalist journalism; concern for the interests of "the people" became synonymous with support for the "national cause." On one level, this was because the war was the *sanmen kiji* story of all time; if sensational news stories sold papers, this was the story to tell. On another level, it was because the lower-class urban readers themselves, first tutored in the spreading emperor system orthodoxy, then inspired by the war, had become more attuned to nationalistic issues. Ariyama Teruo notes that *Yorozu* and *Niroku*, papers that had built their circulations on opposition to political regimes, "now became mobilizers of citizen consciousness" *(kokumin ishiki no dōin).*[169] And Yamamoto Fumio points out that in the fall of 1905, the "identification of the people and the press had become complete."[170] Nationalism and populism had, for writers and readers alike, joined forces.

The second feature of this new chauvinism was the fact that populist patriotism made life no easier for the government. Patriotism was as potent an antigovernment emotion as social indignation had been. The antiwar Kuroiwa, who damned the "present government" because "people are starving" in the spring of 1903,[171] helped to bring it down for compromising at the peace table in 1905. People have argued long over whether or not the riots at Hibiya represented a class uprising, whether the people were anti- or pro-establishment, whether their violence was spontaneous or instigated, whether the episode marked the beginning of "Taishō democracy" or, in Andrew Gordon's phrase, "imperial democracy."[172] While I will touch on some of those questions in a later chapter, the important point here is that, regardless of who instigated the incident, the riots demonstrated dramatically the private sector's propensity for being more aggressive about foreign policy than its governors were. Carol Gluck has written cogently about the "ideological denial of politics" by private opinion leaders engaged in "positive efforts at citizen-making concentrated on the sense of nation."[173] For many writers, that tension was at the heart of the summer struggle: negotiators had sullied the national honor by making *political* decisions. "The riot," says Okamoto Shumpei, thus became a " 'loyalty contest' between the people and government leaders."[174] Nationalism, it turned out, was as lethal a weapon for fighting one's own leaders as for fighting foreigners.

The third chauvinistic development involves the press' own leadership role in stimulating the imperialistic nationalism of this period. Much has been made of the crowd's explosive passions, particularly after the Osaka and Hibiya rallies—and of the role government censorship played in sparking those passions. The government kept the people uninformed of war's ambiguous realities, the argument goes, and as a result those same people were unprepared to react rationally to a strong but incomplete victory package. While there is a great deal of truth in that analysis, the press' own history in this period shows that it is inadequate. The leading journalists played an active (and not so uninformed) role in misleading the public. Correspondents and editors proved capable of fighting the censors quite effectively when it served their own nationalistic view of the war: pressuring officials to let foreign correspondents go to the continent, agitating for relaxed rules about which reporters should be allowed to cover what, working hard to get stories past the transmission bottlenecks, and sending news illegally by code. But hardly any journalist fought the authorities when it came to reporting war's darker or more ambiguous side.

Expansionist editors and writers cried for Japan to go to war in 1903, they published an endless succession of emotional, patriotic stories in 1904 and 1905, and they wrote of little else but Japan's "right" to insist on massive Russian concessions at the peace table. And they did more than write. The journalists also helped create nationalist organizations such as the Black Dragon Society; they took to the speech circuit in behalf of a strong treaty, and they helped lead the activist groups that organized the antitreaty rallies. What is more, most editors and writers did all this with full knowledge that the losses were greater, the expenses higher, and the results muddier than their patriotic articles and essays ever suggested. It was, in other words, not just popular ignorance that ignited violent passions; it was a decision by relatively well informed correspondents and editors that the "cause of Japan" transcended all other journalistic necessities. They tailored their editorials and news stories to that belief. And as a result, by the fall of 1905 they had brought the press and the people together as never before, giving new meaning to the phrase "popular journalism," even as they helped to trigger patriotic riots based at least in part on the inadequate transmission of information.

CHAPTER 10

LEADING A PUBLIC
1905 to 1912

A newspaper is like a morning glory.
. . . It lives only for a morning; in
the afternoon it becomes wastepaper.

Kuroiwa Shūroku[1]

Newspapers today are commercial products
. . . their aim is to increase sales
and profits.

Yamaji Aizan[2]

The citizens of Tokyo massed again on their city streets late in October 1905, 250,000 strong this time and with quite a different purpose than they had had at Hibiya. Responding now to an imperial call, they walked through triumphal arches and rode festooned streetcars to another "people's park," the one at Ueno, where they officially welcomed the imperial navy home from battle. Meiji himself presided over the ceremonies; Mayor Ozaki Yukio led the cheers; Admiral Tōgō Heihachirō of Tsushima naval fame thanked the masses for their wartime support, and the people indulged in a feast of thanksgiving, more organized but nearly as fervent as their angry outbursts seven weeks earlier.[3]

Something strange surely must have occurred, as citizens who had cursed and spit at the authorities in September joined them in praising the troops in October. Or had it? At one level, these urban *minshū* were making it clear that their protests had not been against the establishment per se, that while they might cry out bitterly against "corrupt politicians" and "vacillating officials," they supported the same national causes as those officials did. At another level, they were demonstrating just how quickly "normal" times could be expected to return in modern, urban Japan. Like the political upheaval of 1881 and the outcry over the Tripartite Intervention in 1895, the Hibiya outburst seemed, at least in the short run, to be all the venting the people needed. Catharsis accomplished, they returned to the usual routine of making a living during the week and celebrating when given an opportunity. It was almost as if the Hibiya tumult had not occurred.

For the press, that meant a new normalcy of its own journalistic type, a return to the profit-oriented, news-based, *minshū*-centered journalism that had emerged during the fourth Meiji decade. This is not to say that things went back to the pre-1904 status quo. We already have seen how much the war changed the press, how it increased readership and demanded more expensive newsgathering methods, the way it undermined some of the livelier but less well endowed papers, the role it played in bringing populism and nationalism together. Those changes were not ephemeral. But as the wartime frenzy passed, the editors were able to resume, somewhat more reflectively, what had become the standard day-to-day tasks of journalism by now: fine-tuning the methods and institutions for producing, selling, and delivering the daily "news" package, finding an editorial-reportorial blend that would satisfy popular tastes without wholly abandoning ideas of the "public good," and struggling with the authorities to influence policy and obtain wider freedom for their own writers.

MODERN TIMES, SHIFTING VALUES

The most important reason the papers did not return to the prewar status quo was that society would not let them do so. All the forces of change that we observed in the 1890s continued now, with enough momentum that contemporary observers began to describe the Russo-Japanese War in grand historical terms, as the beginning of a frenetic, often frightening, kind of modernity that had to be confronted lest the country lose its way. Several features of the new era merely marked an acceleration of prewar trends: movement of people from the provinces to the cities, the appearance of new jobs, the maturation of the educational system. Another of the changes, however, was relatively new. As never before, these years saw the breathtaking transformation of urban material culture—and, most alarmingly for many old-timers, of the commoners' value systems.

The migration into the urban centers, from "villages that have been bled for all they are worth," was particularly striking to many of the intellectuals. "Everyone and his brother is setting out for the city," said Yokoi Tokiyoshi in 1907, "as if gripped by a kind of fever." And he was right about the brothers at least, as younger sons and their friends moved into Tokyo and Osaka at rates approaching 40,000 a year (109 a day) now, pushing Tokyo past the two million mark in 1906.[4] They moved not only to escape rural poverty but because jobs were expanding in both number and type. The factory labor force in Tokyo tripled, for example, in the first fifteen years of the century, to nearly 90,000, and while the bulk of the new jobs were in traditional industries such as cotton and silk production, there also were employment opportunities in new areas as diverse as iron production, ship building, printing, pulling rickshaws, driving streetcars, and making pencils. The jobs did not pay much—not much more than 30 *sen* a day in 1904, if a *Heimin Shimbun* survey was correct—and most people had to work ten- to twelve-hour days in dirty, unhealthy conditions. But the very possibility of finding work was enough to siphon thousands of people monthly from villages where wretched conditions were the norm.[5]

While the expanding worker pool provided greater numbers of people to whom newspaper editors might appeal, the changes in education made it certain that increasing numbers of them would become readers. When compulsory education was raised from four to six years in 1907, it really did not make much difference, because by then expanding numbers of Japanese families already were sending their children on to middle schools, convinced that to "let a child grow up ignorant and illiterate" was to assure a life of "misfortune." Local governments were typically spending nearly half of their budgets on education by then, and while 10,000 youths graduated from higher schools for girls in 1900, 30,000 did so in 1905.[6] School attendance rates across the nation also had risen past 95 percent by the beginning of this period. And the number of students in the higher schools and universities increased by 14.4 percent between 1908 and 1913, while expenditures on higher education jumped in those years, from 1.7 to 2.6 million yen annually.[7]

None of this automatically produced citizens capable of reading newspapers, but literacy studies of military recruits in the Osaka region showed that school graduates at all levels also were increasingly capable of reading the kind of newspapers editors were putting out in the last Meiji years. Whereas more than one in four recruits failed the literacy tests in 1903, only one in eighteen failed in 1912. And a *Heimin* survey in 1904 found that even in the tenements of Honjo, Tokyo's most heavily industrialized ward, where "beggars and street urchins confronted the beholder with the darker side of life" and "petty thieves undermined the efforts of hardworking residents to achieve prosperity," there were as many newspaper subscriptions as there were apartments.[8] "If the quantitative rise in literacy broadened the reading classes," notes Yamamoto Taketoshi, "the qualitative rise deepened them."[9]

One of the most dramatic features of this new era was the explosion of material culture: the nationalization of the rail system in 1906, cutting the Shinbashi-Kobe travel time from fifteen hours to a mere thirteen hours and forty minutes; the new department stores that created appetites even as they sold goods; electricity that moved now into even the poorer areas, and, for a few, automobiles. While the number of Tokyo houses with electricity had risen to a then-impressive 14,969 by the end of the Russo-Japanese War, it skyrocketed now, to more than 360,000 (with more than two million light bulbs installed) in the year Meiji died.[10] Mitsubishi opened a restaurant in its Tokyo store on April 1, 1907, offering coffee for five *sen* and Western candy for ten. More than fifty movie theaters opened in Tokyo during the last four years of the era, and in 1908 the country's first movie studio began producing silent films in Meguro, a year before the appearance of *Katsudō Shashin Kai* (Moving picture world), Japan's first movie magazine. And for the truly rich, there was the horseless carriage, with seventy cars running alongside the Tokyo streetcars by 1910 and five beside those of Osaka.[11] It still would have looked rather spartan to the *ero-guro-nansensu* dandies of the 1920s (only seventy automobiles! just fifty theaters!), but to people who had grown up in a premodern time, the pace of material change was breathtaking.

At least as breathtaking to the country's writers was the impact the changes were having on popular values. Indeed, the transformation that more than any other set the postwar years apart from the previous decade was a growing sense of crisis among the nation's cultural and intellectual arbiters over where society's norms and beliefs were headed. When newspaper and journal writers talked about "city fevers" and "business fevers" and "success fevers" and "enterprise fevers," as they did endlessly now, the reference was not so much to fads as to inflammation and illness, as Carol Gluck has pointed out so vividly in her study of Meiji ideology.[12]

With new classes of citizens going to school (and going longer), new city residents freed from the anchors and nets of rural life, new magazines and novels pouring forth with titles like "Broken Commandment," "Broken Fence," and "Broken Bridge," and socialist writers calling for ideas such as pacifism and "the liberation of male-female relationships,"[13] it was inevitable that popular attitudes would take on new and, for many, forbidding hues.

Even the schools had developed a threatening side, since ambitious parents all too often regarded education as a ladder to success rather than the incubator for Confucian values that Monbushō officials thought it should be; the fact that schooling drove some rural young people to the cities, others to nonagricultural careers like doctoring, and a few women away from marriage was all the worse. That was what Education Minister Makino Nobuaki had in mind when he asserted in 1906 that "wholesome thought and enterprises are fostered on the battlefield, while the nation's many ills are born of peace" and when he added in 1907 that "we are faced with the evil of too many people harboring hopes of higher education." His solution was for the schools to spend more time teaching "wholesome thoughts."[14]

There also was the problem of lower-class city residents— people infected by the lovers of the silent screen and the money-grubbing protagonists of magazine stories—who seemed to have no sense of how to behave in public. *Tōkyō Niroku Shimbun*, itself no paragon of virtue in the view of mainstream editors, reported agitatedly in the summer of 1908 on young women streetcar riders who "looked for chances to seduce male riders, while pretending to be engrossed in reading a newspaper."[15] And *Yomiuri* despaired of the fact that "Hibiya Park has been taken over wholly on recent nights by the illicit cohabitation of depraved men and women"; on any evening, said the writer (who obviously had paid close attention), at least ten such couples could be seen.[16]

The root of the depravity, in Tokutomi Sohō's mind, lay in a loss of civic-mindedness and purpose on the part of urban youth. Whereas early-Meiji success *(risshin shusse)* had meant making a name for the family, now success *(seikō)* meant getting rich and enjoying oneself. Youths, he said, sought pleasures of the moment, and the result was a breakdown in social cohesion. "People today are not satisfied with anything," he wrote; "they want to destroy the status quo *(genjō daha)* and nothing more. But after they unthinkingly have destroyed it, then what?"[17]

Others saw the roots of the problems in the socialists and anarchists who introduced "dangerous ideas"; in the naturalist novelists whose hallmark lay in writing almost clinically about the dark complexity of human nature; in women who chose independent careers and published journals such as *Blue Stocking (Seitō)*; in labor leaders who pitted workers against managers; in school teachers and professors who planted useless or antisocial ideas in innocent minds; in journalists who pandered to the plebeian taste for salacious news. But no matter where they placed the causes, mainstream intellectuals almost all saw these democratic tendencies as a "surging force,"[18] and few thought them good. As Tokutomi wrote, "Intoxication with idleness, profligacy, and indifference toward national affairs . . . nothing could be worse at a time of great trials for the nation."[19] The national policies that apprehensions of this sort stimulated will be discussed later; for now, it is enough to note the powerful impact this combination of change and fear had on the press. The challenges of this new milieu would produce livelier journalistic styles; the worries induced by the shifting values would have more troublesome results.

COMPETING FOR A MASS READERSHIP

As any set of statistics makes clear, the end-of-Meiji press was as dynamic institutionally as the years it attempted to chronicle. From 1905 to 1909, for example, the total number of newspapers and magazines leapt from 1,590 to 2,768, before leveling off at 2,077 at the end of the era, and the number of larger, more stable publications with security deposits rose in every year but one: from 906 at the end of the Russo-Japanese War to 1,326 in 1911. Even more impressive than the totals is the virility of the publishing business now, which produced an average of 622 *new* newspapers and magazines a year, in contrast to the 581 that died. Most of these were ephemeral, cheap sheets or journals with limited impact and shaky finances; that was why so many died. But the sheer numbers of starts—nearly a dozen a week across the entire period—say volumes about the period's intellectual and entrepreneurial zeal.[20]

Almost as striking are numerous sets of figures, presented here at random, bearing evidence not only of the growth and energy of individual papers but of the impact those papers were exerting on citizens and officials as a whole. They show

- *how important speed had become:* in the 546.4 telegrams sent and received by newspapers every single day in 1908.

- *the large labor pool now required to put out papers:* in the growth in the numbers of printers *Tōkyō Asahi* had to employ, from seventy in 1908 to ninety-six in 1912—and in the 140 plant workers *Kokumin Shimbun* needed to print its daily editions in 1910.

- *the importance of gimmicks and promotions:* in the sixteen-page editions *Jiji Shinpō* published every Sunday and the 224-page edition it printed on March 1, 1907, to celebrate its twenty-fifth anniversary.

- *what a huge business enterprise journalism had become:* in the 297,017 yen *Ōsaka Asahi* earned in ad revenue in 1910, compared to the mere 126,472 it took in just five years earlier—and in the 657,000 yen in total revenue it collected in 1910.

- *how crucial newspapers had become to the daily lives of the urban workers:* in the 69 percent of factory workers who told Home Ministry survey takers in 1911 that newspapers were their main form of reading.

- *how much the press worried the authorities:* in the 14,697 legal cases pursued by the police against journalists in 1911 alone.

- *how poorly paid young journalists still were:* in the eighteen-yen-a-month salary that Ishibashi Tanzan (who later became prime minister) earned as a reporter for *Tōkyō Keizai Shinpō* in 1911—compared to forty yen a month made by provincial teachers, twenty-five to forty by civil service workers, ten to fifteen by bankers, and fifteen by an editor of *Waseda Bungaku* journal.[21]

The most impressive figures probably lay in the area of circulation, where the leading papers at last reached mass status. Late-Meiji circulation figures are notoriously hard to pin down, because papers often fudged totals to attract advertisers, but by any reckoning the dominant papers in terms of circulation were *Asahi* and *Mainichi* in Osaka and *Hōchi Shimbun* in Tokyo, now that the war had diminished the *Yorozu* and *Niroku* followings. In 1906, according to the best figures available, the eight largest Japanese papers *averaged* more than 110,000 subscribers each, well above even the largest paper (with the possible exception of *Niroku*) in the pre–Russo-Japanese War years. Their readerships were

Ōsaka Mainichi	216,044
Hōchi	176,090
Ōsaka Asahi	123,566
Tōkyō Asahi	96,475
Yorozu	88,000
Denpō Shimbun	85,000
Miyako	63,350
Tōkyō Niroku	62,000[22]

And just half a decade later, in 1911, the rank order had shifted—with *Ōsaka Mainichi* (269,260) followed by *Ōsaka Asahi* (210,049), *Hōchi* (150,000), and *Kokumin Shimbun* (130,000)—but the totals for the press as a whole were even more impressive. The eight largest papers now averaged nearly 140,000 daily readers, and the fifteen largest Tokyo-Osaka dailies boasted more than 1,365,000 total readers.[23] The Taishō years (1912–1926) would dwarf these figures, with the Osaka giants reaching 350,000 in 1914, but already at the close of Meiji the leading papers had become true mass opinion leaders, boasting daily readerships on the same scale as the influential London and New York papers.[24]

Behind these numbing figures lay several more substantial characteristics. For one thing, editing in these years lost its last vestiges of the old Confucian attitude that newspapers should be opinion leaders above all and that money-making was unseemly. Even the elitist Tokutomi decided after the war that, with "the power of democracy . . . growing daily," *Kokumin Shimbun* would have to popularize if it were to remain profitable; so, grumbling, he let his subordinates take the paper in a less highbrow direction; "vulgarized" was his own word. They broadened news content, added a local page to regional editions, deemphasized editorials, lowered the price—and watched the circulation grow by a full 100,000 in the next five years.[25] To be a mass medium now was to "regard both the newspaper and the public as commodities and thus to compete with all your energy to create services for the reader."[26]

No company exemplified the commercial approach more fully now than Asahi, which behaved in a coldly rational, supposedly un-Japanese manner in cultivating mammon. What patriotic editor Ikebe Kichitarō called *Asahi*'s "big revolution" in management approaches began during the Russo-Japanese War and continued well into the Taishō era.[27] *Ōsaka Asahi* raised its monthly subscription price from 40 to 48 *sen* and *Tōkyō Asahi* from 33 to 37 *sen* shortly after the war began, to pay for the increased cost of covering such a massive story, and when the April–September 1904 period still showed losses of more than 10,000 yen on each paper,[28] co-owners Murayama Ryōhei and Ueno Riichi decided to abandon the old family-style approach for what some saw as a chilly, cut-throat approach to management. Departments were made more fully accountable for their balance sheets; sentimentality was declared out; and by the end of the year twenty-seven Ōsaka Asahi staff members had been fired, as had a goodly number in Tokyo, many of them people who had been with the firm for years.

The result was that Ōsaka Asahi was back in the black by the end of 1904, but when the red ink continued in the east, Ueno headed for Tokyo to find out personally what was wrong. He discovered among other things that the Konishi Yahee company, one of the paper's five major wholesale distributors, had lost nearly 50,000 yen by discounting papers, even giving some away free, to pump up wartime circulation. So he severed that connection. Then he devised a comprehensive outline for more efficient management: cutting back on the funds designated for expansion, increasing the number and price of ads (Tōkyō Asahi began putting nothing but ads on page one in 1905), cutting the editorial department budget, and shifting telephone and telegraph costs to the more stable Osaka office. In 1907, he severed ties with the paper's four other sales agents and had Tōkyō Asahi take over its own distribution system. And in 1910 he and Murayama reorganized the entire management structure, creating a pyramidlike organization headed by ten-person boards of trustees (hyōgikai) in Osaka and Tokyo. The culmination of the process came in mid-Taishō (1919), when the trustees turned Asahi into a joint stock company, with 1.5 million yen in capital, and Murayama as president and Ueno as executive director.[29]

The lesson of such changes was that the most wrenching decisions were no longer editorial but financial. It is highly significant that when hard times struck, Ueno took charge. Murayama, the moralistic sportsman who always wore a black hakama and refused to vote lest he compromise his journalistic independence, long had been Asahi's soul, and when it came time to start a Tokyo branch, he had headed east to get it going. But now, at the end of the era, when that eastern brother stumbled, the businessman Ueno was called on to prescribe the remedy. That was the way these times were everywhere. Venerable political editors such as Shimada Saburō and Kuga Katsunan were lumbering along in the shadows—or gone from journalism altogether—replaced in the leadership by entrepreneurs like *Hōchi*'s Miki Zenpachi, who happily had pronounced the death of "prestige journalism" in 1894, and *Ōsaka Mainichi*'s Motoyama Hikoichi, who boasted that the "aim of a newspaper is to make money."

Evidence of the new norm was everywhere. At *Ōsaka Mainichi*, for example, the capital base was soaring, from 100,000 yen in 1897 to 500,000 at the end of Meiji.[30] At *Jiji*, Fukuzawa Yukichi's more earthy son, Sutejirō, was busy trying to expand into the Kansai region and to bring Colonel Robert McCormick's *Chicago Tribune* brand of journalism, complete with beauty contests and endless promotions, to Japan. At *Tōkyō Keizai Shinpō*, the editors were pioneering journalistic business structures by making their journal into a joint stock company in 1907, a full dozen years ahead of Asahi. *Hōchi* was at work in 1906 creating a precedent-setting evening edition. And most of the papers were dramatically increasing both the price and numbers of ads: from 45 to 60 *sen* a line in the 1906–1912 period at *Tōkyō Nichi Nichi*, for example, and from 50 to 75 *sen* at *Ōsaka Asahi*. *Nichi Nichi* also ran the country's first two-page ad (for *Daiei Encyclopedia*) on November 29, 1905; *Ōsaka Mainichi*, which began running photo ads in 1906, passed the million mark in ad linage in 1910; *Kokumin* saw its ad revenues increase 2.6 times between 1905 and 1907. And all of the papers experienced significant growth in advertisements for toiletries, medicines, and money-making schemes, with the result that advertising revenue began to rival subscription fees in importance.[31]

Many papers also were buying new presses in these years, in their effort to meet the seemingly endless demands created by expanding circulations and new approaches to newsgathering. In fact, this period saw the biggest jump in print technology since the introduction of the cylinder presses in the early 1890s. In 1906, Ishikawa Kakuzō perfected the Ishikawa Rotary Press, a Tokyo-built machine superior to the reliable old Marinoni that had given the Osaka papers such an advantage before the Sino-Japanese War. Locally made, it was cheaper and more accessible; so after early trials by *Kobe Yūshin Nippō* and *Hōchi*, papers all across the country began to purchase it.[32] By 1911, *Tōkyō Nichi Nichi* and *Ōsaka Mainichi* had five rotary presses each; *Tōkyō Asahi, Yamato, Kokumin, Jiji*, and *Chūgai Shōgyō* four each—and *Tōkyō Asahi* seven.[33] Even more telling was the fact that a number of the provincial papers also had become affluent enough to buy Ishikawa or Marinoni presses. And when they did so, they let their readers know it. When *Kahoku Shinpō* in the northeast secured a Marinoni in the spring of 1909, the editors paraded it through town behind a band, on a cart drawn by five flower-bedecked oxen. And when *Kōchi Shimbun* in Shikoku purchased an Ishikawa press in August 1910, fifty people marched into town wearing red headbands and carrying banners that read "the *Kōchi Shimbun* rotary press." At least ninety-four of the cylinder presses were in use nationally by the end of 1911, according to the estimate of press historian Uchikawa Yoshimi.[34] And with photoengraving techniques also having been perfected at *Ōsaka Mainichi* that year, the papers were ready not only to produce bigger issues faster but to put out the liveliest columns yet.

Unabashed commercialism also meant ever-increasing competition for sales—to drive those circulations and profits up and up. To that end, a number of the papers took tighter control of their delivery and sales organizations now, creating their own networks of directly controlled retail shops *(chokueiten)*, based on the system that *Hōchi* had pioneered in 1903. *Chūō Shimbun*, for example, had a *chokueiten* system in place throughout the country within three years after the end of the Russo-Japanese War, as did *Nihon* in most of the regions where it was sold. *Yorozu Chōhō* set up a group of shops with names like Yorozu Gensha and Yorozu Seisha to sell its papers; *Tōkyō Nichi Nichi* went to a similar system after being purchased by *Ōsaka Mainichi* in 1911; and we already have seen *Tōkyō Asahi*'s move in that direction after the Ueno reforms.[35]

Competition for hawking contracts also grew increasingly intense in these years, with a typical agent purchasing a large number of papers, then sending his own small army of students, disabled people, and "intellectual" ne'er-do-wells out to the street corners with a hundred or so copies each, to ring bells and shout "Paper! Paper!" as pedestrians walked by. Most of the sales people worked on a commission, although the permanent ones often bought their own copies from the agent, then sold the remainders back at a reduced rate. The papers were heavy, the work was hard, downright miserable on rainy days, and the competition was intense. But there was enough profit in it for newspaper companies and agents alike to make street hawking a staple of urban journalism for years to come.[36]

Papers also began publishing a greater number of special editions for specific groups of readers and tailoring prices to the regions in which they were sold, on the basis of local competition or the perceived ability of people to pay. In 1908–1909, for example, *Yamato Shimbun*'s daily price ranged from four *rin* in Chiba to six in Saitama and Gunma, while the pricey *Jiji* charged 8.7 *rin* in Chiba and nine in most other places.[37] A number of papers began publishing regional editions, with at least one page of local news inserted to supplement the regular mix of national and international coverage.[38] And for the first time ever, the major papers began launching successful evening editions. Several of them had experimented with evening papers in the 1880s and 1890s, as we have seen, but those all had failed. Now, the enterprising *Hōchi* decided to try again and announced on October 27, 1906, that it would put out a cheap evening edition every day to inform the reader about anything of importance that happened up until 4:00 P.M. Drawing on the market created by *Maiyū Shimbun* and the numberless "evening extras" of the war period, as well as on swifter delivery methods made possible by combining train, bicycle, and coach, it attracted readers by the thousands. And by the end of Meiji, its evening editions had been copied by *Ōsaka Jiji* (1908), *Chūō* (1910), *Yamato, Niroku,* and *Teikoku Shinpō* (all 1911). *Yamato* went so far as to put out morning, noon, and evening editions.[39]

If one had asked a typical reader how she knew publishers were trying to push up sales in this period, she undoubtedly would have cited the unending proliferation of promotion schemes. For if editing policies, pricing plans, and the creation of new editions represented the proper way to compete, gimmicks and promotions certainly were the most interesting. And the exploding technology and changing social mores made them more entertaining than ever. Editors took every special event or dramatic news development as a chance to attract readers with some kind of splashy production. Hence *Jiji*'s 224-page twenty-fifth anniversary issue; *Hōchi*'s heavy use of red, yellow, blue, and green borders and its colorful sketches and maps at New Year; *Ōsaka Mainichi*'s eighty pages of ads and offers of free streetcar rides on the date of its ten thousandth issue (June 22, 1911); and rival *Ōsaka Asahi*'s awards of literary prizes for the same anniversary on January 3, 1910. Contests also became a staple, as did tours, art exhibits, excursions, and sponsorship of lectures.[40]

In the contest field, no paper got more publicity now than Fukuzawa Sutejirō's *Jiji*. Already in 1904, three years after the death his father, Sutejirō had drawn wide comment, not much of it favorable, for staging a race to see who could run nonstop for the longest time around Ueno's Shinobazu Pond—twelve hours, it turned out. Now, on September 15, 1907, the paper announced in a sensational two-page ad that it would sponsor Japan's first beauty contest, based on photos submitted by papers from across the country. Sales rose when it began running photos in October from the twenty-two papers that submitted entries. And they peaked when it announced

the following March 5 that the winner was Gakushūin student Suehiro Hiroko, daughter of the Kokura mayor. Unfortunately for Suehiro, the straight-laced Gakushūin principal, General Nogi Maresuke, took beauty contests as a sign of the era's moral decline, and
within days Suehiro was a student no more. Neither a sixth-place
finish in a subsequent world beauty contest nor lengthy editorial
pleas from Fukuzawa could get her readmitted, but the entire episode proved wondrously helpful to *Jiji*'s sales.[41]

Some promotion schemes involved athletics: *Yomiuri*'s creation of the country's first sports column, "Undōkai" (Sports world),
on October 10, 1907, and *Ōsaka Mainichi*'s promotion of Japan's
first marathon race in 1909. A few offered trips to readers: an *Ōsaka
Asahi* excursion for 374 people to the battlefield sites of Manchuria
and Korea in the summer of 1906, another for fifty-seven readers
(three of them women) to Washington, London, Paris, Rome, Berlin,
and Moscow in 1908, and still a third round-the-world trip in 1910.
And other promotion schemes used the latest technological developments to attract readers. *Yamato*, for example, sponsored a provincial moving picture tour; *Ōsaka Mainichi* organized its own
movie production unit to tout its nine thousandth anniversary
issue in 1908, and in 1910 *Tōkyō Asahi* raised funds and sponsored
rallies to support an expedition by Army First Lieutenant Shirase
Nobu to the South Pole.[42] Even the newly "vulgarized" *Kokumin*
got into the promotion game in 1911, with a typically Tokutomi-
style offer of 10,000 yen to the first Japanese who could fly an airplane from the Meguro race tracks to the Chiba coast.[43] None of the
editors would have admitted to crass commercial motives in sponsoring these stunts. For the record, they wanted to promote modernization, to give their land a place in the community of nations,
or to "encourage the development of aeroplanes in Japan," as Tokutomi put it.[44] The truth was that journalists now were businessmen
first, engaged in frantic competition to pull in ads and readers. And
promotion schemes were among the easiest ways to accomplish
those ends. American press historians have accused the U.S. press
of using "superheated campaigns for increased circulations" in the
1920s, with lotteries, giveaways, and dance contests.[45] One wonders
if the West was borrowing from the East.

STRUCTURES TO SUIT A NEW ERA

The drive for profits led not only to feverish promotion but to significant changes in the structures and makeup of the press world: to

the decline of some papers and the growth of others, to expansions in business and society sections at the expense of political and editorial departments, to increased coordination between editorial and business sides, to the creation of several new newsgathering agencies and reporters' organizations,[46] and to a good deal of consolidation and merger. One of the more significant structural changes was an increase in the numbers of women employees, both in the reporting operation and on the mechanical side. The increase hardly threatened male dominance in the journalistic world; what Kanno Suga called an "invisible iron fence"[47] still kept all but the exceptionally talented and courageous on the outside. But if editors no longer could ignore balance sheets, neither could they disregard the growing numbers of women readers, the ever-rising popularity of family-oriented materials, or the ability of women to cover some stories with a sensitivity impossible to men.

As a result, by the end of Meiji nearly every major paper had at least one or two women on its reportorial staff as well as several operating the presses on the plant floor and a large number working in distribution.[48] Several, including *Hōchi, Ōsaka Mainichi*, and the provincial *Chūgoku Shimbun*, also had begun running regular family-oriented articles and columns with titles such as "Katei no shiori" (Family guide), "Katei ran" (Family column), and "Gofujin" (Wives). And by the early 1910s, the success of these features had prompted *Yomiuri*—which now promoted itself as a "literary newspaper, a family newspaper, an educational newspaper, a newspaper of taste"—to create the country's first complete women's section.[49]

The women reporters were as varied in their styles and contributions as any male group of similar size. Shimoyama Kyōko, for example, gained her reputation through a gossipy insider's style, causing scandals first at Fukuzawa Sutejirō's *Ōsaka Jiji*, then in Tokyo, by disguising her occupation to win the confidence of celebrities, then reporting on their inner worlds. Isomura Haruko, by contrast, caught people's attention through sheer hard work and humane reporting. A native of Fukushima and a mother of eight, she joined the *Hōchi* staff in 1905 and wrote on everything from the ideas of famous women and conditions in the Tokyo slums to the lives of switchboard operators and the working situations of women printers. She also wrote novels, translated Japanese literature into English, filled two trunks with unpublished manuscripts—and died before she reached forty. The forte of her *Tōkyō Asahi* peer Takenaka Shige was English. Hired in 1911, she published Japan's first interview with a foreign woman, then moved to the arts section, where she became known as the "dean of women reporters" *(fujin kisha no genrō)* before retiring in 1930.[50]

Surely the most controversial woman reporter in these years was Kanno, known best for her radical ideas. Kanno started newspaper work in 1902 at *Ōsaka Chōhō*, where she raised local eyebrows with a series of attacks on the prostitution industry; then in 1905 she joined the staff of the Wakayama socialist paper *Murō Shinpō* and wrote that the most pressing task for women was "to develop our own self-awareness," to overcome age-old customs that had turned the typical woman into a "form of maternal property." Even socialism, important as it was, would have to await the achievement of self-awareness, she said.[51] When *Murō* editor Mōri Shian went to jail for slandering an official, Kanno served for the better part of a year as acting editor, the first Japanese woman to fill that role. She went to Tokyo in 1906 as a writer for *Mainichi Denpō*, but when she was arrested for involvement in the 1908 Red Flag incident that signaled the beginning of an official crackdown on socialists, the paper fired her. She continued to write for leftist journals, particularly for *Jiyū Shisō*, but implication in 1910 in the notorious High Treason case resulted in her execution by hanging. The dramatic character of Kanno's career as a socialist leader has consigned her journalistic career to the shadows, even in the work of those who have studied her life. The fact was, however, that newspapers served as her first, probably her most important, stage. It was on daily newspapers that she honed her ideas and developed her understanding of society, in papers and journals that she found her primary mouthpiece for disseminating those ideas. The effectiveness of her use of the press as a personal medium highlighted the beachhead women had established in this once male world.[52]

An even larger contribution by late-Meiji women journalists was made outside the daily newspaper realm, at magazines and journals. Of particular importance was the establishment of *Seitō* or *Blue Stocking* in the fall of 1911 by Hiratsuka Raichō, Nakano Hatsuko, and other activists, with the ringing, now famous declaration: "In the beginning, woman was the sun. She was the authentic human being. Today, woman is the moon, dependent on others for her birth, radiant only in others' light."[53] As the first Japanese journal edited solely by women, *Seitō* outraged much of the male-dominated establishment, particularly when several of its writers engaged in widely publicized extramarital affairs. Male journalists accused its staff of harboring "a deep despair and resentment toward the male sex" and worried darkly about "the disruptive influence it will have upon the family and society in general."[54] There was an outcry when *Seitō* published a special "New Women" *(Atarashii onna)* issue in which Katō Midori wrote: "A modern woman travels a new path. She does not rely on men; rather, she takes her own initiative regarding work. But she always senses that something is missing. . . . It is the modern woman's fate to spend her entire life seeking, seeking to find what that something is."[55] The attack on conventional ideas about proper female roles was too direct for most Japanese to take, and the criticisms of *Seitō* were scathing. The fact, however, that significant numbers of subscribers, both to women's magazines and to newspapers more generally, wanted to read the kinds of things these women had to write meant that their voices no longer could be blocked. Capitalist, male editors may not have liked what these women wrote, and many of them hated the idea of helping women become professionals. But their profit-oriented instincts told them that if a market lurked out there, they had no choice but to find it.

The second major structural development in the end-of-Meiji press was a move toward consolidation and nationalization of the country's leading papers, accompanied by increasing uniformity in the content and style of all leading papers. If one of the hallmarks of the 1890s and early 1900s had been the eruption of individualistic journalistic approaches and philosophies—Kuga Katsunan's intellectual nationalism, Kuroiwa Shūroku's sensational populism, Shimada Saburō's Christian humanism, Kōtoku Shūsui's pacifist socialism— a prime characteristic of these years was quite the opposite. Even as new technologies made it possible to communicate more quickly over larger and larger geographical expanses, the costs of those technologies rendered it impossible to stay in business without huge resource bases, particularly when the country's postwar economic woes cut seriously into advertising revenues.[56] As a result, some of the country's most distinctive papers died; others were swallowed up by rich rivals; and the strongest of the dailies began to seem more and more like interchangeable national papers, emptied of the regional and individual flavors that had marked their early years. At the same time, the creative energies that had produced one new paper after another for more than three and a half decades withered; the papers that survived the end-of-Meiji shakedown were *it*—all there was to be—for Japanese journalism. With the exception of the early-Shōwa financial trade paper *Nihon Kōgyō Shimbun*, no major new daily appeared after 1906.[57]

Several of the embattled papers survived these years, but with a limp. The once-dominant *Niroku*, for example, went from nearly 150,000 subscribers in 1903 to 60,000 in 1907 and even fewer in the early-Taishō years; *Miyako* struggled along at the 30,000 to 50,000 level; *Yomiuri*, plagued by weak editorial leadership, did the same. And *Tōkyō Nichi Nichi* suffered an even worse (though more temporary) fate, plunging to a mere 24,000 daily readers by 1907.[58] Other papers with proud traditions lost their independence altogether or simply vanished. Kuga's once-haughty and influential *Nihon* was turned over to the former *Jiji* reporter Itō Kinryō in 1906 and in 1914 was shut down completely after two dozen writers quit to protest Itō's new, party-oriented editorial policies. Similarly, Shimada Saburō sold his enfeebled *Mainichi Shimbun* to the family-centered *Hōchi* in 1908, announcing in a December 31 editorial to his "beloved readers" that "I no longer have the resolution needed for the newspaper enterprise." *Hōchi* editors dreamed of turning the paper into a political counterpart to the apolitical parent paper but had little success, and though *Mainichi* survived the era, it did so with fewer than 30,000 readers, a staff of just thirty, and a single printing press. Another of the onetime powers, *Chūō*, was purchased by the Seiyūkai in 1910 as a party organ,[59] and *Denpō Shimbun* went out of business altogether, as we shall see shortly.

The major stimulant to consolidation was the activism of the powerful papers: *Hōchi*'s purchase of *Mainichi*, Fukuzawa Sutejirō's ambitious (though ill-fated) creation of *Ōsaka Jiji*,[60] regional power *Fukuoka Nichi Nichi*'s spreading monopoly over other Kyushu papers such as *Saga Nichi Nichi* and *Kumamoto Nichi Nichi*,[61] and, especially, *Ōsaka Mainichi*'s aggressive assault on the Tokyo market. Convinced that his paper would have to establish a Kantō base in order to be more than a regional force, president Motoyama began looking for a voice in the capital at the middle of the decade, provoking rumors of an imminent takeover of Shimada's struggling *Mainichi*. When Shimada signaled his opposition to such a move by changing the paper's name to *Tōkyō Mainichi Shimbun*, the Osaka forces began looking elsewhere and in December 1906 purchased the poorly regarded *Denpō Shimbun* and renamed it *Mainichi Denpō*. Neither *Mainichi*'s resources nor the editors' innovations could keep *Denpō* from losing three thousand yen a month in the competitive Tokyo market, however, so Motoyama began looking for another target, which he found in the financially embattled *Tōkyō Nichi Nichi*. On March 1, 1911, he announced that *Ōsaka Mainichi* would purchase what for many years had been the country's most powerful paper and merge it with *Mainichi Denpō* under the *Nichi Nichi* name. Ignoring the irony of bringing Japan's earliest and most vocal government ally together with one of the country's first popular rights mouthpieces, he wrote in an editorial that only through merger could he make his voice heard in the capital. As he put it:

> Despite the development of railroads and steamships, we still lack adequate methods of transportation to prevent the slow delivery of news. If you want to get your ideas to the entire country quickly, you have to put out more than a single newspaper. . . . Fortunately, the shareholders of the oldest paper in the world of journalism, the independent and highly trusted *Tōkyō Nichi Nichi Shimbun*, agree; so that enterprise has come under our joint management.

He concluded with a promise of "great things for the newspaper world."[62] One might argue about Motoyama's promise, about whether or not *Ōsaka Mainichi* was indeed furthering the cause of Japanese journalism by quieting two highly divergent voices. There was no arguing about the importance of the move, however. The amalgamated *Tōkyō Nichi Nichi* again became one of the city's larger papers, with a combined *Denpō–Nichi Nichi* circulation of about 70,000 and a new base that would catapult it back to the top during the Taishō years. The Mainichi Company now had a voice in the capital that made its rivalry with *Asahi* national in scope.

Osaka had become the wellspring of the country's press. That city's journalistic entrepreneurs had given Japan one of the world's most thoroughgoing national presses, dominated by two companies whose influence now extended into mountain valleys and harbor towns from north to south. Over the next three decades, these Osaka companies would threaten nearly every provincial paper in the country, driving more than a few of them out of existence altogether. And they would use their powerful Kansai-Kantō base to control the daily news intake of citizens in nearly every hamlet and town, to a degree unparalleled in large modern countries. So dominant had they become already by 1912 that a provincial reporter sent to cover the emperor's death would feel no embarrassment at all about simply copying a *Tōkyō Asahi* article and phoning it back to his editors at the *Shinano Mainichi*.[63] The implications of this kind of concentration would engage scholars for decades to come, but there would be no debating its reality. The old *ōshimbun-koshimbun* dichotomy was back. This time, however, the distinctions had nothing to do with content and everything to do with circulation and capital. And the big, national papers were more dominant than ever.

LEADING THE MINSHŪ

If commercialism had changed the structure of Japanese journalism by the time the Emperor Meiji entered his last months, it also had transformed the way in which editors looked at society and, as a result, the narrative they put together for their daily readers. Sensitive to their heavy working-class readership (and to the fact that even elite readers preferred more lively articles), editors not only elevated news over editorials now but moved the "third-page news" of scandal and daily life to page one, though they still called it *sanmen kiji*. They expanded the assignments of what once had been called the "soft faction" *(nanpa)* reporters from pure police beat work to economics and to what were known as "society stories" on the ins and outs of daily life, and they stopped hiring illiterate *tanbōsha* to gather any news at all.[64]

The result was that news columns became livelier, more varied, and often coarser than ever before. As the Russo-Japanese War neared its conclusion, tales of naval victory were edged out by "shocking" stories about a man who murdered an eleven-year-old boy in order to concoct an antileprosy "flesh soup."[65] Articles in 1906 included not only plans to nationalize the railroads and the death of the newspaper world's first dominating voice, Fukuchi Gen'ichirō, who loathed the new brand of journalism,[66] but graphic accounts of citizen protests over streetcar fare increases. The year 1908 would produce sensational reports in Fukuchi's old paper, the once-lofty *Tōkyō Nichi Nichi,* of a twenty-five-year-old Tokyo gardener named Ikeda who snooped on a woman in the local bath, then murdered her on the way home.[67] Two years later, capital papers would be full of predictions that Halley's Comet was headed for a collision with Earth, along with accounts of a dozen students who drowned while boating in Zushi and breathless reports about the first Japanese to fly in an airplane.[68] And two years after that, in 1912, the papers competed fiercely to scoop each other with every trivial particular (including defecation details) about the condition of the dying emperor as well as the name of the new era.[69] Serious news still may have been dominant, but it had to compete now with the sensational and the merely interesting for space, even in the proudest of papers.

There was nothing new about human-interest journalism. The *koshimbun* specialized in it in the early Meiji years, prestige papers such as *Yūbin Hōchi* began to give space to it under editors like Miki in the early 1890s, and the fastidious *Nihon* complained in the late 1890s that editors were contradicting themselves when they claimed that "photographlike" *(shashinteki)* portrayals of society's dark corners had no negative consequences: "If newspapers have the power to disturb public order, they also can be used to undermine morals; . . . if a newspaper can produce assassins, today's realistic, society-oriented papers can just as well instigate crimes such as adultery, theft, and murder."[70] What changed after the Russo-Japanese War was the pervasiveness of this kind of news as well as the editors' attitudes toward printing it. Even the most highly respected papers were filled with these items in the last Meiji decade, to the point that some upper-class fathers reportedly refused to let women and children in their families see a newspaper. And, as Ariyama Teruo points out, the social conscience that had prompted the raw-edged *Yorozu* and *Niroku Shinpō* crusades at the turn of the century largely had vanished by now. In a 1909 survey, editors at all papers defended police blotter and human-interest articles on the simple economic grounds that they were the readers' favorite part of the paper, with the *Hokkai Taimusu* describing a full 70 percent of its readers as "lovers of *sanmen kiji*."[71] Public tastes, noted another analyst of the press, "ran rather to multiple murders and adultery than to moral uplift," a point he thought press critics should keep in mind when asking for "a socially beneficial press."[72]

The public also demanded—and got—an abundance of success stories in these years. If urbanization and the postwar letdown produced hedonism and disillusionment in the popular sphere, socialism in politics, and individualistic naturalism in literature, it also produced what one writer calls a "tireless repetition by newspapers and magazines of 'success stories' built around men of distinction."[73] Even a socialist like Kinoshita Naoe would deplore now the "age of almighty gold" that had taken the place of the long-anticipated "golden age of peace and freedom." And *Chūō Kōron* spoke for most intellectuals when it warned that "the advance of civilization is corrupting morals." But there was no gainsaying that the individualistic new readers, depraved or not, loved articles about the exciting possibilities of the new age: tales of revolutionary inventions, evidence that Japan had become an international power, and, above all, accounts of people who had struggled their way to wealth, fame, or ease. The writers "repeat over and over the principles of success," wrote Kuroiwa. "Even then, however, the readers never tire of it. They pore over such material. . . . Their eyes are like saucers as they read."[74]

And the papers fed that appetite, telling the tale of Shimoda Utako, who made five thousand yen a year (more than any other woman in Japan) as dean of the Peeress' School for Girls, of the discovery in 1907 of a typewriter for Chinese characters, of the use of the automobile to deliver mail, of astronomer Kimura Hisashi's latitude variation discoveries that "brought worldwide recognition to Japanese science," of Captain Hino's maiden airplane flight at Yoyogi field, of novelist Natsume Sōseki's dramatic decision to leave academia and join the *Tōkyō Asahi* staff.[75] Late Meiji might or might not be an "age of success," observed Tokutomi, "but it certainly is the age of success stories." Added Ukita Kazutami, writing in the popular journal *Taiyō:* "Never since the dawn of world history has the growth of the individual been so respected and material happiness so sought after as in present-day Japan."[76] And never, he could have added, had publishers been more eager to satisfy the searchers.

The late-Meiji papers did more than pander to the masses, however; they also led them, sometimes in tumultuous directions. Editors may not have been as concerned about exposing the "social problems" of poverty and labor abuse as Shimada and Kinoshita had been at the beginning of the century, but as the identification between journalists and plebeian readers had grown stronger, the papers had come more and more to accept an expanding role as articulators of the issues that agitated working-class readers: wages, streetcar fare increases, taxes, voting rights. And when the *minshū* began challenging the system with increasing frequency in these years, when "imperial democracy" began gathering steam in what some call the Age of Urban Riots *(toshi bōdō jidai)*,[77] many of the country's most important journalists were there with them, shovels in hand, heaping coal into the engine of discontent. Indeed, no role more fully dramatized what had happened to late-Meiji journalism than the press' assumption of leadership in the struggle to make the "people's voice" heard.

The late-Meiji, early-Taishō urban discontent too often gets lost in mainstream studies of Meiji modernization. At odds with the standard image of successful nation building, the unruly crowds and burning police boxes are described as blips, if they are seen at all. The truth, however, is that the decade and a half after the Russo-Japanese War was a tumultuous time, marked by what the unapproachable Yamagata Aritomo described to Tokutomi as the people "thrashing about in blind courage" until "it is too late, and . . . the nation is beyond rescue,"[78] as much as by expanding empires and new inventions. Led by coalitions of journalists, lawyers, businessmen, and politicians, crowds of thousands—sometimes tens of thousands—took to the streets at least nine times between 1905 and 1918 to protest weak foreign policy, autocratic politics, official corruption, and, especially, rising fares and prices. Their targets included the police, the Home Ministry, the clique-oriented cabinet, and business elites (particularly streetcar companies and rice merchants) that threatened to throw them out of work or charge them more. And their ranks included nearly every group identifiable as *minshū:* factory laborers, shopkeepers, students, rickshaw pullers, transportation workers, craftsmen, and the unemployed, many of them newly arrived in the city, profoundly distanced, in W. Dean Kinzley's phrase, "from the social rhythms of rural life."[79]

They had an impact too, creating enough disruption to bring down cabinets and force numerous policy changes. In the four riots that occurred before the end of Meiji, nearly five hundred people were arrested, more than 130 streetcars and trams were damaged, and hundreds of police boxes were destroyed. And, as Andrew Gordon tells us, the widely publicized city riots represented only the surface of a much broader and deeper world of social discontent, the "apex of a huge pyramid of collective actions comprising in addition several near riots and hundreds of commonplace peaceful instances of assembly and action."[80]

Of particular importance here is the central role played by leading journalists in these episodes. Though the rioting itself normally was unplanned, these were not purely spontaneous crowds. In each case, action was precipitated by rallies called by small professional groups with "a vision of the political order at odds with that of the elite."[81] And both the committees and the speakers always included more than a few journalists. Nor was it merely the working reporters who involved themselves in these movements; on more than one occasion, the editors themselves took the initiative, setting up the rallies, writing or encouraging supportive editorials, and reporting on the events with "instigating words" *(sendōteki genji)* designed to get as many people as possible fighting for the particular cause.[82] The journalists' motives varied, from building circulation and increasing profits to nurturing the press' political influence. But in every case, they saw themselves quite consciously as managers of the people's struggles, a point that an examination of several specific episodes should make clear.

The struggles over streetcar fares in 1906 and 1911 show the varied facets of the press' popular role with particular force. At the beginning of March 1906, *Tōkyō Asahi* informed its readers that the city's three streetcar companies, Densha, Kaitetsu, and Denki, were planning to request a fare increase from the current three *sen* to at least four *sen* and that two company officials had resigned to protest the increases.[83] A few days later, it reported on the companies' actual petition for a two-*sen*, or 67 percent, increase; and a week after that it had an even bigger story to tell—of the citizens' explosive reactions to the proposed increases.[84] A relatively peaceful opposition rally was held on March 11, but a second demonstration, on March 15, ended in violence. As *Asahi* told the story, some two thousand people gathered at Hibiya Park that day beneath a flag-bedecked platform to hear denunciations of the increases by most of the socialist movement's luminaries. They approved (with cheers, of course) a three-part statement rejecting the increases "to the bitter end," demanding that public welfare be placed ahead of private profit, and announcing another rally three days later at Ueno Park.[85] And then hundreds headed for the streets, where things turned ugly.

Picking up supporters as they marched, the demonstrators stopped in front of the Kaitetsu headquarters near the Imperial Hotel and shouted "in a raging wave of voices": "Increases unjust! Increases unjust!" *(neage futō),* hurling stones and breaking windows as they shouted. Others headed toward the Marunouchi financial district and the Tokyo city offices, where a riotous melee drew growing numbers of police. Still others returned to Hibiya, shouting insults and assaulting any streetcar foolish enough to pull into the area. By late afternoon, more than 150 mounted policemen, dozens of riot police, and nearly five hundred regular patrolmen had been called on to restore order, but not before scores of streetcars had been damaged. Kaitetsu not only locked its offices; it stopped its streetcars after 5:00 p.m. "It all looked like an armed camp," said one reporter.

Though the papers' coverage was professional and serious in tone, it was significant that the accounts noted the presence of numerous journalists among the rally leaders and contained little condemnation of the rioters. There was no criticism of the many socialists arrested following the flareup either. And when the city rejected the rate increase petition a week later, on March 23, the papers positively rejoiced. "Streetcar increases rejected; a victory song for the people!" shouted *Tōkyō Asahi.* It credited the "public seething" with helping determine the outcome and noted that "the officials, whose vacillating, noncommittal positions let this grievous public debate go on for more than twenty days, must bear half of the responsibility" for the troubles.[86] The reporters and editorialists made it clear, in other words, that they identified with the *minshū*—the readers.

That sympathy was equally apparent when the public victory over fares proved short-lived, prompting an even larger outburst late that summer. As in the antitreaty episode a year earlier, the papers began publishing ominous reports early in August, writing at the beginning of the month that Home Minister Hara Kei and Tokyo governor Ozaki Yukio had approved a merger of the streetcar companies and a one-*sen* fare increase.[87] In contrast to the previous year, however, the *minshū* themselves, prodded by the socialists (many of them journalists), showed the greater indignation this time. An initial rally was held on August 7, and by late August crowds of up to a thousand were gathering nightly at various spots in the city to protest the increases.[88] The opponents reserved the anniversary date of September 5 to begin the major protest activities, with an outdoor rally at Hibiya Park. "Students, merchants, officials, white-haired old men, and even blind people" began filling the seats a full three hours before the 1:00 P.M. starting time, and by noon their mood was "ripe for an explosion," according to a *Jiji* reporter. Once again, the rally led to riots, three days of them this time. Typically, crowds numbering in the thousands would seek out streetcars, surround them with shouts of *"Banzai waāi,"* then yell, "Get off! Get off!" to the passengers inside. On the night of the fifth, riot police were compelled to shoot blanks into the air along Ginza Street to disperse the rioters. An Asakusa-bound car was "pelted with stones like rain" as the clock neared midnight in Nihonbashi. And similar attacks consumed the Shiba, Kōjimachi, Kanda, Asakusa, and Shinjuku areas. When officials ignored visits from the Anti-Increase Committee (Neage Hantai Iin), the tumult continued, and for several days the streetcars stopped running and "the only transportation available was *jinrikisha.*"

Order largely had been restored by the time an indoor citizens rally was held at the Kanda Kinkikan on September 11, but not before more than 10,000 had taken to the streets, 113 had been arrested (with rally spokesman Matsumoto Junkichi receiving an unusually severe four-year prison sentence),[89] and, again, scores of streetcars and police boxes had been damaged or destroyed. One of the more significant developments was the citizenlike mindset evidenced by many in the crowd now. Not only did they employ many of the dramatic, theatrical methods typical of such uprisings across the centuries, they showed a "national political awareness"[90] that was quite new. The decision to meet at the "people's park" on the anniversary of the 1905 riots was not accidental. Nor was the adoption of a Kinkikan resolution that spoke to political and quality-of-life issues far broader than mere fare increases: the need for student and worker discounts, improved safety features, and more cars to reduce crowding; the irresponsibility of officials who "neglected their duties" and "disregarded the people's interests"—and the "unconstitutionality" of raising fees in defiance of the popular will.[91] Home Minister Hara, said *Yorozu*, must "consider the interest of the masses before that of a few moneyed people."[92] Their rhetoric, in other words, had turned public; they had come to see themselves not as customers or ciphers but as part of a body politic, with rights enshrined in a constitutional system. And the press' own discussions of both popular conditions and what the government *owed* the people lay at the heart of that new consciousness. That was the reason that *Yorozu* noted on September 11 that "not one of the Tokyo papers ranges itself with the government . . . concerning the present question," the reason that its September 13 report on the actual implementation of the four-*sen* fare had such a tone of anger; the government had let its citizens down.[93]

The next several years saw similarly intensive, *minshū*-oriented coverage of many other expressions of citizen discontent. In 1907, for example, there were seemingly endless reports on the sixty strikes that shocked the country—a fourfold increase over the previous year that included two hundred postal workers seeking higher wages in Kyoto, a thousand miners walking off the job in Okayama, two thousand stopping work at the Osaka Yūzen firm, and nearly nine hundred miners torching buildings and tearing up *shōji*-papered windows in Ashio. "The force of the violence at the Ashio copper mine raged with ever greater fury yesterday," *Hōchi* told its readers on February 7; *Tōkyō Asahi* described looting workers dynamiting soil storage facilities and the resultant deaths of numerous strikers on February 8; and *Jiji* reported three hundred arrests on February 9.[94] The tone of most reportage on the strikes was less sympathetic, especially when the protests turned violent or when the revived daily *Heimin Shimbun* raised the specter of a coming "fine morning" when Tokyo would "find itself utterly paralyzed by the sudden stoppage of businesses of street cars, of railways . . . of post and telegraph," just as in "the great strike of Paris."[95] But a significant proportion of mainstream journalists sympathized with Katayama Sen's general descriptions of worker conditions, if not with the socialists' ideology and methods, when he wrote in *Shakai*

Shimbun the next year that managers treated employees "in the most cruel manner," requiring permission to go to the restroom, fining them heavily for minor mistakes, and allowing them to drink hot water only at mealtime.[96]

When new taxes were levied on several consumer commodities early in 1908, the press' populist sympathies again were fully in evidence. *Tōkyō Mainichi*,[97] in particular, not only joined the other major papers in reporting on the February 11 antitax rally attended by 10,000 or more people, but reprinted with all its original zest the inflammatory rally announcement warning people sarcastically *not to:* "bring any dangerous weapons," "fight with the police," "smash any police boxes," "smash any streetcars," or "attack pro-tax or Seiyūkai M.P.'s."[98] Similarly, when the city moved to take over the operation of the streetcars in 1911, the press went well beyond editorial opposition to overt, active leadership of a skeptical public.[99] *Yorozu* was at the front of the line this time, writing about apparent complicity between the companies and city government and predicting an increased tax burden if city ownership were approved. On the afternoon of July 7, a day before the city council was to take final action, Editor Kuroiwa described the proposal to a large, thunderous audience at Kanda Kinkikan as "cunning and outrageous in the extreme."[100]

The next morning, his paper issued a call for its own afternoon citizens' rally "to exhaust every legitimate means possible" to get the proposal quashed, declaring in the politically attuned rhetoric of the day: "Let all citizens who agree that the constitutional system belongs rightfully to us gather at Hibiya Park at 3:00 P.M." And at least 10,000 people (20,000 by *Yorozu*'s count) responded, despite heavy humidity and strong southerly winds that "blew up a dust storm."[101] The rally was peaceful this time, thanks in part to the five hundred police officers who mingled with the crowd, but the situation teetered on the brink until well into the evening, as the next day's *Tōkyō Asahi* story on post-rally activities at city hall made abundantly clear. Using the detail-filled, occasionally overblown journalistic style of the day, the reporter wrote:

> A crowd gathered in front of the main gate of the Tokyo city building. Uniformed officers and plainclothesmen came in tens and twenties, to keep these fugitive Hibiya zealots in check. A sign before the gate said that all visitors' seats were full and that people without tickets would not be permitted to enter the building. So the large street in front of city hall began at once to swarm with people, to the

point that one could not even move for a time. At about 4:30, several Shiba Ward opponents of city ownership raised an eighteen-by-two-foot white remonstrance banner. There was a good deal of shouting and pressing to enter. The police resisted firmly, and the people jostled about noisily. . . . When several council members on their way out shouted, "There are empty visitors' seats, come on in!" the crowd in front of the gate . . . began to yell, "Push! Push!" They decided to shove their way in just as they were, dust-covered clothes and all. But the police were determined to keep them out. The situation grew more turbulent by the moment.

Only with reinforcements from Hibiya police headquarters was the tumult quieted and another riot avoided.[102]

Once again during this episode, editorials and articles supportive of "the people" were filled with the rhetoric of "unconstitutionality," with discussions about the necessity of consulting city residents on matters that affected their livelihood, and with powerful evidence of the editors' own sense of responsibility for helping the minshū demand redress from capricious officials. Some editors dramatized their point by printing photographs of those behind the city takeover, with their heads wrapped in serpents or being pecked by crows, alongside the label "enemy of the people."[103] Not until the early Taishō years would these assertions of popular initiative gain true gale force, in the crises over constitutional government (1912), naval corruption (1913), and rice prices (1918) that brought down three governments. Still, already before Meiji died in the summer of 1912, his people had become politicized to the point of making frequent, often riotous incursions into the streets on behalf of such once-foreign concepts as "official responsibility" and "constitutionality." Thousands of urban commoners had left the realm of the subject and entered the arena of the citizen, not perhaps in the quieter, more responsible ways Fukuzawa envisioned when he talked decades before about a shimin kokka (citizen-centered nation) but as self-perceived participants in the civil sphere nonetheless. And their most visible, vocal allies, their leaders and frequent managers, were the journalists.

GLORIFYING THE NATION

How "liberal" Japan's leading journalists must have seemed to outside observers in July 1911, placing themselves so vocally on the side of the city's working classes, defying the authorities in the name of constitutionalism. But there was another side to their activism, a side with marked potential for circumscribing the freedoms they now championed. The very editors who smiled at rioters and gave the *minshū* their *sanmen kiji* also took a more and more narrowly nationalistic—and, in many ways, increasingly establishment—view of things, even in these years of urban riots and consumer culture. The cessation of war may have lowered the volume on nationalist rhetoric, but it did not diminish its underlying tone. In fact, the commitment to *tennōsei* or emperor-system ideology at home and aggressive behavior abroad grew even firmer in these years. To write of the late-Meiji years without discussing what Gregory Ornatowski calls "the close interaction between nationalist and populist ideologies" would be to describe but half of the institution.[104]

The emperor, not surprisingly, formed one of the prominent news and editorial topics of these years and the grounding for much of the nationalist rhetoric. When Meiji attended the University of Tokyo graduation ceremonies, when his majesty visited the far-flung city of Kagoshima, or even when dancing women *(maiko)* came to the palace, it was news, just as it was when he drank coffee heated in an "honorable tea kettle made of gold."[105] The editorialists also joined *minkan* nationalists in bemoaning from time to time the insufficient patriotism of "the people": the lack of loyalty among local military reservist groups or the inadequacy of the Imperial Rescript on Education for inculcating true loyalty and morality.[106] And writers would cry fairly regularly for "the recovery of our lost national spirit."[107]

The editors also devoted much space to the proper bounds and expressions of loyalty, particularly after the 1911 suicide of a Kyushu railroad official when the touring emperor was delayed for an hour by a train mishap. The incident occurred at Moji station on November 11, when the emperor, on his way to observe military maneuvers at Kurume, was held up by a metal strip caught in the wheels of his train. When Kiyomizu Shōjirō, the Moji stationmaster, took his own life to accept responsibility for slowing the emperor down, the press generally showered him with praise. The *Kyūshū Nippō*, for example, expressed admiration for "the brilliance of the national character, the loyalty and patriotism of the warrior's way *(bushidō)*" that would prompt such self-sacrifice. When President Yamakawa Kenjirō of Kyushu Imperial University questioned the suicide during an interview with a *Fukuoka Nichi Nichi* reporter, suggesting that it might have been better for this "child of the emperor" to have "exhausted himself in the service of the nation," the majority of journalists in Tokyo and Kyushu declared Yamakawa too "heartless" to appreciate the nobility of Kiyomizu's deed.[108] Suicide of this sort represented the height of patriotism, an unquestionable virtue. The writers might cheer on protesters against the emperor's political advisors, but for the *tennō heika* himself only loyalty to the death sufficed.

Treatment of foreign affairs in these years showed a similar single-mindedness, with consistent support for expansion on the Asian continent. When the Asahi company issued a three-plank set of guiding principles in 1908, the first pledged the company to promote the people's welfare *and national profit,* and the second promised to work for world culture and peace, on the basis of "respect for our national polity" *(kokutai).*[109] The place where the contours of this peace were being worked out most aggressively was Korea, where Japan had developed a stranglehold after the Russo-Japanese War—and where Itō Hirobumi's 1909 assassination would lead to annexation as part of Japan. In the first years after the war, journalists wrote a good deal about Korean backwardness, corruption, and its need for civilized leadership, but most papers expressed caution about annexation, lest it become "an economic burden for Japan" or stir up foreign criticism.[110] When the annexation was announced on August 22, 1910, however, the press rejoiced. The moderate *Tōkyō Mainichi* declared, under the headline "Happiness of the World," that "the world can enjoy peace only when all countries reach the same level of civilization. . . . It cannot permit such a thing as low-civilization countries." *Jiji* published a special August 27 edition commemorating the annexation. *Tōkyō Nichi Nichi* said the only reason to hold back on full celebrations was that "there have been bad floods in the Kantō area and the sufferers will not be pleased at so much happiness." And lest anyone think the press' concern about commoners extended to colonial peoples, an *Ōsaka Asahi* writer noted that "the purpose for which a country has a colony is not for the interests of the inhabitants of the colony but for the interest of the mother country"; the Korean people should not be given constitutional rights.[111]

The best illustration of the press' commitment to *kokutai* and national strength, even at the expense of intellectual freedom, was its response in these years to the sputtering socialist movement. With the inauguration of the Saionji Kinmochi cabinet following the war, the socialists enjoyed a brief respite from government harassment. A new Socialist Party was formed in 1906 and several socialist papers and journals were launched, including *Hikari,* put out by Nishikawa Kōjirō and Yamaguchi Yoshizō; *Shin Kigen,* by Kinoshita Naoe and Abe Isoo; the radical *Ōsaka Heimin Shimbun* and *Kumamoto Hyōron;* the more parliamentarian *Shakai Shimbun* and *Tōkyō Shakai Shimbun;* and on January 15, 1907, Kōtoku Shūsui's revived, now-daily *Heimin Shimbun.*[112] The socialists hardly were unified, as this diversity of organs showed; indeed, they split bitterly in 1907 when moderates like Katayama Sen refused to accept Kōtoku's increasingly aggressive calls for " 'direct action' of the workers" as the only viable means of struggle—and his insistence on a "fundamental revolution of the economic order and the abolition of the wage system."[113] Even the rancorous public debates surrounding the splits, however, suggested the relative freedom of the early Saionji months.

The relaxation did not last long though. Small or not, the authorities saw the movement as dangerous. Even the loosening moral climate discussed above was blamed on socialist literature by conservative officials like Katsura and his education minister (and onetime antigovernment journalist) Komatsubara Eitarō. Katsura expressed the attitude of most authorities with the statement: "Socialism is today no more than a wisp of smoke, but if it is ignored it will some day have the force of wildfire and there will be nothing to stop it." He called for social programs to assist the poor as an antidote to radicalism and made it clear that the socialist threat should not be tolerated.[114]

It was hardly surprising then that even Saionji, under heavy pressure from Katsura and Yamagata, began cracking down on the socialists during 1907, his second year in office. Blaming the socialists for fomenting the city riots and the strikes, and warning of potential attacks on the imperial system itself, the government increased surveillance of socialist meetings and started banning left-wing literature. On February 22, 1907, Saionji had the Socialist Party banned; in mid-April *Heimin Shimbun* shut its own doors after the government began legal actions to ban it; and on August 21, 1908, a *hakkō kinshi* order was enforced against the *Tōkyō Shakai Shimbun.*[115] *Heimin Shimbun* articulated the mood of most socialists in its last issue, with a statement that showed considerably more determination to look to the long run than its morose farewell had during the Russo-Japanese War two years before:

> The treacherous power-holding classes finally have achieved their goal.... Only three months have passed, a little more than thirty issues; *Heimin Shimbun*'s life has been exceedingly short. But brev-

ity has not rendered it useless. If *Heimin Shimbun* had lasted only for a day, it would have used that day. Confucius wrote the *Spring and Autumn Annals* and overawed the traitors; during *Heimin Shimbun*'s days we have frightened the powerful classes. People do not live for a century; *Heimin Shimbun* already has done what it set out to do. . . . Some day before long, some place, through someone's efforts, another socialist organ will appear, and then another. We wait confidently for this.[116]

That day would be farther off than the writer realized. When Katsura came back to power in the summer of 1908, the crackdown became total. His government handed down harsh prison sentences to a dozen radical socialists who had clashed with police in the dramatic Akahata (Red Flag) incident in June of that year, and from that point he ordered the "arrests of anyone who publicly espoused socialism." Even to be "marked by the police as a socialist meant to immediately lose one's job" now, noted one of the arrestees.[117] And when the government used shaky evidence to execute a dozen leading socialists, including Kōtoku and Kanno, for an alleged plot against the emperor's life in the High Treason affair of 1910–1911, the socialist movement went into a prolonged winter freeze.[118]

Our key concern is the mainstream urban press' treatment of their leftist comrades, and the first thing to be noted is that none of the mainstream papers ignored the socialists. Kōtoku and his comrades were as controversial as any group in the country; so their activities were in the papers constantly. The mainstream press reported at length on the creation and dissolution of the party. During the urban riots, the papers made repeated references, most of them neutral, to socialist leadership. Their coverage of the violent 1907 strikes in Ashio, similarly, was typified by the *Jiji* observation that "the cause of yesterday's commotion is not yet clear, but the troubles would appear to have resulted from the formation of the Shisei Kai (Sincerity Club) after Minami Sukematsu came here recently propounding socialism."[119] Moreover, there was a modicum of sympathetic coverage, particularly after Katsura (a villain of many editors) began his harsh crackdowns. In the fall of 1910, for example, Uozumi Setsurō ran a stinging attack in *Tōkyō Asahi* on the danger socialist censorship posed for all independent writers. And after the High Treason indictments, the same paper did a caricature of the government's excessive security measures and provided space for Tokutomi Roka to defend the accused.[120]

But support was not the press' primary response to the social-

ists or to the equally maligned naturalist writers in the world of literature, who insisted that the darker side of human nature was valid
artistic material. If hard news stories remained fairly neutral, editorial comment on the left-wing and free thinkers was largely negative. Already at the beginning of the decade, when Uchida Roan's
"Broken Fence" was banned for depicting lecherous hypocrisy in
the upper classes, he found it "very strange that both writers and
publishers have greeted this utterly unexplained command from the
government with silence." Later writers might have been pleased,
however, if the mainstream editorialists had merely remained silent;
in 1908, when Ikuta Kizan was tried for injuring public morals with
his story "The City," *Asahi* reporters worked harder, in the words
of Jay Rubin, "at eliciting laughs than at chronicling an authentic
bid for the freedom of the individual conscience." When several
socialists had extramarital affairs, the papers pilloried them. *Yomiuri* hired a new editor in 1910 who hated all new thinkers and fired
the paper's well-known naturalist writer Masamune Hakuchō. Most
papers bitterly attacked Tokutomi Roka for his lack of patriotism
when he spoke out at the First National Higher School in 1911
against the "cold and calculating . . . balding men" who had shown
the high treason defendants no mercy.[121] And the questions about
free speech and thought came only spasmodically, from a few men
like Uozumi and *Tōkyō Asahi*'s Natsume, even when the socialists
and naturalists were being silenced.

The papers might, in other words, support the struggles of
their *minshū* subscribers for a better financial break; they might
even report the people's changing life-styles and record socialist
activities in professional prose. But the right of intellectuals,
whether political or literary, to probe the limits of acceptable discourse—that is, the right of free speech—was not a serious journalistic concern. Uchikawa notes that "it is hard to find a single case
in these years in which the mainstream papers opposed enforcement of the policy to ban socialist newspapers and magazines."
They saw the socialists as a threat to the capitalist, *kokutai* system
and regarded the official suppression as "absolutely necessary."[122]

The High Treason trial provided telling evidence of this fact.
Mere suggestion of "conspiracy against the emperor" was enough to
keep journalists from probing the facts, despite what is generally
regarded as the questionable nature of the evidence. So when the
authorities forbade publication of anything but vague generalities
about the treason charges, the editors complied without serious
complaint. *Tōkyō Nichi Nichi* referred on June 4, 1910, only to "a

big and unprecedentedly shocking plot," and *Tōkyō Asahi* informed
its readers of the arrest of seven individuals (all named) who "were
discovered to have made a bomb and to have planned a radical act,"
then added that "we, of course, cannot divulge now what their purpose was." It also told the readers to rest at ease, because Japan's
remaining anarchists were "all a bunch of idlers"—and officials had
announced that they would rest "only when they can boast that
there is not an anarchist left in the world."[123] One newspaper ran a
photo of Kōtoku over the caption "Face of the Devil"; *Tōkyō Nichi
Nichi* wrote that these "atrocious tyrants" ought to be wiped out;
and *Yorozu* proclaimed its hope that these "great offenders not be
allowed to enter the heavenly kingdom *(tenchi).*"[124]

Even on the question of open trials, which one might have
expected to stimulate free press instincts, the dailies were largely
silent. The anarchists' cases were argued entirely in secret, behind
closed doors guarded by nearly 250 policemen; yet that violation of
constitutional guarantees of open trials was raised not in the Japanese press but in a letter from the editor of the English-language
Japan Chronicle to *The Times* of London. He called "the procedure
adopted by the authorities ... extremely unjust" and noted that "the
mouths of the accused have been shut, and any newspaper which
dared to give publicity to their defence would have been prosecuted
under the Press Law." Another English-language paper, the *Japan
Weekly Mail*, wrote that the authorities ought to "let the public
hear with their own ears the evidence upon which these men are
arraigned," so that "everybody will be convinced that the miscreants
are as criminal as the authorities allege." But while the foreigners'
criticism caused a bit of a stir in the vernacular papers, only *Niroku*
among all the Japanese papers supported open trials. With a crime
so heinous, prejudgment and secrecy evidently could be ignored.
"The verdict upholds national order," said *Yorozu*; "we see nothing
in it worthy of criticism."[125]

There was a déjà vu quality in all this, a replication of the
press' attitudes toward *Heimin* during the Russo-Japanese War.
Then, war and the need for national unity were the reasons; the
national destiny transcended the rights of individuals who might
undermine the cause for which soldiers were dying. Now, it was
kokutai and morality. Moderate socialists were on the edge of the
pale at best; anyone even accused of treason was outside it. No
questions asked. *Niroku* alone raised issues of freedom and censorship with any frequency, and it too was seen as marginal now that
its circulation had declined. The naturalist writer Nagai Kafū ex-

plained his own failure to fight when censors banned *Furansu monogatari* in 1909 as follows: "If an author is going to struggle with the authorities for his rights, he must have sympathy derived from the general drift of society."[126] It was quite clear by now that not many of the urban journalists were going to provide that kind of sympathy.

The last major news story of the Meiji era, the death of the emperor on July 30, 1912, gave the journalists a more constructive opportunity to show their patriotism. In the weeks surrounding Meiji's death, the outpouring of national affection knew few bounds. Geisha stopped wearing bright outfits, dramatic performances were canceled, and temples burned sesame seeds to exorcise the illness. People kept vigil outside the palace and prayed at shrines all across the country by the hundreds of thousands in those last days. On July 29 alone, more than four thousand "swarmed the Tokyo city offices to inquire about the emperor's health."[127] One foreign journalist noted that "places of entertainment in Tokio were closed and their owners and employers went to swell the crowds that waited hour by hour for the bulletins of the Emperor's progress."[128] When Meiji died, millions wore black arm bands; commemorative magazine editions sold by the tens of thousands; it seemed as if the whole city of Tokyo showed up for the funeral procession. And the press covered both the death and the funeral as it had covered no other peacetime story.

During the final ten days of serious illness, when the emperor was in a coma with uremic poisoning, every paper kept reporters on duty outside the palace day and night. Like the rest, *Jiji* reported on July 21, in the most exalted (and bulky) prose that his august, imperial majesty, the divine emperor, who until recently had been in the best of health and actively engaged in working for his beloved people, "had fallen into an honorable illness, and his health [honorable, of course] had become a matter of grave concern." Over the next days, every possible detail was reported: his hourly temperature, how his complexion fluctuated, when his bowels moved and what the feces weighed, the actions taken by his doctors, the color of his tongue, the reactions of the waiting crowds. *Tōkyō Nichi Nichi* worried that "court usages are very badly handicapping the physicians on attendance," since the lighting in the royal chambers was "reported to be deficient" and doctors could neither "approach the Imperial bed standing" nor "look direct into the face of the Imperial patient."[129] The visit of the reverential General Nogi Maresuke was reported, along with his majesty's chronic problems with diabetes

Typical pages from *Tōkyō Nichi Nichi* illustrate the changing format of journalism across the Meiji years. (All courtesy Mainichi Shimbunsha)

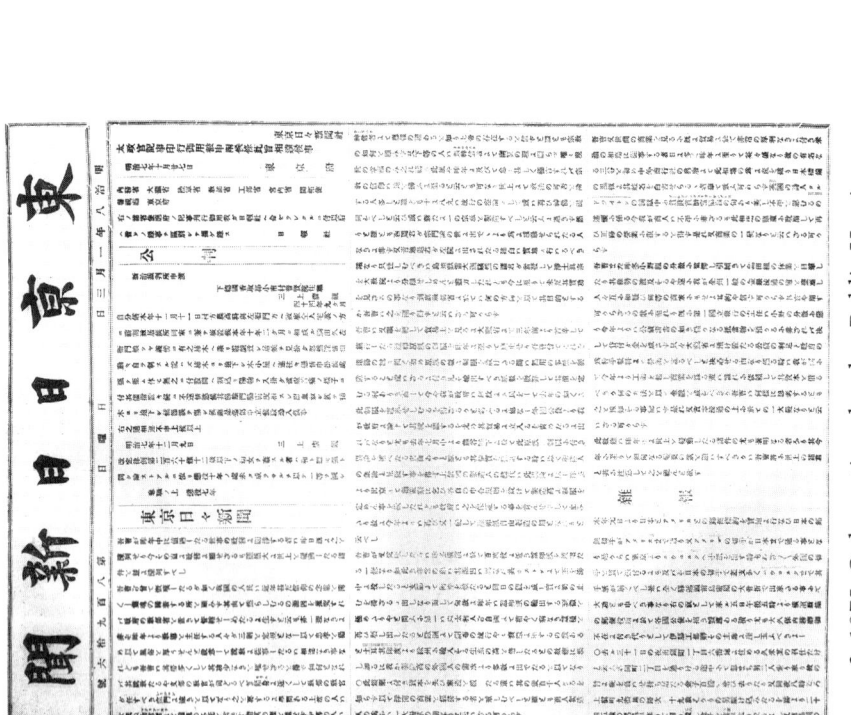

September 6, 1905, page three. Sketches and headlines highlight coverage of the Hibiya riots.

January 3, 1875. Only sections heads—Public Hearing, *Tōkyō Nichi Nichi Shimbun* (i.e., editorial essay), Miscellany (news items)—break up the columns.

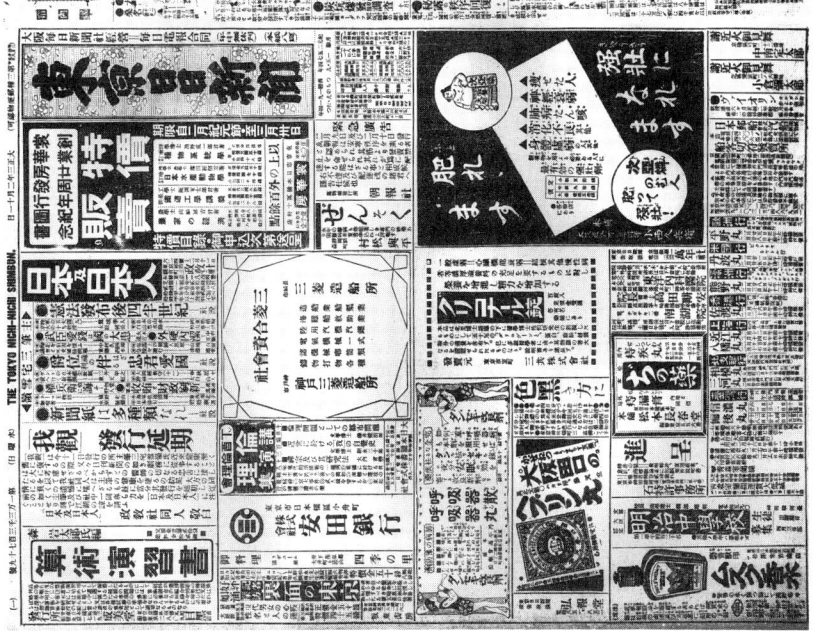

February 11, 1914. By now, page one is given wholly to advertising.

July 30, 1912, page two. The death of Emperor Meiji is marked by varied typefaces, heavy borders, flowery prose, and photographs.

and a hopeful report on the twenty-eighth that the "sincere concern of sixty million loyal subjects had moved heaven" and his condition had improved.[130]

Alas, the improvement was short-lived; so *Yamato* reported on July 30 that "no one, high and low, knows anything but fear now," and when the emperor died later that day, the papers threw every ounce of journalistic knowhow into covering the event. *Tōkyō Nichi Nichi,* which like the other papers wrapped its pages in black borders that day, filled more than half of page one with large pictures of Meiji in full court and military dress under the calligraphy "Mutsuhito" (his given name) and over sketches of the Rising Sun flag. The only headline on the page declared, "Grief Consumes Us; Our Wise and Virtuous Emperor Expires." And the lead story declared: "We the people of the Japanese Empire, hearing the indescribably sad news, are experiencing a depth of grief that is unprecedented." Page two, surrounded by even broader black borders and filled with a confusing mass of headlines and large black type, described the final illness, step by step. The largest headline merely said, "Ah! Alas! Death at Last."

The intense coverage continued in this vein until the evening of September 13, when Meiji's 25,000-person, two-and-a-half-mile-long funeral procession left the Tokyo palace for the trip to Kyoto, where he would be buried in the specially constructed shrines of Momoyama. The stories on the funeral made a bit of history themselves, as the last time Japan's journalists would use the high-flown, poetic (and impossible to understand) prose of the eighth-century *Man'yōshū* in ordinary newspaper articles. "Alas," the *Asahi* reporter said, "the dragon already has flown, astride his horse; the imperial dais is plunged into grief."[131]

The only discordant note to reach the public in these days came in a debate over the appropriateness of the suicide of General Nogi and his wife on the evening of the funeral. *Kokumin* was criticized widely for running the general's original suicide note rather than a sanitized version prepared by the authorities,[132] and debate ensued over whether the suicide was the anachronistic act of a bygone era or a noble expression of the Japanese spirit, appropriate to all ages. *Tōkyō Asahi,* on the one hand, leaned cautiously toward the former, writing the following day: "While we express great *emotional* respect for his act as a fitting climax to Japan's ancient Bushidō, *intellect* tells us to choose differently. We can only hope that it will not have an adverse long-range effect on Japan's morality."[133] Kuroiwa at *Yorozu,* on the other hand, spoke for the majority in likening the suicide to the self-immolation of the medieval war-rior-hero Kusunoki Masashige. The general's death, he wrote, "will inspire us to the end of time. How can we, how can the nation reward him? How can we pass on his great sincerity to our children and grandchildren?" He added a poem of his own composition:

> Until today
> I had thought him
> An excellent man.
> Now I know he was a god
> Born as a man.[134]

This was the very Kuroiwa who had stirred up the *minshū* against the city's takeover of the streetcars twelve months earlier, the Kuroiwa who had reported the nighttime dalliances of the high and mighty a decade and a half before. But he would have admitted of no inconsistency. To have suggested a conflict between antigov-ernment populism and visceral nationalism would have struck him as absurd. Later critics might talk about the capacity of narrow nationalism to restrict the limits of debate and swallow up the democratizing impulses of populism. At the end of Meiji, however, an idea of that sort would have seemed as ludicrous as the social-ists' right to an open trial.

TWIXT STATE AND PEOPLE

So where did the late-Meiji press stand, on the side of the state or on the side of the people? Certainly that was among the era's most important questions. Even to pose it that way, however, was to erect an overly simple duality. Was there indeed such a thing as *the* state? Can one distinguish between "Japan" and its governmental structures, between the structures and the rulers, between the "pure" *kokutai* and the "corrupt" politicians who often were criti-cized for handling their trust so badly? And who were the "people"? The rioters in Hibiya? The docile (or more activist) girls at work on the Osaka spinning machines? The peasants, who still made up the bulk of the population? The strikers at the Ashio and Besshi mines? The professionals who stirred up the strikers? The housewives in Nagoya? There was, in other words, no simple definition of either state or people in late-Meiji Japan. And that being the case, there was no simple answer to where the press stood in its ongoing search for a place as arbiter between people and state. The answer to the question of where the press stood was, in other words, more complex than ever.

But the question cannot be begged, since it speaks to the heart of this study. We must turn once again, quite directly, to the working relationships between the journalists and the authorities who guided—and hounded—them in the last years of Meiji. For there, in the press-government struggles, a good deal of the soul of the end-of-Meiji press lies encapsulated. The press continued, in its own eyes, to be an independent, even an antigovernment, institution. If nothing else, it reported on the unseemly as well as on what the officials considered lofty. It called rallies that sometimes turned into riots. It pandered to plebeian tastes. And it fought the cabinet and Diet quite bitterly, especially when the despised Katsura was prime minister. In February 1910, for example, when a budget compromise resulted in a slight reduction in land taxes, all of the city-based papers except *Kokumin* lambasted the politicians for sacrificing the needs of urban business to the rural prefectures that made up 80 percent of the Diet. And when the government created a Committee on Literature in 1911 to encourage "wholesome" fiction with annual awards to the best writers, many in the press opposed it as a "useless committee," and *Tōkyō Asahi*'s Natsume declined its first award. Writers also used numerous methods, ranging from circumlocutions to the use of *fuseji* (x's and o's in place of sensitive material), to get around censors.[135] Thomas Jefferson complained about enemy journalists who "torture every sentence from me into meanings imagined by their own wickedness only."[136] Katsura and most of the day's other politicians saw their own scribes the same way.

But this was not the whole of the story. Even a generally supportive press seems irascible to officials who prefer sycophancy. And deep patriotism, combined with thoroughgoing capitalism, meant that mainstream editors no longer were likely to wander far from the establishment view of things. That was the main reason, in fact, that a promising 1909 effort to liberalize the press law ended in failure. The revision effort was initiated by friends of the press, at least partly in response to a 1908 call by the Kisha Dōshikai (Association of Like-Minded Reporters) for newspapers to be allowed to publish articles about cases under preliminary court examination and for the abolition of prison terms for press law infractions.[137] A Lower House reform draft, drawn up in March 1909 by the journalist-Dietmen Muramatsu Tsuneichiro of *Ōsaka Asahi* and Suzuki Chi-kara of *Tōyō Hinode Shimbun* in Nagasaki, called for significant, if limited, liberalization of the law, which had been in effect since 1897. It would have lessened the time required between applica-tion for a permit and the first day of publishing from two weeks to three days, permitted publication of materials about cases under pretrial examination, and reduced a number of penalties for violating the law.[138]

By the time the draft became law in May, however, some journalists wished the process never had begun. Police Bureau chief Arimatsu Hideyoshi, speaking for the government, pronounced wholly unacceptable the idea of granting papers permission to run stories on cases under preliminary hearings and suggested that, while they were at the process of revision, the lawmakers should reinstate the right to suspend papers administratively. He also proposed raising the security deposits, ostensibly to assure the ability of papers to pay fines but actually to make sure that small, radical papers be prevented from participating in the public debate. As he put it, "It is exceedingly dangerous for people who cannot even pay a minuscule sum to own such an influential instrument."[139]

Concerned more about their own papers' profitability than about free speech for outsiders, the mainstream journalists who made up nearly half of the special drafting committee wilted during the negotiations over the bill. The revision process reminded one negotiator of bargaining to buy a plant: "The storekeeper begins by giving you an inflated price; then the customer is supposed to throw his heart into getting him to come down." But the journalists threw no heart into the bargaining. Even Muramatsu granted Arimatsu's position on deposits, commenting on how useful they could be in "protecting the stature and quality of the press."[140] As a result, the final bill maintained the prohibition on covering material in pretrial hearings, dropped jail terms for that particular offense (the press' sole victory), and doubled the size of security deposits, to two thousand yen for papers in the Tokyo and Osaka areas, one thousand for those in other cities of 70,000 or more, and five hundred for newspapers in smaller areas.[141] The law gave birth, said journalist-historian Midoro Masaichi, to a "deformed child of a press" *(kikei-jiteki genkō shimbunshi)*.[142] And it remained in effect until the Occupation year of 1949.

The most significant feature of the Diet struggle was the press' reaction to it. No one in the mainstream fought seriously for a more liberal bill, and once it was passed, few journalists had anything negative to say about it. *Ōsaka Asahi* admitted that the reform "was a change for the worse" and called the overall bill "just a useless reform, a half-finished product." As for the prohibition on publishing contents of pretrial hearings: "That is reasonable," as long as courts are "scrupulously fair" in enforcing it. And the officials' right to stop distribution probably was needed to check some writers' tendency to overstep the bounds of propriety.[143] The increase in security deposits did not bother the mainstream papers, since it was aimed at socialist and radical groups for which the commercially oriented, patriotic establishment had scant sympathy anyway. As a result, the editors accepted the new law with only tepid comment. Indeed, the only statement of serious dissatisfaction came from Home Minister Hirata Tōsuke, who complained that it did not give him enough power to control the press, because it still denied his right to suspend and ban papers administratively.[144]

That complacency did not, of course, mean that the press and authorities would work together effortlessly from this point on; the endemic nature of press-official conflicts already has been amply demonstrated. It meant simply that the dance had by now become more complex, that while the mainstream press would continue to fight against its own political villains and for populist causes that attracted *minshū* readers, it would join the authorities almost instinctively in dismissing "extremists" and honoring the *kokutai*. For that reason, its struggles with the authorities most often would relate either to factional political allegiances or to economics, quite often to whether the police would allow the papers to print the things that sold best. The incident that sparked the 1909 press law revision, for example, was the defiant publication by all fourteen of the leading Tokyo papers of the details of a late 1908 brothel murder in Nihonbashi—and the resultant fines against all of them for violating the prohibition on writing about cases in preliminary hearings.

A breakdown of press infractions in the period following the passage of the new law provides telling evidence of the changing character of this press-government struggle. In 1910, the number of suspensions jumped to eleven, the highest since the anti-Portsmouth riots, while the number of prohibitions on sales and distribution doubled to fifty-eight, followed by another sixty-three in 1911. In the same vein, jailings for violation of the press and publication codes stood at six in 1909, jumped to eighteen in 1910 and twenty-eight in 1911, and the number of fines levied increased every year in the post–Russo-Japanese War period, to a huge 13,947 in 1911.[145] But the significant thing is that the suspensions and jailings were levied almost exclusively against the small, socialist journalists, while the sales-distribution penalties and fines usually were enforced against mainstream papers for *sanmen kiji* the editors considered too juicy to hold back until after pretrial hearings.

On June 1, 1909, just weeks after the enactment of the press law, for example, when a murder occurred in eastern Japan, prosecutors forbade newspaper stories under the article on pretrial hearings (Article 19), but four of the papers *(Tōkyō Asahi, Miyako, Nihon,* and *Kokumin)* published anyway, apparently figuring the fifteen-yen fine would be more than matched by additional sales. When Osaka officials invoked a similar prohibition two days later on details about a bribery scandal, the leading papers tried a different tactic; they ran the censorship notice verbatim under the title "Frequent Orders Prohibiting Publication of Articles" *(Iiji sashit-ome meirei hinpin to).* The courts, unimpressed, fined them fifty yen for each time they ran the notices, observing that the prohibition orders themselves included the forbidden information. The Osaka authorities issued a warning to the editors and publishers on June 9, calling attention to the kinds of news about which they should exercise caution, but the editors paid limited attention.[146]

One could argue quite plausibly that official actions of this sort were more like mosquito bites for the mainstream press than serious assaults. Suspensions and jail terms were reserved for radicals; the confiscation of specific issues ordinarily affected no more than a quarter of a given day's sales, since most issues typically had reached the streets before the order could be carried out, and the size of the fines for running *sanmen kiji* paled beside the increased sales revenues. There is no question that the threat of penalties prevented long-term, ongoing discussions of some controversial items or that the frequent fines reinforced the press' self-image as an adversary of the political powers.[147] But their impact was at most limited, because the press no longer needed much supervision on fundamental issues related to national polity and policy. The papers' owners and editors had themselves become a powerful part of the capitalist establishment, more than ready to control themselves on anything that might threaten profits or undermine national strength, as two less formal, evolving arrangements between journalists and the national political leadership now made clear.

It was these years, first of all, that gave rise to rudimentary *kisha kurabu* or press clubs, those cozy reporter-source relationships that would come under such heavy fire in the second half of the century.[148] The roots of the clubs stretched all the way back to the late 1870s and early 1880s, when officials at some government

bureaus began providing special offices, called waiting rooms
(tamaridokoro, hikaejo, hikaeshitsu), with tables, tea, and even
press releases or interview arrangements for journalists working
there. By the middle of the 1880s press rooms of this sort had
become commonplace in Tokyo and were appearing in provincial
government bureaus, and by the beginning of the 1890s, many such
rooms had taken on a clubbish atmosphere, with regular reporters
at a given hikaejo working to keep out newcomers and potential
rivals. In 1888, for example, correspondents for the *Shinonome
Shimbun* were excluded from certain Osaka press offices because of
the paper's feisty antigovernment stands.[149] And when the new Diet
established a pass system in 1890, initially allowing only twenty
reporters into the chambers, the anointed few formed their own
association, the Gikai De-iri Kisha Dan (Diet Reporters Association), and began working not just to help each other but to maintain
their newsgathering advantage over outsiders, especially those from
the provinces. Several temporary "clubs" also were established for
military correspondents during the 1900 Boxer Rebellion and the
Russo-Japanese War.

The most important momentum toward the development of
insider groups, however, came after the advent of the second
Katsura cabinet in 1908. By now, some officials, recognizing that
censorship was not the most effective way to keep large and powerful papers in line, had begun to encourage organizations to facilitate
government-press cooperation. Thus, the Kokusai Shimbun Kyōkai
(International Newspaper Association) was formed in 1909 to bring
newspaper executives and governmental officials together for discussions of mutual concerns, and the Shunshūkai (Spring and
Autumn Club) was created to allow company presidents and editorialists to have background sessions with top officials. Tokutomi
sarcastically described the latter as a club where prominent journalists would "stand at attention, like a group of soldiers, before
Katsura . . . or the police chief, repeating tirelessly, Your Excellency, Your Excellency."[150] And he might have added that that was
exactly what Katsura and his men had in mind when they created it.

Even more important, in terms of editorial impact, was the
fact that by 1910 quite a number of government bureaus had begun
creating actual *kisha kurabu* to encourage not only increased but
more sympathetic coverage. Not all bureaucrats liked the idea;
these "clubs" necessitated substantial budget outlays for room fur-
nishings, telephone lines, tea service, *igo* boards, and people to

assist the reporters—and fawning over writers who might not return the graciousness offended many civil servants. But Katsura had decided by the time he took office in 1908 that reporters were less likely to publish embarrassing or critical stories if they felt indebted to the people they were covering. So he adopted a policy of establishing rooms where only insiders were welcome, where officials would provide access to important news sources and hold back-scratching receptions several times a year, and where news releases would be readily available. As a result, *Shin Kōron* would report in June 1911 that "where there is a bureau there certainly will be a reporters club."

There is little question that these new arrangements facilitated the flow of news; nor is there any question that they encouraged reporters to be careful about what they wrote so as not to cut off sources. Yamamoto Taketoshi uses only slight hyperbole in calling this new form of government assistance "emasculation charity" *(kyosei hodokoshimono)*.[151] Quite clearly, the clubs launched an insiders' approach to mainstream journalism that not only would have disturbed those feisty early-Meiji government adversaries like Narushima Ryūhoku and Suehiro Tetchō but would plague efforts to make the press independent for decades to come.

Less obvious to the casual observer but equally significant were the close ties nearly all leading journalists had nurtured by now with factions in the ruling elites. This practice, like the *kisha kurabu,* already was of long standing by the late-Meiji years, rooted in cases as varied as Fukuchi's friendship with officials from Chō-shū, Shimada Saburō's heavy personal involvement in Diet politics, and Tokutomi's cozy relationship with Katsura. But it had become such a pervasive part of the press by the end of Meiji as to demand a brief discussion here. These relationships are not always easy to document. They tended to be informal, based on personal and financial connections that typically were neither recorded nor meant to be public. Moreover, they shifted from time to time, as both newspaper company leadership and government officials changed. And the links could be highly complex: some were to business elites, some to political parties and groups, some to factions in the bureaucracy.

Nevertheless, these ties were so pervasive that hardly a paper escaped fairly close identification with at least one government or business group as the era drew to a close. The journal *Shin Kōron* took up this issue in 1906, listing the ties of that period as follows:

- Government voice: *Kokumin*

- Semi-official government voice: *Chūō, Yamato, Ōsaka Mainichi*

- Progressive Party (Shinpotō): *Hōchi*

- Semi-official voice of Shinpotō: *Nihon, Niroku, Yomiuri*

- Constitutional Government Party (Seiyūkai): *Jinmin*

- Iwasaki financial clique: *Tōkyō Nichi Nichi*

- Mitsui financial clique: *Jiji*

Two years later, in another discussion of affiliations, the editors had moved *Chūō* to the Seiyūkai column, while another observer put *Ōsaka Asahi* in the Matsukata Masayoshi or Satsuma faction.[152]

Kokumin was the best known of the factional papers, having jumped in bed with the Matsukata and Katsura administrations early on. By the Russo-Japanese War years, Tokutomi even had turned an office on Kokumin's third floor over to full-time dissemination of administration information to other publishers and newspapers.[153] Similarly, *Hōchi* was long and widely known for its close ties to the progressive political parties, first the Kaishintō, then the Shinpotō (and later the Kenseikai and Minseitō), its oft-repeated claims to neutrality notwithstanding. One of the few major editors regarded as independent by the summer of 1912 was *Yorozu's* Kuroiwa, who had made a career of avoiding close ties to influential people, lest he be "swamped" by their views, and even he would draw so close to the anti-Katsura opposition in the tumultuous months after Meiji's death that by early 1913 *Yorozu* was seen as a pro-Ōkuma factional paper too.[154]

Close ties of this sort should not surprise us. After all, the Japanese journalistic tradition had less to do with independence than with influence, and people seeking influence tend to get it where it can be found. Moreover, these early publishers and editors were part of a Confucian culture in which the cultivation of connections to insiders at the top was part of one's duty as a responsible public servant. And by the 1900s, the papers' most influential decision makers were thoroughgoing capitalists too, men bound by the search for profit to create useful liaisons. It is more surprising that while the factional ties undermined the independence of individual papers, they had the ironic effect of making the press as a whole appear more, rather than less, independent. While individual papers tailored positions to fit their patrons, the multiplicity of the factions meant that a variety of voices always would be heard, with the opposition on any given issue claiming to be speaking for "the people." When the papers attacked the government for lowering land taxes in 1910, for example, a number of them actually were speaking more for urban industry and the anti-Katsura groups than for the urban masses they claimed to represent. Similarly, when so many of the papers arrayed themselves against the cabinet in the 1912–1913 constitutional crisis that marked the transition from Meiji to Taishō, they were serving as mouthpieces for big business and the increasingly powerful Seiyūkai political party more than for the "people's army" whose mantle they assumed.[155] But motives may have been less important than results here. The multiplicity of allegiances meant that some papers would be in the opposition on all issues; thus, the "popular" (i.e., nongovernmental) view always would be articulated. Moreover, since the economic and political factions had more real influence than the *minshū*, the papers were sure, in every case, to have a powerful shield behind which to fight. Indeed, one reason they often were able to stand up so loudly against cabinet policies was just that: even in opposition, editors were articulating the views of powerful forces *inside* the establishment and thus had far more protection than they ever would have had as pure representatives of the "people." Thus, even the fighting pose that papers so often struck bore evidence to just how much journalism had become part of the political, capitalist establishment by the end of the Meiji era.

AT ERA'S END

Time means change, and these years were no different from the others we have looked at in that regard. If the Russo-Japanese War eroded the rich journalistic diversity of previous periods and highlighted the papers' increasingly antigovernment brand of populist nationalism, the seven years after the war intensified those trends and turned the press into an unabashedly commercial medium. And in the process, by some curious twist, it brought the voice of the *minshū* into the public arena as never before, since wealth alone was enough to give the newspaper barons an establishment orientation and make their voices influential, even while the source of that wealth—circulation—forced them to be attentive to the people's tastes and concerns. By the onset of Taishō, in other words, successful dailies had become as thoroughly populist as they were establishment, as wholly establishment as they were populist.

The populism showed up in at least three ways. First, the "people" had become the arbiters of journalistic taste and style. Since circulation was everything and the majority of readers came from the middle and lower classes, formats had to be inviting, prose had to be riveting, and news columns had to be filled with gripping material. Stories of crime and tragedy, so commonplace at the end of the twentieth century, still had had no place in proper journalism at the Meiji midpoint, but by 1910 even the once-lofty *Kokumin* and *Jiji* were running *sanmen kiji* without flinching. As a result, the press' social functions and impact had changed too. No longer could journalists simply look down from the editorial column, disinclined "to follow the masses," in Tokutomi's phrase;[156] they had to be servants, attuned to the tastes and concerns of readers who would make or break the balance book. And the impact of this change on Japan's public sphere was enormous. "Popularized *(heiminka)* newspapers read avidly by the masses serve a wholly different function from independent papers," observed Ariyama in discussing this period. "The readers of popularized papers already have a more important power than suffrage, because public opinion expressed through newspapers cannot be extinguished—though it should be remembered that the strength of popular papers lies not so much in discussing political ideas as in expressing formless discontent."[157] The press, to put it another way, had become better than ever at representing popular moods but had lost some of its ability to carry on reasoned, nuanced political discussion.

A second way in which the new populism showed itself, somewhat paradoxically, was in the press' powerful leadership of the masses toward ideas such as "rights" and "constitutionalism." Something clearly had happened to the relationship between the *minshū* and their political leaders by the time the Russo-Japanese War ended. The causes that aroused people were not new; *minken* activists long had sought many of the very things the people were seeking now: a popular voice in government councils, lower taxes, stronger foreign policy, the right to be heard. But never in early Meiji had urban workers marched in support of their own causes; never had they thrown stones and torn down police boxes to secure "constitutional rights." Now, newspapers might not be publishing such learned discussions, but they were doing something just as potent: alerting readers both to problems that needed fixing and to ways of fixing them. Those same readers, in response, came by the tens of thousands to the "people's parks" at Hibiya and Ueno to demand redress. And there, roused by journalists, lawyers, and other activists, they marched into the streets to do battle. The commoners had found a new political space in this period, a space carved out of "constitutionalism" and rooted in the twin ideas that their governors owed them something and they had a right to demand amends when those governors fell short. "A shrill, populist, nationalistic press with a message accessible to increasing numbers of literate city-dwellers," says Gordon, "helped bring home to the populace the disjunction between obligations and rights, between uncomplaining sacrifice on the one hand and limited participation on the other."[158] In doing that, the journalists had created not only a new press but a new civil sphere.

The populism showed itself, third, in an ongoing journalistic commitment to what might be called *banzai* nationalist values. If editors led the masses toward suffrage and equity, they also led them toward an unthinking devotion to both the emperor and *kokutai* in these years. We saw above how the press willingly helped the officials to create a single, unified value system based on nationalism. As long as the writers made a clear distinction between "our Japan" and the frail politicians and bureaucrats who administered the country, they found their readers more than eager to follow their arguments. Every newspaper rally story was filled with the shouting of *banzai*s, one set for the cause and one set for the emperor. Nagai Kafū wrote that "the state and the police and the people are as close as parents and children." When the people came to rallies, performances, and political events, so did the police. And did the people mind? Hardly (unless they were rioting): "There the police are in their grand uniforms, a source of boundless popular pride."[159] And as so many have observed, there was one thing the people and their journalistic leaders did not oppose—and that was military activity abroad. The idea of *Dainihon teikoku* had captured their souls by this period; the idea that democracy and overseas aggression might somehow conflict would have sounded strange indeed.

Beneath this nationalistic symbiosis, beneath the mutual impact that papers and people exerted on each other, lay the final major characteristic of the late-Meiji years: the overweening establishment orientation that resulted from the triumph of commercialism. Movement toward commercialism was no newer than any of this period's other features, as earlier chapters have shown. But it is fair to argue that the drive toward unalloyed capitalism was completed in Meiji's last half decade. The rising financial base needed for publishing drove independent and idiosyncratic papers out of existence in all but the smaller provincial markets. Concentration, rising circulation, and advertising had become the chief ends of all but the most recalcitrant journalists. A Tokutomi might protest that his real goal was to educate, but the evidence of his paper's editorial changes would give the lie to the protests. Komatsubara wrote to Motoyama in 1906 that it would be a good time to start publishing in Tokyo. Why? Because the masses were ready for leaders? Because the nation needed Ōsaka Mainichi's ideas? No; because "this is a good time to take advantage of the growing profitability of the newspaper business."[160] And Motoyama agreed: "One who would publish a newspaper must sell many copies, and to sell many copies you must get the attention of the masses. And to do that, you have to win public sympathy." "Newspaper publishing," he said, "is practical business."[161] It probably pained Kuga to hear it, but that was where journalism stood in 1912—at the center of Japanese capitalism, exerting as much influence as ever, but doing so more through the manipulation of resource bases than through ideas.

Conclusion

Newspapermen are not fair-minded
social critics so much as they are
selfish capitalists.

Murobushi Kōshin, 1911[1]

Bringing a study of the Japanese press to a conclusion in the summer of 1912 is a bit like stopping at the ninth stage of a climb up
Mt. Fuji. We have seen and felt nearly all of the terrain—the entice-
ment of higher profits on ahead, the energizing winds of populism,
the treacherous, unending threats of the authorities—yet we have
not reached the summit. To stop with the death of the emperor,
just before so many of the late-Meiji trends reached their fullness,
seems artificial. Written history is like that, demanding that one
start and end processes that never begin or conclude neatly, all in
the name of helping ourselves organize and "understand" things
that really are too complex to be managed. Even knowing that,
however, does not make a 1912 ending point quite palatable; so I
have opted for a compromise: a brief glimpse at the major features
of the press in the decade following the Taishō emperor's ascension,
followed by an equally brief discussion of the major patterns that
marked Meiji journalism as a whole.

THE AFTER YEARS

Looking first at the institutional side of the press, the most important single characteristic of the post-Meiji years was the maturation
of the process of commercialization. *Ōsaka Mainichi*'s Motoyama

Hikoichi told his employees early in the 1920s, as he had said so often before, that economics had to figure prominently in any editor's thinking. "A newspaper is a . . . commercial product," he said; "some people speak scornfully of commercialism *(shōhinshugi)* and capitalism *(shihonshugi)* . . . but unless we pursue profits, we will not remain independent." He added on other occasions that while it was important for journalists to provide "leadership in the development of society" *(shakai no shidō keihatsu)*, they could do so only if their product were profitable.[2] It was for this reason that the typical newspaper company had developed a clear division between editorial and business departments by the end of World War I, with the business side carrying the greater weight.[3] It also was for this reason that nearly all of the major newspapers followed *Chūgai Shōgyō Shinpō's* late-Meiji lead and became joint stock companies, often with massive capital bases. Asahi, for example, which became a joint stock company in 1919 with 1.5 million yen in capital, had nearly tripled its holdings to 4 million yen by the end of Taishō. *Kokumin Shimbun* went public after the Great Kantō Earthquake of 1923, with holdings of 3 million yen; Mainichi had 5 million yen of capital then, *Jiji* 4.5 million, *Miyako* 1.35 million, *Hōchi* 1.1 million, and even small local papers between 300,000 and 500,000.[4] With capital on that scale and the interests of public shareholders to guard, editors simply had no choice but to look after the balance sheets.

It was no wonder that Tokutomi, ever the purist at heart if not in practice, worried over how newspapering seemed to have lost its editorial soul by the end of the Taishō. "Once," he said, "the dominant figure in the world of journalism was the newspaperman who wielded the pen; today, it is the businessman who fingers the abacus. . . . Newspapers once served a learned minority; today they are for the masses. The newspaperman was once the leader of the masses; today, he provides them with one more source of amusement."[5] Nor was it any wonder that *Tōkyō Asahi* editorial chief Matsuyama Chūjirō would say in 1914, when informed that Kuroiwa had offered grandly to "sacrifice his paper" for his principles: "I have been entrusted with a paper managed by others; I am not allowed that much conviction."[6]

One of the more dramatic examples of what capitalists the newspaper managers had become was the eruption of labor troubles in the Tokyo press world in 1919. Until then, editorialists consistently had supported the struggles of laborer readers, but when the printers applied the editorialists' principles to their own newspaper companies, the managers' core values became abundantly clear. Printers at all the Tokyo papers organized the country's first newspaper union, the Shimbun Insatsukō Kumiai Kakushinkai (Newspaper Printers Reform Association), in June with nearly eight hundred members, and in late July they decided to go on strike if the companies would not agree to eight-hour, two-shift days, a seventy-yen-per-month base salary, and a day off each week. The newspaper executives responded by forming their own alliance, the Shimbun Renmei, which not only rejected the printers' demands but announced a lockout, with publishing suspended until the dispute was settled and a fine of 10,000 yen to be assessed on any company breaking the agreement. A Kakushinkai manifesto called the publishers' action a "declaration of war," an outrage against a public that was left with no public source of news for five consecutive days.[7] But lacking resources to hold out, the printers accepted half of what they had demanded in wages. And on August 5 the papers resumed publication and fired the Kakushinkai's outspoken leaders.[8]

Many of the country's journalists were uncomfortable with their owners' heavy-handed treatment of the printers. Murobushi Kōshin, a former *Tōkyō Asahi* reporter, called the newspaper executives "autocrats" who masqueraded as "leaders of public opinion."[9] Motoyama, who had tried unsuccessfully to block the papers' alliance, pledged that Mainichi papers would not be party to another such "error . . . as long as I am managing this company." And when another dispute arose in 1920, *Yorozu*'s Kuroiwa broke ranks and formed his own separate agreement with the printers.[10] The entire episode weakened the press' self-proclaimed reputation as a "public trust" *(kōhin sei)* interested in workers' rights; but it enhanced the papers' profits.[11] And that, as Matsuyama would have said, was the bottom line now.

A second institutional feature of the Taishō years was the continued popularization of the daily paper. Ads became bigger, brighter, and more numerous than ever. Editorial cartoons, sketches, and photographs combined with dramatic headlines to make dailies almost as lively in appearance as the mass papers of America and Europe. The division of the paper into sections—news, opinion, entertainment, serials—helped readers organize their reading as well as their sense of how the world operated. And by the 1920s, even the most prestigious papers had dropped completely the classical writing styles of the educated in favor of simplified *kanji* and the speech patterns of commoners.[12] Even the *kinds* of ads bespoke popularization, with nearly two dozen ads on a typical page one at *Tōkyō Nichi Nichi* in 1914 calling readers' attention to banks, deodorants, middle schools, violins, worldwide travel opportunities, medicines, and books, books, books.[13] Moreover, news coverage became both quicker and more comprehensive, as the number of cylinder presses more than doubled now to nearly five hundred, as individual papers established dozens of news bureaus all across the country and as editors worshiped ever more earnestly at the altar of the goddess Scoop.[14]

One of the more salutary results of this eagerness to make the daily product appealing to readers was the increasing professionalization of reporters. We already have seen the discontinuation late in Meiji of the hiring of menial *tanbōsha* to gather news. The Taishō years took that trend farther, as the better papers gave more and more time to both hiring and training well-qualified young people as reporters. By the early 1920s, many of them were giving entrance examinations and hiring largely graduates of the most prestigious universities: Waseda, Tokyo, Keiō. In 1924, Motoyama told his trainees, "A newspaper's prestige lies in direct proportion to the personal qualities of its reporters; so newspapers must acquire reporters who have the qualifications to serve, first of all, as channels of discussion *(genron kikan)* and, second, as teachers of society *(shakai no bokutaku)*. Reporters must be statesmen *(keiseika)*, not merely scholars, or politicians, or businessmen."[15] Not everyone saw a change for the better in the move toward professionalism. Kido Mataichi talks dismissively of the *sararīmanka* or salary-manization of the press,[16] as more and more youths took up newspapering as a career in which they could make money or fame rather than as a platform for changing society. That probably was inevitable in a commercialized press; for as Motoyama added in his address to recruits: "The newspaper is an organ for reporting facts, not a tool for leading."[17] There would be better newswriting but less social commitment.

The third institutional feature of Taishō journalism was an impressive surge in circulations. We saw the beginnings of rapid circulation growth near the end of Meiji, but now the figures soared. *Tōkyō Nichi Nichi*, for example, jumped from under 100,000 at the end of Meiji to 350,000 at the end of World War I—and nearly 800,000 at the end of the Taishō era in 1926. The circulation of *Ōsaka Mainichi*, its Kansai parent, stood at 1.2 million by the end of Taishō, while its rival *Ōsaka Asahi* had 800,000 readers. And the average circulation of Tokyo's eight largest papers, which had been

140,000 when Meiji died, had reached 318,000.[18] Perhaps the most impressive statistic of all was not the million-plus circulation of *Ōsaka Mainichi* but the fact that, by the end of Taishō, the capital's papers were delivering 130,000 more papers daily in the Tokyo region than there were homes there, meaning that tens of thousands of families were taking at least two papers each. Not only had the press become a mass medium; it had reached near-saturation coverage.[19]

With the maturing commercialism on the press' institutional side came ever broader coverage and increasing populism on the content side. The *sanmen kiji* approach of the late-Meiji years continued, with vivid accounts of murders, titillating morality tales about eight drunken Ehime policemen who assaulted innocent citizens with broken tree branches, *Tōkyō Nichi Nichi*'s breathless (and mistaken) report that the new era would be named Kōbun when Taishō died in 1926. International coverage also was broadened and speeded up, with *Jiji* scooping the entire world on the 1921 plans to replace the Anglo-Japanese Alliance with a Four Power Agreement and *Tōkyō Nichi Nichi* getting a much-ballyhooed interview with Lenin, reportedly one of only two the Marxist pioneer ever gave to a capitalist reporter. And while the tone of international reporting retained its late-Meiji chauvinism, most papers supported the government's more conciliatory policies of the 1920s as the right way tactically to expand Japanese interests on the Asian continent.[20]

By far the most significant illustration of both the intensified populism and the broadened coverage came in the press' involvement in these years in the continuing urban protest movements. The period from 1912 to 1918 in particular saw a peak in the journalists' sense of themselves as leaders of the mass-based, anticabinet forces demanding "constitutional government" *(rikken seiji)*. Sometimes the writers worked with political party leaders, but just as often they worked against them in these years, decrying every perceived abuse, from the tax system to the sending of Kyushu girls to southeast Asia as prostitutes, from government by secrecy to the folly of dispatching troops to an unwinnable morass in Siberia in 1918.[21] With even greater frequency than in the post–Russo-Japanese War years, the writers drummed home "democratic" and "constitutional" phrases such as "popular suffrage" *(kokumin no sanseiken)* and the "people's desires" *(kokumin no kibō)*. As one Tokyo editorialist put it when the autocratic Terauchi Masatake was selected prime minister in 1916:

> There is a constitutional problem. The elder statesmen have completely disregarded Lower House forces in asking Count Terauchi to form a transcendental cabinet. . . . The question is whether or not our country's politics will be carried out in accordance with the people's desires. The question is whether or not popular suffrage will be realized. The question, in other words, is whether the spirit of the constitution will be effected.[22]

Gregory Ornatowski, who has studied *Asahi* editorials in this period, concludes that the editors' reasons for taking up the constitutional issue had at least as much to do with the "tremendous public appeal" that "promoted a newspaper's popularity and benefitted its commercial interests" as it did with principle.[23] But the important thing for the period's political environment was the continuing spread among the *minshū* of the idea that commoners had a right to demand official redress of their grievances.

The most dramatic link between press and people was forged in the massive rallies and riots of the 1910s and early 1920s, which felled three cabinets and forced several major policy changes. Early in 1913, the press joined the Seiyūkai and Kokumintō political parties in the *kensei yōgo undō* (movement to protect constitutional government), which brought down the Katsura cabinet over military interference in the government and the prime minister's high-handed manipulation of the imperial symbol.[24] The next year, they did the same to the Yamamoto Gonnohyōe government over naval scandals; in 1918, they forced Terauchi out following eight weeks of riots and demonstrations in more than five hundred different communities; and in the early 1920s, they led the popular movement for universal male suffrage. The factional alliances discussed in the previous chapter kept the newspapers from being unified in any of these episodes, but each time a majority of the leading papers played a significant role in bringing the people to the streets. And while space prevents their full treatment, a glance at two of the episodes should help us to understand just what a political force the press had become.

First, the Siemens scandal. The year 1914 opened with the government already in a state of siege: Yamamoto under unending attacks from the press for his ties to the Satsuma clique, the navy under fire for heavy spending, citizen rallies planned by several groups to oppose high business taxes and demand more aggressive policies in Asia.[25] As a result, when Reuters reported on January 23 that the German Siemens company had made secret payments to several high naval officials in exchange for procurement contracts, the press and the people exploded once more. The old journalist warhorse Shimada Saburō raised the issue in the Diet on February 1,[26] journalists demanded impeachment of the cabinet at a national reporters rally *(zenkoku kisha taikai)* in Tsukiji on February 9, and a public gathering by as many as 40,000 people at Hibiya on February 10 touched off several days of violence, with the usual attacks on progovernment newspapers, streetcars, and police boxes, as well as 435 arrests. The issue dominated the press and the Diet for another six weeks, until a planned naval expansion was rejected and Yamamoto resigned.[27]

The press' role as a leader of the popular forces took on several new or expanded dimensions this time. For one thing, it acted independently of the Seiyūkai, with which it had been allied in the 1913 crisis, because the party was allied now with Yamamoto in the Diet. For another, its rhetoric was used quite directly by rally leaders, who read aloud from newspaper articles to arouse passions at the rallies.[28] And for still another, the antigovernment journalists found themselves on the receiving end of police violence, when officers at the February 10 rally turned their swords on two reporters, Hashimoto Shigeru of *Tōkyō Nichi Nichi* and Matsuzawa Itsuba of the Teikoku Tsūshinsha news agency. The injuries, followed several days later by the pommeling of *Tōkyō Asahi* reporter Haga Eizō by guards at Home Minister Hara Kei's residence, led not only to dramatic pictures of bandaged reporters in the papers,[29] but to the most concerted press campaign against the government in years. The papers screamed with headlines about the "barbaric" cabinet, "Hara the unqualified minister," and "Yamamoto the leader of naval corruption," and demanded, "Students! Get involved!" "Medical community! Get involved!"[30] Even the *Kokumin Shimbun*, the old government ally, climbed on the impeachment wagon with cries about the "travesty of justice" and the "indignation of the whole nation."[31] And beginning on February 18, a series of reporters rallies were held in Tokyo, Osaka, Nagoya, Fukushima, and Fukuoka to criticize Hara for sending his henchmen against Haga. The rally at Tokyo's Kokugikan on March 15 drew a reported 30,000 people, all demanding the resignation of a cabinet that "destroys honor and integrity, imprisons the truth, lacks all political merit, and kills the people's aspirations."[32]

It is worth noting that the Seiyūkai allies *Maiyū* and *Chūō* along with the feisty Shimada's former paper *Tōkyō Mainichi* remained quiet during the turbulence (and drew rioters' attacks as a result)—and that most of the Tokyo papers probably were motivated as much by commercialism and their ties to anti-Seiyūkai parties as by opposition to the entrenched cabinet system. Indeed, according to Haruhara Akihiko, only two of the papers, *Yorozu* and *Tōkyō Asahi*, "called sincerely and consistently for destruction of clique government in both of the 1913 and 1914 crises."[33] But once again actions overwhelmed intent. The papers' words were what the agitated citizens heard; the writers *spoke* about constitutionalism, tyranny, and the people's will—and that was enough to trigger the citizen movements, which in turn helped bring down another cabinet.

The press' experience in the 1918 riots was more reactive than proactive and even less unified. The riots started with an evening meeting of fishermen's wives and women stevedores in the Japan seacoast village of Uozu on July 22 to protest spiraling rice prices, and by September the country had been hit by more than five hundred violent protests involving at least a million (some say ten million) participants and resulting in the dispatch of 100,000 troops, nearly 25,000 arrests, 8,185 prosecutions, numerous deaths, and massive property damage.[34] The papers' role this time generally was less inflammatory than reportorial, although urban papers such as the *Nagoya Shimbun* and *Tōkyō Asahi* did advertise protest rallies,[35] but that fact did not make the papers' involvement any less controversial, particularly when Prime Minister Terauchi's government concluded that "bombastic and inflammatory" news accounts of provincial rioting were "spreading an evil influence everywhere."[36]

On August 14, Home Minister Mizuno Rentarō forbade news coverage of the riots and thus touched off one of the most intense press-government struggles in years. At a mass rally the next day, the Tokyo reporters called Mizuno's prohibition "a suppression of freedom of discussion and the most improper act we ever have observed."[37] The reporters then sent the trustees of the Shunshūkai to demand that the ministry "withdraw said order by 3:00 P.M. of the sixteenth," and when Mizuno responded by announcing that the papers would be allowed to print only the Home Ministry's daily summaries of the disturbances, a Press Defense Movement (*Genron Yōgo Undō*) sprang up, supported by reporters rallies all across the country. *Ōsaka Asahi* headlines on August 17 read: "Tyrannical oppression of the press," "Throw out the Terauchi cabinet," and "We the newspapermen of the Kansai region rise up."[38] The papers won a slight modification in the Home Ministry rules, allowing them to write their own accounts of any turbulence that occurred after the ministry's last report each day, but journalists remained in a white heat for the next month, determined that the Terauchi government had to be toppled.

The most blatant criticism came in *Ōsaka Asahi* on August 26, when the young reporter Onishi Toshio described the previous day's Kansai reporters rally in angry, even revolutionary tones. "The age that dazzled the people with majestic brilliance has long passed," he wrote; "who can respect the crown of a monkey? The people suffer in misery; hungry sparrows weep in empty storehouses." He wondered whether "our great Japan, once so full of flawless pride, is approaching the dreaded day of final judgment." And he described reporters dourly eating lunch at the rally, "thinking silently of the evil omen that the ancients used to mutter, 'a white rainbow pierced the sun.' "[39] This final allusion, to peasants contemplating revolution in premodern China, was intentionally inflammatory, and when *Asahi* hit the streets the next morning, the officials pounced with unprecedented vigor. They obviously had been looking for just such an opportunity; *Ōsaka Asahi* had been their chief nemesis for several years now, and a number of right-wing organizations already were calling for its suspension for "putting a curse on our *kokutai*" and "inspiring treason."[40] As a result, Mizuno's minions not only confiscated the August 26 issue but, in a move with enormous implications for the entire press, began judicial proceedings to shut down the paper altogether.

Asahi survived in the end by submitting to the officials' conditions, issuing a public apology, promising henceforth to be "impartial" and to show "respect for the imperial house" and "support for constitutional government,"[41] and announcing the resignations of president Murayama Ryōhei and managing editor Torii Sosen.[42] But the White Rainbow Incident *(hakkō jiken)*, as it came to be called, had a profound impact on the Taishō press, most of it negative. It highlighted, for one thing, the commercialism that motivated most journalists now, as a few progovernment papers attacked *Asahi* for "a lack of loyalty and patriotism," while the majority either ignored the episode or reported primarily on *Asahi*'s irresponsibility. Not a single Japanese paper came to its colleague's defense or brought up the question of free speech.[43] *Ōsaka Asahi* was a daunting commercial rival, and that apparently was more important than free speech and "the people's right to know."

The episode also appeared to intimidate the other papers. The government had prosecuted the press repeatedly throughout this

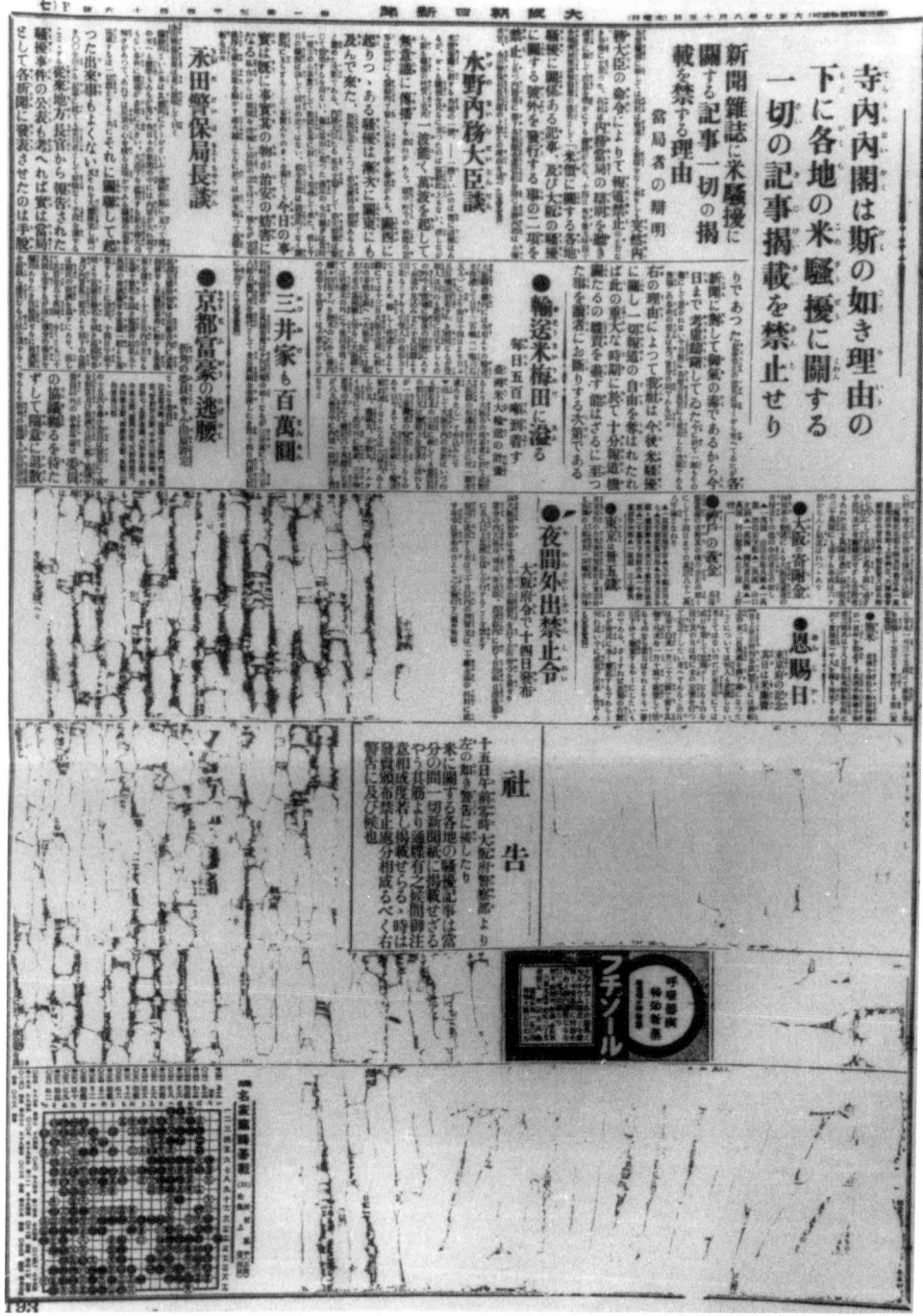

Page seven of *Ōsaka Asahi*, August 15, 1918. The box in the center reprints that morning's official ban on publishing news about the rice riots then under way across Japan. Gouged out columns were retained to underscore the censor's harshness. (Courtesy Asahi Shimbunsha)

Typical page of *Ōsaka Asahi* (September 4, 1923), with photos of the Great
Kantō Earthquake. (Courtesy Asahi Shimbunsha)

era, confiscating more than 550 issues every year between 1915 and 1919, issuing more than a few fines and jail terms.[44] But it had not been able to silence the writers, who had continued to flail away at each administration, sometimes even going to press with gouged-out blank spaces on page one to call attention to the censors' work.[45] As late as August 22, *Yorozu* had published a pugnacious piece asserting that "the final upshot of the rice disturbances is the growth of the popular conviction that the power of the masses can do almost everything" and suggesting that "the people may have come to realize that the power of the masses can destroy the wide gulf separating rich and poor . . . and demolish all that retards the healthy growth and development of constitutionalism."[46]

But belligerent prose of that sort subsided sharply after the White Rainbow scare. The threat to shut down one of the country's two largest papers was sobering, especially to editors whose populism was rooted in the need for profits. They would continue to criticize the government, but not with the same force. Never again would they lead riotous *kokumin* into the streets or make even veiled suggestions of overturning the system. Uchikawa Yoshimi, dean of Japan's press historians, speaks of the rice riots as "the last of the Meiji-style incidents," the beginning of a time when "the newspaper enterprise became synonymous with the capitalist enterprise."[47] The Great Kantō Earthquake would demolish all but three of the major Tokyo newspaper offices in 1923, forever changing the institutional shape of the Japanese press.[48] But the spiritual flattening had come five years earlier, when a white rainbow pierced the profit-bent editors' hearts.

IN RETROSPECT

Middle schoolers in the late Meiji years found this idyllic bit of verse in their authorized language textbook:

Newspapers

City affairs, country affairs,
Affairs in far away lands,
We understand them at a glance:
Newspaper, ah, cherished newspaper!

Making me aware
That fires are many, as are thieves,

That fearful illnesses now are spreading:
Newspaper, ah, kind newspaper!

Conveying good deeds, otherwise unknown,
As well as hidden evils,
Just like a mirror:
Newspaper, ah, bright newspaper![49]

The sentiments were sanitized, the prose more palatable than the targets of Shimada's or Onishi's invective might have thought accurate. The poem suggested nonetheless much of what the Meiji papers actually had become: a conveyor of information from regions both foreign and familiar, a packager of reality-at-a-glance, an educational tool, a publicist for the good and the interesting, a spotlight on the murky backrooms of corruption. To say that this institution, non-existent half a century earlier, had helped to change the world of the average city dweller is to understate the case many times. To explain just how it stimulated change is more difficult. But a few observations about several press characteristics that persisted, and several that underwent a transformation, may prove useful in concluding this analysis.

Let us begin with the press' self-identity, the way Japan's leading journalists perceived their own profession. On one point—the journalists' sense of the press as a defender of the public interest—there never was much wavering. The earliest editors took up the brush as a cudgel, to defend the nation, as they saw it, against the usurping Meiji "rebels." By early Meiji, they were talking about themselves as society's "uncrowned kings," not so much because they sought personal power as because they saw newspapers as tools for shaping political policy. "Newspapers are teachers," wrote *Chōya*'s Narushima Ryūhoku, "the new kings of the imperial court and the friends of all people. They make trouble for the former samurai *(shizoku)* and make light of the nobility *(kazoku).*"[50] And the press' leaders kept on saying such things, with obvious conviction, to the end of the era. The old Confucian types often lamented the onset of vulgarity and commercialization, but no one, not even the most commercial of editors, stopped insisting that journalists must guard the public trust. That is what Kuroiwa had in mind when he told his readers in 1901 that "a newspaper has the power to save the people from confusion, to point out clearly the difference between good and evil in society, between right and wrong ... purity and corruption,"[51] and it is what Tokutomi meant when he called for journalists to be "the script writers of real politics."[52] Whether demanding a popular assembly in 1874, agitating for war in 1903, or promoting rallies to block city ownership of streetcars in 1911, the editors consistently wrapped themselves in the mantle of defenders of the public interest against self-interested politicians and bureaucrats.

On several other points, however, the press' view of itself changed noticeably across the years. A monumental evolution occurred, for example, in the journalists' view of what a newspaper's fundamental purpose should be. There was no question in the minds of the first editors; newspapers were political instruments, no more, no less. That was why intellectual debates over assemblies and constitutions provided most of the press' energy in its early years; it was why *Nisshin Shinjishi* announced in its first issue that it intended to "bring knowledge to the people, assist in spreading enlightenment, and work in everything for the profit of the nation";[53] it was why Fukuchi Gen'ichirō told colleagues that an ambitious public servant who could not become prime minister should become a journalist. It also was why the early editors would have been aghast to hear Motoyama proclaim at the end of this era that "a newspaper is a commercial product"—and why Tokutomi grimaced when noting that journalism had become the domain of the "businessman who fingers the abacus." Such a shift was inevitable, in a modernizing, increasingly literate world that demanded both larger circulations and greater amounts of capital. But it meant that the daily picture of the world that the editors painted would change dramatically over the Meiji decades, from that of a government-dominated society ruled by nuanced, heated debates about political ideas to a hurly-burly world of murders, citizen protest, and international conflict, with political debate thrown in. The Confucian order, in other words, would give way by mid-Meiji to the commercialized world of mass journalism.

Closely related was a shift in the material editors deemed appropriate for newspapers. In the early years, the editorial was front and center in every prestigious paper; editors, educated in the public service rhetoric of Tokugawa Confucianism, saw themselves as "teachers of society," responsible for debating with the elite and enlightening their inferiors. That meant placing government decrees and editorials on page one, relegating news to the miscellany section inside, and publishing only "proper" news that would encourage civilization. That approach was challenged in the 1880s by new-style editors such as Fukuzawa, who once had described a newspaper as simply "a company that investigates new things, records them, and proclaims them to the world."[54] And it was blown to bits in the 1890s by populist editors such as Kuroiwa and Akiyama Teisuke, and by the wars that sandwiched the new century's arrival, until by the Taishō era the *Mainichi* president would be telling his staff, "The newspaper is a vessel for reporting facts, not a teacher of society or a leadership organ."[55] Reporters still used the paper as a political lever sometimes, but the mainstream dailies had become thoroughgoing *news*papers by the end of Meiji, sheets dominated by *sanmen kiji* at the front, hard news and advertisements throughout, and editorials somewhere inside.

A second area that revealed both changes and continuities was the press' relationship to the authorities. Here, the most obvious continuity was unending conflict. On the one side stood the government, which, in Midoro Masaichi's slight exaggeration, "had only one policy for keeping the political situation peaceful: suppression of discussion"—and thus issued no fewer than eighty-three different press decrees and regulations in the first sixteen Meiji years.[56] "The essence of the Meiji state's peace and order system," agrees Okudaira Yasuhiro, was "to suppress antisystem activity *(hantaisei katsudō)* by administrative or police measures."[57] On the other side stood the journalists, government critics who, in the popular mind, were true to their profession only when they were "registering dissent, decrying abuse, and awakening the people to alternative, and generally more liberal, policies and programs for modernization" than those of the officials.[58] The fight between the two sides was unending. Fukuchi launched it by going to jail for his sharp attacks on the new Meiji government at *Kōko Shimbun;* Suehiro Tetchō followed him a few years later with biting *Chōya* articles about "little men" who "toadied to authorities";[59] *Nihon* lost 131 days of publication during the Sino-Japanese War period because of its bitter attacks on what it considered wishy-washy national leadership, and almost all of the leading papers were confiscated repeatedly in the late-Meiji, early-Taishō years for demanding the impeachment of a cabinet or printing something salacious. When Fukuzawa died, Fukuchi wrote rather plaintively: "In 1874, when I was editing *Tōkyō Nichi Nichi,* he said to me, "You have taken up the newspaper business; that is wonderful. Be careful though not to get tied too much to the government. If you become too closely tied, they will mislead you." In the end, they did. . . . Ah, you were a good friend, a trustworthy friend. You did not let me down; I let you down."[60] He was not alone in making that mistake, but he was in the minority, at least until mid-Meiji. No matter the day or the issue, the independent, antigovernment papers were the most popular.

The reverse side of the press-government conflict (and our second point of continuity) was that the editors always were part of the establishment, which meant that the reasons for their antigovernment pose were not always as clear-cut as they appeared. The establishment orientation showed up everywhere: in *Chūgai Shimbun*'s declaration just after the Meiji Restoration that "all the people must follow the government," even as editor Yanagawa Shunsan was railing against the men who were leading it;[61] in editors' constant references to themselves as "teachers" and "managers of the people"; in the large numbers of journalists elected to each Diet; in Tokutomi's participation in the Katsura government and Ikebe Kichitarō's secret 1903 visits with Itō Hirobumi and Yamagata Aritomo to urge war with Russia. Obviously, identification with the elite did not mean that editors would refrain from fighting with the authorities. What it did mean was that editors always would remain close to their own favorite officials, factions, and business leaders; so their positions rarely would range far from the broad center. That was why neither the socialists nor free speech per se ever won much support. The early Meiji writers were Japanese first, Confucian second—and then journalists. By the turn of the century, the categories had changed but not the order; now it was Japanese-businessmen-journalists.

One aspect of the press-government relationship that did change significantly was the nature of the laws under which the press had to operate. Lawrence Beer observes that the harsh, 1930s-style control of "the recesses of the mind . . . did not come about suddenly or in a legally simple manner."[62] And the press' own experience bears him out. The first full-fledged newspaper law was issued in 1875, and for several years after that the primary means of punishment lay in fines and jail terms, which meant that at least 144 journalists went to jail between 1875 and 1877.[63] In 1876, the Council of State added the proviso granting Home Ministers the administrative right to suspend *(hakkō teishi)* or ban *(hakkō kinshi)* any paper that "violated public order" or injured public morals. Then, in 1883, a new press law attempted to squeeze out small, radical papers by requiring that all owners pay a substantial "security deposit" when launching a paper. There was a positive shift in 1891 and 1892, when the Diet refused to allow prepublication censorship except in times of emergency, followed by a major change in 1897 that replaced the government's right to suspend and ban papers administratively with the more limited, though sometimes more expensive, right to prohibit sales and distribution on a given day. And in 1909 the security deposit amount was doubled. Thus, while the right of officials to control speech never was questioned, the acceptable means for doing so underwent a distinct evolution. And the overall impact was a slight liberalization in the last decade and a half of Meiji, at least for the mainstream papers for whom the increased security deposit was no problem.

Closely related to the evolving laws was a significant change, particularly in late Meiji, in the reasons for which journalists were punished. In the first half of the era, punishments typically were political: the jailings of Ueki Emori and Minoura Katsundo for demanding popular rights, a ten-day suspension of *Chōya* in 1878 for publishing the apologia of Ōkubo Toshimichi's assassins, removal from the Tokyo area in 1887 of treaty revision advocates Ozaki Yukio and Nakae Chōmin, the issuance of more than two hundred *hakkō teishi* orders to papers that denounced Japan's "weak" diplomacy in May 1895. By the last Meiji years, however, the pattern had changed. Now that it was no longer possible to suspend papers without recourse to the courts, political punishments had become unusual for any but the socialist papers. In their place had come crackdowns on anything perceived to undermine "public morals." As we saw in the last chapter, these penalties tended generally to be less costly, sometimes involving the confiscation of a day's issues but more often requiring only the payment of a fine, and usually a fairly light one at that. The result was a relatively freer press in the last Meiji decade, a press still subject to harsh penalties in times of emergency like the 1905 Hibiya riots but otherwise constricted as much by its own nationalist, establishment views as by the authoritarian officials.

The third characteristic of the press that demands analysis is the tension in the writers' dual roles as journalists and as Japanese. Hanazono Kanesada began his little 1926 study of pioneer journalists with the observation that "the two salient features of the Japanese press are that it has been struggling for the extension of the people's rights and has always been nationalistic."[64] There is little doubt that he is right, especially about the nationalism. From the day that Yanagawa Shunsan began compiling his *Rich Thicket of News (Shimbun Kaisō)* at the Kaiseijo in 1865, one is hard-pressed to find a single prominent journalist who did not profess to write at least in part out of a deep desire to serve Japan. The writers made a sharp distinction between their beloved nation and its emperor, on the one hand, and the all-too-human politicians and officials, on the other. They also expressed their patriotism in many different ways. But they always expressed it. Even the radically democratic *Hyōron Shimbun* couched its 1876 attacks on the system in terms of what "the emperor would accept."[65] Every paper in the country covered the promulgation of the Meiji Constitution with an unrestrained pride that would have embarrassed journalists in more cynical regions and eras. The most vicious struggles between journalists and the cabinet in the era's last two decades sprang from editors' and writers' assessments that the country's diplomats and oligarchs were weak on backbone and patriotism. The antigovernment demonstrators invariably joined reporters in *banzai*s to the emperor just before they left to smash police boxes. Even the novelist-journalist Futabatei Shimei would comment, "My life is torn between two opposite poles: my innate passion for imperialistic patriotism and my socialist ideals. I alternate constantly between the two."[66]

The impact of this deep-seated patriotism on the press' behavior was complex. There is no question that it undergirded the early journalists' efforts to help their leaders create a nation, "to make the times intelligible even to children," as one put it.[67] It also fueled their debates about the locus of sovereignty, about constitutions, about how the treaties could (and should) be reformed, and it made both the policies and the quality of intellectual life better as a result. And the journalists' deep sense of loyalty touched a chord in the provinces, where a young Tokutomi in Kumamoto would be inspired by Fukuchi's prose to serve his nation, or a school teacher in Gifu would decide to assault the "disloyal" Itagaki Taisuke after reading the Tokyo papers. As the latter incident suggests, however, the nationalism also had a darker side, leading to an uncritical expansionism that led journalists to accept draconian censorship policies during the Russo-Japanese War and prodded them to exult in the war's riotous aftermath. Moreover, it made it easy to ignore universal journalistic principles such as freedom of speech, the people's "right to know," and the need for open trials when officials trampled on those ideals in the name of the *kokutai.* When the populist *Yorozu* declared that Kōtoku's clearly unconstitutional secret trial proceedings contained "nothing . . . worthy of criticism,"[68] the time had come to ask whether the paper's love of the "nation" had blinded it to the need for free discussion.

As all of this suggests, there was one way in which patriotic writing changed significantly across the Meiji years; a distinct evolution took place in the journalists' modes of expressing their nationalism. Essays about love for the country in the early years tended to be less direct. One never could have doubted the commitment of men such as Kurimoto Joun and Yano Fumio to their country. They talked ceaselessly about what would make Japan strong, how it could stand up to the West, the meaning of citizenship, the inviolability of the imperial institution; some grounded their arguments in Japan's special *kokutai*.[69] But patriotism was assumed; it did not need to be exhibited. The struggle over treaty revision and Japan's expanding struggles on the continent led to a change in the rhetoric during the latter 1880s, however, and with the arrival of assertively nationalist papers such as *Nihon* at decade's end, followed by war with China five years later, the tone often turned strident. No longer were mainstream journalists willing to accept as loyal someone who advocated diplomatic moderation or internationalism. If an Uchimura, a Kōtoku, or (for a time) a Kuroiwa were not aggressively expansionist, he was a coward or an opportunist. A cabinet that compromised with the defeated Russians was not only mistaken but traitorous; even torching a fellow editor's offices was acceptable in the name of patriotism. The change in style may have been understandable, given Japan's experiences with the imperialistic world. But it compromised the journalists' capacity for making independent judgments. It also made the writers hypersensitive to unjust treatments from abroad, even as it deadened them to abuses their own fellow citizens inflicted on the Taiwanese and the Koreans. And it clearly restricted the range of acceptable public discourse in Japan at the very time when the writers themselves were demanding a greater voice for the people.[70]

The fourth area that must be reviewed is the press' relationship with the "people," or *minshū*, who have played such a central role in this study. The main point of continuity here was the unending interaction between journalists and the commoners. In every decade, in so many ways, writers indicated their eagerness to meet the needs of the broad populace. The first papers were created in the 1870s to "foster people's knowledge" or because "people need to know the affairs of the world."[71] *Minken* journalists like Nakae, who gave the press so much of its vitality in the early 1880s, were said "never for a moment" to have "doubted that the people were sovereign."[72] By the 1890s Kuroiwa was insisting on low prices and simple prose "to make it convenient for average people to understand the times well—at a glance."[73] And by the Taishō years Baba Tsunego's insistence that a true reporter "recognizes the public as master *(kōshū o shūjin to mitomeru)"* had become a professional cliche.[74] What was more, the phenomenon of commoners responding strongly to the press was equally consistent: 20,000 of them buying up *Tōkyō Nichi Nichi*'s special explanation of the new calendar in 1872, Okayama villagers passing the Tokyo papers from household to household when Inukai Tsuyoshi was a lad, rickshaw pullers hurling stones at the *Kokumin* offices in 1905 because of its support for the Katsura government, Kunikida Doppo talking to strangers on a Tokyo sidewalk about the latest "extra" news from the Manchurian battlefront. Clearly, nothing was closer to the core of Meiji journalism than the symbiotic, ever more intimate relations between journalists and their fellow citizens.

That said, the nature of Meiji journalism is even more fully revealed in the constant evolution that this press-people relationship underwent. Both the press and its commoner readers changed radically across the Meiji decades; the readers grew more educated, more numerous, and more sophisticated politically, while the press became less elitist, more news-oriented, and more influential politically. Looking at these changes from the perspective of the press, two shifts stand out with special clarity, one in the way the journalists viewed the commoners, the other in the impact journalism had on the people's lives.

The transformation in the journalists' assessment of the "people" showed up on one level in an evolution in the very language they used in talking about commoners. In the early Meiji years, the general populace most often was described simply as "people" *(hito, min,* or *jinmin)*, while direct references to those not in the former samurai or noble strata typically employed words with a dismissive quality, such as *heimin* (commoner) or *yōdō fujo* (small children and women).[75] By the 1890s, commoner-oriented editors talked increasingly about the working classes, with relatively neutral labels on the order of Kuroiwa's *futsū ippan no minjin* (common, ordinary people), Tokutomi's *tokai no hito* (city folk), and Akiyama's *ippan kōshū* (general public), or with concrete class designations such as "laborers" *(rōdōsha)* and "poor" *(saimin)*.[76] And from the onset of the new century, the terms of choice became *kokumin* or *shimin* (both normally translated "citizen"), with frequent references to the "public community" *(shakai kōkyō)* or just "the public" *(kōshū)*.[77] Distinctions of this sort are subjective, since individual writers' usage varied considerably in every decade. But my own reading suggests a shift in dominant vocabulary across the Meiji years, from relatively pejorative words that identified the less-educated readers as an undifferentiated mass to respectful terms designating them as fellow actors on the public stage.

That shifting view of the public shows up even more clearly in the content of the articles that typified each period. No one saw it as unusual in the early years when *Yūbin Hōchi* called the *heimin* "powerless fools who live in the realm of servitude" or when *Tōkyō Nichi Nichi* condescendingly urged people to wear clothes in public so foreigners would not laugh.[78] But Kuga Katsunan's haughty dismissal of "people who cannot read without *kana*"[79] had become anachronistic by mid-Meiji. More typical now was *Niroku Shinpō's* sponsorship of labor rallies to attract them, journalist-activist Tanaka Shōzō's declaration that "to kill the people is to kill the nation,"[80] *Hōchi's* initiation of family pages, Motoyama's declaration that "newspapers must earn society's sympathy and the readers' resonance,"[81] and the many efforts to lead the urban working classes into the streets after the Russo-Japanese War. As a *Yomiuri* writer said in 1901, "This is a world in which even rickshaw pullers take newspapers."[82] Even an old elitist such as Tokutomi no longer could fail to do the commoners homage by the end of the era.

The other major evolution in the press-people relationship lay in the dramatic impact journalism had on Japan's *minshū*. This impact can be traced in the shifting content of articles, as reader tastes moved from the political to the technological, literary, and entertaining. It can be seen too in expanding readerships, in *Hōchi's* efforts to help readers get jobs, in women readers who decided that they would like to become reporters themselves, in late-Meiji readers' passion for stories of success and personal achievement. Above all, it can be seen in the changing political messages the papers directed at readers over these years. The era's first people-oriented campaign was the debate over a popular assembly in 1874, in which the commoners were topics of discussion but not objects of persuasion. *Nichi Nichi* argued that the *heimin* should be included in an assembly; *Yūbin Hōchi* and *Chōya* said they should not, and none of them showed an iota of interest in what the commoners themselves thought. The sense of public had expanded somewhat by the 1880s, when *minken* journalists took up popular rights and treaty revision, but even they thought little of "people" outside the circle of property owners and rural leadership classes.

The trigger for change, in the late 1880s and early 1890s, was squeezed first by the urban working classes themselves rather than by the journalists. As more and more people poured out of the schools and into the cities, they became, in the parlance of the papers' increasingly respectable business departments, "circulation targets." And as a result, the newspapers' political activities from the fourth Meiji decade onward were devised, without exception, with an eye on the *minshū*. For editors like Shimada and Akiyama, these masses were the victims of "social problems" that genuinely needed solving; for *Hōchi*'s Miki Zenpachi and *Jiji*'s Fukuzawa Sutejirō, they were potential subscribers; and for everyone they represented a political and economic force too big to be ignored. As a result, by the last years of Meiji, nearly every major paper in the country was talking about the "constitutional" necessity of acting in accordance with the "people's will" and, more than that, the papers were enlisting the working *kokumin* in loud, sometimes riotous, street rallies to demand that officials follow the popular will. Modernization, market forces, and ideology, in other words, had brought the people and the press together. As that autocratic onetime journalist Hara Kei wrote in his diary just two years and a day before Meiji fell into his final coma: "Not only in elections but in other matters as well . . . those who stir up the masses will always win."[83]

Much is made, in the day of postmodernism, of narratives and story lines; so it would be inappropriate to conclude without noting that it was the press that provided the Meiji masses with their daily story, the press more than any other institution that shaped their understanding of what public life was all about. The writers and editors did not, however, create their story line in a vacuum. Their perceptions of reality were shaped by a host of influences: early on by Confucianism and isolationism, later on by challenges and opportunities from the imperialist West, by the political and economic options devised by their own rulers, by stories and values learned at home in Kumamoto, in Tosa, in Niigata—and, as time passed, by the interests and demands of their own readers, the once despised *minshū*, now *kokumin*. It would be safe to say that the journalists' story (at least its political chapters) was dominated by three themes as the Meiji era drew to an end: the inviolability of Japan, the venality of officials, and the people's right to responsive government. It also would be safe to say that this story line was shaped almost as fully by what the *kokumin* readers wanted to hear as it was by the journalists' own worldviews. This, after all, was the era of the customer. The press may have created a public, but it was that public, by 1912, that gave the press its sense of direction.

A Chronology of Leading Tokyo and Osaka Papers

Akebono
Founded as *Shimbun Zasshi*, 1871
Became *Akebono*, January 1875
Became *Tōkyō Akebono Shimbun*, June 1875
Became *Tōyō Shinpō*, 1882
Died December 1883

Asahi Shimbun. See *Ōsaka Asahi Shimbun; Tōkyō Asahi Shimbun*

Chōya Shimbun (Narushima Ryūhoku)
Founded as *Kōbun Tsūshi*, 1872
Became *Chōya Shimbun*, 1874
Died November 1893

Chūgai Shōgyo Shinpō
Founded as *Chūgai Bukka Shinpō*, 1877
Became *Chūgai Shōgyō Shinpō*, 1889
Became *Nihon Sangyō Keizai Shimbun*, 1942
Became *Nihon Keizai Shimbun*, 1946

Chūō Shimbun
Founded as *Eiri Chōya Shimbun*, 1882
Became *Edo Shimbun*, 1889
Became *Tōkyō Chū Shimbun*, 1890
Became *Chūō Shimbun*, 1891
Became *Nihon Sangyō Hōkoku Shimbun*, 1941

Denpō Shimbun
Founded 1903
Became *Mainichi Denpō* (under *Ōsaka Mainichi*), 1906
Merged into *Tōkyō Nichi Nichi Shimbun*, 1911

Eiri Chōya Shimbun. See *Chūō Shimbun*

Hōchi Shimbun. See *Yūbin Hōchi Shimbun*

Heimin Shimbun (Kōtoku Shūsui)
Founded November 1903
Banned January 1905
Revived as daily, January 15, 1907
Folded under pressure April 14, 1907

Jiji Shinpō (Fukuzawa Yukichi)
Founded, 1882
Published *Ōsaka Jiji Shinpō,* 1905–1942
Absorbed by *Tōkyō Nichi Nichi,* 1936
Revived 1946
Absorbed by *Nihon Keizai Shimbun,* 1955

Jiyū no Tomoshibi. See *Tōkyō Asahi Shimbun*

Kokumin Shimbun (Tokutomi Sohō)
Founded February 1890
Merged with *Miyako Shimbun* to become *Tōkyō Shimbun,* 1942

Konnichi Shimbun. See *Miyako Shimbun*

Mainichi Shimbun (for today's *Mainichi,* see *Ōsaka Mainichi*)
Founded as *Yokohama Mainichi Shimbun,* December 1871
Became *Tōkyō-Yokohama Mainichi Shimbun,* 1879
Became *Mainichi Shimbun,* 1886
Became *Tōkyō Mainichi Shimbun,* 1906
Under control of *Hōchi Shimbun,* 1909
Died 1940

Maiyū Shimbun
Founded March 1898
Joined *Chiyoda Nippō* as *Chiyoda Maiyū,* 1899
Became *Maiyū Shimbun* again, 1901
Became *Tōkyō Maiyū Shimbun,* 1911, with ties to *Tōkyō Mainichi*
Absorbed *Yorozu Chōhō,* 1940
Died 1941

Miyako Shimbun
Founded as *Konnichi Shimbun*, 1884
Became *Miyako*, 1888
Merged with *Kokumin Shimbun* to become *Tōkyō Shimbun*, 1942

Nihon (Kuga Katsunan)
Founded as *Tōkyō Shōgyō Denpō*, 1886
Became *Tōkyō Denpō*, 1888
Became *Nihon*, February 1889
Died 1914

Niroku Shinpō (Akiyama Teisuke)
Founded 1893
Folded 1895
Revived 1900
Became *Tōkyō Niroku Shimbun*, 1904, after government shutdown
Became *Niroku Shinpō*, 1909
Banned and became *Sekai Shimbun*, 1914
Revived as *Niroku Shinpō*, 1918
Died 1940

Nisshin Shinjishi (J. R. Black)
Founded 1872
Banned 1875

Ōsaka Asahi Shimbun (Murayama Ryōhei, Ueno Riichi)
Founded as *Asahi Shimbun*, 1879
Created *Tōkyō Asahi Shimbun* from *Mezamashi Shimbun*, 1888
Became *Ōsaka Asahi Shimbun*, 1889
Merged with *Tōkyō Asahi Shimbun* as *Asahi Shimbun*, 1940

Ōsaka Jiji Shinpō. See *Jiji Shinpō*

Ōsaka Mainichi Shimbun
Began as *Ōsaka Nippō*, 1876
Became *Nihon Rikken Seitō Shimbun*, 1882
Became *Ōsaka Nippō* again, 1885
Became *Ōsaka Mainichi Shimbun*, 1888
Purchased *Denpō Shimbun*, 1906; *Tōkyō Nichi Nichi*, 1911
Merged with *Tōkyō Nichi Nichi* to become *Mainichi Shimbun*, 1943

Ōsaka Nippō. See *Ōsaka Mainichi Shimbun*

Shimbun Zasshi. See *Akebono*

Tōkyō Asahi Shimbun
Began as *Jiyū no Tomoshibi,* 1884
Became *Tomoshibi Shimbun,* 1886
Became *Mezamashi Shimbun,* 1887
Purchased by *Ōsaka Asahi* and became *Tōkyō Asahi Shimbun,* 1888
Merged with *Ōsaka Asahi* as *Asahi Shimbun,* 1940

Tōkyō Nichi Nichi Shimbun (Fukuchi Gen'ichirō)
Founded 1872
Purchased by *Ōsaka Mainichi* and merged with *Denpō Shimbun,*
    1911
Merged with *Ōsaka Mainichi* as *Mainichi Shimbun* in 1943

Tōkyō Shōgyō Denpō. See *Nihon*

Tōkyō-Yokohama Mainichi Shimbun. See *Mainichi Shimbun*

Tōyō Jiyū Shimbun (Saionji Kinmochi)
Founded March 1, 1881
Shut down April 30, 1881

Yamato Shimbun
Founded as *Keisatsu Shinpō,* 1884
Became *Yamato Shimbun,* 1886
Died 1944

Yomiuri Shimbun
Founded 1874
Merged with *Hōchi Shimbun* as *Yomiuri Hōchi Shimbun,* 1942
Resumed publishing as *Yomiuri Shimbun,* 1946

Yorozu Chōhō (Kuroiwa Shūroku)
Founded 1892
Merged into *Maiyū Shimbun,* 1940

Yūbin Hōchi Shimbun
Founded 1872
Became *Hōchi Shimbun*, 1894
Merged with *Yomiuri Shimbun* as *Yomiuri Hōchi Shimbun*, 1942
Resumed publishing as *Hōchi Shimbun*, 1946

Yokohama Mainichi Shimbun. See *Mainichi Shimbun*

Circulation of Major Papers, 1875–1915

	1875	1880	1885	1890	1895
Akebono	2,717	7,772	died-83		
Chōya	4,051	9,159	5,121	16,524	died-93
Chūgai Shōgyō			bg-89	12,269	49,031
Chūō				bg-91	80,802
Jiji Shinpō		bg-82	7,402	12,744	18,409
Kokumin			bg-90	8,980	25,949
Mainichi	648	3,494	3,076	13,367	15,333
Miyako			bg-88	14,909	34,640
Nihon			bg-89	15,342	21,124
Ōsaka Asahi	bg-79	9,646	31,935	49,539	102,085
Ōsaka Mainichi			bg-88	13,581	68,475
Tōkyō Asahi			bg-88	23,547	49,512
Tōkyō Nichi Nichi	9,780	8,094	4,284	12,234	18,065
Yamato			bg-86	20,837	28,638
Yomiuri	14,509	20,822	15,453	16,385	15,749
Yorozu Chōhō				bg-92	68,554
Yūbin Hōchi	7,144	8,080	5,717	20,568	21,125

Source: Data compiled from Ukai Shin'ichi, *Chōya Shimbun no ken-kyū,* pp. 22, 26–28; Yamato Taketoshi, *Kindai Nihon no shimbun dokusha sō,* pp. 404–05, 408, 411–412; Ariyama Teruo, *Tokutomi Sohō to Kokumin Shimbun,* pp. 54–55; Ariyama, *Kindai Nihon jiyānarizumu no kōzō,* p. 14; Ōsaka Mainichi Shimbunsha, ed., *Mainichi Shimbun nanajū nen,* p. 612; Yamamoto Fumio, *Nihon shimbun hattatsu shi,* pp. 290–291.

	1899	**1903**	**1907**	**1911**	**1915**
Chūgai Shōgyō	nfa	11,800	18,500	20,000	30,000
Chūō	56,169	41,000	35,000	32,500	100,000
Jiji Shinpō	86,279	41,500	41,000	60,000	70,000
Kokumin	30,176	18,000	34,000	130,000	190,000
Mainichi	24,291	nfa	24,000	30,000	nfa
Miyako	31,908	45,000	nfa	60,000	30,000
Nihon	11,521	10,000	27,000	6,000	died-14
Niroku Shinpō	not pub 1895–1900	142,340	60,000	25,000	50,000
Ōsaka Asahi	113,249	119,816	140,644	182,941	250,326
Ōsaka Mainichi	nfa	92,355	289,699	269,260	321,454
Tōkyō Asahi	47,894	75,388	82,073	120,422	158,209
Tōkyō Nichi Nichi	16,777	11,700	24,000	70,000	120,000
Yamato	nfa	nfa	18,000	100,000	100,000
Yomiuri	14,146	21,500	32,000	25,000	70,000
Yorozu Chōhō	95,876	87,000	87,000	90,000	100,000
(Yūbin) Hōchi	31,000	83,395	175,000	150,000	240,000

Note: Nfa = no figures available; bg = began (indicates year in which paper took that particular name). With the exception of *Yūbin Hōchi* (which became *Hōchi Shimbun* in 1894) and *Mainichi* (which began as Yokohama Mainichi, then switched to *Tōkyō-Yokohama Mainichi*), figures are given only after papers took on the name by which they generally are known to history. Figures should be considered rough approximations since companies tended to inflate figures for advertising purposes, especially in later Meiji years; in early Meiji, when yearly totals alone often were reported, I generally have divided by 300, the average number of issues per year, for a daily approximation.

Selected Subscription Rates (sen per month)

	1874	1881	1890	1899	1904
Akebono		50			
Chōya	50	60			
Jiji			50	50	50
Kokumin			30	35	35
Mainichi		60	25	35	35
Miyako			25	35	
Nihon			30	40	40
Tōkyō Asahi			25	33	37
Tōkyō Nichi Nichi		85	30	40	40
Yomiuri		33	35	35	35
Yorozu Chōhō				24	27
Yūbin Hōchi		83	30	35	35

Source: Compiled from Yamamoto Taketoshi, *Shimbun kisha no tanjō,* pp. 118, 189; Yamamoto, *Kindai Nihon no shimbun dokusha sō;* Ukai Shin'ichi, *Chōya Shimbun no kenkyū,* p. 17; Ariyama Teruo, *Tokutomi Sohō to Kokumin Shimbun,* p. 41; Asahi Shimbunsha, ed., *Asahi Shimbunsha shi; Meiji hen,* p. 487; personal examination.

Note: These were the publicly quoted subscription prices; prices actually charged at sales shops sometimes varied. The *Mainichi* here refers to the *Mainichi* descended from *Yokohama Mainichi,* not to *Ōsaka Mainichi; Yūbin Hōchi* changed its name to *Hōchi Shimbun* in 1894.

Number of Registered Newspapers and Magazines, 1897–1911

	With Security Deposit	Without Deposit	Total
1897			
Tokyo			201
Osaka			56
National			745
1898			
Tokyo			205
Osaka			68
National			829
1899			
Tokyo	149	97	246
Osaka	36	48	84
National	489	489	978
1900			
Tokyo	173	82	255
Osaka	36	50	86
National	535	409	944
1901			
Tokyo	191	116	307
Osaka	42	60	102
National	658	523	1,181
1902			
Tokyo	197	130	327
Osaka	55	66	121
National	744	584	1,328
1903			
Tokyo	207	142	349
Osaka	56	79	135
National	785	714	1,499

	With Security Deposit	Without Deposit	Total
1904			
Tokyo	221	146	367
Osaka	66	93	159
National	817	773	1,590
1905			
Tokyo	259	180	439
Osaka	61	95	156
National	906	869	1,775
1906			
Tokyo	271	193	464
Osaka	88	113	201
National	995	993	1,988
1907			
Tokyo	318	238	556
Osaka	107	110	217
National	1,185	1,115	2,300
1908			
Tokyo	385	329	714
Osaka	109	96	205
National	1,276	1,248	2,524
1909			
Tokyo	443	409	852
Osaka	110	114	224
National	1,379	1,389	2,768
1910			
Tokyo	342	249	591
Osaka	111	63	174
National	1,172	621	1,793
1911			
Tokyo	388	303	691
Osaka	120	69	189
National	1,326	751	2,077

Source: From Uchikawa Yoshimi, *Masu media hō seisaku shi kenkyū*, p. 82. Figures are from *Nihon teikoku tōkei nenkan*, at the end of each year.

Note: No distinction was made between papers with and without security deposits until 1899. Those without deposits were smaller scholarly or special interest journals unlikely to carry controversial material.

Newspapers and the Law

	Suspend	Ban	Distrib.	Fine	Jail
1876		5			86
1877		5			47
1878	5	1		114	15
1879	4	2		199	11
1880	16	2		267	13
1881	58	0		182	15
1882	70	12			
1883	52	4			
1884	38	0			
1885	24	0			
1886	17	0			
1887	30	0			
1888	11	2			
1889	75	0			
1890	19	0			
1891	61	0			
1892	87	0			
1893	87	0			
1894	140	0			
1895	238	0			
1896	25			79	2
1897	0			50	2
1898	0		25	65	1

	Suspend	Ban	Distrib.	Fine	Jail
1899	0		27	90	1
1900	6		25	97	2
1901	0		16	206	9
1902	0		6	155	8
1903	1		10	75	3
1904	1	1	7	645*	10*
1905	2 (+39)**	2	6	449*	3*
1906	2		4	142*	5*
1907	2		8		19*
1908	7	1	46		59*
1909	6		29		6*
1910	11		58		18*
1911	5		63		28*

Source: Jail and fine, 1878–1881, Nishida Taketoshi, *Meiji jidai no shimbun to zasshi*, pp. 92, 95 (in addition to the figures here, Nishida lists sixty-six cases of joint jailing and fines in 1878–1881); suspension, 1878–1880, ban, 1876–1879, Okano Takeo, *Meiji genron shi*, pp. 231–232; ban, 1880, Midoro Masaichi, *Meiji Taishō shi: genron hen*, pp. 86–87; suspension and ban, 1881–1895, Ukai Shin'ichi, *Chōya Shimbun no kenkyū*, p. 37; suspension, 1896–1911, Uchikawa Yoshimi, *Masu medeia hō seisaku shi*, p. 34; jail and fine, 1896–1906, ibid., p. 33; fine, 1907–1911, Uchikawa, "Shimbunshi hō no seitei katei to sono tokushitsu," p. 74; ban, 1904–1908, gleanings from Ono Hideo, *Shimbun no rekishi*, p. 71, Midoro, p. 228, Nishida, pp. 242, 268; I have found no composite records for *hakkō kinshi* after 1896.

Note: Suspend = temporary suspension *(hakkō teishi)*; ban = closing of paper *(hakkō kinshi)*; distrib. = confiscation of issues on a given day *(hatsubai hanpu kinshi)*, a practice that replaced suspensions and bannings, except by court action, after 1897. Records are spotty for fines and jail sentences in early Meiji; thus, blank spaces indicate that I have found no reliable data. The asterisk (*) indicates jailings and fines (1904–1911) under combined newspaper *(shimbunshi)* and publication *(shuppan)* laws; all other figures are for newspaper laws only. The double asterisk (**) indicates that thirty-nine additional papers were suspended in 1905 under Emergency Ordinance 206 for opposition to the Portsmouth treaty; see *Tōkyō Asahi*, December 1, 1905.

Fifty Journalists: Biographical Sketches

Akiyama Teisuke (1868–1950, Okayama). A graduate of Tokyo Imperial University, he founded *Niroku Shinpō* in October 1893, suspended it in 1895 for financial reasons, then revived it in 1900. He resigned as president in 1911 but kept control until its demise in 1940.

Asahina Chisen (1862–1939, Ibaraki). He was founding editor of the Chōshū organ *Tōkyō Shinpō* in 1888, then closed that paper down and assumed the presidency of *Tōkyō Nichi Nichi Shimbun* in 1892. After resigning in 1904, he maintained close ties to *Yamato Shimbun*.

Black, John Reddie (1827–1880, Scotland). A trader, he became editor of A. W. Hansard's *Japan Herald* in 1862, began his own *Japan Gazette* in 1867, then launched the Japanese-language *Nisshin Shinjishi* in 1872. Forced out of journalism by the 1875 newspaper law, which prevented foreigners from editing vernacular papers, he spent his last years writing the two-volume *Young Japan*.

Fujita Mokichi (1852–1892, Ōita). After studying at Keiō Gijuku, he entered *Yūbin Hōchi* in 1874, where, as chief editor, he supported the progressive Kaishintō. He was jailed for his attacks on the government in 1875 and was elected to the Diet in 1890 and 1892.

Fukuchi Gen'ichirō (1841–1906, Nagasaki). He was jailed in 1868 for attacks on the Meiji government at *Kōko Shimbun*, then became the country's most influential editor at the pro-Chōshū *Tōkyō Nichi Nichi Shimbun* in 1874. After retiring in 1888, he became a novelist and kabuki writer. In his latter years, he wrote for *Yamato Shimbun* and was elected to the Diet in 1904.

Fukuzawa Sutejirō (1865–1926, Tokyo). He studied at Keiō Gijuku and Boston University, entered *Jiji Shinpō* in 1981, and assumed the paper's presidency from his father, Yukichi, in 1896. Known for promotional schemes and an emphasis on economic news, he launched the *Ōsaka Jiji Shinpō* in 1905; it never became a strong paper, however.

Fukuzawa Yukichi (1834–1901, Fukuoka). A leading modernizer, he was an important voice on the *Meiroku Zasshi* in the 1870s and launched *Jiji Shinpō* in 1882. The paper specialized in financial reporting and advocated moderately progressive domestic policies and a strong foreign policy.

Hani Motoko (1873–1957, Aomori). She entered *Hōchi Shimbun* in 1898 as a copy editor, then moved to the news side as Japan's first full-fledged woman reporter. Forced to leave *Hōchi* in 1901 for marrying fellow employee Hani Yoshikazu, she later founded *Fujin no Tomo* magazine and the Jiyū Gakuren school.

Hara Kei (Takashi; 1856–1921, Iwate). He became a *Yūbin Hōchi* writer in 1879, then edited *Daitō Nippō* in 1882, before leaving to work in the Foreign Ministry. In 1897, he returned to journalism, as editor, then president (1898) of *Ōsaka Mainichi.* He left *Mainichi* for politics in 1900, as leader of the Seiyūkai. As Home Minister (1906–1908, 1911–1912, 1912–1914), he often oppressed the press. He helped manage two pro-Seiyūkai papers, *Ōsaka Shinpō* and *Chūō Shimbun,* in the early 1900s and was prime minister from 1918 until his assassination.

Heco, Joseph (Hamada Hikozō) (1837–1897, Hyōgō). Shipwrecked in 1850, he was taken to America, then returned to Japan in 1859 as an interpreter. He launched the first Japanese-language paper, *Kaigai Shimbun* (first called *Shimbunshi*) with Kishida Ginkō in 1864; it lasted only a year. He worked for a time in the Finance Ministry, then went into business.

Hiratsuka Raichō (1886–1971, Tokyo). In 1911, she founded *Seitō* (Blue Stocking), the first journal produced entirely by women. After leaving its editorship in 1915, she gave her life to women's and peace issues.

Ikebe Kichitarō (Sanzan; 1864–1912, Kumamoto). He became a writer at *Nihon* in 1890, then after a stint in Paris moved to *Ōsaka Asahi* in 1896. He became chief editor of *Tōkyō Asahi* in 1897, where he was known for advocating strong foreign policies.

Inukai Tsuyoshi (Ki; 1855–1932, Okayama). He wrote for *Yūbin Hōchi* from 1875 onward, then left the paper over differences with Fujita Mokichi, and in 1880 helped found the *Tōkai Keizai Shinpō*. He worked again at *Yūbin Hōchi* from 1882 to 1885, when he left to head *Chōya Shimbun.* He left there in 1890, founded the journal *Minpō* in 1891, then became a *Hōchi* consultant again. His later life was given to politics. He became prime minister in 1931 and was assassinated the next spring.

Isomura Haruko (1879–1918, Fukushima). The mother of eight, she became a *Hōchi* reporter in 1905 and across the next decade was one of the most prolific woman journalists. She moved to *Yamato Shimbun* in 1915 and also wrote novels and translated English-language works into Japanese before dying of heart disease at thirty-nine.

Itō Miyoji (1857–1934, Nagasaki). A protégé of Itō Hirobumi, he hewed to a pro-Chōshū line as president of *Tōkyō Nichi Nichi Shimbun* from 1891 to 1904. He was chief cabinet secretary in 1892 and served as minister in several other cabinets.

Kanno Suga (1881–1911, Osaka). A radical socialist, she took her first newspaper job in 1902 at *Ōsaka Chōhō*, then moved in 1905 to *Murō Shinpō*, where she was acting editor for nearly a year. She became a writer for *Mainichi Denpō* in 1906, was fired in 1908 for her socialist activities, and was executed in 1911 for her role in an alleged conspiracy against the Emperor Meiji.

Katō Takaaki (Kōmei; 1860–1926, Aichi). His life was spent primarily in politics, as foreign minister (three times), head of the Kenseikai, and prime minister (1924–1926). He purchased *Tōkyō Nichi Nichi* with Mitsubishi assistance in 1904 and served as its president until 1908, as part of a plan to spread his own views in society. He played a direct role in editing for a while, until political demands pulled him away from journalism.

Kishida Ginkō (1833–1905, Okayama). With Joseph Heco, he launched the first Japanese-language newspaper, *Kaigai Shimbun*, in 1864; then in Yokohama in 1868 he published *Moshiogusa*, a paper that survived the new Meiji government's press crackdown by focusing on commerce rather than politics. He entered *Tōkyō Nichi Nichi Shimbun* in 1873 and stayed with that paper in various positions until the early 1880s, when he returned to business and the promotion of Chinese-Japanese cultural relations. He covered the 1874 Taiwan expedition as Japan's first war correspondent.

Komatsubara Eitarō (1852–1919, Okayama). In 1875, he became editor of *Hyōron Shimbun* and went to jail for attacking censorship. Later he became a consultant at *Chōya Shimbun* (1878), editor at *San'yō Shinpō* (1879), and president of *Ōsaka Mainichi* (1901–1903). Most of his career after the early 1880s was spent in government, as an increasingly conservative advocate of central control.

Kōtoku Shūsui (1871–1911, Kōchi). A dedicated popular rights advocate, he entered *Jiyū Shimbun* in 1893, then became an editorialist for *Hiroshima Shimbun* in 1895, before going to *Chūō Shimbun* in Tokyo later the same year. He gained prominence as a socialist at *Yorozu Chōhō* after 1898. In 1903, he founded the weekly *Heimin Shimbun*, and after it was banned in 1905, he wrote for several socialist publications before reviving *Heimin* briefly as a daily in 1906. He was executed for involvement in an alleged plot against the emperor in 1911.

Koyasu Takashi (1836–1898, Gifu). He launched Japan's first daily, *Yokohama Mainichi Shimbun*, under government patronage in 1871. Three years later, he joined several others in creating the country's first *koshimbun*, *Yomiuri*. A businessman above all, he also worked in the world of finance and launched *Isami Shimbun* in 1893.

Kubota Beisen (1852–1906, Kyoto). Japan's first major newspaper artist, he did sketches for *Kyoto Nippō*, then went to *Kokumin Shimbun* on its founding in 1890. He was particularly well known for his Sino-Japanese War sketches.

Kuga Katsunan (Minoru; 1857–1907, Aomori). In and out of government in the 1870s and 1880s, he left permanently in 1888 to found the *Tōkyō Denpō* (successor to the *Shōgyō Denpō)*, which he renamed *Nihon* in 1889. He made *Nihon* the country's most consistently nationalist paper and was himself one of Japan's most influential writers.

Kurimoto Jōun (1822–1897, Tokyo). A former shogunal official, he became a writer in 1872 for *Yokohama Mainichi,* then joined *Yūbin Hōchi* in 1873 as chief editor, becoming one of the decade's dominant journalistic voices. He retired in 1885.

Kuroiwa Shūroku (Ruikō; 1862–1920, Kōchi). He moved to Tokyo in 1879, and after dropping out of Keiō Gijuku because he was interested in political affairs, he worked at several papers during the 1880s, including *Konnichi Shimbun* and *Miyako Shimbun* (as editor). In 1892, he founded *Yorozu Chōhō,* which he quickly turned into one of the country's largest papers with a shrewd blend of populism and nationalism. He became active in politics in the Taishō years.

Matsumoto Eiko (1866–1928, Chiba). After entering *Mainichi Shimbun* in 1901, she did a ninety-five-part series on the victims of copper pollution in Ashio, which became such a sensation that authorities forced her out of journalism. She traveled to America immediately thereafter and never returned to Japan.

Miki Zenpachi (1865–1931, Hyōgō). A management genius, he helped found *Kobe Minato Shimbun* (1872), *Awaji Shimbun* (1877), and *Kobe Shinpō* (1880). He entered *Yūbin Hōchi* in 1886, when it was in decline, and turned it into one of Japan's most successful family-oriented papers. He was editor *(shashū)* of *Hōchi* from 1894 to 1924.

Minoura Katsundo (1854–1929, Ōita). He joined *Yūbin Hōchi* after graduating from Keiō Gijuku in 1875 and spent most of his career there, using it as a base to exert political influence. He worked with Miki Zenpachi to popularize *Hōchi* in the 1890s and served as president from 1894 to 1913.

Motoyama Hikoichi (1853–1932, Kumamoto). He began his newspaper career in 1882 at *Ōsaka Shinpō, Yūbin Hōchi's* Kansai ally, then moved in 1883 to *Jiji Shinpō.* In 1888, he assisted in the reorganization of *Ōsaka Mainichi,* and by the 1890s had turned it into one of Japan's largest and most successful papers. He became president in 1903, purchased Tokyo's *Denpō Shimbun* in 1904, and *Tōkyō Nichi Nichi* in 1911.

Murayama Ryōhei (1850–1933, Mie). An Osaka businessman, he helped rescue the failing *Asahi Shimbun* in 1879, then joined Ueno Riichi in purchasing it in 1881. In 1888, he launched an eastern branch, *Tōkyō Asahi*. The combination of solid news and astute management made Asahi the dominant journalistic voice of the late Meiji years.

Nakae Chōmin (1847–1901, Kōchi). One of the era's leading thinkers and an advocate of popular rights, he was a lead writer or editor for numerous papers across the years, among them Saionji Kinmochi's *Tōyō Jiyū Shimbun*, *Jiyū Shimbun*, *Shinonome Shimbun*, *Kōron Shinpō*, *Minken Shimbun*, and *Maiyū Shimbun*.

Narushima Ryūhoku (1837–1884, Tokyo). A former shogunal official, he traveled in Europe after the Meiji Restoration, then returned to edit *Chōya Shimbun* in 1874. Known for a trenchant style, he went to jail twice for opposing official policies. He also served for a time as a consultant to *Yomiuri Shimbun*. *Chōya* went into decline after his death.

Numa Morikazu (1844–1890, Tokyo). He left government service in 1879, in opposition to restrictions on speech, and purchased *Yokohama Mainichi*, which he moved to Tokyo and renamed *Tōkyō-Yokohama Mainichi Shimbun*. He used the paper as a mouthpiece for popular rights issues, supporting first the Jiyūtō, then the more moderate Kaishintō.

Ōsawa Atsuko (1873–1937, Gunma). She entered *Jiji Shinpō* in 1899 as a shorthand writer, soon became a reporter, and stayed there until 1924—the first Japanese woman to spend a full career as a reporter. She also was active in the women's rights movement.

Ozaki Yukio (1858–1954, Kanagawa). He helped edit *Minkan Zasshi* in 1877 and reported for *Niigata Shimbun* from 1878 to 1881. After a brief stint as an official, he entered *Yūbin Hōchi* in 1882, then transferred to *Chōya Shimbun* in 1885. He traveled abroad after being banished from Tokyo in the 1887 *hoan jōrei* episode, wrote for *Chōya* again in 1889–1890, then left newspaper journalism for politics. He maintained close ties to journalists during his long political career.

Saionji Kinmochi (1849–1940, Kyoto). On returning from a decade of study in France, the young prince started the *Tōyō Jiyū Shimbun* in 1881; it was shut down by the government for its popular rights views in less than two months, however. As prime minister (1906–1908, 1911–1912), Saionji enjoyed considerable support from the mainstream press.

Sakai Toshihiko (1871–1933, Fukuoka). He worked for several papers in the 1890s, including *Ōsaka Maiasa Shimbun* and *Fukuoka Nichi Nichi Shimbun*, then entered *Yorozu Chōhō* in 1899, where he became a noted advocate of socialism. He left *Yorozu* in 1903 and helped Kōtoku Shūsui found *Heimin Shimbun*. After it was banned in 1905, he gave himself to numerous socialist causes and journals and helped found the Japan Communist Party in 1922.

Seki Naohiko (1857–1934, Wakayama). He assisted Fukuchi Gen-'ichirō at *Tōkyō Nichi Nichi* in the early 1880s while a student at the University of Tokyo, then entered the paper on graduation, and became its president in 1888. He was pushed out in 1891, after trying to make the paper independent of the government, and gave his subsequent years largely to politics.

Shimada Saburō (1852–1923, Tokyo). He began writing for *Yokohama Mainichi* in 1873, left it for government service in 1875, then rejoined it following the political crisis of 1881. After Numa Morikazu's death, he took control of the paper and became president in 1894, a post he maintained until the paper was taken over by *Hōchi Shimbun* in 1906. The leading supporter of victims of Ashio copper pollution, he never wavered in his support for populist causes.

Suehiro Tetchō (Shigeyasu; 1849–1896, Ehime). He became a writer at *Tōkyō Akebono* in 1875, then moved to *Chōya* the same year, when his writings proved too radical for his editor. Jailed twice for attacks on officials, he remained at *Chōya* for fifteen years, assuming leadership after Narushima Ryūhoku's death in 1884. He left the paper in 1889, following a trip to the West, and affiliated with *Tokyo Kōron, Kansai Nippō, Daidō Shimbun,* and *Kokkai* over the next few years, giving much time to personal writing and politics.

Takekoshi Takeyo (1870–1944, Okayama). She was the first Japanese woman to work as a reporter. In 1890, Tokutomi Sohō engaged her to write at *Kokumin Shimbun,* where she did interviews and other stories for about three months, before moving on to other activities in the women's movement. In the early 1890s, she served as an editor of the journal *Fujin Kyōfū Zasshi.*

Torii Sosen (1867–1928, Kumamoto). Following an early career as a researcher, he entered *Nihon* in 1890 and gained fame as a war correspondent during the Sino-Japanese War. In 1897, he transferred to *Ōsaka Asahi,* where he remained for two decades as a vigorously expansionist, antigovernment writer and editor. After being forced out of *Asahi* by the authorities in 1918 following the controversy over coverage of the rice riots, he launched the *Taishō Nichi Nichi Shimbun;* it never flourished, however, because of competition from the existing Osaka papers.

Tokutomi Sohō (Iichirō; 1863–1957, Kumamoto). After gaining national prominence as a young man with the book *Future Japan (Shōrai no Nihon)* and the journal *Kokumin no Tomo,* he launched *Kokumin Shimbun* in 1890 as a leading voice for populism and expansionism. In the latter 1890s, he became a vocal supporter of the Matsukata Masayoshi and Katsura Tarō cabinets. He reluctantly allowed the paper to be popularized in the late-Meiji years and gave up the company presidency in 1929. He wrote more than 350 works altogether, including the hundred-volume *History of Early Modern Japan (Kinsei Nihon kokumin shi).*

Uchimura Kanzō (1861–1930, Tokyo). The Meiji era's most prominent Christian thinker, he attracted a wide audience as an editorialist at *Yorozu Chōhō* from 1897 to 1903 and later wrote for *Kokumin Shimbun* and for the *Japan Chronicle* in Kobe. He was known in the early 1900s for his pacifism, biblical studies, and advocacy of *mukyōkai* (nonchurch) Christianity.

Ueki Emori (1857–1892, Kōchi). One of the most prolific exponents of popular rights and a leader of the Jiyūtō, he worked as editorialist or reporter for a host of papers, including *Kainan Shinshi, Aikoku Shinshi, Kōchi Shimbun, Jiyū Shimbun, Fukushima Jiyū Shimbun,* and *Izumo Shimbun;* he contributed essays to a large number of other journals and newspapers.

Ueno Iwatarō (1867–1925, Kumamoto). One of the era's best-known war correspondents, he entered *Ōsaka Asahi* in 1890, after a year at *Ōsaka Kōron*, then moved to *Jiyū* (1891) and back to *Asahi* (1893), where he covered the wars with China and Russia as well as the Boxer Rebellion. He later became president of the journal *Shin Kōron*.

Ueno Riichi (1848–1919, Hyōgō). He joined *Ōsaka Asahi* in 1880, helped Murayama Ryōhei purchase the paper in 1881, and played the dominant managerial role for the next thirty-seven years. His reason and moderation balanced Murayama's more passionate, expansive tendencies. From 1908 on, he and Murayama alternated yearly as company president.

Yamaji Aizan (1867–1917, Tokyo). After years as an educator and essayist, he entered *Kokumin Shimbun* in 1892, then became editor of *Shinano Mainichi Shimbun* in 1899. In 1903, he created his own journal, *Dokuritsu Hyōron,* and in 1916 he took the editorship of *Shinano Nichi Nichi Shimbun.* During most of this time, he wrote for numerous journals, espousing eclectic ideas that included bits of nationalism, Confucianism, and Christianity.

Yanagawa Shunsan (1832–1870, Nagoya). The earliest pioneer of Japanese journalism, he entered the *bakufu*'s Kaiseijo in 1863 as a translator of Western newspapers and other writings. While there, he published the *Shimbun Kaisō,* a kind of insider newspaper, then the *Seiyō Zasshi,* Japan's first news-oriented magazine. Immediately after the 1868 Meiji Restoration, he published *Chūgai Shimbun,* one of the best of the anti-Meiji papers. He retired from public life when the government banned the papers that summer.

Yano Fumio (1850–1931, Ōita). He joined *Yūbin Hōchi* in 1876, as assistant editor, then left in 1878 to enter the Finance Ministry. The political crisis of 1881 sent him back to *Hōchi,* where he assumed the presidency and turned the paper into an organ of the progressive Kaishintō. After beginning to popularize *Hōchi* in 1886 following a trip to the West, he resigned as president in 1887, then reassumed that post in 1889, but his interest in the paper soon waned, and he let Miki Zenpachi make *Hōchi* into a less political, more family-oriented paper.

Notes

INTRODUCTION

1. Quoted in Norman Isaacs, *Untended Gates: The Mismanaged Press,* p. 219.

2. James W. Carey, "The Problems of Journalism History," p. 52.

3. Tokutomi Sohō, *Shōrai no Nihon,* p. 106, trans. in Vinh Sinh, *The Future Japan,* p. 169.

4. See Ariyama Teruo, *Tokutomi Sohō to Kokumin Shimbun,* pp. 151–156, for a discussion of this attitude.

5. The most relevant works by these authors are Irokawa Daikichi, *The Culture of the Meiji Period* and *Shinpen Meiji seishin shi;* Mikiso Hane, *Peasants, Rebels and Outcastes: The Underside of Modern Japan;* Patricia Tsurumi, *Factory Girls: Women in the Thread Mills of Meiji Japan;* Okamoto Shumpei, "The Emperor and the Crowd" and *The Japanese Oligarchy and the Russo-Japanese War;* Tetsuo Najita, *Hara Kei in the Politics of Compromise, 1905–1915;* Andrew Gordon, *Labor and Imperial Democracy in Prewar Japan;* Michael Lewis, *Citizens and Rioters: Mass Protest in Imperial Japan;* and Carol Gluck, *Japan's Modern Myths: Ideology in the Late Meiji Period.*

6. See John Pierson, *Tokutomi Sohō, 1863–1957: A Journalist for Modern Japan;* Sinh Vinh, *Tokutomi Sohō (1863–1957): The Later Career;* Kenneth Pyle, *The New Generation in Meiji Japan;* James L. Huffman, *Politics of the Meiji Press: The Life of Fukuchi Gen'ichirō;* D. Eleanor Westney, *Imitation and Innovation: The Transfer of Western Organizational Patterns to Meiji Japan;* and Albert Altman, "The Press and Social Cohe-

sion during a Period of Change: The Case of Early Meiji Japan." The earlier overall histories of the Meiji press are Kisaburō Kawabe, *The Press and Politics in Japan* (1921), and Harry E. Wildes, *The Press and Social Currents in Japan* (1927).

7.   Their works, too numerous to list here, are found in the bibliography. The work that looks most intensely at people-press issues is Yamamoto Taketoshi's *Shimbun to minshū.*

8.   Uchikawa Yoshimi, "Kindai shimbun shi kenkyū hōhō ron," pp. 58–59. The one Western scholar who has treated the role of the Asian press in stimulating nationalism is Benedict Anderson, in *Imagined Communities: Reflections on the Origin and Spread of Nationalism.* He talks a good deal about "print-as-commodity" as "the key to the generation of wholly new ideas of simultaneity" (p. 37) and the "profound fictiveness" of newspapers that enables them to construct stories that stimulate new communities (p. 33), but he makes no direct application of his ideas to the Japanese press.

9.   See Lawrence Beer, *Freedom of Expression in Japan*; Gregory Kasza, *The State and the Mass Media in Japan, 1918–1945* (which deals more with the Meiji era than the title implies); Richard Mitchell, *Censorship in Imperial Japan*; and Jay Rubin, *Injurious to Public Morals: Writers and the Meiji State.*

10.   See especially his *Hikka shi* (1911) as well as his other works in the bibliography.

11.   Okano Takeo, citing Fukuzawa's *Seiyō jijō* (Things Western), in *Meiji genron shi*, p. 9.

12.   Ono Hideo, "Meiji shoki ni okeru shuppan jiyū no gainen," p. 83.

13.   Midoro Masaichi, ed., *Meiji Taishō shi: genron hen*, p. 1. *Genron* can be translated variously as "press," "debate," "expression," "discussion." Midoro uses it in its broader sense here.

14.   Carey, p. 53. Emphasis added.

15.   Douglass Cater, *Power in Washington*, cited in Richard W. Lee, ed., *Politics and the Press*, pp. 108–109.

16.   E. Lloyd Sommerlad, *The Press in Developing Countries*, p. 9.

17.   In Elihu Katz and Tamas Szecsko, eds., *Mass Media and Social Change*, p. 9.

18.   Motoyama Hikoichi, address at *Mainichi*, 1924, quoted in Iwai Hajime, *Shimbun to shimbunjin*, p. 126.

19.   For discussions of the press' role in shaping opinion, see Robin H. Lee, "Media and Change," in J. A. F. Van Zyl and K. G. Tomaselli, eds., *Media and Change*, pp. 51–55; also Richard W. Lee, *Politics and the Press*, pp. 99–100.

20. Quoted in Robert McCormick, *The Freedom of the Press*, p. 11.

21. Wilbur Schramm, *Mass Media and National Development*, pp. 42–44.

22. The subscription number becomes seventy-two million if one counts morning and evening editions separately. Each Japanese household subscribes to an average of 1.24 papers. Figures are for 1994, compiled by the Japan Newspaper Publishers and Editors Association, *The Japanese Press '95*, p. 90. See also Hayashi Toshitaka, "The Japanese Newspaper—Its Past, Present, and Future," p. 108.

23. Katz and Szecsko, p. 14.

24. Baba Tsunego, "Shimbun seisakusha to sono jinseikan," in Tsurumi Shunsuke, ed., *Jiyānarizumu no shisō*, p. 209.

25. *Kōko Shimbun*, May 24, 1868, reprinted in Osatake Takeki, ed., *Bakumatsu Meiji shimbun zenshū*, 1, p. 3.

26. See Tamura Norio, *Nihon no rōkaru shimbun*, pp. 153–161.

27. Ukai Shin'ichi's meticulous, detailed charts in *Chōya Shimbun no kenkyū* show that by 1884, for example, Tokyo had one newspaper subscriber for every 11.9 citizens, while Aichi (Nagoya) had one for 347.4, and Okayama one for 649.2 (p. 41). The lag continued through the pre–World War II era. Nevertheless, as works such as Nihon Shimbun Kyōkai's *Chihōbetsu: Nihon shimbun shi* make clear, there were increasing numbers of solid and influential papers in places as distant as Niigata and Kyushu already by the 1870s.

28. Albert Altman calls the pamphletlike *shimbunshi* that appeared about twice a week in the early-Meiji years "news sheets." See his "Shimbunshi: The Early Meiji Adaptation of the Western-Style Newspaper."

29. Lists of the many and varied magazines that appeared in the Meiji era are found in Nishida Taketoshi, *Meiji jidai no shimbun to zasshi*, pp. 77–94, 132–140, 205–225, 259–264.

30. One other medium, film, did get a start in late Meiji, with the first Kinetoscope showings in 1896, the first Japanese studio opening in 1908, and the first movie magazine appearing in 1909. They were not news-oriented, however.

CHAPTER 1. LEGACY: IN SPITE OF THE AUTHORITIES

1. Cited in John W. Dower, ed., *Origins of the Modern Japanese State: Selected Writings of E. H. Norman*, p. 11.

2. See, for example, "A Dialogue on Poverty," *The Man'yōshū* (New York: Columbia University Press, 1965), pp. 205–207.

3. Quoted in Irokawa Daikichi, *The Culture of the Meiji Period*, p. 116.

4. Haga Eizō, *Meiji Taishō shi*, p. 14. *"Hikka"* refers to any publication or communication that runs afoul of the authorities.

5. I am indebted for this observation to several provocative discussions with South Korean essayist and philosopher Kim Yongkoo. See his "Genron to iu mono," p. 13. Another defense of the relative freedom with which mid-Tokugawa authors wrote is found in Nakano Mitsutoshi, *Edo bunka hyōbanki: gazoku yūwa no sekai* (Tokyo: Chūō Kōronsha, 1992); his argument is summarized in "Revising Edo."

6. Kaneko Kisabu, *Shimbun kenkyū*, p. 259. Translation of the constitution (Article 17) is from Ryusaku Tsunoda et al., eds., *Sources of Japanese Tradition*, 1, p. 51.

7. Minister of Justice, "The Legal System," in Alfred Stead, ed., *Japan by the Japanese: A Survey by Its Highest Authorities*, p. 500; see also Lawrence Beer, *Freedom of Expression in Japan*, p. 46.

8. Yamamoto Taketoshi, *Shimbun kisha no tanjō*, p. 47.

9. Cited in Dower, p. 11.

10. Guido Verbeck, "History of Protestant Missions in Japan," in *Proceedings of the Conference of the Protestant Missionaries: Held at Osaka, Japan, April, 1883* (Yokohama: R. Meiklejohn Company, 1883), p. 31, cited in Gordon Laman, "Our Nagasaki Legacy: An Examination of the Period of Persecution of Christianity and Its Impact on Subsequent Christian Missions in Japan," *The Northeast Asia Journal of Theology*, pp. 119–120.

11. George Sansom, *Japan: A Short Cultural History*, p. 456.

12. Verbeck, p. 31, cited in Laman, p. 120.

13. See Stephen Vlastos, *Peasant Protests and Uprisings in Tokugawa Japan*, p. 59; also see pp. 42–43, 64–65.

14. Futagawa Yoshifumi, *Genron no dan'atsu*, p. 128.

15. One of the fullest discussions of the depth and breadth of the control patterns is found in Futagawa, pp. 9–127.

16. Jay Rubin, *Injurious to Public Morals: Writers and the Meiji State*, p. 17.

17. Futagawa, pp. 28–35; Rubin, p. 17.

18. Futagawa, p. 11.

19. P. F. Kornicki, "The Enmeiin Affair of 1803: The Spread of Information in the Tokugawa Period," pp. 529–530.

20. See Ono Hideo, "Yanagawa Shunsan," pp. 16–19.

21. Zen Nihon Shimbun Renmei, ed., *Shimbun taikan*, p. 26.

22.   The institute was renamed frequently over the next two decades: Bansho Shirabesho (1856), Yōsho Shirabesho (1862), Kaiseijo (1863), Kaisei Gakkō (1868), Daigaku Nankō (1869), and Tōkyō Daigaku (1877). The latter became the national imperial university. The office added instruction in Western studies in 1857. A useful account of the office's evolution is found in ibid., pp. 16–24.

23.   The text, excerpted in Futagawa, p. 11, refers also to earlier censorship actions. Zen Nihon Shimbun Renmei, *Shimbun taikan*, p. 24, refers to a censorship regulation in 1664, as well as in 1713 and 1718. Donald Keene, *World within Walls*, p. 235, refers to a 1644 prohibition against the use of real people's names by playwrights. The first fully developed censorship regulations, however, seem to have been those in 1673.

24.   Quoted in Futagawa, pp. 23–24; also see Yamamoto Fumio, *Nihon shimbun hattatsu shi*, p. 6.

25.   The ordinance is translated in Nakano, "Revising Edo," p. 4. Nakano maintains that the ordinance actually stimulated printing and that it was not so restrictive as subsequent scholars normally have judged it to have been. See also Richard Mitchell, *Censorship in Imperial Japan*, p. 4; Rubin, pp. 17–18; Kornicki, p. 506.

26.   Kornicki, p. 507. Konta Yōzō, *Edo no kinsho*, discusses another 1771 law that proscribed publication of discussion of Christianity, court affairs, the shogunal family, unfounded rumors, speculations, and reports of recent events. He notes that out-of-print books were proscribed and lists more than 150 banned books. See pp. 3–8.

27.   Rubin, p. 18.

28.   Discussed in Donald Keene, *The Japanese Discovery of Europe, 1720–1830*, pp. 39–45, 147–152.

29.   See Futagawa, p. 31, for a citation of the offending passages.

30.   Mitchell, p. 9.

31.   Haga, pp. 16–20.

32.   Rubin, p. 19, citing Konta Yōzō, *Edo no hon'yasan*, pp. 136, 142–143, 191.

33.   Leon Zolbrod, *Takizawa Bakin* (New York: Twayne Publishers, 1967), p. 55, cited in Mitchell, p. 11.

34.   Quoted in Marius B. Jansen, *Japan and Its World*, pp. 7–8.

35.   An insightful discussion of this development is found in M. William Steele, "Goemon's New World View: Popular Representations of the Opening of Japan."

36.   Englebert Kaempfer, *The History of Japan*, 2, p. 1.

37.   See Kim, p. 13.

38.   Ronald P. Dore, *Education in Tokugawa Japan*, p. 321.

39. Conrad Totman, *Japan before Perry*, pp. 197–198.

40. Thomas C. Smith, *Agrarian Origins of Modern Japan*, pp. 81–88.

41. Kornicki, "Enmeiin Affair," p. 532.

42. Donald Keene, *World within Walls*, pp. 2–4. See also his "Japanese Publishing, Yesterday and Today," p. 1. Keene says that the oldest example of printing in the world is Japanese—from the eighth century.

43. See Edward H. House, "Ancient and Modern Periodical Literature of Japan," p. 244; also Ono Hideo, *Nihon shimbun hattatsu shi*, pp. 5–8. Still others find the origins of "news" publishing in the early-Tokugawa storytelling *(kōshaku)* and kabuki performances; see Zen Nihon Shimbun Renmei, p. 5.

44. Zen Nihon Shimbun Renmei, p. 30.

45. See Ono, *Nihon shimbun hattatsu shi*, pp. 8–9; also Kanesada Hanazono, *The Development of Japanese Journalism*, p. 1. There is some question about whether this was indeed the first; see Gerald Groemer, "Singing the News: *Yomiuri* in Japan during the Edo and Meiji Periods," pp. 235–236.

46. Groemer, p. 70.

47. House, p. 244.

48. From *Tenna shōishū*, in Groemer, p. 236.

49. Yamamoto Fumio, *Nihon shimbun hattatsu shi*, p. 5. One of the best collections of broadsides is Nishimaki Yōzaburō, ed., *Kawaraban shimbun: Edo Meiji sanbyaku jiken*, which reprints many of the most important *kawaraban* across three centuries.

50. Official warning in 1684, Groemer, p. 239. Groemer notes that no "all-out prohibition" ever was made on the publication of *yomiuri* (p. 241), though many edicts prohibited specific activities such as printing "groundless rumors."

51. Ono Hideo, *Shimbun no rekishi*, p. 18. The classic study of the *kawaraban* continues to be his *Kawaraban monogatari: Edo jidai masu komi no rekishi*.

52. Steele, pp. 70–71.

53. Zen Nihon Shimbun Renmei, p. 19. The *kawaraban* continued to be hawked on city streets, often right alongside newspaper extras, until the middle of the Meiji era.

54. See Vlastos, p. 68.

55. One of the most complete lists of Edo-era publications is found in Leon Zolbrod, "Mass Media of the Tokugawa Period," pp. 125–131. Zolbrod notes that by the 1840s, there also were more than three hundred recital halls in Japan. An incisive discussion of the subversive nature of

some *kibyōshi* is found in Fumiko Togasaki, "The Assertion of Heterodoxy in Kyōden's Verbal-Visual Art," n.p., 1993; also see her "Santō Kyōden's *Kibyōshi*: Video-Verbal and Contemporary-Classic Intercommunications."

56. Kornicki, "Enmeiin Affair," p. 515.

57. Konta, *Edo no kinsho*, pp. 13–16.

58. See W. G. Aston, *A History of Japanese Literature*, p. 310.

59. Kornicki, "Enmeiin Affair," pp. 503–508; some details also are based on a Kornicki talk at the Asiatic Society of Japan, Tokyo, March 12, 1984.

60. See Dore, *Education in Tokugawa Japan*, p. 20.

61. Ibid., p. 531.

62. Cited in Kōsaka Masaaki, ed., *Japanese Thought in the Meiji Era*, p. 5.

63. Monna Naoki, *Minshū jiyūnarizumu no rekishi*, p. 4.

64. Ono, *Nihon shimbun hattatsu shi*, p. 11.

65. Chikamori Haruyoshi, *Jinbutsu Nihon shimbun shi*, pp. 137–138.

66. Albert Altman, " 'Shimbunshi': The Early Meiji Adaptation of the Western-Style Newspaper," pp. 57–58; Matsumoto Sannosuke and Yamamuro Shin'ichi, eds., *Genron to medeia*, p. 5.

67. Fukuchi Gen'ichirō, *Shimbunshi jitsureki*, p. 326.

68. Chikamori, p. 140. Fukuzawa devoted a whole chapter to "shimbunshi" in his famous *Seiyō jijō* (Things Western).

69. Ono, "Yanagawa Shunsan," p. 21.

70. Dates are in the Western calendar. Conversions from the old Japanese calendar are based on Paul Y. Tsuchihashi, *Japanese Chronological Tables from 601 to 1872 A.D.*

71. There is no relationship between this publication and today's English-language paper of the same title. The latter was launched in 1897.

72. Ono, *Nihon shimbun hattatsu shi*, pp. 16–18.

73. Ono, "Yanagawa Shunsan," p. 16.

74. Ibid.; Ono, *Nihon shimbun hattatsu shi*, p. 11.

75. Ono, "Yanagawa Shunsan," p. 27.

76. For a carefully researched discussion of Hansard's life and work, see Suzuki Yūga, "Aru Eijin hakkōsha o otte: A. W. Hansādo no kiseki," pp. 67–97. One of the best accounts of the paper itself is Hasegawa Shin'ichi, "Nihon saisho eiji shimbun," pp. 37–48. Also see Ono, "Yanagawa Shunsan," p. 30.

77. Suzuki, pp. 98–101.

78. Ono, "Yanagawa Shunsan," p. 32.

79. Ibid., p. 33.

80. See Satow's account in Ernest Satow, *A Diplomat in Japan*, p. 159. Satow reports that he wrote essays for the *Times*, even though it was "doubtless very irregular . . . altogether contrary to the rules of the service."

81. John R. Black, *Young Japan*, 1, p. 377.

82. Black, *Young Japan*, 2, pp. 87–88. Actually, this was Japan's second daily; the *Herald* had published a daily "advertising paper" already in 1863 and had itself been a daily since 1866; see Robert S. Spaulding, "Bibliography of Western-Language Dailies and Weeklies in Japan, 1861–1961," p. 14. Black says the *Herald* followed the *Gazette* in becoming a daily, apparently an error of memory. The *Gazette* lasted until the Great Kantō Earthquake in 1923.

83. Precision regarding numbers is difficult, since different scholars handle papers differently, some counting the *Herald* and *Daily Herald*, for example, as separate titles. Yamamoto Fumio, for example, lists thirteen (*Nihon shimbun hattatsu shi*, pp. 25–26), while Spaulding, typically precise and conservative with his dates, includes just ten. The most thorough study of these papers remains Ebihara Hachirō, *Nihon Ōji shimbun zasshi shi*. Also see the summary of Suzuki Yūga, "Bakumatsu Meiji no Ōji shimbun to gaikokujin jiyānarisuto," pp. 45–50. In English, see J. E. Hoare, "The Foreign Press," in his *Japan's Treaty Ports and Foreign Settlements*, pp. 141–167; also his "British Journalists in Meiji Japan," in Ian Nish, *Britain and Japan*, pp. 20–32.

84. Also worth noting is the appearance early in 1867 of a Japanese-language paper, *Bankoku Shimbunshi*, published by a Britisher, Cambridge-educated Buckworth Bailey, a missionary attached to the British consulate in Yokohama. The paper, a Japanese-language translation from English papers, aimed to "acquaint Japanese with the affairs of all nations" and lasted for a full two years and five months. See Haruhara Akihiko, "Nihon no jiyānarizumu no seisei ni oyobashite dentō to seiō no eikyō," pp. 21–22; and Ishii Kendō, "Bēri no *Bankoku Shimbunshi* to Hiko no *Kaigai Shimbun*," pp. 2–7. Also see Black, *Young Japan*, 2, pp. 60–61.

85. Nishida Taketoshi, *Meiji jidai no shimbun to zasshi*, p. 14. Nishida makes a similar evaluation of *Bankoku Shimbunshi*. Kishida published *Kaigai Shimbun* by himself for some months after Heco left it to take work in Nagasaki; it died finally in 1866. There is some disagreement as to whether *Kaigai Shimbun* represented a mere renaming of *Shimbunshi* or was a new paper, founded after *Shimbunshi* died. See Sugiura Tadashi, *Shimbun koto hajime*, p. 303; Yamamoto Taketoshi, *Shimbun kisha no tanjō*, pp. 77–78. For *Bankoku Shimbunshi*, also see Haruhara Akihiko et al., eds., *Josei kisha*, p. 3.

86. Kishida Ginkō, "Shimbun jitsureki dan," p. 63.

87. See Yamamoto Taketoshi, *Shimbun kisha no tanjō*, p. 67.

88. Ono, "Yanagawa Shunsan," p. 15.

89. Quoted in ibid., pp. 34–35.

90. Ibid., pp. 34–38. Ono's summary of the Roches meeting sheds fascinating light on covert French efforts to aid the bakufu in the late 1860s.

91. Ibid., p. 43.

92. Robert Bellah, *Tokugawa Religion*, p. 13.

93. Tetsuo Najita, *Japan: The Intellectual Foundations of Modern Japanese Politics*, p. 41.

94. Ibid., p. 44.

95. Haga, p. 202.

CHAPTER 2. COMING INTO BEING, 1868

1. Anthony Smith, *The Newspaper: An International History*, p. 36.

2. See Nishida Taketoshi, *Meiji jidai no shimbun to zasshi*, pp. 16–17, for a chronology of these papers. Dates are based on the Western calendar, converted according to Paul Y. Tsuchihashi, *Japanese Chronological Tables from 601 to 1872 a.d.*

3. These Restoration papers are reproduced photographically in Kitane Minoru's 38-volume *Nihon shoki shimbun zenshū* (1986–1992).

4. Fukuchi Gen'ichirō, *Shimbunshi jitsureki*, p. 326.

5. Kishida Ginkō, "Shimbunshi jitsureki dan," p. 63.

6. Lists and names of the papers vary, making precise accounting nearly impossible. The most reliable accounts of these papers include Nishida, pp. 16–24; Okano Takeo, *Meiji genron shi*, p. 216; Nihon Shimbun Renmei, ed., *Nihon shimbun hyakunen shi*, pp. 711–712, and Zen Nihon Shimbun Renmei, ed., *Shimbun taikan*, pp. 43–47.

7. Quoted from *Seiyō Zasshi* in Ono Hideo, "Yanagawa Shunsan," p. 42.

8. See Yamamoto Taketoshi, *Shimbun kisha no tanjō*, p. 70.

9. See Albert A. Altman, " 'Shimbunshi,' " p. 56.

10. See Yamamoto Fumio, *Nihon shimbun hattatsu shi*, p. 40; Nishida, pp. 20–22.

11. Van Reed had met Joseph Heco in the United States, then, in 1859, followed him to Japan, where he engaged in arms sales as an agent for Augustine Heard and Co. and sold arms to Satsuma. He also served as

consul-general in Yokohama for Hawai'i and eventually was asked by the Japanese government to leave the country because of his role in securing workers for Hawaiian plantations. He died en route home in 1873. See Ono Hideo, *Yokohama Shinpō Moshiogusa, Kōko Shimbun,* pp. 11–15. His life is summarized in Albert Altman, "Eugene Van Reed, a Reading Man in Japan, 1859–1872 [sic]," pp. 7–12, 27–31. I am indebted to Uchikawa Yoshimi for calling this piece to my attention.

12.   *Yokohama Shinpō Moshiogusa,* June 1, 1868.

13.   Yamamoto Taketoshi, *Shimbun kisha no tanjō,* p. 77.

14.   Both quotes come from Altman, *"Shimbunshi,"* p. 58, citing Osatake Takeki, ed., *Bakumatsu Meiji shimbun zenshū,* 3, p. 211.

15.   *Kōko Shimbun,* no. 1 (May 24, 1868), in Osatake, *Bakumatsu Meiji shimbun zenshū,* 3, p. 3.

16.   Kishida Ginkō, *Ūsun nikki,* in Tsurumi Shunsuke, ed., *Jiyānarizumu no shisō,* p. 74.

17.   from Naikaku Insatsu Kyoku Hensen, *Naikaku nanajūnen shi* (Tokyo, 1943), p. 188.

18.   Discussed in Yamamoto Taketoshi, *Shimbun kisha no tanjō,* p. 72.

19.   Kishida, "Shimbunshi jitsureki dan," p. 64.

20.   Quoted in Okano, p. 5.

21.   Ono, "Yanagawa Shunsan," p. 40.

22.   Kido Takayoshi commented in his diary on June 1, 1868, that the Nagasaki businessman Thomas Glover had shown him newspaper stories on Meiji army defeats. "These are unreliable," Kido noted, "so we need not bewail the matter." Sidney Brown and Hirota Akiko, trans. *The Diary of Kido Takayoshi,* 1, p. 30.

23.   Ernest Satow, *A Diplomat in Japan,* pp. 366–367.

24.   *Kōko Shimbun,* 16 (June 24, 1868), in Osatake, 2, pp. 61–64. The treatise is analyzed in Okano, p. 7, and in Yamamoto Taketoshi, *Shimbun kisha no tanjō,* pp. 33–34. See also James Huffman, *Politics of the Meiji Press: The Life of Fukuchi Gen'ichirō,* pp. 53–56.

25.   Edwin Emery and Michael Emery, *The Press and America,* p. 1.

26.   Quoted in W. G. Beasley, *The Meiji Restoration,* p. 322.

27.   Many Western scholars give April 28, 1868, as the date of the first Meiji publication decree; that, however, is the date on the old Japanese calendar. The date according to the calendar now in use was June 18. One exception apparently was *Fūka Shimbun,* begun earlier in June and suspended after its very first issue for its slanderous anti-Meiji poetry. See Nishida, p. 20.

28. Quoted, among other places, in Robert M. Spaulding, "The Intent of the Charter Oath," pp. 6–8.

29. Quoted in Okano, p. 6.

30. Anthony Smith, ed., *Newspapers and Democracy: International Essays on a Changing Medium*, p. x.

31. Quoted in Ronald P. Dore, "The Legacy of Tokugawa Education," in Marius B. Jansen, ed., *Changing Japanese Attitudes toward Modernization*, p. 125.

32. *Chūgai Shimbun*, May 2, 1878, cited in Okano, p. 6.

33. *Moshiogusa*, 12 (July 4, 1868); Okano, p. 8.

34. *Kōko Shimbun*, 16 (June 24, 1868); Osatake, 3, p. 64.

35. The most complete compendium of Meiji press regulations is found in Midoro Masaichi, ed., *Meiji Taishō shi: genron hen*, pp. 369–454. This regulation is found on p. 371. Helpful English-language accounts of the 1868 policy are found in Richard Mitchell, *Censorship in Imperial Japan*, pp. 17–22, and Peter Figdor, "Newspapers and Their Regulation in Early Meiji Japan, 1868–1883," pp. 3–5.

36. *Soyofuku Kaze*, 7 (n.d.), quoted in Osatake, p. 408, trans. in M. William Steele, "The Rise and Fall of the Shōgitai: A Social Drama," p. 140.

37. For an account of the episode, see Sugiura Tadashi, *Shimbun koto hajime*, pp. 117–121; Fukuchi, p. 327; Huffman, pp. 57–60.

38. See Nishida, *Meiji jidai no shimbun to zasshi*, pp. 16–17; Midoro, pp. 11–12, 371–72. One paper that escaped the closure was Kishida's *Yokohama Shinpō Moshiogusa*, the reason likely lying in its close ties to the foreign community and the fact that it was published in a treaty port, an area protected by extraterritoriality provisions; see Nishida, pp. 19–20.

39. Midoro, pp. 12, 372.

CHAPTER 3. SERVING THE GOVERNMENT, 1868 TO 1874

1. Kido Takayoshi, *The Diary of Kido Takayoshi*, 1, p. 474.

2. Fukuzawa Yukichi, from *Gakumon no susume*, no. 4, in *Fukuzawa Yukichi on Education*, p. 90.

3. Details from Ono Hideo, "Yanagawa Shunsan," pp. 47–52.

4. Fukuchi Ōchi, *Kaiō jidan*, in Yanagida Izumi, ed., *Fukuchi Ōchi shū*, p. 324. Also see Yanagida Izumi, *Fukuchi Ōchi*, pp. 125–134.

5. See Kishida Ginkō, "Shimbun jitsureki dan," p. 65.

6. Yamamoto Taketoshi, *Shimbun to minshū*, p. 45. Equally telling was the fact that in 1887, only one child in fifty went on to higher primary school, one in 175 to secondary school; see Makoto Aso and Ikuo Amano, *Education and Japan's Modernization*, pp. 24–25.

7. Itō Hirobumi, "Some Reminiscences of the Grant of the New Constitution," in Ōkuma Shigenobu, *Fifty Years of New Japan*, 1, p. 123.

8. Fukuzawa Yukichi, *The Autobiography of Yukichi Fukuzawa*, pp. 243–246.

9. Editorial, *Yūbin Hōchi Shimbun*, April 4, 1875; Sugiura Tadashi, *Shimbun koto hajime*, p. 286.

10. Irokawa Daikichi, "The Survival Struggle of the Japanese Community," p. 475.

11. Cited in Uchikawa Yoshimi and Arai Naoyuki, eds., *Nihon no jiyānarizumu*, pp. 6–7.

12. Cited in Nihon Shimbun Hanbai Kyōkai, ed., *Shimbun hanbai hyakunen*, p. 193.

13. Kido, *Diary*, 1, April 5, 1871, p. 474.

14. Translation from Ryusaku Tsunoda et al., eds., *Sources of Japanese Tradition*, 2, pp. 145–146. Shinagawa's letter is in Midoro Masaichi, ed., *Meiji Taishō shi: genron hen*, pp. 17–18.

15. Kido, *Diary*, 2, July 31, Aug. 1, 1872, pp. 191–192; Oct. 18, 1872, pp. 236–237. Visits included the New York *Tribune, Harpers Weekly,* and the *Scotsman.*

16. An example of Kido's awareness of the social potential of the press is the entry for July 21, 1871, when he noted informing the "newspaper office" of a plague in the Itaku area "in order to warn people to take preventative measures." Kido, *Diary*, 2, p. 46.

17. Quoted in George Akita, *Foundations of Constitutional Government in Modern Japan, 1868–1900*, p. 7.

18. Robert M. Spaulding, Jr., "The Intent of the Charter Oath," pp. 6–7.

19. Midoro, p. 373. See Richard Mitchell, *Censorship in Imperial Japan*, pp. 22–24, for a discussion of the intricacies of the new regulations.

20. Midoro, p. 373.

21. Peter Figdor, "Newspapers and Their Regulation in Early Meiji Japan, 1868–1883," p. 7. Also see Gregory Kasza, *The State and the Mass Media in Japan, 1918–1945*, p. 6.

22. Nearly all the ordinances are printed, verbatim, in Midoro, pp. 369–384. Detailed treatments of the early-Meiji press laws are found in

ibid., pp. 13–46; Okudaira Yasuhiro, "Nihon shuppan keisatsu hōsei no rekishiteki kenkyū josetsu," *Hōritsu Jihō,* April–October 1967; Figdor, pp. 1–44; and Inada Masatsugu, *Meiji kenpō seiritsu shi,* 1, pp. 181–185.

23. See Nishida Taketoshi, *Meiji jidai no shimbun to zasshi,* p. 38; also Albert Altman, " 'Shimbunshi': The Early Meiji Adaptation of the Western-Style Newspaper," p. 62.

24. See Midoro, pp. 32, 383–384. Mitchell's evaluation (pp. 34–37) is useful here.

25. Satō Shōzō notes in *Gendai hikka shi ken dainenpyō,* pp. 1–33, that an annual average of 1.83 press infractions *(hikka)* occurred from 1869 to 1873, compared to fifty-one a year in the following decade.

26. Tamura Hisashi, "Fukuchi Ōchi," in *Sandai genronjin shū,* 3, p. 45.

27. Observation by Ōkuma Shigenobu, cited in Akita, p. 10.

28. See Oka Mitsuo, *Kindai Nihon shimbun koshi,* p. 10; also Sheldon Harsel, "Freedom, Responsibility, and the Intellectual in the Development of Japanese Mass Communication," pp. 142–143.

29. Yamamoto Fumio, ed., *Nihon masu komiyunikēshiyon shi,* p. 15. The Daigaku Nankō was a successor to the Kaiseijo and Kaisei Gakkō; it later became Tokyo Imperial University.

30. There has been dispute about the paper's initial date of publication since there are no extant copies of the first issues, but it appears to have been January 28, 1871 (December 8, 1870 under the old calendar); see Chikamori Haruyoshi, "*Yokohama Mainichi Shimbun* sōkan hi ronsō ni shūshifu," pp. 57–63. Some claim that *Shimbunshi* in 1864 was Japan's first daily, but it lived only two months. Some of the foreign papers in the treaty ports also were dailies. But *Yokohama Mainichi* was the first daily published on a sustained basis in Japanese. Initially called *Yokohama Shimbun,* it changed its name in May to *Yokohama Mainichi Shimbun.* The paper changed its name again in December 1879 to *Tōkyō-Yokohama Mainichi Shimbun,* and once again in April 1886 to *Tōkyō Mainichi Shimbun.* See Nihon Shimbun Renmei, ed., *Nihon shimbun hyakunen shi,* p. 713.

31. Kido Takayoshi letter, in Tsunoda et al., pp. 145–146.

32. Uchikawa and Arai, p. 4. A most helpful account of the paper's founding is in Sugiura, Tadashi, *Shimbun koto hajime,* pp. 138–143. Also see Yomiuri Shimbunsha, ed., Yomiuri Shimbun *hyakunijūnen shi,* p. 44.

33. See Ono Hideo, "Kido Takayoshi to shimbun," p. 3. Talk of the rumors is found in John R. Black, *Young Japan,* 2, pp. 309–310; they are confirmed also in Sidney D. Brown, "Kido Takayoshi and the Meiji Restoration: A Political Biography, 1833–1877," p. 17. A one-*ryō* gold coin was worth one yen, according to the government rate established in 1871.

34.   Recollection of Nishida Densuke, *Tōkyō Nichi Nichi Shimbun,* November 10, 1904, quoted in Imayoshi Ken'ichirō, "Jinmyaku yon'man gō shimbun koto hajime," *Mainichi Shimbun,* August 5, 1987. A six-mat room would be approximately nine feet by twelve feet.

35.   See Kanesada Hanazono, *Journalism in Japan and Its Early Pioneers,* p. 13.

36.   Fukuchi Gen'ichirō, *Shimbunshi jitsureki,* p. 328; also James L. Huffman, *Politics of the Meiji Press,* pp. 83–84.

37.   Fukuchi Gen'ichirō, "Ishin no genkun," *Taiyō,* 2, no. 4, p. 36.

38.   Black, 2, p. 364.

39.   See Black, 2, pp. 364–372; also Uchikawa and Arai, p. 5; Midoro, p. 20.

40.   Kishida Ginkō, "Shimbun jitsureki dan," in Tsurumi Shunsuke, ed., *Jiyānarizumu no shisō,* p. 66.

41.   Free postal delivery of newspaper manuscripts was extended to other newspapers July 1, 1873; see Sugiura, p. 213.

42.   See Chikamori Haruyoshi, *Jinbutsu Nihon shimbun shi,* p. 88; Albert Altman, "The Emergence of the Press in Meiji Japan," pp. 120–121; Uchikawa Yoshimi, *Shimbun shi wa,* p. 143.

43.   Nihon Shimbun Kyōkai, ed., *Chihōbetsu Nihon shimbun shi,* p. 257.

44.   Ibid., p. 204; see also Altman, " 'Shimbunshi,' " p. 64.

45.   Nihon Shimbun Kyōkai, ed., *Chihōbetsu: Nihon shimbun shi,* p. 174.

46.   Ibid., p. 413.

47.   Nishida, *Shimbun to zasshi,* p. 68.

48.   Ibid., p. 66.

49.   Ibid., p. 71.

50.   Uchikawa, *Shimbun shi wa,* pp. 27–28. Maejima also placed ads for the postal service in the newspapers, thus assisting both the papers and his new service; see D. Eleanor Westney, *Imitation and Innovation,* p. 154.

51.   Maejima recounted his role in the founding of the press in an 1899 *Taiyō* article, "Yūbin sōgyō dan," which is quoted extensively in Sugiura, pp. 211–213. Sugiura also discusses Maejima's role as a press founder, along with his memory lapses.

52.   Maejima, "Yūbin sōgyō dan"; Yamamoto Taketoshi, "Meiji shoki ni okeru shimbun no fukyū jokyō," p. 43; Huffman, p. 84.

53.   Sugiura, p. 213.

54.   Kuroda's proposal was to require that all publications *had* to use the national mail system except for local subscriptions; it failed after intense press opposition. See Uchikawa, *Shimbun shi wa*, pp. 28–30.

55.   See Nihon Shimbun Hanbai Kyōkai, ed., *Shimbun hanbai hyakunen shi*, p. 140. On January 28, 1873, responsibility for distribution was shifted to the Home Ministry, and on March 23 that ministry let prefectures begin choosing freely what papers to buy. The purchases of all but *Tōkyō Nichi Nichi Shimbun* ended on January 12, 1874. See also Yamamoto Taketoshi, "Meiji shoki," p. 42; Sasaki Takashi, "Meiji jidai no seijiteki komiyunikēshiyon," pt. 3, p. 110.

56.   The government purchases in 1872 made up 22.5 percent of the total *Tōkyō Nichi Nichi Shimbun* circulation, for example; see Yamamoto Taketoshi, "Meiji shoki," p. 42. Worth noting is that, beginning in October 1873, the government also purchased five hundred copies of each issue of the *Japan Mail* for distribution abroad; see James E. Hoare, "British Journalists in Meiji Japan," p. 25.

57.   Chikamori, *Jinbutsu Nihon shimbun shi*, p. 82.

58.   See *Kindai Nihon sōgō nenpyō*, p. 1872.

59.   Altman, " 'Shimbunshi,' " p. 269.

60.   Donald Read, *Press and People, 1790–1850: Opinion in Three English Cities*, pp. 201–202.

61.   The *Yamanashi Nichi Nichi* is the oldest provincial paper still in existence; see Haruhara Akihiko et al., eds., *Josei kisha*, p. 3.

62.   Translated in Albert Altman, "The Press and Social Cohesion during a Period of Change: The Case of Early Meiji Japan," p. 874; Altman suggests that attendance at such sessions was compulsory. See also Nihon Shimbun Renmei, ed., *Hyakunen shi*, p. 655.

63.   Quoted in Yamamoto Taketoshi, *Shimbun to minshū*, p. 46.

64.   Yamamoto Taketoshi, "Meiji shoki," p. 49; Nihon Shimbun Kyōkai, *Chihōbetsu*, p. 31. For a general treatment of these reading rooms see Hironiwa Motosuke, "Shimbun jūransho shōron," *Toshokan Kai*, 25, no. 3 (October 1973), pp. 84–100, and 25, no. 4 (December 1973), pp. 133–152.

65.   See, for example, Yamamoto Taketoshi, "Meiji shoki," p. 48; John Pierson, *Tokutomi Sohō, 1863–1957: A Journalist for Modern Japan*, p. 65; Irokawa Daikichi, "Freedom and the Concept of People's Rights," p. 194.

66.   Yamamoto Taketoshi, "Meiji shoki," p. 44; Altman, " 'Shimbunshi,' " pp. 60–61.

67.   "Native Press," *Japan Weekly Mail*, April 5, 1879.

68.   Nishida, *Shimbun to zasshi*, p. 176.

69. *Chōya Shimbun*, March 31, 1877, quoted in Chikamori, *Jinbutsu Nihon shimbun shi*, p. 84. A superb reproduction of several of the *nishikie shimbun* is found in Waseda Daigaku Toshokan, ed., *Bakumatsu Meiji no medeia ten*, pp. 41–54.

70. See Nihon Shimbun Hanbai Kyōkai, *Hanbai shi*, p. 135; Chikamori, *Jinbutsu Nihon shimbun shi*, p. 75.

71. Yamamoto Taketoshi, *Shimbun to minshū*, p. 49.

72. Irokawa, p. 194.

73. Yamamoto Taketoshi, *Shimbun to minshū*, p. 48.

74. *Tōkyō Nichi Nichi Shimbun*, February 28, 1876.

75. Black, 2, pp. 370–372.

76. Cited in Westney, p. 163.

77. Kawabe Kisaburō, *The Press and Politics in Japan*, pp. 47, 80; his figure for the latter date is 470. It should be noted that reports on the emperor's move to Tokyo did appear in Yokohama's English-language press.

78. They were, in order, *Yomiuri* (5,457,000), *Chōya Shimbun* (5,320,000), *Tōkyō Nichi Nichi Shimbun* (3,285,000), *Yūbin Hōchi Shimbun* (2,393,000), *Akebono Shimbun* (1,534,000), *Eiri Shimbun* (1,849,000), and *Kanayomi Shimbun* (1,561,000). Figures are for the period July 1, 1877, to June 30, 1877. Papers typically published about three hundred issues a year. See Nishida, *Shimbun to zasshi*, p. 58.

79. Altman, " 'Shimbunshi,' " p. 61.

80. See F. G. Notehelfer, *American Samurai*, p. 174; also Nihon Shimbun Kyōkai, *Chihōbetsu*, p. 468.

81. Nishida, p. 70.

82. *Yūbin Hōchi Shimbun*, October 22, 1878; see Haruhara Akihiko, *Nihon shimbun tsū shi*, p. 42.

83. Nihon Shimbun Kyōkai, *Chihōbetsu*, pp. 365–366.

84. See E. Lloyd Sommerlad, *The Press in Developing Countries*, pp. 54–55: urbanization is defined as the percentage of the population in cities of 50,000 or more.

85. Yamamoto Taketoshi, *Shimbun to minshū*, p. 10. For a discussion of the value *Tōkyō Nichi Nichi Shimbun* placed on the *goyō* label, see my *Politics of the Meiji Press*, pp. 92–95.

86. *Yūbin Hōchi Shimbun*, May 1873, cited in Uchikawa and Arai, p. 8. The sixteenth issue of *Yūbin Hōchi*, in the summer of 1872, called the press a "shortcut to increased knowledge."

87. Quote taken from *Nisshin Shinjishi*, no. 30, June 6, 1872 (May 1 on old calendar). The ad ran at the beginning of each day's issue.

88.　*Yomiuri Shimbun,* April 21, 1876; Yamamoto Fumio, *Nihon shimbun hattatsu shi,* pp. 8–9.

89.　From a company ad in the spring of 1879, quoted in Asahi Shimbunsha, ed., *Asahi Shimbunsha shi: Meiji hen,* p. 11. See also Albert Altman, "Proprietor *versus* Editor: The Case of the *Osaka Asahi Shimbun* in the Late Nineteenth Century," p. 244. Altman effectively discusses the "social utility" of early newspapers in the "The Press and Social Cohesion during a Period of Change: The Case of Early Meiji Japan," pp. 865–876.

90.　Carol Gluck, *Japan's Modern Myths: Ideology in the Late Meiji Period,* p. 9.

91.　Fukuchi Gen'ichirō, *Shimbunshi jitsureki,* p. 328.

92.　Early Meiji journalists who went on to become prime ministers included Inukai Tsuyoshi, Hara Kei, and Saionji Kinmochi. Later parliamentary leaders included Ozaki Yukio, Tanaka Shōzō, Hoshi Tōru, and Shimada Saburō. Numbered among the influential opinion leaders who were journalists: Fukuzawa Yukichi, Tokutomi Sohō, Kuga Katsunan, and Itō Miyōji. A late-Meiji journalist who became prime minister was Katō Takaaki (Kōmei).

93.　Ono Hideo, *Shimbun no rekishi,* p. 64.

94.　Uchikawa Yoshimi, "Shimbun ronsetsu no hensen," pp. 3–4.

95.　An exception to this rule was *Yokohama Mainichi Shimbun,* which gave its first page to shipping lists, ads related to shipping, and other trade-related items. The second and subsequent pages generally were like those of the other *ōshimbun.*

96.　Fukuchi Gen'ichirō, *Shimbunshi jitsureki,* p. 331. *Yūbin Hōchi Shimbun,* October 23, 1878, comments that even the despised *koshimbun* or vulgar papers were more accurate in their news columns than were the *ōshimbun,* because the prestige papers focused so heavily on editorials and paid little attention to the quality of news.

97.　Evaluation of Midoro Masaichi, in *Shundei shimbun wa,* quoted in Chikamori, *Jinbutsu Nihon shimbun shi,* pp. 125–126.

98.　Read, p. 89.

99.　Suehiro Tetchō, *Shimbun keirekidan,* p. 51.

100.　These statistics come from Kido Mataichi, ed., *Kōza gendai jiyānarizumu,* 1 *(Rekishi),* p. 33. A useful discussion of early management and structure is found in Yamamoto Fumio, *Nihon shimbun hattatsu shi,* pp. 126–135.

101.　Figures from Ukai Shin'ichi, *Chōya Shimbun no kenkyū,* p. 22.

102.　"Shimbun dokusha no hensen," *Chūō Kōron,* May 1900, cited in Yamamoto Taketoshi, "Shimbun sangyō no keisei katei," p. 122.

103.   *Chōya Shimbun,* September 7, 1877.

104.   *Tōkyō Nichi Nichi Shimbun,* February 16, 1875.

105.   Both cited in Yamamoto Fumio, *Nihon shimbun hattatsu shi,* p. 128.

106.   Black, 2, p. 449.

107.   See George Sansom, *The Western World and Japan,* pp. 385–386.

108.   *Tōkyō Nichi Nichi Shimbun,* December 9, 1872 (November 9 by the old calendar).

109.   A *sen* equaled .01 yen.

110.   *Yūbin Hōchi Shimbun,* no. 23 (October 1872), cited in Haruhara Akihiko, *Nihon shimbun tsū shi,* pp. 26–27.

111.   *Tōkyō Nichi Nichi Shimbun,* January 1, 1873 (December 3, 1872 on the old calendar). See Chikamori, *Jinbutsu Nihon shimbun shi,* p. 83.

112.   *Tōkyō Nichi Nichi Shimbun,* August 14, 1872 (July 11 by old calendar); Yamamoto Taketoshi, *Shimbun to minshū,* pp. 55–56.

113.   Cited by Altman, " 'Shimbunshi,' " p. 64.

114.   Correspondence column, *Yomiuri Shimbun,* August 7, 1876.

115.   Yamamoto Taketoshi, *Shimbun to minshū,* pp. 59–60.

116.   Ibid., p. 57.

117.   *Yūbin Hōchi,* May 1873; Yamamoto Taketoshi, *Shimbun to minshū,* p. 8.

CHAPTER 4. FINDING ITS OWN VOICE, 1874 TO 1881

1.   Editorial, *Chōya Shimbun,* August 15, 1875; cited in Ono Hideo, *Shimbun no rekishi,* pp. 29–30.

2.   See Zen Nihon Shimbun Renmei, ed., *Shimbun taikan,* 1, p. 75.

3.   See Joyce Lebra, *Ōkuma Shigenobu: Statesman of Meiji Japan,* p. 23. A full account is given in Bernard D. Quinlan, "Inoue Kaoru and the Formation of Economic Policy in Early Meiji Japan," pp. 130–152. An earlier dispute over funding of the military, carried out wholly behind closed government doors, is described in Kyugoro Obata, *An Interpretation of the Life of Viscount Shibusawa,* pp. 75–79.

4. See Peter Figdor, "Newspapers and Their Regulation in Early Meiji Japan, 1868–1883," p. 11.

5. See *Tōkyō Nichi Nichi Shimbun,* May 23, 1873, for example, cited in Takeichi Hideo, *Nichibei shimbun shi wa,* p. 81. Also see Lebra, p. 156, n. 25; Uchikawa Yoshimi, "Shimbun no jiyū no rekishi," p. 52.

6. Yamamoto Fumio, *Nihon shimbun hattatsu shi,* pp. 60–61.

7. For useful accounts of the Korean Crisis, see Roger Hackett, *Yamagata Aritomo in the Rise of Modern Japan, 1838–1922,* pp. 67–76; Hilary Conroy, *The Japanese Seizure of Korea,* pp. 35–55; Marlene Mayo, "The Korean Crisis of 1873 and Early Meiji Foreign Policy," pp. 793–820; Nobutaka Ike, "The Triumph of the Peace Party in Japan in 1873," pp. 286–295.

8. Stephen Koss, *The Rise and Fall of the Political Press in Britain,* 1, p. 4.

9. Midoro Masaichi, ed., *Meiji Taishō shi: Genron hen,* p. 31.

10. Nishida Taketoshi, *Meiji jidai no shimbun to zasshi,* p. 41.

11. The phrase is used in Albert A. Altman, "The Press and Social Cohesion during a Period of Change: The Case of Early Meiji Japan," p. 874.

12. See Nihon Shimbun Hanbai Kyōkai, ed., *Shimbun hanbai hyakunen shi,* p. 140; Figdor, p. 12.

13. Uchikawa Yoshimi and Arai Naoyuki, eds., *Nihon no jiyānarizumu,* p. 9. Also see J. E. Hoare, "The 'Bankoku Shimbun' Affair," p. 293.

14. A fascinating paradox (though hardly a contradiction) lies in the fact that at this very time, on October 13, 1873, the government decided to begin purchasing five hundred copies of the *Japan Mail* to send abroad to publicize Japanese affairs in Europe and America. See *Kindai Nihon sōgō nenpyō,* p. 56.

15. The paper had begun in December 1872 as *Kōbun Tsūshi* and changed its name to *Chōya Shimbun* in September 1874; for its political chronology, see Sasaki Takashi, "Meiji jidai no seijiteki komiyunikēshiyon," pt. 3 (1986), p. 111.

16. Oka Yoshitake, *Five Political Leaders of Modern Japan,* p. 127; see also Nishida, pp. 41–42. Kurimoto entered *Yūbin Hōchi* in June 1873.

17. See Kawabe Shinzō, *Fukuchi Ōchi,* p. 5; Tokutomi Sohō, in Kubota Tatsuhiko, ed., *Nijūichi dai senkaku kisha den,* p. 66.

18. Most scholars see *Meiroku Zasshi,* begun early in 1874, as the first publication to initiate regular, public political discussions. While that journal is not discussed in detail here, since it was a journal intended primarily for intellectual insiders rather than a newspaper, its influence on the daily newspaper press was significant. Indeed, many Meirokusha members wrote essays for the newspapers. See William Braisted, trans., *Meiroku Zasshi: Journal of the Japanese Enlightenment.*

19.   Translated in Ryusaku Tsunoda et al., eds., *Sources of Japanese Tradition*, 2, pp. 176–178. It also is included, among other places, in Midoro, *Meiji Taishō shi*, pp. 33–38. W. W. McLaren, ed., *Japanese Government Documents*, pp. 432–484, includes a number of memorials related to the popular assembly debate.

20.   Yamamoto Taketoshi, *Shimbun to minshū*, p. 16; also see Yamamoto Fumio, *Nihon shimbun hattatsu shi*, p. 65. *Nisshin Shinjishi* published the memorial on January 18, 1864, the day after it was issued.

21.   *Akebono Shimbun* joined *Chōya* and *Yūbin Hōchi* at the forefront of the *kyūshinshugi* (radical) camp at the beginning of 1875, when *Shimbun Zasshi*, which had been founded with Kido's assistance, cut off its ties to the government and chose the new name *Akebono*. It changed its name again, to *Tōkyō Akebono Shimbun*, on June 2, 1875. See Zen Nihon Shimbun Renmei, *Shimbun taikan*, 1, p. 80.

22.   *Tōkyō Nichi Nichi Shimbun*, February 5, 1874; Ōi's essay appeared before *Nichi Nichi* had developed its consistent, progovernment stance.

23.   Katō's response ran in *Tōkyō Nichi Nichi Shimbun*, February 25, 1874. Ōi's rebuttal to Katō is quoted in Okano Takeo, *Meiji genron shi*, p. 27.

24.   *Minkan Zasshi*, January 1875, cited in Okano, pp. 194–196.

25.   *Nisshin Shinjishi*, no. 232; Okano, pp. 24–25.

26.   *Shimbun Zasshi*, February 6, 1874; the essay also ran in *Tōkyō Nichi Nichi Shimbun*, February 2, 1874. A discussion of the *Nichi Nichi* position is found in Sugiura Tadashi, *Shimbun koto hajime*, pp. 242–252. See also Okano, pp. 23–24.

27.   *Tōkyō Nichi Nichi Shimbun*, December 6, 1874.

28.   Ibid., March 23, 1875.

29.   Ibid., March 25, 1875.

30.   Ibid., March 27, 1874.

31.   The decree, issued on April 12, 1875, accomplished little in moving Japan toward genuine popular involvement in affairs of state, but succeeded in quieting the press. It is discussed in George Akita, *Foundations of Constitutional Government in Modern Japan*, pp. 21–24; see also Robert Scalapino, *Democracy and the Party Movement in Prewar Japan*, p. 60.

32.   Quoted in Ono Hideo, *Shimbun no rekishi*, p. 31.

33.   *Nisshin Shinjishi*, no. 232. Cited in Okano, pp. 24–25; discussed at length in Midoro, *Meiji Taishō shi*, pp. 49–52.

34.   For examples of this extremist writing, see Nishida, pp. 92–94.

35.   *Sōmō Zasshi*, June 1, 1876, quoted in Midoro, pp. 66–67.

36. Midoro, pp. 384–385.

37. See Okudaira Yasuhiro, "Nihon shuppan keisatsu hōsei no reki-shiteki kenkyū josetsu," *Hōritsu Johō*, 3, p. 42. The Naimushō, or Home Ministry, which had been created the previous November to maintain public order, took control of the Police Bureau in 1874 and of press control in 1875. See Lawrence W. Beer, *Freedom of Expression in Japan*, p. 49.

38. The law is reprinted, among other places, in *Dajōkan Nisshi*, June 28, 1875, excerpted in Uchikawa Yoshimi and Matsushima Eiichi, eds., *Meiji niyūsu jiten* (hereafter, MNJ), 1, pp. 195–196; Midoro, pp. 385–389; McLaren, pp. 539–543; Nishida, *Meiji jidai no shimbun to zasshi*, pp. 87–91; and Centre for East Asian Cultural Studies, ed., *The Meiji Japan through Contemporary Sources: Basic Documents, 1854–1889*, 3, pp. 30–37. A subsequent law, the *shuppan jōrei* (publication law), was issued on September 3, 1875, dealing primarily with other types of publications; it is reproduced in Midoro, pp. 389–394. An analysis of the law and its impact is found in my article "Japan's First Newspaper Law: The Emergence of an Independent Meiji Press."

39. Many think that Ōkubo Toshimichi also had a hand in the preparation of the law. Yamamoto Fumio, for example, suggests that Ōkubo encouraged a new law after seeing the freedom with which European papers printed officials' private materials and deciding Japan must avoid that; see *Nihon shimbun hattatsu shi*, pp. 75–76. The officials also likely drew on a memorandum submitted to them in 1872 by the missionary Guido F. Verbeck; see Albert Altman, "A Recently Discovered Document on Early Meiji Press Censorship Legislation." Midoro suggests that a group called the Kyōson Dōshū, made up of individuals such as Ono Azusa, Matsudaira Nobumasa, and Iwasaki Kojiro, who had studied in London, helped prompt the libel regulations with a memorial discussing the "serious penalties" the British levied against people who "stained the honor of individuals or groups" (pp. 42–43).

40. Article 8, McLaren, p. 541. The following quotations from the law come from the McLaren translation.

41. Ono, *Shimbun no rekishi*, p. 27.

42. Midoro, p. 43.

43. Suehiro Tetchō, *Shimbun keirekidan*, p. 52.

44. Numerous petitions had been sent to the Sa'in, urging that press freedoms be maintained, and many of these were reprinted in the newspapers. See McLaren, pp. 535–536, for examples; also *Tōkyō Nichi Nichi Shimbun*, June 9, 1875.

45. See figures in Oka Mitsuo, *Kindai Nihon shimbun koshi*, p. 28. He notes that the monthly salary of a police officer then was between six and ten yen a month. Also see Nihon Shimbun Kyōkai, ed., *Chihōbetsu: Nihon shimbun shi*, p. 175.

46. *Yūbin Hōchi Shimbun,* August 30, 1875, reproduced MNJ, 1, p. 196.

47. *Tōkyō Nichi Nichi Shimbun,* September 3, 1875; Yamamoto Taketoshi, *Shimbun to minshū,* p. 12.

48. One of the best discussions of the Meirokusha debate over closing down the journal is in Braisted, pp. xli–xliii. Also see Ivan Hall, *Mori Arinori,* pp. 244–245; Kōsaka Masaaki, ed., *Japanese Thought in the Meiji Era,* pp. 128–129. Fukuzawa Yukichi's rationale, cited here, was spelled out in an editorial he had published in *Yūbin Hōchi Shimbun,* September 4, 1875, reprinted in MNJ, 1, p. 708.

49. *Hyōron Shimbun,* no. 16, reprinted in Miyatake Gaikotsu, "Meiji hikka shi shiryō," no. 2, in Meiji Bunka Kenkyūkai, ed., *Zasshi: Meiji Bunka Kenkyū,* 1, p. 21.

50. Suehiro, *Shimbun kei rekidan,* p. 52.

51. Accounts are found in Suehiro, p. 52; Ono, *Shimbun no rekishi,* p. 28; Chikamori Haruyoshi, *Jinbutsu Nihon shimbun shi,* p. 99.

52. Quoted in Sugiura Tadashi, *Shimbun koto hajime,* p. 292.

53. Reported in *Tōkyō Akebono Shimbun,* August 8, 1875; MNJ, 1, p. 196. See also Nihon Shimbun Renmei, ed., *Nihon shimbun hyakunen shi,* p. 714.

54. The editorial, which ran in *Chōya Shimbun* on December 20, 1875, is reprinted in Maeda Ai, *Narushima Ryūhoku,* p. 238. See also Chikamori, p. 103, and Haga Eizō, *Meiji Taishō hikka shi,* pp. 30–31.

55. *Chōya Shimbun,* August 9, 1875; Chikamori, p. 101.

56. *Chōya Shimbun,* August 15, 1875; see Ono, *Shimbun no rekishi,* pp. 29–30.

57. *Tōkyō Nichi Nichi Shimbun,* July 24, 1875; quoted in Ono Hideo, *Nihon shimbun hattatsu shi,* pp. 75–76.

58. The incident is discussed in Miyatake, no. 4, pp. 31–35. Hasegawa was given a sentence of one month under house arrest and a two-hundred-yen fine. Fujita Mokichi of *Yūbin Hōchi* also received a one-month, two-hundred-yen fine for a similar article about Mishima, who was to become one of the popular rights forces' most hated officials in the 1870s and 1880s, a man known for harsh crackdowns on popular movements.

59. See Nihon Shimbun Renmei, *Hyakunen shi,* p. 715; Haga, p. 30.

60. Suehiro Yasuo, "Suehiro Tetchō," in *Sandai genronjin shū,* 4, p. 137; Chikamori, p. 102.

61. J. R. Black, *Young Japan,* 2, p. 448.

62. Kageyama Saburō, *Dokusha no genron,* pp. 106–109.

63.   One example had been Black's ability to publish news about the Chihōkan Kaigi in June 1875 while the other Japanese-language papers were prevented by authorities from doing so. See Sugiura, p. 176.

64.   Black attempted to start another paper, *Bankoku Shimbun*, on January 6, 1876, but it was shut down within a week. The episode is described in Hoare, "Bankoku Shimbun," pp. 289–302. See also Hazel Jones, *Live Machines: Hired Foreigners and Meiji Japan*, p. 121; Nishida, *Meiji jidai no shimbun to zasshi*, p. 92; Haga, pp. 28–29. Black sought British ambassador Harry Parkes' assistance in securing the right to publish *Bankoku*, but on February 7, 1876, Parkes forbade British subjects from publishing newspapers in Japanese; see Hoare, "British Journalists in Meiji Japan," p. 31. Also see Asaoka Kunio, "*Nisshin Shinjishi* no henshitsu to seifu no shimbun seisaku," pp. 1–16.

65.   See Maeda, *Narushima*, pp. 236–237.

66.   Narushima Ryūhoku, "Gokuchū shirushi," *Chōya Shimbun*, June 13, 1876, reprinted in MNJ, 1, pp. 537–538; also in the same volume, p. 197, see *Hyōron Shimbun*, September 1875. Overall figures are provided by Nishida, p. 92. Similar lists are found in Okano, pp. 226–227; Midoro, *Meiji Taishō shi*, p. 57; and Chiba, p. 54.

67.   A helpful account of his newspaper career is Tomizuka Hideki, "Komatsubara Eitarō to Miyazaki Hachirō *Hyōron Shimbun* de katsuyaku shita futari no minken ka."

68.   These editorials, all from early 1876, are found in issues 62, 78, and 91 of *Hyōron Shimbun*, reprinted in Midoro, pp. 58–59. Other editorials called for a stronger foreign policy (no. 91) and argued that a mean-spirited government likely would self-destruct (no. 97). See also Okano, pp. 32–33.

69.   Midoro, p. 57. For a list of prominent journalists jailed in 1876–1877, see Yamamoto Taketoshi, *Shimbun kisha no tanjō*, pp. 109–110.

70.   *Hyōron Shimbun*, no. 109, July 5, 1876; Midoro, p. 59. Also see pp. 60–64. For discussions of the new Dajōkan regulation regarding suspension of papers, see Okudaira, part 6, p. 56, and Figdor, pp. 18–19.

71.   Quoted in Chikamori, *Jinbutsu Nihon shimbun shi*, p. 100. See also *Akebono*, August 8, 1875; MNJ, 1, p. 196.

72.   Suehiro Tetchō, *Shimbun keirekidan*, pp. 58–59; also Yoshio Iwamoto, "Suehiro Tetchō: A Meiji Political Novelist," p. 87.

73.   Narushima Ryūhoku, *Gokunai banashi*, quoted in Midoro, pp. 56–57. He lists twenty-eight journalists who shared the jail at one time or another. Related material also is found in *Chōya Shimbun*, June 15, 1876; MNJ, 1, p. 538; in Maeda, pp. 242–243, and in Thomas M. Huber, "Numa Morikazu and the Intelligentsia Origins of Japanese Democracy" (unpublished paper presented at American Historical Association, December 28, 1982).

74. His talk, "Matsuri shimbunshi bun," is printed in Midoro, pp. 82–83, and Nihon Shimbun Renmei, *Hyakunen shi*, p. 235, and excerpted in Kageyama, pp. 113–114; my translation relies in part on Jay Rubin, *Injurious to Public Morals: Writers and the Meiji State*, p. 36. The service is described in *Chōya Shimbun*, June 24, 1876.

75. Irokawa Daikichi, *The Culture of the Meiji Period*, p. 119; see especially pp. 185–194 for a discussion of "people's conventional morality."

76. Lawrence Ward Beer, *Freedom of Expression in Japan*, p. 45.

77. Iwamoto, p. 88.

78. Narushima Ryūhoku editorial, reprinted in *Tokio Times*, May 12, 1877, pp. 226–227.

79. See Irwin Scheiner, *Christian Converts and Social Protest in Meiji Japan*, p. 206.

80. Black, 2, pp. 449–450. Similarly, George Sansom wrote: "It was samurai of a nonconforming type who were unwilling to serve the clan coalition and gravitated towards journalism as a means of protest, with the result that almost every newspaper was hostile to, or at least critical of, the government. These circumstances gave a special character to the Japanese press." *The Western World and Japan*, pp. 424–425.

81. Quoted in Kawabe Kisaburō, *The Press and Politics in Japan*, pp. 81–82.

82. See George Boyce et al., eds., *Newspaper History: From the Seventeenth Century to the Present Day*, p. 120.

83. See, for example, Michael Emery and Edwin Emery, *The Press and America*, pp. 131, 141.

84. Ukai Shin'ichi, *Chōya Shimbun no kenkyū*, p. 11. Ukai has pulled together fifty-eight pages (pp. 3–60) of wonderfully helpful statistics on the Meiji press, based on a variety of newspaper and government documents.

85. See D. Eleanor Westney, *Imitation and Innovation*, pp. 168–169; Yamamoto Taketoshi, *Shimbun kisha no tanjō*, p. 125. In contrast, already by the 1850s the better British papers had as many as sixteen reporters covering Parliament alone, a number covering the courts and foreign correspondents throughout Europe; see Boyce et al., p. 109.

86. Ukai, p. 11.

87. Westney, pp. 169–70; Ukai, pp. 11–13; James L. Huffman *Politics of the Meiji Press*, p. 84.

88. Katakozawa Chiyomatsu, "Shimada Saburō," p. 258.

89. For tests, see Albert Altman, "Proprietor *versus* Editor: The Case of the *Osaka Asahi Shimbun* in the Late Nineteenth Century," p. 252; for other employees, Westney, pp. 170–172.

90.   Kawabe Shinzō, p. 156.

91.   Yomiuri Shimbunsha, ed., *Yomiuri Shimbun hyakunijūnen shi*, p. 52.

92.   For "ambitious person," see Kido Mataichi et al., eds., *Kōza gendai jiyānarizumu, 1 (Rekishi)*, p. 33. For "profit," see Yamamoto Fumio, *Nihon Shimbun hattatsu shi*, pp. 126–135; detailed description of costs and profits, on p. 130.

93.   Ukai, pp. 12–13.

94.   Edward S. Morse, *Japan Day by Day*, 2, pp. 112–114.

95.   Ukai, pp. 12–13. *Nichi Nichi* and *Akebono* secured their first steam presses in 1881, the other *ōshimbun* not until later. In 1880, *Chōya* had two hand-operated presses; *Nichi Nichi*, eight; *Akebono*, three; and *Yūbin Hōchi* seven. The commercially oriented *koshimbun Yomiuri*, by contrast, secured its first steam press in 1878 and had twelve hand presses in 1880.

96.   See Ukai, pp. 22–23, 32–33, for detailed circulation charts. Another exception was *Chōya*, which reported an average daily circulation of 17,732 in 1876, perhaps due to Narushima's popularity when he went to jail, but then declined to the 7,000 to 9,000 range thereafter.

97.   *Japan Weekly Mail*, April 5, 1879, p. 419.

98.   Ibid., p. 418.

99.   Ukai, p. 35.

100.   *Japan Weekly Mail*, April 5, 1879, p. 419.

101.   Morse, 1, p. 380, describing the situation in 1878.

102.   The material in this paragraph comes largely form Yamamoto Taketoshi, "Meiji shoki ni okeru shimbun no fukyū jōkyō," pp. 44–47. The first contract by an Osaka shop to sell *Nichi Nichi* came in April 1872. Also see Nihon Shimbun Hanbai Kyōkai, p. 140.

103.   See Yamamoto Taketoshi, "Meiji shoki," pp. 54–55. Kawabe Kisaburō says 225 is the correct figure (p. 47); The *Japan Weekly Mail*, April 5, 1879, suggests that at least one hundred newspapers were being published; Nishida lists the specific names of seventy-seven regional papers publishing in the late 1870s (*Meiji jidai no shimbun to zasshi*, pp. 71–76), a figure that when added to the major urban papers would yield over one hundred.

104.   See Nishida, pp. 72–76; also Nihon Shimbun Hanbai Kyōkai, pp. 143–160, and Nihon Shimbun Kyōkai, *Chihōbetsu*.

105.   Useful descriptions of these magazines are found in Nishida, pp. 33–36, 133–141.

106.   Other *kana*-only papers included Joseph Heco's *Kanagaku Shimbun* (1873) and the *Tōkyō Hiragana Eiri Shimbun*, published in 1875.

Most such efforts had little success, at least partly because of the difficulty of reading in *kana* that has no breaks between words. See Ono, *Shimbun no rekishi*, p. 32; Nishida, pp. 54–56; Kanesada Hanazono, *The Development of Japanese Journalism*, pp. 39–40.

107.   Koyasu was assisted by Motono Morimichi and Shibata Masayoshi, his partners in a firm that published English-Japanese dictionaries.

108.   D. Eleanor Westney argues that *Yomiuri* really was not a *koshimbun* because, among other things, it did not initially run serialized novels and it paid more attention to politics than most *koshimbun* did. However, it adhered to most characteristics generally ascribed to the "small papers" and was generally included in that category.

109.   *Yomiuri Shimbun*, November 2, 1874; translations thanks to Albert Altman, " 'Shimbunshi,' " pp. 245–246.

110.   Yomiuri Shimbunsha, ed., *Yomiuri Shimbun hyakunijūnen shi*, pp. 46, 50.

111.   Ibid., p. 53. The Sakurada fire prompted Japan's first extra *(gogai)*, the November 30, 1875, issue of *Yomiuri*. See Nihon Shimbun Renmei, *Hyakunen shi*, p. 715.

112.   Japan's first serialized novel was begun at *Tōkyō Eiri Shimbun* in November 1875; Nihon Shimbun Renmei, p. 715. *Yomiuri* was the exception among *koshimbun*, not running novels in its early years.

113.   Ono Hideo, *Nihon shimbun hattatsu shi*, pp. 109–110. Other, similar, summaries are found in Nakanowatari Nobuyuki, ed., *Masukomi kindai shi*, pp. 136–139; Nishida, *Meiji jidai no shimbun to zasshi*, pp. 57–58; Chikamori, *Jinbutsu Nihon shimbun shi*, pp. 108–117.

114.   Ukai, pp. 22–23; see also Nishida, pp. 58, 112.

115.   In 1878, for example, *Yomiuri* had net profits of 4,612 yen, compared to 4,550 for *Chōya Shimbun* and 3,609 for *Akebono*. In 1881, it had 4,700 yen profits, *Tōkyō Eiri* had 5,590, *Chōya* had 6,055, and *Yūbin Hōchi* had a mere 3,000. See Ukai, pp. 14–15.

116.   For a colorful account of Tsuda's angry leave taking, see Iwai Hajime, *Shimbun to shimbunjin*, pp. 62–63.

117.   The story of *Asahi*'s first two years is told in Albert Altman, "Proprietor *versus* Editor," pp. 241–253.

118.   Discussed in Julia Meech-Pekarik, *The World of the Meiji Print*, pp. 179–199.

119.   For the first *ōshimbun* coverage of a murder, see *Akebono*, August 9, 1877; Nihon Fūzoku Shi Gakkai, ed., *Genron to masukomi*, p. 100.

120.   Japan sent troops to Taiwan that year to "avenge" the 1871 massacre of fifty-four shipwrecked Ryūkyūans by Taiwanese and thereby to assert Japan's own sovereignty over the Ryūkyū islands. The press' cov-

erage of the Taiwan episode is analyzed in Zen Nihon Shimbun Renmei, *Shimbun taikan*, 3, pp. 315–332; see also Haruhara, pp. 30–31; Nihon Shimbun Renmei, *Hyakunen shi*, pp. 714, 825.

121. Midoro, *Meiji Taishō shi*, pp. 90, 91.

122. Miyatake, "Meiji hikka shi shiryō," no. 7, pp. 22–23. The *Kōmin Shinshi* editor, Yamawaki, had spent a year in jail earlier for his writings at *Hyōron Shimbun*.

123. A *Chōya Shimbun* editorial, reprinted in the *Tokio Times* of May 12, 1877, haughtily dismissed the other papers' writers as "flatterers of government officials" (p. 227). The refusal to cooperate with the authorities led to several inaccurate reports and helped cause a circulation decline, from 17,732 a day in 1876 to 7,067 in 1877. See Ukai, pp. 21–23; also Nishida, *Meiji jidai no shimbun to zasshi*, p. 42; Midoro, p. 91; Yamamoto Fumio, *Hattatsu shi*, p. 93.

124. "Press Censorship Here and Elsewhere," *Akebono Shimbun*, reprinted in translation in *Tokio Times*, February 24, 1877, p. 96.

125. *Tokio Times*, March 3, 1877, p. 99.

126. *Yomiuri Shimbun*, March 15, 1877; Yomiuri Shimbunsha, p. 51.

127. *Tōkyō Nichi Nichi Shimbun*, April 12, 1877.

128. Cited in Oka Yoshitake, *Five Political Leaders of Modern Japan*, p. 128. Oka describes Inukai's prose as "concise, quick and penetrating" (p. 130).

129. They are listed in Yamamoto Fumio, *Hattatsu shi*, pp. 89–90.

130. *Tōkyō Nichi Nichi Shimbun*, March 23, 1877.

131. Fukuzawa Yukichi, *Fukuzawa Yukichi zenshū*, 6, pp. 479–480; Yamamoto Fumio, *Hattatsu shi*, pp. 88–89.

132. Yamamoto Fumio, *Hattatsu shi*, p. 88. The Osaka press also grew significantly in circulation during the war; see Iwai Hajime, *Shimbun to shimbunjin*, p. 66.

133. See *Tōkyō Nichi Nichi Shimbun*, December 26, 1877, as well as July 1874, April 1875; Richard Mitchell, *Janus-Faced Justice*, p. 6.

134. Nishida Taketoshi has painstakingly compiled a complete list of all of *Tōkyō Nichi Nichi Shimbun*'s daily editorials from 1874 to 1887, many of them with brief annotations. The years 1874 through 1877 are published in his "Meiji shoki shimbun ronsetsu sakuin," *Meiji Bunka Kenkyū*, nos. 3, 5, 6 (October–December, 1934), pp. 182–192, 251–260 and 180–189, respectively. Later years are included in unpublished manuscripts graciously made available to me by Professor Nishida.

135. *Minken* advocate Ueki Emori, for example, noted in his diary four letters about political issues that he wrote to newspapers in November

1876 alone; he was twenty at the time; see Yamamoto Taketoshi, *Shimbun no kisha tanjō*, pp. 112–113.

136.   For a description of the incident, see Masakazu Iwata, *Ōkubo Toshimichi: The Bismarck of Japan*, p. 253.

137.   See Miyatake, "Meiji hikka shi shiryō," no. 3, p. 19.

138.   *Chōya Shimbun*, May 15, 1878; reprinted in Haga, p. 43.

139.   Cited in Chikamori, *Jinbutsu Nihon shimbun shi*, pp. 144–145.

140.   Fukuzawa reportedly responded, on hearing that Katō had complied, that it was unacceptable for a journalist to give that kind of promise, noting in a style reminiscent of his call for closing down *Meiroku Zasshi* following the 1875 press law: "You might as well close the paper." Ibid., p. 145.

141.   Haga, p. 43.

142.   Kuga was released in 1889 under the general amnesty granted on the promulgation of the Meiji Constitution.

143.   See Nihon Shimbun Renmei, *Hyakunen shi*, pp. 719–720; also Sidney Brown, "Political Assassination in Early Meiji Japan: The Plot Against Ōkubo Toshimichi," p. 31.

144.   Quoted from Itagaki's speech, "On Liberty," in Robert A. Scalapino, *Democracy and the Party Movement in Prewar Japan*, p. 56. Helpful discussions of the general nature of the *jiyū minken* movement are found in Roger Bowen, *Rebellion and Democracy in Meiji Japan*, pp. 107–115, and Nobutaka Ike, *The Beginnings of Political Democracy in Japan*, pp. 60–71.

145.   *Tōkyō Nichi Nichi Shimbun*, July 28, 1876. Similar evaluations are found in Maruyama Masao, "Meiji kokka no shisō," in *Nihon shakai no shiteki kyūmei*, comp. Rekishigaku Kenkyūkai (Tokyo, 1949), p. 200; Akita, *Foundations*, p. 23; Bowen, *Rebellion and Democracy in Meiji Japan*, pp. 109–111.

146.   See Nishida, *Meiji jidai no shimbun to zasshi*, p. 96, for a list of these groups, particularly those with some connection to journalists. Bowen argues that the movement was a "Kantō-centered and commoner-led affair" (p. 115), but Irokawa argues that while Kantō communities were important in movement leadership, so were those from such rural areas as Nagano, Toyama, Okayama, Shimane, and Kumamoto (*Culture of the Meiji Period*, pp. 201–203). Irokawa is supported forcefully by Monna Naoki, *Minshū jiyānarizumu no rekishi*, pp. 30–39.

147.   Irokawa, p. 107. Irokawa and others note that the foundations for political activism were laid in the peasant movements of the Tokugawa era, which, while localized, provided a tradition of local efforts to change higher-level official policies. See, for example, Stephen Vlastos, *Peasant Protests and Uprisings in Tokugawa Japan*; Herbert Bix, *Peasant Protest in Japan, 1590–1884.*

148.   Quoted in Okano, p. 54. A list of such organizations is found in Nishida, p. 96.

149.   Irokawa, pp. 103–105. The teacher, Chiba Takasaburō from Nishitama, actually rewrote them all, shifting power in each case from the ruler to the people.

150.   Sandra T. W. Davis, "Ono Azusa and the Political Change of 1881," p. 140.

151.   Irokawa, p. 106; for an account of a similar petition with over 80,000 signatures, see Yanagida Izumi, *Fukuchi Ōchi shū*, p. 352.

152.   Irokawa, p. 196.

153.   *Tōkyō Nichi Nichi Shimbun*, January 2, 1881.

154.   *Yokohama Mainichi* was purchased by Numa Morikazu and moved to Tokyo in 1879, where its name was changed to *Tōkyō-Yokohama Mainichi Shimbun*.

155.   *Tōkyō-Yokohama Mainichi Shimbun*, April 20, 1880; Irokawa, pp. 95–96.

156.   *Yūbin Hōchi Shimbun*, September 14, 1877; Yamamoto Take-toshi, *Shimbun to minshū*, p. 59.

157.   Fukuzawa Yukichi, *Fukuo jiden*, 7, pp. 602–603, trans. in Carmen Blacker, *The Japanese Enlightenment*, p. 117.

158.   Anthony Smith, *The Newspaper: An International History*, p. 74.

159.   Quoted in Okano, p. 72.

160.   Michael Lewis has described the Sōeki Sha (Mutual Benefit Society), created by the *Tōkyō Nichi Nichi Shimbun* reporter Umiuchi Hatasu and supported by Inagaki Shimesu in Toyama Prefecture on the Japan Sea; see his "Interest and Ideology in Meiji Politics: Inagaki Shimesu and the Toyama Jiyūtō," p. 87.

161.   Nishida, *Meiji jidai no shimbun to zasshi*, p. 143. For detailed analysis of the press' role in the discussions of *minken* and constitutional issues in this period, see Otsu Jun'ichirō, *Dainihon kensei shi*, 2, pp. 236–265.

162.   See Zen Nihon Shimbun Renmei, *Shimbun taikan*, 1, p. 104; Nishida Taketoshi, "Meiji jūichinen—dō jūyonnen no shimbunkai," p. 373.

163.   Nishida, *Meiji jidai no shimbun to zasshi*, pp. 69–70. Much of the material discussed here is found in ibid., pp. 69–74.

164.   *Hyōron Shimbun*, January 15, 1876; Okano, p. 32.

165.   *Kōkai Shinpō*, March 1876, quoted in Miyatake, "Meiji hikka shi shiryō," no. 7, p. 21.

166.   For civilization and strength, see "Jiyū o ronzu," *Shinano Mainichi Shimbun,* September 2, 1880; Monna Naoki, *Minshū jiyānarizumu no rekishi,* p. 35. For Narushima, *Chōya Shimbun,* July 5, 1877; Inui Teruo, "Meiji jūnendai ni okeru Narushima Ryūhoku no genron katsudō ni tsuite," p. 125; emphasis in original.

167.   Irokawa, *Culture of the Meiji Period,* p. 197.

168.   *Tōkyō Nichi Nichi Shimbun,* July 28, 1876; Yamamoto Taketoshi, *Shimbun to minshū,* pp. 5–6.

169.   In Uchikawa and Arai, eds., *Nihon no jiyānarizumu,* p. 16.

170.   *Tōyō Jiyū Shimbun,* March 18, 1881.

171.   Lengthy excerpts from key articles are found in Okano, pp. 62–71.

172.   *Tōyō Jiyū Shimbun,* April 27, 1881; Okano, pp. 69–71.

173.   *Tōyō Jiyū Shimbun,* April 9, 1881.

174.   The appeal was printed verbatim by *Kōchi* (April 21, 1881) and *Ōsaka Nippō* (April 19), and was summarized by *Yūbin Hōchi Shimbun* (April 15); see Tomizuka Hideki, "Saionji Kinmochi to Matsuzawa Kyūsaku: *Tōyō Jiyū Shimbun* shachō jinin mondai o meguru ikkōsatsu," pp. 1–2.

175.   Saionji Kinmochi, *Saionji Kinmochi jiden* (Tokyo, 1949), p. 203, cited in Oka Yoshitake, p. 181. See also Tetsuo Najita, *Hara Kei and the Politics of Compromise,* p. 19. Other useful accounts of the Saionji affair are found in Midoro, *Meiji Taishō shi,* pp. 98–99; Yamamoto Fumio, *Hattatsu shi,* p. 107; Nishida, *Shimbun to zasshi,* pp. 49–50.

176.   Edward H. House, "Ancient and Modern Periodical Literature of Japan," *The Tokio Times,* May 26, 1877, p. 245.

177.   See Smith, *The Newspaper,* pp. 105–120, especially p. 112.

178.   George Akita argues this point forcefully in "Government and Opposition in Prewar Japan: A Political Success or Embarrassment?"

179.   See Yamamoto Taketoshi, *Shimbun kisha no tanjō,* pp. 304–306; discussed more fully below in Chapter 10.

180.   Translation in *Tokio Times,* February 24, 1877.

181.   Dajōkan Decree No. 98, July 5, 1876; Midoro lists fourteen Dajōkan and Naimushō orders dealing with the press during 1876 on pp. 395–397. The July 5 decree sparked the combative *Hyōron Shimbun* editorial that resulted in the death of that paper.

182.   See Haruhara, p. 43.

183.   Saitō Shōzō, *Meiji Taishō hikka dainenpyō,* pp. 1–12. *Hikka* is an imprecise term used by press historians to indicate some kind of punishment for written materials; it can refer to the punishment of either individuals or press companies.

184. Okano, p. 230; Nishida, *Shimbun to zasshi*, p. 95. For other figures, see Yamamoto Fumio, *Hattatsu shi*, p. 74; Midoro, pp. 73–77; Richard Mitchell, *Censorship in Imperial Japan*, p. 92; Uchikawa and Arai, eds., *Nihon no jiyānarizumu*, p. 12.

185. See Yamamoto Taketoshi, *Shimbun to minshū*, pp. 18–19.

186. December 29, 1876; see Miyatake, "Meiji hikka shi shiryō," no. 2, p. 24.

187. See Midoro, pp. 174–175; Miyatake, "Meiji hikka shi shiryō," no. 7, pp. 24–25. Also *Tōkyō Akebono Shimbun*, February 21, 1880, in MNJ, 2, pp. 469–470.

188. Miyatake, "Meiji hikka shi shiryō," no. 8, pp. 30–34.

189. Ibid., no. 5, pp. 38–39.

190. Ibid., no. 3, p. 23.

191. Jung Bock Lee, *The Political Character of the Japanese Press*, pp. 21–22; another editor was jailed for reporting on drinking among Japanese army officers.

192. Cited in Haruhara, pp. 35–36; at least eighteen of *Hyōron*'s editors were jailed.

193. See Figdor, p. 20; also Miyatake, "Meiji hikka shi shiryō," no. 2, pp. 19–23. *Hyōron*'s successor, *Bunmei Shinshi*, was killed a year later, on June 13, 1877, by a *hakkō kinshi* order; its editor also received a three-month jail term and a fifty-yen fine at that time.

194. For a list, see Midoro, pp. 86–87.

195. See *Chōya Shimbun*, May 15, 25, 1878. The suspension is discussed in Brown, "Political Assassination," p. 31; Haruhara, p. 44; Nishida, *Shimbun to zasshi*, p. 48.

196. Rubin notes that the salary usually was increased to nine to fifteen yen a month during a person's actual incarceration (p. 21).

197. Edwin O. Reischauer, *Japan, the Story of a Nation*, p. 143.

198. A brief but helpful discussion of this problem is found in Lewis, "Interest and Ideology in Meiji Politics," pp. 88–89.

199. *Yūbin Hōchi Shimbun*, December 29, 1877; Yamamoto Taketoshi, *Shimbun to minshū*, p. 20.

CHAPTER 5. SERVING THE POLITICAL PARTIES, 1881 TO 1886

1. Joyce C. Lebra, *Ōkuma Shigenobu: Statesman of Meiji Japan*, pp. 41–42; she discusses Ōkuma's general role in the crisis on pp. 37–54. Useful collections of documents on the crisis are found in Inada Masa-

tsugu, *Meiji kenpō seiritsu shi*, 1, pp. 508–529, and Otsu Jun'ichirō, *Dainihon kensei shi*, 2, pp. 433–448. Also see George Akita, *Foundations of Constitutional Government in Modern Japan*, pp. 31–41.

2.   Mikiso Hane, *Modern Japan: A Historical Survey*, p. 121; Lebra, p. 46.

3.   Hane, pp. 121–122.

4.   Erwin Baelz, *Awakening Japan: The Diary of a German Doctor*, June 21, 1881, p. 66.

5.   Useful accounts are found in Okano Takeo, *Meiji genron shi*, p. 236; Akita, pp. 42–43; Lebra, pp. 47–49; Zen Nihon Shimbun Renmei, ed., *Shimbun taikan*, 1, pp. 102–103. Okano claims that only Ōkuma opposed the sale, but apparently Prince Arisugawa and several lower-ranking officials also opposed it.

6.   Midoro Masaichi, *Meiji Taishō shi: genron hen*, p. 105; Lebra, p. 52. Quote cited in Akita, p. 45.

7.   Meiji Bunka Kenkyūkai, ed., *Meiji bunka zenshū: seishi hen*, pp. 377–405, reprints the entire series, which ran from March 30 to April 16, 1881. Excerpts are found in Inada, 1, pp. 375–388. It is discussed in Joseph Pittau, *Political Thought in Early Meiji Japan*, pp. 99–101, and my *Politics of the Meiji Press*, pp. 110–113.

8.   Inada, 1, pp. 388–389; Pittau, p. 105.

9.   Inada, 1, pp. 401–425.

10.   Irokawa Daikichi, *The Culture of the Meiji Period*, pp. 108–113, discusses the constitutional discussions in rural Japan.

11.   Lebra, pp. 5, 49. She notes also that Ōkuma in his later years tried to moderate the harsh press laws and, as prime minister, initiated cabinet press conferences. Oka Yoshitake agrees about his skill in press relations but sees self-serving motives behind his press policies; *Five Political Leaders of Modern Japan*, p. 58.

12.   See Andrew Fraser, "The Expulsion of Ōkuma from the Government in 1881," p. 225.

13.   Ōkuma himself became closely tied to the editorship of *Yūbin Hōchi* after leaving the government. Yano Fumio, Inukai Tsuyoshi, and Ozaki Yukio all went to that paper, while Shimada Saburō went to *Mainichi*. See Yamamoto Fumio, *Nihon shimbun hattatsu shi*, p. 98; Oka, p. 52.

14.   See Sandra T. W. Davis, "Ono Azusa and the Political Change of 1881," p. 150.

15.   *Tōkyō-Yokohama Mainichi Shimbun*, July 26, 1881. The editorial was continued on July 27 and 28. Portions of the July 26 editorial are reprinted in Haruhara Akihiko, *Nihon shimbun tsū shi*, p. 48.

16.   *Tōkyō-Yokohama Mainichi*, August 2–3, 1881. See also Zen Nihon Shimbun Renmei, *Taikan*, 1, p. 103.

17. *Tōkyō-Yokohama Mainichi,* September 18–19, 1881; see Haruhara, pp. 49–50, for a list of the paper's editorials as well as those that ran in *Tōkyō Akebono Shimbun.*

18. *Tōkyō-Yokohama Mainichi,* October 13, 1881.

19. *Tōkyō Akebono Shimbun,* August 9, 1881.

20. "Kan'yūbutsu haraisage ni giwaku" (Misgivings about the sale of government holdings), *Chōya Shimbun,* August 8, 1881. The most complete collection of newspaper articles on the Hokkaido episode is found in Uchikawa Yoshimi and Matsushima Eiichi eds., *Meiji niyūsu jiten* (hereafter MNJ), 2, pp. 108–124. This editorial is reprinted on pp. 109–110. Newspaper accounts also are discussed in Otsu, 1, pp. 432–449, and in Inada, 1, pp. 508–529.

21. *Tōkyō Nichi Nichi Shimbun,* August 11, 1881.

22. *Tōkyō Nichi Nichi,* August 25, 1881; MNJ, 2, p. 111.

23. "Shintomiza de hantai enzetsukai" (Opposition lecture rally at Shintomiza), *Tōkyō Nichi Nichi,* August 27, 1881; MNJ, 2, pp. 111–112. Applause was calculated from the transcript of Fukuchi's lecture, published in *Tōkyō Nichi Nichi,* August 27–30, 1881; MNJ, 2, pp. 112–115.

24. *Tōkyō Nichi Nichi,* August 27, 1881; MNJ, 2, p. 112.

25. Ibid., August 29, 1881; MNJ, 2, p. 114.

26. Ibid., August 30, 1881; MNJ, 2, p. 115.

27. Fraser, p. 228.

28. From Iwakura Tomomi's diary, cited in Akita, *Foundations,* pp. 25–26; Sasaki invoked fears of the French Revolution in his statement.

29. Akita, p. 32.

30. Ibid., pp. 54 57.

31. Midoro, *Meiji Taishō shi,* p. 103.

32. Haruhara, p. 50.

33. Okano, p. 237.

34. Haga Eizō, *Meiji Taishō hikka shi,* p. 47.

35. John W. Dower, ed., *Origins of the Modern Japanese State: Selected Writings of E. H. Norman,* p. 280 (emphasis mine). Also see Robert Scalapino, *Democracy and the Party Movement in Prewar Japan,* pp. 99–116; Mikiso Hane, "The Movement for Liberty and Popular Rights," pp. 90–97.

36. Shimoyama Saburō, "Jiyū minken undō: sono chiikiteki bunpu," pp. 199–222.

37. Roger Bowen, *Rebellion and Democracy in Meiji Japan: A Study of Commoners in the Popular Rights Movement*, especially pp. 285–313.

38. See Shimura Akiko, "Meiji ki no josei jiyānarisuto," pp. 645–646.

39. Irokawa, *Culture of the Meiji Period*, p. 151. The same point is made repeatedly in his *Shinhen: Meiji seishin shi.*

40. *Tōkyō-Yokohama Mainichi*, February 4, 1882; Irokawa, *Culture of the Meiji Period*, p. 238.

41. Irokawa, *Culture of the Meiji Period*, p. 190.

42. Ibid., p. 237; also *Chōya Shimbun*, May 7, 1882.

43. Irokawa, *Culture of the Meiji Period*, p. 107.

44. Shōji Kichinosuke, ed., *Nihon seisha seitō hattatsu shi* (Tokyo: Ochanomizu Shobō, 1959), pp. 60, 174; Takahashi Tetsuo, *Fukushima jiken* (Tokyo: San'ichi Shobō, 1970), p. 98; both cited in Bowen, pp. 234–235.

45. *Jiyū Shimbun*, July 12, 1882; Uchikawa Yoshimi and Arai Naoyuki, eds., *Nihon no jiyānarizumu: taishū no kokoro o tsukanda ka*, p. 15.

46. *Yayoi Shimbun*, September 2, 1882, cited in Oka Mitsuo, *Kindai Nihon shimbun koshi*, p. 26; also Haga, pp. 59–61.

47. See MNJ, 2, pp. 108, 316–317, 687–690.

48. *Tōkyō Nichi Nichi*, May 23, 1882; MNJ, 2, p. 317.

49. Described in Bowen, pp. 8–31. See also his "Political Protest in Prewar Japan: The Case of Fukushima Prefecture," pp. 22–31. Also *Tōkyō Nichi Nichi*, December 4–5, 14–15, 1882, in Ishida Fumishirō, *Daijiken shi Meiji Taishō shōwa shimbun kiroku shūsei*, pp. 111–118.

50. *Chōya Shimbun*, October 30, 1881; MNJ, 2, pp. 314–315.

51. *Yūbin Hōchi Shimbun*, March 14, 1882; MNJ, 2, pp. 682–683; the party also was analyzed at length in *Tōkyō Nichi Nichi*, March 20–22, 1882; MNJ, 2, pp. 683–685.

52. *Tōkyō Nichi Nichi*, March 18, 1882.

53. Fukuchi Gen'ichirō, *Shimbunshi jitsureki*, p. 337.

54. Stephen Koss, *The Rise and Fall of the Political Press in Britain*, 1, pp. 432–433.

55. *Jiyū Shimbun*, June 25, 1882; MNJ, 2, pp. 313–314; also excerpted in Uchikawa and Arai, *Nihon no jiyānarizumu*, p. 13; Yamamoto Taketoshi, *Shimbun to minshū*, p. 21.

56. Chikamori Haruyoshi, *Jinbutsu Nihon shimbun shi*, pp. 131–132.

57.   *Tōkyō Nichi Nichi*, February 25, 1882; Okano, pp. 108–109.

58.   *Ise Shimbun*, April 13, 1882; Monna Naoki, *Minshū jiyānari-zumu no rekishi*, p. 41.

59.   Nishida Taketoshi, *Meiji jidai no shimbun to zasshi*, p. 98; Ono Hideo, *Nihon shimbun hattatsu shi*, p. 127.

60.   Oka Mitsuo, *Shimbun koshi*, pp. 33–34.

61.   *Tōyō Shinpō*, September 17, 1883; Kōsaka Masaaki, *Meiji bunka shi*, 4, p. 608. The paper listed twenty Teiseitō papers (including itself), eighteen Kaishintō organs, and fifteen papers affiliated with the Jiyūtō. Two major unaffiliated papers, *Jiji Shinpō* and *Ōsaka Asahi*, were not included in the list.

62.   Ono Hideo, *Shimbun no rekishi*, p. 35. Also see Nishida, pp. 99, 125–132; Okano, pp. 239–241; Midoro, pp. 109–113; Monna, pp. 39–44.

63.   Nishida, p. 112. The paper went through several name changes, eventually taking the name *Chūgai Denpō* on October 1, 1884. It was highly political but eschewed ties to a specific party.

64.   Recounted in Nishida, pp. 102–103.

65.   Letter of January 17, 1887, from Inukai to Ōkuma, cited in Lebra, p. 82.

66.   *Tōkyō Nichi Nichi*, June 26, 1883. The story of *Chōya*'s ambivalence is told in Yamamoto Taketoshi, *Shimbun to minshū*, pp. 22–26.

67.   *Chōya Shimbun*, June 28, 1883.

68.   *Jiyū*, July 4, 1883.

69.   *Jiyū Shimbun*, June 25, 1882; MNJ, 2, p. 313.

70.   See Monna, p. 41.

71.   *Tōkyō Nichi Nichi* reported its demise on March 4, 1885; Nishida notes that its last edition appears to have come out on March 15, though the publication data printed on that issue are too unclear to be certain (p. 102).

72.   The *Kokuyū Zasshi*, which had close ties to Baba Tatsui, originally had been named the *Dekinei Sōdan*, a play on words since the characters literally meant "drowning in mud," while the pronunciation suggested the "impossibility" *(dekinai)* of free discussion under current laws; see Nishida, p. 135.

73.   See Ukai Shin'ichi, *Chōya Shimbun no kenkyū*, pp. 26–27. Following the *Eiri Jiyū Shimbun* example, *Jiyū no Tomoshibi* launched an equally successful newspaper career on May 11, 1884, and after several name changes in 1888 became Murayama Ryōhei's base for expanding *Asahi Shimbun* from Osaka into Tokyo; see Nishida, pp. 117–118.

74.   See Nishida, pp. 108–109; soon after it was shut down, it resumed publication as *Osaka Nippō*.

75. See Nishida, *Shimbun to zasshi*, pp. 120–122, for the best list of the most important of these papers. For useful material on *Kōchi Shimbun*, see Nishida Taketoshi, "Kōchi Shimbunsha shiryō," *Shimbun Gaku Hyōron*, 15, pp. 103–110.

76. Ukai, p. 27; also Nishida, *Shimbun to zasshi*, p. 137.

77. Oka Yoshitake, *Five Political Leaders*, p. 88. Oka says that Ōkuma became "proprietor" of *Yūbin Hōchi* after leaving the government, but nowhere have I been able to corroborate that claim. Also see Nishida, *Shimbun to zasshi*, p. 103.

78. Fukuchi was head of the Tokyo *fukai* (assembly) at the time, and Numa accused him of spending funds indiscriminately for the reception. The episode is discussed in Nishida Taketoshi, "Meiji jūichinen—dō jūyonnen no shimbunkai," p. 373.

79. Lebra, p. 64; Nishida, *Shimbun to zasshi*, p. 104. The five were Shimada, Numa, Ono Azusa, Haruki Yoshiaki, and Mudaguchi Gengaku. See also Junesay Iddittie, *Marquis Okuma*, p. 228.

80. See Nishida, *Shimbun to zasshi*, pp. 123–124.

81. Nihon Shimbun Kyōkai, ed., *Chihōbetsu: Nihon shimbun shi*, pp. 175–176.

82. See Jung Bock Lee, *The Political Character of the Japanese Press*, p. 24; also Lebra, p. 75.

83. For a discussion of the origins of the party, see Miyake Setsurei, *Dōjidai shi*, 2, p. 164, as well as Otsu, 2, pp. 550–551, and Huffman, *Politics of the Meiji Press*, pp. 145–154.

84. *Tōkyō Nichi Nichi*, March 20, 1882; MNJ, 2, p. 688. See also Yanagida, pp. 245–246.

85. *Tōkyō Nichi Nichi*, May 6, 1882. For a selection of newspaper accounts of the incident, see MNJ, 2, pp. 32–37. The episode also is recounted in Sakai Kunio, *Ijin ansatsu shi* (Tokyo: Genrindō, 1958), pp. 137–171; Itagaki Taisuke, ed., *Jiyūtō shi*, 2 (Tokyo: Iwanami Shoten, 1953), pp. 105–154; and Nobutaka Ike, *The Beginnings of Political Democracy in Japan*, pp. 150–151.

86. See Nishida, *Shimbun to zasshi*, pp. 49, 106.

87. Ukai, pp. 26–27; Nihon Shimbun Renmei, ed., *Nihon shimbun hyakunen shi*, pp. 725, 729.

88. See Nishida, *Shimbun to zasshi*, p. 111; Yoshitake Oka, *Five Political Leaders*, p. 88; Ukai, p. 26; Kōsaka, *meiji bunka shi*, 4, p. 608.

89. A sense of the space given to different kinds of coverage can be gained by a study of *Tōkyō Nichi Nichi*'s page-one essays in 1882; 113 discussed domestic politics, 53 East Asian affairs (mostly the anti-Japanese riots in Korea); 39 economic issues, and a handful took up other matters. *Nichi Nichi* generally was considered more balanced in its coverage than

most of the other papers. These figures are based on title lists from 1875 through 1887 compiled in Nishida Taketoshi, "*Tōkyō Nichi Nichi* shasetsu sakuin" (unpublished manuscript), pp. 81–117.

90.   See Okano, pp. 58–59, 65–66; for Itagaki's famous lecture "On Liberty," see *Japan Weekly Mail*, June 15, 1882; Walter W. McLaren, "Japanese Government Documents," pp. 605–614.

91.   Ono Hideo, *Shimbun no rekishi*, p. 37.

92.   Summarized at length in Masaaki Kōsaka, ed., *Japanese Thought in the Meiji Era*, pp. 148–150, and Pittau, pp. 106–108. Excerpts from the respective editorial discussions are reprinted in Inada, 1, pp. 599–602, and Inada, 2, pp. 313–317.

93.   Discussions of this series are found in Pittau, pp. 108–110, and Huffman, *Politics of the Meiji Press*, pp. 141–144.

94.   *Tōkyō Nichi Nichi*, January 14–17, 1882; MNJ, 2, pp. 319–322. A major focus of the series was a point-by-point dissection of the arguments of *Nichi Nichi*'s more liberal opponents.

95.   *Tōkyō-Yokohama Mainichi*, January 18–22, 1882; Pittau, p. 109.

96.   *Tōkyō Nichi Nichi*, January 24–28, 1882; the quoted passage ran on January 26; see also Ozawa Ryōzō, *Onnagata konseki dan*, p. 75.

97.   *Tōkyō-Yokohama Mainichi*, January 21; February 1–5, 7, 1882; Pittau, pp. 110–111.

98.   "*Tōkyō Nichi Nichi* o bakusu," *Chōya Shimbun*, February 19, 1882; MNJ, 2, pp. 322–323.

99.   *Kōchi Shimbun*, March 23, 1882; MNJ, 2, pp. 323–324; discussed in Pittau, p. 114.

100.   Quoted in Zen Nihon Shimbun Renmei, *Shimbun taikan*, 1, p. 113.

101.   Seki Naohiko, *Nanajūnana nen no kaiko*, quoted in Yamamoto Fumio, *Hattatsu shi*, pp. 109–110. "Mr. Austin" probably was John Austin (1790–1859), a British jurist who wrote, among other things, *The Province of Jurisprudence Determined* and *Lectures on Jurisprudence*.

102.   *Chōya Shimbun*, February 19, 1882; MNJ, 2, p. 323.

103.   See "Itagaki no tokō o hihan," *Tōkyō-Yokohama Mainichi*, September 24, 1882; MNJ, 2, pp. 30–32. Also see Ono, *Shimbun no rekishi*, p. 39; Yamamoto Fumio, *Hattatsu shi*, p. 113. Roger Hackett, *Yamagata Aritomo in the Rise of Modern Japan*, suggests that their assumptions about government payoffs were correct; see p. 101.

104.   Osatake Takeki, *Nihon kensei shi taikō*, 2, p. 625; Scalapino, p. 137.

105.   Quoted in Scalapino, p. 137.

106.   Lebra, p. 76.

107.   See, for example, an essay by Taguchi Ryūkichi in *Tōkyō Keizai Zasshi*, November 19, 1881, and a similar essay in *Meiji Nippō*, February 20, 1882; Yamamoto Fumio, *Shimbun hattatsu shi*, pp. 113–114.

108.   See especially editorials by Furusawa Uruo in *Jiyū Shimbun*, December 17, 1882 and May 23, 1883; Yamamoto Fumio, *Shimbun hattatsu shi*, p. 114.

109.   Zen Nihon Shimbun Renmei, *Shimbun taikan*, 1, p. 114; Chikamori, *Jinbutsu Nihon shimbun shi*, p. 132.

110.   *Jiji Shinpō*, July 1, 1882; Okano, p. 109.

111.   *Yūbin Hōchi* shifted to prepayment in 1884, a move that seems to have hurt its circulation in the short run but helped its overall finances in the long run; see Uchikawa Yoshimi, *Shimbun shi wa*, p. 28.

112.   Yamamoto Taketoshi, in Uchikawa and Arai, p. 17.

113.   Typical declines from 1882 to 1883 were at *Tōkyō Nichi Nichi* (37 percent), *Yūbin Hōchi* (30 percent), and *Chōya Shimbun* (24 percent). By 1885, *Tōkyō-Yokohama Mainichi* had only 3,094 daily subscribers, while circulations at nonpartisan papers were rising. See Nishida, *Shimbun to zasshi*, pp. 147–148. See Jung Bock Lee, p. 22, for similar figures regarding *Ōsaka Nippō*.

114.   For a useful discussion of *kan* and *min*, see Carol Gluck, *Japan's Modern Myths: Ideology in the Late Meiji Period*, especially p. 60.

115.   Akita, *Foundations*, pp. 26–27.

116.   Cited in Midoro, *Meiji Taishō shi*, p. 113.

117.   Ibid., pp. 118–119. Midoro's figures, based on Naimushō records, show that 14 percent of the 28,496 meeting and speech requests were denied in these years. The largest percentage of denials came in 1884: 17.2 percent (117) of meetings and 21.8 percent (994) of speeches. Saitō Shōzō, in *Meiji Taishō hikka dainenpyō*, cites 1882 as the Meiji year with the greatest number of significant government actions against the press (142), with 1889 coming second (111), 1881 third (97), 1883 fourth (78), 1880 fifth (47), and 1884 sixth (45); see pp. 1–44.

118.   Midoro, p. 113; for a discussion of *taji sōron*, see Ariyama Teruo, " 'Taji sōron' to seifu kikanshi mondai," pp. 133–139.

119.   *Kokumin no Tomo*, November 13, 1892, pp. 3–4, referred to in Gluck, p. 71.

120.   Quoted in Zen Nihon Shimbun Renmei, *Shimbun taikan*, 1, p. 114.

121.   At one point in 1880, Fukuzawa agreed to become editor of a *kanpō*, but that scheme died when agreement could not be reached among the officials planning the gazette. See, for accounts of the various discus-

sions, Shinoda Kinkōzō, *Meiji shimbun kidan*, pp. 191–193; Nishida Take-toshi, "Meiji jūichinen—dō jūyonnen no shimbunkai," p. 372; Lebra, pp. 40–41.

122.   His memorial is published in Kido Mataichi et al., eds., *Kōza gendai jiyānarizumu*, 1 *(Rekishi)*, pp. 32–33; also see Haruhara, p. 56.

123.   For a discussion of Komatsubara's shift, see Yamamoto Take-toshi, *Shimbun kisha no tanjō*, pp. 160–163.

124.   See Kōsaka, *Meiji bunka shi*, 4, pp. 608–609, and Midoro, p. 175; also Okano, pp. 241–242. Government assistance to *Nichi Nichi, Yūbin Hōchi, Tōyō Shinpō, Meiji Nippō*, and others also is detailed in Sasaki Takashi, "Meiji jidai no seijiteki komiyunikēshiyon," part 3, pp. 110–111.

125.   Yanagida, *Fukuchi Ōchi*, p. 214; stockholders included Shibu-sawa Eiichi, Seki Naohiko, and Jōno Denpei, the paper's original owner. See also Fukuchi Gen'ichirō, *Shimbunshi jitsureki*, p. 337, and Ariyama, " 'Taji sōron,' " pp. 139–146.

126.   Sasaki, p. 111. *Asahi* eventually received a total of 25,000 yen from the government, much of it channeled through Mitsui sources; see Asahi Shimbunsha, ed., *Asahi Shimbunsha shi: Meiji hen*, p. 87.

127.   *Tōkyō Nichi Nichi*, December 20, 1881; Fukuchi, p. 337.

128.   See Ariyama Teruo, " 'Chūritsu' shimbun no keisei: Meiji chūki ni okeru seifu to *Asahi Shimbun*," especially pp. 34–37. The *Asahi* company history notes that no internal records shed light on either the gov-ernment's reason for giving the money or the company's reason for accept-ing it but suggests that it was an effort to "use newspapers in creating harmony between government and people *(kan-min)*"; Asahi Shimbunsha, *Meiji hen*, p. 87.

129.   It should be noted that the government was not the only sup-plier of funds to the press at this time. The pro-Kaishintō Mitsubishi firm also apparently did its part to secure a favorable press as it struggled against rival Mitsui early in the 1880s, with payments to *Yūbin Hōchi* (20,000 yen), *Tōkyō Nichi Nichi* (10,000), *Chōya* (5,000), *Akebono* (5,000), *Tōkyō-Yokohama Mainichi* (150 a month), and the Osaka papers; see Fraser, p. 225, and Lebra, p. 50. Mitsui also helped secure the funds for the reorgani-zation of *Nichi Nichi*; see Kōsaka, *Meiji bunka shi*, 4, p. 610.

130.   See Sasaki, "Meiji jidai no seijiteki komiyunikēshiyon," p. 111; Nishida, *Shimbun to zasshi*, pp. 51, 111, 145.

131.   See *Chōya Shimbun*, March 14, 1883; Haruhara, p. 56.

132.   *Jiji Shinpō*, April 17, 1882; Nishida, *Shimbun to zasshi*, p. 144.

133.   See *Jiji Shinpō*, January 19–20, 1885. Similar censorship epi-sodes occurred frequently that spring when Itō traveled to Tianjin to nego-tiate a treaty over the Korean problem; for a discussion of those, see Hilary Conroy, *The Japanese Seizure of Korea, 1868–1910*, pp. 170–171.

134.   *Hikka* figures vary widely in these years, partly because records often failed to distinguish between types of punishments. The figure of six hundred—based on lists in Nishida, *Shimbun to zasshi*, p. 95; Uchikawa and Arai, p. 12; and Saitō, *Meiji Taishō hikka dainenpyō*, pp. 13–33—is on the conservative side.

135.   See Nishida, *Shimbun to zasshi*, p. 141.

136.   Miyatake Gaikotsu, "Meiji hikka shi shiryō," no. 8, p. 33.

137.   Account from *Eiri Jiyū Shimbun*, May 30, 1884; see Miyatake, "Meiji hikka shi shiryō," no. 3, p. 24.

138.   Miyatake, "Meiji hikka shi shiryō," no. 8, p. 29.

139.   The peak year for both suspensions and bannings was 1882. My figure here is based on Ukai, p. 37. Others give even higher totals. Okano, pp. 231–232, lists 216 suspensions (104 in 1882); Uchikawa uses a figure of 238 total suspensions and banishments (in Chiba Yūjirō, ed., *Shimbun*, p. 56), and Oka Mitsuo (*Shimbun koshi*, pp. 34–35) suggests a higher figure yet. The official *Kanpō* began listing *hakkō kinshi* cases after its appearance in 1883. *Yūbin Hōchi* lamented on January 6, 1883, that "newspaper suspensions and bannings in 1882 showed a surprising increase over 1881 and are continuing at a similar level this year"; Ono, *Shimbun no rekishi*, p. 40.

140.   During 1882, *Yūbin Hōchi* and *Chōya* each was suspended at least twice. *Tōkyō-Yokohama Mainichi* was suspended once and *Asahi* twice in 1881, and *Jiji Shinpō* was suspended once, in May 1882; see Kōsaka, *Meiji bunka shi*, 4, pp. 614–617.

141.   Miyatake, "Meiji hikka shi shiryō," no. 5, p. 37.

142.   See Jung Bock Lee, p. 28; Nishida, *Shimbun to zasshi*, pp. 108–109.

143.   Michael Lewis, "Interest and Ideology in Meiji Politics: Inagaki Shimesu and the Toyama Jiyūtō," p. 159.

144.   Cited in Midoro, *Meiji Taishō shi*, p. 127.

145.   *Kōchi Shimbun*, March 17, 1882.

146.   The editorial ran in *Kōchi Shimbun*, July 15, 1882; the episode is recounted in Haruhara, pp. 52–53.

147.   A good description of the use of surrogates is found in Uchikawa, *Shimbun shi wa*, pp. 30–34.

148.   Subsequent press laws were issued in 1887 and 1909, but they made fewer changes and followed the essential philosophy of the 1883 revision. Evaluations are found in ibid.; Midoro, p. 119; Uchikawa and Arai, p. 17; Chiba, *Shimbun*, p. 55. The law is printed in Midoro, pp. 400–405, and Otsu, 2, pp. 781–785. Otsu also summarizes press reactions to the law on pp. 774–781.

149. Uchikawa, *Shimbun shi wa*, p. 44.

150. A helpful chart, comparing the provisions of this law to others, is found in Gregory J. Kasza, *The State and the Mass Media in Japan, 1918–1945*, p. 5. Discussions of the law are found in Richard Mitchell, *Censorship in Imperial Japan*, pp. 80–81; Nishida, *Shimbun to zasshi*, pp. 145–146; and Peter Figdor, "Newspapers and Their Regulation in Early Meiji Japan," p. 26.

151. *Jiji Shinpō*, May 19, 1883; Haruhara, p. 54. A similar report was published in *Nihon Rikken Seitō Shimbun*, May 18, 1883.

152. Yamamoto Fumio, *Nihon shimbun hattatsu shi*, p. 117; Midoro, p. 132; Uchikawa, *Shimbun shi wa*, p. 44.

153. *Tōkyō Nichi Nichi*, May 7, 1883, discussed this "unexpected result" of the new law; Haruhara, p. 55.

154. Lebra, p. 77.

155. Quoted in Midoro, p. 135.

156. Ibid., p. 134.

157. Figures from Ukai, pp. 26–27. Larger papers now included *Yomiuri*, with an annual circulation of 4,635,782, *Jiyū no Tomoshibi* (4,139,739), and *Eiri Chōya* (3,048,641). Daily figures in the text are determined by dividing annual circulation by three hundred, the approximate number of issues a year. *Nichi Nichi* that year had a total of 1,285,324 subscribers, *Chōya* 1,541,448, and *Yūbin Hōchi* 1,715,157.

158. Ukai, p. 19.

159. Yamamoto Fumio, *Nihon shimbun hattatsu shi*, p. 130.

160. Its income in that period was 7,348 yen, its expenditures 9,669; Uchikawa, *Shimbun shi wa*, p. 28.

161. Albert A. Altman, "Proprietor *versus* Editor: The Case of the *Ōsaka Asahi Shimbun* in the Late Nineteenth Century," p. 251.

162. Problems are outlined in Iwai Hajime, *Shimbun to shimbunjin*, pp. 63–64.

163. Asahi Shimbunsha, *Meiji hen*, pp. 43–44. Notice of the suspension, which began on January 25, 1881, and lasted for three weeks, ran in *Tōkyō Nichi Nichi* on January 29.

164. First issue of *Asahi*, January 25, 1879; cited in Uchikawa and Arai, p. 23.

165. Original *Asahi* handbill, reprinted in Asahi Shimbunsha, *Meiji hen*, p. 11.

166. Iwai, p. 70.

167. "Waga Asahi Shimbun no mokuteki," *Asahi Shimbun*, July 1, 1882; Iwai, p. 69.

168.   See Altman, p. 252.

169.   D. Eleanor Westney, *Imitation and Innovation: The Transfer of Western Organizational Patterns to Meiji Japan*, p. 168. Also see Asahi Shimbunsha, *Meiji hen*, pp. 93–94.

170.   Nihon Shimbun Hanbai Kyōkai, ed., *Shimbun hanbai hyaku-nen shi*, p. 219.

171.   Other prices then were *Tōkyō Nichi Nichi* and *Yūbin Hōchi*, four *sen*; *Chōya* and *Tōkyō-Yokohama Mainichi*, three *sen*; *Akebono*, 2.5 *sen*; and *Eiri Shimbun*, 1.5 *sen*. Asahi Shimbunsha, *Meiji hen*, p. 49.

172.   Ukai, pp. 26–27.

173.   Ibid., p. 19. *Jiji* had the second highest income from sales (46,631), and *Chōya* was third with 45,934.

174.   The story of the failed *kanpō*, as noted above, is told in Shinoda, *Meiji shimbun kidan*, pp. 191–93, and Fraser, p. 221.

175.   Yamamoto Taketoshi, *Shimbun to minshū*, discusses these phrases, pp. 70–74.

176.   *Jiji*, March 1, 1882; MNJ, 2, pp. 293–294.

177.   See Iwai, p. 70.

178.   Gluck, p. 59.

179.   Cited in Yamamoto Taketoshi, *Shimbun to minshū*, p. 71.

180.   *Jiji*, October 30, 1882. The articles were prompted by a government decision to tax patent medicines, beginning January 1, 1883. The patent medicine merchants sued Fukuzawa, demanding a retraction and a public apology. In a case that dragged on for two years, the merchants won at the lower-court level, then were reversed by the higher courts. See Chikamori, *Jinbutsu Nihon shimbun shi*, p. 146.

181.   *Jiji*, July 10, 1886; other articles on eating habits were run on December 15–16, 1882, and October 14 and 28, 1886.

182.   See also the evaluations in Nishida, *Shimbun to zasshi*, p. 108; Iwai, p. 70.

183.   Fukuzawa Yukichi, *The Autobiography of Yukichi Fukuzawa*, p. 323.

184.   Letter from Fukuzawa to Ōkuma Shigenobu, October 1, 1881, reprinted in Iwai, p. 94.

185.   Quoted in Yamamoto Fumio, *Shimbun hattatsu shi*, pp. 129–130.

186.   Ibid.

187.   Ukai, pp. 26–27.

188.   The difference was 22,137 yen in 1885; in 1886 it was 6,816, with *Jiji*'s sales revenues having increased to 59,586 while *Asahi*'s dropped to 66,402; ibid., p. 19.

CHAPTER 6. DEVELOPING A NEW PERSONA, 1886 TO 1894

1.   Anthony Smith, *The Newspaper: An International History*, p. 141.

2.   A reference to the Japanese press, reprinted in Uchikawa Yoshimi and Miyaji Masato, eds., *Gaikoku shimbun ni miru Nihon*, 2 *(gen-bun hen)*, p. 380.

3.   The Gunma details come from Ubukata Toshirō, "Kenpō happu to Nisshin sensō," p. 80.

4.   Oka Mitsuo, *Kindai Nihon shimbun koshi*, p. 53.

5.   Ōsaka Asahi Shimbun, *Gojūnen no kaisō*, p. 395; Yamamoto Fumio, *Nihon shimbun hattatsu shi*, pp. 144, 192; Watanabe Kazuo, *Jitsu-roku gogai sensen*, pp. 74–75.

6.   Coverage rights were granted by the government to *Chōya, Jiji, Kaishin, Nihon, Mainichi, Tōkyō Kōron, Tōkyō Nichi Nichi, Tōkyō Shin-pō, Yomiuri,* and *Yūbin Hōchi. Asahi* was represented through *Tōkyō Kōron*, with which it had ties. See Ono Hideo, *Nihon shimbun hattatsu shi*, pp. 208–209.

7.   See, for example, the striking ads in *Tōkyō Nichi Nichi*, February 11, 1889. Yamamoto Fumio gives a vivid description of Japan's "first extra *(gogai)* war" in *Hattatsu shi*, pp. 209–210.

8.   "Kenpō tsui ni happu seraretari," a February 7 to March 4, 1889, series in *Seiron*, excerpted in Inada Masatsugu, *Meiji kenpō seiritsu shi*, 2, p. 936.

9.   Erwin Baelz, *Awakening Japan: The Diary of a German Doctor*, January 29, 1889, p. 81.

10.   *Tōkyō Shinpō*, September 4, 1889, quoted in Carol Gluck, *Japan's Modern Myths: Ideology in the Late Meiji Period*, p. 50.

11.   See Sinh Vinh, *Tokutomi Sohō (1863–1957): The Later Career*, pp. 15–16.

12.   See especially discussions in Roger Bowen, *Rebellion and Democracy in Meiji Japan*, pp. 197–199, and Sharon L. Sievers, *Flowers in Salt: The Beginnings of Feminist Consciousness in Modern Japan*, pp. 26–113.

13.   *Yūbin Hōchi Shimbun*, February 20, 1886; *Tōkyō Nichi Nichi Shimbun*, May 19, 1886; *Nichi Nichi* actually responded in several edito-

rials, beginning March 11, 1886. The debate is discussed in detail in Inada Masatsugu, *Meiji kenpō seiritsu shi*, 2, pp. 452–481.

14.   *Doyō Shimbun*, June 17, 18, 19, 22, 1886, excerpted in Inada, 2, pp. 452–453.

15.   Quoted in Nakae Chōmin, *A Discourse by Three Drunkards on Government*, pp. 60, 75–76.

16.   Quoted in Midoro Masaichi, *Meiji Taishō shi: genron hen*, pp. 140–141. Also see Yamamoto Fumio, *Hattatsu shi*, p. 147; Nishida Taketoshi, *Meiji jidai no shimbun to zasshi*, p. 153.

17.   *Seiron*, vol. 18, described in Haga Eizō, *Meiji Taishō hikka shi*, pp. 93–94. The journal was suspended and Ōishi Masami was jailed for a year and a half over the incident provoked by this article.

18.   For an account of the latter, see *Yūbin Hōchi Shimbun*, May 10, 1889, reprinted in Nakayama Yasuaki, ed., *Shimbun shūsei Meiji hennen shi* (hereafter SSMH), 7, p. 270.

19.   For press accounts of the movement, see Uchikawa Yoshimi and Matsushima Eiichi, eds., *Meiji niyūsu jiten* (hereafter MNJ), 4, pp. 406–409. Particularly useful are *Yūbin Hōchi Shimbun*, July 21, 1888, and *Tōkyō Nichi Nichi Shimbun*, March 20, 1889.

20.   *Shinano Mainichi Shimbun*, quoted in Gluck, p. 49.

21.   Quoted in Inada, 2, pp. 937–938.

22.   Gluck, p. 46.

23.   Useful summaries of this discussion are found in Walter W. McLaren, *A Political History of Japan during the Meiji Era, 1867–1912*, pp. 191–192.

24.   *Tōkyō Asahi Shimbun*, February 17, 1889; Inada, 2, pp. 926–927.

25.   *Kokumin no Tomo*, March 22, 1889; Inada, 2, pp. 927–928.

26.   Coverage is summarized in Haruhara Akihiko, *Nihon shimbun tsū shi*, p. 60.

27.   *Jiji Shinpō*, November 6, 1887; *Tōkyō Nichi Nichi Shimbun*, November 7, 1886, reprinted in ibid., pp. 60–61. Additional accounts of the press' coverage of the episode are found in Haga Eizō, *Meiji Taishō hikka shi*, pp. 84–86. Nearly twenty of the articles are reprinted in MNJ, 3, pp. 630–637.

28.   *The Times*, April 19, 1889; in Uchikawa and Miyaji, 2, p. 381.

29.   See *The Times*, April 19, 1889, p. 6. Also Joyce Lebra, *Ōkuma Shigenobu: Statesman of Meiji Japan*, p. 86, and Yamamoto Fumio, *Hattatsu shi*, p. 148.

30.   Tōgen Haruo, "*Shinonome Shimbun* to jōyaku kaisei mondai," p. 69; they made up 41 percent of all the editorials run by those papers in that period.

31. *Nihon Shimbun,* July 28, 1889; reprinted in Asahi Shimbunsha, ed., *Asahi Shimbunsha shi: Meiji hen,* p. 233. The survey found eleven papers against Ōkuma's approach, eight for it, and four fairly neutral.

32. *Ōsaka Mainichi Shimbun,* December 29, 1889; SSMH, 7, p. 353.

33. Excerpted in Sashihara Yasuzō, *Meiji sei shi,* vol. 10 of *Meiji bunka zenshū* (1956), pp. 82–83. Also see Zen Nihon Shimbun Renmei, ed., *Shimbun taikan,* 1, pp. 133–134.

34. *Fusō,* November 10, 1889; SSMH, 7, p. 338.

35. *Shinonome Shimbun,* July 13, 1889; Tōgen, p. 74.

36. *Shinonome Shimbun,* July 20, 1889; Tōgen, p. 74.

37. *North-China Herald,* August 3, 1889; Uchikawa and Miyaji, 2, p. 391.

38. Several leading papers and journals, including *Tōkyō Nichi Nichi Shimbun* and *Kokumin no Tomo,* remained ambivalent on the issue, though they too engaged in the debates. MNJ, 4, pp. 323–335, focuses on *Tōkyō Nichi Nichi's* editorials on the issue. A detailed discussion also is found in Asahi Shimbunsha, *Meiji hen,* pp. 229–237. See also Keizo Shibusawa, *Japanese Society in the Meiji Era,* pp. 88–90.

39. Baelz, p. 93.

40. *The Times,* April 19, 1889; Uchikawa and Miyaji, 2, p. 381.

41. Shumpei Okamoto, *The Japanese Oligarchy and the Russo-Japanese War,* p. 48.

42. *Hyōron Shimbun,* no. 62, January 15, 1876.

43. The best treatment of this change in generations continues to be Kenneth Pyle, *The New Generation in Meiji Japan.*

44. Nishida, *Shimbun to zasshi,* p. 151.

45. Evaluation of *North-China Herald,* August 3, 1889, regarding the extraterritoriality debates; in Uchikawa and Miyaji, 2, p. 391.

46. See Gluck, pp. 14, 25. For another example of this approach, see *Seiron's* postconstitutional series "Kenpō tsui ni happu seraretari," in Inada, 2, p. 936.

47. Discussed in Margaret Mehl, "Scholarship and Ideology in Conflict: The Kume Affair, 1892," pp. 337–358. *Nihon* received so many angry letters that it could not publish them all; Kume eventually was forced to resign from the university. Also see Kenneth Pyle, "The Emergence of Bureaucratic Conservatism in the Meiji Period," p. 20.

48. *Japan Weekly Mail,* February 5, 1892, in Uchimura Kanzō, *The Complete Works of Kanzō Uchimura,* 5, p. 63.

49. Nishida, *Shimbun to zasshi,* p. 173.

50. Pyle, *New Generation*, p. 75.

51. *Nihon*, February 11, 1889; quoted in Yamamoto Taketoshi, *Shimbun to minshū*, p. 87, and in Uchikawa Yoshimi and Arai Naoyuki, eds., *Nihon no jiyānarizumu*, p. 28. Also see Chikamori Haruyoshi, *Jinbutsu Nihon shimbun shi*, p. 160.

52. *Taiyō*, July 1900, quoted in Yamamoto Taketoshi, *Shimbun to minshū*, p. 89.

53. Chikamori, p. 162.

54. Nihon Shimbun Hanbai Kyōkai, ed., *Shimbun hanbai hyakunen shi*, p. 205. Figures are for 1894. The country's largest paper then, *Ōsaka Asahi*, had a daily circulation of 95,000; the largest Tokyo paper, *Tōkyō Asahi*, had 55,000.

55. Ono Hideo, *Shimbun no rekishi*, p. 48.

56. Pyle, "Emergence of Bureaucratic Conservatism," p. 18.

57. Roger Hackett, *Yamagata Aritomo in the Rise of Modern Japan, 1838–1922*, p. 104.

58. Letter of August 1, 1887, from Yamagata to Kiyoura Keigo, head of the Police Bureau, quoted in Hackett, p. 105. See Inada, 2, pp. 503–512, for the editorials and essays that helped spark the *hoan jōrei*.

59. The ordinance is translated in Centre for East Asian Cultural Studies, ed., *The Meiji Japan through Contemporary Sources*, 3, pp. 43–45. In Japanese, it is reprinted in Midoro, *Meiji Taishō shi*, pp. 143–145. Also see Richard Mitchell, *Censorship in Imperial Japan*, p. 85.

60. These episodes all are recounted in *Jiji Shinpō*, December 30, 1887; MNJ, 3, pp. 705–706.

61. *Jiji Shinpō*, December 28, 1887; reprinted in Ishida Fumishiro, ed., *Daijiken shi Meiji Taishō Shōwa shimbun kiroku shūsei*, p. 148.

62. *Jiji Shinpō*, December 30, 1887; MNJ, 3, p. 705.

63. *Jiji Shinpō*, December 30, 1887; MNJ, 3, p. 706.

64. *Jiji Shinpō*, December 29, 1887; MNJ, 3, p. 704.

65. *Jiji Shinpō*, December 30, 1887; MNJ, 3, p. 707.

66. *Jiji Shinpō*, December 29, 1887; MNJ, 3, p. 704.

67. The fullest list of these evacuees is in Ishida, p. 147, based on the reporting of *Jiji Shinpō*, December 28, 1887. Useful lists also are found in *Tōkyō Nichi Nichi Shimbun*, December 28–29, 1887 (reprinted in MNJ, 3, pp. 702–703; SSMH, 6, pp. 551–552), and Midoro, pp. 143–145.

68. "Chūsei ron," *Chōya Shimbun*, quoted in Nihon Shimbun Hanbai Kyōkai, ed., *Shimbun hanbai hyakunen shi*, p. 236.

69. See Nihon Shimbun Hanbai Kyōkai, p. 236; Nishida, *Shimbun to zasshi*, p. 156.

70. Zen Nihon Shimbun Renmei, ed., *Shimbun taikan,* 1, pp. 131–132.

71. *Shinonome Shimbun* lost strength after Nakae returned to Tokyo following the amnesty of 1889, and it folded in 1891.

72. Taken from the lengthy *Jiji Shinpō* accounts of December 29–30, 1887; MNJ, 3, pp. 703–707.

73. Hackett, p. 106.

74. The law is reprinted in its entirety, along with the thirty-four-article publication law *(shuppan jōrei)* in Midoro, pp. 407–416. He gives a clear summary of the major changes from previous laws on pp. 145–146. See also MNJ, 3, p. 705, for a note on the law in *Jiji Shinpō,* December 30, 1887. Minor revisions were made to the law in 1893 and 1897, but they did not change the direction of press control policy. A more significant revision in 1909 will be discussed below. See also Mitchell, *Censorship,* p. 87.

75. Lawrence W. Beer sees it as somewhat more lenient than the 1883 press code *(Freedom of Expression in Japan,* p. 53), while Midoro calls it a "press extinction" law (p. 145).

76. See analysis of Uchikawa Yoshimi in Chiba Yūjiro, ed., *Shimbun,* p. 57. The best discussion of the law in English is in Jay Rubin, *Injurious to Public Morals: Writers and the Meiji State,* pp. 22–27. A helpful chart, comparing the successive press laws, is found in Gregory J. Kaeza, *The State and the Mass Media in Japan, 1918–1945,* p. 5.

77. Midoro, pp. 162–163.

78. The deliberations are narrated in detail in ibid., pp. 167–172.

79. The proposals provoked a storm in the press, discussed in Uchikawa Yoshimi, *Shimbun shi wa,* pp. 27–30. Haruhara, p. 76, provides a summary of postal regulations from 1871 to 1900, by which time papers were mailed third class at a reduced rate.

80. Yamamoto Fumio, *Hattatsu shi,* p. 160.

81. See Sasaki Takashi, "Daiichiji Matsukata naikaku ki no shimbun sōjū mondai," pp. 29–33; also his "Meiji jidai no seijiteki komiyunikēshiyon," pt. 3, pp. 110–111; and Nishida, *Shimbun to zasshi,* p. 144. A fascinating case of assistance to *Chōya Shimbun* is discussed in Itō Takashi and George Akita, "The Yamagata-Tokutomi Correspondence," p. 402. Often one ministry or faction would support one paper in opposition to other factions. *Kokkai* and *Tōkyō Shinpō,* for example, were close to the Home Ministry, *Tōkyō Nichi Nichi* and *Chōya* to the Itō Hirobumi faction in these years.

82. Seki's resistance and final defeat are discussed in Uchikawa, *Shimbun shi wa,* pp. 24–27. Itō took over in 1892.

83. The *seimu bu* plan is detailed meticulously in Sasaki, "Dai-ichiji Matsukata naikaku," pp. 37–43, quote on p. 37. Even seemingly independent papers like *Nihon, Jiji,* and *Chōya* were courted ceaselessly by leading officials.

84. Arase Yutaka, "Makkureikā no dansei," p. 677; Haga, pp. 105–106.

85. Reported in *North-China Herald,* April 3, 1890; Uchikawa and Miyaji, 2 *(Genbun hen),* p. 402. The writer and publisher of the article also received four-year jail terms.

86. *Hakkō teishi/kinshi* lists in Midoro, *Meiji Taishō shi,* pp. 87, 149; Chiba, p. 56; Okano Takeo, *Meiji genron shi,* pp. 231–232; Ukai, p. 37; Ono, *Shimbun no rekishi,* p. 41. For papers suspended during the Diet, see MNJ, 4, p. 620.

87. Midoro, p. 173.

88. Discussed in Uchikawa, *Shimbun shi wa,* pp. 30–34.

89. *Nihon,* June 27, 1891; Kuga Katsunan, *Kuga Katsunan zenshū,* 3, pp. 166–167.

90. Barbara Teeters, "Press Freedom and the *Twenty-sixth Century* Affair in Meiji Japan," p. 340.

91. *Tōkyō Nichi Nichi* touched off considerable alarm on March 15, 1891, when it reported on rumors that Nicholas was coming to Japan to investigate its geography and military readiness. Papers also reported that spring on rumors that Saigō Takamori had not died but had escaped to Siberia at the end of the Satsuma Rebellion and that he would return in Nicholas' entourage; see *Nihon,* April 8, 1891. These are discussed in Peter Yong-Shik Shin, "The Otsu Incident," pp. 49–50, 71–72.

92. The word for foreign emperors is *kōtei; tennō* (literally, heavenly emperor) is used only for the Japanese imperial family.

93. Saigō's view, from diary of Kojima Iken, May 25, 1891, quoted in Shin, p. 157; for Matsukata's statement, see Barbara Teeters, "The Otsu Affair: The Formation of Japan's Judicial Conscience," pp. 48–49.

94. Taoka Ryōichi, *Ōtsu jiken to saihyōka,* pp. 284–291, provides a useful day-by-day account of the events.

95. Teeters, "Otsu Affair," p. 37.

96. See, for example, *Tōkyō Nichi Nichi Shimbun,* May 12, 1891; Haruhara, p. 75.

97. Based on *Murayama Ryōhei den,* in Uchikawa Yoshimi, *Masu medeia hō seisaku shi kenkyū,* p. 9.

98. Imperial Order 46, reprinted in *Ōsaka Mainichi Shimbun,* May 22, 1891; MNJ, 4, p. 74.

99. Ibid.

100. See, for example, *Yomiuri Shimbun*, May 23, 1891.

101. For copies of *Ōmi Shinpō* extras that were censored, see Ono Hideo, *Gogai hyakunen shi*, p. 20.

102. Quoted in Teeters, "Otsu Affair," p. 42.

103. *Kokumin Shimbun*, May 17, 1891.

104. See *Kokumin Shimbun*, May 24, 1891; Uchikawa, *Hō seisaku shi*, p. 11.

105. Exceptions came during the tumult following the Russo-Japanese War in the fall of 1906 and again after the Great Kantō Earthquake in 1923; see Uchikawa, *Shimbun shi wa*, p. 37.

106. Uchikawa, *Hō seisaku shi*, p. 25. He describes the Diet debates on pp. 14–25. Also see his "Ōtsu jiken no hōdō o meguru tōsei to teikō," pp. 43–66.

107. See D. Eleanor Westney, *Imitation and Innovation: The Transfer of Western Organizational Patterns to Meiji Japan*, pp. 189–190.

108. Figures from Naimushō, ed., *Nihon jinkō tōkei shūsei*, 1–4. Quote from Sheldon Garon, *The State and Labor in Modern Japan*, p. 24.

109. Hugh Patrick, ed., *Japanese Industrialization and Its Social Consequences*, p. 302.

110. Edward Seidensticker, *Low City, High City: Tokyo from Edo to the Earthquake*, p. 110.

111. John Crump, *The Origins of Socialist Thought in Japan*, pp. 8–9.

112. Income figures in Patrick, p. 335; *Chōya* series discussed in Sally Hastings, *Neighborhood and Nation in Tokyo 1905–1937*, pp. 22–23.

113. Figures on communication come from John Pierson, *Tokutomi Soho, 1863–1957: A Journalist for Modern Japan*, p. 169.

114. Kido Mataichi et al., eds., *Kōza gendai jiyānarizumu*, 1 (Rekishi), p. 2.

115. *Teikoku Tōkei nenkan*, in Yamamoto Taketoshi, "Meiji sanjūnendai zenhan no shimbun Nihon no dokusha sō," p. 123. Tokyo school attendance rates often were lower than those in many provincial areas in the early years, because public schools developed very slowly there owing to the larger number of private schools; in 1879 Tokyo had fewer public schools than any prefecture but Okinawa; see Seidensticker, pp. 86–87.

116. Max Pemberton, *Lord Northcliffe: A Memoir*, pp. 29–30.

117. *Yorozu Chōho*, November 1, 1892; Okano, p. 13.

118. Yamamoto Taketoshi, "Shimbun sangyō no keisei katei," pp. 119–120.

119. See Shibusawa Keizo, *Japanese Society in the Meiji Era*, pp. 379–381.

120. Yamamoto Fumio, *Hattatsu shi*, p. 128; Zen Nihon Shimbun Renmei, *Shimbun taikan*, 1, p. 122.

121. Zen Nihon Shimbun Renmei, *Taikan*, 1, p. 130.

122. Murayama noted that it was with the Sino-Japanese War (1894–1895) that *Asahi* began using the telegraph in a substantial way to cover the news. Actually, however, most stories continued to be sent by slower means during that war because of the high cost of transmission. Yamamoto Taketoshi, *Shimbun kisha no tanjō*, p. 176.

123. *Yomiuri Shimbun*, August 8, 1888; see Yomiuri Shimbunsha, ed., *Yomiuri Shimbun hyakunijūnen shi*, p. 8; also discussed in Haruhara, p. 68.

124. See Yamamoto Fumio, *Hattatsu shi*, p. 176.

125. Ibid., p. 181.

126. Zen Nihon Shimbun Renmei, *Taikan*, 1, p. 129.

127. *Tōkyō Nichi Nichi Shimbun* tried to use a Western printing press, then switched back to woodblock, because the metal type it had bought in Shanghai did not have enough of the needed characters; see Westney, pp. 166–167.

128. Ibid., p. 168; Ukai Shin'ichi, *Chōya Shimbun no kenkyū*, pp. 12–13.

129. Westney, p. 169.

130. Uchikawa, *Shimbun shi wa*, pp. 45–46. The press cost about 7,300 yen, and *Mainichi* paid nearly 10,000 yen for its own press in 1893—about a fifth of the company's capital stock.

131. When *Mainichi*'s printing supervisor asked *Asahi* managers for instructions on how to use the new press, they refused to help him; he finally secured assistance from the government printing office. Such was the competitive spirit of the times. See ibid., p. 46.

132. Yamamoto Fumio, *Hattatsu shi*, pp. 175–176; Westney recounts the story of *Mainichi*'s delay in getting its Marinoni press into operation because no one knew how to use it, and neither the government printing bureau nor *Asahi* would share their knowledge (p. 182).

133. Westney, p. 184. Uchikawa Yoshimi discusses the history of the rotary press in *Shimbun shi wa*, pp. 44–47.

134. For figures, see Nishida, *Shimbun to zasshi*, pp. 147–148; Uchikawa and Arai, p. 22; Yamamoto Taketoshi, *Shimbun to minshū*, pp. 43–44.

135. Evaluation based on observation of the papers at Meiji Shimbun Zasshi Bunko, University of Tokyo.

136. Ukai, p. 19.

137. Fukuchi Gen'ichirō, *Shimbunshi jitsureki*, p. 340.

138. Yamamoto Taketoshi, *Shimbun to minshū*, p. 44.

139. Ukai, p. 19.

140. *Minato* was created from the old *Konnichi Shimbun*; both *Yamato* and *Minato* aimed at a more popular audience. Their respective daily circulations in 1888 were 19,512 and 5,804. See Yamamoto Taketoshi, *Shimbun dokusha sō*, pp. 404–405; Nishida, *Shimbun to zasshi*, pp. 166–167.

141. The paper had been founded as *Jiyū no Tomoshibi* in 1884, changed its name to *Tomoshibi* in 1886, and to *Mezamashi Shimbun* in 1887.

142. Yamamoto Taketoshi, *Shimbun dokusha sō*, pp. 404–405; chart based on *Keishichō jimu nenpyō*.

143. Pemberton, p. 54.

144. Uchikawa, *Shimbun shi wa*, p. 28.

145. "Kairyō iken sho," *Yūbin Hōchi Shimbun*, September 1, 1886; Nishida, *Shimbun to zasshi*, p. 150.

146. See Uchikawa, *Shimbun shi wa*, pp. 144–145.

147. Nishida, *Shimbun to zasshi*, p. 150.

148. See Ukai, pp. 26–28.

149. Uchikawa and Arai, p. 49.

150. Yamamoto Fumio, *Hattatsu shi*, p. 132.

151. Home delivery had been started by *Tōkyō Nichi Nichi Shimbun* in 1875 and quickly adopted by most of the major papers.

152. See Westney, pp. 163–165; she notes that the same system applied in Osaka, where already by the early 1880s, 70 percent of *Asahi*'s papers were handled by delivery agents.

153. Ibid., p. 191.

154. Iwai Hajime, *Shimbun to shimbunjin*, p. 72.

155. Gregory Ornatowski, "Press, Politics, and Profits: The 'Asahi Shimbun' and the Prewar Japanese Newspaper," p. 23.

156. The story is told, with useful documentation, in Nihon Shimbun Hanbai Kyōkai, *Hyakunen shi*, pp. 244–246.

157. *Konnichi Shimbun*, May 20, 1885; SSMH, 6, p. 89.

158. Westney, p. 188. An interesting British parallel is found in Lord Northcliffe's 1889 offer of cash to the person who estimated most

closely the amount in the Bank of England on a certain date; the contest sent the circulation of his struggling journal, *Answers*, soaring; Pemberton, pp. 38–39.

159.   Westney, p. 187.

160.   John Hohenberg, *Between Two Worlds: Policy, Press and Public Opinion in Asian-American Relations*, p. 111.

161.   See Yamamoto Fumio, *Hattatsu shi*, p. 131.

162.   Other terms for ads included *hōkoku*, *kokubun*, *kokuchi*, and *kokujō*; the use of *kōkoku* did not become standard until the late 1880s. See Nihon Shimbun Hanbai Kyōkai, *Hyakunen shi*, p. 170.

163.   "Shōjin ni tsuguru bun," *Jiji Shinpō*, October 16, 1883.

164.   See Haruhara, pp. 65–66.

165.   Nihon Shimbun Hanbai Kyōkai, p. 178.

166.   *Jiji Shinpō*, January 1, 1892; the issue was twenty pages long, compared to eight pages on a typical day.

167.   See Chikamori Haruyoshi, *Jinbutsu Nihon shimbun shi*, p. 177. The paper was launched on the twenty-sixth day of the month, in the twenty-sixth year of Meiji, when its owner, Akiyama Teisuke, was twenty-six years old; hence its name.

168.   Westney, p. 197.

169.   Hani Motoko, "Stories of My Life," pp. 338, 346.

170.   Stephen Koss, *The Rise and Fall of the Political Press in Britain*, 1, p. 6.

171.   Discussed in Ono, *Hattatsu shi*, pp. 229–231.

172.   The first evening paper was *Tōkyō Maiyū Shimbun* (1877–1878) and the second *Konnichi Shimbun*; neither was successful. *Tōkyō Nichi Nichi Shimbun* was the first paper to try simultaneous morning and evening editions, on January 1, 1885; it was followed the same year by a similar *Jiji Shinpō* experiment, by *Yūbin Hōchi Shimbun* in 1889, and by *Tōkyō Asahi* in 1898. *San'yō Shinpō* in Okayama also launched an evening edition in 1885. None of these lasted more than a few months. The first successful evening editions came after the Russo-Japanese War. See Haruhara, p. 59; Yamamoto Fumio, *Hattatsu shi*, pp. 182–183.

173.   See Nishida, *Shimbun to zasshi*, p. 234.

174.   Reported in *Jiji Shinpō*, September 30, 1890; Haruhara, p. 73. The literal translation of the group's name is Association of Reporters Coming and Going in the Diet. The practice of establishing press offices is discussed in Yamamoto Taketoshi, *Shimbun kisha no tanjō*, pp. 304–307.

175.   See Roger Purdy, "The Ears and Voice of the Nation: The Dōmei News Agency and Japan's News Network, 1936–1945," p. 31. Also Yamamoto Fumio, *Hattatsu shi*, pp. 177–178.

176. See Haruhara, p. 348; Zen Nihon Shimbun Renmei, *Taikan*, 1, pp. 180–181. The *Mail* apparently received a government subsidy in exchange for letting the domestic press use its Reuters dispatches.

177. Japan's first weather reports were published at *Jiji Shinpō*; see *Jiji*, April 17, 1888; Nihon Fūzoku Shi Gakkai, ed., *Genron to masu komi*, p. 80.

178. Coverage of Tanaka Shōzō's campaign to clean up the pollution problems was found in most of the major papers in the early 1890s; it was only after the Sino-Japanese War, however, that it became a major topic. For an analysis of the early coverage, see Yamamoto Taketoshi, "Ashio kōdoku mondai no hōdō to yoron," pp. 165–169.

179. The coverage is summarized in Haruhara, pp. 78–80. Fukushima's observations in Manchuria played a role in dissuading officials from creating an alliance with China; see Stewart Lone, *Japan's First Modern War*, p. 25.

180. Uchikawa Yoshimi, "Shimbun ronsetsu no hensen," pp. 3–4.

181. Ubukata Toshirō, "Kenpō happu to Nisshin Sensō," p. 86.

182. The first election resulted in 129 progovernment Diet members and 172 from the Jiyūtō and Kaishintō parties; see George Akita, *Foundations of Constitutional Government in Modern Japan*, p. 76.

183. An example of the role factional infighting played in the press-government struggles is found in George Akita's account of Inoue writing Matsukata in 1891 to accuse the prime minister of planting a *Keisei Shinpō* article that accused Inoue of ambitious plotting against Matsukata; "Government and Opposition in Prewar Japan: A Political Success or Embarrassment?" p. 53.

184. See *Yūbin Hōchi Shimbun*, July 7, 1890; Ono Hideo, *Gogai hyakunen shi*, pp. 18–19. Also see *Asahi Shimbun*, July 3, 1890, in Asahi Shimbunsha, ed., *Hyakunen no jūyō shimen*, p. 35.

185. See *Jiyū Shimbun Gogai*, November 25, 1890; Ono, *Gogai*, p. 18.

186. See, for example, *Tōkyō Nichi Nichi Shimbun*, November 28, 30, 1890.

187. See *Tōkyō Nichi Nichi Shimbun*, May 24, 1892; MNJ, 4, pp. 271–272.

188. *Chōya Shimbun*, November 25, 1892; MNJ, 4, p. 272.

189. *Chōya Shimbun*, July 7, 1891; Sasaki Takashi, "Daiichiji Matsukata naikaku ki no shimbun sōjū mondai," p. 36.

190. Oka Yoshitake, *Five Political Leaders of Modern Japan*, p. 20.

191. Inoue Masaaki, ed., *Hakushaku Kiyoura Keigo den*, 1, pp. 168–169, quoted in Yamamoto Fumio, *Hattatsu shi*, p. 160. The Matsukata

cabinet's press control policies are discussed in Sasaki Takashi, "Daiichiji Matsukata naikaku," pp. 16–26.

192.   *Chōya Shimbun,* January 13, 1892, quoted in Akita, *Foundations of Constitutional Government,* p. 82.

193.   Yamamoto Fumio, *Hattatsu shi,* p. 160.

194.   See Uchikawa, *Hō seisaku shi,* p. 17.

195.   In the election, the antigovernment forces won a clear majority with 163 of the three hundred seats.

196.   *Yomiuri Shimbun,* February 3, 1892; *Chōya Shimbun,* February 3, 1892; SSMH, 8, pp. 203–204. Also Nakanowatari Nobuyuki, ed., *Masukomi kindai shi,* pp. 10–11.

197.   *San'in Shimbun,* February 14, 1892, cited in Nakanowatari, p. 11.

198.   *Nihon,* February 12, 1892; SSMH, 6, pp. 207–209.

199.   Police Bureau Chief Kiyoura Keigo recalled that Prime Minister Itō became so distressed by attacks later in 1892 (including a cartoon in "a certain newspaper" [*marumaru chimbun*] suggesting that he was considering making Christianity Japan's official religion) that he wrote several personal letters to the bureau about how to handle the press. See Midoro, *Meiji Taishō shi,* pp. 176–177.

200.   Ibid.; Chiba, p. 58; Mitchell, *Censorship in Imperial Japan,* pp. 116–118; Nishida, *Shimbun to zasshi,* p. 229.

201.   See Ono, *Shimbun no rekishi,* p. 63.

202.   *Chōya Shimbun,* May 2, 3, 1890; *Yomiuri Shimbun,* May 4, 1890; *Nihon,* May 5, 1890; Yamamoto Taketoshi, *Shimbun to minshū,* pp. 89–90.

203.   One of the more remarkable shifts was when the "independent" *Tōkyō Asahi Shimbun* was accused by the formerly progovernment *Tōkyō Nichi Nichi Shimbun* of being a "government paper" during the late 1890s because of its close ties to Ōkuma, who became prime minister in 1898.

204.   List largely based on Nishida, *Shimbun to zasshi,* pp. 154–155; also from Yamamoto Taketoshi, *Shimbun to minshū,* p. 77; Yamamoto Fumio, *Hattatsu shi,* pp. 151–160. See also *Nihon,* October 8, 1890. *Jiyū Shimbun* had been revived on October 2, 1895.

205.   *Japan Weekly Mail,* January 2, 1891, quoted in Akita, *Foundations of Constitutional Government,* p. 62.

206.   Ukai, pp. 28–29. *Asahi* had a total circulation that year of 12,983,254; *Yorozu Chōhō* of 9,077,294; in second place was *Miyako Shimbun* (11,103,979), a paper that put more emphasis on the arts and culture than on politics, though it had Kaishintō ties. *Yūbin Hōchi* had a circulation of 7,352,581, *Tōkyō Nichi Nichi* 4,868,236.

207.   Haruhara, p. 64; Chikamori, *Jinbutsu Nihon shimbun shi*, p. 156.

208.   Yamamoto Taketoshi, *Dokusha sō*, pp. 404–405; Nishida, *Shimbun to zasshi*, pp. 166–167. Kuroiwa was as well known by his pen name, Ruikō, as by his given name, Shūroku. Also see Ono, *Hattatsu shi*, pp. 224–226.

209.   Chikamori, pp. 177–178; *Niroku Shinpō*, October 26, 1893; MNJ, 5, pp. 663–664.

210.   See Uchikawa and Arai, p. 49. Motoyama's career is treated in Zen Nihon Shimbun Renmei, ed., *Kindai Nihon shimbun taikan*, 2, pp. 457–497.

211.   The paper had begun as *Ōsaka Nippō* in 1876, had become *Nihon Rikken Seitō Shimbun* in 1882, and then *Ōsaka Asahi Shimbun* in November 1888. Motoyama became an advisor to the paper in 1889 and president in 1893. See Gotō Fumio, "Shimbun akusesu *Mainichi Shimbun* no shimen kaikaku," p. 220; also Iwai, p. 113; Nihon Shimbun Renmei, ed., *Nihon shimbun hyakunen shi*, pp. 344–346. Motoyama was famous for personally calling on employees at sales shops to encourage circulation; Ono, *Shimbun no rekishi*, p. 67.

212.   See Nihon Shimbun Hanbai Kyōkai, *Hyakunen shi*, p. 244.

213.   Iwai, p. 73.

214.   Ibid., p. 74.

215.   Forty-five of the people who died were bathing at the time, according to *Yomiuri Shimbun*, July 17, 1888. The *Tōkyō Asahi* coverage, which began on July 17, is discussed in Haruhara, pp. 67–68.

216.   *Tōkyō Asahi Shimbun*, July 28, 1889; Ono, *Gogai*, p. 16.

217.   Yamamoto Taketoshi, *Dokusha sō*, pp. 404–405.

218.   Recollection of Tokutomi, quoted in Iwai, p. 81.

219.   *Yūbin Hōchi Shimbun*, January 22, 1890; MNJ, 4, pp. 218–219.

220.   For an account of his success with *Kokumin no Tomo*, see John Pierson, *Tokutomi Sohō*, pp. 164–165, 170–177.

221.   Kanesada Hanazono, *The Development of Japanese Journalism*, p. 45.

222.   Chikamori, p. 164.

223.   Quoted by Iwai, p. 155.

224.   See Haruhara Akihiko, Yoneda Sayoko, et al., eds., *Josei kisha*, p. 10. Takekoshi sometimes is called Japan's first woman journalist, though she seems to have written only occasionally for *Kokumin*, giving her time primarily to activism in behalf of women's and popular rights issues. Also see Shimura Akiko in Tanaka Hiroshi, *Kindai Nihon no jiyānarisuto*, pp. 656–657.

225.   See Pierson, p. 176; Tokutomi created a good deal of resentment when he hired Kubota in 1890 for one hundred yen a month—three times the salary of most staffers.

226.   Iwai, p. 171.

227.   Kido Mataichi et al., eds., *Kōza gendai jiyānarizumu, 1 (Rekishi)*, p. 39.

228.   *Kokumin no Tomo*, January 3, 1890, quoted in Okano, p. 112.

229.   Pierson, p. 252; see, for example, "Itō naikaku," *Kokumin no Tomo*, February 1, 1896. By the late 1890s, Tokutomi had become a vocal supporter of the government's Chōshū faction, especially of Katsura Tarō, a point that will be discussed later.

230.   Ono, *Hattatsu shi*, p. 216.

231.   The first issue of *Kokumin Shimbun* showed the hand of an editor who was as good at promotion as he was at editorials. It included impressive artwork, several pages of ads, and congratulatory messages from some of the country's most popular figures, including Itagaki Taisuke, Ozaki Yukio, Yano Fumio, and Nakae Chōmin; see *Kokumin Shimbun*, February 1, 1890.

232.   Ukai, pp. 32–34.

233.   All told, he translated at least fifty novels, including Victor Hugo's *Les Misérables.*

234.   Actually, Kuroiwa changed the name of *Yoron Nippō* to *Nihon Taimusu* (with "Times" in *hiragana*); see Ono Hideo, "Kuroiwa Shūroku," p. 16. The paper received an unusually long eight-week suspension because of Kuroiwa's writings and never recovered.

235.   Ibid., pp. 16–18.

236.   Kuroiwa Shūroku, "Yo ga shimbun no kokorozashita dōki," p. 114.

237.   Ibid., p. 116.

238.   Ono, "Kuroiwa Shūroku," pp. 20–21.

239.   See announcement in *Mainichi Shimbun*, October 19, 1892; MNJ, 4, pp. 778.

240.   *Yorozu Chōhō*, February 1, 1892, in Okano, p. 12.

241.   Pemberton, p. 41.

242.   *Yorozu Chōhō*, November 1, 1892; Okano, p. 113.

243.   Kuroiwa, p. 119.

244.   Yamamoto Taketoshi, *Dokusha sō*, pp. 406–407.

245. *Yorozu Chōhō*, November 1, 1892; Iwai, pp. 205–206. Also see Ono, "Kuroiwa," p. 25; Nishida, *Shimbun to zasshi*, p. 176. Actually, newspaper prices had come down sharply at all the *ōshimbun*, for reasons described in this chapter. Even *Yomiuri*, the *koshimbun*, charged only 35 *sen* a month in 1890, compared to 33 *sen* in 1881. *Yorozu Chōhō* was nonetheless much cheaper than the others.

246. For a comparison of 1896 prices, see Iwai, p. 210.

247. Ibid., p. 22; the patron, taken aback, reportedly responded by paying for a full ten years in advance.

248. *Yorozu Chōhō*, November 1, 1892; Ono, "Kuroiwa," p. 25.

249. See Ono Hideo, "Shimbun kenkyū gojūnen," p. 25; also Chikamori, p. 171. He also said writing should be short, easy to understand, and interesting; Iwai, p. 215.

250. *Yorozu Chōhō*, November 1, 1892, in Ono, "Kuroiwa," p. 25.

251. Ibid., p. 85.

252. See Michael Emery and Edwin Emery, *The Press and America*, pp. 97–102. Day's *New York Sun* also was a four-page paper, which focused on sensational news and gained almost immediate success; Bennett's *New York Morning Herald* was more successful yet and like Kuroiwa even had the temerity to take on religious institutions.

253. *Yorozu Chōhō*, November 1, 1892; Okano, p. 113.

254. The episode is discussed in Ono, "Kuroiwa Shūroku," pp. 30–34.

255. He vigorously denied such charges, and I know of no credible support for them, at least in the early *Yorozu Chōhō* years; Kuroiwa, p. 117. Sasaki Takashi's list of papers receiving government assistance in this period includes no mention of *Yorozu Chōhō*; "Meiji jidai no seijiteki komiyunikēshiyon," 3, pp. 110–112.

256. Discussed at length in ibid., pp. 319–321; also Uchikawa and Arai, p. 38; Iwai, p. 215; Chikamori, p. 170.

257. Ono, "Kuroiwa Shūroku," p. 28.

258. Kubota Tatsuhiko, ed., *Nijūichi dai senkaku kisha den*, p. 310.

259. Nishida, *Shimbun to zasshi*, pp. 175–176.

260. Yamamoto Fumio notes that Ōkuma loved it and Itō read it each morning, afraid to miss what the masses might be learning; *Hattatsu shi*, p. 171.

261. Itō Michiumi, later head of the Buddhist sect Sōdōshū, about his days at Sōdōshū Daigaku, quoted in Iwai, p. 201. The reference to the "red newspaper" refers to the fact that *Yorozu Chōhō* was published for a time on red paper; see Kubota, pp. 310, 321.

262.   Ono Hideo, *Hattatsu shi*, pp. 150–152; his list: the decline of editorials, the addition of brief reviews, an increase in society news, greater coverage of business and the arts, the use of the telegraph, the addition of artwork, an increase in the size of the paper itself, the use of vertical mast-heads, the introduction of larger typefaces for headlines, the spread of promotion campaigns, increased reliance on ads for revenue.

263.   See Nishida, *Shimbun to zasshi*, p. 152, for an evaluation of this development.

264.   *Kokumin no Tomo*, January 3, 1890.

CHAPTER 7. REPORTING A WAR, 1894 TO 1895

1.   Ubukata Toshirō, "Kenpō happu to Nisshin Sensō," p. 88.

2.   China notified Japan on June 7 that it was sending troops, in keeping with the Tianjin Convention, but many Japanese maintained that the unilateral dispatch of forces violated the Convention's spirit. See Kamikawa Hikomatsu and Kimura Michiko, eds., *Japanese-American Diplomatic Relations in the Meiji-Taishō Era*, pp. 157–158. Actually, the Convention itself had left hawkish papers such as *Jiji Shinpō, Tōkyō-Yokohama Mainichi*, and *Yūbin Hōchi* unhappy back in 1885, since it permitted a nonmilitary Chinese presence in Seoul. They had not complained in print though, possibly because of censorship; see Hilary Conroy, *The Japanese Seizure of Korea, 1868–1910*, pp. 170–171.

3.   Tokutomi's leadership of an organized anti-Itō, pro-expansion press early in 1894 is analyzed in Komiya Kazuo, "Zenkoku Dōshi Shimbun Zasshi Kisha Dōmei to Meiji nijūnen zenhan no seikyoku," pp. 116–134; also Kajita Akihiro, "Meiji nijūnananen taigaikō undō to Tokutomi Sohō," pp. 59–75.

4.   The phrase was used in the official notification of China's decision to send troops; Kamikawa and Kimura, p. 158.

5.   Conroy concludes that the government's decision actually to go to war did not come until the middle of July, by which time events on the continent and public opinion at home had precluded other options. He notes, "Caution died hard in the oligarchs, especially Itō"; p. 254. Peter Duus sees the cabinet as fairly eager to support the idea of war, "determined not to let a golden opportunity slip"; see his *The Abacus and the Sword*, pp. 66–69.

6.   See, for example, Duus, pp. 90–91. Various Western powers tried unsuccessfully to negotiate an agreement between China and Japan in June and July, but nearly all thought China would win if war came; see Kamikawa and Kimura, pp. 159–163.

7.   See *Jiji Shinpō* editorial, May 22, 1894; Conroy, p. 228.

8. Reprinted in Uchikawa Yoshimi and Matsushima Eiichi, eds., *Meiji niyūsu jiten* (hereafter MNJ), 7, p. 43.

9. *Jiji Shinpō*, June 8, 1894; Nakayama Yasuaki, ed., *Shimbun shūsei Meiji hennenshi* (hereafter SSMH), 9, p. 81.

10. Yamamoto Fumio, *Nihon shimbun hattatsu shi*, p. 165; the dates are mistakenly reported as March 9 and 16 in Zen Nihon Shimbun Renmei, ed., *Shimbun taikan*, 1, p. 148.

11. Muramatsu Shōfū, ed., *Akiyama Teisuke wa kataru*, p. 94. See also Sakurada Kurabu, ed., *Akiyama Teisuke den*, p. 69.

12. Quoted in Haruhara Akihiko, *Nihon shimbun tsū shi*, pp. 83–84.

13. *Jiji*, June 14, 1894; SSMN, 9, p. 84.

14. *Jiji*, June 20, 26, 1894; SSMH, 9, pp. 87, 90.

15. *Yūbin Hōchi*, July 4, 1894; SSMH, 9, p. 95.

16. *Tōkyō Nichi Nichi Shimbun*, July 7, 1894; SSMH, 9, pp. 95–96.

17. *Yūbin Hōchi*, July 10, 1894; SSMH, 9, p. 97.

18. *Nihon*, July 12, 1894; SSMH, 9, p. 97.

19. *Jiji*, July 29, 1894; SSMH, 9, p. 106. Emphasis added.

20. Conroy, p. 463.

21. "Kōki," *Kokumin Shimbun*, July 23, 1894, quoted in John Pierson, *Tokutomi Soho, 1863–1957: A Journalist for Modern Japan*, p. 233.

22. *Tōkyō Keizai Zasshi*, June 16, 1894, quoted in Conroy, p. 446.

23. *Gifu Nichi Nichi Shimbun*, July 11, 1894, cited in Stewart Lone, *Japan's First Modern War*, p. 27.

24. *Jiji*, July 13, 1894; SSMH, 9, p. 98. Evaluation of *Jiji* stance by Uchikawa Yoshimi, MNJ, 7, p. 33.

25. *Jiji*, July 27, 1894; MNJ, 5, p. 33. Also excerpted in Yamamoto Fumio, *Hattatsu shi*, p. 166.

26. *Jiji*, July 29, 1894, quoted in Conroy, p. 255.

27. *Ōsaka Asahi Shimbun*, June 6, 1894; Yamamoto, *Hattatsu shi*, p. 165.

28. *Kokumin Shimbun*, June 9, 1894; SSMH, 9, p. 82.

29. *Tōkyō Nichi Nichi Shimbun* extra, June 7, 1894; MNJ, 5, p. 43.

30. Statements about the papers' suspensions are reproduced in Haruhara Akihiko, *Tsū shi*, pp. 81–82.

31. Reprinted in Ono Hideo, *Gogai hyakunen shi*, p. 22.

32.   "Kaitei dewanaku seifu no kaika—Tōnichi" (Not a release from suspension but a government apology to *Tōkyō Nichi Nichi*), *Tōkyō Nichi Nichi*, June 12, 1894; MNJ, 5, pp. 622–623. The editorial writer chided the writers at *Kokumin Shimbun* who had gloated in print about *Nichi Nichi*'s "errors."

33.   Ubukata, p. 89.

34.   *Tōkyō Nichi Nichi*, July 26, 1894; Yamamoto Fumio, *Hattatsu shi*, p. 166.

35.   *The Illustrated London News*, October 20, 1894, p. 491; quoted in Yamamoto Fumio, *Hattatsu shi*, p. 132. Emphasis in original.

36.   Ubukata, pp. 90–91.

37.   Donald Keene, "The Sino-Japanese War of 1894–95 and Its Cultural Effects in Japan," p. 126.

38.   One possible exception was the journal *Fuhei* (Discontent), banned after its maiden issue in August; *Yomiuri Shimbun*, August 16, 1894; SSMH, 9, p. 117; also Lone, p. 100.

39.   *Yorozu Chōhō*, October 18, 1894.

40.   Kenneth Pyle, *The New Generation in Meiji Japan: Problems of Cultural Identity, 1885–1895*, p. 199.

41.   *Kokumin Shimbun*, December 5, 1894; quoted in Nishida Taketoshi, *Meiji jidai no shimbun to zasshi*, p. 235.

42.   *Kokumin no Tomo*, August 23, 1894; translated as "Justification of the Corean War," in Uchimura Kanzō, *The Complete Works of Kanzō Uchimura*, 5, pp. 66–75. Emphasis in the original.

43.   *Jiji*, August 14, 1894, reprinted in Zen Nihon Shimbun Renmei, *Taikan*, 1, pp. 147–148. Similar *Jiji* editorials are discussed in Conroy, p. 255, and Carmen Blacker, *The Japanese Enlightenment: A Study of the Writings of Fukuzawa Yukichi*, p. 137.

44.   "Nihon shinmin no kakugo" (The resolution of the Japanese people), *Jiji*, August 28–29, 1894; MNJ, 5, pp. 586–588. Also Zen Nihon Shimbun Renmei, *Shimbun taikan*, 1, p. 148.

45.   The decree is reprinted in Midoro Masaichi, *Meiji Taishō shi: genron hen*, pp. 193–194. See also Yamamoto Fumio, *Hattatsu shi*, p. 168; Nishida, *Shimbun to zasshi*, pp. 229–230.

46.   Oka Mitsuo, *Kindai Nihon shimbun koshi*, p. 57.

47.   See Nishida, *Shimbun to zasshi*, p. 230; Yamamoto Fumio, *Hattatsu shi*, p. 168; Midoro, p. 194.

48.   The number in the tumultuous Diet years of 1892 and 1893 had been eighty-seven each; see Ukai Shin'ichi, *Chōya Shimbun no kenkyū*, p. 37.

49.   "The Press," *Yorozu Chōhō*, October 13, 1894.

50.   On July 23, Japanese Ambassador Otori had entered the Korean court, driven out the pro-Chinese Queen Min, and placed the pliable Taewongun in power.

51.   See Oka Mitsuo, p. 58. The Treaty of Alliance is reprinted in Conroy, pp. 266–267.

52.   *Tōkyō Nichi Nichi*, September 7, 1894; MNJ, 5, p. 624.

53.   Pyle, *New Generation*, p. 176.

54.   Takeichi Hideo, *Nichibei shimbun shi wa*, p. 107.

55.   Yomiuri Shimbunsha, ed., *Yomiuri Shimbun hyakunijūnen shi*, p. 72.

56.   See Takeichi, p. 107; Midoro, p. 193.

57.   See Yamamoto Fumio, *Hattatsu shi*, for a list of prominent correspondents.

58.   For the first military regulations for war correspondents, see Zen Nihon Shimbun Renmei, ed., *Kindai Nihon shimbun taikan*, 3, pp. 397–398.

59.   "Heijō jūgun kikō" (Traveling with the troops to Pyongyang), *Yomiuri*; quoted in Yomiuri Shimbunsha, p. 72.

60.   Oka Mitsuo, *Ōsaka no jiyānarizumu*, p. 102.

61.   Killed on September 15, 1894, near Pyongyang, Yamashita was the first Japanese ever to lose his life as a war correspondent. See Nihon Shimbun Renmei, *Nihon shimbun hyakunen shi*, p. 734. His name is mistakenly rendered Shimoyama in Oka Mitsuo, *Ōsaka no jiyānarizumu*, p. 102.

62.   Reporters from twenty-seven papers held a special meeting in Hiroshima during the war to demand that a system of compensation be set up; see Yomiuri Shimbunsha, p. 72.

63.   Before the war was out Tanaka Sadakichi was appointed to create Japan's first field operations postal service *(yasen yūbin kyoku)*; Yamamoto Fumio, *Hattatsu shi*, p. 168.

64.   *Asahi*'s Murayama Ryōhei reported that at *Asahi* the telegraph "became highly useful in reporting during the Sino-Japanese War of 1894–1895 and the Boxer Rebellion of 1900"; Yamamoto Taketoshi, *Shimbun kisha no tanjō*, p. 176. Yamamoto shows, however, that it was not until after the Russo-Japanese War of 1904–1905 that most papers had the capital to use the telegraph extensively; pp. 175–181.

65.   The Western papers experienced similar problems, especially when Reuter's chief Chinese correspondent, "an aged auctioneer in Shanghai, who is not a newspaper man," failed to cable news of most of the war's major events, causing what the *New York Times* gloatingly called a "break-

down of Reuter's service in the East in connection with news regarding the Japanese-Chinese war." See *New York Times*, September 19, 1894, reprinted in Uchikawa Yoshimi and Miyaji Masato, eds., *Gaikoku shimbun ni miru Nihon*, 2 *(Genbun hen)*, pp. 528–529.

66.   Zen Nihon Shimbun Renmei, *Shimbun taikan*, 1, p. 150.

67.   Yomiuri Shimbunsha, p. 73.

68.   See *Yūbin Hōchi*, February 22, 1895, on two French reporters' evaluation of Japanese troops, reprinted at length in Zen Nihon Shimbun Renmei, *Kindai Nihon shimbun taikan*, 3, pp. 398–400.

69.   Kuroda Kōshirō, *Tōkyō Nichi Nichi*, October 1, 1894; Lone, p. 36.

70.   The account is heavily excerpted in Lone, pp. 307–309.

71.   See Zen Nihon Shimbun Renmei, *Shimbun taikan*, 1, p. 149.

72.   *Yomiuri*, December 1–2, 1894; Yomiuri Shimbunsha, p. 73.

73.   "Yashū Kansenki" (An observer's record of a night battle), *Tōkyō Asahi*, February 17, 1895; described in Oka Mitsuo, *Ōsaka no jiyānarizumu*, p. 101.

74.   Both stories recorded in Keene, "Sino-Japanese War," pp. 138–139.

75.   Ibid., p. 133.

76.   The novel, begun in October 1894, was titled *Yobihei* (Reserve soldier); it is summarized in Keene, p. 180.

77.   Ibid., p. 129; Tokutomi Sohō's brother Roka also wrote serialized fiction about the war for *Kokumin Shimbun*.

78.   Keene, p. 131.

79.   Ubukata, p. 90. The stories and treatment of these heroes are recounted in Keene, pp. 143–155; the anonymous sailor's words are quoted on p. 153.

80.   Diaries of Japanese soldiers, quoted in Lone, p. 155.

81.   *Yorozu Chōhō*, October 17, 1894.

82.   The play was *Kairiku renshō asahi no mihata* (The rising sun flag, triumphant on land and sea); *Tōkyō Nichi Nichi*, November 7, 1894; MNJ, 5, p. 590. Fukuchi had helped to build the Kabukiza, which still stands in central Tokyo, and had become Japan's leading kabuki playwright since leaving the world of journalism. See my *Politics of the Meiji Press*, pp. 179–181. The play was a failure, though other plays related to the war were more successful; Keene, pp. 157–160.

83.   *Jiji*, December 11, 1894; MNJ, 5, pp. 591–592.

84. *Kokumin Shimbun*, December 5, 1894, in Pierson, pp. 235, 236; the quotation on the word "Japanese" is translated in Pyle, *New Generation*, pp. 175, 177.

85. *Yomiuri*, January 14, 1895; territorial gains also were discussed in a December 19, 1894, editorial. See Yomiuri Shimbunsha, p. 73.

86. *Jiji*, July 25, 1894; Watanabe Kazuo, *Jitsuroku gogai sensen*, pp. 111–113.

87. Oka Mitsuru, *Ōsaka no jiyānarizumu*, p. 101.

88. See Nihon Shimbun Renmei, *Hyakunen shi*, p. 273.

89. For a good example of both varied typefaces and maps, see *Ōsaka Asahi*, September 21, 1894, p. 2, in Asahi Shimbunsha, ed., *Asahi hyakunen no jūyō shimen*, p. 42.

90. *Jiji*, February 15, 1895; the cartoon was reprinted from the *New York World*.

91. *Yūbin Hōchi*, November 26, 1894; see discussion in Yamamoto Taketoshi, *Shimbun to minshū*, p. 74; also Yamamoto Fumio, *Hattatsu shi*, p. 172. The actual format changed more gradually after that than the paper's bold assertions might have led one to expect.

92. Ubukata, p. 95.

93. Quote from Pyle, *New Generation*, p. 180. Also see Pierson, pp. 237–238; Tokutomi returned home on the first ship available after hearing Japan had acquiesced to Russia, Germany, and France on May 5 and returned Liaodong to China; he kept the gravel in a box for years as a reminder of the humiliation he felt.

94. Mutsu Munemitsu, *Kenkenroku: A Diplomatic Record of the Sino-Japanese War, 1894–95*, pp. 251–252.

95. See Richard Mitchell, *Censorship in Imperial Japan*, p. 121.

96. *Ōsaka Asahi*, April 21, 1895; Asahi Shimbunsha, *Meiji hen*, p. 320. This was two days before Russia actually made its "advice" official.

97. *Niroku Shinpō*, April 24, 26, 1895; Sakurada Kurabu, *Akiyama Teisuke den*, 1, pp. 210–211.

98. Ubukata, p. 96; the original reads, "Oi, Nihon," with the *furigana* gloss "Jiyappu" beside Nihon.

99. *Tōkyō Nichi Nichi*, May 14, 1895.

100. *Nihon*, May 14, 1895.

101. See the article by Nishimura Tenshū, *Ōsaka Asahi*, May 14, 1895; Asahi Shimbunsha, *Meiji hen*, pp. 321–322.

102. *Ōsaka Asahi shimbun*, May 15, 1895; Asahi Shimbunsha, *Meiji hen*, p. 322. Also see Oka Mitsuo, *Kindai Nihon shimbun koshi*, p. 63.

103. Mutsu, pp. 248–229.

104. *Niroku Shinpō*, May 4, 1895, in Sakurada Kurabu, 1, p. 212.

105. *Niroku Shinpō*, May 29, 1895, in Sakurada Kurabu, 1, p. 215.

106. *Nihon*, May 27, 1895, quoted in Ono Hideo, *Shimbun no rekishi*, p. 58.

107. Several of these are discussed and quoted in Haruhara, pp. 85–86; Miyake's editorial ran in *Nihon*, May 15, 1895. It resulted in a lengthy ten-day suspension.

108. *Niroku Shinpō*, May 28, 1895, in Sakurada Kurabu, 1, p. 215.

109. *Kokumin Shimbun*, July 28, 1895; Pierson, pp. 237, 240.

110. Pierson, p. 238.

111. Quoted in Zen Nihon Shimbun Renmei, *Kindai Nihon shimbun taikan*, 3, p. 402.

112. *Yorozu Chōhō*, August 18, 1894. *Yorozu* complained again on August 28, 1894—a day after the paper failed to appear on the newsstands—about government censorship as an infringement on press freedom. I have not been able to ascertain if it was suspended on the twenty-seventh, though it likely was.

113. Based on examination of the actual papers. *Nihon* was suspended again after its May 27 issue and did not reappear until June 3; see Haruhara, p. 86.

114. See Sakurada Kurabu, 1, pp. 209–217.

115. See Yamamoto Taketoshi, *Shimbun to minshū*, p. 95.

116. See *Nihon*, May 27, June 3, 1895; the offending May 27 editorial by Kuga was titled "Ryōtō kanchi no jikyoku ni taisuru shigi" (Personal opinion of the circumstances of the Liaodong retrocession).

117. The figure for the decade was 729: 238 in 1895, 140 in 1894, 87 each in 1892 and 1893, 61 in 1891—and 25 or fewer in all other years. See Ukai, p. 37. Also Uchikawa Yoshimi, *Shimbun shi wa*, pp. 32–33; Midoro, *Meiji Taishō shi*, p. 180; Ono, *Shimbun no rekishi*, p. 60. After 1897, suspensions required judicial approval, and their numbers declined dramatically; see Gregory Kasza, *The State and the Mass Media in Japan, 1918–1945*, p. 15.

118. Kuga Katsunan, *Kuga Katsunan zenshū*, 4, p. 515.

119. Nishida, *Shimbun to zasshi*, p. 269.

120. At Ōsaka Asahi, the newspaper operation during the last half of 1894 cost 188,000 yen, compared to 106,000 during the first half of 1893, while profits went from 26,000 yen in the former period to 7,000 in the latter; *Ōsaka Mainichi*'s early 1893 profits of 4,985 yen decreased to 983 yen in the last half of 1894. See Ariyama Teruo, *Tokutomi Sohō to Kokumin Shimbun*, p. 80.

121.   Annual circulation for several papers in 1895: *Tōkyō Nichi Nichi*, 5,347,245; *Yūbin Hōchi*, 6,274,326; *Minato Shimbun*, 10,531,893; *Tōkyō Asahi*, 16,191,070; *Kokumin Shimbun*, 7,784,776; *Yorozu*, 19,812,240; *Ōsaka Mainichi*, 20,542,533; *Ōsaka Asahi*, 25,242,171. See Ukai, pp. 28–31.

122.   Oka Mitsuo, *Koshi*, p. 60.

123.   Midoro, p. 191.

124.   Michael Emery and Edwin Emery, *The Press and America*, p. 198.

125.   Ubukata, p. 87.

126.   See evaluations of Yamamoto Fumio, *Hattatsu shi*, p. 169; Nishida, *Shimbun to zasshi*, p. 269.

127.   They were, in order from largest to smallest, *Ōsaka Asahi*, *Ōsaka Mainichi*, *Tōkyō Asahi*, *Miyako*, *Yorozu*, *Yamato*, *Yūbin Hōchi*, and *Chūgai Shōgyō Shinpō*; Ukai, pp. 28–29.

128.   Figures are computed from Ukai, pp. 28–31, based on a rough average of three hundred issues a year.

CHAPTER 8. BUILDING A MASS BASE, 1895 TO 1903

1.   Letter, March 29, 1801, quoted in James E. Pollard, *The Presidents and the Press*, p. 74.

2.   Postcard correspondence to *Nihon*, July 18, 1898, quoted in Yamamoto Taketoshi, *Kindai Nihon no shimbun dokusha sō*, p. 144.

3.   Quoted in Oka Mitsuo, *Kindai Nihon shimbun koshi*, p. 65.

4.   Andrew Gordon, *Labor and Imperial Democracy in Prewar Japan*, p. 63; Uchikawa Yoshimi, "Shimbunshi hō no seitei katei to sono tokushitsu," p. 67.

5.   See Gordon, p. 70.

6.   Kanesada Hanazono, *The Development of Japanese Journalism*, p. 47.

7.   See George C. Allen, *A Short Economic History of Modern Japan*, pp. 231–232.

8.   Eighty-four percent of 8,612 companies; Sheldon Garon, *The State and Labor in Modern Japan*, p. 10.

9.   See Kazushi Okawa, *The Growth Rate of the Japanese Economy since 1878*, pp. 26–28.

10.   The labor demand is discussed in Garon, p. 14.

11.   Gordon, p. 63; by 1917, there were 140,940 industrial workers in Tokyo.

12.   Carol Gluck notes that by 1911, only 40 percent of Tokyo's residents had been born there; *Japan's Modern Myths: Ideology in the Late Meiji Period*, p. 33.

13.   Monthly wages based on survey by Yokohama Gennosuke of Tokyo's commoners cited in ibid., p. 151.

14.   Janet Hunter, *The Emergence of Modern Japan*, p. 93.

15.   Yamamoto Taketoshi, "Meiji sanjūnendai zenhan no shimbun dokusha sō," p. 123; also see his *Kindai Nihon shimbun dokusha sō*, pp. 115–16.

16.   Yamamoto Taketoshi, "Meiji sanjūnendai zenhan," p. 121.

17.   Gordon, p. 18.

18.   Gluck, p. 30.

19.   Hugh Patrick, *Japanese Industrialization and Its Social Consequences*, p. 31; Garon, p. 15. Garon notes that worker instability continued until well past the Meiji era.

20.   See chart by Gordon, p. 66.

21.   Uchikawa, "Seitei katei," p. 67; also see John Crump, *The Origins of Socialist Thought in Japan*, p. 22.

22.   Gordon, pp. 68, 72.

23.   The Association for the Promotion of Labor Unions (Rōdō Kumiai Keiseikai) was founded in 1897 to encourage the formation of other unions. The Union for Industrial Progress, founded in 1889, lasted but briefly, and the most successful attempt at organizing, the Ironworkers Union, lasted three years until it was felled in 1900 by the combined effect of the new Peace Police Law and changing economic conditions. Other temporary unions of the 1890s included the Printers Union and the Japan Railway Workers Reform Society.

24.   In Uchikawa Yoshimi and Arai Naoyuki, eds., *Nihon no jiyānarizumu: taishū no kokoro o tsukanda ka*, p. 37.

25.   *Chūō Kōron*, May 1899, quoted in Yamamoto Taketoshi, *Kindai Nihon no shimbun dokusha sō*, p. 93.

26.   See Ariyama Teruo in Uchikawa and Arai, p. 34.

27.   Nishida Taketoshi, *Meiji jidai no shimbun to zasshi*, p. 234.

28.   Hanazono, p. 47.

29.   Kuroiwa's quote about his aims is from Kuroiwa Shūroku, "Yo ga shimbun no kokorozashita dōki," p. 119. He was sensitive about the *"akashimbun"* (red newspaper) charge and took pains to note that redness was not a *Yorozu Chōhō* "characteristic" and that *Jiji Shinpō* used red

paper first (although I have gone through *Jiji* from 1882 to 1907 and find no evidence of red paper). He also says he discontinued the use of red paper in 1904, but my examination of original issues in the Meiji Shimbun Zasshi Bunkō shows the *Yorozu* using red paper from early 1897 (white is used on January 7, and issues are missing from then until February 18, by which time red was being used) until December 13, 1898; it is possible that dyes of other issues have faded, but paper for these dates clearly was red. Regarding the reasons for discontinuation, see *Yorozu* editorial, October 23, 1904; *furigana* in the editorial used the phrase *"iero jiyānaru"* in discussing the accusations of others that *Yorozu* was a "scandal sheet"; it is quoted in Yamamoto Taketoshi, *Shimbun kisha no tanjō*, p. 201.

30.   Nihon Shimbun Renmei, ed., *Nihon shimbun hyakunen shi*, pp. 546–547; D. Eleanor Westney, *Imitation and Innovation: The Transfer of Western Organizational Patterns to Meiji Japan*, pp. 183–184.

31.   *Yorozu Chōhō*, which had started with seven, increased to nine columns; Kuroiwa, p. 119.

32.   See chart in Ariyama Teruo, *Tokutomi Sohō to Kokumin Shimbun*, pp. 54–55.

33.   *Hōchi Shimbun*, January 27, 1902.

34.   On press purchases, see *Yorozu Chōhō*, February 9, 11, 1902, cited in Yamamoto Taketoshi, *Shimbun kisha no tanjō*, pp. 200–201; see also Yamamoto's *Kindai Nihon no shimbun dokusha sō*, p. 357. Regarding *Fukuoka Nichi Nichi*, see Uchikawa Yoshimi, *Shimbun shi wa*, p. 34.

35.   Nihon Shimbun Renmei, *Hyakunen shi*, p. 517; also Westney, p. 183.

36.   Westney, p. 184; *Ōsaka Asahi* went to ten pages in 1899. *Jiji*, by contrast, was publishing twelve-page editions by late in the 1890s; see Ariyama, *Tokutomi Sohō*, p. 100.

37.   See Yamamoto Fumio, *Nihon shimbun hattatsu shi*, p. 183.

38.   For a description of Ueno Riichi's ideas for twice-daily editions at *Asahi*, see Yamamoto Taketoshi, *Kindai Nihon no shimbun dokusha sō*, p. 128; also see Westney, p. 185. The idea was revived when distribution improved after the Russo-Japanese War, laying the groundwork for the two issues per day that most Japanese papers have today.

39.   From chart in Yamamoto Taketoshi, *Dokusha sō*, p. 332.

40.   Ibid., pp. 110, 133 (quote from p. 133).

41.   Yamamoto Fumio, *Hattatsu shi*, pp. 181–182.

42.   Ibid., pp. 205–206.

43.   See Yamamoto Taketoshi, *Dokusha sō*, p. 96, for circulation rates of six leading papers in 1899; the monthly and daily rates (in *sen*, with daily rates in parentheses) were *Jiji Shinpō*, 50 (2.5); *Nihon*, 40 (2); *Yomiuri*

Shimbun, 35 (2); *Hōchi Shimbun*, 35 (1.5); *Tōkyō Asahi Shimbun*, 33 (1.5); *Yorozu Chōhō*, 24 (1).

44.   Ōsugi Sakae, *The Autobiography of Ōsugi Sakae*, p. 96.

45.   Yamamoto Taketoshi, *Dokusha sō*, p. 96.

46.   See Iwai Hajime, *Shimbun to shimbunjin*, pp. 210–211.

47.   Reader interest in this contest is recounted in Tayama Katai's novel *Country Teacher*, pp. 157–158; the answer was 73,250.

48.   Stunts are discussed in Ono Hideo, *Shimbun no rekishi*, pp. 65–66; Hanazono, *Development*, p. 47; Yamamoto Fumio, *Hattatsu shi*, pp. 174–175; *Yorozu Chōhō's* gold coin was found at the Black Gate in Ueno Park.

49.   See, for example, Uchikawa and Arai, pp. 40–41.

50.   See especially Kuroiwa, pp. 50–52; also *Yorozu Chōhō*, July 2, 1901, reprinted in Nakayama Yasuaki, ed., *Shimbun shūsei Meiji hennen shi* (hereafter SSMH), 11, pp. 277–279. It also is discussed in F. G. Notehelfer, *Kōtoku Shūsui: Portrait of a Japanese Radical*, pp. 70, 101.

51.   Yamamoto Taketoshi, *Kisha no tanjō*, p. 183; these associations are discussed at length in his *Dokusha sō*, pp. 293–323. His charts on Risōdan and Nihon Seinenkai membership by regions and professions are especially useful; pp. 296, 302–303, 308.

52.   These postcards form the basis of much of Yamamoto Taketoshi's research in *Dokusha sō*; a chart breaking down the correspondents by class is found on p. 129. Also see Sharon Nolte, *Liberalism in Modern Japan: Ishibashi Tanzan and His Teachers*, p. 25.

53.   *Tōkyō Asahi*, June 17, 1899; Yamamoto Taketoshi, *Dokusha sō*, p. 117, n 3.

54.   Uchikawa and Arai, p. 32.

55.   In Kido Mataichi et al., eds., *Kōza gendai jiyānarizumu*, 1 *(Rekishi)*, p. 2.

56.   See Yamamoto Fumio, *Hattatsu shi*, p. 215; the 410-person staff included 48 in the business department and 107 workers in areas such as typesetting and printing. Also see the recollection of Kiryū Yūyū, in "Omoideru mama," 18 (March 20, 1940), *Tazan no ishi*, 4, p. 43.

57.   Chart reproduced in Yamamoto Taketoshi, *Kisha no tanjō*, p. 41.

58.   *Jiji Shinpō*, January 28–29, 1902.

59.   The *Nihon* circulation went from 21,124 a day in 1895 to 11,521 in 1899; it held its own after that, then rose in the Russo-Japanese War period; see Ariyama, *Tokutomi Sohō*, pp. 55, 139, 149.

60.   Quoted in Chikamori Haruyoshi, *Jinbutsu Nihon shimbun shi*, p. 185.

61. The first permanent family column actually was started by Hara Kei at *Ōsaka Mainichi* in May 1900; see Nijūseiki Kenkyūjo, ed., *Masu komiyunikēshiyon kōza*, 6 *(Masu komiyunikēshiyon jiten)*, p. 32.

62. Hara's policies are described in Ono, *Shimbun no rekishi*, pp. 66–67; also see Yamamoto Fumio, *Hattatsu shi*, p. 215, and Nijūseiki Kenkyūjo, 6, p. 30.

63. See Haruhara Akihiko, *Nihon shimbun tsū shi*, p. 90. Carrier pigeons were used by many of the Japanese papers until World War II.

64. See Roger Purdy, "The Ears and Voice of the Nation: The Dōmei News Agency and Japan's News Network, 1936–1945," p. 31. Others formed in these years included Jiyū Tsūshinsha (1899), Chūya Tsūshinsha and Taishō Tsūshinsha (1901), Tōkyō Kyūhōsha (1903), and Maiyū Tsūshinsha (1903).

65. *Kokumin Shimbun*, no. 5, February 1890, quoted in Haruhara Akihiko, Yoneda Sayoko, et al., eds., *Josei kisha*, p. 10. See also Ariyama, *Tokutomi Sohō*, pp. 18, 20. Even earlier, *Yomiuri* began the first newspaper serialization of a female novel in January 1889, the seventeen-year-old Kimura Akebono's *Fujin no kagami* (A woman's mirror); it described a woman who studied at Cambridge, then returned to Japan, where she ran a factory that hired the poor and established a nursery; see Chieko Mulhern, "Japan's First Newspaperwoman, Hani Motoko," p. 312.

66. She reported for that paper from 1889 until she was fired by editor Walter Dening; then the owner released Dening and made her editor; she left the paper in 1893 and became a journalist in China and a correspondent for the *London Standard*. See James Hoare, "British Journalists in Meiji Japan," p. 22.

67. Kishida Toshiko became a consultant to *Nihon Rikken Seitō Shimbun* and a contributor to women's journals in the 1880s. Useful treatment of the press' discussions of women's issues is found in Okano Takeo, *Meiji genron shi*, pp. 169–193. A number of women's monthly magazines also appeared in the 1880s, the most prominent being Iwamoto Yoshiharu's *Jogaku Zasshi*, founded in 1885. Others included *Jokan*, *Tōkyō Fujin Kyōfūkai Zasshi*, and Tokutomi's *Katei Zasshi*. Among the more important later-Meiji women's magazines were the socialist, liberationist *Sekai Fujin* of Fukuda Hideko; Hiratsuka Raichō's *Blue Stocking (Seitō)*, the first Japanese magazine published exclusively by women; and Hani Motoko's own *Fujin no Tomo*. See Katō Keiko, "Josei to jōhō: Meiji ki no fujin zasshi kōkoku o tōshite," pp. 31–33. The first women's "newspaper," the weekly *Fujin Shimbun*, was founded in 1900 and survived for forty-three years; Haruhara, Yoneda, et al., p. i.

68. Others give the title of "first woman journalist" to Takekoshi Takeyo, noted above. Her work as a journalist seems, however, to have been secondary to her primary efforts as an activist for women's issues and popular rights. The first to give herself to reporting as a profession was Hani. See Shimura Akiko, "Meiji ki no jiyānarisuto," pp. 656–657.

69.   Hani Motoko, "Stories of My Life," p. 346.

70.   Ibid., p. 349.

71.   Mulhern, p. 322.

72.   See Hani, p. 350.

73.   Shimura p. 655. The list that follows is taken largely from here and from Haruhara, Yoneda, et al., pp. 15–18.

74.   "Katei no shiori" (Family guidebook); it was renamed "Katei ran" (Family column) in July 1900, four month after Ōta's entry.

75.   See Haruhara, *Nihon shimbun tsū shi*, p. 97; Uchikawa, *Shimbun shi wa*, p. 81. Honjō also called herself Japan's "first woman reporter" (see Shimura, p. 656), but there seems to be no evidence to support the claim.

76.   By 1897, only 50.9 percent of school-aged girls were attending school, compared with 80.7 percent of all children; five years later, the figure for girls was up to 87 percent. See Katō Keiko, p. 31; Yamamoto Taketoshi, *Dokusha sō*, p. 168.

77.   Hani, p. 347; "zoo" was the slang term commonly used for the newsroom then.

78.   Cited in Mulhern, pp. 321–322.

79.   *Tōkyō Asahi*, October 11, 1909; Haruhara, Yoneda, et al., p. 17.

80.   This approach is discussed in detail in Nakanowatari Naoyuki, ed., *Masukomi kindai shi*, pp. 69–124; also see Yamamoto Taketoshi, *Shimbun to minshū*, pp. 100–130, on the development of reporting in these years.

81.   See Ono Hideo, *Nihon shimbun hattatsu shi*, p. 252.

82.   See Shōwa Joshi Daigaku Kindai Bungaku Kenkyūshitsu, ed., *Kindai bungaku kenkyū sōsho*, 7 ("Fukuchi Ōchi"), pp. 333–338; Uchikawa, *Shimbun shi wa*, pp. 173–174.

83.   See Nishida, *Shimbun to zasshi*, pp. 238–239; Hanazono, *Development*, p. 48.

84.   He actually entered the Matsukata cabinet (1896–1898); in the early 1900s, he was especially close to Prime Minister Katsura Tarō. The best treatment of *Kokumin Shimbun* in these years is Ariyama, *Tokutomi Sohō*, pp. 91–135.

85.   Kuga Katsunan, *Nihon oyobi Nihonjin*, April 1930, quoted in Yamamoto Taketoshi, *Dokusha sō*, p. 141.

86.   See Uchikawa, *Shimbun shi wa*, pp. 154–155.

87.   *Maiyū* changed its name to *Tōkyō Maiyū Shimbun* in 1910 and published until 1941; its strengths were market prices and *sanmen kiji*.

The best study of this generally overlooked paper is Yamamoto Taketoshi, *Dokusha sō,* pp. 254–262.

88.   The paper had begun as *Yokohama Mainichi,* then had become *Tōkyō-Yokohama Mainichi* in 1879, and had changed its name to the simple *Mainichi Shimbun* in 1886; Shimada took over as editor after the death of Numa Morikazu in 1890; it was not related to the *Ōsaka Mainichi Shimbun* or to today's *Mainichi Shimbun.*

89.   The episode is discussed in Katakozawa Chiyomatsu, "Shimada Saburō," pp. 276–278; Shimada called Hoshi "the great public thief."

90.   *Mainichi Shimbun,* December 9, 1901; Yamamoto Taketoshi, *Dokusha sō,* p. 156.

91.   See Ariyama, *Tokutomi Sohō,* pp. 54–55; *Mainichi's* circulation declined again in the early 1900s, at least in part because Shimada's antimilitarism was not in sync with the anti-Russian expansionism sweeping the country. Shimada was among the last editors to come out in favor of war.

92.   Ibid.

93.   See Iwai, p. 97.

94.   See the chart in Yamamoto Taketoshi, *Dokusha sō,* pp. 406–407; in 1899, for example, *Jiji* had 20,412,383 non-Tokyo readers (about two-thirds of its total circulation), compared to 13,822,792 for *Yorozu Chōhō,* the paper with the second highest total.

95.   The monthly rates (in *sen*) of six leading papers in 1899: *Jiji,* 50; *Nihon,* 40; *Hōchi,* 35; *Yomiuri,* 35; *Tōkyō Asahi,* 33; *Yorozu,* 24. Ibid., p. 96; see pp. 110–111 and 132–133 for an evaluation of the *Jiji* readership.

96.   *Taiyō,* July 1900; Yamamoto Taketoshi, *Dokusha sō,* p. 131.

97.   Yamamoto Taketoshi, *Dokusha sō,* pp. 128–132, quote on p. 132.

98.   The Shinpotō (Progressive Party) was founded in 1896 by ninety-nine Diet members to advocate an active foreign policy and a government responsible to the Diet. For a discussion of *Hōchi's* political ties, see Uchikawa, *Shimbun shi wa,* pp. 144–145.

99.   Quoted in Yamamoto Taketoshi, *Dokusha sō,* p. 101.

100.   See *Hōchi Shimbun,* January 14, 1901; also Yamamoto Taketoshi, *Dokusha sō,* pp. 103–104.

101.   Correspondence column, *Hōchi,* December 6, 1899; Yamamoto Taketoshi, *Dokusha sō,* p. 103.

102.   See Christiane Seguy, *Histoire de la presse Japonaise,* p. 261; also Yamamoto Taketoshi, *Kisha no tanjō,* p. 170. Reader classifications are based on Yamamoto's *Dokusha sō,* p. 129; it is worth noting that *Hōchi's* approach still remained too serious for the lowest classes of readers; it was taken by very limited numbers of the laboring classes.

103.   See Ariyama, *Tokutomi Sohō*, pp. 54–55; Uchikawa and Arai, p. 50. By the early 1900s, *Yorozu* was no longer Tokyo's circulation leader, however; its place was taken by *Niroku Shinpō*, which was revived on February 1, 1900, then shut down by the government again on April 4, 1904.

104.   See Yamamoto Taketoshi, *Dokusha sō*, p. 129.

105.   *Chūō Kōron*, January 1903; Ono, *Shimbun no rekishi*, p. 65.

106.   Masaoka Geiyō, *Shimbunsha no uramen*, cited in Ono Hideo, "Kuroiwa Shūroku," p. 41.

107.   Norman Isaacs, *Untended Gates: The Mismanaged Press*, p. 47.

108.   It was translation that first gained Kuroiwa a name as a journalist; he translated nearly sixty novels into Japanese during his lifetime. See Kuroiwa, p. 85.

109.   *Yorozu*, November 19, 1899; also see Nobuya Bamba and John Howes, eds., *Pacifism in Japan: The Christian Socialist Tradition*, p. 131. Kawakami is discussed in the unpublished manuscript by William D. Hoover, "Journalist Kawakami Kiyoshi Interprets Japan's Relations with the United States," Association for Asian Studies, Honolulu, Hawaii, 1996.

110.   Writing in *Yonjūgonen kisha seikatsu*, quoted in Ono, "Kuroiwa Shūroku," p. 48.

111.   *Yorozu*, June 5, 1899, reprinted in Uchimura Kanzō, *The Complete Works of Kanzō Uchimura*, 7, p. 103.

112.   *Yorozu*, June 12, 1899; in Uchimura, *Complete Works*, 7, p. 104.

113.   *Yorozu*, June 19–25, 1901; reprinted in SSMH, 11, pp. 266–269, 271–276.

114.   *Yorozu*, June 19, 1901; SSMH, 11, p. 266.

115.   *Yorozu*, June 21, 1901; SSMH, 11, p. 268.

116.   *Yorozu*, June 24, 1901; SSMH, 11, p. 274.

117.   Phrase from Yamamoto Taketoshi, *Shimbun to minshū*, p. 97.

118.   Masaoka Un'yō, quoted in Ono, "Kuroiwa Shūroku," p. 41.

119.   See, for example, Uchikawa Yoshimi, "Shimbun dokusha no hensen," p. 24.

120.   Ōita, Yamaguchi, and Toyama had six each; Aichi had nine and Hokkaidō thirteen; Saitama had none; Iwate, Fukui, Miyazaki, Kagoshima, and Okinawa had one each; and another seven had just two each.

121.   Figures here are based on Ukai Shin'ichi, *Chōya Shimbun no kenkyū*, pp. 44–45.

122.   See Nishida, *Shimbun to zasshi*, pp. 152–159.

123. See charts, Yamamoto Taketoshi, *Dokusha sō*, pp. 406–407; Ukai, pp. 44–45.

124. The precise figure going to Kyushu was 7,872; see chart, Yamamoto Taketoshi, *Dokusha sō*, p. 273.

125. Also see Yamamoto Taketoshi, "Shimbun sangyō no keisei katei," p. 168. Though it lies outside the parameters of this study, it should be noted that the magazine world also became commercialized after the late 1890s, especially under the influence of the powerful publisher Hakubunkan, founded by Ōhashi Sahei in 1887. One of its most influential early magazines was *Taiyō*, sometimes called Japan's first *sōgō zasshi* or all-purpose magazine. See Nishida, *Shimbun to zasshi*, pp. 259–265, for a general discussion of magazines of this period.

126. In Uchikawa and Arai, pp. 31–59, esp. pp. 31–32. Uchikawa Yoshimi argues that the "campaign journalism" label is too narrow, that while campaigns were important, use of the label causes scholars to miss many of the more important facets of the era; interview with him, November 29, 1983.

127. See *Yorozu*, October 9, 10, and 19, 1902, reprinted in Uchikawa Yoshimi and Matsushima Eiichi, eds., *Meiji niyūsu jiten* (hereafter MNJ), 6, pp. 53–54.

128. *Niroku Shinpō*, November 2, 1903.

129. The articles ran from April 29 to July 25, 1900, and are discussed in Sakurada Kurabu, ed., *Akiyama Teisuke den*, 1, pp. 153–155; Yamamoto Fumio, *Hattatsu shi*, p. 172; Inoue Kaoru eventually intervened to bring the attacks to a close.

130. *Niroku Shinpō*, October 26, 1901; Haruhara, *Tsū shi*, pp. 105–106.

131. *Yorozu*, July 7, 1898; MNJ, 6, p. 740.

132. The more notable sketches are reprinted in MNJ, 6, pp. 740–755.

133. Chikamori, *Jinbutsu Nihon shimbun shi*, p. 170.

134. *Mainichi Shimbun*, October 15, 1900.

135. *Mainichi Shimbun*, November 3–10, 1900; the accusation ran, along with lists of other council members, at the top of page three, for eight successive days. This episode is detailed in Haruhara, *Tsū shi*, pp. 102–105.

136. *Mainichi Shimbun*, December 22, 1900.

137. Katakozawa Chiyomatsu, "Shimada Saburō," p. 278.

138. See Tanaka, *Kindai Nihon no jiyānarisuto*, pp. 453–672, for a journalist-by-journalist treatment of this topic.

139. Yokoyama Gennosuke, *Nihon no kasō shakai* (1899), from *Yokoyama Gennosuke zenshū*, 1 (Meiji Bunken, 1972), pp. 139–140, trans-

lated in Garon, p. 27. See Nishida Taketoshi, *Nihon jiyānarizumu shi ken-kyū*, pp. 359–459, 508–525, for detailed treatment of Yokoyama and his writings.

140. *Niroku Shinpō*, April 1, 1901; MNJ, 6, p. 799.

141. Described in Chikamori, *Jinbutsu Nihon shimbun shi*, p. 180; also see Crump, p. 24.

142. *Niroku Shinpō*, April 4, 1901; MNJ, 6, pp. 800–801; Katayama also thanked *Niroku Shinpō* profusely for its efforts on behalf of workers.

143. *Jiji*, March 17, 1902; *Kokumin Shimbun*, March 19, 1902; *Niroku Shinpō*, March 30, 1902; MNJ, 6, pp. 802–803.

144. Quoted in Haga Eizō, *Meiji Taishō hikka shi*, p. 124. Murphy's role is discussed in Katakozawa, pp. 283–284. The 1872 law is reprinted and analyzed in Ishikawa Iwao, "Meiji gonen shōgi kaihō rei," pp. 55–60. For a discussion of earlier press treatment of the problem of Japanese girls being sold as prostitutes abroad, see Nishida, *Nihon jiyānarizumu shi*, pp. 344–358. The *Japan Evangelist*, published by the Conference of Federated Missions, was a forerunner of the *Japan Christian Quarterly*; see Charles W. Iglehart, *A Century of Protestant Christianity in Japan*, pp. 145–146.

145. *Niroku Shinpō*, September 4, 1900; MNJ, 6, pp. 294–295.

146. Muramatsu Shōfū, ed., *Akiyama Teisuke wa kataru*, p. 185.

147. See, for example, *Jiji*, September 11, 1900; MNJ, 6, pp. 310–312.

148. Home Ministry ordinance 44, *Kanpō*, October 2, 1900; SSMH, 11, p. 131.

149. Former figure, *Jiji*, October 31, 1900; MNJ, 6, p. 314; latter figure, William Mensendiek, "Protestant Missionary Perceptions of Meiji Japan," p. 243.

150. Kenneth Pyle, F. G. Notehelfer, and Alan Stone, "Symposium: The Ashio Copper Mine Pollution Case," p. 363 (Notehelfer quote); these three articles (pp. 347–408) contain a particularly useful summary of the entire Ashio episode.

151. The early leader in coverage was *Nihon*, which sent a reporter to investigate reports of village suffering in the spring of 1891 (see May 12, 1891); the early coverage is discussed in Tamura Norio, "Nōmin undō to komiyunikēshiyon," pp. 165–169.

152. This "press war," which Yamamoto Taketoshi calls the most intense of the period, is described in his "Ashio kōdoku mondai no hōdō to yoron," pp. 175–178. The fiercest opponents were *Yomiuri*, on the side of the victims, and *Nichi Nichi*.

153. Kōuchi Saburō, "Iwayuru kōgai hōdō no rekishi: Ashio kōdoku jiken no issokumen," p. 28.

154. See Pyle et al., "Symposium," pp. 376–381. In the initial trial, which ended December 22, 1900, twenty-nine were found guilty of resist-

ing public officials, while twenty-two were found innocent. The appeals to the Tokyo Court of Appeals, which drew even more press coverage than the initial trial, overthrew all but three of the convictions. The Court of Cassation then remanded the whole case to the Miyagi Court of Appeals, where it was thrown out on December 25, 1902.

155.   Ibid., p. 396.

156.   *Jiji* editorials: October 5, 1901 ("shifting in spirit"), January 19, 1902 ("excessive exaggeration"), March 22, 1902 ("scientific"); Kōuchi, pp. 30–32.

157.   See *Hōchi*, October 5, 1901; Kōuchi, p. 33.

158.   Particularly helpful here is Yamamoto Taketoshi, "Ashio dōtoku mondai," pp. 248–250; Yamamoto notes that a number of individual reporters were quite sympathetic to the Ashio farmers even when their papers were not. On this point, also see Okano, pp. 211–213, for an account of *Yorozu* reporter Kōtoku Shūsui's support of Tanaka.

159.   Kenneth Strong, *Ox against the Storm: A Biography of Tanaka Shōzō*, p. 116.

160.   *Yorozu*, December 3, 1901. Kōuchi notes that while it is not clear whether Furukawa did indeed have seven concubines, he did not refute the allegation; p. 35.

161.   See Pyle et al., "Symposium," p. 397.

162.   Kōuchi Saburō sees these January 1902 editorials breaking important ground in moving the issue away from simple concern about victims and farmer-official clashes to the broader, systemic question of democracy and official attitudes toward the "people"; see especially pp. 29–30.

163.   See Strong, p. 124 (Pollution Group), p. 118 (Tanaka response); Yamamoto Taketoshi, "Ashio kōdoku mondai," pp. 248–249 (commission).

164.   Alan Stone in Pyle et al., "Symposium," pp. 396, 398. Kiryū Yūyū supports this assessment with the comment in his memoirs that it was the newspapers that acquainted him, as a student who knew nothing about national matters, with the Ashio problem; *Omoideru mama*, 17 (March 5, 1940), in *Tazan no ishi*, 4, p. 36.

165.   *Yorozu*, December 30, 1901, probably written by Kōtoku Shūsui; Kōuchi, p. 16.

166.   Richard Mitchell, *Censorship in Imperial Japan*, p. 17.

167.   Figures from Uchikawa Yoshimi, "Shimbunshi hō no seitei katei," p. 63.

168.   Peter Duus, "Liberal Intellectuals and Social Conflict in Taishō Japan," p. 438.

169.   This account relies a good deal on Barbara Teeters, "Press Freedom and the *Twenty-sixth Century* Affair in Meiji Japan," pp. 337–351. Also see Sasaki Takashi, "Nijūseiki jiken to hanbatsu," pp. 15–28; Midoro, *Meiji Taishō shi*, p. 184, Haruhara, *Tsū shi*, pp. 88–89; Haga, pp. 122–123.

170.   Quoted in Midoro, p. 182.

171.   See Teeters, pp. 342, 344.

172.   Numerous papers, including *Yorozu, Yomiuri, Tōkyō Asahi, Tōkyō Shimbun, Mainichi, Hōchi,* and *Kokumin,* were ordered by the Imperial Household Ministry to retract articles about this episode; see Yamamoto Taketoshi, *Dokusha sō,* p. 389.

173.   *Nihon,* December 18, 1896; reprinted in Kuga Katsunan, *Kuga Katsunan zenshū,* 5, p. 477.

174.   These measures are discussed, among other places, in Nishida, *Shimbun to zasshi,* p. 230; Gregory Kasza, *The State and the Mass Media in Japan, 1918–1945,* pp. 14–15; Mitchell, *Censorship,* pp. 112–113; and, most extensively, in Midoro, pp. 177–182. Midoro gives a useful summary of each Diet's actions on pp. 189–190.

175.   See Lawrence Beer, *Freedom of Expression in Japan,* p. 58; Uchikawa, "Seitei katei," p. 61; Jay Rubin, *Injurious to Public Morals: Writers and the Meiji State,* p. 26. Pertinent portions of the law are reprinted in Midoro, pp. 423–424.

176.   Exceptions were *Tōkyō Nichi Nichi* and *Kokumin Shimbun.*

177.   Uchikawa Yoshimi, *Masu medeiya hō seisaku shi kenkyū,* p. 41.

178.   Midoro, p. 231.

179.   The author of this memo is unclear, but it is written on Privy Council paper, and Yamamoto Fumio speculates that it was Itō Miyoji, who was both president of *Tōkyō Nichi Nichi* (1891–1904) and, after 1899, a member of the Privy Council; *Hattatsu shi,* pp. 161–162.

180.   Douglass Cater, *The Fourth Branch of Government,* p. 76.

181.   According to a list drawn up by *Nihon,* late in 1896, only *Yorozu* and *Nihon* were independent; *Jiji* was tied to business interests and *Chūō Shimbun* to the Kokumin Kyōkai; Nishida, *Shimbun to zasshi,* p. 244. By 1900, Ōkuma's reception room was described by one observer as "something like a school for reporters" and his party headquarters as "a social club of revered reporters," so close had the relationship between party and many reporters become; see Yamamoto Taketoshi, *Kisha no tanjō,* p. 307.

182.   Yamamoto Taketoshi, *Shimbun to minshū,* p. 82. Reader cynicism was heightened by rumors, apparently well founded, about government subsidies to certain papers, including four hundred yen a month to *Kokumin,* an unknown amount to *Yamato,* and various kinds of assistance to *Tōkyō Nichi Nichi.* See Itō Takashi and George Akita, "The Yamagata-Tokutomi Correspondence: Press and Politics in Meiji-Taishō Japan," p. 402; they also cite as indirect subsidies the provision of news scoops to favored journalists and giving favored reporters the calligraphy of famous people, which could then be framed and sold at high prices. It is worth noting that the English-language *Japan Times* was founded in 1897 with finan-

cial and other assistance from powerful political and business leaders such as Itō Hirobumi and Shibusawa Eiichi.

183.   He declined a higher-profile post as cabinet secretary because of the time it would have taken away from his work as a journalist.

184.   See John Pierson, *Tokutomi Sohō, 1863–1957: A Journalist for Modern Japan,* pp. 253–274 (260–261 for the quote).

185.   See Itō and Akita, pp. 399, 401, for example. Rubin notes a telling example of the effect of Tokutomi's liaison with the government; in 1902 his brother, the well-known writer Roka, broke with the paper because its editors on their own removed antigovernment phrases from one of his articles; p. 170.

186.   Pierson, pp. 274–275.

187.   Yamamoto Taketoshi notes that demands for papers to correct errors or retract materials peaked before the Sino-Japanese War, then declined, partly because papers became more careful about what they wrote and partly because the officials and the courts grew more lenient, particularly as the papers learned what kinds of things were and were not allowed; *Dokusha sō,* pp. 387–389.

188.   From charts in Uchikawa, *Masu medeiya hō,* p. 33, developed from *Nihon teikoku tōkei nenkan;* in the same years, 676 more were fined and one jailed under the Publication Law.

189.   The sentence was overturned on trial and he was released early; see Nobuya Bamba and John Howes, eds., *Pacifism in Japan: The Christian Socialist Tradition,* pp. 7–71.

190.   See Rubin, p. 48.

191.   See, for example, Katakozawa, p. 281; Uchikawa, *Masu medeiya hō,* p. 44.

192.   Sakurada Kurabu, 1, p. 285; also Uchikawa and Arai, pp. 43–44. Akiyama asserted that the investigations all were complete fabrications, aimed at intimidation.

193.   See Beer, p. 58; the Home Ministry did keep lists until 1910 of papers that had received *hatsubai hanpu kinshi* orders, which publishers could consult for guidance.

194.   Uchikawa, *Masu medeiya hō* chart, p. 34, compiled from *Nihon teikoku tōkei nenkan.*

195.   *Hansei Zasshi,* quoted in Ono, *Shimbun no rekishi,* p. 62.

196.   *Hakkō teishi* cases between 1897 and 1903 totaled just seven: six in 1900 and one in 1903; Uchikawa, *Masu medeiya hō,* p. 34. Also see evaluation of Yamamoto Taketoshi, *Shimbun to minshū,* p. 95.

197.   The actual number that year was 1,499; in a typical year, about three hundred publications died and five hundred new ones were born. See Uchikawa, "Seitei katei," p. 87.

198.   *Hōchi's* circulation was 86,279, *Yorozu's* 95,876, *Ōsaka Asahi's* 113,249; see Uchikawa and Arai, p. 39; Yamamoto Taketoshi, *Dokusha sō,* p. 411.

199.   In 1903, according to Police Bureau statistics, *Ōsaka Asahi, Ōsaka Mainichi, Tōkyō Asahi, Hōchi,* and *Yorozu* all had more than 70,000 subscribers. Precise figures are difficult to obtain at the beginning of the 1900s, because highly competitive editors tended to guard circulation information; no one disputes that these figures are approximately correct. See Uchikawa and Arai, p. 39; Yamamoto Taketoshi, *Kisha no tanjō,* p. 170, Ariyama, *Tokutomi Sohō,* p. 139.

200.   The largest in 1904 were *Shin Aichi* (40,000), *Chūkyō Shinpō* (25,000), and *Fukuoka Nichi Nichi Shimbun* (20,000); see Yamamoto Fumio, *Hattatsu shi,* pp. 201–203.

201.   The *New York Times* did not pass the 100,000 mark until 1901; see Michael Emery and Edwin Emery, *The Press and America,* pp. 135, 198.

202.   Quoted in Norman Isaacs, *Untended Gates: The Mismanaged Press,* p. 3.

203.   Editorial campaign, *Yorozu,* June 19–25, 1901; also see Ono, "Kuroiwa Shūroku," pp. 53–58.

204.   Hanazono, *Development,* p. 47.

205.   "Seitō naikaku," *Ōsaka Mainichi Shimbun,* July 4–14, 1898; excerpted and discussed in Haruhara, *Tsū shi,* pp. 94–95.

206.   Gluck, p. 27.

207.   Interview, February 8, 1995.

208.   Peter Duus, *Party Rivalry and Political Change in Taishō Japan,* p. 25.

209.   Ōsugi, p. 97. Also see Kōuchi, pp. 8–17, for a discussion of the rising social consciousness in the press.

210.   *Jiji,* September 1, 1897.

CHAPTER 9. COVERING A BIGGER WAR, 1903 TO 1905

1.   Tayama Katai, *Country Teacher,* p. 202.

2.   *Yorozu Chōhō,* October 9, 1903.

3.   Their editorials are reprinted or excerpted in Okano Takeo, *Meiji genron shi,* p. 139; Nakayama Yasuaki, ed., *Shimbun shūsei Meiji hennen shi* (hereafter SSMH), 12, pp. 117–118; Haga Eizō, *Meiji Taishō hikka shi,* pp. 128–130; Araki Masayasu, ed., *Shimbun ga kataru Meiji shi,* 2, p. 264;

Uchikawa Yoshimi and Matsushima Eiichi, eds., *Meiji niyūsu jiten* (hereafter MNJ), 7, pp. 747–779.

4. The timing of this episode related directly to the fact that October 8 had been set as the deadline for Russia to withdraw the last of its troops from Manchuria, and it had not done so. Kuroiwa first announced his decision to shift to a prowar stance in *Yorozu* on that day, and Uchimura, Kōtoku, and Sakai made their decision to resign that night. See Uchikawa Yoshimi, *Shimbun shi wa,* p. 51.

5. *Yorozu,* October 13, 1903; SSMH, 12, p. 120.

6. *Taiyō,* October 20, 1897, p. 59, quoted in Carol Gluck, *Japan's Imperial Myths: Ideology in the Late Meiji Period,* p. 25.

7. Ivan Hall, *Mori Arinori,* p. 408.

8. A useful discussion of this development, particularly in the periodical press, is found in Okano, pp. 118–130.

9. *Asahi Shimbun* was especially vigorous in covering the rebellion and Japan's participation in the international force that put it down; see discussions in Nishida Taketoshi, *Meiji jidai no shimbun to zasshi,* p. 246; Yamamoto Fumio, *Nihon shimbun hattatsu shi,* pp. 186–187.

10. See Oka Yoshitake, *Five Political Leaders of Modern Japan,* pp. 185–186.

11. Nishida, p. 237.

12. He was responding to suggestions of Takekoshi Yosaburō that his calls for an alliance with Great Britain were "impractical"; quoted in Chikamori Haruyoshi, *Jinbutsu Nihon shimbun shi,* p. 141.

13. It is significant that the *Asahi*s and *Yomiuri* were supporters of the Kenseihontō political party, which had descended from Ōkuma Shigenobu's Kaishintō and Shinpotō, while *Jiji* and *Ōsaka Mainichi* were neutral; the only pro-Kenseihontō paper not to call for war was Shimada Saburō's *Mainichi Shimbun.* See discussion in Shumpei Okamoto, *The Japanese Oligarchy and the Russo-Japanese War,* p. 67. It also was significant that both *Asahi*s had close ties to the nationalist *Nihon,* having quite consciously hired away several hawkish *Nihon* writers (Takahashi Kenzō, Ikebe Kichitarō, and Torii Sōsen). A direct side effect of the Japanese reportage was the stimulation of anti-Manchu protests by Chinese students studying in Japan against what they saw as Yuan Shikai's weak policies toward Russia; see Mary B. Rankin, *Early Chinese Revolutionaries,* p. 22.

14. "Nichiro kaisen setsu shikiri ni" (Repeated explanations of the opening of a Japanese-Russian war), *Tōkyō Asahi,* April 19, 1903; SSMH, 12, p. 53.

15. *Tōkyō Asahi,* May 1, 1903; SSMH, 12, p. 58.

16. *Tōkyō Asahi,* April 15, 1903; MNJ, 7, p. 490.

17. See Okamoto, pp. 63–64.

18. *Tōkyō Nichi Nichi*, June 21, 1903; MNJ, 7, p. 491; *Nichi Nichi* also reported an admonition Education Minister Kikuchi Dairoku gave the seven on June 28; p. 493.

19. Account in *Tōkyō Asahi*, June 24, 1904; MNJ, 7, pp. 491–492. A good account in English of the seven professors incident is Byron Marshall, "Professors and Politics: The Meiji Academic Elite," pp. 86–97. The tensions between the professors continued until after the Russo-Japanese War, when Tomizu was suspended from the Tokyo University faculty and large numbers of faculty members there and at Kyoto University threatened to resign, forcing the government to capitulate. The professors included Kanai Noboru, Onozuka, Terao Tōru, and Tomii Masaaki. Also see Araki, 2, pp. 249–251.

20. *Niroku Shinpō*, English column, June 15, 1903.

21. See Gregory Ornatowski, "Press, Politics, and Profits: The 'Asahi Shimbun' and the Prewar Japanese Newspaper," pp. 67–68.

22. See *Tōkyō Asahi*, September 12, 1903 (note: Ikebe, who also was active behind the scenes in the summer of 1903, talking privately with Katsura, Itō, and Yamagata in behalf of war, wrote under the alias Sanzan); "Manshū mondai kōshō shinten sezu," (No progress in negotiations about the Manchurian problem), *Jiji*, September 9, 1903, in MNJ, 7, p. 493; *Yorozu*, September 15, 1903, quoted in Okamoto, p. 86.

23. *Yorozu*, October 14, 1903, reprinted in *Japan Weekly Mail*, October 17, 1903; see Okamoto, p. 86.

24. See Zen Nihon Shimbun Renmei, ed., *Kindai nihon shimbun taikan*, 3, p. 435.

25. See Uchikawa Yoshimi and Arai Naoyuki, eds., *Nihon no jiyānarizumu: taishū no kokoro o tsukanda ka*, p. 42; Nishida, *Shimbun to Zasshi*, p. 236; Ornatowski, pp. 59–60. More than two-thirds of the country's papers also supported the Kokumin Dōmeikai (National People's League), also formed in 1900 to advocate sending Japanese troops to Korea to counter the Russian presence in Manchuria; see Okamoto, p. 58.

26. Described in Itō Masanori, *Shimbun gojūnen shi*, p. 77; Midoro Masaichi, *Meiji Taishō shi: genron hen*, pp. 194–195.

27. Yamamoto Fumio, *Hattatsu shi*, p. 189.

28. *Tōkyō Asahi*, December 12, 1903; Asahi Shimbunsha, ed., *Asahi Shimbunsha shi*, 1, p. 442.

29. See editorials by Uchimura Kanzō ("murder"), June 30, 1903, and Kōtoku Shūsui ("consequences"), June 19, 1903; Uchikawa, *Shimbun shi wa*, pp. 49–50.

30. *Yorozu*, April 24, 1903, quoted in Okamoto, p. 67.

31. See Katakozawa Chiyomatsu, "Shimada Saburō," p. 94, for a discussion of Shimada's reasons; Uchikawa argues that Shimada's opposi-

tion to war sprang less from his Christianity than from his philosophical belief in the idea of dividing Manchuria and Korea between Russia and Japan; *Shimbun shi wa*, p. 49.

32.   Tokutomi's biographer John Pierson notes that Tokutomi sympathized with the prowar faction, but that he no longer was free to write as he felt; see *Tokutomi Sohō, 1863–1957: A Journalist for Modern Japan*, p. 277.

33.   Okamoto, p. 87; also Ono Hideo, *Nihon shimbun hattatsu shi*, p. 287.

34.   *Tōkyō Keizai Zasshi*, February 1904, p. 3, quoted by Ornatowski, p. 55.

35.   See Meirion Harries and Susie Harries, *Soldiers of the Sun*, p. 90.

36.   Nakae Chōmin, *A Discourse by Three Drunkards on Government*, p. 11 (quoted from Kōno Kenji, *Nakae Chōmin*, in *Chūō Kōron, Nihon no meishō*, 36, p. 36).

37.   Chamoto Shigemasa, *Sensō to jiyānarizumu*, p. 112.

38.   Tayama, pp. 166 ("separate newspaper"), 171 ("newspaper extras"), 203 ("five minutes").

39.   Frank Luther Mott, *Journalism in Wartime*, p. 10; Roberts was managing editor of the *Kansas City Star* and president of the American Society of Newspaper Editors during World War II.

40.   Uchikawa and Arai, p. 45; Itō Masanori, *Shimbun gojūnen shi*, p. 80.

41.   See Zen Nihon Shimbun Renmei, *Kindai Nihon shimbun taikan*, 3, p. 424. The total actually is less than the sixty-six papers reported to have sent correspondents to the Sino-Japanese War; it would appear, however, that figures for that war included all publications (not just dailies); the significant change in the Russo-Japanese War lay in the much more extensive coverage by the strongest papers. Also see Yamamoto Fumio, *Hattatsu shi*, p. 190; Itō Masanori, p. 80.

42.   Okumura became *Ōsaka Mainichi* president in 1936.

43.   See Zen Nihon Shimbun Renmei, *Kindai Nihon shimbun taikan*, 3, pp. 434–435.

44.   Wireless to Japan would not be available at all for another decade, until 1916; Japan did not become fully linked to the rest of the world by wireless until the establishment of the Japan Wireless Telegraph Company in 1925. See Chugo Kōito, "The Press and National Affairs in Recent Japan," p. 203.

45.   *Ōsaka Mainichi Shimbun*, May 12–13, 1904; MNJ, 7, pp. 438–442; the story of Okumura's strategies for getting his news to the paper quickly is recounted in Zen Nihon Shimbun Renmei, *Kindai Nihon shimbun taikan*, 3, p. 433.

46. Zen Nihon Shimbun Renmei, *Kindai Nihon shimbun taikan,* 3, p. 433.

47. Midoro, *Meiji Taishō shi,* pp. 199–200; if Japan had lost the battle, the reporter would have cabled: "What products did you buy?" *(nan no shōhin o katta).*

48. Zen Nihon Shimbun Renmei, *Kindai Nihon shimbun taikan,* 3, pp. 437–439; also Yamamoto Fumio, *Hattatsu shi,* p. 191.

49. Uchikawa, *Shimbun shi wa,* p. 53.

50. The naval officer aboard, a Lieutenant Colonel Tonami, was granted special recognition by the government for his intelligence work while aboard the *Haimun;* see *Tōkyō Asahi,* May 10, 1904; SSMH, 12, p. 245.

51. Chamoto Shigemasa, *Sensō to jiyānarizumu,* p. 109.

52. Haruhara Akihiko, *Nihon shimbun tsū shi,* p. 113.

53. Chamoto, p. 109.

54. Quoted by Ariyama Teruo, *Kindai Nihon jiyānarizumu no kōzō,* p. 41, from Kunikida Doppō, *Zen shū,* 3 (Gakushū Kenkyūsha, 1964).

55. See *Shin Kōron,* February 1904; Yamamoto Taketoshi, *Kisha no tanjō,* p. 180.

56. See Yamamoto, *Kisha no tanjō,* p. 134; Zen Nihon Shimbun Renmei, *Kindai Nihon shimbun taikan,* 3, p. 434; Itō Masanori, *Shimbun gojūnen shi,* p. 81.

57. Discussed in Watanabe Kazuo, *Jitsuroku gogai sensen,* pp. 135–136.

58. Chamoto, p. 111, from *Bungei Shunjū,* July 1948.

59. Kiryū Yūyū (Seishi), "Omoideru mama," 21 (May 5, 1940), in *Tazan no ishi,* 4, p. 67.

60. Nihon Shimbun Hanbai Kyōkai, ed., *Shimbun hanbai hyaku-nen shi,* p. 316.

61. See Chamoto, pp. 110, 112. The Osaka papers distributed the extras free, but the Tokyo papers normally sold them for one or two *sen* per copy (and for even more in the central city). They were sold to the sellers, however, at an average 25 *sen* for one hundred copies; so the profit margin was considerable. Subscribers in Tokyo received the extras for a delivery fee of five *rin* each; see Nihon Shimbun Hanbai Kyōkai, *Hyakunen shi,* pp. 100, 315. For *Kōchi Shimbun,* see Nihon Shimbun Kyōkai, ed., *Chihōbetsu: Nihon shimbun shi,* p. 432.

62. Kiryū, 4, p. 67.

63. Michael and Edwin Emery, *The Press and America,* p. 190; the *New York Tribune* pioneered the regular printing of photographs in 1897.

64. For accounts of the development of photography in the press, see Asahi Shimbunsha, ed., *Meiji hen*, pp. 460–461; Yamamoto Fumio, *Hattatsu shi*, pp. 176–177; Nishida Taketoshi, *Meiji jidai no shimbun to zasshi*, p. 233; Zen Nihon Shimbun Renmei, *Kindai Nihon shimbun taikan*, 3, p. 441.

65. Zen Nihon Shimbun Renmei, *Taikan*, 3, pp. 439–440; for *Jiji's* April 9 article on this sighting see MNJ, 7, pp. 805–806. Also see Asahi Shimbunsha, *Meiji hen*, pp. 469–470.

66. Chamoto, p. 110.

67. The first reporter killed in battle was Kawashima Junkichi of *Shinano Shinpō*, who was struck down by a bullet in Liaodong in October 1904; see Asahi Shimbunsha, *Meiji hen*, p. 461.

68. *Yorozu*, English column, August 25, 1904.

69. *Kokumin Shimbun*, April 25, 1905; MNJ, 7, p. 434; *Yorozu*, English column, May 2, 1904. The *Yorozu* correspondent was particularly impressed by the "fine strapping Jinrikisha men" who "could stand fatigue in a long campaign."

70. See, for example, *Jiji*, January 1, 1905; these are playing cards based on a "hundred poems by a hundred poets," much used in Japanese homes at the New Year.

71. See *Yorozu*, August 4, 1904, for example.

72. *Jiji*, May 18, 1904; MNJ, 7, p. 430.

73. *Yorozu*, December 5, 1904; MNJ, 7, pp. 433–434. According to the story, the soldiers received eight *monme* of beef at lunch and dinner on November 23, or 1.06 ounces at each meal.

74. These and other extras are reproduced photographically in Ono Hideo, *Gogai hyakunen shi*, p. 33.

75. Harries, p. 85.

76. *Jiji*, May 30, 1904; MNJ, 7, p. 507.

77. See Konishi, *Tōkyō Asahi*, July 1, 1904.

78. *Ōsaka Asahi*, May 14, 1904, quoted in Zen Nihon Shimbun Renmei, *Kindai Nihon shimbun taikan*, 3, p. 436; also *Taikan*, 1, pp. 159–160.

79. *Yomiuri Shimbun*, February 13, 1904, quoted in Yomiuri Shimbunsha, ed., *Yomiuri Shimbun hyakunijūnen shi*, p. 81.

80. For "fervent patriotism," see Tayama, p. 175; for "no embarrassment," *The Times* (London), February 9, 1905, p. 3.

81. *Ōsaka Asahi* editorial after the May 26, 1904, victory at Nanshan; reprinted in Asahi Shimbunsha, *Meiji hen*, p. 455.

82. Quoted in ibid., p. 449.

83. "Whole country" in Okamoto, p. 128, quoting B. L. Putnam Weale, *The Re-Shaping of the Far East*, 1 (New York: The Macmillan Company, 1911), p. 423; "no newspaper" in Okamoto, p. 266, n. 3.

84. Quoted in Mott, p. 42.

85. Tokutomi Iichirō, *Sohō jiden*, p. 396.

86. The prewar decree was issued February 5, 1904; see Zen Nihon Shimbun Renmei, *Kindai Nihon shimbun taikan*, 3, p. 445. The codes—Army Ministry Notice 3, February 10, 1903; Navy Ministry Notice 8, February 12, 1904—also are reprinted in Midoro, *Meiji Taishō shi*, pp. 197–198.

87. Foreign correspondents residing in Japan had to register through their own embassy or consulate general with the Foreign Ministry (Article 1).

88. Erwin Baelz, *Awakening Japan: The Diary of a German Doctor*, p. 283; he also comments on censorship on pp. 271, 282–283, 289–291.

89. John Hohenberg, *Foreign Correspondence: The Great Reporters and Their Times*, pp. 178–179; Roger Purdy, "The Ears and Voice of the Nation," pp. 3–4. A useful account of foreign reporters' frustrations also is found in Asahi Shimbunsha, *Meiji hen*, pp. 455–456. Baelz, pp. 290–291, reports that twenty foreign correspondents, frustrated over being kept in Tokyo, agreed that each would send a cable home asking to be recalled. The military censors, shocked and worried about foreign criticism, refused to send the cables, but—Baelz relates—the reporters soon were on their way to the battlefront.

90. Quoted in Okamoto, p. 267, n. 4.

91. Quoted in Haruhara, *Tsū shi*, p. 114; the papers whose reporters joined the club included *Nihon*, both *Asahi*s, *Jiji*, *Yomiuri*, *Kokumin*, *Mainichi*, *Tōkyō Nichi Nichi*, *Senji Gahō*, *Ōsaka Mainichi*, *Ōsaka Shimbun*, *Geibi Nichi Nichi Shimbun*, and *Chūgoku*.

92. For Yugeta, see Asahi Shimbunsha, *Meiji hen*, p. 456; for *Yorozu*, Zen Nihon Shimbun Renmei, *Kindai Nihon shimbun taikan*, 3, p. 448.

93. Akiyama later claimed that others wrote the offending text but admitted that his schemes were behind it; see Sakurada Kurabu, ed., *Akiyama Teisuke den*, 1, pp. 106–107.

94. Muramatsu Shōfū, ed., *Akiyama Teisuke wa kataru*, p. 253.

95. "Naikaku dangai mondai," *Niroku Shinpō*, March 16, 1904; discussed in Uchikawa and Arai, p. 44; Oka Mitsuo, *Kindai Nihon shimbun koshi*, p. 34; Midoro, *Meiji Taishō shi*, p. 207. Rumors that Akiyama was a spy had begun to spread during the election campaign.

96. Muramatsu, p. 255.

97. See "Nichiro wayaku," *Niroku Shinpō*, June 17, 1903.

98. "No evidence," in Uchikawa, *Shimbun shi wa*, p. 57; "beneficial," in Zen Nihon Shimbun Renmei, *Shimbun taikan*, 1, p. 156.

99. His speech is reprinted in Muramatsu, pp. 260–261. Akiyama said Itō Hirobumi had told him about the expenditure of Home Ministry funds to defeat him.

100. Muramatsu, pp. 257, 262. Akiyama also said that Itō Hirobumi defended him and once refused to drink a toast with Akiyama's antagonist Ogawa because of Ogawa's role in the episode. When Ogawa proposed the toast, Itō reportedly said, "I'll not drink a toast with you; don't you make a toast to me!" Itō also told Akiyama he was ashamed that a "bastard *(yatsu)* like that" came from his home fief of Chōshū (pp. 264–265). For press accounts of the incident, see MNJ, 7, pp. 4–7; also Sakurada Kurabu, 1, pp. 326–329.

101. In Uchikawa and Arai, p. 44.

102. The November 1904 purchase, with borrowed money from Mitsubishi powers Iwasaki Yaroku and Toyokawa Ryōhei, resulted in part from cabinet dissatisfaction with *Nichi Nichi's* mild criticism of government programs to collect money for bereaved war families. Negotiations for the sale involved many of the country's leading officials, including Itō Hirobumi, Yamagata Aritomo, and Katsura himself. As time passed, the paper under Katō became a sharp Katsura critic, particularly during the Portsmouth treaty negotiations. See Zen Nihon Shimbun Renmei, *Kindai Nihon shimbun taikan,* 3, pp. 440–441; Peter Duus, *Party Rivalry and Political Change in Taishō Japan,* pp. 38, 57.

103. Pierson, p. 281; Tokutomi served as Katsura's press advisor during the war (pp. 278–280). Hara Kei's diary in the spring of 1903 notes that four hundred yen a month of government money was allocated for *Kokumin,* and correspondence between Tokutomi and Yamagata shows the oligarch directly helping Tokutomi get news scoops; Itō Takashi and George Akita, "The Yamagata-Tokutomi Correspondence: Press and Politics in Meiji Japan," pp. 401–402.

104. See Ariyama, *Kōzō,* p. 14, for relevant circulation charts.

105. Ornatowski, p. 79.

106. *Myōjō,* September 4, 1904; discussed in Jay Rubin, *Injurious to Public Morals: Writers and the Meiji State,* pp. 56–57.

107. *Otaru Shimbun,* October 2, 1904; reprinted in Monna Naoki, *Minshū jiyānarizumu no rekishi,* pp. 50–51.

108. *Kanhan Kaigai Shimbun,* January 2, 1863 (by the old calendar, it was December 2 of Bunkyū 1); reprinted in Osatake Takeki, ed., *Bakumatsu Meiji shimbun zenshū,* 2, p. 109.

109. See Germain Hoston, *The State, Identity, and the National Question in China and Japan,* p. 183. Accounts of the early press discussions of socialism are found in Midoro, *Meiji Taishō shi,* pp. 156–158; Okano, pp. 143–168; and Nishida, *Shimbun to zasshi,* pp. 174, 181–182. On Tokutomi's early *heiminshugi* (people-ism) views, which often are seen as a precursor of Japanese socialism, see Pierson, pp. 177–180.

110.   Several papers, including *Yorozu*, ran the party's manifesto. The authorities also brought charges against Katayama Sen and others for violating the press law's provisions about disturbing order, but the courts found the defendants innocent. See Midoro, p. 214. The party's treatment also is discussed in Haga, pp. 125–128, and Monna, pp. 53–72. For the general development of Japanese socialist thought in the third decade of Meiji, see John Crump, *The Origins of Socialist Thought in Japan*, and Hoston, pp. 105–112.

111.   "People's Column" (English language), *Niroku Shinpō*, March 21, 1902; the rally finally was prohibited by the authorities, as discussed in the previous chapter. During this period, *Niroku* ran articles about labor day after day, on nearly every page.

112.   "Innocent people," *Mainichi Shimbun*, January 2, 1902, quoted in Kōuchi Saburō, "Iwayuru kōgai hōdō no rekishi," p. 29; "construct a new era," Masaaki Kōsaka, ed., *Japanese Thought in the Meiji Era*, p. 352; "heart of God," quoted in Crump, p. 95. On *Mainichi*, also see Nobuya Bamba and John Howes, eds., *Pacifism in Japan*, pp. 69–72, 78.

113.   See discussions in F. G. Notehelfer, *Kōtoku Shūsui: Portrait of a Japanese Radical*, pp. 58–61; the "requiem" ran in *Yorozu* August 30, 1900.

114.   *Yorozu*, August 7, 1900; Okano, p. 133.

115.   *Kanson jiden* (Ronsōsha, 1960), p. 16; Yamamoto Taketoshi, *Kindai Nihon shimbun dokusha sō*, p. 100.

116.   Sakai Toshihiko, *Shakaishugi undō shi wa*, in *Sakai Toshihiko zenshū*, 6, pp. 181–182; he lists as socialist writers at the paper Kōtoku, Shiba Teikichi, Kawakami Kiyoshi, Ishikawa Sanshirō, himself, "and others."

117.   There were exceptions to the benign neglect policy; on August 10, 1901, for example, the Home Minister forbade sale and distribution of Osaka's *Banzai Shimbun* for the article "Shakaishugi" (Socialism); see *Jiji*, August 11, 1901; MNJ, 6, p. 627.

118.   The other defector from *Yorozu*, Uchimura Kanzō, could not accept his fellows' socialism and gave his time to his own Christian journal, *Seisho no Kenkyū*, to preaching, and to freelance writing. He wrote several strong antiwar essays, primarily for the English-language *Japan Chronicle* in Kobe. Typical was his declaration in the November 18, 1904, issue: "What would I personally not have given to prevent this saddest of all explosions! But I am only a worm in this country, and a worm, however it may wriggle and lament, has no power to stop an explosion of this kind. . . . I deplore this Russo-Japanese War, because I believe it is in one sense a war between brothers. . . . Are not Russians half-Orientals, and Japanese half-Occidentals?" Reprinted in Uchimura Kanzō, *The Complete Works of Kanzō Uchimura*, 7, pp. 119–122.

119.   Midoro, *Meiji Taishō shi*, p. 246.

120.   Quoted in Midoro, p. 217; he also reprints the manifesto itself (pp. 217–218), as do Araki Masayasu, ed., *Shimbun ga kataru Meiji shi*, p. 267; MNJ, 7, p. 682; and SSMH, 12, pp. 134–135. Discussions of the first issue also are found in Crump, p. 103, and Notehelfer, *Kōtoku Shūsui*, p. 94. The entire newspaper is reprinted in Hattori Shisō and Konishi Shirō, eds., *Shūkan Heimin Shimbun*, 4 vols.

121.   Quoted in Masaaki Kōsaka, p. 354.

122.   See Mikiso Hane, *Reflections on the Way to the Gallows*, pp. 19, 31–32, 52–53.

123.   "Monied interests," *Heimin Shimbun*, February 7, 1904 (see Notehelfer, p. 96); "millions, nay trillions," February 14, 1904; "dear comrades," March 20, 1904, English-language column.

124.   Circulation data from Bamba and Howes, p. 139; for advertising, see, for example, *Heimin Shimbun*, May 29, 1904, pp. 235–242 of Hattori and Konishi, eds., *Shūkan Heimin*, 1. The ads now were for speech rallies, for other journals, and for Heiminsha, the paper's publisher; ads for general products disappeared completely.

125.   The offending editorial, titled "Aa zōzei" (Alas, the rising taxes), ran on March 28, 1904. *Heimin*'s account of the banning and appeal ran on April 10, 1904; MNJ, 7, p. 683. On other harassment, see Notehelfer, p. 97.

126.   *Heimin Shimbun*, English-language column, June 12, 1904, in Rōdō Undō Shi Kenkyūkai, ed., *Shūkan Heimin Shimbun*, 1, p. 251.

127.   The episode is recounted in Notehelfer, pp. 105–107; the court disposition is printed in Midoro, pp. 221–228.

128.   *Heimin Shimbun*, January 29, 1905, in Rōdō Undō Shi Kenkyūkai, 2, p. 517. The entire editorial also is reprinted in Midoro, pp. 228–230.

129.   *Tōkyō Asahi*, January 30, 1905; SSMH, 12, p. 375. The press had reported on the *hakkō kinshi* order in November, again briefly; see *Jiji*, November 14, 1904, in MNJ, 7, p. 683; *Tōkyō Asahi*, November 14, 1904, in SSMH, 12, pp. 334–335.

130.   *Heimin Shimbun*, English-language column, November 20, 1904, in Rōdō Undō Shi Kenkyūkai, 2, p. 437. Several other socialist publications were brought out later, including another *Heimin Shimbun* (this time as a daily), but none lasted long; see Nishida, *Shimbun to zasshi*, p. 267.

131.   The demands were outlined by Tomizu and his cohorts at a June 11 meeting, reported in *Nihon*, June 14, 1905; MNJ, 7, p. 412. Also see *Ōsaka Asahi* editorials, June 16, 17, 1905; *Tōkyō Asahi*, June 12, July 8, 1905; Asahi Shimbunsha, *Meiji hen*, p. 475. See also Byron K. Marshall, "Professors and Politics," pp. 88–91.

132.   His press policy is outlined in Midoro, pp. 203–205. He and Japanese plenipotentiary Komura reportedly agreed to keep information about the negotiations secret, but Witte disregarded the agreement; see Okamoto, p. 157.

133.   Hikomatsu Kamikawa and Michiko Kimura, *Japanese-American Diplomatic Relations in the Meiji-Taishō Era*, p. 237.

134.   See *Ōsaka Mainichi*, August 3, 1905 (MNJ, 7, p. 697), for an example of an interview Witte gave to the Japanese reporters.

135.   See Ono Hideo, *Nihon shimbun hattatsu shi*, p. 298; through O'Laughlin, *Ōsaka Mainichi* secured a scoop about Roosevelt's agreement to serve as mediator in the peace talks. *Ōsaka Mainichi* and *Kokumin Shimbun* worked together in covering the talks; see *Ōsaka Mainichi*, June 2, 1905; MNJ, 7, p. 693.

136.   Reprinted in *Japan Daily Herald*, August 4, 1905; Okamoto, p. 156.

137.   The fact that the demands were made available to Japanese reporters by Witte not only dramatized the secretive style of the Japanese diplomats but made journalists more suspicious of their countrymen than they otherwise might have been; see Okamoto, p. 159. For the demands, see *Tōkyō Asahi*, August 13, 1905; MNJ, 7, pp. 697–698.

138.   *Jiji* statement reprinted in *Japan Weekly Mail*, August 26, 1905; reporters' resolution, August 31, 1905, quoted in Ornatowski, p. 84.

139.   Asahi Shimbunsha, *Meiji hen*, pp. 478–479; Yamamoto Fumio, *Hattatsu shi*, pp. 193–194.

140.   The first reports of Japan's compromise actually were made without comment in bold-faced extras on August 30; the editorial fury erupted on August 31.

141.   *Yorozu*, August 31, 1905; Okamoto, p. 167.

142.   "We must," *Ōsaka Asahi*, September 1, 1905, reproduced in Asahi Shimbunsha, ed., *Asahi Shimbun hyakunen no jūyō shimen*, p. 58; "delay after delay," *Ōsaka Mainichi*, September 1, 1905; MNJ, 7, pp. 412–413. A *New York Times* piece on August 30, 1905, suggests that the Japanese journalists were not wholly off base in their evaluations of what their diplomats gave up. Under the headline "Witte Rejoices In His Victory," the paper quoted the Russian plenipotentiary as saying: "I have told the Japanese that I would not recede one inch, and I have not done so. . . . I did not believe any other man in my place would have dared to hope for the possibility of peace on the conditions to which we have just agreed. . . . At this morning's meeting I presented my written proposition, which was the Russian ultimatum. It was accepted by the Japanese. I was amazed." When the *Times* correspondent suggested to a Russian official that his country had won a "great diplomatic achievement," the official replied: "Yes, but it is better than that. It is a great stroke of genius, and there is only one man in the whole world who could have done it, and that is M. Witte." The report

ended, "The weather here to-day was superb. It was like an Autumn day. The sea was bathed in a flood of golden sunshine, the air was cool and bracing, and the whole landscape breathed the spirit of peace on earth and good will to men." Reprinted in Uchikawa Yoshimi and Miyaji Masato, eds., *Gaikoku shimbun ni miru Nihon, 1896–1905,* 3, pp. 837–839.

143. "Half mast," *Yorozu,* September 2, 1905; Uchikawa and Arai, p. 46; "never before," *Yorozu,* September 3, 1905; letters, Okamoto, pp. 179–181 (a number of letters are reprinted here); "debauchery," *Hōchi,* September 3, 1905; Akiyama, *Kōzō,* p. 44; "if this is," *Jiji,* September 4, 1904; MNJ, 7, pp. 417–418. Summaries of key editorials are found in Ono, *Hattatsu shi,* pp. 301–304.

144. Based on a study by Okamoto; *Japanese Oligarchy,* pp. 197–203. The organization was a revival of the prewar Tairo Dōshikai (Society of Fellow Activists against Russia). See also Okamoto Shumpei, "The Emperor and the Crowd: The Historical Significance of the Hibiya Riot," p. 260.

145. See accounts in *Ōsaka Mainichi* and *Ōsaka Asahi,* September 4, 1905; MNJ, 7, pp. 418–419.

146. See Ornatowski, p. 88.

147. See Okamoto, "Emperor and the Crowd," pp. 261–262; Okamoto, *Japanese Oligarchy,* pp. 208–215.

148. Andrew Gordon, *Labor and Imperial Democracy in Prewar Japan,* p. 54.

149. See, for example, *Tōkyō Nichi Nichi,* September 7, 1905, which goes over the riots by region on pp. 3–4.

150. *Ōsaka Asahi,* September 6, 1905.

151. *Kokumin Shimbun,* September 10, 1905, quoted in Ornatowski, p. 91.

152. Articles from *Ōsaka Mainichi, Jiji, Tōkyō Nichi Nichi,* September 7–27, 1905, in MNJ, 7, pp. 420–423.

153. *Kokumin Shimbun,* September 2, 1905.

154. Tokutomi, *Sohō Jiden,* p. 398. The attacks on *Kokumin Shimbun* are described vividly in Pierson, pp. 183–184. Detailed accounts by the paper itself are reprinted in MNJ, 7, pp. 653–655, and SSMH, 12, pp. 489–490.

155. Tokutomi, *Sohō jiden,* p. 397.

156. Ariyama, *Tokutomi Sohō,* pp. 140, 143; for a breakdown of the circulation loss by region, see Wada Mamoru, *Kindai Nihon to Tokutomi Sohō,* pp. 176–177.

157. Quoted by Pierson, p. 283.

158. The same day, Ordinance 207 permitted police to: (1) forbid newspapers, magazines, or assemblics likely to disturb the public peace, (2)

search suspicious private homes and buildings, and (3) remove people from "inappropriate" places; it also permitted the Tokyo post office to inspect suspicious pieces of mail. Both ordinances are reprinted in Uchikawa, *Masu medeia hō seisaku shi kenkyū*, pp. 46–47; also see Midoro, *Meiji Taishō shi*, p. 441; Richard Mitchell, *Censorship in Imperial Japan*, p. 138.

159.   Kansai and provincial cases (twenty-one, for a total of 199 days) were handled by the Home Minister's office, Kantō cases (seventeen, for 134 days) by the Police Inspector. Other significant papers suspended at least once included *Yorozu, Nihon, Tōkyō Asahi, Yomiuri, Tōkyō Shimbun, Tōhoku Hyōron, Otaru Chōhō, Nihon Shimbun*, and *Yamanashi Minpō*. See *Tōkyō Asahi*, December 1, 1905; SSMH, 12, p. 534. When papers resumed publication, they typically apologized and explained the circumstances of the order to their readers; see, for example, *Yorozu*, September 11, 1905.

160.   Yamamoto Fumio, *Hattatsu shi*, p. 198. The two abstainers were *Kokumin Shimbun* and *Chūō Shimbun*.

161.   *Tōkyō Nichi Nichi* and both *Asahi*s, for example, remained relatively gray in these years, attracting readers more through the quality of their news than by their formats; even they, however, steadily increased their use of headlines and varied typefaces. And their ads were lively. *Jiji*, by contrast, had developed quite a popular, appealing format by this time, though section headings remained fairly small.

162.   See Yamamoto Fumio, *Hattatsu shi*, p. 205.

163.   *Chūō Kōron*, January 1903; Yamamoto Taketoshi, *Kisha no tanjō*, p. 175.

164.   Yamamoto Fumio, *Hattatsu shi*, p. 203. Precise circulation figures are impossible to obtain for the early 1900s; among the most useful charts is Ariyama, *Kōzō*, p. 14.

165.   Discussed in Uchikawa and Arai, p. 51.

166.   *Shin Kōron*, February 1904; Yamamoto Taketoshi, *Kisha no tanjō*, p. 177.

167.   Yamamoto Taketoshi, *Kisha no tanjō*, p. 176.

168.   Yamamoto Fumio, *Hattatsu shi*, p. 192.

169.   Ariyama, *Kōzō*, p. 42.

170.   Yamamoto Fumio, *Hattatsu shi*, p. 198.

171.   *Yorozu*, April 20, 1903, quoted in Bamba and Howes, p. 137.

172.   See, for example, Okamoto, "The Emperor and the Crowd"; Andrew Gordon, *Labor and Imperial Democracy*, esp. pp. 1–10; Matsuo Takayoshi, *Taishō demakurashii no kenkyū* (Aoki Shoten, 1966); Eguchi Keiichi, *Toshi shoburujoa undō shi no kenkyū* (Miraisha, 1976).

173.   Carol Gluck, *Japan's Modern Myths*, p. 72.

174.   Okamoto, "Emperor and the Crowd," p. 271.

CHAPTER 10. LEADING A PUBLIC, 1905 TO 1912

1. Quoted in Iwai Hajime, *Shimbun to shimbunjin*, p. 211.

2. *Taiyō*, February 1, 1910, p. 39.

3. The rally is described in *Tōkyō Asahi Shimbun*, October 25, 1905; Nakayama Yasuaki, ed., *Shimbun shūsei Meiji hennen shi* (hereafter SSMH), 12, pp. 516–517. Also see Okamoto Shumpei, "The Emperor and the Crowd: The Historical Significance of the Hibiya Riot," pp. 274–275.

4. "Bled," Kaneko Fumiko, *Prison Memoirs of a Japanese Woman*, pp. 40–41; "everyone and his brother" and figures, Carol Gluck, *Japan's Modern Myths: Ideology in the Late Meiji Period*, p. 159; the estimates (for the 1898–1907 decade) were 40,000 to 60,000 for Tokyo and 20,000 to 40,000 for Osaka. For Tokyo population, see Ariyama Teruo, *Kindai jiyā-narizumu no kōzō*, p. 20.

5. For job numbers, see Andrew Gordon, *Labor and Imperial Democracy in Prewar Japan*, p. 85; for analysis of jobs, Gordon, p. 21, W. Dean Kinzley, *Industrial Harmony in Modern Japan*, pp. 11–12; for wages and working hours, *Heimin Shimbun*, February 7, 1904, which found the highest wage in cotton spinning, the lowest (15 *sen*) in soap making; Gluck suggests an average monthly wage of twenty yen near the end of Meiji (p. 175).

6. For middle school rates, Ronald Dore, "Mobility, Equality, and Individuation in Modern Japan," p. 131; for attitudes about a child's education and budgets, Gluck, pp. 164–166; for girls' school graduation rates, Tanaka Hiroshi, *Kindai Nihon no jiyānarisuto*, p. 656.

7. Byron K. Marshall, "Growth and Conflict: Japanese Higher Education, 1905–1930," p. 279.

8. See Gordon, p. 19. For a description of life in Honjo, see Sally Hastings, *Neighborhood and Nation in Tokyo, 1905–1937*, pp. 20–59; quote from p. 16.

9. For charts on school attendance and literacy rates, see Yamamoto Taketoshi, *Kindai Nihon no shimbun dokusha sō*, pp. 168, 167, respectively; his statement is on p. 164.

10. Homes with electricity, Uchikawa Yoshimi, "Shimbun dokusha no hensen," p. 24; bulbs, Hugh Patrick, ed., *Japanese Industrialization and Its Social Consequences*, p. 303.

11. For these and other accounts of the new city life, see Oka Mitsuo, *Kindai Nihon shimbun koshi*, pp. 97–98, 123. Regarding theaters, also Gordon, p. 30.

12. Gluck, pp. 157–178.

13. *Heimin Shimbun*, January 26, 1907.

14. "Battlefield," April 1906 speech, quoted in Oka Yoshitake, "Generational Conflict after the Russo-Japanese War," p. 216; "we are faced" in Gluck, p. 167.

15. *Tōkyō Niroku Shimbun,* June 28, 1908; Oka Mitsuo, p. 105.

16. *Yomiuri,* July 11, 1908; Oka Mitsuo, p. 105.

17. *Kokumin Shimbun,* December 29, 1912, quoted in Ariyama, *Kōzō,* p. 36.

18. See *Chūō Kōron,* March 3, 1908, p. 9; also John Pierson, *Tokutomi Sohō, 1863–1975: A Journalist for Modern Japan,* p. 288.

19. Writing in 1906, quoted in Oka Yoshitake, "Generational Conflict," p. 209.

20. Figures from *Tōkei nenkan,* in Uchikawa Yoshimi, "Shimbunshi hō no seitei katei to sono tokushitsu," p. 87. His figures (pp. 88–89) also show that until 1908 provincial publications increased more rapidly than those in Tokyo; after that the capital's publications soared past their regional counterparts—one more sign of the impact of urbanization in these years.

21. For telegrams, see Uchikawa Yoshimi, *Masu medeia hō seisaku kenkyū,* pp. 81–83; for *Tōkyō Asahi* printers, Yamamoto Taketoshi, *Shimbun kisha no tanjō,* p. 215; for *Kokumin Shimbun* workers and *Jiji* pages, ibid., p. 179; for *Ōsaka Asahi* income, Yamamoto Taketoshi, *Dokusha sō,* p. 332; for factory workers, Ariyama, *Kōzō,* p. 22; for legal cases, Uchikawa Yoshimi, *Masu medeia hō,* p. 54; for salaries, Sharon Nolte, *Liberalism in Modern Japan: Ishibashi Tanzan and His Teachers,* pp. 10–11.

22. Compiled from Ariyama Teruo, *Tokutomi Sohō to Kokumin Shimbun,* p. 149; Yamamoto Taketoshi, *Dokusha sō,* p. 411; Mainichi Shimbunsha, ed., *Mainichi Shimbun nanajūnen shi,* p. 612; figures should be taken as rough approximations, as computation methods varied from paper to paper. The next papers dropped sharply in circulation: *Yomiuri,* 38,000; *Jiji,* 35,500; *Kokumin Shimbun,* 32,000; *Tōkyō Nichi Nichi,* 31,000; and *Nihon,* 30,000. In 1903, *Niroku Shinpō* was the largest paper, with 142,340 subscribers, followed by *Ōsaka Asahi* with 104,000; all others had fewer than 100,000; see Yamamoto Taketoshi, *Kisha no tanjō,* p. 170.

23. From Mainichi Shimbunsha, p. 612; Yamamoto Taketoshi, *Dokusha sō,* p. 412; also Nishida Taketoshi, *Meiji jidai no shimbun to zasshi,* p. 272. It is worth noting that *Niroku Shimbun* by now had dropped to a mere 25,000, while *Tōkyō Nichi Nichi Shimbun* and *Jiji* had jumped to nearly 70,000. *Nihon* now had a mere 6,000, while Tokyo's *Mainichi* had recovered from postwar slumps to 30,000. Also see Ariyama, *Kōzō,* p. 14, for 1912 figures. Even higher figures for 1911 (*Ōsaka Asahi,* 350,000; *Ōsaka Mainichi,* 320,000–330,000; *Hōchi,* 200,000) are given by Zen Nihon Shimbun Renmei, ed., *Shimbun taikan,* 1, pp. 172–173; the more conservative figures, however, are safer, because those from *Taikan* are derived from the papers' own claims for advertising purposes.

24.   The *New York Times*, for example, did not reach 330,000 daily circulation until 1921; see Michael Emery and Edwin Emery, *The Press and America*, p. 239. At the same time, no Japanese paper yet had the circulation of the largest working-class papers of the West. Britain's *News of the World*, for example, reached 1.5 million in 1909, and in 1898, during the Spanish-American War, Joseph Pulitzer's *World* reached a circulation of one million; see Anthony Smith, *The Newspaper: An International History*, pp. 156, 160.

25.   See Pierson, pp. 286–288, 306; Zen Nihon Shimbun Renmei, *Shimbun taikan*, 1, p. 174; quote from *Chūō Kōron*, May 3, 1908. Also Ariyama, *Tokutomi Sohō*, pp. 151–156. One wag quipped that its name should be changed to *Zokumin Shimbun* (paper of the vulgar people).

26.   Zen Nihon Shimbun Renmei, *Shimbun taikan*, 1, pp. 173–174.

27.   This account is based primarily on Asahi Shimbunsha, ed., *Asahi shimbun shi, Meiji hen*, pp. 487–490. Ikebe was an editor at *Tōkyō Asahi*.

28.   *Ōsaka Asahi* lost 10,317 yen, compared to a 6,382 yen profit the previous six months; *Tōkyō Asahi* fared even worse, with losses of 11,634 yen, compared to profits of 9,893 yen in the earlier period.

29.   See Iwai, p. 75.

30.   See Yamamoto Taketoshi, *Kisha no tanjō*, p. 175.

31.   See Yamamoto Fumio, *Nihon shimbun hattatsu shi*, pp. 207–210; also Zen Nihon Shimbun Renmei, *Shimbun taikan*, 1, pp. 176–178, and Ono Hideo, *Nihon shimbun hattatsu shi*, pp. 343–348. *Kokumin Shimbun* figures from Ariyama, *Tokutomi Sohō*, p. 161; *Tōkyō Asahi* ad revenues jumped 1.8 times in the same period.

32.   Zen Nihon Shimbun Renmei, *Shimbun taikan*, 1, p. 180; by 1914, seventy of the Ishikawa presses were in operation in Japan.

33.   Nishida, *Shimbun to zasshi*, pp. 271–272.

34.   Uchikawa Yoshimi, *Shimbun shi wa*, p. 47.

35.   Zen Nihon Shimbun Renmei, *Shimbun taikan*, 1, pp. 175–176; many papers continued to use the more indirect system of letting wholesalers handle distribution to shops *(toritsugi hanbai)*, but the movement in this year was strongly toward direct management. For *Chūō Shimbun* and *Nihon*, see Nihon Shimbun Hanbai Kyōkai, ed., *Shimbun hanbai hyakunen shi*, p. 486.

36.   See Nihon Shimbun Hanbai Kyōkai, *Hyakunen shi*, p. 426; for a vivid description of the hawker's life in the Taishō years, see Kaneko Fumiko, *The Prison Memoirs of a Japanese Woman*, pp. 175–193.

37.   See Nihon Shimbun Hanbai Kyōkai, *Hyakunen shi*, pp. 485–486. The price to retailers did not always determine what customers would be charged; so actual newspaper prices often varied considerably.

38.   *Chūō, Yamato, Hōchi, Tōkyō Asahi, Kokumin,* and both Osaka papers all had regional editions in this period. An excellent account of *Kokumin*'s discussions and strategies in creating a Yokohama edition is found in Ariyama, *Tokutomi Sohō,* pp. 156–159. Also useful is Ono Hideo, *Shimbun no rekishi,* p. 75.

39.   Yamamoto Fumio, *Nihon masu komiyunikēshiyon shi,* pp. 89–90. In the Taishō years, *Ōsaka Mainichi, Ōsaka Asahi, Tōkyō Asahi, Kokumin Shimbun, Yorozu Chōhō,* and *Jiji* also came out with evening editions.

40.   The *Jiji* anniversary issue is discussed in Haruhara Akihiko, *Nihon shimbun tsū shi,* p. 121. For *Ōsaka Mainichi* and *Ōsaka Asahi,* see Oka Mitsuo, p. 119.

41.   For the announcement of the winner, see *Jiji,* March 5, 1908; for the paper's lengthy response to the Gakushūin dismissal of Suehiro, see March 29, 1908; the dismissal itself is reported in *Ōsaka Mainichi,* March 22, 1908; all in Uchikawa Yoshimi and Matsushima Eiichi, eds., *Meiji niyūsu jiten* (hereafter MNJ), 14, pp. 681–686. The episode also is discussed in Haruhara, *Tsū shi,* pp. 122–123.

42.   See Iwai, p. 75. Shirase's initial plans fell through and the *Asahi* debate over whether to continue supporting the lieutenant led finally to the resignation of his champion, editor Ikebe Sanzan. The official *Asahi* story version is in Asahi Shimbunsha, *Meiji hen,* pp. 563–568.

43.   These promotions are described in Oka Mitsuo, pp. 101–103. No one succeeded in making the thirty-six-kilometer flight by the deadline of November 30, 1911.

44.   *Kokumin Shimbun,* November 19, 1910; Oka Mitsuo, p. 103.

45.   See Norman Isaacs, *Untended Gates: The Mismanaged Press,* pp. 48–49.

46.   Major increases in news agencies would not come until the Taishō era, but new organizations in late Meiji included the Seiyūkai-oriented Chōya Tsūshinsha (1906) and Tōyō Tsūshinsha (1907), and the Nihon Keizai Tsūshinsha, formed in 1908 to gather economic news. It is worth noting that Associated Press General Manager Melville Stone made a speech in Tokyo calling for the creation of a "national news agency" *(kokka daihyō tsūshinsha)* in 1910 to assist the Japanese press in getting its perspectives reported more effectively around the world; this is regarded as the first time the idea had been raised. Other early proponents of a national news agency were the businessman Shibusawa Eiichi and Associated Press Tokyo bureau chief John Russell Kennedy. The first attempt at a national agency, Kokusai Tsūshinsha, was launched in 1914. See Roger Purdy, "The Ears and Voice of the Nation," pp. 36, 74–84.

47.   Essay at *Murō Shinpō,* quoted in Mikiso Hane, *Reflections on the Way to the Gallows,* p. 53.

48. The large majority of printers were men, but by the end of Meiji as many as 15 percent at some papers were women. This was not entirely a sign of progress, however, since printers tended to be part-time or short-contract workers at the low end of the pay scale. In 1912, five of *Yorozu's* seventy printers were women; their pay averaged 42 *sen* a day, compared to 68 *sen* for the men. See Yamamoto Taketoshi, *Kisha no tanjō*, pp. 215–216; Haruhara Akihiko, Yoneda Sayoko, et al., eds., *Josei kisha*, pp. 25–27.

49. Haruhara, Yoneda, et al., pp. 21–22; the section, launched in 1914, was modeled after a women's section in the Paris newspaper *Figaro*.

50. For Isomura, see Shimura Akiko, in Tanaka Hiroshi, ed., *Kindai Nihon no jiyānarisuto*, pp. 659–660; for Takenaka, Haruhara, Yoneda, et al., p. 17. In the office, Isomura was called "Rubitsuki no kisha," the reporter who carries her *furigana* around, because she so often went around the office carrying her eldest son, Eiichi; Eiichi later became president of Tōyō Daigaku.

51. Quoted in Hane, *Gallows*, p. 53.

52. Material on Kanno is taken primarily from Shimura, pp. 664–666, and Uchikawa, *Shimbun shi wa*, pp. 81–82. Uchikawa (pp. 82–83) also lists a number of other female reporters in the late-Meiji, early-Taishō era. The Taishō years also saw the establishment of Japan's first women reporters association, the Fujin Kisha Kurabu, and it is noteworthy that in 1917–1918, Ichikawa Fusae, the famous reporter-politician, joined the staff of *Nagoya Shimbun*; see Haruhara, Yoneda, et al., pp. 17–18.

53. *Seitō*, September 1911; Shimura, p. 667.

54. Quoted in Miyamoto Ken, "Itō Noe and the Bluestockings," p. 195.

55. Shimura, p. 671.

56. See Uchikawa, *Masu medeia hō*, p. 85.

57. Formed in Osaka in 1933, it was renamed *Sangyō Keizai Shimbun* in 1942, and in 1955 it joined *Jiji* and became *Sankei Jiji*; in 1958 it changed its name to *Sankei Shimbun* and developed into one of Japan's "big five" papers. Two other Osaka papers were started in the Taishō years: *Taishō Nichi Nichi Shimbun*, begun by *Asahi* defector Torii Sosen following the infamous 1918 "White Rainbow *(hakkō)* Incident," and *Mainichi Ōsaka Shimbun* (1922), which later changed its name to *Yūkan Ōsaka Shimbun*. Neither paper ever developed a strong base, however. See Uchikawa, *Shimbun shi wa*, pp. 192–195.

58. See Ariyama, *Kōzō*, p. 14; also Yomiuri Shimbunsha, ed., *Yomiuri Shimbun hyakunijūnen shi*, pp. 88–89.

59. For *Nihon*, see Uchikawa, *Shimbun shi wa*, p. 155; Itō first aligned it with the Seiyūkai, then folded it after fire destroyed its building in 1914. For *Mainichi*, Nishida, *Shimbun to zasshi*, pp. 270–273; Shimada had changed its name to *Tōkyō Mainichi Shimbun* in July 1906; the paper

actually survived until 1941; Shimada editorial from Yamamoto Taketoshi, *Kisha no tanjō*, p. 242. For *Chūō*, see Ono, *Hattatsu shi*, pp. 314–325, and Uchikawa, *Shimbun shi wa*, pp. 176–177.

60.　The paper was created in March 1905, as a result of Sutejirō's eagerness to make *Jiji* a national paper as well as his belief that the many Keiō graduates in the Kansai business world would provide a natural constituency. The parent firm poured heavy resources into it, holding a railway exposition to promote it in 1906 and launching an evening edition in 1908, but the paper proved an unending financial drain, and in 1923 Tokyo *Jiji* cut it off. *Ōsaka Jiji* continued to struggle along under various owners until 1941. See Uchikawa, *Shimbun shi wa*, pp. 195–198.

61.　Nishida, *Shimbun to zasshi*, p. 250.

62.　*Tōkyō Nichi Nichi Shimbun*, March 1, 1911, reprinted in Araki Masayasu, ed., *Shimbun ga kataru Meiji shi*, 2, pp. 559–560. Also see Nishida, *Shimbun to zasshi*, p. 270; Iwai, pp. 130–133.

63.　Kiryū Yūyū, "Omoideru mama," no. 34, in *Tazan no ishi*, 4, p. 166.

64.　*Tōkyō Asahi*, for example, discontinued the practice in 1907, firing four of its remaining *tanbōsha*, elevating the other four to the society section, and hiring four graduates of Waseda and Tokyo universities as replacements; see Asahi Shimbunsha, *Meiji hen*, p. 541.

65.　*Tōkyō Asahi*, July 6, 1905; Nihon Fūzoku Shi Gakkai, ed., *Genron to masu komi*, p. 106.

66.　A spate of these articles appeared in March; see, for examples, *Tōkyō Asahi*, March 2, 4, 15, 16, 28, 1906; SSMH, 13, pp. 56–57, 60, 68.

67.　*Tōkyō Nichi Nichi*, March 24, 1908; SSMH, 13, pp. 106–107.

68.　See *Ōsaka Asahi*, May 20, 1910 (Halley's Comet); *Yomiuri*, January 25, 1910 (capsized boat); *Tōkyō Nichi Nichi*, December 20, 1910 (first flight); Haruhara, *Tsū shi*, pp. 133–134.

69.　*Tōkyō Asahi* was first to report that the new era would be named Taishō; Haruhara, *Tsū shi*, p. 138.

70.　*Nihon*, June 7, 1897; Ariyama, *Kōzō*, pp. 34–35.

71.　Ibid., pp. 33, 35; the survey appeared in the September 1909 issue of *Shin Kōron*.

72.　From *Chūō Kōron*, January 1914, in Gluck, p. 171.

73.　Oka Yoshitake, "Generational Conflict," p. 198.

74.　Kinoshita, quoted in Kenneth Pyle, F. G. Notehelfer, and Alan Stone, "Symposium: The Ashio Copper Mine Pollution Case," p. 404; *Chūō Kōron*, January 1909, p. 17, in ibid.; Kuroiwa, in Oka Yoshitake, p. 199.

75. These particular items are gleaned from Araki, *Shimbun ga kataru Meiji shi*, 2: Shimoda, *Nihon*, February 15, 1906 (p. 369); typewriter, *Yorozu*, December 13, 1907 (412); automobile, *Hōchi Shimbun*, December 25, 1908 (456); Kimura, *Kokumin Shimbun*, June 15, 1911 (567); Hino, *Tōkyō Nichi Nichi*, December 20, 1912 (532); Natsume, *Tōkyō Asahi*, May 3, 1907 (396); a great deal of shock was expressed in the press over Natsume's decision to leave a prestigious position at the University of Tokyo and enter journalism—just as it was when Fukuchi left government for the press thirty-three years earlier.

76. Tokutomi Sohō, "Daiko hon'i" (1911), quoted in Oka Yoshitake, p. 198; Ukita, *Taiyō*, June 1910, in ibid., p. 197. The plethora of success stories also is discussed in Jay Rubin, *Injurious to Public Morals: Writers and the Meiji State*, pp. 59–60.

77. See Uchikawa Yoshimi and Arai Naoyuki, eds., *Nihon no jiyānarizumu: taishū no kokoro o tsukanda ka*, p. 48. The years of this phenomenon generally are seen as 1905–1918, also known as the "era of popular violence" (*minshū sōjō ki*).

78. Letter, January 27, 1914, quoted in Itō Takashi and George Akita, "The Yamagata-Tokutomi Correspondence: Press and Politics in Meiji-Taishō Japan," p. 420.

79. Kinzley, *Industrial Harmony*, p. 13.

80. Figures based largely on chart compiled by Gordon, pp. 28–29; this book's chapter "The Urban Crowd and Politics, 1905–18" (pp. 26–62) is perhaps the best treatment of this subject in English. The riots occurred in 1905 (anti–peace treaty), 1906 (twice, both over streetcar fare increases), 1908 (against tax increases), 1913 (against the Katsura cabinet's "unconstitutional" policies), 1914 (against naval scandals), and 1918 (twice, for universal suffrage and against soaring rice prices); quote from p. 27.

81. Ibid., p. 27.

82. Phrase of Ariyama Teruo in Uchikawa and Arai, p. 56.

83. *Tōkyō Asahi*, March 4, 1906; SSMH, 13, p. 57.

84. Increase request, *Tōkyō Asahi*, March 8, 1906; MNJ, 7, p. 364. Unless otherwise noted, accounts of the March riot are taken largely from *Tōkyō Asahi* articles on March 16, 1906; SSMH, 13, pp. 61–62; and from *Jiji*, March 16, 1906; MNJ, 7, pp. 364–365.

85. The Police Bureau issued a proclamation on March 17 prohibiting the rally; *Jiji*, March 18, 1906; MNJ, 7, p. 365.

86. Report on socialists arrested, *Tōkyō Asahi*, March 17, 1906, in SSMH, 13, p. 62; for sentences, see *Tōkyō Asahi*, July 10, 1906, in MNJ, 7, p. 367; "streetcar increases," *Tōkyō Asahi*, March 24, 1906, in SSMH, 13, pp. 67–68.

87. See *Jiji*, August 2, 1906; MNJ, 7, p. 367.

88. See, for example, *Tōkyō Asahi*, August 7, 10, 1906, in MNJ, 8, pp. 368–369; also Gordon, pp. 40–41. Material for the subsequent description comes from *Jiji*, September 6–12, and *Nihon*, September 10, 1906, in MNJ, 7, pp. 369–376; also *Tōkyō Asahi*, September 6, 1906, in SSMH, 13, pp. 140–141.

89. *Jiji*, December 29, 1906; MNJ, 7, p. 376. The 1906 anti–fare increase riots also gave Ōsugi Sakae his first encounter with socialist activism (and jail); see his *Autobiography of Ōsugi Sakae,* p. 109. Material comes too from *Yorozu*, September 6, 1906, which also described an indoor rally at the Hongoza.

90. Phrase of Gordon, p. 31.

91. See report in *Jiji*, September 12, 1906; MNJ, 7, p. 376.

92. *Yorozu*, September 10, 1906. The front page of the issue in which this statement ran contained a large space where an article, apparently censored, had been gouged out prior to publication.

93. Reprinted in SSMH, 13, p. 142.

94. Sheldon Garon, *The State and Labor in Modern Japan,* p. 249, notes that 11,483 workers participated in strikes in 1907; for slightly lower figures, see Uchikawa, "Shimbunshi hō no seitei katei," p. 67. For February 7 and 9, see articles reprinted in MNJ, 7, pp. 245–247; for February 8, see article excerpted in Araki, 2, pp. 390–391.

95. *Nikkan Heimin Shimbun*, English column, April 14, 1907.

96. *Shakai Shimbun*, English column, March 8, 1908, quoted in Gordon, pp. 74–75.

97. Formerly Shimada Saburō's paper, which had added *Tokyo* to its name in 1906 in fending off purchase by *Ōsaka Mainichi.*

98. Leaflet reprinted February 10, 1908; reprinted in Gordon, p. 49. For accounts of the rallies and the violence, see *Tōkyō Nichi Nichi*, February 12, 1908; SSMH, 13, pp. 384–385.

99. This was not the first time the issue had come up; the Home and Finance ministries had refused to approve a city takeover proposal three years earlier, for example; see *Tōkyō Nichi Nichi*, June 28, 1908; MNJ, 8, pp. 563–564. The Home Ministry approved such a move on July 31, 1911; *Jiji*, August 1, 1911; MNJ, 8, p. 567.

100. Reported in *Jiji*, July 8, 1911; MNJ, 8, p. 566.

101. *Yorozu*, July 8, 1911; MNJ, 8, p. 566. The note about the wind is from *Jiji*, July 9, 1911; reprinted in ibid.

102. *Tōkyō Asahi*, July 9, 1911; SSMH, 14, p. 440. Also see *Yorozu*, July 9, 1911.

103. See *Yorozu*, July 9, 10, 11, 1911.

104.   Gregory Ornatowski, "Press, Politics, and Profits: The 'Asahi Shimbun' and the Prewar Japanese Newspaper," p. 99.

105.   For the coffee story, *Jiji*, August 21, 1906; distant visits, *Tōkyō Asahi*, October 24, 1906; *maiko, Tōkyō Asahi*, November 13, 1903. Attendance at the graduation ceremony *(Tōkyō Asahi*, July 11, 1912) occurred only two days before he fell seriously ill and less than three weeks before his death.

106.   See examples from the press of 1909–1910 in Carol Gluck, *Japan's Modern Myths*, pp. 154, 206, taken from *Shimin*, April 1911, and *Tōkyō Asahi*, April 18, 1909.

107.   See Ono, *Shimbun no rekishi*, p. 48.

108.   "Brilliance," *Kyūshū Nippō*, November 28, 1911; "heartless," in *Nippō* articles, December 5–8, 1911. For supportive editorials elsewhere, see, for example, *Tōkyō Asahi*, November 14, and *Yomiuri*, November 23, 1911. Material here is largely from Omata Noriaki, "Moji ekiin no inseki jisatsu to Yamakawa Kenjirō genseki jiken," pp. 39–69; Haruhara, *Tsū shi*, pp. 135–136.

109.   Nishida, *Shimbun to zasshi*, p. 246; emphasis mine.

110.   For detailed accounts of Japanese attitudes toward Koreans, see Peter Duus, *The Abacus and the Sword*, pp. 397–423.

111.   Press accounts taken from Hilary Conroy, *The Japanese Seizure of Korea*, pp. 388–392: "happiness," *Tōkyō Mainichi*, August 23, 1910; "bad floods," *Tōkyō Nichi Nichi*, August 25, 1910; "purpose for which," *Ōsaka Asahi*, October 12, 1910. Also see Asahi Shimbunsha, *Genron hen*, pp. 583–586.

112.   For accounts of these, see Midoro Masaichi, *Meiji Taishō shi: genron hen*, p. 246; Nishida, *Shimbun to zasshi*, p. 268. In 1910, Kōtoku and Kanno Suga began the journal *Jiyū Shisō*; it lasted but two issues, and both were fined one thousand yen; see F. G. Notehelfer, *Kōtoku Shūsui: Portrait of a Japanese Radical*, p. 174.

113.   *Nikkan Heimin Shimbun*, February 5, 1907, quoted in Notehelfer, *Kōtoku Shūsui*, pp. 141–142. The debates between the parliamentary socialists and the direct actionists were carried out in the *Heimin Shimbun* and later in the *Shakai Shimbun*. Also see Kōuchi Saburō, "Iwayuru kōgai hōdō no rekishi: Ashio kōdoku jiken no issokumen," p. 26.

114.   Kenneth Pyle, "The Emergence of Bureaucratic Conservatism in the Meiji Period," pp. 26–27.

115.   See Uchikawa, "Shimbunshi hō no seitei katei," pp. 72–74; Notehelfer, *Kōtoku Shūsui*, pp. 145–146; Nishida, *Shimbun to zasshi*, p. 268. At the time of its closing, *Heimin Shimbun* was under litigation for four different articles, including publication of the Socialist Party's resolutions at its February conference and a March 27 essay titled "Kick your Parents"; *Heimin Shimbun*, April 14, 1907, p. 2.

116.   *Nikkan Heimin Shimbun*, April 14, 1907; Midoro, pp. 249–250.

117.   "Espoused socialism," Richard Mitchell, *Censorship in Imperial Japan*, p. 140; "marked by the police," Yamakawa Hitoshi, quoted in John Crump, *The Origins of Socialist Thought in Japan*, p. 23.

118.   Censorship and other aspects of this episode are treated in Mitchell, pp. 158–159; Notehelfer, *Kōtoku Shūsui*, pp. 196–200; Rubin, pp. 155–162; Haga Eizō, *Meiji Taishō hikka shi*, pp. 159–161.

119.   *Jiji*, February 5, 1907; MNJ, 7, p. 244.

120.   Uozumi, *Tokyo Asahi*, September 16, 1910, in Rubin, p. 146; caricature, *Tokyo Asahi*, December 11, 1910, in Notehelfer, p. 188; Tokutomi, discussed in Rubin, p. 171.

121.   Uchida Roan, in Rubin, p. 49; Ikuta's "The City," ibid., p. 83; for extramarital affairs, *Tōkyō Asahi*, June 28, 1909, and *Hōchi Shimbun*, September 6, 1909, reprinted in Araki, 2, pp. 471–472, 477–478; *Yomiuri* editor, in Masaaki Kōsaka, ed., *Japanese Thought in the Meiji Era*, p. 459; Tokutomi Roka, in Rubin, pp. 170–175.

122.   Uchikawa, *Masu medeia hō*, p. 66.

123.   *Tōkyō Asahi*, June 5, 1910; Asahi Shimbunsha, *Meiji hen*, p. 579, and Oka Mitsuo, *Shimbun koshi*, p. 112.

124.   Kōtoku, in Rubin, p. 167; *Tōkyō Nichi Nichi* (January 1, 1911) and *Yorozu* (January 18, 1911), from Oka Mitsuo, *Shimbun koshi*, pp. 112–113.

125.   The *Japan Chronicle* editor was Robert Young; his letter appeared on January 6, 1911; the *Japan Weekly Mail* editorial, titled "The Socialists," was run on November 19, 1910; they are reprinted at length in Notehelfer, pp. 196, 186; *Yorozu* editorial, January 18, 1911; Oka Mitsuo, *Shimbun koshi*, p. 113.

126.   In *Yomiuri*, April, 11, 1909; Rubin, p. 120.

127.   *Yamato Shimbun*, July 30, 1912; Haruhara, *Tsū shi*, p. 138. Vivid accounts are found in Edward Seidensticker, *Low City, High City*, pp. 252–253.

128.   *North-China Herald*, August 3, 1912; Uchikawa Yoshimi and Miyaji Masato, eds., *Gaikoku shimbun ni miru Nihon*, 4 *(Genbun hen)*, pp. 348–349.

129.   *Tōkyō Nichi Nichi*, English column, July 28, 1912; the report also expressed surprising concern that court physicians' skills might not be wholly "up to date" medically.

130.   *Kokumin Shimbun*, July 28, 1912; MNJ, 8, p. 759.

131.   *Tōkyō Asahi*, September 14, 1912; Haruhara, *Tsū shi*, p. 138.

132. This episode is described in Chikamori Haruyoshi, *Jinbutsu Nihon shimbun shi*, pp. 226–227.

133. *Tōkyō Asahi*, September 14, 1912; translated in Rubin, p. 223.

134. Quoted and analyzed in Ono Hideo, "Kuroiwa Shūroku," p. 68.

135. For Committee on Literature, Rubin, pp. 197–205; discussion of getting around censors in Mitchell, *Censorship*, pp. 163–166.

136. Letter to John Nowell, June 11, 1807, in Walter Brasch and Dana Ulloth, *The Press and the State*, p. 116.

137. Ono, *Shimbun no rekishi*, pp. 72–74; Midoro, *Meiji Taishō shi*, p. 231.

138. Summary of changes, along with the following summary of the process, is taken largely from Uchikawa, *Masu medeiya hō*, pp. 51–78. The Muramatsu-Suzuki draft is given on pp. 89–92.

139. See quote in Uchikawa, *Shimbun shi wa*, pp. 42–43.

140. Uchikawa, *Masu medeiya hō*, pp. 73–74. Eight of the eighteen members of the committee, including Muramatsu and Suzuki, were editors or presidents of newspapers.

141. The law is largely reprinted in Haruhara, *Tsū shi*, pp. 124–129; it is translated into English in Koito Chūgo, "The Press and National Affairs in Recent Japan," pp. i–vi. It also is discussed in Gregory Kasza, *The State and the Mass Media in Japan, 1918–1945*, pp. 15–20; his summary on pp. 18–19 is especially useful.

142. Midoro, p. 241.

143. *Ōsaka Asahi*, May 15, 1909; Haruhara, *Tsū shi*, p. 131; also discussed in Kasza, p. 16.

144. Uchikawa, *Masu medeiya hō*, p. 78.

145. Ibid., p. 42; for fines, Uchikawa, "Hō seitei katei," p. 74. Lawrence Beer notes that the number of times papers lost an issue owing to the prevention of sales and distribution soared to 1,100 in 1913; I have not found figures for 1910–1911; *Freedom of Expression in Japan*, p. 58.

146. Material on the legal struggles from Asahi Shimbunsha, *Meiji hen*, pp. 576–578; also see Haruhara, *Tsū shi*, pp. 131–132.

147. For a discussion of the effectiveness of confiscation in preventing long-term discussion as well as its ineffectiveness in halting actual distribution, see Kasza, pp. 36–37.

148. Material for this section relies heavily on Yamamoto Taketoshi, *Kisha no tanjō*, pp. 298–327. For discussion of press clubs in the 1990s, see Ofer Feldman, *Politics and the News Media in Japan.*

149. See *Tōkyō Nichi Nichi*, April 17, 1882; *Chōya Shimbun*, February 21, March 16, 1882; *Tōkyō Eiri Shimbun*, January 11, 1883; *Ōsaka Asahi*, November 5, 1887; *Shinano Shimbun*, May 1, 1888; Yamamoto Taketoshi, *Kisha no tanjō*, pp. 304–306.

150. Comment by Tokutomi Sohō, himself no slouch at bowing and scraping before certain officials; ibid., p. 315.

151. Ibid., p. 314.

152. *Shin Kōron*, January 1906, May 1908, in Yamamoto Taketoshi, *Shimbun to minshū*, pp. 83–85. The other observer was Yamaji Aizan.

153. See Pierson, pp. 297–298.

154. Discussed in Chikamori, *Jinbutsu Nihon shimbun shi*, p. 176. When Ōkuma was named prime minister in 1914, Kuroiwa reportedly gave three *banzais* at the palace; he also was in the first group of journalists to be decorated by the government; the others were *Asahi*'s Murayama, *Mainichi*'s Motoyama, and *Kokumin*'s Tokutomi; they received the Order of Merit Third Class.

155. Arase Yutaka, "Taishō seihen to jiyānarizumu," pp. 1–17; p. 5 for "people's army." *Hōchi Shimbun*, an anti-Seiyūkai paper, supported the government position by and large.

156. Quoted by Pierson regarding Tokutomi, when he popularized *Kokumin Shimbun* in 1906; p. 289.

157. Ariyama, *Kōzō*, pp. 36–37.

158. Gordon, pp. 50 ("political space"), 105.

159. Edwin Seidensticker, *Kafū the Scribbler*, p. 27; Rubin, pp. 118–119.

160. Letter from Komatsubara Eitarō to Motoyama Hikoichi, quoted in Uchikawa, *Masu medeiya hō*, p. 84.

161. Quoted in Uchikawa and Arai, p. 49.

CONCLUSION

1. *Chūō Kōron*, September 1919, p. 120.

2. For "commercial product," see Motoyama Hikoichi, "My personal newspaper policy" *(Kojin toshite no yo no shimbun seisaku)*, in Iwai Hajime, *Shimbun to shimbunjin*, p. 126. For a discussion of Motoyama's views on leading society, see Ariyama Teruo in Tanaka Hiroshi, *Kindai Nihon no jiyānarisuto*, pp. 704–709; quote from p. 705.

3. See Uchikawa Yoshimi and Arai Naoyuki, eds., *Nihon no jiyānarizumu: taishū no kokoro o tsukanda ka*, p. 270.

4. Figures from Yamamoto Fumio, *Nihon shimbun hattatsu shi*, pp. 265–266; Ono Hideo, *Shimbun no rekishi*, p. 94. For *Kokumin Shimbun*, see John Pierson, *Tokutomi Sohō, 1863–1957: A Journalist for Modern Japan*, p. 346.

5. In *Shimbun oyobi kisha no hensen* (1929), translated in Albert Altman, "The Emergence of the Press in Meiji Japan," p. 66.

6. Quoted in Ono, *Shimbun no rekishi*, pp. 81–82.

7. Zen Nihon Shimbun Renmei, ed., *Shimbun taikan*, 1, p. 224.

8. For firings, see ibid.; for the settlement, see Yamamoto Fumio, *Hattatsu shi*, p. 261. The strike also is treated in Haruhara Akihiko, *Nihon shimbun tsū shi*, pp. 160–161; Nihon Shimbun Hanbai Kyōkai, ed., *Shimbun hanbai hyakunen shi*, pp. 419–422; Gregory Ornatowski, "Press, Politics, and Profits: The 'Asahi Shimbun' and the Prewar Japanese Newspaper," pp. 155–161. Only at *Tōkyō Asahi* were the printers able to resist the firing of strike leaders.

9. Murobushi Kōshin, "Shimbun insatsu shokkō no higyō to shimbun kyūkan jiken," p. 120.

10. Motoyama's position is discussed by Arai Naoyuki in Kido Mataichi et al., eds., *Kōza gendai jiyānarizumu: rekishi*, p. 81. For the 1920 dispute, see Ornatowski, pp. 161–165.

11. Arai, in Kido, p. 81. It was not only the printers who were paid poorly; by 1926, the average starting wage for reporters was about seventy yen a month, at weak papers as little as fifty yen; editors in chief *(henshūchō)* at all but the top papers tended to receive between two hundred and three hundred yen a month; see Baba Tsunego, "Shimbun seisakusha to sono jinseikan," p. 211.

12. In 1925, ten leading papers adopted a standard list of 2,108 kanji that would be used in newspapers; Uchikawa and Arai, p. 264.

13. *Tōkyō Nichi Nichi*, February 11, 1914, p. 1.

14. Total rotary presses in Japan increased from 224 in 1918 to 462 in 1926, and *Asahi*, for example, had twenty-nine bureaus across the country in 1920; see Yamamoto Fumio, *Hattatsu shi*, pp. 274–275; Haruhara calls this the era of "scoop battles" *(sukūpu kassen)*; *Tsū shi*, p. 140.

15. Quoted in Iwai, p. 126.

16. Kido Mataichi, in Kido et al., eds., p. 7.

17. Iwai, p. 124.

18. The eight, in order, were *Tōkyō Nichi Nichi, Tōkyō Asahi, Hōchi, Jiji, Kokumin, Maiyū, Chūgai Shōgyō*, and *Miyako*; see figures in Yamamoto Fumio, *Hattatsu shi*, pp. 291–292, and Yamamoto Taketoshi, *Kindai Nihon no shimbun dokusha sō*, p. 410.

19.   According to Yamamoto Fumio, 920,000 dailies were delivered to a region with 792,834 households (Tokyo and environs); calculating that 100,000 households took no paper at all, he estimates that nearly a quarter of a million took two papers; *Hattatsu shi,* p. 292.

20.   For drunken policemen, see *Kainan Shimbun,* continuing articles, April 7–15, 1915, summarized in Haruhara, *Tsū shi,* pp. 147–149. For Kōbun scoop, *Tōkyō Nichi Nichi,* December 25, 1926. According to some accounts, Kōbun had been selected and the era name was hurriedly changed to Shōwa when *Nichi Nichi* printed its scoop before an official announcement could be made; Kido Motosuke resigned as chief editor as a result of the episode; see ibid., pp. 174–175. For Four Power scoop, Ono Hideo, *Nihon shimbun hattatsu shi,* p. 416; Midoro Masaichi, *Meiji Taishō shi: genron hen,* p. 285. For Lenin interview, *Tōkyō Nichi Nichi,* June 10, 1920, in Uchikawa and Arai, p. 268; sales of the paper were banned temporarily for running it. The chauvinism of the press was illustrated by *Ōsaka Asahi*'s threat of war if China did not accept the infamous Twenty-one Demands on March 12, 1915; translated in Ornatowski, pp. 194–195; both *Asahi*s secured scoops on the demands.

21.   Regarding taxes, see editorials in Uchikawa Yoshimi and Matsushima Eiichi, eds., *Taishō niyūsu jiten* (hereafter TNJ), 1, pp. 633–641; on Kyushu girls, see *Fukuoka Nichi Nichi Shimbun,* December 26, 1909; also James Warren, *Ah Ku and Karayuki-san: Prostitution in Singapore, 1870–1940* (Oxford University Press, 1993), pp. 211, 222–223; on secrecy (a constant theme), *Tōkyō Asahi,* October 6, 1916, and Kido Mataichi et al., pp. 60–61; on Siberia, Midoro, p. 270. In contrast to all other foreign issues, papers split on the Siberian incursion, with *Yorozu* supporting it (see English-language column, August 25, 1918) and most joining *Tōkyō Asahi* in saying the "people are being lured, step by step, into dangerous territory" (see Iwai, p. 77).

22.   *Tōkyō Asahi,* October 7, 1916; Kido et al., p. 61.

23.   Ornatowski, p. 111.

24.   The best sources on the press' role in the Taishō crisis of 1912–1913 are Arase Yutaka, "Taishō seihen to jiyānarizumu," pp. 10–17; Ornatowski, pp. 111–24; Midoro, pp. 254–261; TNJ, 1, pp. 448–463.

25.   See discussion in Andrew Gordon, *Labor and Imperial Democracy in Prewar Japan,* pp. 52–53.

26.   See report in *Tōkyō Nichi Nichi,* February 3, 1914.

27.   His resignation came on March 24. Useful accounts of the crisis are found in Yamamoto Fumio, *Hattatsu shi,* pp. 237–245; Haga Eizō, *Meiji Taishō hikka shi,* pp. 165–167; Otsu Jun'ichirō, *Dainihon kensei shi,* 7, pp. 196–283; A. Morgan Young, *Japan in Recent Times,* pp. 42–48.

28.   See example in Gordon, pp. 39–40.

29.   See *Tōkyō Nichi Nichi,* February 11, 1914, p. 5; the caption beneath Hashimoto's picture was "police draw swords and slash our employee."

30.   Phrases respectively from *Hōchi*, February 24, 28, March 13, 8, 10, 1914; Haruhara, *Tsū shi*, p. 146.

31.   *Kokumin Shimbun*, February 6, 7, 1914, respectively; Uchikawa and Arai, p. 55.

32.   From rally resolution of March 22, 1914; Yamamoto Fumio, *Hattatsu shi*, pp. 244–245. Issues of most of the leading papers were confiscated by authorities several times during this controversy.

33.   In Kido Mataichi et al., p. 59.

34.   See especially Michael Lewis, *Rioters and Citizens: Mass Protest in Imperial Japan*, particularly pp. 1–33, 45–65.

35.   Gordon notes, for example, that the one instance of press involvement prior to the Tokyo riots, which began on August 13, was a *Tōkyō Asahi* ad (August 10) calling for a rally on the twelfth; about two hundred came, and police broke it up without incident; p. 60. Lewis notes that the *Nagoya Shimbun* called for a citizens' meeting at Tsurumai Park prior to rioting there in early August (p. 118); he also gives several examples of exaggeration or distortion in the press accounts of the riots; see pp. 126–127, 191.

36.   Quoted from Mizuno statement to newspaper executives, August 16, 1918, in Midoro, p. 272.

37.   Yamamoto Fumio, *Hattatsu shi*, p. 246.

38.   Translated in Ornatowski, p. 137.

39.   *Ōsaka Asahi*, August 26, 1918, quoted in Asahi Shimbunsha, ed., *Taishō Shōwa senzen hen*, p. 96; also in Uchikawa and Arai, p. 57, and Haruhara, *Tsū shi*, pp. 154–155. The white rainbow allusion arises in *The Tale of Genji* in connection with questions about Genji's own loyalty to the emperor; see Murasaki Shikibu (Edward Seidensticker, trans.), *The Tale of Genji* (New York: Vintage Classics, 1990), p. 213.

40.   The right-wing attack is discussed in Zen Nihon Shimbun Renmei, *Shimbun taikan*, 1, pp. 204–205. Members of the Kokuryūkai went so far as to beat up *Ōsaka Asahi* president Murayama in an Osaka park on September 28, and they continued an intimidation campaign against the paper well into October; see Ornatowski, pp. 144–145.

41.   *Ōsaka Asahi*, November 1, 1918; Ornatowski, p. 147.

42.   Torii later founded the *Taishō Nichi Nichi Shimbun*, which lasted only two years, mainly because of the intense competition from the two established Osaka papers. A number of liberal writers, including Kawakami Hajime, also left the paper.

43.   See Haga, pp. 170–175; Ornatowski, pp. 149–151. The English-language *Kobe Chronicle* was the one paper to raise the question of what implications the *Ōsaka Asahi* suppression might have for other papers. Also see Lawrence Beer, *Freedom of Expression in Japan*, p. 63, for *Tōkyō*

Asahi's response. It is worth noting that most papers continued their anti-leftist, establishment approach even in reporting the riots. The Seiyūkai's *Chūō Shimbun* inaccurately suggested that up to 70 percent of the rioters were *burakumin*, and *Kōbe Shimbun* blamed leftists (again inaccurately); see Lewis, pp. 125–127.

44.   Haga, p. 206.

45.   See, for example, *Ōsaka Asahi*, August 14, 15, 1918.

46.   *Yorozu*, August 22, 1918.

47.   In Chiba Yūjirō, ed., *Shimbun*, p. 63; also conversation with Uchikawa, May 2, 1984.

48.   The three were *Tōkyō Nichi Nichi*, *Hōchi*, and *Miyako*. See especially, Nihon Shimbun Hanbai Kyōkai, *Hyakunen shi*, pp. 443–447; Midoro, pp. 296–303. *Yomiuri*, which had begun modernizing in mid-Taishō, had scheduled opening ceremonies for September 1, 1923, the day of the earthquake; Jung Bock Lee, *The Political Character of the Japanese Press*, p. 33.

49.   *Authorized National Language Text No. 8 (Kokutei kokugo kyōkasho dai hachi)*, 1904–1909, reprinted in Oka Mitsuo, *Kindai Nihon shimbun koshi*, p. 107.

50.   "Shimbun shō," in Okano Takeo, *Meiji genron shi*, p. 106.

51.   *Yorozu*, June 19, 1901; SSMH, 11, p. 266.

52.   Tokutomi Sohō, *Sohō jiden*, p. 224.

53.   *Nisshin Shinjishi*, March 17, 1872; Matsumoto Sannosuke and Yamamuro Shin'ichi, eds., *Genron to medeia*, p. 117.

54.   *Seiyō jijō*; Matsumoto and Yamamuro, p. 3.

55.   Motoyama to *Mainichi* trainees, 1924, in Iwai, p. 124.

56.   Midoro, p. 115; see also his analysis on p. 367. The government issued twenty-one more decrees and regulations in the remaining Meiji years and another twelve in Taishō; most are reprinted wholly in Midoro, pp. 369–458. He also reprints other press-related draft laws and ordinances proposed to the Diet; pp. 459–480.

57.   Okudaira Yasuhiro, *Jian iji hō shōshi*, p. 1.

58.   Pierson, p. 265.

59.   *Chōya Shimbun*, December 20, 1875; Maeda Ai, *Kindai doku-sha no seiritsu*, p. 238.

60.   *Yamato Shimbun*, February 4, 1901; reprinted in Chikamori Haruyoshi, *Jinbutsu Nihon shimbun shi*, p. 139.

61.   *Chūgai Shimbun*, April 10, 1868, quoted in Okano Takeo, *Meiji genron shi*, p. 6.

62. Beer, p. 56.

63. See Nishida Taketoshi, *Meiji jidai no shimbun to zasshi*, p. 93.

64. Kanesada Hanazono, *Journalism in Japan and Its Early Pioneers*, p. 2.

65. *Hyōron Shimbun*, January 15, 1876.

66. In *Yo ga hansei no zange*, translated in Irokawa Daikichi, *The Culture of the Meiji Period*, p. 216.

67. Statement by Fukuchi Gen'ichirō, in *Kōko Shimbun*, May 24, 1868; Osatake Takeki, ed., *Bakumatsu Meiji shimbun zenshū*, 1, p. 3.

68. *Yorozu*, January 18, 1911; Oka Mitsuo, *Koshi*, p. 113.

69. See, for example, Fukuchi's discussion of a constitution, *Tōkyō Nichi Nichi*, March 30–April 16, 1881; also my *Politics of the Meiji Press*, pp. 110–112.

70. A telling example of the direction in which this unquestioning allegiance to "the country" was leading was this statement in the 1932 *Nihon Shimbun Nenkan* (Japanese newspaper yearbook): "The worse Japan's foreign relations get, the more nationalistic does the press have to be in accordance with its readers' demands and surrounding circumstances." In another example of press activism in behalf of the state, the previous fall the Nihon Shimbun Kyōkai, the professional association of the national press, had wired the League of Nations, defending Japan's actions in the Manchurian Incident. See Koito Chūgo, "The Press and National Affairs in Recent Japan," pp. 62–63, 58.

71. Uchikawa and Arai, p. 6; Nihon Shimbun Hanbai Kyōkai, Hyakunen shi, p. 193.

72. Kuwabara Takeo, in introduction to *Nakae Chōmin, A Discourse by Three Drunkards on Government*, p. 19.

73. *Yorozu*, November 1, 1892.

74. Baba, p. 209.

75. *Heimin* was used with particular frequency in the 1874–1875 debates over a popular assembly; references to "children and women" were commonplace in newspaper descriptions of the classes they wished to reach; for examples, see Nihon Shimbun Hanbai Kyōkai, *Hyakunen shi*, p. 193. Hayashi Mokichi was fond of the term *min*; see, for example, *Minkan Zasshi*, January 1875; Okano, pp. 194–196.

76. See, for example, *Yorozu*, November 1, 1892; *Niroku Shinpō*, March 22, 1901; MNJ, 6, 798.

77. For typical references to public, see *Mainichi Shimbun* editorial series, January 1902, in Kōuchi Saburō, "Iwayuru kōgai hōdō no rekishi," pp. 29–30; Baba, p. 209.

78.   *Yūbin Hōchi*, April 4, 1875, in Sugiura Tadashi, *Shimbun koto hajime*, p. 286; *Tōkyō Nichi Nichi*, December 9, 1872.

79.   Yamamoto Taketoshi, *Kindai Nihon no shimbun dokusha sō*, p. 141.

80.   Speech, February 17, 1900, quoted in Kenneth Strong, *Ox against the Storm*, p. 119.

81.   Iwai, p. 125.

82.   *Yomiuri Shimbun*, July 3, 1901; Yamamoto Taketoshi, *Dokusha sō*, p. 193.

83.   *Hara nikki*, July 12, 1910, in Tetsuo Najita, *Hara Kei in the Politics of Compromise*, p. 161.

BIBLIOGRAPHY

Note: Japanese-language books are published in Tokyo, unless otherwise noted.

Able, Elie. "On Journalistic Freedom," *Dialogue*, 55 (January 1982), pp. 2–5.

Akebono Shimbun. (Tōkyō Akebono Shimbun).

Akita, George. *Foundations of Constitutional Government in Modern Japan, 1868–1900.* Cambridge: Harvard University Press, 1967.

———. "Government and Opposition in Prewar Japan: A Political Success or Embarrassment?" *Transactions of the Asiatic Society of Japan,* third series, 18 (July 1983), pp. 39–70.

Allen, George C. *A Short Economic History of Modern Japan, 1868–1937.* New York: Frederick A. Praeger, 1962.

Altman, Albert A. "The Emergence of the Press in Meiji Japan." Ph.D. dissertation, Princeton University, 1965.

———. "Eugene Van Reed, a Reading Man in Japan, 1859–1872." *Historical Review of Berks County,* 30, no. 1 (Winter 1964–1965), pp. 6–12, 27–31.

———. "The Press." In *Japan in Transition: From Tokugawa to Meiji,* ed. Marius B. Jansen and Gilbert Rozman, pp. 231–247. Princeton: Princeton University Press, 1986.

———. "The Press and Social Cohesion during a Period of Change: The Case of Early Meiji Japan." *Modern Asian Studies,* 15, no. 4 (1981), pp. 865–876.

———. "Proprietor *versus* Editor: The Case of the *Osaka Asahi Shimbun* in the Late Nineteenth Century." *Asian and African Studies,* 14, no. 3 (November 1980), pp. 241–253.

————. "A Recently Discovered Document on Early Meiji Press Censorship Legislation." *Gazette,* 17 (November 4, 1971), pp. 220–223.

————. " '*Shimbunshi':* The Early Meiji Adaptation of the Western-Style Newspaper." In *Modern Japan: Aspects of History, Literature and Society,* ed. W. G. Beasley, pp. 52–66. Berkeley: University of California Press, 1975.

Amari Shōhachi. *Nyūsu pēpā jōriku su: Nihon no shimbun no yoake* (The newspapers disembark: the dawn of the Japanese press). Shinjinbutsu Ōraisha, 1987.

Anderson, Benedict. *Imagined Communities: Reflections on the Origin and Spread of Nationalism.* London: Verso, 1991.

Araki Masayasu, ed. *Shimbun ga kataru Meiji shi* (A history of Meiji through newspapers). 2 vols. Hara Shobō, 1976.

Arase Yutaka. "Makkureikā no dansei" (Flexibility of the muckrakers). In *Miyatake Gaikotsu chosakushū,* II. Kawade Shobō Shinsha, 1986.

————. "Taishō seihen to jiyānarizumu" (Journalism and the Taishō political change), *Tōkyō Daigaku Shimbun Kenkyūjo Kiyō,* no. 28 (1980), pp. 1–17.

Ariyama Teruo. " 'Chūritsu' shimbun no keisei: Meiji chūki ni okeru seifu to *Asahi Shimbun*" (The composition of "neutral" newspapers: *Asahi Shimbun* and the mid-Meiji government). *Seijō Bungei,* 117 (December 1986), pp. 30–54.

————. *Kindai Nihon jiyānarizumu no kōzō* (Structure of modern Japanese journalism). Tokyo Shuppan, 1995.

————. "Taishō shoki ni okeru 'kokumin no jikaku' ron" (On the "people's consciousness" in the early-Taishō era). *Shimbun Gaku Hyōron,* 21 (1972), pp. 26–35.

————. " 'Taji sōron' to seifu kikanshi mondai" (The problem of contentious debates and government organs). In *Jiyū rekishi medeia* (Freedom, history, media), ed. Arase Yutaka, et al., pp. 133–52. Nihon Hyōronsha, 1988.

————. *Tokutomi Sohō to Kokumin Shimbun* (Tokutomi Sohō and *Kokumin Shimbun*). Yoshikawa Kōbunkan, 1992.

Asahi Shimbun. (Ōsaka Asahi Shimbun, Tokyo Asahi Shimbun).

Asahi Shimbun Japan Almanac 1993. Asahi Shimbun Publishing Company, 1992.

Asahi Shimbunsha, ed. *Asahi Shimbun hyakunen no jūyō shimen, 1879–1979* (A century of *Asahi Shimbun:* important pages). Asahi Shimbunsha, 1979.

————. *Asahi Shimbun jūyū shimen de miru: Asahi Shimbun kyūjū nen (1879–1969)* (Ninety years of Asahi Shimbun, as seen through important pages in *Asahi Shimbun*). Asahi Shimbunsha, 1969.

————. *Asahi Shimbunsha shi: Meiji hen, Taishō Shōwa senzen hen* (History of the *Asahi Shimbun* Company: Meiji, Taishō, prewar Shōwa volumes). 2 vols. Asahi Shimbunsha, 1990.

————. *Murayama Ryōhei den* (Biography of Murayama Ryōhei). Osaka: Asahi Shimbunsha, 1953.

Asaoka Kunio. "*Nisshin Shinjishi* no henshitsu to seifu no shimbun seisaku" (The decline of *Nisshin Shinjishi* and government newspaper policy). *Medeiya Shi Kenkyū*, 1 (March 1994), pp. 1–16.

Aso, Makoto, and Ikuo Amano. *Education and Japan's Modernization.* Tokyo: Ministry of Foreign Affairs, 1972.

Aspinall, A. *Politics and the Press, c. 1780–1850.* New York: Barnes and Noble, 1974.

Aston, W. G. *A History of Japanese Literature.* Tokyo: Charles E. Tuttle Company, 1972.

Baba Tsunego. "Shimbun seisakusha to sono jinseikan" (Newspaper producers and their view of life). In Tsurumi Shunsuke, pp. 209–212.

Baelz, Erwin. *Awakening Japan: The Diary of a German Doctor: Erwin Baelz.* Bloomington: Indiana University Press, 1974.

Bamba, Nobuya, and John Howes, eds. *Pacifism in Japan: The Christian Socialist Tradition.* Kyoto: Minerva Press, 1978.

Barr, Pat. *The Deer Cry Pavilion. A Story of Westerners in Japan, 1868–1905.* London: Macmillan, 1968.

Beasley, W. G. *The Meiji Restoration.* Stanford: Stanford University Press, 1972.

Beckmann, George. M. *The Making of the Meiji Constitution.* Lawrence: The University Press of Kansas, 1957.

Beer, Lawrence Ward. *Freedom of Expression in Japan.* Tokyo: Kodansha International, 1984.

Bellah, Robert N. *Tokugawa Religion: The Values of Preindustrial Japan.* Boston: Beacon Press, 1957.

Beniger, James R., and D. Eleanor Westney. "The Social Role of the Newspaper as Reflected in Statistical and Didactic Graphics: A Comparison of the *Asahi Shimbun* and the *New York Times.*" Unpublished manuscript, 1980.

Bix, Herbert. *Peasant Protest in Japan, 1590–1884.* New Haven: Yale University Press, 1986.

Black, John R. *Young Japan: Yokohama and Yedo, 1858–79.* 2 vols. London: Oxford University Press, 1968.

Blacker, Carmen. *The Japanese Enlightenment: A Study of the Writings of Fukuzawa Yukichi.* Cambridge: Cambridge University Press, 1964.

Bowen, Roger W. "Political Protest in Prewar Japan: The Case of Fukushima Prefecture," *Bulletin of Concerned Asian Scholars,* 16 no. 2 (April–June 1984), pp. 22–31.

———. *Rebellion and Democracy in Meiji Japan: A Study of Commoners in the Popular Rights Movement.* Berkeley: University of California Press, 1980.

Boyce, George, James Curran, and Pauline Wingate, eds. *Newspaper History: From the Seventeenth Century to the Present Day.* London: Constable, 1978.

Braisted, William R., trans. *Meiroku Zasshi: Journal of Japanese Enlightenment.* University of Tokyo Press, 1976.

Brasch, Walter, and Dana Ulloth. *The Press and the State: Sociohistorical and Contemporary Interpretations.* New York: University Press of America, 1986.

Brown, Sidney D. "Kido Takayoshi and the Meiji Restoration: A Political Biography, 1833–1877." Ph.D. dissertation, University of Wisconsin, 1952.

———. "Political Assassination in Early Meiji Japan: The Plot Against Ōkubo Toshimichi." In Wurfel, pp. 18–35.

Carey, James W. "The Problems of Journalism History," *Journalism History,* 12, no. 2 (Summer 1985), pp. 51–53.

Cater, Douglass. *The Fourth Branch of Government.* Boston: Houghton-Mifflin, 1959.

Centre for East Asian Cultural Studies, ed. *The Meiji Japan through Contemporary Sources.* 3 vols. Toyo Bunko, 1969–1972.

Chamoto Shigemasa. *Sensō to jiyānarizumu* (War and journalism). San'ichi Shobō, 1984.

Chiba Yūjirō, ed. *Shimbun* (Newspapers). Yūhikaku, 1955.

Chikamori Haruyoshi. *Jinbutsu Nihon shimbun shi* (Human history of Japanese journalism). Shinjinbutsu Ōraisha, 1970.

———. *Jiyosefu Hiko* (Joseph Heco). Yoshikawa Kōbunkan, 1963.

———. "*Yokohama Mainichi Shimbun* sōkan hi ronsō ni shūshifu" (Settling the dispute over the founding date of *Yokohama Mainichi Shimbun*), *Sōgō Jiyānarizumu Kenkyū,* 42 (February 1968), pp. 57–63.

Chōya Shimbun. Facsimile edition. Vols. 1–38 (1874–1893). Perikansha, 1981–1984.

Conroy, Hilary. *The Japanese Seizure of Korea, 1868–1910: A Study of Realism and Idealism in International Relations.* Philadelphia: University of Pennsylvania Press, 1960.

Conroy, Hilary, Sandra T. W. Davis, and Wayne Patterson, eds. *Japan in Transition: Thought and Action in the Meiji Era, 1868–1912.* Toronto: Associated University Press, 1984.

Craig, Albert M., and Donald H. Shively, eds. *Personality in Japanese History.* Berkeley: University of California Press, 1970.

Crump, John. *The Origins of Socialist Thought in Japan.* New York: St. Martin's Press, 1983.

"A Cry for Light," *Hyōron Shimbun,* in *Tokio Times,* March 3, 1877, pp. 107–108.

Davis, Sandra T. W. "Ono Azusa and the Political Change of 1881." *Monumenta Nipponica,* 25, nos. 1–2, pp. 137–154.

Davison, W. Phillips. "The Role of Communication in Democracies." In Fischer, Heinz-Dietrich, and Merrill, pp. 29–36.

DeFleur, Melvin L. *Theories of Mass Communication.* New York: David McKay Company, 1966.

Devine, Richard. "The Way of the King: An Early Meiji Essay on Government." *Monumenta Nipponica,* 34, no. 1, pp. 49–72.

Dominick, Joseph R. *The Dynamics of Mass Communication.* 2d ed. New York: Random House, 1987.

Dore, Ronald P. *Education in Tokugawa Japan.* Berkeley: University of California Press, 1965.

———. "The Legacy of Tokugawa Education." In *Changing Japanese Attitudes Toward Modernization,* ed. Marius B. Jansen, pp. 99–131. Princeton: Princeton University Press, 1965.

———. "Mobility, Equality, and Individuation in Modern Japan." In *Aspects of Social Change in Modern Japan,* ed. Ronald Dore, pp. 113–150. Princeton: Princeton University Press, 1979.

Dower, John W., ed. *Origins of the Modern Japanese State: Selected Writings of E. H. Norman.* New York: Random House, 1975.

Duus, Peter. *The Abacus and the Sword: The Japanese Penetration of Korea, 1895–1910.* Berkeley: University of California Press, 1995.

———. "Liberal Intellectuals and Social Conflict in Taishō Japan." In Najita and Koschmann, pp. 412–440.

———. *Party Rivalry and Political Change in Taishō Japan.* Cambridge: Harvard University Press, 1968.

Ebihara Hachirō. *Nihon Ōji shimbun zasshi shi* (History of Japan's English-language newspapers and magazines). Taikaidō, 1934.

Emery, Michael, and Edwin Emery. *The Press and America.* 7th ed. Englewood Cliffs, N.J.: Prentice Hall, 1992.

Feldman, Ober. *Politics and the News Media in Japan.* Ann Arbor: University of Michigan Press, 1993.

Figdor, Peter. "Newspapers and Their Regulation in Early Meiji Japan, 1868–1883." *Papers on Japan* (Cambridge: Harvard East Asian Research Center), 6 (1972).

Fischer, Heinz-Dietrich, and John C. Merrill, eds. *International and Intercultural Communication.* New York: Hastings House Publishers, 1970.

Fraser, Andrew. "The Expulsion of Ōkuma from the Government in 1881." *Journal of Asian Studies,* 26, no. 2 (February 1967), pp. 213–236.

Fukuchi Gen'ichirō. "Ishin no genkun" (Elder statesmen of the Restoration). *Taiyō,* 1 (April 1895), pp. 31–37.

———. *Moshiya sōshi* (What if?). In *Fukuchi Ōchi shū,* ed. Yanagida Izumi, pp. 3–91.

———. *Shimbunshi jitsureki* (My career in the newspaper). In *Fukuchi Ōchi shū,* ed. Yanagida Izumi, pp. 325–341.

Fukuda Tsuneari. *Genron no jiyū to iu koto* (Freedom of the press). Shinchōsha, 1973.

Fukuzawa Yukichi. *The Autobiography of Yukichi Fukuzawa.* Trans. Eiichi Kiyooka. New York: Columbia University Press, 1966.

———. *An Encouragement of Learning.* Sophia University Press, 1969.

———. *Fukuzawa Yukichi on Education.* Trans. Eiichi Kiyooka. University of Tokyo Press, 1985.

———. *Fukuzawa Yukichi zenshū* (Complete works of Fukuzawa Yukichi). 21 vols. Keiō Gijiku Hensan, 1958–1963.

Futagawa Yoshifumi. *Genron no dan'atsu* (Suppression of speech). Hōsei Daigaku Shuppankyoku, 1959.

Garon, Sheldon. *The State and Labor in Modern Japan.* Berkeley: University of California Press, 1987.

Gluck, Carol. *Japan's Modern Myths: Ideology in the Late Meiji Period.* Princeton: Princeton University Press, 1985.

Gordon, Andrew. *Labor and Imperial Democracy in Prewar Japan.* Berkeley: University of California Press, 1991.

Gotō Fumio. "Shimbun akusesu *Mainichi Shimbun* no shimen kaikaku," (Newspaper access: reforming the *Mainichi* format). *Sekai,* January 1992, pp. 220–221.

Gotō Takao, ed. *Nakae Chōmin shū* (Collected works of Nakae Chōmin). Vol. 10 of *Meiji Taishū genron shiryō.* Misuzu Shobō, 1984.

Groemer, Gerald. "Singing the News: *Yomiuri* in Japan during the Edo and Meiji Periods," *Harvard Journal of Asiatic Studies,* 54, no. 1 (June 1994), pp. 233–261.

Hackett, Roger. "The Meiji Leaders and Modernization: The Case of Yamagata Aritomo." In *Changing Japanese Attitudes Toward Modernization*, ed. Marius Jansen, pp. 243–281.

———. *Yamagata Aritomo in the Rise of Modern Japan, 1838–1922.* Cambridge: Harvard University Press, 1971.

Haga Eizō. *Meiji Taishō hikka shi* (A history of Meiji-Taishō press infractions). Shikōsha Shobō, 1924.

Haisei Gaikotsu. *See* Miyatake Gaikotsu.

Hall, Ivan. *Mori Arinori.* Cambridge: Harvard University Press, 1973.

Halloran, Richard. "Japanese Newspapers." *Asahi Evening News*, December 6–7, 1973.

Hanazono, Kanesada. *The Development of Japanese Journalism.* Osaka: Osaka Mainichi Shimbunsha, 1924.

———. *Journalism in Japan and Its Early Pioneers.* Osaka: Osaka Mainichi Shuppansha, 1926.

Hane, Mikiso. *Modern Japan: A Historical Survey.* Boulder, Co.: Westview Press, 1992.

———. "The Movement for Liberty and Popular Rights." In *Japan Examined: Perspectives on Modern Japanese History*, ed. Harry Wray and Hilary Conroy, pp. 90–97. Honolulu: University of Hawai'i Press, 1983.

———. *Peasants, Rebels, and Outcastes: The Underside of Modern Japan.* New York: Pantheon, 1982.

———. *Reflections on the Way to the Gallows.* Berkeley: University of California Press, 1988.

Hani Motoko. "Memoirs of a Successful Woman." In *As the Japanese See It: Past and Present*, ed. Michiko Aoki and Margaret Dardess, pp. 137–146. Honolulu: University of Hawaii Press, 1981.

———. "Stories of My Life." *Japan Interpreter*, 12, nos. 3–4 (Summer 1979), pp. 330–354.

Haratane Akira. "Saifū kisha Katō kun ni tsuite futatabi" (More about the *Saifū* reporter Katō). *Shinkyū Jidai (Meiji Bunka Kenkyū)*, 3, no. 6 (June 1927), pp. 24–29.

Harries, Meirion, and Susie Harries. *Soldiers of the Sun: The Rise and Fall of the Imperial Japanese Army.* New York: Random House, 1991.

Harsel, Sheldon M. "Freedom, Responsibility, and the Intellectual in the Development of Japanese Mass Communication." Ph.D. dissertation, University of Iowa, 1979.

Haruhara Akihiko. "Nihon no jiyānarizumu no seisei ni oyobashite dentō to seiō no eikyō" (The influence of tradition and the West in the creation of Japanese journalism). *Komiyunikēshiyon Kenkyū,* 21 (1992), pp. 21–22.

———. *Nihon shimbun tsū shi: 1861–1986* (General history of the Japanese press, 1861–1986). Niizumisha, 1987.

Haruhara Akihiko, Yoneda Sayoko, Iwasaki Chieko, Ikeda Emiko, and Hirano Kyōko, eds. *Josei kisha* (Women reporters). Sekai Shisōsha, 1993.

Harumura Sen'ichi. *Shimbunshi hōsei ron* (A discussion of press laws). Nihon Hyōronsha, 1933.

Hasegawa Shin'ichi. "Nihon saisho eiji shimbun" (Japan's first English-language newspaper). *Shimbun Gaku Hyōron,* 13 (1963), pp. 37–48.

———. *The Japan Times monogatari* (The story of *The Japan Times*). Japan Times, 1966.

Hastings, Sally A. *Neighborhood and Nation in Tokyo, 1905–1937.* Pittsburgh: University of Pittsburgh Press, 1995.

Hattori Shisō and Konishi Shirō, eds. *Shūkan Heimin Shimbun (Heimin Shimbun Weekly).* 4 vols. Tokyo, 1953–1958.

Hayashi, Toshitaka. "The Japanese Newspaper—Its Past, Present, and Future." *Nihon Shimbun Kyōkai Kenkyūjo Nenpō,* 9 (1970), pp. 108–116.

Heco, Joseph. *The Narrative of a Japanese.* 2 vols. Yokohama: Yokohama Printing and Publishing Company, n.d.

Herd, Harold. *The March of Journalism.* London: George Allen and Unwin, 1952.

Heimin Shimbun. See Hattori Shisō; Rōdō Undō Shi Kenkyūkai.

Havens, Thomas R. H. *Nishi Amane and Modern Japanese Thought.* Princeton: Princeton University Press, 1970.

Hess, Stephen. *The Washington Reporters: Newswork.* Washington, D.C.: Brookings Institute, 1981.

Hironiwa Motosuke. "Shimbun jūransho shōron" (Discussion of newspaper reading rooms). *Toshokan Kai,* 25, no. 3 (October 1973), pp. 84–100, and 25, no. 4 (December 1973), pp. 133–152.

Hoarc, James E. "The 'Bankoku Shimbun' Affair: Foreigners, the Japanese Press and Extraterritoriality in Early Meiji Japan," *Modern Asian Studies,* 9, no. 3 (1975), pp. 289–302.

———. "British Journalists in Meiji Japan." In Nish, pp. 20–32.

———. "Extraterritoriality in Japan, 1858–1899." *Transactions of the Asiatic Society of Japan,* third series, 18 (July 1983), pp. 71–97.

———. *Japan's Treaty Ports and Foreign Settlements.* Kent: Japan Library, 1994.

Hōchi Shimbun. (Yūbin Hōchi Shimbun).

Hohenberg, John. *Between Two Worlds: Policy, Press, and Public Opinion in Asian-American Relations.* New York: Frederick A. Praeger, 1967.

———. *Foreign Correspondence: The Great Reporters and Their Times.* New York: Columbia University Press, 1964.

———. *Free Press/Free People.* New York: Columbia University Press, 1971.

Hoston, Germaine A. *The State, Identity, and the National Question in China and Japan.* Princeton: Princeton University Press, 1994.

House, Edward H. "Ancient and Modern Periodical Literature of Japan." *The Tokio Times,* 1, no. 21 (May 26, 1877), pp. 244–245.

Howes, John F. "Modernization vs. Marx: Canadian Ideas and Japanese History." *Queen's Quarterly,* 90, no. 2 (Summer 1983), pp. 414–427.

Huber, Thomas. "Suehiro Tetchō versus the Press Law of 1875." Unpublished paper, Durham, North Carolina, July 1981.

Huffman, James L. "Edward Howard House: In the Service of Meiji Japan." *Pacific Historical Review,* 56, no. 2 (May 1987), pp. 231–258.

———. "Freedom and the Press in Meiji-Taishō Japan." *The Transactions of the Asiatic Society of Japan,* third series, 19 (1984), pp. 137–171.

———. "Japan's First Newspaper Law: The Emergence of an Independent Meiji Press." *The American ASIAN REVIEW,* 7, no. 4 (Winter 1989), pp. 29–46.

———. "Managing the News: Fukuchi Gen'ichirō Attempts to Balance Two Worlds." In Conroy, Davis, and Patterson, pp. 50–74.

———. "The Meiji Roots and Contemporary Practice of the Japanese Press." *Japan Interpreter,* Spring 1977, pp. 448–466.

———. *Politics of the Meiji Press: The Life of Fukuchi Gen'ichirō.* Honolulu: University Press of Hawai'i, 1980.

Hulteng, John L., and Roy P. Nelson. *The Fourth Estate: An Informal Approach to the News and Opinion Media.* New York: Harper and Row, 1971.

Hyōron Shimbun.

Iddittie, Junesay. *Marquis Okuma.* Tokyo: Hokuseido Press, 1956.

Iglehart, Charles W. *A Century of Protestant Christianity in Japan.* Tokyo: Charles Tuttle, 1959.

Ike Nobutaka. *The Beginnings of Political Democracy in Japan.* Baltimore: The Johns Hopkins University Press, 1950.

———. "The Triumph of the Peace Party in Japan in 1873." *Far Eastern Quarterly,* 2, no. 3 (May 1943), pp. 286–295.

Ikeuchi Hiroshi. "*Hokuriku Jiyū Shimbun* no shisō kempō" (Private draft constitution of the *Hokuriku Jiyū Shimbun*). *Nihon Rekishi*, 419 (April 1983), pp. 1–16.

Ikuta Masaki. "Shimbun shijō ni okeru *Jiji Shinpō* no ichi to seikaku" (The character and standing of *Jiji Shinpō* in press history). *Hōgaku kenkyū*, 37, no. 12 (December 1964), pp. 263–287.

Imayoshi Ken'ichirō. "Jinmyaku—yon'man gō: shimbun koto hajime" (Forty thousand issues: press beginnings—the human connections). *Mainichi Shimbun*. 61 articles. August 4–November 24, 1988.

———. *Mainichi Shimbun no genryū: Edo kara Meiji kakumei o yomu* (Finding the sources of *Mainichi Shimbun* in the years prior to the Meiji transformation). 62 articles. Mainichi Shimbunsha, 1988.

Inada Masatsugu. *Meiji kenpō seiritsu shi* (History of the framing of the Meiji Constitution). 2 vols. Yūhikaku, 1960–1962.

Inoue Kiyoshi, ed. *Taishō ki no seiji to shakai* (Politics and society in the Taishō era). Iwanami Shoten, 1969.

Inui Teruo. "Meiji jūnendai ni okeru Narushima Ryūhoku no genron katsudō ni tsuite" (Narushima Ryūhoku's press-related activities, 1877–1884). *Kai Jōhō Kagaku*, 6, no. 2 (August 1993), pp. 117–161.

Irokawa Daikichi. *The Culture of the Meiji Period*. Princeton: Princeton University Press, 1985.

———. "Freedom and the Concept of People's Rights." In *Modern Japan: An Interpretive Anthology*, ed. Irwin Scheiner, pp. 190–201. New York: Macmillan Publishing Company, 1974.

———. *Shinpen Meiji seishin shi* (History of the spirit of Meiji: revised edition). Chūō Kōronsha, 1973.

———. "The Survival Struggle of the Japanese Community." *Japan Interpreter*, 9, no. 4 (Spring 1975), pp. 465–494.

Isaacs, Norman. *Untended Gates: The Mismanaged Press*. New York: Columbia University Press, 1986.

Ishida Fumishirō. *Daijiken shi: Meiji Taishō Shōwa shimbun kiroku shūsei* (History of major incidents: collected newspaper records—the Meiji, Taishō, and Shōwa eras). Kinshosha, 1964.

Ishii Kendō. "Bēri no *Bankoku Shimbun* to Hiko no *Kaigai Shimbun*" (Bailey's *Bankoku Shimbun* and Heco's *Kaigai Shimbun*). *Meiji Bunka*, 5, no. 10 (October 1929), pp. 2–7.

Ishikawa Iwao. "Meiji gonen shōgi kaihō rei" (Law to liberate prostitutes in 1872). *Shinkyū Jidai (Meiji Bunka Kenkyū)*, 1, nos. 11–12 (special edition 1926), pp. 55–60.

Itagaki Taisuke, ed. *Jiyūtō shi* (History of the Liberal Party). Revised by Tōyama Shigeki and Satō Shigerō. 3 vols. Iwanami Shoten, 1958.

Itō Hideo. *Kuroiwa Shūroku sono shosetsu no subete* (Complete novels of Kuroiwa Shūroku). Tōgensha, 1971.

Itō Hirobumi. *Commentaries on the Constitution of the Empire of Japan.* Chūō Daigaku, 1906.

Itō Masanori. "History of the Japanese Press." In *The Japanese Press, Past and Present,* ed. Nihon Shimbun Kyōkai, pp. 4–15. Tokyo: Nihon Shimbun Kyōkai, 1948.

———. *Shimbun gojūnen shi* (Fifty years of press history). Revised ed. Masu Shobō, 1947.

———. *Shimbun seikatsu nijū nen* (Twenty years of newspaper life). Chūō Kōronsha, 1933.

Itō Shin'ichi et al. *Shimbun no jiten* (Dictionary of the press). Tōyōsha, 1955.

Itō Takashi and George Akita. "The Yamagata-Tokutomi Correspondence: Press and Politics in Meiji-Taishō Japan." *Monumenta Nipponica,* 36, no. 4 (1981), pp. 391–423.

Iwai Hajime. *Shimbun to shimbunjin* (Newspapers and journalists). Gendai Jiyānarizumu Shuppankai, 1974.

Iwamoto Yoshio. "Suehiro Tetchō: A Meiji Political Novelist." In *Japan's Modern Century,* ed. Edmund Skrzypczak, pp. 83–114. Monumenta Nipponica, 1968.

Iwano Seiichi, ed. *Biographical Dictionary of Japanese History.* Kodansha, 1978.

Iwata, Masakazu. *Ōkubo Toshimichi: The Bismarck of Japan.* Berkeley: University of California Press, 1964.

Jansen, Marius B. *Japan and Its World: Two Centuries of Change.* Princeton: Princeton University Press, 1980.

———. "The Meiji Restoration." In Wurfel, pp. 2–17.

The Japan Mail.

Japan Newspaper Publishers and Editors Association. *The Japanese Press '95.* Nihon Shimbun Kyokai, 1995.

Japan's Mass Media. Revised ed. Tokyo: Foreign Press Center, 1986.

The Japan Times.

Jibun Taikan Kankōkai, ed. *Ouchi Bunshū* (Works of Fukuchi Ōchi). Vol. 2 of *Jibun taikan.* Jibun Taikan Kankō, 1910.

Jiji Shinpō.

Jō Ichirō. *Hakkinbon hyakunen* (A century of prohibited books). Tōgensha, 1969.

Jones, F. C. *Extraterritoriality in Japan.* New York: AMS Press, 1970.

Jones, Hazel. *Live Machines: Hired Foreigners and Meiji Japan.* Vancouver: University of British Columbia Press, 1980.

Kaempfer, Englebert. *The History of Japan.* 3 vols. Glasgow: J. Maclehose, 1906.

Kageyama Saburō. *Dokusha no genron* (Readers' communication). Revised ed. Gendai Jiyānarizumu Shuppankai, 1976.

Kaji Ryūichi. *Meiji igo no go daikisha* (Five great reporters since the Meiji era). Asahi Shimbunsha, 1973.

Kajita Akihiro. "Miyake Setsurei no 'Kōzen to Jiyū' " (Miyake Setsurei's "Freedom and Broadmindedness"). *Medeiya Shi Kenkyū,* 1 (March 1994), pp. 55–74.

———. "Meiji nijūnananen taigaikō undō to Tokutomi Sohō" (Tokutomi Sohō and the expansionist movement of 1894). *Nihon Rekishi,* 242 (September 1983), pp. 59–75.

Kakegawa Tomiko. "Jiyūnarisuto toshite no Fukuzawa Yukichi: Fukuzawa seishin to gendai" (Fukuzawa Yukichi as a journalist: Fukuzawa's spirit and the present age). *Sangyō Seminā,* 1984, pp. 106–124.

Kamikawa, Hikomatsu, and Michiko Kimura, eds. *Japanese-American Diplomatic Relations in the Meiji-Taishō Era.* Tokyo: Pan-Pacific Press, 1958.

Kaneko Fumiko. *The Prison Memoirs of a Japanese Woman.* Trans. Mikiso Hane. London: M. E. Sharpe, 1991.

Kaneko Kisabu. *Shimbun kenkyū* (Newspaper research). Asahi Shobō, 1976.

Kasuya Kazuki, ed. *Genron wa Nihon o ugokasu* (The press moves Japan). Kodansha, 1985.

Kasza, Gregory J. *The State and the Mass Media in Japan, 1918–1945.* Berkeley: University of California Press, 1988.

Katakozawa Chiyomatsu. "Shimada Saburō" (Shimada Saburō). *Sandai genronjin shū,* 4, pp. 143–362. Jiji Shimbunsha, 1963.

Kato Hidetoshi. *Japanese Research on Mass Communication: Selected Abstracts.* Honolulu: University Press of Hawai'i, 1974.

Katō Keiko. "Josei to jōhō: Meiji ki no fujin zasshi kōkoku o tōshite" (Women and information: looking at ads in Meiji-era women's magazines). *Shimbun Kenkyūjo Nenpō* (Keiō Gijuku Daigaku), 32 (1989), pp. 31–58.

Katō Shūichi. "The Mass Media, Japan." In *Political Modernization in Japan and Turkey,* ed. Robert E. Ward and Dankwert A. Rustow, pp. 236–254. Princeton: Princeton University Press, 1964.

Katsuda Magoya. *Ōkubo Toshimichi den* (Biography of Ōkubo Toshimichi). 3 vols. Dōbunkan, 1910–1911.

Katz, Elihu, and Tamas Szecsko, eds. *Mass Media and Social Change.* London: SAGE Publications, 1981.

Kawabe, Kisaburō. *The Press and Politics in Japan.* Chicago: University of Chicago Press, 1921.

Kawabe Shinzō. *Fukuchi Ōchi* (Fukuchi Ōchi). Sanseidō, 1942.

Kawashima Yūji. "Jiyosefu Hiko ni tsuite" (Regarding Joseph Heco), *Meiji Bunka Kenkyū,* 5 (June 1929), pp. 57–59.

Keene, Donald. *Dawn to the West: Japanese Literature in the Modern Era.* 2 vols. New York: Henry Holt and Company, 1984.

———. *The Japanese Discovery of Europe, 1720–1830.* Revised ed. Stanford: Stanford University Press, 1969.

———. "Japanese Publishing, Yesterday and Today," *IHJ Bulletin,* 9, no. 2 (Spring 1989), pp. 1–3.

———. "The Sino-Japanese War of 1894–95 and Its Cultural Effects in Japan." In *Tradition and Modernization in Japanese Culture,* ed. Donald Shively, pp. 121–175. Princeton: Princeton University Press, 1971.

———. *World within Walls: Japanese Literature of the Premodern Era, 1600–1867.* New York: Holt, Rinehart and Winston, 1976.

Kido Mataichi et al., eds. *Kōza gendai Jiyānarizumu* (Lectures: modern journalism). Vols. 1, 2: *Rekishi* (History), *Shimbun* (Newspapers). Jiji Tsūshinsha, 1974.

Kido Takayoshi. *The Diary of Kido Takayoshi.* 3 vols. Trans. Sidney D. Brown and Hirota Akiko. University of Tokyo Press, 1983–1985.

Kim Yongkoo. "Genron to iu mono" (This thing called speech). *Chūgai Nippō,* Oct. 31, 1984, p. 13.

———. "Wide Open Path of Speech." In *Continuity and Change in Communications in Post-Industrial Society,* pp. 285–292. Vol. 2 of *Proceedings, World Academic Conference of the Seoul Olympiad.* 6 vols. 1988.

Kindai Nihon sōgō nenpyō (Comprehensive chronology of modern Japan). Iwanami Shoten, 1968.

Kinsei Haruyoshi. *Jinbutsu: Nihon shimbun shi* (History of the Japanese press: the people). Shin Jinbutsu Ōraisha, 1970.

Kinzley, W. Dean. *Industrial Harmony in Modern Japan: The Invention of a Tradition.* London: Routledge, 1991.

Kiryū Yūyū (Seishi). "Omoideru mama" (As I remember it). *Tazan no ishi,* vols. 3, 4. Facsimile edition. Fuji Shuppan, 1987.

Kishida Ginkō. "Shimbun jitsureki dan" (Talk about my newspaper career). In Tsurumi Shunsuke, pp. 63–66.

Kitane Minoru, ed. *Nihon shoki shimbun zenshū* (Complete compilation of Japan's early newspapers). 38 vols. Perikansha, 1986–1992.

Koito, Chūgo. "The Press and National Affairs in Recent Japan." M.A. thesis, University of Minnesota, 1941.

———. *Sekai no shimbun tsūshinsha* (The World's newspapers and news agencies). Risō Shuppansha, 1980.

———. *Shimbun no rekishi: kenryoku to no tatakai* (Newspaper history: influence and the fight for it). Shinchōsha, 1992.

Kōko Shimbun.

Kokumin Shimbun.

Komatsubara Hisao. "Japan." In Lent, pp. 95–125.

Komiya Kazuo. "Zenkoku Dōshi Shimbun Zasshi Kisha Dōmei to Meiji nijūnen zenhan no seikyoku" (National Federation of Newspaper and Magazine Journalists and the early 1890s political situation). *Medeiya Shi Kenkyū,* 2 (February 1995), pp. 116–134.

Konta Yōzō. *Edo no hon'yasan* (Booksellers of Edo). Nippon Hōsō Shuppan Kyōkai, 1977.

———. *Edo no kinsho* (Prohibited books of the Edo era). Yoshikawa Kyōbunkan, 1981.

Kornicki, P. F. "The Enmeiin Affair of 1803: The Spread of Information in the Tokugawa Period." *Harvard Journal of Asiatic Studies,* 42, no. 2 (December 1982), pp. 503–533.

———. "Nishiki no Ura: An Instance of Censorship and the Structure of *Sharebon.*" *Monumenta Nipponica,* 32, no. 2 (Summer 1977), pp. 153–188.

———. *The Reform of Fiction in Meiji Japan.* London: Ithaca Press, 1982.

Kōsaka, Masaaki, ed. *Japanese Thought in the Meiji Era.* Tokyo: Pan-Pacific Press, 1958.

———. *Meiji bunka shi* (History of Meiji culture). Vol. 4, *Shisō genron hen* (Ideas and expression). Yoyosha, 1955.

Koss, Stephen. *The Rise and Fall of the Political Press in Britain.* Vol. 1: *The Nineteenth Century.* London: Hamish Hamilton, 1981.

Kōuchi Saburō. "Iwayuru kōgai hōdō no rekishi: Ashio kōdoku jiken no issokumen" (A history of reporting on environmental pollution: one aspect of the Ashio Copper Mine pollution incident). *Shimbun Gaku Hyōron,* 20 (1971), pp. 6–38.

Koyama Fumio. *Meiji no isai Fukuchi Ōchi: wasurerareta daikisha* (Meiji genius Fukuchi Ōchi, forgotten journalist). Chūō Kōronsha, 1984.

Kubota Tatsuhiko, ed. *Nijūichi dai senkaku kisha den* (Biographies of twenty-one pioneer reporters). Osaka: Ōsaka Mainichi Shimbunsha, 1930.

Kuga Katsunan. *Kuga Katsunan zenshū* (Complete works of Kuga Katsunan). 5 vols. Misuzu Shobō, 1970.

Kuroiwa Shūroku. "Yo ga shimbun no kokorozashita dōki" (My motives in planning a newspaper). In Tsurumi Shunsuke, pp. 114–120.

Laman, Gordon. "Our Nagasaki Legacy: An Examination of the Period of Persecution of Christianity and its Impact on Subsequent Christian Mission in Japan." *The Northeast Asia Journal of Theology*, 28–29 (March–September 1982), pp. 94–141.

Lebra, Joyce. *Ōkuma Shigenobu: Statesman of Meiji Japan.* Canberra: Australian National University Press, 1973.

———. "Yano Fumio: Meiji Intellectual, Party Leader, and Bureaucrat." *Monumenta Nipponica*, 20, nos. 1/2 (1965), pp. 1–14.

Lee, Alan. *The Origins of the Popular Press in England, 1855–1914.* London: Croom Helm, 1976.

Lee, Jung Bock. *The Political Character of the Japanese Press.* Seoul: Seoul National University Press, 1985.

Lee, Richard W. *Politics and the Press.* Washington, D.C.: Acropolis Books, 1970.

Lee, Robin Henry. "Media and Change." In Van Zyl and Tomaselli, pp. 49–57.

Lent, John A. *The Asian Newspaper, Reluctant Revolution.* Ames: Iowa State University Press, 1971.

———. *Newspapers in Asia: Contemporary Trends and Problems.* Hong Kong: Heinemann Asia, 1982.

Lewis, Michael. *Rioters and Citizens: Mass Protest in Imperial Japan.* Berkeley: University of California Press, 1990.

———. "Interest and Ideology in Meiji Politics: Inagaki Shimesu and the Toyama Jiyūtō," *Asian Cultural Studies, International Christian University*, 3-A, no. 18 (February 1992), pp. 157–176.

Lone, Stewart. *Japan's First Modern War.* London: St. Martin's Press, 1994.

Lowenstein, Ralph L. "Press Freedom as a Barometer of Political Democracy." In Fischer, Heinz-Dietrich, and Merrill, pp. 136–147.

Maeda Ai. *Kindai dokusha no seiritsu* (The formation of modern readership). Yuseidō, 1973.

———. *Narushima Ryūhoku* (Narushima Ryūhoku). Asahi Shimbunsha, 1976.

Mainichi Shimbun.

Mainichi Shimbunsha: Fifty Years of Light and Dark: The Hirohito Era. Mainichi Newspapers, 1975.

Mainichi Shimbunsha, ed. *Mainichi Shimbun hyakunen shi* (One-hundred-year history of *Mainichi Shimbun*). Mainichi Shimbunsha, 1972.

———. *Mainichi Shimbun nanajūnen shi* (Seventy-year history of *Mainichi Shimbun*). Mainichi Shimbunsha, 1952.

Marshall, Byron K. *Academic Freedom and the Japanese Imperial University.* New York: Peter Lang, 1990.

———. "Growth and Conflict in Japanese Higher Education, 1905–1930." In Najita and Koschmann, pp. 276–294.

———. "Professors and Politics: The Meiji Academic Elite." *Journal of Japanese Studies,* 3, no. 2 (Winter 1977), pp. 71–98.

Masumi Junnosuke. *Nihon seitō shi ron* (On the history of Japan's political parties). 4 vols. Tōkyō Daigaku Shuppankai, 1965–1968.

Matsumoto Sannosuke, and Yamamuro Shin'ichi, eds. *Genron to medeia* (Press and media). Vol. 11 of *Nihon shisō taikei* (Comprehensive outline of Japanese thought). Iwanami Shoten, 1990.

Mayo, Marlene. "The Foreign Crisis of 1873 and Early Meiji Foreign Policy." *Journal of Asian Studies,* 31, no. 4 (August 1972), pp. 793–820.

McCormick, Robert. *The Freedom of the Press.* New York: D. Appleton-Century Company, 1936.

McLaren, Walter W. "Japanese Government Documents." *Transactions of the Asiatic Society of Japan,* 42, no. 1 (1914), pp. 1–681.

———. *A Political History of Japan during the Meiji Era, 1867–1912.* New York: Russell and Russell, 1965.

Meech-Pekarik, Julia. *The World of the Meiji Print: Impressions of a New Civilization.* New York: Weatherhill, 1986.

Mehl, Margaret. "Scholarship and Ideology in Conflict: The Kume Affair, 1892." *Monumenta Nipponica,* 48, no. 3 (Autumn 1993), pp. 337–358.

Meiji Bunka Kenkyū. Originally published as the journal *Shinkyū Jidai;* title changed in 1927.

Meiji Bunka Kenkyūkai, ed. *Meiji bunka zenshū* (Collected works on Meiji culture). 31 vols. Volume 1, *Kensei* (Constitutional government); 4, *Shimbun* (Newspapers); 9–10, *Seishi* (Political history). Nihon Hyōronsha, 1968. Originally edited by Yoshino Sakuzō in 1928–30, the series was expanded and reissued in 1968 by Meiji Bunka Kenkyūkai.

———. *Zasshi: Meiji bunka kenkyū* (Periodicals: research in Meiji culture). Vols. 1–2. Kōbunko, 1972. This journal reprints the thirteen installments of Miyatake Gaikotsu's "Meiji hikka shi shiryō" (Materials on the history of Meiji press infractions), which appeared originally in the 1925 editions of *Shinkyū Jidai.*

Meiji Taishō genron shiryō (Materials on the Meiji-Taishō press). 20 vols. projected. Misuzu Shobō, 1984– .

Meiji Taishō Shōwa Kenkyūkai, ed. *Shimbun shūsei Taishō hennen shi* (Chronological compilation of Taishō-era press articles). 43 vols. Hirakawa Kogyojo, 1978.

Mensendiek, C. William. "Protestant Missionary Perceptions of Meiji Japan" *Kyōkai to Shingaku* (Church and theology). (Tōhoku Daigaku) March 1986, pp. 233–273.

Merrill, John C. "A Conceptual Overview of World Journalism." In Fischer, Heinz-Dietrich, and Merrill, pp. 18–28.

———. "Media and National Development." In Fischer, Heinz-Dietrich, and Merrill, pp. 186–199.

Midoro Masaichi. *Meiji Taishō shi: genron hen* (History of the Meiji and Taishō eras: the press). Asahi Shimbunsha, 1930.

———. *Shakai to shimbun* (Society and the press). Asahi Shimbunsha, 1929.

Millard, Thomas. "The Fruits of Japan's Victory." *Scribner's Magazine,* 2 (August 1905), pp. 240–251.

Mitchell, Richard. *Censorship in Imperial Japan.* Princeton: Princeton University Press, 1983.

———. *Janus-Faced Justice: Political Criminals in Imperial Japan.* Honolulu: University of Hawaii Press, 1992.

———. *Thought Control in Prewar Japan.* Ithaca: Cornell University Press, 1976.

Miyake Setsurei. *Dōjidai shi* (An account of my times). 6 vols. Iwanami Shoten, 1954.

Miyamoto Ken. "Itō Noe and the Bluestockings," *Japan Interpreter,* 10, no. 2 (Autumn 1975), pp. 190–204.

Miyatake Gaikotsu. *Hikka shi* (History of press infractions). Hankyōdō, 1911.

———. "Meiji hikka shi shiryō" (The history of Meiji press infractions). Installments 1–13. *Zasshi: Meiji Bunka Kenkyū,* 1 (1972).

———. "Meiji kinbatsu tosho mokuroku naka no bakki" (Selected index of works that drew official punishment in the Meiji era). *Zasshi: Meiji Bunka Kenkyū,* 3, no. 5 (1972), pp. 2–5.

Miyatake Gaikotsu and Nishida Taketoshi, eds. *Shimbun zasshi kankei sha ryakuden* (Brief biographies of newspaper and magazine journalists). Misuzu Shobō, 1985.

MNJ. See Uchikawa and Matsushima, eds., *Meiji niyūsu jiten.*

Moeller, Leslie G. "Mass Media and National Goals." In Fischer, Heinz-Dietrich, and Merrill, pp. 200–209.

Monna Naoki. *Minshū jiyānarizumu no rekishi* (History of the popular press). San'ichi Shobō, 1983.

Mori Kyōzō. "Freedom of the Press and Asia," *Japan Quarterly,* 22, no. 2 (April–June 1975), pp. 119–125.

Mori Shina. "Meiji gannen Fukuchi Ōchi gokuchū benmeisho" (Fukuchi Ōchi's prison defense, 1868). *Bungaku,* November 1968, pp. 86–91.

Morse, Edward S. *Japan Day by Day.* 2 vols. Boston: Houghton Mifflin Company, 1917.

Mott, Frank Luther, ed. *Journalism in Wartime.* Westport, Conn.: Greenwood Press, 1984.

Mulhern, Chieko Irie. "Japan's First Newspaperwoman, Hani Motoko." *Japan Interpreter,* 12, nos. 3–4 (Summer 1979), pp. 310–329.

Muramatsu Shōfū, ed. *Akiyama Teisuke wa kataru* (Akiyama Teisuke speaks). Dai Nihon Yūbenkai Kōdansha, 1938.

Murobushi Kōshin. "Shimbun insatsu shokkō no higyō to shimbun kyūkan jiken" (Newspaper printers' strike and the newspapers' suspension of publication). *Chūō Kōron,* September 1919, pp. 115–121.

Mutsu Munemitsu. *Kenkenroku: A Diplomatic Record of the Sino-Japanese War, 1894–95.* Trans. Gordon Berger. Tokyo: University of Tokyo Press, 1982.

Nagai Michio and Miguel Urrutia, eds. *Meiji Ishin: Restoration and Revolution.* Tokyo: United Nations University, 1985.

Naimushō Keihōkyoku, ed. *Zenkoku shimbun shichō* (National survey of the history of newspapers). Naimushō, 1925.

Najita, Tetsuo. *Hara Kei and the Politics of Compromise, 1905–1915.* Cambridge: Harvard University Press, 1967.

———. *Japan: The Intellectual Foundations of Modern Japanese Politics.* Chicago: University of Chicago Press, 1974.

Najita, Tetsuo, and J. Victor Koschmann, eds. *Conflict in Japanese History: The Neglected Tradition.* Princeton: Princeton University Press, 1982.

Nakae Chōmin. *A Discourse by Three Drunkards on Government.* Trans. Tsukui Nobuko. Tokyo: Weatherhill, 1984.

Nakamura Masanori. "The Emperor System of the 1900s." *Bulletin of Concerned Asian Scholars,* 16, no. 2 (1984), pp. 2–11.

Nakano Mitsutoshi. "Revising Edo." *Japan Foundation Newsletter,* 21, no. 1 (July 1993), pp. 1–8.

Nakanowatari Nobuyuki, ed. *Masukomi kindai shi* (Recent history of mass communications). Yūsankaku Shuppan, 1969.

Nakayama Yasuaki, ed. *Shimbun shūsei Meiji hennen shi* (Chronological compilation of Meiji-era press articles). 15 vols. Honpō Shoseki, 1982.

Narushima Ryūhoku. "A Defence of the Press." *Tokio Times*, May 12, 1877, pp. 226–227. Originally published in Japanese in *Chōya Shimbun.*

"The Native Press." *The Japan Weekly Mail*, April 5, 1879, pp. 418–419.

Nihon.

Nihon Fūzoku Shi Gakkai, ed. *Kindai Nihon fūzoku shi* (History of modern Japanese customs). Vol. 8, *Genron to masu komi* (Press and mass media). Yūsankaku Shuppan, 1968.

Nihon Shimbun Hanbai Kyōkai, ed. *Shimbun hanbai hyakunen shi* (One-hundred-year history of newspaper management). Nihon Shimbun Hanbai Kyōkai, 1969.

Nihon Shimbun Kyōkai, ed. *Chihōbetsu: Nihon shimbun shi* (History of the Japanese press: the provinces). Nihon Shimbun Kyōkai, 1956.

Nihon Shimbun Renmei, ed. *Nihon shimbun hyakunen shi* (One-hundred-year history of the Japanese press). Nihon Shimbun Renmei, 1961.

Nijū Seiki Kenkyūjo, ed. *Masu komiyunikēshiyon kōza* (Studies in mass communications). Vol. 6, *Masu komiyunikēshiyon jiten* (Dictionary of mass communications). Kawade Shobō, 1955.

Niroku Shinpō. Facsimile edition. Vols. 1–8 (1897–1900). Fuji Shuppan, 1992.

Nish, Ian, ed. *Britain and Japan: Biographical Portraits.* Kent: Japan Library, 1994.

Nishida Taketoshi. "*Chōya Shimbun* shasetsu mokuroku" (Index of *Chōya Shimbun* editorials). *Shimbun Gaku Hyōron*, 26 (1977), pp. 146–207.

———. "*Heimin Shimbun* to sono jidai" (*Heimin Shimbun* and its era). *Bungaku*, 21, no. 10 (1953), pp. 976–982.

———. *Meiji jidai no shimbun to zasshi* (Newspapers and magazines of the Meiji period). Shibundō, 1966.

———. "Meiji jūichinen dō jūyonnen no shimbunkai" (The newspaper world, 1877–1881). In *Meiji bunka no shinkenkyū* (New research on Meiji culture), ed. Osatake Takeki, pp. 367–415. Meiji Bunka Kenkyūkai, 1944.

———. "Meiji shoki shimbun ronsetsu sakuin" (Index of early Meiji newspaper editorials). *Meiji Bunka Kenkyū*, vols. 3, 5–6 (October 1934–November 1935), pp. 182–190, 250–260, 180–189 respectively.

————. *Nihon Jiyānarizumu shi kenkyū* (Research on the history of Japanese journalism). Misuzu Shobō, 1989.

————. "*Tōkyō Nichi Shimbun* shasetsu sakuin" (Index of *Tōkyō Nichi Nichi Shimbun* editorials). Mimeographed from Nishida's personal collection.

————. ed. *Tōyō Jiyū Shimbun (Tōyō Jiyū Shimbun).* Facsimile edition. Tokyo Daigaku Shuppankai, 1964.

Nishimaki Yōzaburō, ed. *Kawaraban shimbun: Edo Meiji sanbyaku jiken* (Kawaraban newspapers: Three hundred Edo and Meiji incidents). 4 vols. Heibonsha, 1978.

Nolte, Sharon. *Liberalism in Modern Japan: Ishibashi Tanzan and His Teachers.* Berkeley: University of California Press, 1986.

Notehelfer, F. G. *American Samurai: Captain L. L. Janes and Japan.* Princeton: Princeton University Press, 1985.

————. *Kōtoku Shūsui: Portrait of a Japanese Radical.* Cambridge: University Press, 1971.

Obata, Kyugoro. *An Interpretation of the Life of Viscount Shibusawa.* Tōkyō Insatsu Kabushiki Kaisha, 1936.

Oka Mitsuo. *Kindai Nihon shimbun koshi* (Brief history of Japan's modern press). Mineruba Shobō, 1969.

————. *Ōsaka no Jiyānarizumu* (Journalism in Osaka). Osaka: Ōsaka Shobō, 1987.

Oka Yoshitake. *Five Political Leaders of Modern Japan: Itō Hirobumi, Ōkuma Shigenobu, Hara Takashi, Inukai Tsuyoshi, and Saionji Kimmochi.* Tokyo: University of Tokyo Press, 1986.

————. "Generational Conflict after the Russo-Japanese War." In Najita and Koschmann, pp. 197–225.

Okamoto, Shumpei. "The Emperor and the Crowd: The Historical Significance of the Hibiya Riot." In Najita and Koschmann, pp. 258–275.

————. *The Japanese Oligarchy and the Russo-Japanese War.* New York: Columbia University Press, 1970.

Okano Takeo. *Meiji genron shi* (History of the Meiji press). Hō Shuppan, 1974.

Okawa, Kazushi. *The Growth Rate of the Japanese Economy since 1878.* Tokyo: Kinokuniya, 1957.

Okudaira Yasuhiro. *Jian iji hō shōshi* (Short history of the peace preservation law). Echima Shobō, 1977.

————. "Nihon shuppan keisatsu hōsei no rekishiteki kenkyū josetsu" (Introduction to historical research on Japan's police regulations regarding publication). *Hōritsu Jihō,* 1 (April 1967), pp. 54–63; 2 (May

1967), pp. 101–108; 3 (June 1967), pp. 36–53; 4 (July 1967) pp. 66–73; 5 (August 1967), pp. 73–80; 6 (September 1967), pp. 56–63; 7 (October 1967), pp. 96–104.

———. *Political Censorship in Japan from 1931 to 1945.* Philadelphia: Institute of Legal Research, University of Pennsylvania, 1962.

Ōkuma Shigenobu, ed. *Fifty Years of New Japan.* 2 vols. London: Smith, Elders, 1910.

Omata Noriaki. "Moji ekiin no inseki jisatsu to Yamakawa Kenjirō genseki jiken" (The episode in which Yamakawa Kenjirō commented on the sacrificial suicide of a Moji station employee). *Jinbun Gakuhō*, 72 (March 1993), pp. 39–70.

Omura Bunji. *The Last Genro: Prince Saionji, the Man Who Westernized Japan.* New York: J. B. Lippincott, 1938.

Ono Hideo. *Gogai hyakunen shi* (One hundred years of newspaper extras). Yomiuri Shimbunsha, 1969.

———. *Kawaraban monogatari: Edo jidai masu komi no rekishi* (The *kawaraban* story: history of mass communiations in the Edo period). Yūzankaku, 1960.

———. "Kido Takayoshi to shimbun" (Kido Takayoshi and the press). *Shinkyū Jidai*, 1, no. 8 (October 1925), pp. 3–6.

———. "Kuroiwa shi no shimbun kisha gikō" (Mr. Kuroiwa's skill as a journalist), *Meiji Bunka*, 5, no. 9 (September 1929), pp. 9–12.

———. "Kuroiwa Shūroku." In *Sandai genronjin shū*, 6, pp. 11–126.

———. "Meiji shoki ni okeru shuppan jiyū no gainen" (The early-Meiji concept of press freedom). *Shinkyū Jidai*, 2, nos. 4–5 (April–May 1926), pp. 83–92.

———. "Meiji shoki no handō shisō no shimbun" (Reactionary early-Meiji newspapers). *Shinkyū Jidai*, 3, no. 1 (January 1927), pp. 30–42.

———. *Naigai shimbun shi* (History of the foreign and domestic press). Nihon Shimbun Kyōkai, 1966.

———. *Nihon shimbun hattatsu shi* (History of the development of the Japanese press). Gogatsu Shobō, 1982.

———. "Ōsaka no migawari shimbun" (Surrogate newspapers of Osaka). *Meiji Bunka Kenkyū*, 1, no. 2 (1928), pp. 29–32.

———. *Shimbun kenkyū gojūnen* (Fifty years of newspaper research). Mainichi Shimbunsha, 1971.

———. *Shimbun no rekishi* (History of the press). Risōsha, 1961.

———. "Yanagawa Shunsan." In *Sandai genronjin shu*, 1, pp. 9–105.

———. *Yokohama Shinpō Moshiogusa, Kōko Shimbun* (*Yokohama Shinpō Moshiogusa* and *Kōko Shimbun*). Meiji Bunka Kenkyūkai, 1926.

Ornatowsky, Gregory. "Press, Politics, and Profits: The 'Asahi Shimbun' and the Prewar Japanese Newspaper." Ph.D. dissertation, Harvard University, 1985.

Ōsaka Asahi Shimbun.

Ōsaka Mainichi Shimbun.

Osatake Takeki. *Nihon kensei shi taikō* (Outline of Japanese constitutional history). 2 vols. Nihon Hyōronsha, 1939.

———. *Shimbun zasshi to sōshisha Yanagawa Shunsan* (Yanagawa Shunsan, press pioneer). Nagoya: Nagoya Chūdankai, 1920.

Osatake Takeki, ed. *Bakumatsu Meiji shimbun zenshū* (Collected papers of the Bakumatsu-Meiji period). 6 vols. Taiseidō, 1934–1935.

Ōsugi Sakae. *The Autobiography of Ōsugi Sakae.* Trans. Byron Marshall. Berkeley: University of California Press, 1992.

Ōta Masao. *Kiryū Yūyū* (Kiryū Yūyū). Kinokuniya Shoten, 1972.

Otsu Jun'ichirō. *Dainihon kensei shi* (Constitutional history of Japan). 10 vols. Hara Shobō, 1970.

Ozawa Ryōzō. *Onnagata konseki dan* (On female impersonators, past and present). Chikuma, 1941.

Patrick, Hugh, ed. *Japanese Industrialization and Its Social Consequences.* Berkeley: University of California Press, 1976.

Pemberton, Max. *Lord Northcliffe: A Memoir.* London: Hodder and Stoughton, 1922.

Pierson, John. *Tokutomi Sohō, 1863–1957: A Journalist for Modern Japan.* Princeton: Princeton University Press, 1980.

Pittau, Joseph. *Political Thought in Early Meiji Japan, 1868–1889.* Cambridge: Harvard University Press, 1967.

Pollard, James E. *The Presidents and the Press.* New York: The Macmillan Company, 1947.

"Press Censorship Here and Elsewhere." *Tokio Times,* February 24, 1877, p. 96.

Purdy, Roger. "The Ears and Voice of the Nation: The Dōmei News Agency and Japan's News Network, 1936–1945." Ph.D. dissertation, University of California at Santa Barbara, 1987.

"Putting the World at Peril: A Conversation with James W. Carey." *Journalism History,* 7, no. 2 (Summer 1986), pp. 38–53.

Pyle, Kenneth B. "The Emergence of Bureaucratic Conservatism in the Meiji Period." *Undercurrent,* 1 (March 1983), pp. 13–29.

———. *The New Generation in Meiji Japan: Problems of Cultural Identity, 1885–1895.* Stanford: Stanford University Press, 1965.

Pyle, Kenneth B., F. G. Notehelfer, and Alan Stone. "Symposium: The Ashio Copper Mine Pollution Case," *Journal of Japanese Studies*, 1, no. 2 (Spring 1975), pp. 347–408.

Quinlan, Bernard D. "Inoue Kaoru and the Formation of Economic Policy in Early Meiji Japan." Ph.D. dissertation, University of Hawai'i, 1978.

Rankin, Mary B. *Early Chinese Revolutionaries: Radical Intellectuals in Shanghai and Chekiang, 1902–1911*. Cambridge: Harvard University Press, 1975.

Read, Donald. *Press and People, 1790–1850: Opinion in Three English Cities*. London: Edward Arnold Publishers, 1961.

Reischauer, Edwin O. *Japan, the Story of a Nation*. New York: Alfred A. Knopf, 1974.

Rōdō Undō Shi Kenkyūkai, ed. *Shūkan Heimin Shimbun* (The Weekly *Heimin Shimbun*). 2 vols. In *Meiji shakaishugi shiryō shū* (Collected historical records of Meiji socialism). Meiji Bunko Shiryō Kankōkai, 1962.

Rogers, Everett. *Modernization among Peasants: The Impact of Communications*. New York: Holt, Rinehart and Winston, 1969.

Rosten, Leo. *The Washington Correspondents*. New York: Harcourt, Brace and Company, 1937.

Rubin, Jay. *Injurious to Public Morals: Writers and the Meiji State*. Seattle: University of Washington Press, 1984.

Ruikō Kai, ed. *Kuroiwa Ruikō* (Kuroiwa Ruikō). Fusō Hakkō, 1922.

Saitō Shōzō. *Meiji Taishō hikka dainenpyō* (Chronology of Meiji-Taishō press infractions). Shisōsha, 1932.

———. "Shimbun jōrei shisho" (Documents on press laws). *Meiji Bunka Kenkyū*, 5, no. 1 (January 1929), pp. 28–34.

Sakai Kunio. *Ijin ansatsu shi* (History of the assassination of great men). Genrindō, 1937.

Sakai Toshihiko. *Sakai Toshihiko zenshū* (Complete works of Sakai Toshihiko). 6 vols. Kyoto: Hōritsu Bunkasha, 1970.

Sakurada Kurabu, ed. *Akiyama Teisuke den* (Biography of Akiyama Teisuke). 3 vols. Sakurada Kurabu, 1977.

Sandai genronjin shū (The works of three generations of journalists). 8 vols. Jiji Tsūshinsha, 1962.

Sansom, George. *Japan: A Short Cultural History*. New York: Appleton-Century-Crofts, 1962.

———. *The Western World and Japan*. New York: Alfred A. Knopf, 1968.

Sasaki Takashi. "Daiichiji Matsukata naikaku ki no shimbun sōjū mondai" (A study of press control during the first Matsukata cabinet). *Tōkyō Daigaku Shimbun Kenkyūjo Kiyō*, 31 (1983), pp. 13–100.

———. "Kanshō senkyō saikō: dai nikai sōsenkyō to Kuki Ryūichi" (A record of election interference: Kuki Ryūichi and the second general election). *Nihon Rekishi*, 395 (April 1981), pp. 57–74.

———. "Meiji jidai no seijiteki komiyunikēshiyon" (Political communication in the Meiji era), *Tōkyō Daigaku Shimbun Kenkyūjo Kiyō*, 33–35 (1984–1986), pp. 221–235, 117–193, 99–156.

———. "Meiji seijika no seiji jōhō katsudō: Meiji zenchūki no Itō Miyoji" (Meiji politicians and political information strategies: Itō Miyoji in early/middle Meiji). *Medeiya Shi Kenkyū*, 1 (March 1994), pp. 35–54.

———. "*Nijūseiki* jiken to hanbatsu" (Clique government and the *Twenty-sixth Century* affair). *Shimbun Gaku Hyōron*, 36 (1987), pp. 15–28.

Sashihara Yasuzō, ed. *Meiji sei shi* (A political history of the Meiji period). 3 vols. Fuzanbō Shoten, 1893. Reprinted as vol. 2 of *Meiji bunka zenshū, sei shi hen* (Collected works of Meiji culture, political history). Nihon Hyōronsha, 1956.

Satō Shōzō. *Gendai hikka shi ken dainenpyō* (Chronology of modern press infractions). Risōsha, 1933.

———. "Kokkai ni kansuru hikka jiken" (Press infractions related to the Diet), *Meiji Bunka Kenkyū*, 4, no. 7 (July 1928), pp. 56–58.

———. *Nihon hakkin bungeikō* (Literary works prohibited in Japan). Amatoraisha, 1955.

Satow, Ernest. *A Diplomat in Japan.* London: Seeley, Service and Company, 1921.

Scalapino, Robert A. *Democracy and the Party Movement in Prewar Japan: The Failure of the First Attempt.* Berkeley: University of California Press, 1967.

Scheiner, Irwin. *Christian Converts and Social Protest in Meiji Japan.* Berkeley: University of California Press, 1970.

Schramm, Wilbur. *Mass Media and National Development.* Stanford: Stanford University Press, 1964.

———. *Responsibility in Mass Communication.* New York: Harper and Row, 1957.

Seguy, Christiane. *Histoire de la presse Japonaise.* Paris: Publications Orientalistes de France, 1993.

Seidensticker, Edward. *Kafū the Scribbler: The Life and Writings of Nagai Kafū, 1879–1959.* Stanford: Stanford University Press, 1965.

———. *Low City, High City: Tokyo from Edo to the Earthquake.* Rutland, Vt.: Charles E. Tuttle, 1983.

Seki Naohiko. *Nanajūnananen no kaiko* (A seventy-seven-year retrospective). Sanseidō, 1933.

Sherill, Robert. "News Ethics, Press, and Jerks," *Grand Street*, 5, no. 2 (Winter 1986), pp. 115–133.

Shibusawa, Keizo. *Japanese Society in the Meiji Era.* Tokyo: Obunsha, 1958.

Shik, Edward. *Political Development in the New States.* The Hague: Mouton, 1966.

Shimada Saburō. *Shimada Saburō zenshū* (Complete works of Shimada Saburō). Keiseisha, 1924–1925.

Shimazaki Ken'ichi. *Shimbun sōseiki* (Genesis of the press). Kōseidō, 1968.

Shimbun Henshū Kankei Hōsei Kenkyūkai, ed. *Hō to shimbun* (Law and the press). Nihon Shimbun Kyōkai, 1972.

Shimizu Hideo. *Hō to masu komyunikeshon* (mass communication and the law). Shakaisōsha, 1970.

Shimoyama Saburō. "Jiyū minken undō: sono chiikiteki bunpu" (The regional distribution of the freedom and rights movement). *Tōkyō Keidai Gakkai Shi (Shiryō)*, 37 (December 1962), pp. 199–222.

Shimura Akiko. "Meiji ki no josei jiyānarisuto" (Women journalists in the Meiji era). In *Kindai Nihon no jiyānarisuto* (Modern Japanese journalists), ed. Tanaka Hiroshi, pp. 645–672. Ochanomizu no Shobō, 1987.

Shin, Peter Yong-Shik. "The Otsu Incident: Japan's Hidden History of the Atempted Assassination of Future Emperor Nicholas II of Russia in the Town of Otsu, Japan, May 11, 1891 and Its Implications for Historical Analysis." Ph.D. dissertation, University of Pennsylvania, 1989.

Shinkyū Jidai. At vol. 3, no. 3 (1927), this becomes *Meiji Bunka Kenkyū.*

Shinoda Kōzō. *Meiji shimbun kidan* (Strange stories of Meiji newspapers). Meiseidō, 1943.

Shioda Shōbee. "Ashio kōdoku mondai narabi ni: Tanaka Shōzō ni kansuru kenmokuroku" (Index of works related to Tanaka Shōzō, in connection with the Ashio Copper Mine problem), *Tōkyō Toritsu Daigaku Jinbun Gakuhō*, 20 (March 1959), pp. 125–149.

Shōwa Joshi Daigaku Kindai Bungaku Kenkyūshitsu, ed. *Kindai bungaku kenkyū sōsho* (Studies in modern literature). Vols. 1, 5, 8. Shōwa Joshi Daigaku, 1956–1958.

Shūroku Kai, ed. *Kuroiwa Shūroku* (Kuroiwa Shūroku). Aiyûsha, 1922.

Silberman, Bernard, and H. D. Harootunian, eds. *Japan in Crisis: Essays on Taishō Democracy.* Princeton: Princeton University Press, 1974.

Sievers, Sharon L. *Flowers in Salt: The Beginnings of Feminist Consciousness in Modern Japan.* Stanford: Stanford University Press, 1983.

Smith, Anthony. *The Newspaper: An International History.* London: Thames and Hudson, 1979.

——, ed. *Newspapers and Democracy: International Essays on a Changing Medium.* Cambridge: MIT Press, 1980.

Smith, Henry Dewitt II. *Japan's First Student Radicals.* Cambridge: Harvard University Press, 1972.

Smith, Thomas C. *The Agrarian Origins of Modern Japan.* Stanford: Stanford University Press, 1959.

Sōgō Jiyānarizumu Kenkyūjo, ed. *Masukomi bunkenshū taisei* (Collected works on mass communications). Shadan Hōjin Tokyosha, 1974.

Sommerlad, E. Lloyd. *The Press in Developing Countries.* Sydney: Sydney University Press, 1966.

Soviak, Eugene. "An Early Meiji Intellectual in Politics: Baba Tatsui and the Jiyūtō" In *Modern Japanese Leadership,* ed. Bernard Silberman and H. D. Harootunian, pp. 121–170. Tucson: University of Arizona Press, 1966.

Spaulding, Robert. "Bibliography of Western-Language Dailies and Weeklies in Japan, 1861–1961." Unpublished manuscript, University of Michigan, n.d.

——. "The Intent of the Charter Oath." In *Studies in Japanese History and Politics,* ed. Richard K. Beardsley, pp. 3–36. Ann Arbor: University of Michigan Press, 1967.

SSMH. *See* Nakayama Yasuaki.

Stead, Alfred, ed. *Japan by the Japanese: A Survey by Its Highest Authorities.* London: Dodd Mead and Company, 1904.

Steele, M. William. "Goemon's New World View: Popular Representations of the Opening of Japan." *Asian Cultural Studies, International Christian University,* 3-A, 17 (March 1989), pp. 69–83.

——. "The Rise and Fall of the Shōgitai: A Social Drama." In Najita and Koschmann, pp. 128–144.

Stewart, Kenneth. *News Is What We Make It.* Boston: Houghton Mifflin, 1943.

Strong, Kenneth. *Ox against the Storm: A Biography of Tanaka Shōzō, Japan's Conservationist Pioneer.* Vancouver: University of British Columbia Press, 1977.

Suehiro Tetchō. "Shimbun keirekidan" (My newspaper experiences). In *Meiji bunka zenshū* (Complete works of Meiji culture), ed. Meiji Bunka Kenkyūkai, 4: *Shimbun hen* (Newspapers) , pp. 49–68. Hyōronsha, 1968.

Sugiura Tadashi. *Shimbun koto hajime* (Newspaper beginnings). Mainichi Shimbunsha, 1971.

Suzuki Yūga. "Aru Eijin hakkōsha o otte: A. W. Hansādo no kiseki" (Pursuing an English publisher: the legacy of A. W. Hansard). *Komiyunikēshiyon Kenkyū,* 23 (1993), pp. 67–102.

———. "Bakumatsu Meiji no Ōji shimbun to gaikokujin jiyānarisuto" (Foreign journalists and the late-Tokugawa, Meiji English-language press). *Komiyunikēshiyon Kenkyū,* 21 (1991), pp. 45–50.

Takagi Takeo. *Shimbun shōsetsu shi* (A history of newspaper novels). Tosho Kankōkai, 1974.

Takahashi Yasuo. *Medeiya no akebono* (Dawn of the media). Nihon Keizai Shimbunsha, 1994.

Takeichi Hideo. *Nichibei shimbun shi wa* (Discussion of the history of the Japanese and American press). Fukumi Shobò, 1984.

Takeuchi Saburō. "Iwayuru kōgai hōdō no rekishi" (The history of pollution reporting). *Shimbun Gaku Hyōron,* 20 (1971), pp. 6–38.

Tamura Norio. *Nihon no rōkaru shimbun* (Japan's local newspapers). Gendai Jiyānarizumu Shuppankai, 1968.

Tamura Tsunao. "Nōmin undō to komiyunikēshiyon" (Farmers' movements and communications). *Tōkyō Daigaku Shimbun Kenkyūjo Kiyō,* 20 (1971), pp. 105–161.

Tanaka Hiroshi, ed. *Kindai Nihon no Jiyūnarisuto* (Modern Japanese journalists). Ochanomizu no Shobō, 1987.

Taoka Ryōichi. *Ōtsu jiken to saihyōka* (A reevaluation of the Ōtsu incident). Egusa Tadaatsu, 1976.

Tayama Katai. *Country Teacher.* Honolulu: University of Hawaiʻi Press, 1984.

Teeters, Barbara. "The Otsu Affair: The Formation of Japan's Judicial Conscience." In Wurfel, pp. 36–62.

———. "Press Freedom and the *Twenty-sixth Century* Affair in Meiji Japan," *Modern Asian Studies,* 6, no. 3 (1972), pp. 337–351.

The Times (London).

TNJ. *See* Uchikawa and Matsushima, eds., *Taishō niyūsu jiten.*

Tocqueville, Alexis de. *Democracy in America.* New York: A. S. Barnes and Company, 1873.

Togasaki, Fumiko. "The Assertion of Heterodoxy in Kyōden's Verbal-Visual Art." Springfield, Ohio, unpublished manuscript, 1993.

———. "Santō Kyōden's *Kibyōshi:* Video-Verbal and Contemporary-Classic Intercommunications." Ph.D. dissertation, Indiana University, 1995.

Tōgen Haruo. "*Shinonome Shimbun* to jōyaku kaisei mondai" (The *Shinonome Shimbun* and the treaty revision problem). *Shimbun Gaku Hyōron*, 27 (1978), pp. 68–78.

The Tokio Times.

"Tokushū: Nichikan genron no hassei ni oyobashita dentō to seiō no eikyō" (Special issue: the beginnings of the Japanese and Korean presses and the influence of the West). *Komiyunikēshiyon Kenkyū*, 21 (1991), pp. 3–88.

Tokutomi Iichirō (Sohō). "Hausu sensei no omoide" (Recollections of Mr. House). In *Shimbun kisha to shimbun* (Newspapers and journalists), pp. 105–126. Min'yūsha, 1929.

———. *Shōrai no Nihon* (The Future Japan). In Tokutomi Sohō, *Tokutomi Sohō shū* (Collected works of Tokutomi Sohō), *Meiji bungaku zenshū* (Complete works of Meiji literature), 34, pp. 50–112. Echima Shobō, 1974. English translation by Sinh Vinh. *The Future Japan.* Edmonton: University of Alberta Press, 1989.

———. *Sohō jiden* (Autobiography of Tokutomi Sohō). Chūō Kōronsha, 1935.

Tōkyō Akebono Shimbun.

Tōkyō Asahi Shimbun.

Tōkyō Daigaku Hōgakubu, ed. *Meiji shimbun zasshi bunka hen, Chōya Shimbun shukusatsu han, 1874–1893* (Meiji newspaper/periodical archives: small-print editions of *Chōya Shimbun*, 1874–1893). 38 vols. Perikansha, 1980–1984.

Tōkyō Nichi Nichi Shimbun.

Tōkyō-Yokohama Mainichi Shimbun.

Tomizuka Hideki. "Komatsubara Eitarō to Miyazaki Hachirō *Hyōron Shimbun* de katsuyaku shita futari no minken ka" (Komatsubara Eitarō and Miyazaki Hachirō: two democratic activists from *Hyōron Shimbun* and their post-newspaper lives), *Shimbun Gaku*, 11 (1992), pp. 1–14.

———. "Saionji Kinmochi to Matsuzawa Kyūsaku: *Tōyō Jiyū Shimbun* shachō jinin mondai o meguru ikkōsatsu" (Saionji Kimmochi and Matsuzawa Masakazu: a consideration of problems related to the resignation of the *Tōyō Jiyū Shimbun* president). *Shimbun Gaku*, 10 (1989), pp. 1–11.

Tosaka Jun. "Shimbun genshō no bunseki" (Analysis of the newspaper phenomenon). In Tsurumi Shunsuke, pp. 236–272.

Totman, Conrad. *Japan before Perry: A Short History.* Berkeley: University of California Press, 1981.

Tōyama Shigeki, ed. *Meiji no ninai te* (Shapers of the Meiji era). Vol. 11 of *Jinbutsu: Nihon no rekishi* (Japanese history: its people). Yomiuri Shimbunsha, 1973.

Tōyō Jiyū Shimbun. See Nishida Taketoshi, ed.

Treat, Payson J. *Japan and the United States, 1853–1921.* Boston: Houghton Mifflin, 1921.

———. *Diplomatic Relations between the United States and Japan, 1853–1895.* 2 vols. Gloucester, Mass.: Peter Smith, 1963.

Tsuchihashi, Paul Y. *Japanese Chronological Tables, from 601 to 1872 A.D.* Tokyo: Sophia University Press, 1952.

Tsuchiya Reiko. "Meiji shoki no genron tōsei to koshimbun no hikka" (The early Meiji government's press policy and popular press infractions). *Medeiya Shi Kenkyū*, 1 (March 1994), pp. 17–34.

———. *Ōsaka no nishikie shimbun* (Osaka's colored woodblock newspapers). Sangensha, 1995.

Tsunoda, Ryusaku, Wm. Theodore deBary, and Donald Keene, eds. *Sources of Japanese Tradition,* vol. 2. New York: Columbia University Press, 1958.

Tsurumi, E. Patricia. *Factory Girls: Women in the Thread Mills of Meiji Japan.* Princeton: Princeton University Press, 1990.

Tsurumi Shunsuke, ed. *Jiyānarizumu no shisō* (Philosophy of the press). Vol. 12 of *Gendai Nihon shisō taikei* (Comprehensive outline of modern Japanese thought), ed. Matsumoto Sannosuke. Chikuma Shobō, 1965.

Ubukata Toshirō. "Kenpō happu to Nisshin Sensō" (Promulgation of the constitution and the Sino-Japanese War). In Tsurumi Shunsuke, pp. 80–112.

Uchikawa Yoshimi. "Kindai shimbun shi kenkyū hōhō ron" (An introduction to the methodology of modern press history studies), *Tōkyō Daigaku Shimbun Kenkyūjo Kiyō,* 3 (1954), pp. 57–66.

———. *Masu medeia hō seisaku shi kenkyū* (Studies in the formation of mass media law). Yūhikaku, 1989.

———. "Meiji shoki no shimbun to dokusha" (Newspapers and their readers in early Meiji). *Gengo Seikatsu,* December 1959, pp. 18–25.

———. "Ōtsu jiken no hōdō o meguru tōsei to teikō" (Control and resistance regarding reporting of the Ōtsu incident). *Shimbun Gaku Hyōron,* 4 (1955), pp. 43–66.

———. "Shimbun dokusha no hensen" (Changes in newspaper readership). *Shimbun Kenkyū,* 126 (July 1961), pp. 19–27.

———. "Shimbun no jiyū no rekishi" (History of press freedom). In Chiba Yūjiro, pp. 1–74.

————. "Shimbun ronsetsu no hensen" (Changes in newspaper editorials). *Gendai Nihon Shisō Taikei, Geppō*, 25 (June 1965), pp. 3–5.

————. "Shimbunshi hō no kaisei no katei to sono kiketsu" (Results of the process of developing newspaper laws). *Tōkyō Daigaku Shimbun Kenkyūjo Kiyō*, 13 (1965), pp. 1–31.

————. "Shimbunshi hō no seitei katei to sono tokushitsu" (Special characteristics of the process of developing newspapers laws). *Tōkyō Daigaku Shimbun Kenkyūjo Kiyō*, 5 (1956), pp. 59–95.

————. *Shimbun shi wa* (Historical anecdotes from the press). Shakai Shisōsha, 1967.

————. ed. *Nihon kōkoku hattatsu shi* (The development of Japanese advertising). 2 vols. Dentsū, 1976.

Uchikawa Yoshimi et al., eds. *Kōza gendai shakai to komiyunikēshiyon* (Studies: communication and modern society). 5 vols. Tōkyō Daigaku, 1974.

Uchikawa Yoshimi and Arai Naoyuki, eds. *Nihon no Jiyānarizumu: taishō no kokoro o tsukanda ka* (Japanese journalism: has it captured the spirit of the masses?). Yūhikaku, 1983.

Uchikawa Yoshimi and Matsushima Eiichi, eds. *Meiji niyūsu jiten* (Encyclopedia of Meiji news). 9 vols. Mainichi Komiyunikēshiyon Shuppanbu, 1983–1986.

————. *Taishō niyūsu jiten* (Encyclopedia of Taishō news). 7 vols. Mainichi Komiyunikēshiyon Shuppanbu, 1986–1989.

Uchikawa Yoshimi and Miyaji Masato, eds. *Gaikoku shimbun ni miru Nihon* (Japan as seen in foreign newspapers). 4 vols. Mainichi Komiyunikēshiyon, 1990.

Uchimura Kanzō. *The Complete Works of Kanzō Uchimura.* 7 vols. Kyobunkwan, 1973.

Ukai Shin'ichi. *Chōya Shimbun no kenkyū* (Research on *Chōya Shimbun*). Misuzu Shobō, 1984.

Uyehara, George E. *The Political Development of Japan, 1867–1909.* London: Constable and Company, 1910.

Van Zyl, J. A. F., and K. G. Tomaselli, eds. *Media and Change.* Johannesburg: McGraw-Hill Book Company, 1977.

Vinh, Sinh. *Tokutomi Sohō (1863–1957): The Later Career.* Toronto: University of Toronto–York University Joint Centre on Modern East Asia, 1986.

Vlastos, Stephen. *Peasant Protests and Uprisings in Tokugawa Japan.* Berkeley: University of California Press, 1986.

Wada Mamoru. *Kindai Nihon to Tokutomi Sohō* (Tokutomi Sohō and modern Japan). Ochanomizu Shobō, 1990.

Wada Yōishi. "Meiji Taishō ki no jiyānarizumu" (Journalism of the Meiji and Taishō eras). *Shimbun Gaku Hyōron*, 18 (March 1969), pp. 70–76.

Waseda Daigaku Toshokan, ed. *Bakumatsu Meiji no medeia ten* (Exhibit of Bakumatsu and Meiji era media). Waseda Daigaku Shuppanbu, 1987.

Watanabe Kazuo. *Jitsuroku gogai sensen* (Fighting with extras: a true record). Shimbun Jidaisha, 1963.

Wataru Ichikawa. "A Confused Account of a Trip to Europe, like a Fly on a Horse's Tail." Trans. Henry Satow. *Chinese and Japanese Repository of Facts and Events: Science, History, and Art, Relating to Eastern Asia*, July–December 1865.

Westney, D. Eleanor. *Imitation and Innovation: The Transfer of Western Organizational Patterns to Meiji Japan.* Cambridge: Harvard University Press, 1987.

Wildes, Harry Emerson. *Aliens in the East: A New History of Japan's Foreign Intercourse.* Reprint ed. Wilmington, Del.: Scholarly Resources, 1973.

———. *The Press and Social Currents in Japan.* Chicago: University of Chicago Press, 1927.

———. "Press Freedom in Japan." *American Journal of Sociology*, 32 (1927), pp. 601–614.

Williams, Harold S. *Foreigners in Mikadoland.* Rutland, Vt.: Tuttle, 1963.

Wurfel, David, ed. *Meiji Japan's Centennial: Aspects of Political Thought and Action.* Lawrence: University Press of Kansas, 1971.

Yamamoto Fumio, ed. *Nihon masu komiyunikēshiyon shi* (History of mass communications in Japan). Tōkai Daigaku Shuppankai, 1970.

———. *Nihon shimbun hattatsu shi* (Evolution of the Japanese press). Itō Shoten, 1944.

Yamamoto Taketoshi. "Ashio kōdoku mondai no hōdō to yoron" (Public opinion and news coverage of the Ashio copper mine pollution problem), *Tōkyō Daigaku Shimbun Kenkyūjo Kiyō*, 20 (1971), pp. 163–282.

———. *Kindai Nihon no shimbun dokusha sō* (Structure of newspaper readership in modern Japan). Hōsei Daigaku Shuppankyoku, 1981.

———. *Kōgai hōdō no genten Tanaka Shōzō to seiron keisei* (Tanaka Shōzō and the formation of political debate: basic principles of pollution reporting). Ochanomizu Shobō, 1986.

———. "Meiji sanjūnendai zenhan no shimbun dokusha sō" (Newspaper readership structure at the turn of the century). *Shimbun Gaku Hyōron*, 16 (March 1967), pp. 98–123.

———. "Meiji sanjūnendai zenhan no shimbun *Nihon* no dokusha sō chishikijin dokusha no 'shimbun ishiki' o megutte" (Readership structure of the newspaper *Nihon* at the turn of the century, focusing on the "newspaper consciousness" of the intellectual class). *Hitotsubashi Ronsō*, 58, no. 4 (October 1967), pp. 510–516.

———. "Meiji sanjūnendai zenhan no *Tōasa Jiji* no dokusha sō shōkō dokusha sō o chūshin ni" (The readership structure of *Tōkyō Asahi* and *Jiji* at the turn of the century: focusing on the business of readers). *Hitotsubashi Kenkyū*, 14 (1967), pp. 1–10.

———. "Meiji shoki ni okeru shimbun no fukyū jōkyō" (Aspects of the spread of newspapers in early Meiji). *Shimbun Gaku Hyōron*, 9 (March 1959), pp. 42–58.

———. *Shimbun kisha no tanjō: Nihon no medeia o tsukutta hitobito* (Birth of news reporters: the people who formed Japan's media). Shin-'yōsha, 1990.

———. "Shimbun sangyō no keisei katei" (Formative processes of the newspaper industry). *Tōkyō Daigaku Shimbun Kenkyūjo Kiyō*, 19 (1970), pp. 117–194.

———. *Shimbun to minshû* (Newspapers and the masses). Kinokuniya, 1973.

———. "Shūkan *Heimin Shimbun* no dokusha sō no keifu" (Genealogy of the readership structure of the weekly *Heimin Shimbun*). *Hitotsubashi Ronsō*, 61, no. 5 (May 1969), pp. 632–640.

Yamanaka, Hayato, et al., comps. *Japanese Communication Studies of the 1970s: Bibliographic Abstracts of Studies Published Only in Japanese.* Honolulu: East-West Center, 1986.

Yanagida Izumi. *Fukuchi Ōchi* (Fukuchi Ōchi). Nihon Rekishi Gakkai, 1965.

———, ed. *Fukuchi Ōchi shū* (The works of Fukuchi Ōchi). Vol. 11 of *Meiji bungaku zenshū* (Collected works of Meiji literature). Chikuma Shobō, 1966.

Yokohama Mainichi Shimbun. Vols. 1–34 (1871–1880). Facsimile reproductions. Fuji Shuppan, 1989–1992. Also *Mainichi Shimbun.*

Yomiuri Shimbun.

Yomiuri Shimbunsha, ed. *Yomiuri Shimbun hyakunijūnen shi* (One hundred twenty years of *Yomiuri Shimbun*). Yomiuri Shimbunsha, 1994.

Yorozu Chōhō.

Yoshino Takao. *Miyatake Gaikotsu* (Miyatake Gaikotsu). Kawade Shobō, 1980.

Young, A. Morgan. *Japan in Recent Times, 1912–1926.* Westport, Conn.: Greenwood Press, 1973.

Yūbin Hōchi Shimbun.

Zen Nihon Shimbun Renmei, ed. *Kindai Nihon shimbun taikan* (Overview of the modern Japanese press). 3 vols. Zen Nihon Shimbun Renmei, 1980–1982. (Note: the word Kindai is omitted from vol. 3.)

———. *Shimbun taikan* (Overview of the press). 3 vols. Zen Nihon Shimbun Renmei, 1975–1981.

Zinn, Howard. *Politics of History.* Boston: Beacon Press, 1970.

Zolbrod, Leon M. "Mass Media of the Tokugawa Period: Background of Japanese Popular Literature and Journalism." In *Asian Studies at Hawaii: East Asian Occasional Papers (II)*, ed. Harry J. Lamley, 4 (July 1970), pp. 123–143.

Index

Subentries in this index are listed in chronological order. Dates are italicized.

War, 203, 208, 211, 214, 219, 220; interwar years, 229–231, 233, 236–239, 247, 254, 257, 262, 265, 380; advocating war with Russia, 274–275; Russo-Japanese War, 279, 282–283, 285; Portsmouth Treaty, 301, 304; late-Meiji, 316–317, 319– 321, 323, 326, 334, 354; Taishō era, 360

Yugeta Seiichi, 290

Yūkan Ōsaka Shimbun, 497 n 57

zappō, zatsuwa. See miscellany section

zuihitsu (miscellanies), 21

About the Author

James L. Huffman is professor of history at Wittenberg University. A former reporter for the *Minneapolis Tribune,* he holds degrees from Indiana Wesleyan University (A.B.), Northwestern University (M.S. Journalism), and the University of Michigan (M.A., Ph.D.). He has taught at the University of Nebraska–Lincoln (1972–1975), Indiana Wesleyan (1975–1977), and Wittenberg (1977–present) and has been a visiting researcher at the University of Tokyo's Jōhō Shakai Kenkyūjo (1983–1984, 1994–1995) and Japan's National Institute of Multimedia Education (1994–1995). A lifelong student of the press, his publications include *Politics of the Meiji Press: The Life of Fukuchi Gen'ichirō* (University of Hawai'i Press, 1980) and *Japan: An Encyclopedia of History, Culture, and Nationalism* (editor; Garland, 1997).